BUSINESS LAW

FOR

BTEC NATIONAL

JOHN ELLISON, LL.B(Hons), P.G.C.E., M.A.(Ed)
Senior Lecturer in Law,
New College Durham

JIM BEDINGFIELD, B.A.(Hons), P.G.C.E. Solicitor
Lecturer in Law,
New College Durham

TOM HARRISON, B.A. (Hons), P.G.C.E., LL.M (Lond)
Senior Lecturer in Law,
New College Durham

BUSINESS EDUCATION PUBLISHERS
1987

Published in Great Britain by Business Education Publishers Ltd.,
Leighton House 10 Grange Crescent Stockton Road Sunderland
Tyne and Wear SR2 7BN Tel: 091 567 4963

Reprinted 1989,1990

ISBN 0 907679 17 X

Printed in Great Britain by Thomson Litho Ltd, East Kilbride, Scotland

PREFACE

This book has been written to provide a comprehensive coverage of the Business Law option unit at BTEC National level. It assumes no previous legal knowledge on the part of the reader. The text has been structured to take the student on a logical journey through the legal environment in which the business community operates, beginning with the nature of the legal system and its significance to business activity, and finishing with an examination of the methods used to resolve legal disputes. The text covers in depth the internal and external legal framework of business: the acquisition and use of resources; the nature of transacting; the rights and obligations of a business.

The inclusion of a range of practical, work related problem based assignments provides an opportunity for students to engage in active learning activities. It also provides a basis for the in-course assessment programme.

The book complements the main text 'Core Studies for BTEC National' also published by B.E.P. Ltd.

The text should also prove of value for the study of Business Law under other syllabuses, including those at the BTEC Higher level, and those of many of the professional bodies.

A free lecturers manual is available from the publishers for colleges which adopt the book for student use.

The authors are all staff at New College Durham.

ACKNOWLEDGEMENTS

We would like to thank the staff at City Printers and Business Education Publishers for all the assistance they have provided in the production of this book. Most especially we must record our thanks to our tolerant and long suffering wives (and children).

All errors and ommissions remain the responsibility of the authors.

The law is stated as at 1st July 1987.

JE
JB
TH

Durham
September 1987

CONTENTS

TABLE OF CASES

TABLE OF STATUTES

Chapter 1

AN INTRODUCTION TO BUSINESS LAW

THE NATURE AND PURPOSE OF LAW

The principle objective of a legal system is the establishment of rules which, in the broadest sense, are designed to regulate relationships. Human societies are highly complex social structures. Without systems of rules or codes of conduct to control them, such societies would find it difficult to maintain their cohesion, and would gradually break up. The interdependance of each member of the community with its other members brings people into constant social contact and this contact sometimes leads to disagreement and conflict. It is unrealistic to expect that in a culture which encourages people to express their individualism, there will never be occasions when the activities of one person clash with those of another. Someone who wishes to paint political slogans on the side of his house, play loud music during the night and use hard drugs may take the view that these activities are the exercise of his personal rights. But they may well give rise to conflict if his neighbour is not of the same political viewpoint, is a light sleeper and regards the use of drugs as immoral. What the law seeks to do in circumstances where interests conflict in this way is to attempt to reconcile differences by referring their solutions to established rules which have been developed to clarify individual rights and obligations.

The relationship between neighbours are but a small part of the complex pattern of relationships most people find themselves part of, and a book devoted to the study of business law inevitably concentrates upon those legal relationships that are a product of business activity. The task of defining what is meant by business activity is dealt with in the next chaper, but we can briefly note at this stage that businesses are organisations providing goods and services to whoever requires them. The customers of a business are usually referred to as consumers. They may be other businesses themselves, but they also include individuals, ultimate consumers who use the goods and services for their own private benefit. Once we enter the business world we begin to see that there is far more to legal relationships than the simple neighbour example given earlier. We find an environment in which an enormously diverse range of transactions are constantly taking place, resources of labour, capital, and land are being acquired and disposed of, information and advice is being given and sought, and decisions are regularly being made which have an impact on the owners, managers and customers of the organisations with which they are concerned. It is fair to say that no one can avoid entering into or being affected by business relationships during their lives.

One relatively simple way to begin to analyse the relationships enjoyed by a business organisation is to consider firstly its internal environment, looking at it on a 'micro' level, and secondly the external environment in which it operates, viewing it on a 'macro' level. Figures 1.1 and 1.2 provide a brief diagrammatic illustration.

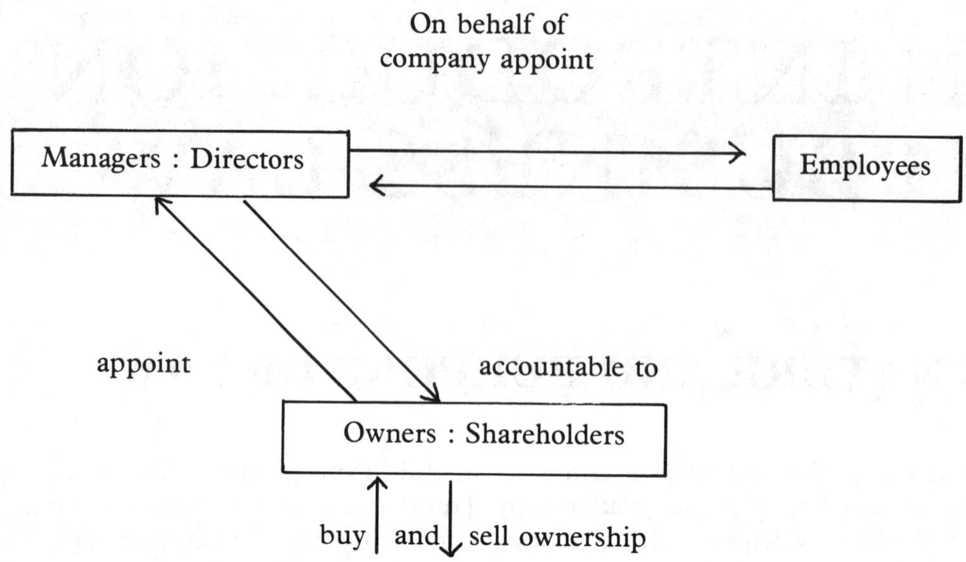

Fig. 1.1 The internal dimensions of a business organisation — the limited company.

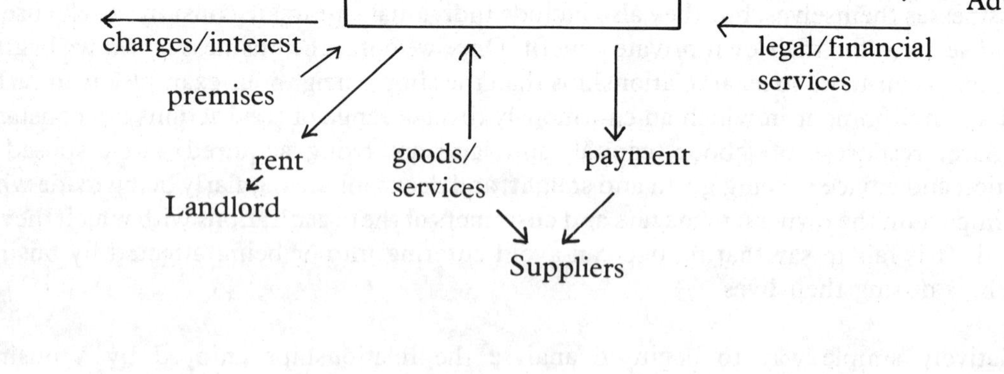

Fig. 1.2 The external dimensions of a business organisation

It will be appreciated that even at the superficial level of analysis these figures provide, business organisations are at the centre of a web of relationships all of which have a strong legal dimension to them. For instance, a business may take decisions on the basis of expert advise provided by a professional advisor in return for payment of a fee or charge. Inaccurate or incomplete advice relied upon by the business may cause it to suffer commercial harm. If this occurs the business may have a legal remedy against the advisor, and will seek to recover any losses it has sustained. Similarly, within the organisation relationships exist between managers, owners and staff. Directors of a limited company are accountable to the shareholders in general meeting, and may be dismissed from their office by a company resolution in circumstances where they have been guilty of commercial incompetence or malpractice. It is the primary task of a business law book to examine the legal framework within which all businesses, from the multinational corporations to the one man businesses, pursue their commercial objectives. We have noted that this framework has to do with the relationships their business activity gives rise to. What we must next do is to ascertain more precisely the purposes which underpin the legal regulation of business affairs.

Complex, affluent, property owning societies develop detailed and sophisticated rules to regulate themselves, and in the United Kingdom as in most modern states almost every aspect of human activity is either directly or indirectly affected by law. Such laws will be designed to achieve different purposes. One major classification of any legal system involves distinguishing between legal rules which are concerned with private rights and obligations, a branch of law referred to as civil law, and those whose primary purpose is the well-being of society at large, and its protection by means of rules that seek to prevent anti-social forms of behaviour, and to punish those who break them. This is the criminal law. The following list indicates the primary purposes being served by imposing legal rules:

(i) the remedying of private grievances. Various branches of law are concerned with recognising rights, which can be enforced by means of legal proceedings where they have been infringed, or even where there is simply a threat to infringe them. For instance the law of tort is based upon the existence of a set of obligations (torts) which are imposed by law, rather than arising by agreement between the parties. To commit a tort is to be in breach of a general duty imposed by law. In effect the law of tort grants legal rights, which entitle anyone whose rights have been infringed to sue for compensation. Examples of torts include trespass, nuisance, defamation, and negligence, which is considered in detail in Chapter 6.

The law of contract is a further example of a branch of law dealing in private rights and obligations. Contractual agreements involve the making of promises which are legally enforceable. A party to a contract therefore has the right to take legal action against the other party to the agreement in the event of that person being in breach of his contractual obligations.

Both the law of contract and the law of tort have an impact upon the business environment. Without the ability to enter into binding agreements businesses would not be able to function, for buying and selling is their life. Without the ability to seek compensation and redress for wrongs committed against them they could suffer economic ruin. Imagine for example, a situation where a small business could obtain no compensation following the total destruction of its stock and premises due to negligent repair work carried out to an adjoining gas main by the gas board;

(ii) the control of anti-social activities. This is the task of the criminal law. Whilst it is not possible to prevent crimes from being committed, the presence of penal sanctions, such as imprisonment and fining, which are used to support the criminal code, can act as a deterrent to the commission of an offence.

There is no adquate definition of a crime. Lord Diplock in *Knuller v. Director of Public Prosecutions (1972)* attempted to pinpoint the essential differences between civil and criminal law when he said "Civil liability is concerned with the relationship of one citizen to another; criminal liability is concerned with the relationship of a citizen to society organised as a state."

Businesses, like individuals, are subject to the criminal law. Of the wide range of offences than an organisation might commit in the course of its business, the following provide some illustrations:

(i) Offences in the field of consumer protection, such as offences connected with trade descriptions, consumer credit matters such as engaging in activities requiring a licence where no licence has been granted, and consumer safety regarding certain manufactured items, among them oil heaters and electric blankets, which must satisfy safety standards laid down under government regulations (Consumer Protection Act 1987).

(ii) Offences in the field of employment, such as contravention of the obligations owed to employees under health and safety legislation.

(iii) Offences connected with the operation of registered companies, such as a failure to file accounts or the insertion of untrue statements in a prospectus.

(iv) Offences in relation to tax liability, such as the making of false returns.

Since a business is an organisation and cannot be imprisoned, it can only be held criminally liable for offences which are punishable by a fine.

(iii) the regulation of harmful activities. Methods of legal regulation include licencing, registration and inspection, and these can be useful mechanisms for exercising effective control over a range of activities, which, if uncontrolled, could be physically, economically and socially harmful. Thus powers of inspection, supported by enforcement mechanisms, are granted to factory inspectors working for the Health and Safety Executive. The inspection of work places such as factories and building sites enables inspectors to ascertain whether safety legislation is being complied with, and that employee's physical requirements are thus being met. Certain types of trading practices which are potentially anti-competitive can only be pursued legitimately if the agreements in which they are contained are registered with the Director General of Fair Trading, under the Restrictive Trade Practices Act 1976. Even then they are only legally permissable if they are approved by the Restrictive Trade Practices Court. Additionally anyone in the business of providing credit facilities is obliged to register under the Consumer Credit Act 1974 with the Director General of Fair Trading before being legally permitted to lend money. The aim is to eliminate unscrupulous finance dealers from the credit market, overcoming the social problems which arise when poorer members of society borrow at high rates of interest which they are unable to afford, often in an effort to extricate themselves from other debts.

THE IMPORTANCE OF LAW TO BUSINESS

The legal system affects businesses just as it does individuals. Every aspect of business life, from formation and operation to dissolution is conducted within an environment of legal regulation. Many purposes are being served in applying legal regulation to business activity. The underlying features of business law are the dual aims of

(a) providing a practical and comprehensive framework of legal rules and principles to assist the organisation in its commercial affairs, whilst at the same time;

(b) ensuring a sufficient level of protection for the legitimate interests of those who come into direct contact with it. This includes not only members of the public in their capacity as consumers, but also business creditors and the employees and owners of business enterprises.

There is one fundamental reason why business organisations are likely to seek to comply with the law. If they fail to do so it will affect them financially. A business which is in breach of law, whether the civil law or the criminal law, will suffer from the breach commercially. The commercial consequences of breaking the law can include:

(i) an action for damages, seeking financial compensation for a breach of contract committed by the business, or in respect of some form of tortious liability; an alternative claim brought against it could be an injunction restraining it from pursuing a particular course of action;

(ii) a claim that the action of the business is devoid of legal effect because it has failed to follow procedures which bind it. For instance, a limited company cannot act unless it has correctly followed the registration procedures laid down by statute, and has received a certificate of incorporation. Nor can it alter its own constitution (its articles of association) unless this is done in accordance with the procedures, in good faith and for the benefit of the company as a whole;

(iii) the loss of an opportunity to take some form of legal action, because the time limit for doing so has passed, for instance bringing a late appeal against an unfavourable planning decision;

(iv) a prosecution brought against it alleging breach of the criminal law, resulting in a fine;

(v) the exercise of enforcement action against it for its failure to comply with some legal requirement, for example to take steps to remedy a serious hazard to health, as a result of which its business operations are suspended.

Thus there is a sound commercial reason for keeping properly informed about and complying with the law as it affects business, quite apart from any moral or social responsibility for doing so.

Legal proceedings often attract public attention and result in adverse publicity to the organisations. Individuals engaged in managing a business may find themselves dismissed if they are responsible for serious errors of judgment which carry legal consequences.

It may not be possible for people in business to find the time or develop the skills to cope with all the legal demands of operating a business, however there will remain strong reasons for at least acquiring a basic level of legal knowledge and skills and devoting some time to legal issues as and when they arise. This is because:

(i) many straightforward legal problems can be resolved simply by means of a letter or a telephone call to the other party involved. Legal advice has to be paid for, and in some situations will be an unnecessary expense, and a time consuming activity;

(ii) certain legal problems require immediate action, for example what rights the employer has to dismiss an employee caught in the act of damaging the employers property;

(iii) the daily routine of a business involves frequent encounters with matters of a legal nature, such as examining contracts, signing cheques, negotiating transactions and so on;

(iv) many business activities are closely legally regulated, and a working knowledge of them is essential if the business is to function effectively. For example a business providing credit facilities needs to employ staff who are fully aware of the strict legal requirements regulating such transactions;

(v) when expert advice and assistance is being sought the effectiveness of the process of consultation is assisted if the precise issues can be identified from the outset, and relevant records and materials can be presented at the time. In addition, when the advice is given it will be of little value in the possession of someone who can make no real sense of it.

Obtaining and using legal information

Having established the importance of legal rules and procedures in the running of a business, the next question which arises is how to obtain and apply relevant legal principles, so that the process of business decision making and practical operation is informed and guided by the legal environment in which it functions. Large organisations employ their own professional advisors. Public companies and local authorities will have departments specialising in legal, financial and other areas of professional work. In such organisations it will be the role of staff in the legal department to deal with the routine legal aspects of the work of the business, and it may be expected of them to produce and distribute to relevant personnel details of legal changes which are likely to have an effect on the way in which the business works. For example, following the introduction of the Health and Safety at Work Act 1974, employers were required to fulfil a number of general duties set out by the Act to ensure the health, safety and welfare of their employees whilst at work. The Act specifically stated that these duties were to include providing staff with any necessary information, instruction, training and supervision. Smaller organisations, whose scale of business operations is insufficient to make the employment of a full time lawyer financially viable will instead rely for their legal needs on the services of a law firm, which will probably be locally based, to deal with legal matters as and when they arise. The nature of such an arrangement makes it unlikely that legal changes affecting the business will always be picked up by their legal advisers and fed into the business in advance of the change. Most of the legal work performed will be as a response to matters which are routinely passed on to the firm, such as the renewal of the business lease, actions for the recovery of debts and financial borrowing by means of the use of a security such as a mortgage or debenture.

In the smallest organisations, such as one man businesses, there may be reluctance to seek legal services at all, unless it is absolutely necessary for the business to do so. Professional advice costs money, and time is taken up in meetings with professional advisors. Whilst this may be a shortsighted view, and one which can result in the organisation getting itself into greater difficulty in the long term, it is nevertheless the case that such organisations will occassionally try to 'go it alone'.

It is clear that the nature of advice and assistance that organisations have need of to operate satisfactorily, is often of a detailed and technical kind which only accountants, lawyers and other professionals are capable of providing. However it would be quite wrong to assume that in consequence there is little value to be gained from employing staff who have a basic knowledge and appreciation of principles of bookkeeping, or how the Sale of Goods Act 1979 works. Daily, practical business operations raise a range of issues, many of which, whilst broadly located in areas of technical expertise of which staff have no deep knowledge, can be easily dealt with by people with only a general level of expertise. There is no reason why a small trading organisation should not be able to cope with most of the contractual disagreements that will arise from time to time between it and its suppliers and customers in the ordinary course of business.

Whatever method a business uses to obtain legal support, it is quite clear that business managers are not doing their jobs properly if they are ignorant of the legal implications inherent in the daily activities carried out by their organisations. How they manage their premises, their staff, their financial affairs and their trading operations should be guided by their business ability, and part of this ability involves recognising the legal implications inherent in pursuing different courses of action. Certainly the failure of management to identify and respond to changes in the law which directly affects the business will prevent it from adapting its operations to accommodate and comply with these changes. An example of how significant such a failure might be is usefully illustrated by referring to a recently introduced statute, the Consumer Protection Act 1987. This legislative enactment is of considerable importance to any business, which is a producer of goods that will ultimately be purchased by consumers. The Act significantly alters the basis of a producers liability for defective products, and as is the case in respect of many modern legal changes, the failure of the organisation to recognise the change and reassess its production processes in the light of it, can result in the payment of large sums by way of compensation. Legal changes can produce immediate alterations to the extent of an organisation's liabilities, affecting the very heart of its commercial activities. In these circumstances it is essential that information is fed into the organisation to enable appropriate action to be taken.

There are two stages involved in reacting to legal change: obtaining the relevant information and applying it. The primary sources of English law are statute and precedents (case law). Both these sources are published, and are available in law libraries. Statutes, or Acts of Parliament as they are usually known, can also be purchased from branches of HMSO.

In order to understand these two sources of law it is useful to examine them in outline and consider the processes by which they are created.

Sources of English Law

The two major sources of English law are the Common Law (case-law) and Statute (Acts of Parliament and delegated legislation). The rules relating to different areas of law are found by examining both statutory provisions and the judgments of the courts. Some areas of law are essentially common law in nature, such as the law of tort and the law of contract, while others are mainly embodied in statute, for instance company law and criminal law. However if a dispute arises as to the meaning of a statutory provision it may be interpreted by the courts who by their judgment will create a precedent (a rule of law) as to the provision's meaning. Before considering the operation of statute and case law it is useful first to briefly outline the contribution and origin of earlier sources of English law.

The meaning of 'common law'

In its modern day usage the expression 'common law' means all law other than statutory provisions. Thus common law in this sense means judge made law embodied in case decisions. The expression 'common law system' however is a reference to the type of legal system that operates in England and Wales and indeed has been adopted by countries all over the world and particularly in the Commonweath. The common law of England dates back as far as the Norman Conquest and has its origins in the decisions of the royal judges who attempted to apply law which was 'common' to the whole country. This they did by modifying and adapting rules of Norman law, and rules contained in Saxon local custom. The development of the common law was a long process evolving over hundreds of years.

Judicial Precedent

While it is still true to say English law has the common law as its base, over the centuries common law rules have become embodied in precedent (case decisions) and so today the expression common law and case-law are virtually synonymous and may be referred to as 'judge-made' law. Judge-made law is found in the law reports and when you consider that there are well over half a million reported cases, it is not difficult to appreciate that the rules relating to many areas of law are contained in precedents. Under the doctrine of judicial precedent, judges when deciding cases must take into account previous past precedents in the same area of law. The superior courts form a hierarchy and, as a general rule, decisions of higher courts will bind lower courts in the hierarchy.

CIVIL COURTS

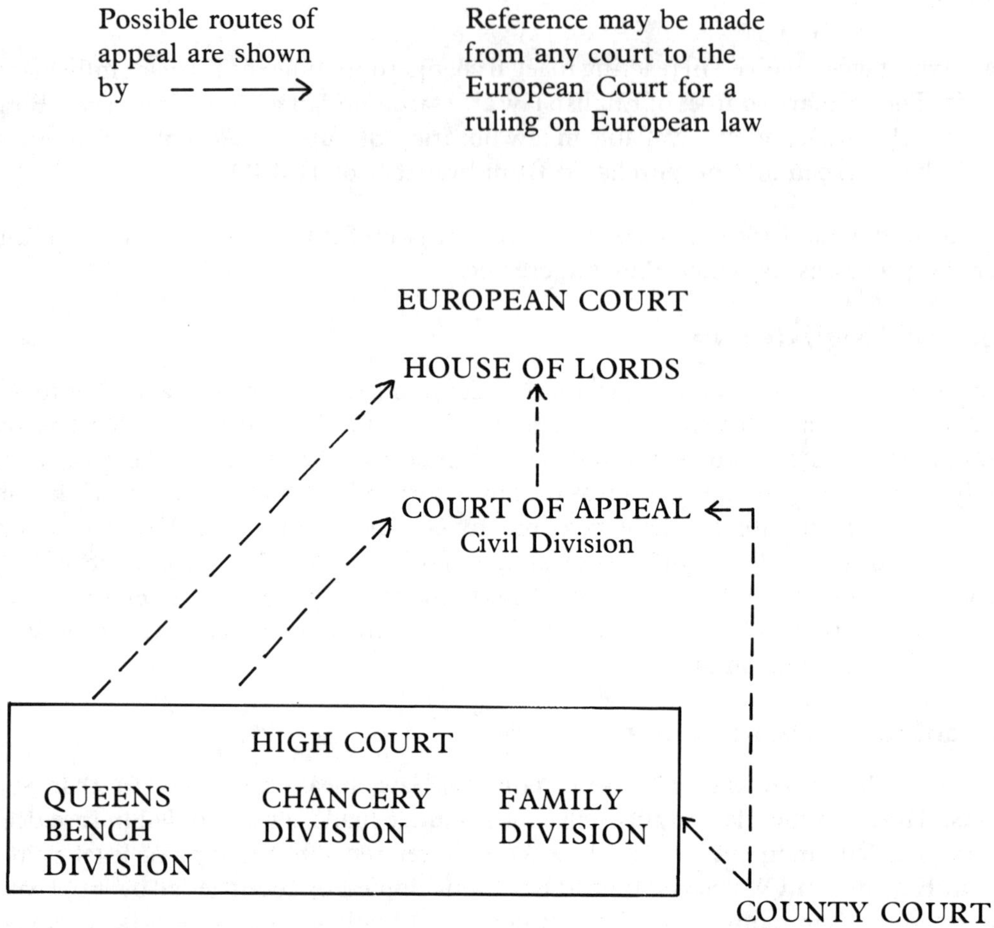

CRIMINAL COURTS

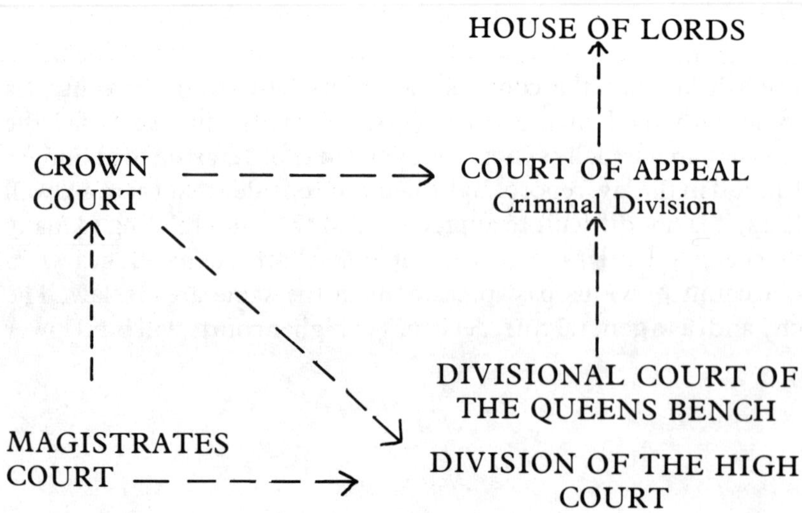

The binding element of a judgment. When a decision is reached on a dispute before a superior court, the judges will make their decision known by making speeches (the judgment). Within a judgment, the judges will refer to numerous matters such as the relevant legal principles which are drawn from cases or statutes, a review of the facts of the case, their opinion on the relevant law, the actual decisions and the reasons for it. As far as the parties to a dispute are concerned the matter they are most concerned with is the actual decision, that is who has won the case. The main matter of relevance to the law, however, is the reason for the decision. This is known under the law as the 'ratio decidendi' (the reason for deciding). The 'ratio' forms the underlying legal principle relied on in reaching the decision and it is this that constitutes the binding precedent. All this means is that if a lower court in a later case is faced with a similar dispute they would be bound to apply the earlier 'ratio decidendi.'

The persuasive element of a judgment. All other matters referred to in a judgment are called 'obiter dicta' (things said by the way). The 'obiter' forms persuasive precedent and should be taken into account by a lower court in a later similar case although the lower court is not bound to follow it.

THE LEGISLATURE

The legislature, Parliament, sits at Westminster. It consists of a lower house, the Commons, in which M.Ps sit and the upper house, the Lords, which has a non elected membership that includes hereditary and life peers, law Lords and the Archbishop and Bishops of the Church of England. The primary responsibilities of Parliament are the enactment of legislation which amongst other things involves the task of granting consent to the spending of public revenue, and the guardianship of the interests of the nation, which involves attempting to control the activities of the government when they are believed to conflict with the national interest. The control mechanism relies upon the accountability of Ministers to Parliament. They can be called upon to provide public answers during question time and during debates on proposed legislation. Furthermore they can be summonsed to appear before Parliamentary Select Committees for more detailed and rigorous questioning. Undoubtably the broadcasting on radio of Parliamentary proceedings has increased the public awareness of the role of the legislature. Nowadays when the Government faces a severe test during Prime Minister's question time the occasion is built up into a significant media event.

What is legislation?

Technically, legislation is defined as the formulation of law by the Queen in Parliament, thus the Monarch and both Houses are involved in creating it. The Monarch's role is limited to the granting of assent which is a formality; the real legislative power lies with the two Houses of Parliament of whom the House of Commons is constitutionally the most powerful. During this century two Acts, the Parliament Acts of 1911 and 1949 have reduced the power of the House of Lords. The 1911 Act provides that a money Bill (eg the Finance Bill) must be passed through the Lords without amendment, within one month following its passage through the Commons, whilst under the 1949 provisions the Lords are unable to 'block' any public Bill which has passed the Commons in two successive sessions. A Bill is the name given to legislation whilst it proceeds through the various stages which culminate in it becoming an Act after the Royal Assent is given.

A classification of Bills is contained in Fig. 1.3 below.

Something in the region of sixty or seventy Bills become law annually. Creating legislation is the most obvious way in which governments are able to implement their policies, whether they be fiscal, economic or social. The process by which governments arrive at Parliament is beyond the scope of this book, but it is certainly possible to note that some of the most significant factors which influence legislation.

(a) Royal Commissions.

(b) pressure groups, such as MIND, the Friends of the Earth.

Fig. 1.3 The Classification of Parliamentary Bills

Public Bills
(to alter the general law)

these may be sponsored by:

- The Government as a means of implementing its policies: most Bills are **Government Bills**
- Private members: all M.P.s and members of the Lords can present their own Bills, although little time is available for them

  Such Bills are called **Private Members Bills**

Private Bills
(application limited to an organisation eg local authority or an individual)

sponsored by the promoter.

(c) UK membership of international organisations, such as the EEC. EEC policy decisions have a direct impact upon legislative activity in the United Kingdom. For instance the Competition Act 1980 (see Chapter 4) was passed as a response to EEC requirements.

(d) public opinion and the media.

(e) Government reports.

Thus before a bill is presented to Parliament many events may have occured leading to its drafting. One possibility is given below (fig. 1.4).

Fig. 1.4 The stages leading to the Proposal of Legislation

Pressure for change in the law builds up: eg: Various members of the majority party express major concern about an indentified issue during the party conference.

↓

Prime Minister and the Cabinet consider the issue and identify a strategy.

↓

Opinions of interested groups invited through the issue of a Green Paper.

↓

Evidence collated and Government policy expressed through the issue of a White Paper.

↓

Specific legislative proposals are drafted by government lawyers (called Parliamentary Counsel to the Treasury).

↓

The bill is then pased to Parliament, usually to the Commons although if it is non-controversial it may begin in the House of Lords.

The process by which legislation is created is illustrated in fig. 1.5.

The procedure followed in both Houses is the same where public bills are being considered.

First reading — a formal notification of the bill to the House.

↓

Second Reading — a general debate on the principles of the bill.

↓

Committee Stage — detailed discussion of the bills in committee, amendments are proposed.

↓

Report stage — bill, as amended, passed back to whole House for consideration.

↓

Third reading — a formal final debate, only verbal amendments permitted.

↓

House of Lords — (or the House of Commons, if the bill began in the Lords)

↓

The Royal Assent — the bill is now an Act of Parliament and enforceable by the Courts.

Fig. 1.5 The passage of legislation.

Delegated or Subordinate legislation

It is not possible for Parliament to cope with all the legislative demands placed upon it. For one thing it lacks time due to its slow procedures; for another it does not always possess the technical expertise necessary to create detailed rules in specialised fields of knowledge. A further difficulty lies in anticipating, in the legislation being enacted today, what might develop in the future.

Parliament overcomes these inadequacies by delegating law making power to subordinates. These include organisations — local authorities are a prime example — as well as individuals, especially Minister. Thus much of our statute law merely lays down general principles, while specifically granting the power to a Minister, in liaison with his or her department, to "finish the job" by legislatively filling in the details. Without such a system effective government could not be carried out in a country as complex as ours, but this does not mean that this method of legislating escapes criticism. Constitutionally the role of Parliament is weakened, as the executive obtains a law making capacity for itself; delegated legislation does not attract publicity sometimes the subordinate can legislate on matters principle. These criticisms are dealt with by control mechanism which help us to maintain a proper balance between effective government on the one hand and accountability on the other. The courts can be resorted to where it is believed that the delegated powers have been exceeded and, if this is established, the action taken by the subordinate will be declared ultra vires (beyond the powers) and void. Additionally Parliament has its own 'Scrutiny Committee' which examines statutory instruments (one form of delegated legislation) in order to report to Parliament on any matters requiring special attention such as lack of clarity in the instrument.

CHANGE AND THE LAW

Legal rules are not made simply for their own sake. They are made because there is a need for them. It may not always be easy to recognise why particular areas of law, or specific legal rules have become necessary. Nor will people always agree that a particular need has been properly established, or that legal rule making is the best way to respond to an identified problem or issue. However it remains true that all laws orginate out of some sense of need for formal regulation or control of a particular situation. We have already seen the variety of purposes these legal rules are designed to fulfil, each purpose being an area of need for rule creation. One way of expressing these ideas is to say that legal rules are an effect rather than a cause.

Although certain fundamental needs are constant, such as food and shelter, others are more variable. Whilst our need for law to regulate human conduct is always present the form and content of the law varies over time, altering and adapting to take account of the dynamic nature of modern society. We have always had a need for laws to provide for order in society, and the criminal law is the outcome. Crimes have been recognised since earliest times as offences against the well-being of society, which if allowed to pass unchecked would undermine the fabric of society. Criminal laws have thus been created to protect the individual and property. However whilst crimes such as murder and theft have always been regarded as an essential part of the criminal code, the means by which we define these crimes today, and the legal penalties that are attached to them are not exactly as they were a hundred years ago, or even thirty years ago. Law evolves as society evolves, and this is entirely appropriate for law is the servant of society rather than its master.

It is possible to identify certain general causes of legal change, and the following list indicates what these may be:

(i) social requirements, for example to provide tenants with legal protection from unscrupulous landlords who threaten eviction if the tenant refuses to pay unjustifiable rent increases;

(ii) economic requirements. Within a free market economy trading practices often develop which may be harmful to general economic needs. For example, dominant suppliers who use their market dominance to restrict competition in the supply of such goods are distorting market conditions. Governments may find it necessary to intervene by means of legislation to curb the growth of dominant market suppliers;

(iii) political needs, for instance a government may feel it appropriate to introduce legislation to penalise councils who overspend;

(iv) technological and scientific developments. Technological change has from time to time created problems which require legal regulations to control. The growth in the use of computers over the past twenty years as a means of storing personal data, has given rise to concern over the apparent loss of rights of individuals whose lives are recorded in this way and who may have little or no control over the use to which such information is put. Legislation now seeks to provide an measure of security for individuals in this situation.

In reality the change factors listed here overlap to a considerable extent with each other. For example, the decision to join the European Economic Community was both political and economic. Legally it was achieved by passing the European Communities Act 1972. Potentially it also had social implications, since for example, the Community was pledged to move towards enabling a free movement of labour between the member states. A more specific example of the overlap is provided by various aspects of modern employment legislation. The creation of the right of employees not to be unfairly dismissed by their employees, which is at present contained in the Employment Protection (Consolidation) Act 1978 (as amended) illustrates the use of a legal devise (statute) to achieve a social objective (job security), which has political implications (electorally popular) and includes an economic dimension (restriction on employers freedom to reduce the size of the workforce).

The protection of the interests of the buying public has produced a spate of legal change over the past two decades. It is a recognition by Parliament that consumers rights are a matter of national interest and debate, making them a part of the political agenda. Increases in the spending power of the nation, together with great technological advances in the production of consumer durables from compact discs to microwave ovens have led to an enormous growth in the demand for goods from consumers, and producers have responded accordingly. As 'consumerism' has expanded, and the demand for consumer rights has increased, so the law has been invoked as the means of achieving an appropriate level of consumer protection. Statutory changes have sought to regulate this particular market.

An illuminating illustration of the change process in operation is provided by one facet of modern consumer law. Back in 1893 the Sale of Goods Act was passed, as a means of codifying the law of sale. Codification involves bringing all the law in a specific field together in a single statute. It is a way of clarifying the law, and it assists the task of discovering the law on a particular subject if it is primarily contained in a single statute. The rules that were expressed in the Act were based upon the need for a clear legal framework within which trade could be effectively conducted between businesses. At that time the interests of private consumers of goods were given little consideration. One of the provisions of the Act stipulated that in any sale of goods transaction between a buyer and a business seller, the seller would be treated as impliedly promising the buyer that the goods were of a certain standard, known technically as the standard of 'merchantable quality'. The seller was however at liberty to exclude this implied promise if he did so clearly, a right eagerly grasped by most sellers, who had no desire to increase their liabilities unnecessarily. At this time the predominant business philosophy was 'caveat emptor', let the buyer beware. It was essentially the buyers task to satisfy himself that what he was buying was suitable and fit.

By the 1970's it was felt that the interests of private consumers were being largely overridden by the majority of sellers, who simply avoided their legal obligations to provide merchantable goods by the use of contractual clauses excluding liability. This, of course, they were perfectly legally entitled to do, but it was felt that consumers were being treated harshly by being denied the opportunity to reject defective goods, from whose sale the seller had made a profit. In 1973 legislation was introduced which invalidated any attempt by a seller to exclude liability for breach of the merchantable quality provisions.

Sellers however continued to exclude, confident that private consumers were largely unaware of their rights, and that in any event attempting to exclude was not unlawful, simply invalid. This subsequently lead to further statutory intervention, so that since 1978 an attempt to exclude liability has constituted a criminal offence, under the Consumer Transactions (Restrictions on Statements) Order. The order has proved an effective deterrent to most traders, and consumer rights have been fully secured in this field.

One other cause of legal change requires brief mention, that of legal clarity. Legislation is introduced from time to time as an attempt at simply clarifying legal rules, rather than creating new ones. The codified Sale of Goods Act, mentioned above provides an example.

Chapter 2

BUSINESS ORGANISATIONS

INTRODUCTION

The logical starting point in a study of business law is to examine the business organisations which are responsible for conducting business activity. To do so we need to be clear about what we mean by the expression "business organisations". The problem this raises is that business is an economic concept rather than a legal one. The law does on occasion find it necessary to define the meaning of business, but only in specific situations limited to the context of a particular problem. For instance tax liability may depend upon deciding whether a person who has bought and sold three cars during the year is trading, and is thus in business as a car dealer. But the answer to such a question would tell us very little about the nature and quality of businesses in general.

In order then to appreciate fully the law as it applies to business organisations it is helpful to draw briefly from economics, and summarise what an economist sees as making up a business organisation. It should be remembered that the decision to form a business is a commercial rather than a legal one, and that those who set up businesses will treat the legal form the business is to take as a secondary rather than a primary consideration. First you decide your business aims and objectives. Then you decide on the form of business appropriate to achieve them. As we shall see, examining the general economic background to business organisations is also useful because it helps to explain why substantial parts of business law have evolved, either as an aid to the business community in achieving commercial aims, or as a means of regulating business activities and curbing undesirable practices.

CHARACTERISTICS COMMON TO BUSINESS ORGANISATIONS

Most business organisations will display the following characteristics:

(i) They will establish their business aims. In general organisations are set up for a specific purpose; selling particular products, providing a service, and so on. Of course businesses are also likely to evolve as the commercial environment changes and new commercial opportunities present themselves.

(ii) The identity of the organisations will be distinct. It will, for example, be possible to establish who are the owners of the organisation, and who it employs.

(iii) There will be some form of leadership in the organisation. Leadership will be provided in the form of a system of management of the organisation.

(iv) There will be accountability within the organisation. The organisation will have accountability. It will be accountable to those who own it, those whom it employs, and those with whom it trades.

It is the commercial aim of the business enterprise which distinguishes this type of organisation from others. For instance some organisations have scientific, educational, or social goals, and are not primarily concerned with the profit motive in the same way as business organisations; examples include the National Trust, BTEC, and sports and social clubs. Local authorities are not commercial organisations either. The expression 'business' is however a wide one, and used in some senses would certainly apply to the organisations just mentioned even though they are non-commercial. The expression is often used in a general sense to describe the way in which an organisation is run, a 'business-like operation', meaning it is run efficiently. It is also used to characterise the type of organisational activity being carried out, thus someone may refer to BTEC as being 'in the education business'. For our purposes we will be using business in its commercial sense, looking at organisations which aim to make a profit for their owners, and which are owned privately, rather than by the state.

THE CLASSIFICATION OF BUSINESS ORGANISATIONS

It is easy to get bogged down in charts and diagrams which classify business organisations in different ways, but it is helpful to take a birds-eye view of how these organisations relate to each other. Fig. 2.1 below provides a broad classification, which firstly distinguishes the organisations according to ownership, and then breaks down private sector business organisations, which form the subject matter of this chapter, by reference to their legal status.

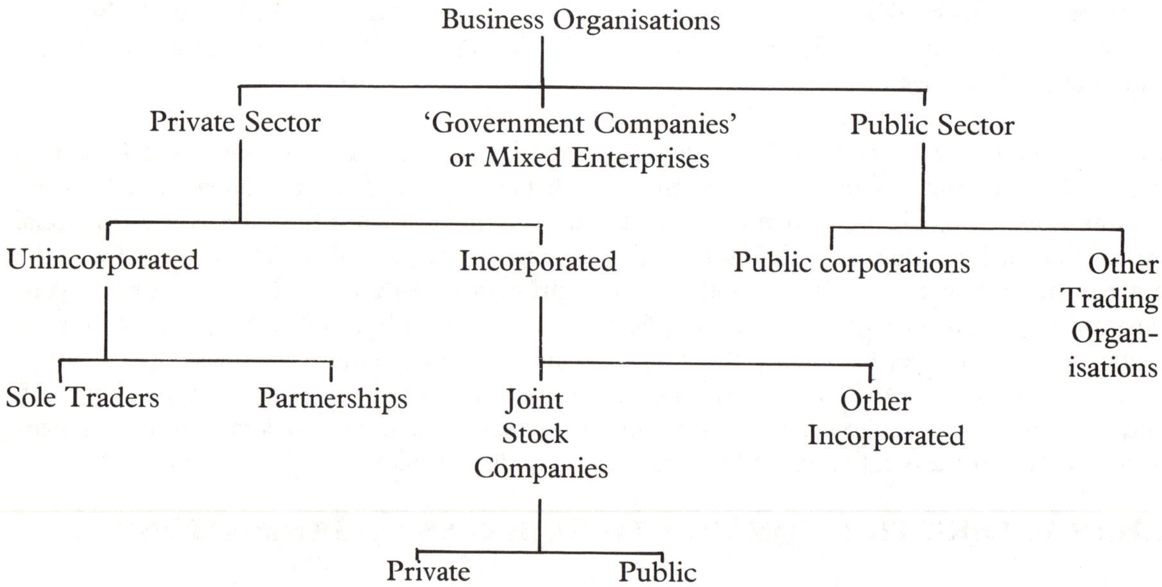

Fig. 2.1 **Classification of business organisations**

Two features of the figure above require special attention:

(i) The distinction exists between corporate and unincorporated bodies, and

(ii) The distinction between private and public sector organisations.

It is outside the scope of this book to examine the differences between public and private sector organisations in any detail, however it is important to be clear as to the significance of the distinction. Essentially what distinguishes a public sector from a private sector organisation is who owns, and therefore controls it. In the case of the public sector this will be the state; in the private sector individuals. Much of the work carried out by organisations in the public sector has nothing to do with the commercial trading, but is concerned with the provision of public services such as health and social welfare benefits such as pensions. The state does however engage in commercial trading in certain areas. British Rail is a state trading organisation; so to is Her Majesty's Stationery Office (HMSO). Much of the law contained in this book is as applicable to these state organisations as to those trading in the private sector.

A further distinguishing feature is the method used to create public sector organisations. Usually they are created by a specific Act of Parliament, thus British Coal, which is state owned, was created by the Coal Industry Nationalisation Act, 1946. The use of an Act of Parliament to create a private sector organisation is most unusual.

CORPORATE AND UNINCORPORATED BODIES

All business enterprises can be classified into two basic legal forms. They are either unincorporated bodies or corporate bodies. An unincorporated body is either an individual, or more usually a group of individuals, who have joined together to pursue a common business purpose. The body and the individuals who compose it are not separate from each other under the law, even though they may trade under a business name, not using their own names, thus superficially at least making it appear that the business is a separate entity. A corporate body, or corporation, is also made up of a group of individuals who have joined together for a common purpose, but by the process of legal incorporation they have created an artificial legal person which has a separate legal identity from the members who compose it.

The corporation has proved itself to be a vital business form in the evolution of commercial activity in the United Kingdom, for reasons that are explained below. Two basic types of corporation exist, the corporation sole and the corporation aggregate.

Corporations Sole

These consist of a single person and all the successors of that person. The bishops are corporations sole and so is the Crown. The Bishop of Durham is not only an individual but an office, and the office itself continues to exist despite one bishop being replaced by another. This is known as perpetual succession and can be a useful legal device because it can mean, for example, that property held by the office of the Bishop of Durham does not have to be transferred from one holder of the office to the next. Corporations sole are not primarily commercial organisations.

Corporations aggregate

These are by far the most numerous type of corporation, and they consist of a number of people who combine to form or constitute the corporation, such as the elected members of a county or district council or the shareholders of a limited company.

Corporations may be created in the following ways:

(1) by Royal Charter. Charter, or common law corporations, are rarely used today as a means of acquiring corporate status, although many of the early trading organisations such as the Hudson's Bay Company were created in this way. The charter is granted by the Monarch acting under the royal prerogative upon the advice of the Privy Council. Examples of twentieth century charter corporations include the BBC and the more modern universities.

(2) by particular statute. Here an Act of Parliament creates and grants powers to the corporation. Public corporations such as the Independent Broadcasting Authority have been created in this way, and, outside London, the corporate status and powers of all local authorities in England and Wales are contained in the Local Government Act 1972.

(3) by registration under the Companies Act 1985. The 1985 Act recognises two basic forms of registered company, public companies and private companies.

The liability of the members of a company may be limited or in rare cases unlimited. Under s.1(2) a company may be:

(i) limited by shares, where the liability of the company members, the shareholders, is limited to any amount as yet unpaid on their shares; or

(ii) limited by guarantee, where the members' liability is limited to an amount they have guaranteed to contribute in the event of the company being brought to an end i.e. a process known technically as winding up; or

(iii) unlimited, where the members are fully liable for the debts of the company.

At the time of writing there are approximately 6,000 public companies and 816,000 private companies in England and Wales. Unlimited companies can only operate as private ones, and there are around 4,000 of them. They operate primarily as service and investment companies. Although the number of public limited companies is relatively small, they are certainly of great commercial importance. They include the major banks, and multinational organisations such as I.C.I., British Airways and Lloyds Bank. It is usual to find that public companies have begun life as private companies which have become sufficiently successful commercially to warrant 'going public', that is offering their shares to the general public.

The classification of companies registerable under the Companies Act 1985 is contained in Fig. 2.2 below.

Public Limited Companies	Private Companies
limited by shares	limited by shares
limited by guarantee	limited by guarantee
	unlimited

Fig. 2.2 **Classification of registerable companies under the Companies Act 1985**

Certain other statutes allow for incorporation by registration, for example working mens' clubs and organisations such as workers' co-operatives, can incorporate by registration under the Industrial and Provident Society Acts 1965-1975. The latter group, which have grown in number over recent years and now total about 1,000, can also be registered as companies limited by guarantee, or may operate as partnerships (see later).

Statutory registration was first introduced under the Companies Act 1844, to provide a method of forming corporations which was less expensive and cumbersome than obtaining a charter or sponsoring legislation through Parliament. The system of statutory registration proved immediately popular and helped to provide the capital which the growth of business activity at that time urgently needed. Capital was provided by investors attracted not only by the investment prospects offered by newly formed registered companies but also by the financial protection available through limited liability. The registered company remains just as popular with investors today, and has been further stimulated by the privatisation programme of the Thatcher Government, under which many previously state owned businesses have been sold off to the public for example Jaguar Cars, British Telecom and British Airways.

Later we will consider in more detail the legal implications of trading as a corporate body, but before so doing, it is helpful to look first at business organisations which function as unincorporated bodies, and examine their legal status. As we shall see, the legal status of a business is a matter of considerable importance to its members, not least because it is largely responsible for describing what their rights and responsibilities are, and hence their relationship to the organisation and to each other.

The two types of unincorporated businesses we need to consider are the sole trader and the partnership.

SOLE TRADERS

The term 'sole trader' is an expression used to describe an individual who is self employed, operating a business alone and who has sole responsibility for its management. In practice, of course, sole traders rarely work alone and will usually employ staff to assist them in the operation of the business. There are no specific legal formalities relating to the creation of such a business. However operating as a sole trader will necessarily involve the owner in buying and selling, employing staff and acquiring business premises. As an employer, a sole trader is subject to the law relating to employment contained in the common law, (that is law defined by the courts) and numerous statutes, (law determined by Parliament), the most important of which is the Employment Protection (Consolidation) Act 1978 (as amended). In addition, as a supplier of goods or services, a sole trader must comply with the law relating to consumer protection, for example the Sale of Goods Act 1979, the Trade Descriptions Act 1972 and the Supply of Goods and Services Act 1982. Some types of business enterprise must also acquire a licence to permit them to operate. For example a publican requires a licence to sell intoxicating drinks and a turf accountant a betting and gaming licence.

A sole trader's business will normally be financed by the owner himself, which means that the opportunities for raising business capital are necessarily limited. Whilst the sole owner is entitled to all the profits of the business, he has unlimited liability in relation to its losses and so must bear them personally. The sole trader form of business is therefore most suitable for an individual who wishes to retain absolute control of the sort of business enterprise which requires only a modest amount of financial investment. Obvious examples include retail shops and service trades such as plumbing, hairdressing and farming. Collectively, sole traders provide a valuable service to the community by making a wide range of goods and services available in a personal way, meeting needs which might otherwise be unfulfilled.

The responsibility for decision making in such a business rests with the owner, and there is no individual or group to which he is made directly accountable. This is very attractive to those who wish to 'be their own boss'. Of course there are groups who will be affected by the owner's actions such as the customers or clients, the creditors to whom the business owes money, and especially the employees of the business. Such groups have a valid interest in the decisions made by the sole trader and may ultimately seek to hold him accountable for his actions. For instance an employee may complain that employment rights have been infringed, or a customer that consumer rights have been abused. Accountability is perhaps at its most extreme level in the event of the sole trader becoming insolvent.

Over recent years there has been a substantial increase in the number of one-man businesses being established and this trend has been encouraged by the government by giving grants and tax advantages to small businesses. The present climate of unemployment has resulted in large numbers of skilled and unskilled workers losing their jobs and many receive lump sum payments as compensation. There is evidence that increasing numbers of such individuals have been willing to use their redundancy payments as initial capital to set up a business in which they will be their own employer.

PARTNERSHIPS

An alternative form of unincorporated business organisation is a partnership. Partnerships are commonly referred to as 'firms'. The Partnership Act 1980 states under s.4 that: "Persons who have entered into a partnership with one another for the purposes of this Act called collectively 'a firm', and the name under which their business is carried on is called the firm-name". There are no detailed legal formalities required when individuals agree to operate a business together and thus form a partnership, and the advantages to a business enterprise of forming a partnership are somewhat similar to those enjoyed by the sole trader. The partners are capable of managing their own firm as they see fit, of sharing the profits and being able to deal directly with their customers or clients.

The partnership provides the compromise of allowing an extension of skill and expertise and the possible influx of additional capital by the introduction of extra partners. This extra potential for capital allows many partnerships to grow to become substantial business enterprises.

Although it has always tended to be overshadowed by the limited company, the partnership remains a significant form of business organisation in the United Kingdom, and is the choice of many people either setting up a new business or modifying an existing one. There are in fact over two million businesses operated either as partnerships or under sole trader arrangements, a clear indication of their popularity as a business form.

An agreement between two or more persons to form a partnership will constitute a contract but there is no legal requirement as to its specific form. It may be oral, in writing, contained in a deed, or even implied by the law from the surrounding circumstances. The Partnership Act 1890, which contains most of the legal rules relating to partnerships, defines a partnership under s.1 simply as the "relation which subsists between persons carrying on business in common with a view of profit". It follows from this definition that it is quite possible for a business to be run as a joint venture without the participants ever being aware that their business is in law a partnership. Whilst this may be of no consequence to them for as long as they are able to work together in harmony, in the event of a dispute it is important to them to ascertain whether their relationship constitutes a partnership. If it does the provisions of the 1890 Act will apply, and as we shall see the effect of this statute on the partnership business in terms of the rights and obligations it lays down is substantial.

The main risk in operating a business as a firm is that if the business should get into financial difficulties, the liability of the partners is not limited in any way. The individual members are liable to the extent of their personal wealth to pay off partnership debts.

Partnership formalities

As noted earlier, a partnership agreement can be created in many ways. The 1890 Act lays down no formalities. It is of course commercially desirable, and is common practice for partners to execute a deed of partnership, in which they provide for matters such as the capital contribution required from each member of the firm, and how profits and losses are to be divided. If the partners do not agree such details then the rights and duties laid down under the Act will apply to the partnership.

By s.716 Companies Act 1985, a partnership cannot validly consist of more than twenty members. An exception is made however for certain professions, such as accountants and solicitors, who are prevented by statute from practicing as limited companies. No restriction is placed upon the size of such firms. As a result some of the larger firms now have in excess of a hundred partners.

The partners may choose any name they please for the firm provided it is not similar to an existing name and therefore not likely to mislead others. Also, there is a legal restriction that the last name must not be the word "limited" or any abbreviation of it, for this would indicate that the organisation is a company having limited liability. The words "and Co" at the end of the partnership name refer to the fact that there are partners in the firm whose names do not appear in the firm name. Under the Business Names Act 1985 when a firm carries on business using a trading name which does not consist of the surnames of all the partners then their names must appear on their business stationery, and their true names and addresses must be prominently displayed at their business premises in a place to which the public have access. Non-compliance with these statutory provisions as to size and name is a criminal offence.

The definition of 'partnership'

It will be recalled that the definition of a partnership under s.1 requires there to be

(i) a business,

(ii) carried on in common by its members,

(iii) with a view to making a profit.

Under the Act 'business' includes every trade, occupation or profession. Although business is a broad term it does seem that it involves the carrying on of some form of commercial activity. This may be for a single purpose.

> In *Spicer (Keith) Ltd. v. Mansell* (1970), the Court of Appeal held that two persons who were working together for the purpose of forming a limited company, and had opened a bank account and ordered goods in this connection were not in partnership prior to the incorporation of the company (which in fact was never formed). The reason was that at that time, they were preparing for business, rather than operating an existing one.

Further examples of how the courts have approached the question of determining a business are provided by the following two cases. They in fact involve individuals rather than firms, but they provide a useful illustration of the thin line that often exists between a mere hobby and a business.

> In *Eiman v. London Borough of Waltham Forest (1982)*, the issue was whether the defendant had been rightly convicted in the Crown Court of the offence of making a demand for unsolicited goods "in the course of a trade or business", contrary to the Unsolicited Goods and Services Act 1971. As a full time employee of the local authority the accused had, as a hobby, composed and published a book of verse. He had then sent out copies of the book to local libraries and made a demand for payment. The High Court held that the Crown Court was entitled to convict the defendant as what had started as a hobby, had become a 'business' as defined by the Act and therefore the Unsolicited Goods and Services Act did apply. The court found it possible to reach such a conclusion despite the fact that this was an isolated incident without any intention to make a profit.
>
> A further example is provided by the decision in *Blakemore v. Bellamy (1983)*. Here the question was whether the accused's spare time activity of buying and selling motor cars through advertisements, contravened the Fair Trading Act 1973, and the Business Advertisements

(Disclosure) Order 1977. This is because in the course of a business it is an offence to "advertise goods for sale" without making it clear that the goods were sold in the course of a business. Offences under the Trade Descriptions Act, 1968 were also alleged which involved applying false trade descriptions to two of the vehicles "in the course of a business". Despite the number of transactions involved, eight in all, the High Court agreed with the Magistrates' finding that the defendant's activity was merely a hobby rather than a business. Accordingly the statutory provisions had not been infringed, for the sales were merely private bargains. This was despite the fact that the defendant's objective in making the sales was to achieve gain or reward and as a seller he had clearly demonstrated skill and expertise in the business of buying and selling cars.

The business must be a joint venture, which implies mutual rights and obligations existing between the members of it. There may still be a joint venture even though one (or more) of its members is a 'sleeping partner' who does not take an active part in the management of the business but simply contributes capital.

There must be a profit motive underlying the business. It will be a question of fact whether the partners aim to make a profit.

Help in determining when a business may be treated as a partnership is provided by s.2. It states that where a person receives a share in the profits of a business, this will be prima facie evidence that he is a partner, although the presumption can be shifted by other conflicting evidence. The section goes on to state a list of situations which do not, of themselves, make a person a partner, namely where a person:

(i) receives a debt or other liquidated amount out of the profits of a business, whether or not by instalments;

(ii) being a servant or agent is paid out of a share of the profits of the business;

(iii) being the widow or child of a deceased partner receives an annuity (an annual set payment) out of a portion of the profits of the business in which the deceased was a partner;

(iv) lends money to a person engaged or about to engage in business, on a written contract signed by, or on behalf of the parties to it that the lender shall be repaid either at a rate of interest varying with the profits, or as a share of the profits;

(v) receives by way of annuity or otherwise a portion of the profits of a business in consideration of the sale by the person of the goodwill of the business.

In *Pratt v. Strick (1932)* a situation of the kind described in (v) above occurred. A doctor sold his medical practice together with its goodwill, on terms that for the following three months he would remain living at the practice, introducing patients, and sharing profits and losses equally with the purchaser. It was held that the practice was the purchaser's as soon as he bought it.

Two further situations are specified by s.2 which it indicates do not automatically give rise to a partnership. Firstly co-ownership of land, even where profits are shared from the use of the land. Secondly the sharing of gross returns even if the people sharing the returns have a common right or interest in the property which is yielding the income. This draws a distinction between returns and profit. A return is the revenue obtained by some business activity, such as the receipts obtained from the sale of a book over a fixed period, whilst the profit is the sum left after deducting costs from revenue. In the example these would include printing and transport costs.

A partner's authority to bind the firm.

There are obvious problems inherent in attempting to reach the sort of joint decisions which are necessary to successfully manage a partnership and it is not uncommon for partners to disagree. There are also risks involved, both in having unlimited liability and in the fact that individual partners may be responsible for the acts and defaults of their co-partners. Each partner is an agent of the co-partners and as such has an agent's power to bind the partnership by his acts undertaken within the ordinary course of the business. It is crucial therefore that each partner has trust and confidence in his co-partners, the relationship being one of the utmost good faith. This is sometimes given its latin name and is known as a relationship of 'uberrimae fidei'. Each partner is therefore under a duty to make a full and frank disclosure to the firm of any matters affecting it that come to the partner's attention.

The power of a partner to bind the other members of the firm by his actions illustrates how important it is that each partner should trust and have confidence in his co-partners, not only in regard to their business ability but also as to their business ethics. In *Helmore v. Smith (1886)* Bacon V-C remarked that, "mutual confidence is the life-blood" of the firm, whilst in *Baird's Case (1870)* James LJ stated:

> "Ordinary partnerships are by the law assumed and presumed to be based upon the mutual trust and confidence of each partner in the skill, knowledge and integrity of every other partner. As between the partners and the outside world (whatever may be their private arrangements between themselves), each partner is the unlimited agent of every other in every matter connected with the partnership business, or which he represents as the partnership business, and not being in its nature beyond the scope of the partnership".

In the course of business, partnerships enter into transactions with other organisations and individuals and inevitably such transactions are negotiated and executed for the partnership by individual partners, rather than by the firm as a whole. It has already been noted that each partner is an agent of his co-partners. "In English law a firm as such has no existence; partners carry on business both as principals and as agents for each other within the scope of the partnership business; the firm-name is a mere expression, not a legal entity", stated Lord Justice Farwell in *Sadler v. Whiteman (1910).*

Under the law of agency, an agent will bind the principal (i.e. the person who has appointed the agent to act) by contracts made within the agent's *actual* and *apparent* authority. If the agent acts within either of these two spheres the contract concluded between the agent and the third party becomes the principal's contract, and hence it is the principal and the third party who become bound to each other. The actual authority of an agent is the express power given by the principal. A firm may for instance expressly resolve in a partnership meeting that each partner shall have the power to employ staff. Actual authority may also arise where the agent's power to make a particular contract or class of contracts can be implied from the conduct of the parties or the circumstances of the case. The apparent, or ostensible authority of an agent is the power which the agent appears to others to hold. Of a partner's apparent authority s.5 Partnership Act, 1890, says:

> "Every partner is an agent of the firm and his other partners for the purpose of the business of the partnership; and the acts of every partner who does any act for the carrying on in the usual way business of the kind carried on by the firm of which he is a member bind the firm and his partners, unless the partner so acting has in fact no authority to act for the firm in the particular matter, and the person with whom he is dealing either knows that he has not authority, or does not know or believe him to be a partner".

Whether a particular contract is one 'carrying on in the usual way business of the kind carried on by the firm' is a question of fact.

> In *Mercantile Credit Co. Ltd v. Garrod (1962)*, the court had to decide what would be considered as an act of a 'like kind' to the business of persons who ran a garage. It was held that the sale of a car to a third party by one of the partners bound the other partners. This was despite an agreement between them that provided for the carrying out of repair work, and the letting of garages, but expressly excluded car sales.

The agency position of a partnership is contained diagramatically in Figs. 2.3 and 2.4 below.

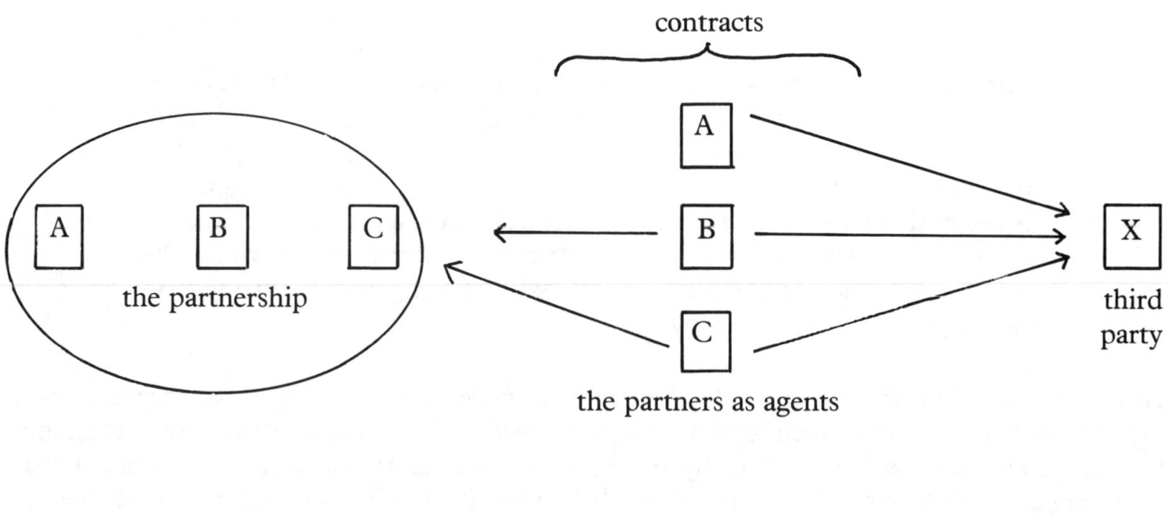

Fig. 2.3 **Ability of each partner to bind the firm**

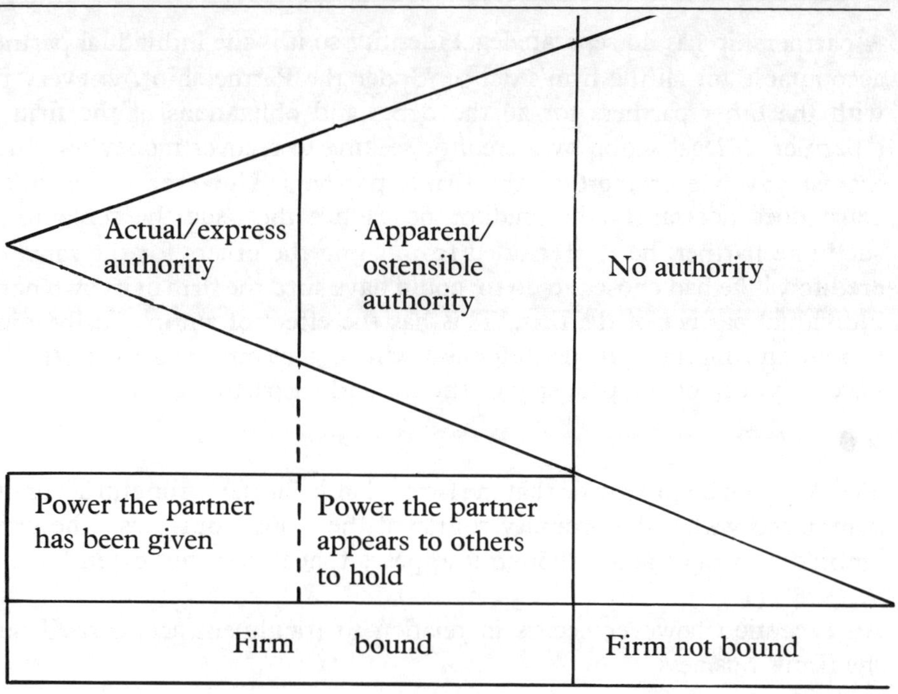

Fig. 2.4 **Capacity of a partner to bind the firm**

Clearly a private exclusion of the powers of an agent is not an effective way to bring the restriction to the notice of an outsider dealing with the agent, and the law recognises this. Thus for example, when a partner has acted as an agent for his firm in the past with a particular third party, and he carries out a further transaction of a similar kind with the third party after the firm has taken away this particular agency power, the third party can nevertheless hold the firm bound unless he knew at the time of contracting of the partner's lack of authority.

The exact scope of an agent's apparent authority under s.5 has been the subject of much litigation, and the following powers will usually fall within the agent's apparent authority:

(a) in the case of all types of partnership the power to:

   (i) sell the goods or personal property of the firm;

   (ii) purchase in the firm's name goods usually or necessarily used in the firm's business;

   (iii) receive payments due to the firm;

   (iv) employ staff to work for the firm.

(b) in the case of a partnership whose business is the buying and selling of goods (i.e. a trading partnership), the following additional powers are within the partner's authority:

   (i) to borrow money for a purpose connected with the business of the firm;

   (ii) to deal with payments to and from the firm.

A partnership has no separate legal identity so it is the individual partners who are ultimately accountable for all the firm's debts. Under the Partnership Act every partner is jointly liable with the other partners for all the debts and obligations of the firm incurred whilst being a partner. A legal action by a creditor seeking to recover money owed to him may be brought against any one or more of the firm's partners. However if the judgment obtained in the court does not satisfy the creditor he cannot then sue the remaining partners for, having sued one partner, he is precluded from suing the others for the same debt. Nevertheless the creditor, if he had chosen to do so, could have sued the firm in its own name rather than suing an individual partner of the firm. This has the effect of automatically joining all the partners in action, and means that the judgment will be met out of assets of the firm as a whole and, if necessary, out of the property of the individual partners.

The Act goes on to provide that the firm is liable for the 'wrongful act or omission of any partner' committed within the ordinary course of the firms's business. The term 'wrongful' certainly embraces tortious acts although it appears that it does not extend to criminal acts.

An exception however occurs in relation to fraudulent acts carried out within the scope of the firm's business.

> In *Hamlyn v. Houston & Co. (1903)*, the defendant firm was run by two partners as a grain merchants. One of the partners bribed the clerk of a rival grain merchant, and obtained information from him which enabled the firm to compete at greater advantage. The Court of Appeal held that both partners were liable for this tortious act. Obtaining information about rivals was within the general scope of the partner's authority, and therefore it did not matter that the method used to obtain it was unlawful. In the words of Collins, M.R.
>
> > "It is too well established by the authorities to be now disputed that a principal may be liable for the fraud or other illegal act committed by his agent within the general scope of the authority given to him, and even the fact that the act of the agent is criminal does not necessarily take it out of the scope of his authority".

It is no defence for a firm to show that it did not benefit from the unlawful act of its agent.

> The House of Lords in *Lloyd v. Grace, Smith & Co.* (1912) held a solicitor's firm liable for the fraud of its managing clerk who induced one of the firm's clients to transfer certain properties into his name. In advising the client the clerk was acting within the scope of his authority, and that alone made the firm liable for his acts.

Although the Act does not apply to criminal matters two points should be noted. Firstly, there may be occasions when one partner may be held *vicariously liable* for an offence committed by another (see Chapter 7). Secondly, a partner may be a party to an offence committed by another simply because it is in the nature of that partnership that they work together.

> In *Parsons v. Barnes* (1973) where two partners worked together in a roof-repairing business, one of them was convicted of an offence under the Trade Descriptions Act 1968, by being present when his co-partner made a false statement to a customer.

If a partner acting within the scope of his apparent authority receives and misapplies the property of a third person while it is in the firm's custody the firm is liable to meet the third person's loss. Similarly when the firm has received property of a third person in the course of its business, and the property has been misapplied by a partner while in the firm's custody, it must make good the loss. The liability of partners for misapplications of property, or wrongs of the firm, is stated by the Act to be joint and several. This means that if a judgment is obtained by a plaintiff against one partner, this does not operate as bar to bringing a further action against all or any of the others if the judgment remains unsatisfied. Where liability is merely joint this is not possible.

> In *Plumer v. Gregory* (1874) two of the partners in a firm consisting of three solicitors accepted on the firm's behalf and subsequently misappropriated money entrusted to them by the plaintiff, a client of the firm. The third member of the firm was unaware of these events, which only came to light after the other partners had died. The plaintiff's action against the remaining partner succeeded, for the firm was liable to make good the loss, and liability of the members was joint and several.

Changes in membership

The membership of a firm will normally alter from time to time. It may wish to expand its business by bringing in new partners to provide the benefit of additional capital or fresh expertise. Existing partners may leave the partnership to join a new business, or to retire. A changing membership poses the question of the extent to which incoming and outgoing partners are responsible for the debts and liabilities of the firm. Although partners are responsible for any matters arising during their membership of the firm, incoming partners are not liable for the debts incurred before they joined, nor outgoing partners for those incurred after they leave, provided the retiring partner advertises the fact that he is no longer a member of the firm. This involves sending notice to all customers of the firm while that person was a partner, and advertising the retirement in a publication known as the 'London Gazette'. If this is not done a person dealing with the firm after a change in its membership can treat all apparent members of the old firm as still being members of the firm. With regard to existing liabilities the partner may be discharged from them when he retires through the agreement of the new firm and the creditors.

Rights and duties of the partners

Ideally the partnership relationship should be regulated by a comprehensive partnership agreement. Although the provisions of the Partnership Act will apply when the parties are in dispute as to the nature of their duties and are unable to reach agreement amongst themselves, in a business enterprise of this sort, where a member's entire wealth lies at stake, it is clearly of great value to execute a detailed agreement setting out in precise form the powers and responsibilities of the members. For instance it would be prudent for the agreement to provide grounds for the removal of partners, since the Act makes no such provision. Because the members of the firm have the freedom to make their own agreement, without the statutory controls imposed upon other forms of business organisation, such as the registered company, the partnership stands out as a most flexible form of organisation.

The duties that the Act sets out are based upon a single foundation of fundamental importance to all partnerships, namely that the relationship between the parties is of the utmost good faith.

> This principle can be seen in *Law v. Law* (1905). A partner sold his share in the business to another partner for £21,000, but the purchasing partner failed to disclose to his co-partner certain facts about the partnership assets, of which he alone was aware. When the vendor realised that he had sold his share at below its true value he sought to have the sale

> set aside. The Court of Appeal held that in such circumstances the sale was voidable, and could be set aside.

A partner is under a duty to his co-partners to render true accounts and full information of all things affecting the partnership. Personal benefits can only be retained with the consent of the other partners.

> In *Bentley v. Craven* (1853), one of the partners in a firm of sugar refiners, who acted as the firm's buyer, was able to purchase a large quantity of sugar at below market price. He resold it to the firm at the true market price. His co-partners were unaware that he was selling on his own account. When they discovered this they sued him for the profit he had made, and were held to be entitled to it. It was a 'secret profit' and belonged to the firm.

A partner is under a duty not to compete with his firm by carrying on another business of the same nature unless the other partners have consented. If a partner is in breach of this duty he must account to the firm for all the profits made and pay them over. If the partnership agreement prohibits the carrying on of a competing business, the court may grant an injuction to stop a partner who disregards the limitation.

Further rights and duties set out in the Act state that, in the absence of a contrary agreement:-

(i) all partners are entitled to take part in the management of the partnership business;

(ii) any differences arising as to ordinary matters connected with the partnership business are to be decided by a majority of the partners, but no change can be made in the nature of the partnership business without the consent of all the partners;

(iii) no person may be introduced as a partner without the consent of all existing partners;

(iv) all partners are entitled to share equally in the profits of the business irrespective of the amount of time they have given to it, and must contribute equally towards any losses. The Act does not require the firm to keep books of account, although this will normally be provided for in the partnership agreement, together with specific reference to the proportions of the profits each partner is entitled to. If however there are partnership books they have to be kept at the principal place of business, where every partner is entitled to have access to them for the purpose of inspection and copying;

(v) if a partner makes a payment or advance beyond the agreed capital contribution he is entitled to interest at 5% p.a.;

(vi) a partner is not entitled to payment of interest on his capital until profits have been ascertained;

(vii) the firm must indemnify a partner in respect of payments made and personal liabilities incurred in the ordinary and proper conduct of the business of the firm, or in or about anything necessarily done for the preservation of the business or property of the firm (e.g. paying an insurance premium);

(viii) a partner is not entitled to remuneration for acting in the partnership business.

In cases where the firm consists of *active* and *sleeping* partners the partnership agreement will often provide that as well as taking a share of the profits the active partners shall be entitled to the payment of a salary.

If any of the terms of the partnership agreement are broken, damages will be available as a remedy, and where appropriate an injunction may be granted.

Partnership property

It can be of importance, particularly to the partners themselves, to establish which assets used by the partnership actually belong to the firm itself, rather than to an individual partner. Mere use of property for partnership purposes does not automatically transfer ownership in it to the business.

In *Miles v. Clarke* (1953) the defendant started up a photography business which involved him in acquiring a lease and photographic equipment. After trading unsuccessfully he was joined by the plaintiff, a free-lance photographer, who brought into the firm his business connection which was of considerable value. The partners traded profitably for some time, on the basis of equal profit sharing. Later, as a result of personal difficulties, it became necessary to wind up the firm. The plaintiff claimed a share in all the assets of the business. The Court held that the assets of the business, other than the stock-in-trade which had become partnership property, belonged to the particular partner who had brought them in.

The Act provides that all property and rights and interests in property originally brought into the partnership or subsequently acquired by purchase or otherwise on account of the firm, must be held and applied by the partners exclusively for the purposes of the partnership and in accordance with the partnership agreement. Such property is called 'partnership property' and will normally be jointly owned by the partners. Because a partner is a co-owner of partnership property, rather than a sole owner of any particular part of the partnership's assets, he may be guilty of theft of partnership property if it can be established that his intention was to permanently deprive the other partners of their share.

Under the Act property bought with money belonging to the firm is deemed to have been bought on account of the firm, unless a contrary intention appears. There is nothing to prevent an individual partner taking out of the partnership a particular asset, provided the co-partners' consent is obtained. The asset may be purchased by the partner either by making payment, or by accepting a reduction in his capital. However if at the time of the transaction the firm is insolvent then the removal of the asset will not affect the interests of the firm's creditors, for they can require the asset to be returned.

Limited partnerships

Unlike the liability of members of a limited company for its debts, the liability of partners for partnership debts is unlimited. If the partnership assets are insufficient to meet them, the personal property of the partners can be legitimately realised by the firm's creditors to meet the liability. It is however possible to trade using a business organisation known as a limited partnership, which is a cross between the ordinary partnerships we have considered so far, and the limited companies which are examined later in the chapter.

Limited partnerships are permitted under the Limited Partnerships Act 1907 and must consist of:

(a) one or more persons called general partners, who are liable for all the debts and obligations of the firm in the ordinary way; and

(b) one or more persons, called limited partners, who have contributed at the time of entering into the partnership a sum or sums as capital or property of a stated value who are not liable for the debts or obligations of the firm beyond the amount contributed.

The Act allows a limited partner to be a *body corporate*. Once the limited partner has made the capital contribution he cannot withdraw any part of it, either directly or indirectly, without becoming liable for the firm's debts and liabilities up to the amount withdrawn.

Limited partnerships must be registered with the Registrar of Companies. This is achieved by sending to the Registrar a statement signed by the partners containing details of the firm's name, the general nature of its business, the principal place of business, the full name of each partner, the date of commencement and length of term of the partnership (if any), a statement that the partnership is limited, and particulars of each limited partner and the amount contributed by each whether in cash or otherwise. The registered statement is available for public inspection. If the partnership fails to register the limited partner becomes fully liable as a general partner. It will be appreciated that the principal difference between a limited partnership and a general partnership lies in the accountability of the partners of these respective organisations for the debts and liabilities of the firm. In a general partnership each partner has an unlimited liability for the debts and other liabilities of the firm, whereas in a limited partnership there must by definition be at least one member who, like a shareholder in a limited company, has a fixed or limited liability. Unlike a shareholder, however, the limited partner has no *right* to take part in the management of the organisation; a partner who does so becomes fully responsible for all liabilities incurred by the firm while acting as its manager. Nor does the limited partner have power to bind the firm. The limited partner is however granted the right to inspect the firm's books.

The limited partnership has been an unsuccessful rival to the private limited company largely, it would seem because of its non-corporate status. The total number of partnerships registered in this way numbers approximately 4,000 whereas there are almost $^3/_4$ million private limited companies.

REGISTERED COMPANIES

As we have already seen the registered company limited by shares is a corporate body, an artificial person recognised by the law, which has an identity separate and distinct from the members which compose it. The members of such an organisation are referred to as its shareholders. The limited company is the most common type of business enterprise operated as a corporation, although there were of course many other types of corporation in existence. These are considered earlier in the chapter.

There are many thousands of registered limited companies in this country and between them they employ the majority of the nation's workforce and comprise about two thirds of the income made by the private sector. Companies can be formed which have only two members. They can also develop into the massive multi-national UK registered enterprises which have thousands of shareholders. Such is the diversity of these organisations that it is difficult to generalise on their structure and behaviour but most have been formed with the expectation of future expansion financed by the raising of capital through the issue of shares. As separate legal entities they also give the owners the protection of limited liability and it is this feature more than any other that has contributed to their popularity. Another appealing feature is that ownership can be divorced from management, thus an investor can stake capital in a company without having to be involved in the actual running of it whilst maintaining control over the managers by means of accountability in the general meeting.

Limited liability means that in the event of the company facing financial difficulty the shareholders' legal liability to contribute to the payment of debts is limited to the amount, if any, unpaid on their shares. For instance, if an individual purchases 20 £1 shares in a company and pays 25p on each share (these are called partly paid shares) he is only liable to contribute the amount of the share value remaining unpaid, in this case 20 × 75p, a total of £15.

Companies can thus expand and diversify by raising additional capital when it is needed through the issue of more shares, and hence large scale commercial organisations have evolved with thousands of shareholders holding between them millions of shares. The growth of this form of business enterprise and the recognition of the company as a separate legal entity has however posed many problems and led to many abuses. The law has recognised these difficulties. Various Companies Acts, now consolidated in the Companies Act 1985, have attempted to regulate corporate behaviour, bearing in mind not only the interest of the shareholders themselves but also the interests of outsiders who trade with the companies.

CORPORATE PERSONALITY

As we have seen the limited company is an artificial legal person, and has some although not all the powers and responsibilities of a natural person. It is capable therefore of owning property, entering into contracts such as trading contracts and contracts of employment, and of suing or being sued in its own name. But its artificial nature imposes some obvious limitations upon its legal capacity. It cannot generally be held liable for criminal acts, since most crimes involve proving a mental element such as intention or recklessness and a corporation has as such no mind. Nevertheless there may occur circumstances in which the collective intention of the Board of Directors can be regarded as expressing the will of the corporation. Lord Denning has spoken of the company as having human body, the employees being the hands that carry out its work while "others are directors and managers who represent the directing mind and will of the company and control what it does".

Since the membership of a company is distinct from the corporate body this means that the company shareholders are separate from the company which has a legal personality of its own. Changes in its membership, including the death or bankruptcy of members will have no effect upon the company, which may have an almost perpetual life span if there remain investors willing to become or to remain members of it.

> The separation of a company from its members was confirmed in the famous case of *Salomon v. Salomon & Co. (1897)*. The plaintiff sold his leather business to the defendant company which he had formed himself, and received in return the majority of the company's shares and a number of debentures. (These are a form of loan capital which entitle the holder to re-payment before other ordinary creditors in the event of a company being liquidated). Eventually the company went into liquidation owing £8,000 to ordinary creditors and having only £6,000 worth of assets. The plaintiff claimed that as a debenture holder with £10,000 worth of debentures he was a secured creditor and entitled to repayment before the ordinary unsecured creditors. The unsecured creditors did not agree. The Court held that despite the fact that following the company's formation, Salomon had continued to run the business in the same manner and with the same control as he had done when it was unincorporated, the company formed was a separate person from Salomon himself. When the company was liquidated, therefore, Salomon, like any other debenture

holder, was a secured creditor and entitled to repayment before ordinary creditors. The court thus upheld the principle that a company has a separate legal existence from its membership even where one individual holds the majority of shares and effectively runs the company as his own.

A company is also the owner of its own property in which its members have no legal interest, although clearly they have a financial interest.

In *Macaura v. Northern Assurance Co. Ltd (1925)* it was held that a majority shareholder has no insurable interest in the company's property. A fire insurance policy over the company's timber estate was therefore invalid as it has been issued in the plaintiff shareholder's name and not the company's name.

Both the Courts and Parliament have accepted that situations may arise in which it is right and proper to prevent the members from escaping liability by hiding behind the company, and so there are cases where the "corporate veil", as it is called, can be lifted. The main thinking behind such exceptions has been to give effect to the economic reality of the particular case.

So for example if a company is wound up and the court is satisfied that the directors have carried on the business with an intention to defraud the creditors, they may be made personally liable for all the company's debts. This would cover trading and incurring debts, where they knew that there was no reasonable prospect that the creditors would be paid.

In rare cases, the courts will disregard the separate legal personality of a company because it was formed or used to facilitate the evasion of legal obligations. This is sometimes referred to as 'lifting the veil of incorporation', meaning that the court is able to look behind the corporate, formal identity of the organisation to the individual ones which make it up. Clearly this is a very significant step, since it is effectively denying the protection which the members have sought to obtain by incorporation.

In *Gilford Motor Co. Ltd v. Horne (1933)*, the defendant had been employed by the plaintiff motor company and had entered into a valid agreement not to solicit the plaintiff's customers or to compete with it for a certain time after leaving the company's employment. Shortly after leaving the employment of the motor company, the defendant formed a new company to carry on a similar business to that of his former employers and sent out circulars to the customers he had previously dealt with while working for the motor company. In an action to enforce the restraint clause against the new company the court held that as the defendant in fact controlled the new company, its formation was a mere 'cloak or sham' to enable him to break the restraint clause. Accordingly an injunction was granted against the defendant and against the company he had formed, to enforce the restraint clause.

Similarly in *Jones v. Lipman (1962)*, the defendant agreed to sell land to the plaintiff and then decided not to complete the sale. To avoid the possibility of an order of specific performance to enforce the sale the defendant bought a company, by purchasing a majority shareholding in an existing company to which he then sold the land. The plaintiff applied to the court for an order against the defendant and the company to enforce the sale. It was held that the formation of the company was a mere sham to avoid a contract of sale, and specific performance was ordered against the vendor and company.

The courts are also prepared to lift the veil in order to discover the relationship within groups of companies. It is a common commercial practice for one company to acquire shares in another, often holding sufficient shares to give it total control over the other. In these circumstances the controlling company is referred to as a holding company, and the other company its subsidiary. In appropriate cases a holding company can be regarded as an agent of its subsidiary, although it is more usual to find the subsidiary acting as an agent for the holding company.

> In *D.H.N. Food Distributors Ltd v. Tower Hamlets L.B.C. (1976)*, an arrangement under which two subsidiaries of the holding company were wholly owned by it and had no separate business operations from it, was held by the court to constitute a single corporate body rather than three separate ones.

> In: *Re Bugle Press Ltd. (1961)* two of the three shareholders in an existing company, formed a new company which then made a 'take-over bid' for the shares of the first company. Not surprisingly the two shareholders who had formed the new company accepted the bid. The third did not. However since he only held $^1/_{10}$ of the total shareholding, under what is now s. 428 Companies Act 1985, the new company was able to compulsorily acquire the shares. The Court of Appeal however held that this represented an abuse of the section. The minority shareholder was in effect being evicted from the company. The veil of the new company was lifted and, in the words of Harman L.J.: this revealed a "hollow sham", for it was "nothing but a little hut built round" the majority shareholders. Their action was unsuccessful.

> In *Firestone Tyre & Rubber Co. Ltd v. Llewellin (Inspector of Taxes) (1957)* the appellant company was a subsidiary of an American company which made and sold branded tyres and had a world-wide organisation. The British subsidiary manufactured and sold tyres in Europe. The House of Lords held that the appellant company was in fact not trading on its own behalf but as agent of the parent company and the parent company was consequently liable to pay United Kingdom income tax.

In some cases the courts have disregarded the separate legal personality of a company and have in the public interest investigated the personal qualities of the shareholders. It is in the public interest that an enemy alien is unable to sue in British courts.

> In *Daimler Co. Ltd v. Continental Tyre and Rubber Co. (Gt. Britain) Ltd (1916)* the tyre company, which was registered in England, and had its registered office there, sued Daimler for debts incurred before the war with Germany had been declared. Daimler claimed that as all of the membership of the tyre company except one were German nationals and the directors were German nationals resident in Germany the claim should be struck out because to pay the debt would be to trade with the enemy.

> The House of Lords held that although the nationality of a company is normally decided by where it is incorporated, in some cases the court has power to consider who was in control of the company's business and assets in order that it might determine its status. Here, those in control of the company were enemy aliens and the action was struck out.

In addition there are a number of provisions contained in the Companies Act 1985 which have the effect of lifting the veil. They include the following:

(i) a fall in the membership of a company to below 2, under s. 24. In these circumstances the sole shareholder become personally liable for the company's affairs. Note that to be a member of a company it is only necessary to hold a single share.

(ii) Under s. 349(4) if an officer of a company or any person on its behalf:

(a) uses the company seal and the company name is not engraved on it;

(b) issues or authorises the issue of a business letter or signs a negotiable instrument and the company name is not mentioned;

(c) issues or authorises the issue of any invoice, receipt or letter of credit of the company and again the company name is not mentioned;

that person shall be *personally* liable for debts incurred unless they are paid by the company.

In *Penrose v. Martyr* (1858) a bill of exchange was drawn up with the word 'limited' omitted after the company's name and the company secretary who had signed the bill on the company's behalf was held to be personally liable for it.

(iii) Under powers granted to the Department of Trade and Industry to investigate the affairs of any company within the same group as one primarily under investigation by a DTI Inspector s. 442(1) provides that where there appears to be good reason to do so, the Department may appoint inspectors to investigate and report on the membership of any company in order to determine the true persons financially interested in its success or failure, or able to control or materially influence its policy.

(iv) Under s. 214 Insolvency Act 1986, which provides that a director guilty of wrongful trading may be required by the court to make such a contribution to the assets of the company as the court considers appropriate in the circumstances. The idea underlying this provision is that a director whose company goes into liquidation through insolvency will be responsible to make a contribution as indicated above, if he is unable to satisfy the court that when he became aware or should have been aware that the company could not avoid insolvency, he failed to take appropriate steps to minimise the potential loss to the company's creditors. Insolvency is simply a situation in which the company's assets are insufficient to meet its liabilities.

Contributions may also be required under s.213 Insolvency Act 1986 in cases of fraudulent trading. If, when a company is wound up, the court is satisfied that its business has been carried on with intent to defraud its creditors or the creditors of another person, or for any fraudulent purpose, the court may declare that any persons who were knowingly parties to carrying on its business in that way shall be personally liable for all the company's debts and liabilities. Under this provision therefore, personal liability may be imposed on any persons responsible for managing the company's business who have been guilty of dishonesty. Certainly, if a company carries on business and incurs debts when the directors are aware that there is no reasonable prospect of the creditors ever receiving payment, then it is a proper inference that the company is carrying on business with intent to defraud.

To be liable under the section a person must have acted positively in carrying on the business fraudulently.

In *Re: Gerald Cooper Chemicals Ltd (1978)* the court held that a creditor who accepts money from the company knowing it has been procured by carrying on business with the intent to defraud other creditors by the act of paying him, will be liable under s. 213. Templeman, J. stated "A man who warms himself with the fire of fraud cannot complain if he is singed".

CLASSIFICATION OF COMPANIES

Under s. 1 the Companies Act 1985, the two main categories of company are the public limited company and the private limited company. The main distinction between the two categories is that a public company has the authority to place advertisements which invite the public to subscribe for shares which can then be freely bought and sold whenever the shareholder wishes. A private company cannot advertise in this way and will also normally restrict the transfer of the shares by requiring the directors' consent to be given before a sale to an outsider can take place, or a further offer of the sale of shares to existing shareholders can happen. To register as a public limited company, the corporation's public documents must state that it is a public limited company, the company must have a minimum share capital of £50,000 of which one quarter is fully paid up before the company commences trading, and the company name must end with the words "public limited company" or "p.l.c." It is possible for a private company to re-register as public and vice versa under the 1985 Act.

The nominal share capital is the amount that the company is legally authorised to raise by the issue of shares, the paid-up share capital is the amount the company has received from the shares it has issued, and the uncalled capital is the amount remaining unpaid by shareholders for the shares they hold; e.g. a company may issue £1 shares but require those to whom they are allotted to pay only 50p per share for the present. Any registered company not satisfying the above requirements will be a private company and, unlike a PLC, will be unable to offer its shares for sale to the public.

Public Limited companies	*Private companies*
A company whose a) memorandum states that the company is a public company b) authorised share capital is £50,000 with at least one-quarter paid up.	A company that is not registered as a public company and cannot invite the public to invest.

Fig 2.5 **Classification of public and private limited companies**

FORMATION OF A REGISTERED COMPANY

A company is incorporated and so comes into being when the Registrar of Companies issues a document called the Certificate of Incorporation. This certificate is issued following an application by the persons who wish to form the company. They are known as the company's promoters. Two of the main documents which must be included in the application are the memorandum of association and the articles of association.

The Memorandum of Association

The memordandum of association, together with the articles of association set out the constitution of a registered company, is one of a group of documents to be sent to the Registrar of Companies prior to incorporation. A memorandum is required by the Companies Act 1985 which specifies that the memorandum must include the following matters:-

(i) the name of the company with "limited" as the last word in the case of a private company, or "public limited company" in the case of a public company;

(ii) the situation of the registered office identifying whether the company is situated in England or Scotland;

(iii) the objects of the company;

(iv) the liability of the members;

(v) the nominal capital of the company and its division into numbers of shares and denominations.

The Registrar of Companies maintains a file for all registered companies, which is open to public inspection on payment of a fee. The file for each company includes the company memorandum. The contents of the memorandum are of importance to the members of the company itself (the shareholders), and especially to those who deal with the company commercially. The indication that the company is a corporate body shown by the inclusion of the word "limited", serves as a warning to outsiders that in the event of the company being unable to meet its financial liabilities at any time, its shareholders, as we have previously seen, can only be called upon to make good any loss, up to the value which remains unpaid to the company on their shares. Once however the shares have been fully paid the shareholders' financial liability ceases.

Stating the country in which the company is situated determines whether it is an English or Scottish company. Usually a Notice of Situation of Registered Office, giving the company's full address is sent to the Registrar together with the Memorandum. It must, in any event, be sent to him within fourteen days of incorporation of the company. The registered office is important since documents must be effectively served on the company by posting or delivering them to this address. Thus a writ (a document used to commence legal proceedings) served on the company will be effectively served if delivered to the registered office.

The objects clause sets the contractual limits within which the company can validly operate. Contracts falling outside the scope of the objects clause are not binding on the company, for they are beyond its powers (known as ultra vires). The need to state the company's objects may be seen as a protection to shareholders by giving them some reassurance as to the ways in which their capital may be spent. A company, can, however, resolve to alter its objects, and in any event it is usual to draft the objects clause very widely. Furthermore a transaction decided upon by all the directors can bind the company even though the transaction is ultra vires, provided the other party to the transaction is not aware of this and is acting in good faith. This matter is considered in more details below.

The liability clause is a formality which merely states the nature of the shareholders' liability.

The capital clause sets out the amount of capital the company is authorised to raise by the issue of shares, and the way in which the shares are to be divided. This amount can be raised by the agreement of the shareholders without difficulty, although a reduction in the share capital, whilst possible, is more of a problem to achieve.

The subscribers for the shares in the memorandum will often be appointed as directors. As the statutory minimum membership of a company is two, two subscribers to the memorandum will suffice to form the company.

COMPANY NAME

Generally a company is free to choose the name it wishes to adopt, although the word 'limited' for a private company or 'plc' for a public company must be inserted at the end of the company name. This is provided for by s.26 Companies Act 1985. The section also provides that the name cannot be the same as one already held on the index of company names kept by the registrar. Nor can a name be used which would in the opinion of the Secretary of State constitute a criminal offence or be offensive.

It is a tort for one person to represent his business as that of another and thereby obtain profit from that other's business goodwill. In such circumstances the innocent business could maintain the tort action of 'passing off' against the business guilty of the deception and recover damages and/or an injunction to prevent future trading as a remedy.

> In *Ewing v. Buttercup Margarine Co. Ltd* (1917) the plaintiff, who carried on business using the name Buttercup Dairy Co. obtained an injunction against the defendant company on the grounds that the public might be confused as to the identify of the two organisations.

It makes no difference whether the name is real or invented.

> In *Exxon Corporation v. Exxon Insurance Consultants International Ltd* (1981) the plaintiffs obtained an injunction to prevent the defendants from passing off its goods as the defendant's by the use of the word 'Exxon'. The plaintiffs, formerly the Esso Company, had invented the word Exxon as a replacement name. They were however unsuccessful in seeking an injunction for breach of copyright. The court held that the word 'Exxon' was not an "orginal literary word" under the Copyright Act 1956, since, in the words of Stephenson LJ a "literary work is something intended to afford either information and instruction or pleasure in the form of literary enjoyment".

THE OBJECTS CLAUSE AND THE ULTRA VIRES DOCTRINE

A fundamental feature of all statutory corporations is that their activities must be restricted in their constitution. In the case of a registered company this is achieved by requiring that its objects clause sets out the purpose for which it is formed and the kind of business or activities that it intends to carry on. The purpose of having restrictions on a company's activities is to protect investors and creditors. It is reasonable that an investor should know the purposes for which the investment is to be used and similarly a creditor is entitled to expect that the company's funds are not used for unauthorised activities. If a company purports to do anything beyond the limit of its permissible activities as expressed in the objects clause it is acting *ultra vires* (beyond the powers) and may be restrained by one of its members securing a court injunction. Prior to the European Communities Act 1972 the courts would also treat a transaction between a company and another, which was ultra vires the company, as being automatically void. This was the case even if a contracting party was unaware that the company was exceeding its powers as expressed in the memorandum of association, for such a contracting party was taken to have constructive notice of its content.

> These principles were clearly established by the House of Lords in the case of *Ashbury Railway Carriage and Iron Co. v. Riche* (1875). Here the plaintiff company's objects included the power to manufacture or sell rail rolling stock and carry on business as mechanical engineers and general contractors. The company purchased a concession to finance the building of a railway in Belgium, but later the directors repudiated the contract.

> In an action for breach of contract against the company, the court held that the contract was 'ultra vires' and void from the outset. Lord Cairns expressed the law when he said, 'This contract was entirely beyond the objects in the memorandum . . . If it was a contract void at its beginning, it was void because the company could not make the contract'.

It is important to draw a distinction between the objects of the company and the powers given to achieve those objects. It has always been the intention of the courts that they should assist a company to achieve its expressed objects by implying all the powers necessary for it to do so. Thus, for example, it will be unnecessary for a company whose objects are trading activities to specifically state that it also has the power to employ staff.

To avoid the restriction placed upon a company by the ultra vires rule it became the practice to frame the object clause of a company in very wide terms, so as to state all the possible things that the company might wish to do at any time in the future. At one time the courts would interpret such object clauses containing wide powers in a very narrow manner by restricting all such powers only to the achievement of the company's main objects. This became known as the 'main objects rule' and was eventually circumvented by a declaration in the memorandum that each part of the objects clause was to be regarded as an *'independent main object'*. Where this is the clear intention of the memorandum the courts will interpret it in this manner.

> In *Cotman v. Brougham (1918)* the memorandum clearly stated that each of a rubber company's many objects were to be regarded as independent. The main clause was to develop rubber estates abroad but another subclause authorised the company to deal with the shares of any company. When the company underwrote shares in an oil company the action was challenged as ultra vires.The court held that the power to underwrite was clearly provided for in the memorandum and the action was therefore *intra vires* and valid.
>
> Another method of conferring wide powers in the memorandum is to include a clause similar to the one included in *Bell Houses Ltd v. City Wall Properties Ltd (1966).* Here the main object of the company was to develop housing estates, but another clause allowed the company to carry on 'any other trade or business whatsoever which can, in the opinion of the board of directors, be advantageously carried on by the company with, or as ancillary to, any of the above businesses or the general business of the company'. The Court of Appeal held that such a clause was valid provided that the directors in forming their opinion acted in good faith.

In addition s.9 Companies Act 1985 provides for a company by *special resolution* (a three-quarter majority of voting shareholders) to alter or extend its objects clause to enable the company to achieve any of the following stated ends:

(i) to carry on business more economically or more efficiently,

(ii) to attain its main purpose by new or improved means,

(iii) to enlarge or change the local area of its operations,

(iv) to carry on some business which may be conveniently combined with its own,

(v) to restrict or abandon any of its objects,

(vi) to sell its undertaking, or

(vii) to amalgamate with another company.

Enforcement of ultra vires transactions

As part of the aim of harmonising the company law of member states of the European Economic Community, s.35 Companies Act 1985 provides that in favour of a person dealing in good faith with a company, any transaction decided on by its directors shall be deemed to be within the capacity of the company to enter into validly and the other party to the transaction shall not be bound to enquire about the capacity of the company to engage in it and shall be presumed to have acted in good faith unless the contrary is proved.

This provision of course does not abolish the ultra vires rule but merely enables the other party to an ultra vires transaction to enforce it if certain requirements are met. A member may still secure an injunction to prevent a company entering into an intended ultra vires transaction, and the Companies act 1985 confers no right on a company itself to enforce an ultra vires transaction. As a result of the Act however, the rule that an outsider dealing with a company is presumed to have constructive knowledge of the contents of the memorandum has been abolished. To enforce an otherwise ultra vires transaction against a company, an outsider, presumed by the Act to have acted in good faith, will have to show that:

(i) the transaction has been decided upon by the board of directors or

(ii) the transaction has been authorised, effected or ratified by resolution of the board.

The effect of this limitation is that relatively few transactions will come within s.35 for in most companies it is only the most important contracts which are formally resolved at board meetings.

THE ARTICLES OF ASSOCIATION

The articles of association of a registered company must be supplied to the Registrar of Companies prior to incorporation. Like the memorandum of association the articles will then be included in the company's files kept at Companies House in Cardiff.

The articles are concerned with the internal administration of the company, and it is for those setting up the company (its promoters) to determine the rules they consider appropriate for inclusion within the articles. The Companies Act 1985 does however provide a set of model articles which a company can adopt in whole or in part if it wishes. If a company fails to provide a set of articles then the model articles contained in the 1985 Act automatically apply to the company. They are known as 'Table A' Articles. Matters which are normally dealt with in the Articles include the appointment and powers of the board of directors, the rules in relation to members' meetings and voting and the types of shares and rights attaching to the share categories.

Once the company has been incorporated the articles may be altered or added to by means of a special resolution which requires a 75% majority of the members voting. Such alterations must however be made bona fide (in good faith) and for the benefit of the company as a whole. This is an important feature of the law regulating companies, for articles constitute a contract between the company and its members and identify members' rights, such as the right to vote. Clearly the ability of the company to change the terms of this contract at some future time may have the effect of placing individual members who might be harmed by such changes, in a disadvantageous position. Thus the courts reserve the power to refuse an alteration to the articles which has such an effect, unless there is a benefit to the company as a whole and the alteration has been made in good faith.

In *Brown v. British Abrasive Wheel Co. (1919)* a majority of the shareholders (98%) were willing to provide the company with much needed extra capital if they could buy the 2% minority. As the minority were unwilling to sell, the majority proposed to alter the Articles so as to enable nine-tenths of the shareholders to buy out any other shareholders. The plaintiff, representing the minority, brought an action to restrain the majority. It was held by the Court that the alteration would be restrained as it was not for the benefit of the company as a whole but rather for the benefit of the majority shareholding.

The rule that the articles and the memorandum of a company constitute a binding contract between the company and its members is contained in s.14 of the 1985 Act. It is a provision which has caused some difficulty for the courts in the past, in their attempts at precisely identifying its effects. The section states that the company and its members are bound to each other as though each shareholder has covenanted to observe the provisions of the memorandum and articles, and it also provides that any money owed by a member to the company is a specialty debt. This means the company has twelve years in which to recover the debt. In the case of debts arising from a simple contract the period is six years.

The effect of the articles can be summarised as follows:

(i) the company is bound to the members in their capacity as members, and they are bound to it in the same way; and

(ii) the members are contractually bound to each other, under the terms of the articles.

An illustration of (i) above is provided by *Salmon v. Quin & Axtens Ltd (1909)*. Here the articles gave directors full management powers, but prevented the directors from purchasing or letting any premises if the managing director dissented. The directors however resolved to deal in premises, despite the dissent of the managing director, and an extraordinary meeting of shareholders affirmed this action by a simple majority. The managing director sought an order from the court that the resolutions were invalid. The Court of Appeal agreed. The resolutions conflicted with the articles, and the company was bound by the articles. It could be restrained from its proposed action.

In *Hickman v. Kent and Romney Marsh Sheepbreeders Association (1915)* the articles of the association stipulated that disputes between itself and its members should be referred to arbitration. The plaintiff, a member, brought court action against the association in relation to a number of matters. It was held that in accordance with the articles these matters must be referred to arbitration.

The position regarding the contractual position as between the members themselves is dealt with later *see Foss v. Harbottle (1843)*. It is relevant to note in the context of alteration of the articles that a company has two principal sources of control over its affairs. These are the shareholders in general meeting, and the directors. The most important matters affecting the company, for example changes in its constitution, rest with the shareholders in general meeting. Decisions reached at such meetings are arrived at through the putting of resolutions, which are then voted on. Generally a simple majority vote is sufficient to carry them, although some matters of special significance require a 75% majority. Since voting power plays such an important role in company matters the type of shares the company has issued is of considerable significance. Some shares, for example ordinary shares, usually carry full voting rights.

However other classes of share, such as preference shares, may carry no voting rights at all and therefore exclude shareholders of that class from effectively influencing the company.

Since all public companies and many private companies consist of numerous members it is impractical to operate the company on a daily basis by means of general meetings. The articles will therefore provide for directors to be responsible for the daily running of the company and usually grant them the right to exercise all the powers of the company. They will remain answerable to the members in a general meeting although acts carried out by the directors within the powers delegated to them under the articles cannot be affected by decisions of a general meeting. So, if the directors have acted contrary to the wishes of the members, the ultimate sanction is to dismiss them or to change the articles and so bring in provisions that restrict the powers of the directors. In small companies the directors will often be the principal or only shareholders, so that such considerations will not be relevant.

OTHER REGISTRATION DOCUMENTS

In addition to the memorandum and articles of association there are certain other documents which must be supplied to the Registrar prior to incorporation. These include a Statutory Declaration that all the requirements of the Act have been complied with. Fees must also be paid.

Having examined all the documents filed and ensured that they are in order, the Registrar then issues a certificate under official seal which certifies that the company is incorporated. The certificate is conclusive evidence that all the requirements of the Companies Act have been complied with and that the company is a company authorised to be registered and duly registered under the Act. A private company can enter into contracts, borrow money, and carry on business immediately on incorporation. However a public limited company registered under the 1985 Act cannot commence business until a certificate is issued by the Registrar that the share capital of the company is not less than the authorised minimum (i.e. £50,000 with at least one-quarter paid up). If more than a year after the incorporation of a public company it has not been issued with such a certificate the Secretary of State may petition the court for the company to be wound up.

THE CONDUCT OF COMPANY AFFAIRS

We have seen that a partnership is subject to few statutory regulations and the partners are free to decide for themselves such matters as the conduct of meetings, the keeping of records and accounting methods.

Registered companies limited by shares however, are different. The fundamental principle of accountability of the directors to the members necessarily involves stricter regulation of the company's operation. The Companies Act provides therefore that every company must, in each year, hold an annual general meeting and that every member is entitled to notice of this meeting. In addition, the holders of one-tenth or more of paid-up shares with voting rights may at any time compel the directors to call an extra-ordinary general meeting. The articles usually regulate the procedures to be adopted at these meetings, but in any case the minutes of all meetings must be strictly recorded.

Decisions at general meetings are usually taken by ordinary resolution, that is a majority of voting members present. For some types of business, usually related to the company's constitution such as the alteration of the articles or objects of the company, a special resolution is necessary which requires a three-quarters majority of voting members.

Form of Meetings

Types	Business	When Called	Notice
Annual General Meeting	Declaring Dividends, Directors, Auditors Reports Appointment of Directors.	Within 18 months of incorporation then once a year with no more than 15 months between each.	At least 21 days Items of ordinary business need not be mentioned in notice
Extra-ordinary General Meeting	All business is 'special' — e.g. alteration of articles, memordandum, removal of directors	Whenever directors think fit, or if demanded by holders of $^1/_{10}$ or most of paid-up shares.	At least 14 days. If called by members, they must state why they want it.

Resolutions

Type	Majority	Notice	Use
Ordinary	Simple i.e. over 50%	At the meeting	For matters not covered below
Extraordinary	75% of votes cast	At the time the meeting was called	Where required by the Companies Act or the articles
Special	75% of votes cast	21 days	Where required by law e.g. alteration of articles.
		Sometimes 'special notice' giving 28 days is required e.g.: to dismiss a director	

Each year a company must submit an annual return to the Registrar of Companies which has to include details of the company's share capital, share division, debts secured by mortgages, and a list of members and directors. Also company legislation contains detailed provisions relating to the preparation of accounts, the information to be included in these accounts, and the need for submission of annual accounts to the general meeting and the Registrar of Companies. Generally the accounting records must be kept at the registered office of the company and must be available for inspection by shareholders. Company accounts must also be audited, and the auditor's report must be read out to the company in general meeting, and must be open to inspection by any member. Other documents which a company is obliged to keep include a register of the interests of directors and their service contracts, a register of the company members and debenture holders, and a register of members who have substantial interests in the company, that is, of those who have one-tenth or more of the share capital of the company.

These requirements not only ensure the members are kept informed, but also assist outsiders in assessing the strength of the company prior to investing in it or doing business with it. Investments in a company can be undertaken in two distinct ways:

(a) By lending money to the company in return for an issue of debentures. A debenture holder is a secured creditor of the company who is entitled to a fixed rate of interest on the investment.

(b) By taking up shares and becoming a company member. The rights of a shareholder depend upon the type of shares involved but generally a shareholder has the right to receive a proportion of the profits of a company, vote in general meetings and share in the capital of the company if it is wound up.

FINANCING A LIMITED COMPANY

There are various methods used by companies to raise capital, the issue of shares and debentures being two of the most significant methods. Before considering them in more detail, it will be helpful to recap and expand upon the meaning of the expression 'capital', which we encountered earlier in the chapter whilst examining the contents of the memorandum of association. Capital is unfortunately a broad expression carrying a number of meanings, however in relation to limited companies the following are the most common uses of the expression:

(i) *Nominal (or authorised) capital*
This expression refers to the value of shares that a company is authorised to issue, and is included in the capital clause of its memorandum of association.

(ii) *Issued capital*
This refers to the value of capital in the form of shares which have been actually issued to the shareholders.

(iii) *Paid-up capital*
This is the amount of capital which has actually been paid up on the shares issued, or the amount of capital that the company has actually raised and received. Under s.351 Companies Act 1985 if a company makes a reference to share capital on its business stationery or order forms, it must refer to its paid-up capital.

(iv) *Unpaid capital*
If shares which have been issued are not fully paid for, the amount outstanding is referred to as unpaid capital, e.g. if 5,000 shares issued have a nominal value of £1 each and only 50p has been paid up on them, then the paid up capital is £2,500 and the unpaid capital is £2,500. Shareholders may be required to pay up the unpaid amount on their shares by the company making a '*call*' on them to do so.

(v) *Reserve capital*
A company, by special resolution (75% majority vote) may declare that any portion of its unpaid capital shall not be called up except if the company is being brought to an end (liquidated) by a winding up. This is called reserve capital and cannot be converted into ordinary capital for use in the operation of the company without the court's permission.

It is important to note that the references to capital being made here are to share capital. The law regards capital as something positive, a financial contribution to the company which it can use for the purposes of its business. For instance it purchases business premises, which are then regarded as fixed capital, and stock, which becomes circulating capital. Accountants see capital in a different way. They regard it as something the company owes: the members are owed the company's share capital; the debenture holders are owed the loan capital. To the economist capital again has a different meaning. In the context of any discussion concerning capital it is clearly important to establish in which sense the term is being used. Here we are using the term in the legal sense.

SHARES

The nature of shares has been considered both by Parliament and the courts. Thus s.182 Companies Act 1985 provides that shares are personal property and that they are transferrable in accordance with the provisions in the articles, whilst in *Borland's Trustee v. Steel Bros. & Co. Ltd* (1901) Farwell J stated that; "A share is the interest of a shareholder in the company measured by a sum of money, for the purpose of liability in the first place, and of interest in the second". This is a helpful definition. It indicates that a member:

(i) has a liability to pay the company, which arises when he applies for the shares, or when they are alloted to him, or when having received them he is called upon to pay for them; and

(ii) has an interest in the company which grants him rights. These rights are determined by the class or type of shares he acquires and what the articles identify as the rights attached to the class, such as voting rights, and rights to dividends. Whatever these rights may be the shareholder is a part owner of the company. It is of course impossible to say which part is owned. The shareholders collectively own the undertaking of the company, and the company is a single person, thus the company is in effect the agent of the shareholders. It is they who ultimately determine the actions of the company through shareholders' meetings. Invariably the company will appoint directors to carry out the management of the company. The directors will be responsible to the shareholders for their actions, and in carrying out the business of the company will themselves be agents of it (see Fig. 2).

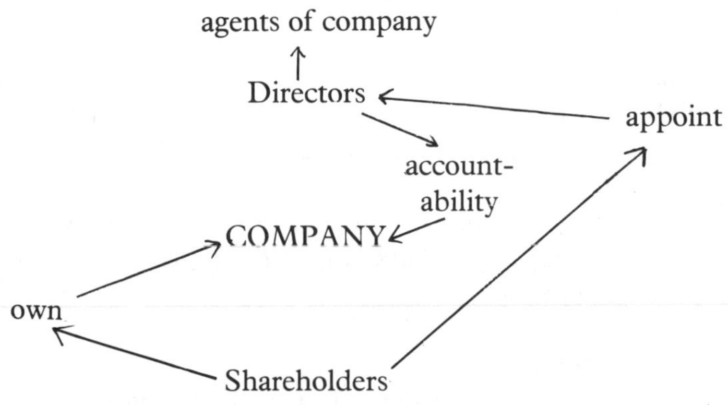

Fig. 2 **Shareholders as company controllers**

A shareholder can transfer his shares by selling them or giving them away, for instance as a gift during his lifetime or under his will after his death. S.183 Companies Act 1985 requires a 'proper instrument of transfer' to be delivered to the company for a valid assignment of ownership to occur. All this means is that a written document is necessary. It does not need to be a deed unless the articles require one. The shareholders' document of title to the shares is a share certificate, issued by the company. The shareholder obtains legal title to the shares when his name is entered by the company onto its register of shareholders. The share certificate is a document of considerable importance. Although physically transferring it from one person to another does not pass legal ownership in the shares (registration is required), s.186 of the 1985 Act states that the certificate is prima facie evidence of the shareholder's ownership in the shares. It is in other words a statement by the company that at the time it was issued the person named on it was the owner, and had paid for the shares to the extent stated. The company is bound by this statement in respect of those who have relied upon its accuracy.

CLASSES OF SHARES

There is nothing to prevent a registered company limited by shares from issuing one class of shares with equal rights. Usually, however, different classes of shares are issued with varying rights attaching to them relating to such matters as voting, payment of dividends and return of capital on liquidation. The three main types of shares are:

(i) *Preference shares*
The main characteristic of a preference share is that it will have the right to a preferred fixed dividend. This means that the holder of a preference share is entitled to a fixed amount of dividend, e.g. 6% on the value of each share, before other shareholders are paid any dividend. They are presumed to be cumulative which means that if in any year the company fails to declare a dividend, the shortfall must be made up out of profits of subsequent years. A preference share is therefore a safe investment with fixed interest, no matter how small or large is the company's profit. As far as return of capital on a winding up is concerned, the preference shareholder will rank equally with ordinary shareholders for any payment due, unless the preference shares are made 'preferential as to capital'. Normally, preference shares do not carry voting rights and therefore the preference shareholder has little influence over the company's activities.

(ii) *Ordinary shares*
Ordinary shares are often referred to as the 'equity share capital' of a company. When a company declares a dividend and the preference shareholders have been paid, the holders of ordinary shares are entitled to the remainder. It follows therefore that an ordinary shareholder in a well-managed company, making high profits will receive a good return on his investment and consequently the value of his share will rise, e.g. a £1 ordinary share could have a market value of £1.25. Unfortunately, the reverse is also true and they may fall in market value so that ordinary shares inevitably involve a certain risk. This risk is reflected in the amount of control that an ordinary shareholder has over the company's business. While voting rights are not normally attached to preference shares, they are attached to ordinary shares enabling the ordinary shareholder to voice an opinion in a general meeting and vote on major issues involving the running of the company.

(iii) *Founders shares (or deferred ordinary shares)*
Such shares are now uncommon but were originally granted to the founders of a company, the company promoters. Their main characteristics was to confer on the holder the right to the remainder of the distributed profit after a dividend had been paid on the ordinary shares.

A private company, it will be recalled, is unable to issue its shares publicly. If it does so it loses its status as a private company. A public company can publicly advertise its shares which it may do either to acquire initial capital or more commonly to increase its existing capital. The methods used by a public company to raise capital from the public are:

(i) through direct invitation to the public, through the issue of a prospectus;

(ii) by an offer for sale. This involves the company selling the total number of shares it hopes to issue to an organisation which specialises in financial transactions of this kind. Such organisations are known, not surprisingly, as 'issuing houses'. They resell to the public at a higher price, by publishing a document called an 'offer for sale', which contains an application form for the prospective shareholder to complete and return to the issuing house; and

(iii) by placing. Again an issuing house is involved. It may subscribe for the share issued itself, reselling as in (ii) usually inviting its own clients to purchase the shares, or it may simply seek persons interested in purchasing the shares acting merely as an agent for the company, which will pay a fee for the service provided. This is called 'brokerage'. The most common method used is (ii) above.

There are detailed legal provisions dealing with the public sale of shares. They are designed to protect the investing public, and are contained in the Financial Services Act 1986. One of the most important features of this statutory protection relates to the obligation on the company to disclose specific information of relevance to investors in reaching a decision as to whether to buy. Aspects of this protection are considered in Chapter 4.

Shareholders' rights

As we have already seen the rights enjoyed by a member of a company are primarily contractual, arising from the class of shares acquired and the rights attached to them as specified in the articles. Unlike a partner, who will always possess the right to take part in the management of the firm, a shareholder will not always be involved in the daily management of the company, unless the organisation has a very small membership and its shareholders are also its directors. Companies' articles usually confer power on directors to operate the business, which they will perform on behalf of the members. The effect of such an arrangement is that ownership and management are separated. Nevertheless, ultimate control of the business is in the hands of the shareholders by the exercise of voting power in the general meeting. Where appropriate they can vote to remove a director.

In any vote which does not produce a unanimous outcome there will be two groups, the majority shareholders and the minority shareholders. In effect it is the majority that make the company decisions. If the minority have a grievance, legally there is little they can do to redress it. The courts have been reluctant to assist minority shareholders who are claiming they have been oppressed or have had their interests prejudiced by the majority. Since it is the majority who rule the company it is not for the court to thwart their actions.

The case of *Foss v. Harbottle (1843)* laid down as a general principle that the courts will not interfere in the internal management of a company at the insistance of the minority shareholders. Here an action had been brought by the minority alleging that the directors were responsible for losses that had occurred when they sold some of their own land to the company, at what was alleged to be an overvaluation. The Court held that the action must fail as the proper plaintiff in such circumstances was the company itself. As the action to which the minority shareholders objected could have been ratified by the majority then it was the majority shareholders who should decide whether an action should be brought in the company name. The Court saw no merit in interferring in the internal management of a company by passing judgment on its commercial decisions.

In *Pavlides v. Jenson and others (1956)*, a company sold an asbestos mine for £182,000 when its real value was close to £1,000,000. A minority shareholder brought an action for damages against three directors who were responsible for the sale and against the company, alleging gross negligence. The Court held that the action could not be brought by a minority shareholder because it was the company itself which should decide whether to redress the wrong that had been committed.

It should be remembered that the process of incorporation, having invested a company with a separate legal personality, dictates that the company and individual members are separate. If a wrong is committed against the company it is the company, by virtue of a decision made by the Board of Directors that should redress it.

The rule in *Foss v. Harbottle* does not however apply to every type of action taken by the majority. In certain situations the court will hear a claim brought by minority shareholders, even though the majority do not wish it. Thus:

(i) Ultra vires activities can never be ratified by the majority. A member with a single share can bring proceedings to restrain an ultra vires act.

(ii) Where directors attempt to do something requiring a special resolution (i.e. a ¾ majority and prior notice) which they do not obtain, then action cannot be ratified by an ordinary resolution (i.e. a simple majority). Were this to be otherwise, the protection for minorities granted in circumstances where a ¾ majority is needed would be avoided.

(iii) Where a wrong is suffered to a member in his personal capacity, through the action of the directors.

For instance in *Pender v. Lushington* (1877) the company chairman wrongfully refused to accept the votes cast by certain shareholders. The resolution they opposed was in consequence able to be carried. The court held that the company could be restrained from carrying out the proposed resolution.

(iv) When a fraud has been committed against the minority. This does not mean fraud in the criminal sense, rather conduct which is grossly unfair.

An example is provided by *Daniels v. Daniels* (1978). Here two company directors, in 1970, instructed the company to sell land to one of them for £4,250. In 1974 the land was resold for £120,000 and a minority shareholder brought an action claiming that damages should be payable to the company. The Court held that despite no allegation of fraud the action by the individual shareholders should be allowed to proceed.

In addition to the common law, the Companies Act confers certain statutory rights on minority shareholders.

An important example of this is s. 459 which gives a member the right to apply to the court for an order on the ground that the affairs of the company are being or have been conducted in a manner which is unfairly prejudicial to some members (including at least himself), or that any actual or proposed act or omission of the company is or would be prejudicial.

If the case is proved the court may issue a court order which could:

(i) regulate the company's affairs for the future;

(ii) require the company to act or refrain from acting in a particular way;

(iii) authorise civil proceedings in the name and on behalf of the company by a person; or

(iv) require the purchase of any member's shares by the company or by other members.

An example of a court order regulating a company's future affairs is seen in *Re: H R Harmer Limited* (1959). The company was run by an elderly father acting as chairman and his two sons as directors. The father had voting control. He largely ignored the wishes of the board of directors and ran the business as his own. On an application by the sons as minority shareholders, alleging oppression, the Court held that relief should be granted. The father was appointed life president of the company without rights, duties or powers and was ordered not to interfere with the company's affairs.

DEBENTURES

A trading company may, as an alternative to a share issue, raise money by means of issuing a debenture or series of debentures. These may be secured or unsecured. The definition of *'debenture'* is very wide and includes all forms of securities (undertakings to repay money borrowed) which may or may not be secured by a charge on the company's assets. Indeed a mortgage of the company's property to a single individual may be regarded as a debenture within the definition. Debentures are usually made by means of a trust deed which will create a *fixed charge* over specific company property by mortgage and/or a *floating charge* over the rest of the company assets. The distinction between a fixed and floating charge is essentially that a company is not free to deal with assets subject to a fixed charge, i.e. by selling or mortgaging, but is free to deal with any of its assets covered by a floating charge. However, on the occurrence of a particular event, a floating charge is said to *crystallise* and is then converted into a fixed charge. Such an event occurs when money becomes payable under a condition in the debenture such as repayment of interest, and the debenture holder takes some steps to enforce his security because the interest due is unpaid.

The principal rights of a debenture holder are contained in the debenture deed. They will include:

(i) the date of repayment of the loan and the rate of interest;

(ii) a statement of the assets of the company which are subject to fixed or floating charges;

(iii) the rights of the company to redeem the whole or part of the monies owing;

(iv) the circumstances in which the loan becomes immediately repayable, i.e. if the company defaults in repayment of interest;

(v) the powers of the debenture holder to appoint a receiver and manager of the assets charged.

OTHER FORMS OF FINANCING

Loans

All trading companies have an implied power to borrow finance for the purposes of their business activities. In the case of non-trading companies, there is no such power unless expressly provided for in the memorandum of association. Power to borrow money is usually conferred on the company directors in the articles of association. However there is nothing to prevent a company from restricting its own borrowing powers to a specific amount stated in the memorandum, e.g. borrow an amount which is no more than two-thirds of the value of the company's paid-up capital. If a power to borrow has been conferred, then this will also carry with it an implied power to offer company property as security for a loan. As we have seen, if a company borrows beyond its powers then the loan and any security given for it is void on the grounds of ultra vires. The lender cannot sue for the return of the loan unless he can invoke s.35. Under the rule in *Royal British Bank v. Turquand (1856)* the facts of which are considered later, if the company has power to borrow money, the lender is under no obligation to discover the purpose for which the money is to be used.

In the short term, registered companies make use of overdraft facilities offered by the commercial banks to finance a temporary cash flow difficulty. This type of borrowing is increasingly used during temporary financial and economic recession, when the cash receipts of the company are anticipated to rise in the future.

Longer term loans may be borrowed either through the commercial banks or on the capital market and are normally secured against some collateral offered by the company which may be realised by the lender in the event of a default on the loan.

Factoring

A further means of raising capital open to organisations facing a cash flow problem is *factoring.* Essentially this means that an organisation with outstanding monies owed to it, sells the right to this money to a *factor* (an organisation willing to provide immediate cash in return for the right to collect and keep the monies owed from the organisation's debtors). The factor will usually pay the organisation less than the face value of the debts and so if the debt can be collected in full, this percentage is the factor's profit on the transaction.

THE ACQUISITION OF ASSETS

It may be briefly noted here that a limited company is able to acquire property and property rights in the same way as an individual. Companies frequently take leased property such as vehicles and land (see Chapter 8) under which they acquire limited rights of ownership. They also obtain goods on credit terms (see Chapter 5).

MANAGEMENT OF THE COMPANY

THE POSITION OF DIRECTORS

The management of a registered company is carried on by the directors who are responsible for policy making, contract making and supervising the company property. Company directors are normally appointed in a manner prescribed in the articles of association, for example by the company in general meeting or by the existing directors. The Companies Act 1985 specifically provides, however, that despite anything in the articles to the contrary, a director may be removed by an ordinary resolution. There is nothing to prevent the articles conferring special voting rights on certain occasions.

> In *Bushell v. Faith (1970)*, the company had an issued share capital of £300 equally divided between three members. Each share carried one vote. The Articles provided, however, that on a resolution to remove a director, the directors' individual shares should carry three votes per share. Two of the members voted to remove the third from his position as director but were defeated because their 200 votes were cancelled by the individual director's 300 votes. The court held this to be in order.

DIRECTORS' POWERS AND DUTIES

The specific powers of directors are stated in the articles but in addition to this actual authority to carry out functions, the directors will also have an authority to act which is implied under the law. This is because the director is an agent of the company and can bind it whether he acts within his actual or apparent authority.

Of course if a director enters into an ultra vires transaction on the company's behalf, then whatever his agency powers are the transaction is invalid (unless s.35 of the Companies Act 1985 applies to the transaction.) This is because it is beyond the company's power to complete the transaction, and the director gains his powers from the company. But if the director merely fails to comply with the internal rules of the company when making a transaction this does not amount to an ultra vires act and the company will be bound.

> This principle can be seen in the leading case of *Royal British Bank v. Turquand (1856)*. Here a company conferred power on the directors to borrow such sums as were authorised by an ordinary resolution of the general meeting. The directors borrowed money without such a resolution being passed. The court held that the company was bound by the loan and laid down the following basic principles:-
>
> (a) An outsider who is dealing with a company is not bound to inquire whether the internal regulations of the company have been complied with, such as passing resolutions to authorise specific acts. Basically, therefore, an outsider is entitled to assume that the directors have acted properly.
>
> (b) An outsider is not entitled to rely on this presumption if he is aware of the irregularity or ought in the circumstances to have made inquiries.

This aspect of the principle can be seen operating in the following cases.

> In *Howard v. Patent Ivory Manufacturing Co. (1888)*, the directors of the company had power to borrow up to £1,000, with larger amounts having to be authorised by the general meeting. The company borrowed £3,500 from the directors without a resolution being passed. The court held that as the directors were aware of the procedural irregularity the borrowing was only valid up to £1,000.
>
> In *Underwood Ltd. v. Bank of Liverpool (1924)*, the director of a company paid cheques, made payable to the company, into his personal account. An action was brought against the bank to recover the sums paid. The court held that the bank was not entitled to assume that the director was acting properly, as the circumstances were so unusual that the bank ought to have been suspicious.

Even if an individual has not been actually appointed as director or managing director, should the company, through the directors, expressly or impliedly represent him as such, then as far as the outsider is concerned the individual will have all the apparent authority of a director.

> In *Freeman Lockyer v. Buckhurst Properties (1964)*, an individual director, with the consent of his fellow directors, employed the plaintiff architects to do some work. The director had been held out as managing director although he had not been appointed to this post, and the contract of employment was held to be binding. To enter into such a contract was within the apparent scope of a managing director's power.

Since it is the directors who are responsible for managing the company, it is of great concern to establish what they are legally capable of carrying out in the company's name, and to what extent they are accountable to the company for their actions.

Their powers are conferred on them by the articles, and in general these powers cannot be removed from them by resolution in a general meeting. Alteration of the articles themselves will be necessary.

The Companies Act 1985 does not define the term 'director' in a way which is very helpful. It says simply, a director is "any person occupying the position of director, by whatever name called". This is contained in s. 741. The courts however have provided some useful indications as to the nature of the director, variously describing such a person as a trustee, agent and managing partner.

> However Lord Jessel stated in *Re: Forest of Dean Coal Mining Co. (1878)*, "It does not matter much what you call them, so long as you understand what their true position is which is that they are merely commercial men, managing a trading concern for the benefit of themselves and all other shareholders in it".

It is clear that a director stands in a fiduciary capacity to the company, and like an agent for a principal, must act in good faith and not make personal use of his position. The nature of a director's fiduciary duty can be broken down into the following components:

(a) *A director must act bona fide in what he considers is the interest of the company* The powers that are invested in directors are to be used for the benefit of the company as a whole, that is all the shareholders, rather than some sectional interest such as a class of shareholders, the company employees, the directors, a holding or subsidiary company. Thus a breach of duty will occur where the directors:

(i) issue new shares to themselves, not because the company needs more capital but merely to increase their voting power.

In *Piercy v. S. Mills & Co. Ltd. (1920)*, the directors used their powers to issue new voting shares to themselves, solely to acquire majority voting power. The court held that the directors had abused their powers and the allotment was declared void.

(ii) approve a transfer of their own partly-paid shares to escape liability for a call they intend to make. A call is a request for payment on the shares.

In *Alexander v. Automatic Telephone Co. (1900)* the directors used their position to require all shareholders to pay 3s 6d on each share excluding themselves. The Court held that this was a clear abuse of power and the directors were required to pay to the company the same amount.

(ii) negotiate a new service agreement between the company and its managing director simply in order to confer additional benefits on him or his dependants.

In *Re: W and M Roith (1967)* it was held that a new service contract negotiated between a managing director and his company was unlawful as it was solely to make a pension provision for his widow and that no regard had been taken as to whether this was for the benefit of the company.

(iv) abdicate responsibility for the running of the company and appoint a manager with full powers (i.e. no board control), or obey the majority shareholder without exercising their own judgment or discretion.

(v) being directors of a subsidiary company use their powers exclusively in the interests of the holding company to the detriment of the minority shareholders of the subsidiary.

(b) A director must not place himself in a position where there is likely to be conflict between personal interests and duty to the company.
Directors act as agents on behalf of the company they represent and in such a capacity they must not enter into engagements where there is, or is likely to be, a conflict between the interests of the company and their own personal interests. The Companies Act therefore requires a director to give notice at the board meeting of a personal interest — direct or indirect — in any contracts or proposed contracts in which the company is involved. Failure to disclose such an interest can result in fines being imposed. In addition any director who uses position to make personal profit may be made to account for such a profit to the company.

In *Cook v. Deeks (1916)* the directors of a railway company having negotiated a contract on behalf of the company decided to make the contract in their own names. The Court held that the benefit of the contract belonged to the company and the directors should account to the company for any profit made. The extent of the duty is also illustrated by the case of *Regal Hastings v. Gulliver (1942)*. Here the company owned a cinema and decided to purchase two others with the intention of selling the whole undertaking as a going concern. A subsidiary company was formed which acquired the other cinemas, however the shares of the subsidiary were allocated between the company and its directors. Following a sale of the whole undertaking, involving a transfer of the shares of the company and its subsidiary, the purchasers brought an action to recover the profit on the sale by the directors of their shares in the subsidiary. Despite the fact that the purchasers had freely agreed to pay the share price, the House of Lords held that the former directors must deliver up to the company the profit they had made. It was by the use of their special knowledge and opportunities as directors that they had made the profit.

If a director uses his position to make a secret profit for himself, he will be in breach of his contract of employment, and may also be made to hand over such profit to the company.

In *Boston Deep Sea Fishing & Ice Co. v. Ansell (1888)*, the managing director of a trawling business received a secret commission on placing an order for the construction of fishing boats. The court held that the company was entitled to the commission.

The Financial Services Act 1986 makes it a criminal offence for an "insider", that is an individual connected with a company as a director, officer, employer or someone having a professional or business relationship with it, to deal on a recognised stock exchange in the company's shares in prescribed circumstances. These are that the insider has information obtained through his connection with the company which it would be reasonable to expect him not to disclose and which he knows to be price sensitive unpublished information. Obviously many people who deal with and work in companies are ideally placed to either purchase or dispose of shares having obtained confidential information about such matters as possible takeovers, trading difficulties and so on.

The Act carries a maximum penalty of two years imprisonment (which is likely to be increased to seven) and an unlimited fine. However a prosecution can only be brought by the Secretary of State, or by or with the consent of the Director of Public Prosecutions.

A further duty imposed upon a director is the obligation to exercise care and skill in performing his work. This duty is a variable one. In *Re: City Equitable Fire Insurance Co. Ltd. (1926)* Romer J commented:

> "The position of a director of a company carrying on a small retail business is very different from that of a director of a railway company. The duties of a bank director may differ widely from those of an insurance director, and the duties of a director of one insurance company may differ from those of another . . . The larger the business carried on by the Company the more numerous, and the more important the matters that must of necessity be left to the managers, the accountants and the rest of the staff".

Provided the directors act honestly this will normally be sufficient to fulfil the duty.

> In *Re: New Marshanalond Exploration Co. (1892)* the directors approved a loan of £1,250 and failed to ensure that security was given. The Court held that in the absence of fraud the directors were not liable for this 'error of judgment'.

> In *Re: Denham & Co. (1883)* a situation had arisen where, for four years, a company's dividend was negligently paid out of capital. As the powers of management of the company had been vested in one individual, another director who rarely attended board meetings and had no reason to suspect misconduct, was held not liable for the negligence.

Clearly however there are circumstances in which a director can fall short of what the law expects. The standard of care is a subjective one that is of a variable standard based upon the skill and knowledge of the individual in question. A highly paid professional director of a public limited company is expected to demonstrate a high level of business acumen.

REMOVAL OF DIRECTORS

If the directors have voting control of the company they cannot be removed. Where this does not apply s.303 of the 1985 Act provides that a company may by means of an ordinary resolution remove a director before his term of office expires, despite anything in the articles or in any agreement made between the company and the director. The section does not deprive the director of his right to sue for breach of contract on removal, if he has this right.

A public company must have at least two directors, a private company must have at least one. Directors of public companies must normally retire at 70, although the articles may provide otherwise. It is not a legal requirement that directors hold shares in the company, although articles commonly specify that such 'qualification' shares be held.

A common provision in articles is that directors hold office for three years, after which time they must either retire or offer themselves for re-election. Any changes in the directors must be notified to the Registrar of Companies. The company must keep a register at its office, available for public inspection, containing a list of the directors and the company secretary. Directors are also required by statute to disclose to the company and its members matters such as their financial interests in the company and connected companies.

The company secretary is the senior administrative officer, responsible for meetings, notices, resolutions, registers, and the company accounts. A director can and usually does fulfil this function, although if there is only one director there must be a separate company secretary.

THE TERMINATION OF BUSINESS ORGANISATIONS

INTRODUCTION

The life of a business organisation can come to an end for many reasons. It may have achieved what its members required of it, so that it no longer has any useful value. It is not, for instance, unknown for a group of people to form a limited company for the purpose of carrying out a specific business venture, and inserting a provision in the company's articles of association making it clear that the business is to last for a fixed period, or that it will expire on the happening of a certain event. A group of businessmen may contribute capital to a company they have formed, with the aim that the company will purchase, renovate and then sell certain industrial premises, or a large country house. The company will end when the sale takes place.

A business may also come to an end because the commercial foundations upon which it was based have ceased to exist, or it has become no longer commercially viable to continue. If this occurs there is nothing to prevent the organisation from diversifying if this is acceptable to the members, thus prolonging the life of the business.

> An interesting illustration of this process, and the legal consequences which can attach to it, is provided by *Prudential Assurance Co v. Chatterley-Whitfield Collieries Ltd (1949)*. The colliery company's main business interest was in coal mining, although it had other business interests as well. Following the nationalisation of the coal industry in 1946, the company, in common with other colliery companies, received a large payment by way of compensation. It decided to continue to operate its other business activities, but had more capital than it needed for these, and so it passed a special resolution to repay all its preference shareholders. Under the articles they had the right to priority of repayment of capital in the event of the company being brought to an end. The preference shareholders objected, claiming they would lose the opportunity to share in future profit.
>
> The Companies Act strictly controls the power of a company to reduce its capital, in order to protect creditors, shareholders and the public. The court must sanction the reductions, which it will not do if the reduction is not fair and equitable as between different classes of shareholders. The House of Lords nevertheless held that this reduction was fair and equitable on the basis that surplus capital should first be returned to the class of shareholders having priority to repayment in the event of the company being brought to an end.

Most businesses which are terminated however, do not end their own lives out of choice, but because such action has been forced on them by their creditors. This occurs when the creditors loose confidence in the capacity of the organisation to repay them. It is a common feature of commercial life that when a business develops financial ill-health, its creditors will seek to reduce their losses by dissolving the business whilst there are still assets remaining in it.

Thus in considering the law as it affects the dissolution of businesses it is helpful to bear in mind the health of the organisation at the time it is being dissolved. The law, quite understandably, exerts far greater control over businesses which are terminated in circumstances of financial failure, than in cases where they are brought to an end fit and healthy, and nobody will lose money. Dissolution is important to the members of the business, who will be concerned as to what share of the assets they are entitled to, and for much the same reason it will be of concern to the creditors; they will want to know what the assets of the business are, and how they are to be distributed.

THE PROCESS OF DISSOLUTION

The process laid down for terminating or dissolving a business depends upon two factors:

(a) what the type of business is; and

(b) what its financial condition is.

We have previously seen that business organisations can be classified according to their legal status. Some are corporate bodies, some are unincorporated associations, whilst others are simple one man businesses. By now it should be clear that there are significant differences between these alternative business forms. This is reflected in the procedures for dissolving them. In the case of a limited company the procedure by which it is dissolved is referred to as a winding-up. Bankruptcy is the term used to describe the process by which an insolvent individual's assets are collected in, converted into money and distributed between his creditors. There is no technical term to describe the process for terminating a partnership. It is simply referred to as dissolution.

DISSOLUTION OF A PARTNERSHIP

When the commercial activity of a partnership ceases so does the business itself, for it is no longer being 'carried on' as required under the Partnership Act 1890. In such circumstances the partnership will be dissolved, and its assets disposed of to those legally entitled to them. Alternatively a partnership may still be in operation, but be dissolved on any one of a number of different grounds.

Dissolution can occur either with or without the intervention of the court. Under the Partnership Act 1890 a partnership is dissolved without the intervention of the court, in any of the following circumstances:

(i) if it was entered into for a fixed term, when that term expires;

(ii) if it was entered into for a single venture, when that venture has been completed, for example, where the aim of the business is to acquire a single piece of property and resell it;

(iii) if entered into for an undefined time, by any partner giving notice to the other or others of his intention to dissolve the partnership. If such a notice is served then the partnership is dissolved from the date mentioned in the notice as the date of dissolution. If no date has been given dissolution operates from the time the notice was received, subject to the Articles providing for some other date;

(iv) by the death or bankruptcy of any partner. The Articles will often provide that in such an event the partnership will continue to be run by the remaining partners. In the case of the death of a partner the Articles may provide that the surviving partners will continue to run the business in partnership with the personal representative of the deceased;

(v) if a partner's share of the business is charged to secure a separate judgment debt, the other partners may dissolve the business;

(vi) by the happening of an event which makes it unlawful for the business of the firm to be carried on, or for the members of the firm to carry it on in partnership. This may occur, for example, where there is a partnership between a British partner and a foreign partner, the business is carried on in the United Kingdom, and war breaks out between the countries of the respective partners.

Dissolution can be granted by the court on an application to dissolve, made by a partner, in any of the following cases:

(i) where a partner is suffering from a mental disorder;

(ii) where a partner other than the partner petitioning

(a) becomes in any way permanently incapable of performing their part of the partnership contract, eg through physical illness, or

(b) has been guilty of misconduct in business or private life, as in the opinion of the court, bearing in mind the nature of the partnership business, is calculated to be prejudicial to the carrying on of the business, or

(c) wilfully or persistently commits a breach of the partnership agreement, or otherwise behaves in a way in matters relating to the partnership business that it is impractical for the other partners to carry on in business with that partner.

Cases on dissolution on these grounds have included a refusal to meet for discussions on business matters, the keeping of erroneous accounts, persistent disagreement between the parties, and in *Anderson v. Anderson (1857)* where a father and son were in partnership together, the opening by the father of all his son's corrrespondence.

(d) where the business of the partnership can only be carried on at a loss;

(e) if circumstances have arisen which, in the opinion of the court, render it just and equitable that the partnership be dissolved.

In *Re: Yenidje Tobacco Co Ltd (1916)* although the company was trading profitably the court held that it was just and equitable to wind it up, on the basis that its two directors had become so hostile towards each other that they would only communicate by means of messages passed to each other via the Secretary, and that this amounted to a position of deadlock. It was pointed out that a private limited company is similar to a partnership, and that had the directors been partners in a partnership, there would have been sufficient grounds for dissolution. Lord Justice Warrington stated:

'. . . I am prepared to say that in a case like the present, where there are only two persons interested, and there are no shareholders other than those two, where there are no means of over-ruling by the action of a general meeting of shareholders the trouble which is occasioned by the quarrels of the two directors and shareholders, the company ought to be wound up if there exists such a ground as would be sufficient for the dissolution of a private partnership at the suit of one of the partners against the other. Such grounds exist in the present case.'

The partnership and bankruptcy

Two distinct insolvency situations may arise which affect the partnership:

(a) one of the partners is declared personally bankrupt, whilst the remaining partners are personally solvent. This automatically brings the partnership to an end, although a new one may well be formed, without the bankrupt partner. The reason the firm automatically dissolves in such circumstances is because the bankrupt party's share passes to his trustee in bankruptcy, and thus in effect he is withdrawing his contribution and his stake in the business.

(b) the partnership itself is insolvent. If this is so, all the partners will normally have bankruptcy proceedings brought against them. It should be remembered that since a partnership does not grant limited liability to its members, they become personally liable for the debts which cannot be met by the assets of the firm.

The administration and distribution of assets

If the partnership is dissolved its property is gathered in, and used to pay all debts and liabilities. If after this is done a surplus is left it is distributed between the partners. What they receive will depend upon what their partnership agreement says. If it makes no provision for such a situation, the following rules are laid down by the 1890 Act:

(a) if there is no loss suffered by the firm, the surplus is used firstly to repay the capital contribution of the partners, and then to the partners in equal shares. Thus if the firm has three partners, A, B and C, whose respective capital contributions were £2,000, £1,000 and £500, and on dissolution the firm has debts of £3,000 and assets of £8,000, the distribution to the partners will be as follows:

	£
Assets available for distribution	8,000
Firms debts	3,000
Surplus assets available for distribution	5,000
Repayment of capital contributions: A	2,000
B	1,000
C	500
	3,500
Remaining surplus to be equally distributed	1,500

The share of net assets taken by each partner will be A £2,500, B £1,500, C £1,000

(b) if there are losses these are met in the following order:

(i) out of profits;

(ii) out of capital;

(iii) by the partners individually according to the proportions by which they shared profits.

Using the example of A, B and C above, if the partnership assets on dissolution were £5,000 and the debts £3,000, then assuming profits were shared equally, the distribution to each partner would be as follows:

	£
Assets available for distribution	5,000
Firms debts	3,000
Surplus assets available for distribution	2,000
Repayment of total capital contribution	3,500
Shortfall	1,500
Losses shared equally	500

A receives £2,000 - £500 = £1,500

B receives £1,000 - £500 =£ 500

C receives £500 - £500 = £ 0

Where there has been a bankruptcy situation with either a partner or the firm itself being adjudicated bankrupt, there will be two groups of creditors; those of the partners personally, and those of the firm itself. It is important therefore that the personal debts and property of the partners can be kept separate from those of the partnership itself.

DISSOLUTION OF A REGISTERED COMPANY

We have already seen that the process by which a registered company can be brought to an end is known as a winding-up or a liquidation. The process is a detailed and complex one. It is regulated by the Insolvency Act 1986, a statute based upon the report of Sir Kenneth Cork. Shortly before the Royal Assent was granted, the Insolvency Bill as it then was, came back to the House of Lords for approval, where Lord Denning remarked, "In 1977 Sir Kenneth Cork and his Committee entered upon a review of the insolvency law. They sat for five years and heard the most expert evidence. It is the most technical subject you can imagine. Both lawyers and accountants hate it. Most of them know nothing about it."

The main aspects of it will be considered shortly, but before doing so two further points need to be made regarding dissolution. The first is that there are other methods by which a company can be dissolved that do not involve winding-up procedures. The second is that where the threat of dissolution is based upon company insolvency, alternatives to the drastic step of terminating the company by winding it up and realising its assets are available to creditors. A creditors composition may be entered into, or an administration order may be made by the court. These points are considered below.

(a) Methods of dissolution

A company is created by incorporation through registration. It can therefore only come to an end when the registration is discharged. Once this happens the contractual relationship between the company and its members, based upon the memorandum and articles of the company, also comes to an end.

A company can be dissolved:

(a) by proceedings brought by the Attorney-General for cancellation of the registration, on the grounds that the company's objects are illegal.

In *Attorney-General v. Lindi St. Claire (Personal Services) Ltd (1980)*, a lady, Miss St. Claire, formed the defendant company for the purposes of prostitution. The registrar had granted it a certificate of incorporation, after refusing to register it under various names submitted by Miss St. Claire, including Hookers Ltd, Prostitutes Ltd and even Lindi St. Claire French Lessons Ltd. The court however granted the cancellation on the grounds that the objects of the company were illegal;

(b) by an order of the court where the company is transferring its undertaking to another company under a scheme of reconstruction or reorganisation;

(c) by the registrar, who under s.652 Companies Act 1985 may strike off the register a company that is defunct. A defunct company is one which is no longer carrying on business. The section lays down a procedure to be followed by the registrar before he can validly exercise the power to remove the company from the register. This has become a very common method of dissolution, for it is cheap and easy; and

(d) by being wound-up, which may be either voluntary or compulsory. The legal provisions relating to company liquidations are contained in the Insolvency Act 1986. The title of this statute is perhaps rather misleading, since it contains provisions which regulate not only companies which are being dissolved on the basis of their insolvency, but also companies which, for a variety of reasons, are being wound up fully able to meet their liabilities.

Winding-up

Like a partnership, a limited company can be wound up as mentioned above either voluntarily, or compulsorily by order of the court. The grounds for winding up, whether on a voluntary or compulsory basis, are set out in the Insolvency Act 1986. They recognise that winding up is a step which may become necessary not only in cases of financial instability, but also because the company, which is of course a creature of statute, has failed to comply with the statutory provisions which bind it, or simply because the members no longer wish to trade together. When examining the operation of the limited company it is common to draw an analogy with natural persons. Thus the company is said to be born when its certificate of incorporation is granted, and henceforth its brain, the board of directors, guides its actions and formulates it decisions, which are executed through those it employs. Following this analogy through to its conclusion the process of winding-up is akin to the process of administering the estate of a deceased person. Assets are collected and used to satisfy debts owing, after which any property remaining can be distributed to those lawfully entitled, in the case of a company to its members. However the process of administering the estate of a deceased person commences with death, whereas winding-up is a process which culminates in the dissolution of the company, the administration being completed before the life of the company ends.

Terminology

A number of technical expressions are used in liquidation and it is helpful to briefly identify and describe them before proceeding further.

A 'petition' is an application to the court requesting the court to exercise its jurisdiction over company liquidations. A petition is presented where the liquidation is compulsory. In such cases the court has a major role to play. This is not so however in voluntary liquidations, where the liquidation is under the control of either the members or the creditors of the company.

A 'contributory' is a person liable to contribute to the assets of a company if it is wound-up. Existing members whose shares have not been fully paid fall within the definition of a contributory, and so to do similarly placed past members, whose shareholding ceased within the year preceding the winding-up. However a past member is not liable in respect of any debt contracted after his membership ceased. Nor is he required to make a contribution if the existing members are able to satisfy the contributions required of them.

A 'liquidator' is a person appointed to take control of the company, collect its assets, pay its debts, and distribute any surplus to the members according to their rights as shareholders. The liquidator therefore holds a position of great responsibility, and it is important to ensure that only individuals of integrity are qualified to hold such a post. In recent years some disquiet has been felt as a result of company liquidations in which the liquidator has been found to be conducting the winding-up for the benefit of directors, rather than the company's creditors. The Insolvency Act 1986 copes with this by requiring that only an 'insolvency practitioner', a term covering liquidators, can act in a winding-up. He must be authorised to do so by his own professional body (these include accountancy bodies and the Law Society), or by the Department of Trade and Industry. Certain people are completely excluded. An applicant must be shown to be a fit and proper person, and must provide security, to become an insolvency practitioner.

The 'Official Receiver' is appointed by the Department of Trade, and is concerned both with personal insolvency and with corporate insolvency. Official receivers are attached to courts with insolvency jurisdiction, and they act in the capacity of liquidators in the case of compulsory liquidations, being appointed automatically when a 'winding-up order' is made, that is when the court issues an order that the company be wound up. The Official Receiver (OR) remains in this office until another liquidator is appointed. Finally the London Gazette is an official publication used to satisfy the requirement of providing public notice of certain legal events, in the case of a liquidation for example, notice of a creditors meeting.

The basic aspects of a company liquidation

We have already noted that when the process of winding-up has been completed the company will be struck off the register of companies and will cease to exist. Of course no further claims can then be made against it. Consequently for anyone who is connected with the company, whether as an investor, creditor or employee, winding-up is of great significance.

Although statutory winding-up provisions are detailed, and sometimes complex, there are basically three aspects to a liquidation:

(a) who has the ability to institute and control the winding-up, and on what grounds;

(b) what are the legal provisions to be fulfilled during the procedure; and

(c) in what order are claims made against the company for payment met?

Methods of winding-up

Under s.73 Insolvency Act 1986 two methods of winding-up are recognised. These are:

(a) a voluntary winding-up, which according to s.90 may be either:

- (i) a members voluntary winding-up, or
- (ii) a creditors voluntary winding-up; and

(b) a winding up by the court, usually referred to as a compulsory winding-up.

Voluntary winding-up is more common than compulsory liquidation. It is a less formal procedure, and is therefore cheaper.

(a) Voluntary winding-up

Shareholders can at any time resolve to end the company. They initiate the procedure by passing a resolution to wind-up, either a special resolution if the company is solvent, or, in the case of insolvency, an extraordinary resolution that it cannot continue in business by reason of its liabilities. An ordinary resolution is sufficient where the time period fixed in the articles for the life of the company has passed, or an event stipulated in the articles as giving rise to dissolution has taken place.

Under s.86 when the resolution is passed the liquidation procedure begins. The consequences are that:

(i) the company ceases to carry on business, other than to enable it to wind up;

(ii) the company's corporate status remains intact until dissolution;

(iii) transfers of shares, and changes in member's rights are void unless sanctioned by the liquidator;

(iv) the director's powers cease when the liquidator is appointed, although he, or in a creditor's voluntary winding up they themselves, may permit the directors to continue; and

(v) if the liquidation is due to insolvency, company employees, who may include directors, will be dismissed. The liquidator may however employ them under a new contract.

Notice of the resolution must be advertised in the London Gazette within 14 days of it being passed. If a majority of the directors within five weeks of the passing of the resolution make a statutory declaration that the company is solvent, then the company members manage the winding-up. This includes the appointment of their own liquidator. This is a valuable power for the person appointed will be under their control, rather than the control of the creditors or the court. The court can nevertheless remove a liquidator on the basis of unfitness for office. The declaration of solvency states that the directors have examined the company's affairs and formed the opinion that within a stated period (up to a maximum of twelve months) the company will be able to pay its debts in full. If a declaration of solvency is not made the winding-up is a creditors winding-up. A creditors meeting must be summoned by the company. Details of this meeting must be posted to creditors and members giving them at least seven days notice, and be advertised in the London Gazette and two local newspapers.

The business of the creditors' meeting is to receive from the directors a full statement of the company's affairs, to draw up a list of creditors with estimates of their claims, to appoint a liquidator who will insert a notice in the London Gazette notifying other creditors to send in claims and if considered necessary appoint a committee of inspection.

(b) Compulsory winding-up

A compulsory winding-up is carried out by the court. This is either the High Court or, if the company's paid-up share capital does not exceed £120,000 the County Court in whose district the company has its registered office. Not all County Courts however, possess the necessary insolvency jurisdiction.

Proceedings are commenced by a person presenting a petition to the appropriate court. The petitioner may be the company itself, by resolution, the Secretary of State following an investigation or, in most cases, a creditor.

> In *Re: Othery Construction Ltd (1966)* Lord Buckley stated that if a fully paid up shareholder is to successfully petition to wind up:
>
> ". . . he must show either that there will be a surplus available for distribution amongst the shareholders or that the affairs of the company require investigation in respects which are likely to produce such a surplus".

Under s.122 a company may be wound-up by the court if:

(i) the company has passed a special resolution requesting it; or

(ii) in the case of a company registered as a public company, the company has been registered for more than a year, but as yet no certificate of ability to commence business has been issued. This certificate, which is issued by the Registrar, can only be obtained when certain financial details have been given to him. The company cannot commence business until the certificate, which is required under s.117 Companies Act 1985, has been issued. Private Companies do not require such a certificate and can commence business immediately on incorporation; or

(iii) the company does not commence business in the first year of its incorporation, or suspends business at any time for a whole year. An order will only be granted on this ground if the company has no intention of carrying on business again.

In *Re: Middlesbrough Assembly Rooms Co (1880)* a shareholder petitioned for winding-up where the company had suspended trading for over three years, because of a trade depression. The majority shareholders opposed the petition on the basis that the company intended to recommence trading when the economic situation improved. It was held that in the circumstances the petition should be dismissed;

(iv) if the membership has fallen below two; or

(v) if the company is unable to pay its debts. This is the ground most commonly relied upon. The company is deemed to be unable to pay its debts if a creditor who is owed a sum exceeding £750 by the company has left a written demand for it at the company's registered office, and the demand has remained unpaid for a period of three clear weeks. The company is not however regarded as neglecting the debt if it bone fide disputes the payment of it. Alternatively the company is deemed unable to pay its debts if:

   (a) execution has been issued on a judgment in favour of a creditor which is returned either wholly or partially unsatisfied (see Chapter 9); or

   (b) it is proved to the satisfaction of the court that the company is unable to pay its debts as they fall due.

In *Re: A Company (1986)* it was held that a company can be regarded as unable to pay its debts under this ground, where it has funds but persistently fails or neglects to pay its debts unless it is forced to do so. Many companies have a deliberate policy of holding back payment for as long as possible, and for some this may be their means of survival; or

   (c) where the court is satisfied that taking into account the company's present and future liabilities, the value of its assets is less than the amount of its liabilities; or

(vi) the court is of the opinion that it is just and equitable that the company should be wound-up. This ground covers a number of situations. For instance it covers cases where the substratum of the company has been destroyed.

In *Re: German Date Coffee Co (1882)* the company was wound up on the basis that it had become impossible to carry out the main object in the memorandum of association, namely the acquisition and working of a German patent to make coffee from dates, because the patent could not be obtained.

It also extends to circumstances in which the company has been formed for a fraudulent purpose; where the company is a sham, having no business or property; or where the rights of members are being flouted.

In *Loch v. John Blackwood Ltd (1924)* a director with voting control refused to hold meetings, produce accounts or pay dividends. The court held that the company could be wound up.

In *Ebrahami v. Westbourne Galleries (1972)* two individuals E and N had operated successfully in partnership together for many years. Later they converted the business to a company, with themselves as sole shareholders and directors, and after a time N's son was allowed into the business. This was granted as a favour by the plaintiff, who transferred some of his shares to the son. Unfortunately his generosity was met by N and his son combining their interests to force the plaintiff out of the business. The court granted the plaintiff's application to wind up. Commenting on the expression 'just and equitable' Lord Wilberforce said:

> 'The words are a recognition of the fact that a limited company is more than a mere legal entity, with a personality in law of its own; that there is room in company law for the recognition of the fact that behind it, or amongst it, there are individuals, with rights, expectations and obligations . . . which are not necessarily submerged in the company structure'.

The petition to wind up is presented to the Registrar of the court who fixes a time and place for the hearing. The petition must be advertised in the London Gazette at least seven clear days (excluding Saturday and Sunday) before the hearing. Rules of Court set out the form in which this advertised information must be provided; if they are not complied with the petitioner may have to meet all the court costs. The aim of the advertisement is to invite interested parties, the company's creditors and contributories, to oppose or support the petition. A person intending to appear at the hearing must give notice of this to the petitioner. After presentation of the petition a provisional liquidator may be appointed who is generally the Official Receiver. In any event when the hearing takes place, and the court makes a winding-up order, the Official Receiver becomes provisional liquidator by statute, and continues as liquidator unless the meeting of the creditors and contributories agree to the appointment of some other liquidator. This person must be an insolvency practitioner. The 1986 Act sets out the liquidator's powers. Essentially his task is to collect and realise the company's assets, including unpaid sums due to the company from contributories for their shares, to settle the lists of creditors and contributories, pay the company's debts in a fixed order, and finally to adjust the rights of the contributories distributing any surplus assets amongst them. At meetings of creditors and contributories it may be decided to apply to the court to form a committee of inspection. Having fulfilled these responsibilities the liquidator applies to the court for an order that the company be dissolved, and is then released from his or her role. The court, it should be noted, has a complete and unfettered discretion as to whether to make an order for winding-up. It may as an alternative conditionally or unconditionally adjourn the hearing, make an interim order, or dismiss the petition altogether.

The order of priorities

On dissolution there are likely to be many claims against the assets of the company. Provided the company is solvent this does not create any problems, but if it is insolvent the question which arises is how the shortfall is dealt with. Do all the companies creditors absorb the loss according to the proportion of credit they have provided, or do some creditors rank before others, so that whilst those at the top of the list may be repaid in full, those at the bottom could find themselves with nothing?

The answer is that the Insolvency Act 1986 lays down an order of priorities for the distribution of assets. The relevant provisions are contained in ss.175 and 176, which lays down the following order:

(i) the costs of winding-up (for example the liquidator's fees;

(ii) preferential debts. These include: income tax deducted from the pay of company employees under the PAYE system over the past year; VAT payments owed by the company that have accrued over the past six months; wages and salaries of employees outstanding for the previous four months, up to a present maximum figure of £800 per employee. A director may be a salaried employee, and thus qualifies under this head, however a director's fee rather than a salary will not rank as a preferential debt. If assets are sufficient, preferential debts are paid in full. If not, the available assets are distributed rateably between the preferential creditors, and in these circumstances property subject to a floating charge must be applied first in the payment of preferential debts, the holder being entitled only to the balance. Creditors who have the security of a fixed charge over assets of the company are, of course, able to realise the assets charged to meet the company's liability towards them;

(iii) ordinary unsecured debts, such as sums owing to trade creditors. If these cannot be paid in full they are paid rateably amongst the creditors;

(iv) the members according to their rights under the memorandum and articles. It may be that one class of shareholders is entitled to repayment of a certain amount of the surplus before the others, thus preference shareholders may receive repayment of their paid up capital in priority to ordinary shareholders.

ALTERNATIVES TO WINDING-UP

Whilst as we have seen, a company may be dissolved for reasons other than financial difficulty, many dissolutions are the result of a financial crisis. Directors faced with this situation may have the future affairs of the company taken out of their hands in a compulsory or creditors liquidation, the result of which will be that the life of the company will come to an end, and some creditors at least will be left with their debts unsatisfied. One of the aims of the Insolvency Act 1986 was to provide alternatives to this drastic outcome, which would act as financial rescue packages for companies in difficulty.

(a) Corporate voluntary arrangements — compositions with creditors

These are provided for by ss1 - 7 Insolvency Act 1986. They enable a company which is solvent or partially insolvent to follow a procedure which will result in a legally binding arrangement with its creditors. In outline the following stages have to be followed. The directors, or the liquidator if a winding-up is in progress, choose an insolvency practitioner to act as a 'nominee', and help them produce proposals to put to the creditors. These may be a composition (see Chapter 3) or a scheme of arrangement for the company i.e. the revision of its financial affairs in some way, such as alterations to class rights, or the extension of time for payment given by debenture notices.

The proposals are reported to the court and a meeting of creditors and shareholders is called both of which must approve them. The outcome is reported to the court. If approved, the proposals bind all the creditors and shareholders having notice of them, under s.5.

(b) Administration orders.

One of the problems with a voluntary arrangement is of course the difficulty of obtaining the agreement of large creditors, such as banks. They will want greater control over the organisation of the company's affairs. In such circumstances an administration order may be a useful device. Such an order can be made by the court once it is satisfied that the company is, or is likely to become, unable to pay its debts, and that an administration order would be likely to achieve:

(i) the survival of the company, and the whole or any part of its undertaking as a going concern; or

(ii) the approval of a voluntary arrangement (i.e. because of the appointment of an administrator); or

(iii) a more advantageous realisation of the company's assets than in a winding-up.

The company itself, its directors, a creditor or creditors may petition the court for such an order, and if granted the court will appoint the receiver who will be responsible for the management of the affairs, business and property of the company for the duration of the order. This can include the calling of meetings and the appointment and removal of directors. Any winding-up petition previously presented must be dismissed on the grant of an administration order. It remains to be seen how much use will be made of the administration order as an alternative to liquidation.

INDIVIDUAL INSOLVENCY

Personal insolvency occurs when an individual finds himself in serious financial difficulties and is unable to pay his creditors when debts fall due. If the creditors are unwilling or unable to wait for payment, the debtor may face bankruptcy proceedings under the Insolvency Act 1986. Broadly the purpose of bankruptcy is to ensure a fair distribution of assets to creditors and to allow the debtor to make a fresh start after his discharge.

The law relating to individual insolvency has undergone substantial change in recent years. The procedures under the Bankruptcy Act 1914 have been abolished and replaced with simpler procedures first introduced by the Insolvency Act 1985 and now contained in the Insolvency Act 1986. The new legislation was introduced with two main aims:

(a) to encourage voluntary arrangements between debtors and creditors; and

(b) to simplify and update bankruptcy procedures and bring them into line with the procedures applicable to company liquidations.

Under the 1986 Act there are two possible outcomes of individual insolvency: a voluntary arrangement or a bankruptcy order.

VOLUNTARY ARRANGEMENTS

Where an individual is facing insolvency, he may try to avoid a bankruptcy order by proposing a voluntary arrangement with his creditors. The advantages from the debtor's point of view of such an arrangement are that he avoids the stigma, loss of status and adverse publicity associated with a bankruptcy order, and avoids the disabilities to which an undischarged bankrupt is subject. The benefit of a voluntary arrangement for the creditor is that it should be less expensive, leaving more assets available for payment to him; and it will usually be quicker than bankruptcy procedure, which means that he will be paid sooner. The disadvantage from the creditors point of view is that the supervisor of a voluntary arrangement will not have as many powers as a trustee in bankruptcy, for example to set aside transactions at an undervalue or preferences.

The option of making a voluntary arrangement existed under the old bankruptcy law. Such an arrangement could be made under the Deeds of Arrangement Act 1914. In practice, however, deeds of arrangement are not used to any great extent, mainly because any one creditor, no matter how small the sum owed to him, could petition for bankruptcy if he did not accept the debtor's proposals. He could do this even though all of the other creditors were prepared to accept them. Under the 1986 Act, as we shall see, a dissenting creditor must accept a voluntary arrangement if more than 75% by value of creditors agree to it.

PROCEDURE FOR MAKING A VOLUNTARY ARRANGEMENT UNDER PART VIII OF THE INSOLVENCY ACT 1986

If a debtor wishes to make a voluntary arrangement he must choose an insolvency practitioner to help him draw up a proposal which can be presented to his creditors. An insolvency practitioner, usually an accountant or a solicitor, must be qualified in relation to insolvency and must be authorised by the Department of Trade to act in that capacity. The insolvency practitioner will have an important role to play in the voluntary arrangement, first as a 'nominee' preparing and presenting the proposal; and later as supervisor, implementing the proposal if it is accepted by the creditors.

PROCEDURE FOR MAKING A VOLUNTARY ARRANGEMENT

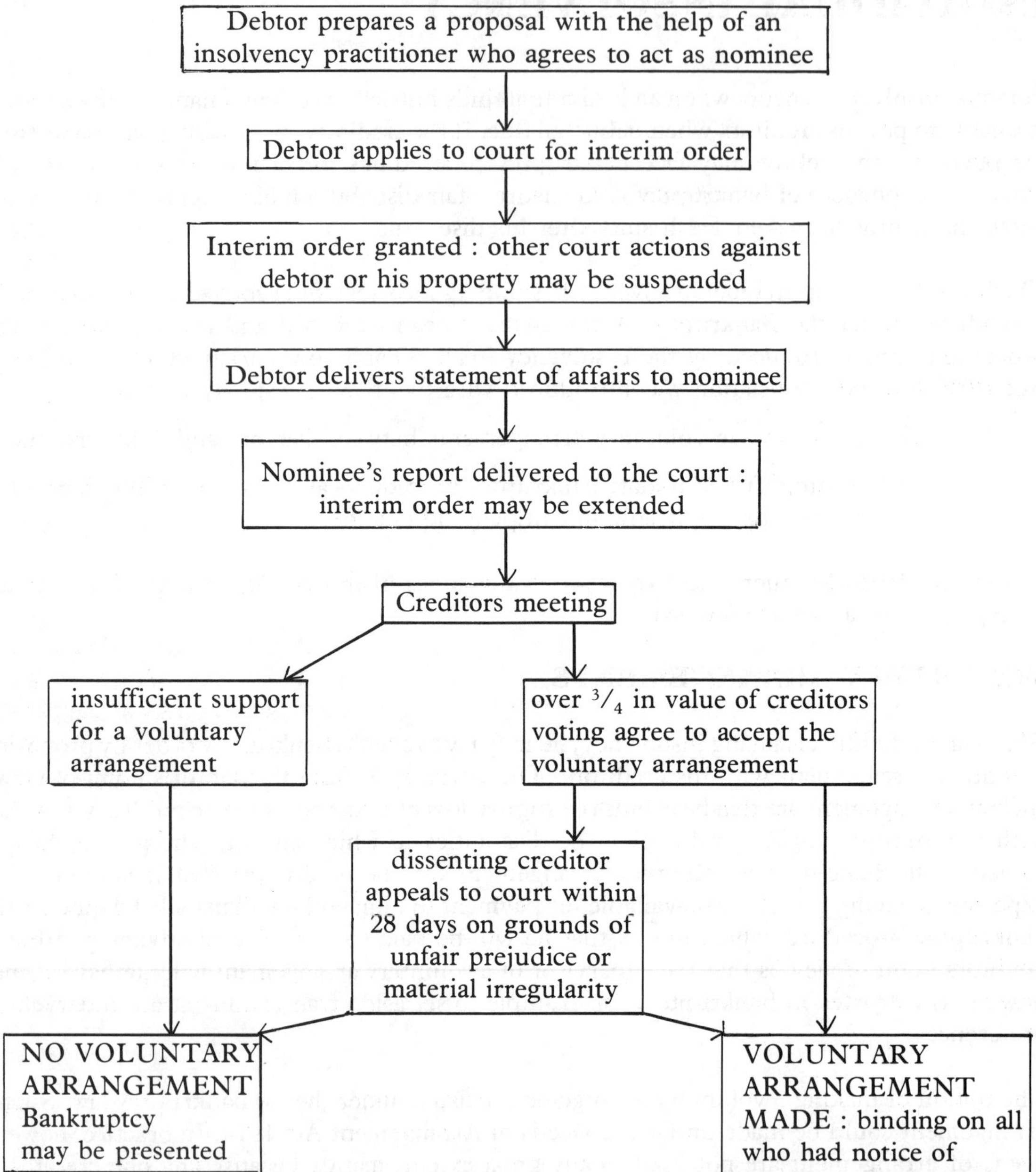

When the proposal is prepared, and an insolvency practitioner has agreed to act as nominee, the debtor must apply to the court for an interim order. Once this application is made, the court has power to suspend any legal proceedings against the debtor or his property.

The court will make an interim order if it is satisfied that it would be appropriate to do so, in order to allow the debtor to go ahead and make his proposal. If the court believes that the debtor is not acting in good faith or that the proposal is wholly unrealistic it may refuse to make the order. If an interim order is made, it will last for 14 days unless it is extended by the court. The effect of the order is that no bankruptcy petition can be presented against the debtor and no other legal proceedings may be commenced or continued against him without the court's permission.

Before the interim order expires, the nominee must report to the court stating whether he thinks that a meeting of creditors ought to be summoned to consider the debtor's proposal. To enable the nominee to make his report, the debtor has a duty to deliver a statement of affairs to him, together with the details of his proposal.

After receiving the nominee's report, the court will extend the interim order to allow the creditors to consider the debtor's proposal. The nominee must call a meeting of creditors. He must inform every creditor of whom he is aware about the meeting.

The purpose of the creditors meeting is to decide whether or not to accept the debtor's proposals for a voluntary arrangement, either in the form put forward by the debtor or in a modified form.

If the creditors are unable to agree to the proposal, the court can discharge the interim order and normal bankruptcy proceedings will probably follow. If a scheme is approved by over 75% in value of creditors voting at the meeting, the voluntary arrangement will be binding upon all creditors who had notice of the meeting and were entitled to vote.

The voluntary arrangement may be challenged by a dissatisfied creditor who must apply to the court to set it aside within 28 days. His application can be made on the grounds that there was a material irregularity in the calling or conduct of the creditors meeting; or that the voluntary arrangements unfairly prejudice his interests as a creditor.

If the proposal is approved at the creditors meeting, the nominee becomes its supervisor. The debtor must hand over his property to the supervisor, who will then carry out the arrangements. During the implementation of the voluntary arrangement by the supervisor, any of the parties, including the debtor, any creditors or the supervisor himself may apply to the court for directions to resolve any problems that may arise. When the task of supervision has been completed, the supervisor must notify all creditors and the debtor.

BANKRUPTCY PETITION BY A CREDITOR

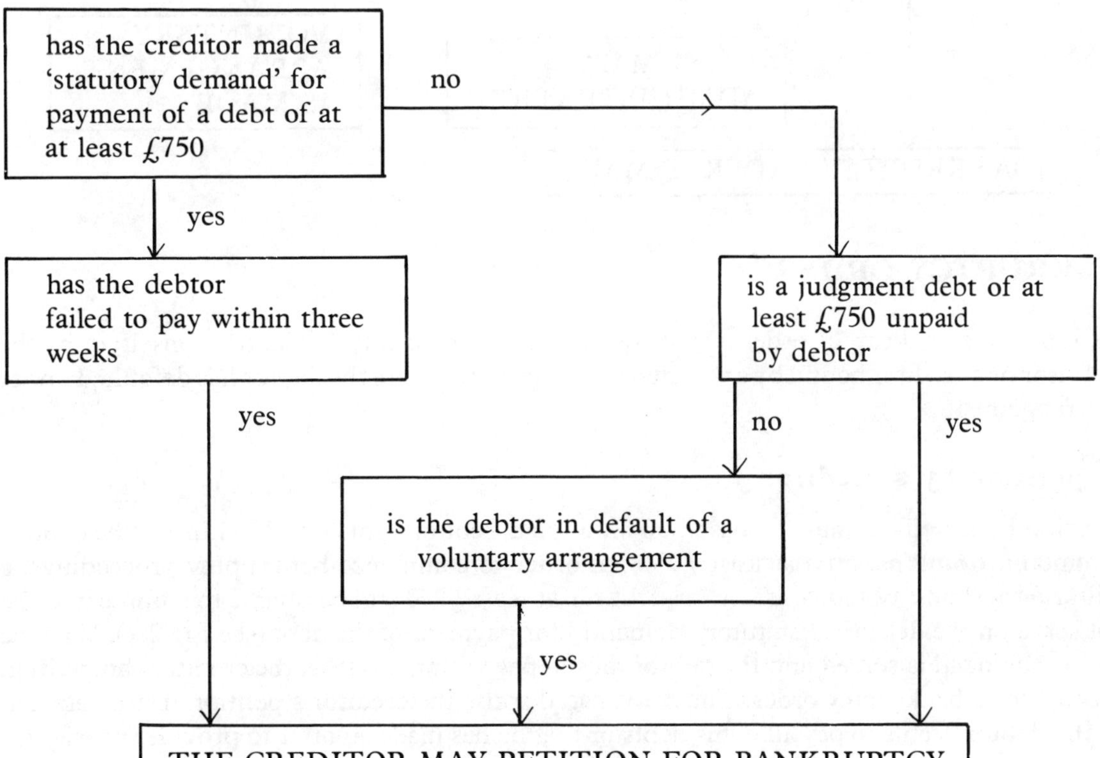

BANKRUPTCY PETITION BY A DEBTOR

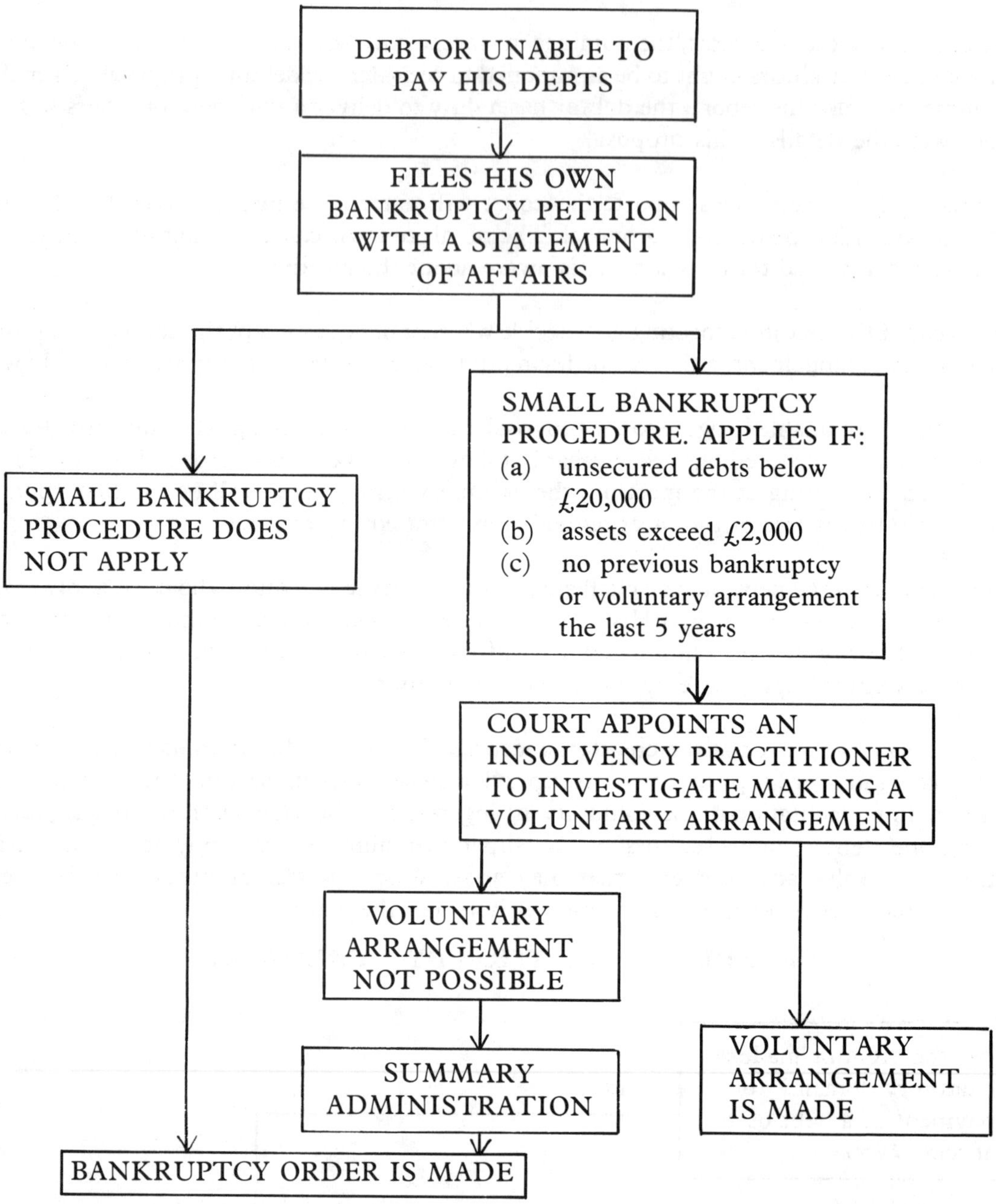

BANKRUPTCY ORDERS

A petition for a bankruptcy order may be presented by a creditor; the debtor himself; or by the supervisor or a creditor bound by a voluntary arrangement where the debtor has defaulted under the arrangement.

(a) petition by a creditor

A petition by a creditor must be based on an unpaid debt or debts owed to him by the debtor. The amount owing must be at least £750. In order to commence bankruptcy proceedings, a creditor either must obtain a judgment debt for at least £750 and be unable to enforce it; or he must serve on the debtor a "statutory demand" for payment of the debt (see Fig 2.x). Where a statutory demand is served and the debtor fails to pay within 3 weeks, the creditor can petition the court for a bankruptcy order. The court can dismiss the creditor's petition if it is satisfied that the debtor is able to pay all of his debts or that he has made an offer to provide security for the payment of the debt or to enter into a voluntary arrangement and the creditor has unreasonably refused to accept his offer.

(b) petition by the debtor

The sole ground on which a debtor may petition for his own bankruptcy is that he is unable to pay his debts. His petition must be accompanied by a "statement of affairs" setting out details of his assets and liabilities.

Where the debtor's unsecured debts are less than £20,000, his assets are £2,000 or more and he has not been bankrupt or made a voluntary arrangement within the last 5 years, the court will appoint an insolvency practitioner to investigate the possibility of a voluntary arrangement and prepare a report. If the report is favourable the court will make an interim order with a view to a creditors meeting and a voluntary arrangement. If the report of the insolvency practitioner indicates that a voluntary arrangement would be unlikely to succeed, the court, if it agrees, will make a bankruptcy order. In these circumstances the order will be by way of a summary administration of the bankrupt's estate.

The advantages of a summary administration are that the procedures are simpler and, from the debtor's point of view, he will be discharged from the bankruptcy after 2 years.

THE TRUSTEE IN BANKRUPTCY

The function of the trustee in bankruptcy is to collect in the assets of the bankrupt and distribute them in accordance with the rules in the Insolvency Act. The order of priority for repayment of debts is similar to that described for the winding-up of companies. All of the bankrupts property vests in the trustee in bankruptcy, with the exception of tools, vehicles and equipment for use by the bankrupt in his employment or business; and such clothing, bedding, furniture and household equipment as are necessary to satisfy the basic domestic needs of the bankrupt and his family.

Any property which is acquired by the bankrupt before he is discharged can be claimed by the trustee. The trustee may also apply to the court for an "income payments order". Under the terms of such an order part of any income to which the bankrupt is entitled whilst undischarged will be transferred to the trustee for the benefit of the creditors.

Creditors must submit proof of any debts to the trustee in bankruptcy. When the trustee has collected in all the bankrupts property he can declare and distribute a final dividend to creditors. After this has been done he will call a final general meeting of creditors and report on the administration of the estate.

Two further powers of the trustee enable him to apply to the court for an order to overcome certain types of transaction entered into by the bankrupt prior to the presentation of the bankruptcy petition. These are transaction at 'an undervalue', meaning a transaction in which the consideration received by the bankrupt is significantly less than that he has given (or is non existent), and 'preferences', which involves the bankrupt putting a creditor in a better financial position than he would have been in for the purpose of distributing the assets of the bankrupt's estate; in other words advancing the interests of one or more creditors to the disadvantage of others.

Almost identical powers are available to a liquidator in the event of a company winding-up, in cases where prior to the winding-up, the company, through its directors, has entered into individual transactions or has given preference to certain of its creditors. Although such activities may be fraudulent, fraud does not need to be established for the court to consider the issue of an order to set aside such transactions.

DURATION OF BANKRUPTCY

The bankruptcy continues until an individual is discharged from it. If a person is bankrupt for the first time, he will be discharged automatically after 3 years from the date of the Bankruptcy Order. In a summary administration, as we have seen, discharge will occur after 2 years. In either case, the period can be extended by the court if the bankrupt has failed to comply with any of his obligations under the Insolvency Act 1986. If the bankrupt has previously been an undischarged bankrupt during the previous 15 years, he will not automatically be discharged. He must apply to the court for discharge after 5 years from the making of the Bankruptcy Order. Where such an application is made, the court may refuse to discharge the bankrupt. It may grant a discharge, either unconditionally or upon condition that he, for example, makes further payments to his creditors.

An undischarged bankrupt is subject to certain legal disabilities. He cannot obtain credit; or become a member of parliament, a justice of the peace or a councillor.

Discharge from bankruptcy releases the bankrupt from the debts which existed at the commencement of his bankruptcy. A discharge from bankruptcy, however, does not affect his liability for fines imposed by a court for any criminal offence, or the enforcement of any security by a secured creditor.

ASSIGNMENT — WESTBOROUGH ROCK CONCERT

During the summer Westborough City Council organised a series of rock concerts over a three day period. The concerts were very succesful, however the event has given rise to certain legal issues, and a file dealing with them has been passed to the City Solicitor. You work in the City's Legal Department and the file has been referred to you from the City solicitor with a covering internal memorandum from him. The letters are included below:

> "The Chief Executive
> Westborough City Council
> City Hall
> WESTBOROUGH
>
> Dear Sir,
>
> **Westborough Rock Concert**
>
> I am the managing director of Starburst Enterprises Limited, and I am writing to you regarding the contract under which we agreed to provide you with a supporting band, The Roadcrash, for each of the three performances organised by you at the concert. The agreement was negotiated on our side by Ralph Jacobs, a director of the company, for a fee of £6,000. Ralph informs me that due to the non appearance of the band for the first night's performance, you are seeking to invoke clause 8 of our agreement with you which states:
>
> > "In the event of the artists failing to perform on stage for any one or more of the agreed performances, the council shall have the right, at its absolute discretion, to claim damages of an amount not to exceed one and a half times the total appearance fee due to the company."
>
> I must point out to you that my company intends to strenously resist any attempt by you to release this sum. It is indeed the company's view that the agreement itself is invalid since the company's articles of association require all contracts over £5,000 to be agreed by the full board, and Mr. Jacobs neither sought nor received such approval.
>
> Yours faithfully,
>
> Jack Soames
>
> JACK SOAMES
> Managing Director."

A S GILBERT ACCA
Chartered Accountant

Breams Buildings
West End
Denton Grove
Westborough WH1 2AC

The Chief Executive
Westborough City Council
City Hall
Westborough BM1 1AA

Dear Sir,

I have been appointed as Liquidator of Happy Jack Records Ltd. I understand that you are owed the sum of £400 by the company for a licence you granted to it to operate a small sales unit at the Westborough Rock Concert, from which it sold tee shirts, badges and similar items.

It is my view that the company lacked the authority to enter into this licence agreement. Its objects clause provides that:

> *"The objects for which the company is established are: to carry on and undertake the business of phonographic materials retailers; and to carry on any trade, business or mercantile operation which in the opinion of the directors may be incident, auxilliary or conducive to the above objects."*

In these circumstances I must reject all liability for the licence fee due.

Yours faithfully,

A S Gilbert
Liquidator

TASKS

1. (a) Draft a letter of reply to the Managing Director of Starburst Enterprises in which you argue the legal merits of the council's claim against the Company

   (b) Produce notes to append to the file which identify any weaknesses in the Council's claim.

2. Draft an internal memorandum to the City Solicitor indicating whether, in your view, the liquidator's denial of liability for payment of the licence fee is a valid one.

ASSIGNMENT — TROUBLE AT MILLS

In 1980 Mark Mills, together with his cousin Bryan and a business associate of Bryan's, an accountant called Peter Marshall, decided to form a company to deal in personal insurance services. The company received its certificate of incorporation at the end of 1980. It was called Mills & Co. (Insurance Services) Ltd and its premises were in Leeds. Mark and Bryan took up 35% of the shares each, Peter took the remainder. The company objects stated that it could carry on the business of providing "personal insurance of any kind".

In 1983 Peter was anxious that his wife should join the company, and each of the existing shareholders agreed to transfer some of their shares to her. As a result she obtained a 25% stake, Mark, Bryan and Peter's shareholding being reduced to 25% each.

Mark was happy with the company structure, since Peter's wife brought to the business considerable commercial expertise, and he recevied a large sum for the shares he transferred to her. Within a year however the relationship between the shareholders had deteriorated. In particular Mark felt increasingly isolated. He was anxious that the company expand its insurance business to provide insurance facilities for commercial as well as personal customers. The other shareholders however were of the view that the company, which was suffering a reduced level of profit, should diversify, and move into the lucrative field of marketing, the area in which Peter's wife had previously worked.

By 1986 Mark had decided to form a separate business to offer a complete range of insurance facilities. He formed a partnership with James Blake-Smith, an old schoolfriend, to carry on the additional business. He did not reveal the existence of this business to his fellow shareholders in Mills & Co. Ltd, assuming that since it was based in Barnsley, a town twenty miles away from the company's place of business in Leeds, it had nothing to do with them. No partnership articles were drawn up.

The other members of Mills & Co Ltd recently discovered the existence of Mark's new firm. They responded by calling a company meeting, at which, during very stormy business they resolved to alter the company articles to enable it to pursue marketing work, to sell off the company's present business undertaking at a figure well below what Mark believes to be its true value, and to remove him as a director. In addition they are threatening to take away his voting rights. Marks problems have been compounded by problems in the partnership. He has discovered that James Blake-Smith has been in financial difficulties, and that bankruptcy proceedings have been commenced against him this week. He has also purchased, in the firm's name, an expensive computer system, despite a recent partnership meeting at which it was agreed to defer the expendiutre until the next financial year.

In an effort to clarify the legal position in relation to these business difficulties Mark has sought your help. As someone with a business of your own and a knowledge of the legal principles applicable to business organisations. Prior to meeting Mark in a couple of days time, you have decided to analyse the legal position he has found himself in, in order to fully advise him as to the extent of his rights and liabilities.

TASK

Draft an outline report which you can give to Mark at your meeting with him, that expresses your considered legal opinion on his present business problems.

TASK

Chapter 3

BUSINESS CONTRACTING

Economic activity, which we may regard as the acquisition, use and disposal of resources, is one of the most fundamental characteristics of human patterns of behaviour. Organisations and individuals all participate to a greater or lesser extent in this activity, and a nation's material well-being is usually judged in terms of its economic fitness, in other words how economically active it is. There are many factors contributing towards a fit and flourishing economy. They include the presence of natural physical resources, the skills and mobility of the labour force, and the devices used by government to manage the economy. These factors are not matters for consideration in a book of this kind. What we are concerned with, however, is a less obvious but nontheless indispensable component of the economic process. It is the rules and principles which govern the conduct of the participants engaged in negotiating and and carrying out the millions of tranactions by which economic objectives are achieved. This body of rules and principles is collectively referred to as the law of contract.

Without an effective legal framework to regulate the enormous number of transactions which an industrialised economy demands each day to function effectively, economic activity would rapidly decline. The reason for this is that most industrial and commercial organisations would be unwilling to take the financial risks inherent in trading, if it were not for the existence of well established, formalised rules of trading, supported by legal sanctions if they are broken. Although it is not possible to prevent a fellow trader from breaking promises if the promises are included in a contract, at least you have the reassurance of knowing that a legal obligation has been broken. If necessary court action can be taken to obtain redress. The remedy is usually in the form of an award of damages, which is monetary compensation. The process which describes a person bringing legal action against another is called litigation. A litigant is said to bring a legal action or sue. Thus for a bank to lend money, a civil engineering company to construct a motorway, a landowner to grant a lease of land or an employer to take on staff, there needs to be a measure of confidence underlying such agreements so that if they are broken in some way a legal remedy is available to the injured party. Without the security of a binding contract there would be little confidence in forming trading bonds. The only security that might exist would depend upon whether the other party

(i) felt a moral obligation to meet the promises given, or

(ii) believed it could be damaging to his business reputation and standing if it became known that he did not honour his agreements.

It is not only in the economic interest that ground rules are important. There may be social implications too. If a manufacturer of childrens toys produces items which are dangerous to their users, or an employer dismisses an employee out of spite, or a tour operator sells holidays which it knows do not meet the claims made in the brochure, most people will see this as socially unacceptable conduct in terms of the consequences that result from it. As a society it concerns us if children are hurt when playing with dangerous toys whose design faults could not have been discovered at the time their parents purchased them. We would conclude, no doubt, that whatever the manufacturers legal responsibilities may be, he is without doubt socially irresponsible. Similarly it concerns us that the employee has lost his job without good cause, and the family on holiday with young children find the beach is not 100 yards away from the hotel as they were promised, but 1000 yards away. In each case there is a social cost, not merely a financial one. The employee is unable to find alternative employment nearby, and is obliged to move with the family to another part of the country, disturbing his childrens education and creating a stressful situation. The family on holiday suffer considerable disappointment and inconvenience.

Sometimes particular forms of contractual activity may appear to be both economically and socially undesirable. Suppose a major UK employer were to insist that all employees sign an undertaking not to seek further employment with any rival organisation anywhere in the UK, for a period of ten years after leaving the present employer. The effect is like to be

(i) to create an unfair trading advantage to the present employer, gained by excluding similar employers who may operate their business more efficiently, from the full pool of skilled labour potentially available;

(ii) to prevent employees from exercising the opportunity to obtain the best salaries that their skills can command; and

(iii) in general economic terms to distort the mobility of labour.

It is clear then that rules are necessary to regulate the agreements used in transacting, in order:

(a) to provide a legal framework that offers security and enables commercial activity to expand and prosper;

(b) to restrict activities which are economically harmful;

(c) to pursue the aims of social justice where appropriate; and

(d) to identify the technical means by which parties who wish to do so can make agreements which the law will enforce. An agreement which is legally enforceable is known as a contract.

Before examining the concept of the contract in more depth it is helpful to say a little about the thinking which has guided the lawmakers in creating and developing the principles and rules which make up this body of law.

THE CONCEPT OF FREEDOM OF CONTRACT.

Historically there has never been a time at which contracting parties have enjoyed complete freedom to make whatever bargain they choose. Throughout the long development of the English law of contract, which has taken place over many centuries, restrictions have always been applied. No court, for example has ever been prepared to enforce a contract whose purpose is unlawful, such as an agreement to commit a criminal offence. However the extent of contractual regulation has varied over time, reflecting the thinking current during different periods.

Under the capitalist philosophy of the nineteenth century a laissez-faire approach to the development of the economy was advocated. This involved leaving the markets for goods and services, as far as reasonably practicable, to regulate themselves. The idea of a free market, which should be left to control itself unhindered by the interventions of the Courts or Parliament, helped to reinforce the view that had been influential since the eighteenth century of 'freedom of contract.' The advocates of freedom of contract considered that as few restrictions as possible should be placed upon the liberty of individuals to make agreements. There appear to be some compelling reasons for supporting this view. Firstly the law of contract is a part of private law, which means that the creation and performance of contracts is the responsibility of the parties themselves. As we shall see later contractual rights and obligations only attach to the parties entering the contract, although this principle is subject to certain exceptions. Consequently these rights and obligations are purely personal. If a contract is broken the only person with the right to a remedy is the injured party; no one else can sue the contract breaker. Secondly it is the parties themselves who are best able to judge their own contractual needs. If their negotiations are not concluded to their mutual satisfaction then they will not go ahead and make the contract. If on the other hand they are both in agreement they will be happy to bind themselves formally, and incur contractual obligations. They should be left alone to make the contracts that suit them, free from external interference.

The underlying reasons then, for allowing a wide measure of contractual freedom are:

> **a. market needs:** in the interests of healthy markets the participants in market activity should be allowed to trade unhindered. The able will survive and the weak will flounder. External intervention in this process will tend to weaken rather than strengthen economic performance by the artificial distribution of the bargaining process.
>
> **b. personal liberty:** interference in contract making is an infringement of individual liberty. In the same way that a person chooses when to marry, or for whom to vote, they should be allowed the freedom to make the contracts of their choosing. If subsequently the choice turns out to be a bad one it is of concern to nobody but the contract maker. The contract is a private, not a public event.
>
> **c. knowledge:** contracting parties can be assumed to know what they are doing. They act in a rational manner and will therefore ensure that the contract they make is the contract they want. Nobody else is better placed to identify contractual wants and needs than the parties who are making the contract.

On closer analysis however, it is possible to identify major weaknesses inherent in the factors listed above. In simple terms the underlying flaw in all of them is that they do not reflect the reality of modern contract making. It is important to an understanding of the law of contract to appreciate why the ideas upon which the notion of freedom of contract are based, are in reality largely myths.

THE REALITY OF BUSINESS CONTRACTING

In one sense there is complete contractual freedom. Individuals and organisations alike are free to choose whether to enter into a contracual relationship. It cannot be forced on them for consent is a pre-requirement of the relationship. But what precisely does consent mean? To answer this question we need to examine how the courts discriminate between situations where there is a genuine consent, and those in which the consent is in reality artificial. Where the consent is unreal there is no "consensus ad idem", or meeting of the minds of the parties, even though on a superficial level they have gone through the motions of reaching an agreement. Circumstances in which the courts will be prepared to consider a claim that the consent is unreal are in cases of misrepresentation, mistake, fraud, duress or undue influence. They are referred to technically as vitiating (invalidating) elements. Once established they have the effect of either invalidating the contract in its entirety in which case the contract is said to be void, or of entitling the injured party to escape from the contract if he or she wishes to do so. In such circumstances the contract is said to be voidable in their favour. To vitiate literally means to make invalid or ineffectual. We will return to void and voidable contracts later.

The vitiating elements are dealt with in the next chapter, but we may note here that by granting relief where consent is a sham because a person has been misled, tricked, coerced or mistaken, the courts are demonstrating that they will look at what the parties believed they were agreeing when the contract was made. Equally of course, the notion of freedom carries with it responsibility, and it is certainly not the role of the courts to repair bad bargains made through lack of prudence. The balance between intervening in an attempt to right legitimate wrongs, and leaving the parties to learn from their trading mistakes is not easily achieved. The point is that the courts are prepared in the right circumstances to untie the bond that has been made, thereby protecting parties in a limited way from the consequences that complete freedom of contract would otherwise produce.

A further important element in examining the concept of freedom of contract is the matter of bargaining power. True consensus is only possible where the parties meet as bargaining equals, but it is commonplace to find that there is an inequality of bargaining power so that one party is able to dominate the other. The result is that far from arriving at agreement through a process of negotiation, the contract is a one sided arrangement in which the dominant party presents terms to the weaker party on a take-it-or-leave it basis. Commonly the dominant party will only be prepared to do business on the basis of standard terms designed to provide him with a high level of commercial protection (see figure 5.2). If the dominant party is a monopoly supplier, like British Gas or British Rail, the consumer is unable to shop around for a better deal. Even in a reasonably competitive market situation, however, it is often the case that suppliers of goods or services trade on the same or very similar terms, for instance by using a contract designed by the trade association of which they are a member. To help redress the imbalance Parliament has used legislation to bolster the rights of consumers, whether they be businessess or individuals. This legislation is considered elsewhere in the book, but the most notable examples are the Consumer Credit Act 1974, the Unfair Contract Terms Act 1977, and Sale of Goods Act 1979, the Supply of Goods & Services Act 1982 and the Consumer Protection Act 1987.

Even the courts have been prepared to intervene in circumstances of exceptional exploitation. To do so they have applied an equitable principle known as undue influence.

> A good illustration is provided by the decision of the Court of Appeal in *Lloyds Bank Ltd. v. Bundy (1975)*. Here an elderly farmer, who was ill and had little business knowledge, agreed with the bank to guarantee the account of his son's company. The company was in difficulties, and over a period of time the father increased the size of the guarantee, which was secured by a mortgage on his house, so that eventually the mortgage on the property was for more than the property was worth. This arrangement had been made by the father in consultation with the bank manager, upon whom he implicitly relied. The company's debts remained outstanding, and the bank sought to sell the father's house in order to realise the guarantee. The Court of Appeal unanimously set aside the agreement between the father and the bank. In the course of his judgment Lord Denning M.R. made the following important observations: "No bargain will be upset which is the result of the ordinary interplay of forces. There are many hard cases which are caught by this rule . . . Yet there are exceptions to this general rule . . . in which the courts will set aside a contract, or a transfer of property, when the parties have not met on equal terms, when the one is so strong in bargaining power and the other so weak that, as a matter of common fairness, it is not right that the strong should be allowed to push the weak to the wall . . . English law gives relief to one who, without independent advise, enters into a contract on terms which are very unfair or transfer property for a consideration which is grossly inadquate . . . "

Finally both Parliament and the courts have been prepared to intervene in cases where the effect of a contract is to act as a restraint of trade. In the words of Lord McNaghten in *Nordenfelt v Maxim Nordenfelt Gun & Ammunition Co. Ltd. (1894)*, "The public have an interest in every person's carrying on his trade freely; so has the individual. All interference with individual liberty of action in trading, and all restraints of trade themselves, if there is nothing more, are contrary to public policy, and are therefore void."

Of the many types of restraint of trade recognised, the following are the most common:

(i) restraints on employment. These usually appear as terms inserted in the contract of employment by the employer, designed to prevent employees from setting up in competition when they leave the employment.

(ii) agreements between suppliers and retailers under which the retailer agrees to sell only the supplied goods. The best example of such arrangements can be seen in the practices of the petrol industry. Petrol companies impose 'solus' agreements upon petrol stations, requiring them to sell only the petrol and other products of that particular petrol company.

(iii) price fixing agreements and agreements which seek to regulate or limit supplies of goods.

The essence of a contract in restraint of trade is that it contains an undertaking by one of the parties to restrict that persons freedom of trading action with others in the future. The grounds for legal interference in such arrangements are those of public policy: what the courts and Parliament are seeking to prevent are practices which restrict competition to the detriment of the public.

It can be seen that despite a general desire to allow parties freedom to make the bargains of their choosing, intervention is exercised in a variety of situations which appear to demand it. In summary these are:

(i) where consent is not a true consent;

(ii) in circumstances of significant bargaining inequality; and

(iii) where the best interests of trade are not being achieved by specific market practices, through the use of anti-competitive devices.

Having examined some of the ideas underlying the concept of what a contract is, we now turn to consider whether any formalities are prescribed by law for creating a contract, and how classifications of contracts are made according to their form and nature.

CONTRACTUAL FORMALITIES

It is a commonly held view that a contract is not valid unless it is written. This is simply not the case, as can be illustrated by the number of times we make purchases of goods or pay for services without even contemplating the need for a written contract. Indeed contracts are invariably carried out by parties who are not even aware that they have been involved in a legal relationship at all. If written contracts were necessary to effect all transactions a moments reflection will demonstrate how time consuming, wasteful of paper and largely irrelevant to our needs such an enterprise would be. There are, however, some sound reasons in support of the view that a written contract may be worthwhile;

(i) because the writing would stand as evidence of the transaction should anyone challenge its existence, and

(ii) because the task of reducing an agreement into writing would presumably prompt the parties into expressing themselves clearly, and thinking about the nature of the transaction they are involved in. It would indicate the rights and obligations of the people making it.

SIMPLE CONTRACTS AND DEEDS.

The law recognises a legally enforceable transaction if it is contained in the form of a simple contract, or alternatively in the form of a deed. The latter is far less common.

Simple Contracts

At common law parties are free to express a simple contract in any way, hence the term 'simple' meaning non-technical. The simple contract may be oral, written, or even established by inference based upon the conduct of the parties. Most simple contracts are oral agreements; buying food, petrol, a record or tape, clothes and so on. Those that are commonly expressed in writing include taking a package holiday, arranging for double glazing, central heating, or some other substantial work to be carried out to a property, joining a bookclub, employing staff, and opening a bank account, but there are many more. Sometimes the contract may be part written and part oral. Contracts arising out of conduct are not common. An example will help to illustrate how such a situation can arise. Let us suppose a supplier of oil provides a customer with a fixed quantity of the oil each month, under an agreement to run for a year. In the event that the supplier delivers the same quantity of oil in the first month of the following year, which is then used by the customer, a new contract would be inferred from the conduct of the parties, even though they have not met face to face. The terms of the new contract will be those of the original.

> In *Brogden v. Metropolitan Railway Co. (1877)*, the railway company had been supplied with coal from Brogden for many years. The company was keen to have a formal agreement. It drew up a draft agreement, which was sent to Brogden, and was returned by him to the company marked "approved", although he had inserted a new term to the draft. For the next two years coal was supplied and paid for between the parties in accordance with the draft agreement, although the company never gave notification that they had accepted it. In fact over the two years it lay in a desk draw. Then a dispute arose between the parties. Brogden alleged there was no contract binding them. The House of Lords disagreed, taking the view that there was a contract, based upon conduct. This occurred when the order was placed for the coal on the terms of the draft agreement, although it had never been formally accepted. The Lord Chancellor, Lord Cairns, remarked, "there may be a consensus between the parties far short of a mode of expressing it, and that consensus may be discovered from letters or from other documents of an imperfect and incomplete description."

All that is required in order to establish a simple contract is:

a. an agreement between the contracting parties;

b. the provision of consideration to support the contract;

c. an intention to become legally bound; and

d. legal capacity held by the parties.

These four vital components are essential. The absence of any one of them will prevent the creation of a contract. However a simple contract which meets these requirements may still fail for some other reason. This aspect of contract making is investigated in Chapter 4. Whatever the reason for the failure, it is of the greatest importance to be certain of the effect it has on the contract. The specific nature of the failure determines whether, and if so how, the contract survives, and this in turn tells us about the liabilities of the parties.

Void, voidable and unenforceable contracts.

Sometimes a contract will fail in such a fundamental way as to render it void. A void contract carries no contractual rights or obligations, so if the goods have been transferred under such a contract, ownership in them will not pass and they can be recovered from the person in possession of them. Money paid under a void contract may be reclaimed in a form of contractual action.

> This occurred in *Craven-Ellis v. Canons Ltd (1936)*, where it was found that the plaintiff, who had worked for some time as the managing director of the defendant company, had in fact been employed under a deed which was void because he had failed to take up shares in the company as required by the company's articles. Nevertheless, he was entitled to remuneration for the work he had done.

The term 'void contract' is really a contradiction in terms, since if the contract is void there is no legally enforceable agreement amounting to a contract. An example of a void contract is one whose purpose is illegal, such as an agreement to commit a criminal act, or trade with an enemy alien during time of war.

Sometimes the contract will not be void but merely voidable. Where this is so, one of the parties has the option of avoiding the contract, but until this is done the contract still stands. An example is provided in the case of contracts induced by fraud, where the deceived party can avoid the contract.

Finally, a contract may be unenforceable and where this is so the court is unable to enforce it, although in other respects it is still valid. The unenforceability can occur because of a failure to satisfy some technical requirement, such as the need for written evidence to support certain types of contract.

There is a significant difference between merely requiring written evidence of an agreement, and requiring the entire contract to be in writing. The burden of satisfying the former requirement is less onerous than satisfying the latter.

Contracts where writing is necessary.

Statute requires that certain contracts be made in writing. The reason for demanding this is in some cases to provide the consumer with a measure of protection, but more usually it is required in an effort to oblige parties involved in technical transactions to record their respective obligations. Examples include:

(a) Hire purchase and conditional sale agreements Consumer Credit Act 1974. Under s.65(1) of the Consumer Credit Act 1974 such an agreement cannot be enforced unless it is properly executed. It is properly executed when a legible document containing all the express terms of the agreement and in the prescribed form is signed by the parties.

(b) The transfer of shares in a registered company. This is required under s.183 Companies Act 1985, which states that a "proper instrument of transfer" must be delivered to the company. The company cannot register the transfer until this is done.

(c) An acknowledgement of a debt which has become statute-bound, under the Limitation Act 1980.

(d) An assignment of a copyright, under the Copyright Act 1956.

Failure to comply with these statutory requirements will render the contract void.

In respect of two further catagories of contract, one of great practical significance, the other less so, a court can only enforce the contract if it is evidenced in writing. These are:

(e) Contracts for the sale or other disposition of land under s.40 Law of Property Act 1925. All that is required here is sufficient written evidence to support the alleged contract. Under s.40(1) of the Law of Property Act 1925, this will involve identifying the property concerned, the parties to the agreement and the price to be paid. The written evidence can be in any form, although in any action the party against whom the action is brought must have signed the document. Note that the contract itself does not have to be in writing, although as a matter of practice such contracts almost always are.

(f) Contracts of guarantee under the Statute of Frauds 1677 (as amended). A contract of guarantee is a "promise to answer for the debt, default or miscarriage of another person", and the guarantor's liability arises only upon the failure of the debtor to pay.

Deeds.

A deed is a formal legal document, which must be in writing, be signed and sealed by the parties, and brought into operation by delivery i.e. dating it or physically transferring it. A deed is required under the law, by statute (the Law of Property Act 1925) to transfer legal ownership in freehold land, and to create a lease of more than three years duration. Although most deeds will arise out of agreements between parties who have exchanged promises of value, a deed is valid without the need for consideration to support it. Validity is achieved by the technical form of the document. Although it was originally necessary for corporate bodies to contract using the corporate seal, the Corporate Bodies Contracts Act 1960 specifies that a corporation can make contracts as though it were an individual, thus there are no longer any special formal requirements attached to corporations and their contract making.

Deeds are referred to technically as specialty contracts.

Having considered the formalities that are attached to contracting, we now need to look in some depth at the elements involved in forming a valid contract.

FORMATION OF CONTRACTS.

AGREEMENT

A contract cannot be created without the parties reaching an agreement. The idea of agreement is therefore central to an understanding of the law of contract. In the business context there are two basic legal questions which arise in respect of all transactions. These are firstly whether a legally enforceable agreement has been made, and secondly what are the terms upon which it is based.

The answer to the second question will reveal the specific obligations each party has towards the other, a matter of considerable importance to them both. It is only by identifying the content and extent of their mutual undertakings that the parties are able to know when they have discharged their responsibilities under the contract, and freed themselves from their legal bond. The two questions are, of course, very closely connected, because it is through the process of reaching their agreement that the parties will expressly fix the terms that are to regulate their contract. In other words agreements are arrângements to do, or possibly refrain from doing, specific things, and these specific things are the terms of the contract.

It may be true that most people can instinctively tell whether they have an agreement or not, however for legal purposes it is not sufficient to rely upon subjective judgments to decide such significant events. If a disputed agreement comes before a court, obviously the court cannot get inside the minds of the parties to discover their actual intentions. At best all that can be achieved is to look at the way they have conducted themselves, examining what they have said and done, in order to decide the issue on the basis of what a reasonable person would assume.

What the courts do is objectively to assess the evidence and to apply criteria to help resolve contractual disputes. These criteria take the form of fixed and certain rules, developed and refined by the judiciary which are used by all courts to determine what constitutes an enforceable agreement. It follows that a person may find himself legally bound by an agreement, which, in his own mind, he does not consider he has made. How important then, for organisations and individuals alike, to know and understand these rules. Certainly no business can effectively conduct its affairs without the benefit of such knowledge.

For the sake of convenience agreements can be divided into two separate components:

(i) an offer, made by one party to the other; and

(ii) an acceptance by the other of the terms contained in the offer.

If a court cannot identify the presence of these two components in a transaction, a simple contract will not have materialised, although as we have seen a person can become bound contractually by expressing a promise in the form of a deed. This is not a common practice, and all we need to note here is that the validity of a deed lies in the specialised form in which the promise is made, rather than in the need for agreement.

The process of negotiation

The person making an offer is referred to as the offeror, and the person to whom it is addressed is the offeree. In business it is common to find the parties reaching agreement following a period of negotiation. Such negotiations will be concerned with the details of the proposed transaction, and is likely to include matters such as price, the specifications regarding the subject matter of the agreement, and the time and place for performing it. Often during these negotiations offers will be made by one party to the other which are rejected, or met by a fresh offer. Thus either of the parties to the transaction is able to make an offer, not just the one who wishes to sell the goods or services in question or is the owner or supplier of them.

Examining the negotiating process is important for four reasons:

(i) because it enables us to identify which party made the final offer;

(ii) because it enables us to identify the time at which the contract is made;

(iii) because having established who made the offer we can identify the terms upon which the offer was based, and hence on which the contract is founded;

(iv) because during negotiations false statements are sometimes made by one of the parties which induce the other to enter into the contract. These are referred to as misrepresentations.

CHARACTERISTICS OF A VALID OFFER

To be legally effective an offer must satisfy the following requirements:

1. An offer must be firmly made

(2) An offer must be communicated

(3) The terms of an offer must be certain

(4) The offer must not have terminated.

1. FIRM OFFER OR INVITATION TO TREAT

The offeror must intend his offer to be unequivocal, so that when acceptance occurs he will be bound. The difficulty that can arise here lies in distinguishing firm offers from statements which do not carry the legal status of offers. Sometimes what appears to be a firm offer is merely an incentive or encouragement designed by the person making it to encourage the making of offers to him and is certainly not intended to be legally binding. A statement of this kind is known as an invitation to treat. It is an indication that the person is willing to do business with anyone who is interested.

> In *Pharmaceutical Society of Great Britain v. Boots Cash Chemists (Southern) Ltd (1953)* one of the shops in the company's chain had been converted into a self-service supermarket. Some of the shelves carried poisons which by statute were required to be sold in the presence of a qualified chemist. The chemist was in attendance at the checkout. The Pharmaceutical Society which had a duty to enforce the statutory provisions claimed that the company was in breach of them. The Society argued that the contract was made at the shelves where there was no pharmacist in attendance. The court however held that the goods displayed on the shelves were merely invitations to treat. The contract was made at the checkout. The customers made the offer when presenting the goods for payment and the offer was accepted by the cashier.
>
> Clearly there can be no real distinction between goods displayed on shelves inside a shop and goods displayed in the window. Thus in *Fisher v. Bell (1961)* a shop keeper was prosecuted for displaying a flick-knife inside his shop window with a price ticket attached. He was found by the court not to have committed the offence of offering for sale an offensive weapon contrary to the Restriction of Offensive Weapons Act 1959. The display was simply an invitation to treat.
>
> Advertisements are also generally regarded as constituting invitations to treat. In *Partridge v. Crittenden (1968)* the Divisional Court of the Queens Bench Division were asked to determine whether an advertisement in a magazine which read, "Bramblefinch cocks, bramblefinch hens 25/- each," constituted the offence of offering to sell wild birds contrary to the Protection of Birds Act 1954. The court quoshed the conviction against the defendant which had been issued in the Magistrates Court. The advertisement was simply an encouragement to stimulate the market into making offers. Members of the public responding to the advert made the offers, but of course they could not commit an offence since they were offering to buy, not to sell. The defendant should have been charged with the separate offence contained in the Act of selling wild birds.

The legal inference that advertisements will not normally amount to firm offers to sell is of some value to businesses that sell on a mail-order basis. For instance a company that takes out advertising in a newspaper or colour supplement cannot be sure of the demand for its goods that will result. If the advertisement were to constitute an offer, then the response of a member of the public in sending a cheque or postal order to buy the advertised goods would amount to an acceptance. The company could find itself overwhelmed by the demand, and under a legal obligation to supply goods it simply does not have if it's stocks are exhausted.

Perhaps the clearest example of an invitation to treat can be seen in an auction sale. This occurs when the auctioneer presents items in the auction, and asks for bids from those who are present, using expressions such as "how much am I bid for . . . " and "do I see £20." The auctioneer is testing demand, and having assessed it will try to increase it and push the price up. The auctioneer is certainly not offering to sell. The bids themselves constitute offers which the auctioneer is able to accept or reject.

> As can be seen in the cases above, it is usually in connection with criminal offences that the question of what constitutes an offer will arise. In relation to auction sales an illustration of this position is provided by *British Car Auctions Ltd v. Wright (1972)*. An unroadworthy car had been sold at auction. The auctioneers were convicted in the magistrates court of offering to sell an unroadworthy vehicle, contrary to the Road Traffic Act 1972. In quashing the conviction Widgery L.C.J. stated: "The auctioneer when he stands on his rostrum does not make an offer to sell the goods on behalf of the vendor; he stands there making an invitation to those present at the auction themselves to make offers to buy".

Further examples of the invitation to treat are advertisements inviting suppliers of goods and services to submit tenders, and prospectuses issued by limited companies inviting members of the public to subscribe for shares.

The use of tenders is a common commercial practice. Indeed local authorities are required by the Local Government Act 1972 to contract in this way. Under s.135 a contract made by an authority must comply with its standing orders and that the standing orders must include provisions for securing competition and for regulating the manner in which tenders are invited, in the case of contracts for the supply of goods or materials or for the execution of works. This is usually satisfied by inviting tenders from contractors on an approved list maintained by the authority. Under the tendering process a tender is an offer and an an invitation to tender is an invitation to treat. It is merely an invitation by an individual or organisation wishing to purchase goods or services to request suppliers to submit a contractual offer in the form of a tender. If the invitation to tender stipulates expressly or impliedly that the goods or services will be required, then an acceptance of the tender will create a binding contrct. Alternatively, the invitation may stipulate that the goods or services may be required, in which case an acceptance of the tender results in a standing offer to supply as and when required. A failure to order by the buyer in those circumstances will not result in a breach of contract.

> In *Harvela Investments Ltd v. Royal Trust Co. of Canada Ltd (1985)* the House of Lords was required to examine the nature of an invitation to tender in the context of the sale of shares. Royal Trust of Canada was prepared to sell some of its shares, and invited two companys, Harvela and Outerbridge to tender for them. The invitation to do so stipulated that the tender should contain a single offer price, and be sealed i.e. be made privately. It also stated that the highest bid would be accepted. Harvela's bid was $2,175,000. Outerbridge offered $2,100,000 or $101,000 in excess of any other higher bid, whichever was the higher. A bid of this kind is known as a referential bid. The seller informed both parties that the shares had been purchased by Outerbridge, at a price of $2,276,000. Harvela challenged this claim. The court held that on the facts the referential bid by Outerbridge was invalid. It took the view that presumed intention of the sellers should be deduced from the terms of the invitation read as a whole, and this was they intended to create a fixed bidding scale. In support of this presumed intention were the facts that they had undertaken to accept the highest offer which they had extended to both bidders thus giving them an equal opportunity to purchase the shares. The fact that they insisted on confidentiality in the submission of bids to provoke the best price that each party was prepared to pay was consistant with the presumed intention to create a fixed bidding scale. Accordingly Outerbridge had not been entitled to submit a referential bid and the sellers had not been entitled to accept it. The court ordered the transfer of the shares to Harvela at the price of $2,175,000.

It should be noted however that the invitation to treat is not devoid of legal effect. It can give rise to legal liability in the following ways:

(a) As a statement it can amount to an actionable misrepresentation (see later).

(b) It may also give rise to criminal liability under the Trade Descriptions Acts 1968, 1972 if it constitutes a false trade description, or under the Consumer Protection Act 1987 if it gives a false or misleading indication as to the price of goods or services.

(c) Under specific legislation it may give rise to legal liability. For instance in the case of a company prospectus s.166 Companies Act 1985 provides that the person responsible for a prospectus is liable to compensate anyone acquiring shares to which the prospectus relates, if they suffer loss as a result of an untrue or misleading statement in it.

2 AN OFFER MUST BE COMMUNICATED

The party to whom an offer is directed must be aware of it. An offer will normally be made to a single individual or organisation, however there is nothing to prevent an offer being directed to a specific group of individuals, anyone or more of whom may choose to accept it. For instance a private limited company that is going public may offer some of its shares at favourable rates to the members of its workforce.

It is possible to make an offer to the public generally, where the offeror is not able at the time the offer is made to identify who the possible recipients are. This principle has been in existence for a long time, and seems to be derived from the willingness of the courts to recognise a contractual obligation on the part of someone offering to pay any member of the public a reward, for example in return for information or the return of property. It is not uncommon to find banks offering financial rewards for information leading to the conviction of bank robbers by displaying notices inside the banks. In such circumstances anyone who satisfies the terms of the offer will be entitled to the reward, as long as they were aware of the offer beforehand.

One of the most celebrated instances of an offer made to the public at large, occurred in *Carlill v. Carbolic Smokeball Co. (1893),* which is considered below.

What constitutes communication is a question of fact for the court.

3. THE TERMS OF AN OFFER MUST BE CERTAIN.

In the event of a dispute between the parties as to the meaning of a term it will ultimately fall to the court to decide the question. The courts will always endeavour to find certainty so that the contract is able to survive wherever possible but if a term is obscure or meaningless then it will fail. This may not prove fatal to the contract if the term constitutes only a minor part of the overall obligations, but where the term is central to the functioning of the contract uncertainty as to its meaning will defeat the contract as a whole.

The following cases illustrate the position.

> In *Loftus v. Roberts (1902)* an agreement provided for the appointment of an actress by another person at a "West End salary to be mutually agreed between us." Subsequently the parties were unable to arrive at a salary which satisfied them both. The court held that the contract must fail. Even if it were possible to assess a suitable salary by reference to West End rates of pay, the court could not impose such a figure since the parties had

already stated that it had to be mutually agreed, something they had been unable to achieve. What they had was an agreement to agree at a further date. The contract failed.

In *Scammel v. Ouston (1941)* a agreement for the sale of a van where the balance of the price was to be met "on hire-purchase terms over a period of two years" also failed. Since there was no previous course of dealing between the parties to enable the court to identify what these "hire purchase" terms might be, the only alternative would have been to treat the terms as standard hire purchase terms. Unfortunately, as the court observed, hire purchase terms are not standardised and identical, but vary from agreement to agreement so that for example rates of interest will vary from company to company.

A meaningless term can however often be ignored.

In *Nicolene Ltd. v. Simmonds (1953)* a contract was made for the sale of 3000 tons of steel bars. The seller then broke the contract, and when the buyer sued for damages the seller argued there was no contract between them, relying on a statement in one of the contractual documents that, "we are in agreement that the usual conditions of acceptance apply." The court, whilst recognising that there were no "usual conditions of acceptance," between the parties, found that the contract was in every other respect clear as to the obligations of the parties. The meaningless term could be cut out from the rest of the contract. In the course of his judgment Lord Denning M.R. commented that, "A clause which is meaningless can often be ignored . . . ; whereas a clause which has yet to be agreed may mean there is no contract at all."

Probably the most common example of a clause or term which the parties have yet to agree is price, and price is obviously a vital term in any contract. In the unlikely event that the parties have reached agreement whilst overlooking the question of price altogether how will this affect their agreement? In such circumstances it may still be possible to enforce the agreement. In the case of sales of goods the Sale of Goods Act 1979 provides under s.8 that if the parties have not agreed price, or arranged a method for fixing price, or previously dealt with each other so that there is a price level in existence, then the buyer is bound to pay a reasonable price. This will usually be the market price. A similar rule applies in relation to those contracts which are covered by the Supply of Goods & Services Act 1982. As we saw in *Loftus v. Roberts* the most difficult situation to overcome is one in which an agreement has been made to settle price at a later date. In *May and Butcher v. R (1929)* Lord Buckmaster said of this situation "It has long been a well-recognised principle of contract law that an agreement between two parties to enter into an agreement in which some critical part of the contract is left undetermined is no contract at all." It is an entirely different matter however if machinery has been agreed which can be used to fix the price, or indeed resolve any other aspect of uncertainty.

In *Sykes (F & G) Wessex v. Fine Fare (1967)* a supplier of chickens undertook to supply a supermarket chain with between 30,000 and 80,000 birds each week over a period of 1 year. The agreement also provided that for a further four years the supplier would provide chickens in quantities "as might be agreed." The court held that since the contract provided for arbitration to settle disagreements, the contract was not void on the basis of the uncertainty of the term as to quantity.

In the context of arbitration arrangments of this kind the decision in *Sudbrook Trading Estate Ltd v. Eggleton (1982)* is worth noting. Here the tenant of some land had the right to buy the freehold before the lease ran out. The purchase price was to be determined by two arbitrators, one appointed by the tenant and the other by the landlord. The tenant exercised his option, but later the landlord refused to appoint an arbitrator. The House of Lords held that in these circumstances the court itself would order the transfer and make separate arrangements to fix the price.

When the sale of land is being negotiated it is usual practice for parties initially to reach an agreement "subject to contract." Transactions involving land are considered in detail in Chapter 8, and here all we are concerned with are general observations regarding issues of offer and acceptance in the sale of land. Agreement on a "subject to contract" basis usually achieves no more than to demonstrate a willingness on the part of the prospective purchaser to proceed towards a formal agreement if his professional advisors make no adverse discoveries concerning the property in question. The technical nature of land transactions makes it extremely unwise for a purchaser to enter into a binding agreement without first making inquiries regarding the property. Thus a purchaser will seek to show the vendor that it is his intention to purchase provided the inquiries that are made prove satisfactory. To achieve this he will make a 'conditional offer,' or a 'conditional acceptance' by using an expression like 'subject to contract'. It is well settled that this creates no binding obligation on the parties. The agreement is a legal nullity, even where the purchaser has paid a deposit. If however it is possible to ascertain the terms of the anticipated contract the parties will be bound, even though the formal document has not yet been executed. This occurred in *Filby v. Hounsell (1896),* where an offer was made to purchase some property which remained unsold after an auction, on terms that if the offer was accepted the formal contract would be based upon the published auction particulars. Since these particulars were identifiable the court held the parties bound even though the formal agreement was yet to be made.

4. THE OFFER MUST NOT HAVE TERMINATED

If the offer has come to an end in some way before the offeree accepts it, the acceptance is of no legal effect for there is no longer an offer to accept. However we need to look closely at how offers once made can legally be regarded as at an end. This can occur in the following ways:

(a) where the offeror has revoked the offer

(b) where the offer has lapsed

(c) where the offer has been accepted or met with a counter offer

(a) Where the offeror has revoked the offer. Revocation is permissable at any time before the offeree has accepted it, and the revocation can be effective even if it is not communicated directly by the offeror, provided it is communicated through some reliable channel. However, like an offer, a revocation will only be effective when it is actually communicated by being brought to the attention of the offeree. The following cases illustrate these points.

In *Dickinson v. Dodds (1876)* an offer to sell some houses was expressed to remain open until 9 a.m. on Friday. The offeree however learnt from a reliable third party on Thursday that the offeror had negotiated a sale to another purchaser. This was held to be sufficient to amount to a revocation.

In *Byrne & Co. v. Leon Van Tienhoven & Co. (1880)* an offer to sell tin plate was received by the offeree on 11 October, and immediately accepted by telegram. The offeror however had posted a revocation which the offeree received on 20 October. It was held the revocation was only effective when actually received, and was therefore too late.

Does actual receipt mean physical delivery to the business premises of the offeree or must it in addition be opened and read? The House of Lords has suggested that it will be effective even if it has not been opened provided that it would have been opened "if the ordinary course of business was followed." This comment, which was made in *Eaglehill Ltd v. J. Needham (Builders) Ltd (1972)*, makes clear that a business which for whatever reason fails to promptly deal with its mail may nonetheless find itself bound by the contents of any letters of revocation it has received. If the offeror seeks to revoke an offer made to the world at large, although there is no decided case on the point, it is likely that the revocation can be effected by using the same publicity as that afforded to the original offer. For instance if a new supermarket which is to open next week advertised in the local paper that the first twenty customers taking goods to the checkout on opening day will receive a free bottle of champagne, then a further advertisement in the same paper informing the public that no champagne will be available should be a sufficient act of revocation. It may however do little for business goodwill.

Sometimes an offeror may seek to revoke the offer after the offeree has started to perform the act required by the offeror, but has not yet completed it. Suppose for example that in an attempt to increase the sales, a national newspaper offers £100,000 to the first person to produce a pollution free petrol engine by a certain date. Before this date the newspaper, which is in financial difficulties announces that it is withdrawing its offer. In the meantime an engineer has made considerable progress on a pollution free engine design. It seems that the revocation will not be effective as regards the engineer, on the grounds that the offer carried with it an implied undertaking that it will remain open until the specified date, and that in any event once the engineer starts to carry out the work he has accepted the offer which cannot be revoked.

(b) Where the offer has lapsed. An offer will lapse automatically in the following circumstances:

(i) after a stated time limit which it was to be held open has passed;

(ii) if there is no such time limit, after a reasonable time;

In *Ramsgate Victoria Hotel Co. Ltd v. Montefiore (1866)* the defendant offered by letter on 8 June to buy shares in the company, and was allotted the shares on 23 November. It was held that the defendant was entitled to refuse the shares, since his offer had lapsed before the company had made the allotment. Clearly the market value of shares can fluctuate widely over a period of six months.

(iii) if the situation on which it was based has fundamentally changed as for example where the property which has been offered for sale has been destroyed by fire, or has been stolen before acceptance occurs;

(iv) where the offeror has died, if this is known to the offeree before acceptance. If the offeree is unaware of the offeror's death the latter's estate will be bound by the contract.

There is no legal obligation on an offeror to keep the offer open for any particular length of time, unless some separate contract has been entered into between the offeror and the offeree to this effect.

(c) where the offer has been accepted, or has been met by a counter offer (see below).

CHARACTERISTICS OF A VALID ACCEPTANCE

Acceptance is defined as the unconditional assent to all the terms of the offer. It must therefore be unequivocal. As we have already seen a conditional acceptance occurs when a potential purchaser of land agrees to buy it subject to contract. This is acceptance subject to happening of a future event which may or may not occur, and is not therefore binding.

The following points provide an indication of how to determine whether an acceptance is valid:

1. IT MUST BE UNCONDITIONAL

It is surprisingly common to find a person believing that they have accepted the offer, when in fact they have made a fresh offer themselves by accepting on conditions. The general position regarding the need for unconditional assent is as follows:

(a) a conditional acceptance will constitute a counter offer. Thus a conditional acceptance does not complete the transaction but rather continues the negotiations.

(b) a counter-offer both rejects and extinguishes an original offer.

In *Hyde v. Wrench (1840)* the defendant offered his farm to the plaintiff for £1000. The plaintiff replied offering £950. The defendant subsequently rejected this, so the plaintiff purported to accept the original £1000 offer. It was held that there was no contract since the original offer had been extinguished by the counter offer. Although expressed as an acceptance, it was in fact a fresh offer.

(c) any alteration to the terms of the offer will render the acceptance invalid.

For instance in *Northland Airlines Ltd v. Dennis Ferranti Meters Ltd (1970)*, which involved negotiations for the purchase of an aircraft by Northland from Ferranti, a telegram from Ferranti stated, "Confirming sale to you — aircraft — £27,000. Winnipeg. Please remit £5,000 for account of . . . " to which Northland replied by telegram, "This is to confirm your cable and my purchase — aircraft on terms set out in your cable. Price £27,000 delivered Winnipeg. £5,000 forwarded to your bank in trust for your account pending delivery. Balance payable on delivery. Please confirm delivery to be made 30 days within this date." This was held by the Court of Appeal to be a counter offer, for it contained new terms — provisions regarding delivery, and payment of the deposit in trust rather than outright, so that it did not transfer to the seller until physical delivery had occurred.

(d) in commercial dealings between parties each trading on their standard terms, the terms which apply to the contract will often be those belonging to the party who fired the last shot. This situation has become known as the "battle of the forms".

In *Butler Machine Tool Co. v. Ex-Cell-O Corporation (England) Ltd (1979)* the plaintiffs offered to sell a machine tool to the defendants in a quotation. This contained a price variation clause, which by means of a specific formula enabled the plaintiffs to raise the quoted price between contract and delivery if their own costs rose. The defendants ordered the goods but

> on their own standard terms which did not include a price variation clause. The plaintiffs, on receipt of the order form, signed and returned an acknowledgement slip which it contained. The plaintiff's costs rose considerably between contract and delivery. The Court of Appeal regarded the defendants order as a counter offer, and the return of the acknowledgement slip as the plaintiff's acceptance. The contract between them did not therefore contain a price variation clause.

2. THE ACCEPTANCE MUST BE COMMUNICATED

It is open to the offeror to stipulate the method by which acceptance may be made. If no stipulation is made anything that achieves communication will suffice; words, writing or conduct. If it is clear that the offeror demands a particular method of acceptance only, then no other method will be effective. In most cases however the offeror is likely to do little more than to give a general indication of the form of acceptance to be used. Where this occurs but the offeree adopts a different method of acceptance which is as quick or quicker than the specified method the acceptance will be effective, since no disadvantage will have been caused to the offeror.

> Consequently the Court of Appeal in *Yates Building Co. v. R.J. Pulleyn & Son (York) (1976)* held that an acceptance by means of ordinary post was effective, despite the offeror directing that registered post or recorded delivery should be used.

Given the need for positive action in communicating it follows that silence can never amount to an effective acceptance of the offer. This holds true even if the parties have, in advance, agreed upon such procedure. For instance, if following an interview, an employer says to the interviewee that the job is his or hers if they hear nothing from the employer in the next 5 days, the interviewee agrees this arrangement, and the 5 days elapse without word from the employer, a binding contract will not have come into existence. What the law requires is some positive act.

> In *Felthouse v. Bindley (1862)* an uncle wrote to his nephew offering to buy the nephew's horse for £30.15s. and stating 'If I hear no more about him I shall consider the horse mine at that price'. The nephew gave instructions to the defendant, an auctioneer, not to sell the horse as he intended it for his uncle. The defendant inadvertently sold the horse, and the uncle sued him in the tort of conversion. The court held that action must fail. The horse had not become the uncle's for there was not a contract.

The existence of this common law principle did not in the past act as a disincentive to curb the practice of inertia selling, and it was not until the passing of the Unsolicited Goods and Services Act 1971 (as amended) that the practice was effectively controlled. Inertia selling involves sending goods by post to recipients who have not requested them. Usually an accompanying letter will indicate that if the goods are not wanted they should be returned, but that if the recipient retains possession of them beyond a stated period (usually between 7 and 21 days) this will be treated as acceptance, and payment should then be made. Prior to 1971 this type of "hard sell" was widespread: it is an example of the way in which the less scrupulous try to take advantage of the public's absence of legal knowledge and awareness. The 1971 Act provides that the recipient of unsolicited goods can treat them as an unconditional gift after six months have elapsed. The period is reduced to 30 days if the recipient serves notice on the sender asking that that goods be collected and the sender fails to do this.

There are two circumstances in which acceptance can operate without communication occuring at the same time, firstly in cases where the post is used to create the contract and secondly where the nature of the offer makes formal notification of acceptance unrealistic.

(a) transactions using the post.

Transactions effected by means of corrrespondence in the form of letters, invoices, quotations and share applications are obviously very common in commercial life. From a practical standpoint a business organisation will wish to keep records of its business activities, and the use of written correspondence is an effective way of achieving this.

Where the post is used there will always be a period during which the letter is in transit when the person to whom it is addressed is unaware of its contents. In the case of an offer or revocation of an offer made by post the communication is effective only when it is received by the party to whom it is sent. However, in the case of an *acceptance* by post the courts have laid down a rule that the letter is effective at the time and place of posting, provided it was correctly addressed and pre-paid. This rule applies even if the letter of acceptance is lost or destroyed in the post.

> The case of *Henthorn v. Fraser (1892)* illustrates the practical application of the post rules. Fraser offered to sell some houses to Henthorn and gave him 14 days to consider. The following day Fraser decided the price he had quoted was too low and wrote to Henthorn revoking the offer. After the letter of revocation had been posted but before he had received it, Henthorn decided to buy the houses, and posted his letter of acceptance at 3.50 p.m. It was held that a binding contract had come into existence at 3.50 p.m. The letter of revocation was ineffective, for it had arrived too late.

> This position was confirmed in the case of *Brinkibon Ltd v. Stahag Stahl und Stahlwarenhandel (1983)*. The parties had contracted using telex facilities. The plaintiffs were in London and the defendants in Vienna. The acceptance was telexed from London to Vienna. The defendants were alleged by the plaintiffs to be in breach of contract and the plaintiffs sought leave to serve a writ on the defendants. Since the defendants were outside the jurisdiction of the English Courts, having their business in Austria, the only way the writ could be served under the Rules of the Supreme Court was if the contract had been made in England. The House of Lords held that the contract had been made in Vienna.

It is, of course, open to the parties to vary these rules if they wish to do so, and it may be prudent for an offeror to stipulate that an acceptance in writing which is posted to him shall not be effective until it is actually received. It is common to find terms in standard form business contracts to this effect, and the courts seem willing to infer a variation of the post rules whenever possible.

> In *Holwell Securities Ltd. v. Hughes (1974)* an option (offer) provided that it should be exercisable 'by notice in writing'. The court held that this requirement effectively excluded the postal rule and that actual receipt of the letter of acceptance was necessary to conclude a contract.

> The consequences of the post rules can be remarkable. In *Household Fire Insurance Co v. Grant (1879)* the defendant applied for 100 shares in the plaintiff company. The company received his application form, and the company secretary in consequence completed and posted a letter of allotment to the defendant, and entered his name on the register of shareholders. The letter never arrived. Some time later the company went into liquidation, and the liquidator claimed the payment outstanding on the shares from the defendant. By a majority the Court of Appeal held that the defendant was liable for this sum. The shares became his when the letter of allotment was posted.

(b) formal acceptance unrealistic.

Sometimes the circumstances of the offer are such that the courts will regard conduct which occurs without the knowledge of the offeror as a sufficient method of acceptance. Although in a sense this is not the same as silence, from the offeror's point of view it amounts to the same thing since if the offeree does not have to make contact with the offeror the offeror remains in the dark. Where an offer has been made to the public at large the courts may take the view that the offeror could not possibly have expected to receive an acceptance from every person who has decided to take up the offer. This would be a commercial nonsense.

> In *Carlill v. Carbolic Smoke Ball Co. (1893)* the defendant company advertised a medical preparation which they manufactured, and claimed in the advertisement that they would pay £100 reward to anybody who contracted 'the increasing epidemic of influenza' after purchasing and using the product as directed. The advertisement added that £1000 was deposited with the Alliance Bank 'showing our sincerity in the matter'. The plaintiff purchased a smoke ball, used it as directed, then caught influenza. She sued for her £100 reward. The court held that the advertisement constituted a firm offer intended to be legally binding, since the bank deposit indicated an intention to meet claims; the offer could be made to the public at large, and acceptance of the offer in such circumstances could be implied by the conduct of those like the plaintiff, who performed the stated conditions. In consequence the company were held liable.

It is only when the parties have reached an agreement which satisfies the common law requirements relating to offer and acceptance that a contract can be said to have been made. One of the traditional views of contracting sees the contract in terms of a meeting of minds or consensus ad idem. An examination of the law relating to agreement reveals that sometimes a binding agreement can occur where the minds of the parties are not entirely at one. This situation will be seen even more clearly in the next chapter, which considers the effect of circumstances where consent to the agreement is not a true consent. Sometimes, however, even the presence of a consensus between the parties will not be enough for an agreement to be treated as legally valid if the fundamental principles of offer and acceptance have not been met.

> In *Gibson v. Manchester City Council (1979)* the parties were engaged in negotiations for the sale of a council house to the plaintiff, a council tenant. The plaintiff, having completed a request for information received a letter from the council saying it might be prepared to sell the house to him for £2,180 freehold and that if he wished to make a formal application to purchase he should return the application form. This the tenant did. Unfortunately he left the purchase price blank requesting that the price should take into account defects in the path of the property. A further letter from the council stated that defects in the path had been taken into account in fixing the price. In interpreting the above correspondence a majority of the Court of Appeal held that a contract of sale had indeed been entered into. Lord Denning MR put forward the view that in such circumstances there was no need to look for a strict offer and acceptance rather, "you should look at the correspondence as a whole and at the conduct of the parties and see therefrom whether the parties have come to an agreement on everything that was material". This decision was later reversed following a further appeal to the House of Lords in 1979. The Law Lords adopted the more traditional approach by analysing each piece of correspondence and held that no firm offer had been made or accepted by the council. The words the council "may be prepared to sell" only amounted to an invitation to treat and thus no contract of sale had resulted.

It is clear in Gibson that whilst no contract actually resulted from their negotiations, both sides were, at least initially, willing to contract over the sale of the property. There are other authorities by way of contrast which suggest that under suitable conditions a contract may arise where there is clearly no consensus between the parties, but where logic or common-sense seems to demand that the court read one into the situation.

> In *Clarke v. Dunraven (1897)* the parties were yacht owners who entered their vessel for a yacht club regatta. Each owner who took part in the regatta undertook in a letter sent to the yacht club to obey its rules. These included an obligation to pay "all damages" caused by fouling another vessel. Whilst preparing for a race Clarke's yacht, the Satanita, fouled Dunraven's vessel, which sank. Under statute Clarke was liable to pay only limited damages of £8 per ton of the registered tonnage of the vessel, however Dunraven claimed the existence of a contract between the parties, on the terms of the club rules, and sought to recover full damages. The House of Lords accepted his argument that a contract existed, even though the parties had not dealt contractually with each other. Lord Herschell stated, "The effect of their entering for the race, and undertaking to be bound by the rules to the knowledge of each other . . . is to indicate a liability on the part of the one to the other . . . to create a contractual obligation to discharge that liability."

> In *Rayfield v. Hands (1960)*, a case involving the transfer of shares in a registered company, Vaisey. J applied the principle laid down by Clarke v. Dunraven. He took the view that the taking up of shares not only creates a contract between the shareholder and the company, but also, at least in the case of a private limited company, gives rise to a contract between the shareholder and all the other members of the company. The terms of this contract are the provisions contained in the articles.

CONSIDERATION

Under English law the simple contract has always been seen in terms of a bargain struck between the parties. The bargain is arrived at by negotiations and concluded when a definite and certain offer has been made which has been met with an unequivocal acceptance. Millions of transactions of this kind are made each day.

Making an agreement, as we have already seen, involves giving undertakings or promises. The offeror makes his promise, and indicates what the offeree must do in return. For instance the seller of goods undertakes to transfer ownership in the goods, and specifies the price to be paid by the buyers for acquiring ownership. The employer indicates the type of work the employee will be required to perform, and promises a certain wage rate or salary for doing it. The idea of a contract as an exchange of promises is fundamental to an understanding of the simple contract. We have already encountered a basic definition of a contract as being a legally enforceable agreement. There are others however. A definition provided by Sir Frederick Pollock, a leading legal writer, described the contract as "a promise or set of promises which the law will enforce". Pollock was seeing the 'agreement' of our first definition as something always made up of promises.

If promises are exchanged the contract is said to be bilateral. This is the most common type of arrangement. For instance, if a partnership offers a person a place in the business if they are prepared to contribute £5,000 to the capital of the business, and the prospective partner undertakes to do so the contract is a bilateral one. If however the offeror, rather than requiring a promise in return requires of the offeree some other act, then the contract is said to be unilateral. An example of a unilateral contract occurs where a company promises to make a payment or provide goods to any of its customers who collect a certain number of tokens from buying the company's products. Petrol companies frequently use this type of device to compete with their rivals, so that by the time a customer has purchased a specific quantity of petrol they become entitled to items such as glasses or cutlery. The customer has made no promise to the garage, but is certainly entitled to the advertised items if he satisfies the requirements stipulated by the petrol company to qualify for the 'gifts'.

Executory and executed consideration

Consideration, and hence the contract itself, is said to be executory where the promises that have been made are to be performed in the future. An example is an agreement whereby the seller promises to deliver goods next week, and the buyer agrees to pay for them on delivery. Consideration is said to be executed where in return for a promise the offeree provides the required consideration which also acts as acceptance of the offer. This would occur, for instance, in the case of a member of the public who provides the Post Office with information that leads to the conviction of those responsible for an armed robbery at a sub-post office, where the Post Office has offered a reward for such information.

An agreement in which the consideration exchanged is entirely executory is fully enforceable, although legal action for breach of contract can only be commenced after the date for performance has passed, or if before this time one of the parties has made clear that they will not perform their obligations when they fall due. This is referred to as anticipatory breach of contract. Where a contract is entirely executory, legal action on it may prove difficult to sustain if there is no written evidence and the other party disputes the existence of the alleged agreement.

1. CONSIDERATION IS NEEDED TO SUPPORT ALL SIMPLE CONTRACTS.

In the absence of valid consideration passing between the parties the general rule is the agreement they have made will be of no legal effect. If however their agreement is expressed in the form of a deed, the absence of a valuable promise made by the promisee to the promisor does not invalidate the contract. If a person executes a deed under which he promises to make a payment or transfer property to someone else at a future date, the promise will bind him, and be enforceable by the promisee, despite the absence of any consideration provided by that person.

2. CONSIDERATION NEED NOT BE ADEQUATE BUT MUST HAVE SOME VALUE.

The word *adequate* in this context means equal to the promise given. The principle of adequacy of consideration has developed to cope with contractual disputes in which one of the parties is arguing that the contract is bad because the value of the consideration provided by the other party is not the economic equivalent of the value of the promise he or she has made.

The courts are not prepared to defeat an agreement merely on the grounds that one of the parties has, in effect, made a bad bargain. Bad bargains are a fact of commercial life. A deal that is struck where one of the parties has entered it in haste, or without proper enquiry, or has been swayed by convincing salesmanship, may be bitterly regretted subsequently, but it is certainly not possible in such circumstances to escape liability on the grounds that "I gave more than I got". Consequently there is no relief for the business or the individual who is at the receiving end of a hard bargain. For instance, suppose a company is in urgent need of a specific item of machinery without which the manufacturing process cannot function. It eventually locates suitable machinery owned by the seller, with whom the company negotiates to make a purchase. The seller is aware of the company's pressing need, and responds by raising the price to a figure well beyond the usual selling price. The company agrees to buy at this price, but before receiving delivery discovers another machine of the same type which is available at the usual selling price. Can the company escape from its original contract on the grounds that the cost of the machinery was well in excess of the usual market price, and therefore that the consideration it has received (the machinery) is not adequate to sustain the promise of payment it has made? The answer is a clear no. The parties fixed their price by agreement. The company received what it wanted, and the price level merely reflected the sellers bargaining strength and the buyers urgent need.

> The case of *Haigh v. Brooks (1839)*, provides a useful illustration of the idea of the bargain taken to its most extreme position. The plaintiffs were owed large sums of money by a third party, and the defendant agreed to guarantee these debts. He later asked the plaintiffs if they would cancel the guarantee. This they agreed to, provided that in return the defendant would pay off certain debts they owed. He agreed, and the guarantee was returned to him. On examination the defendant discovered that because the written guarantee failed to meet certain statutory requirements it was unenforceable, and indeed always had been. He refused to pay the debts on the grounds that all he had received in return was a worthless piece of paper. The court held that the agreement was binding. Even though the guarantee was legally invalid the defendant had received what he bargained for — his release from the supposed liability. Lord Chief Justice Denman remarked, "The plaintiffs were induced by the defendant's promise to part with something they might have kept, and the defendant obtained what he desired by means of that promise".

> Similarly in *Mountford v. Scott (1975)*, the defendant made an agreement with the plaintiff, granting the plantiff an option to purchase the defendant's house for £10,000 within six months. The plaintiff paid £1 for the option, and later sought to exercise it. The value of the defendant's property had risen by this time and he refused to sell. The court was prepared to grant an order for specific performance (see Chapter 4), compelling the defendant to transfer the property for the agreed price. It was for the defendant to fix the value of the option. Some consideration was provided and this was enough. The trial judge commented: "It is only necessary, as I see it, that the option should have been validly created".

However apparently insignificant the consideration may be, as long as it has some discernible value it will be valid.

> In *Chappell and Co Ltd v. Nestlé Co Ltd (1960)*, the defendants, as part of a sales promotion, offered a record at a reduced price if their chocolate bar wrappers accompanied the payment. The plaintiffs held the copyright in the record, and argued that the royalties they were entitled to should be assessed on the price of the record plus the value of the wrappers, which the defendants in fact simply threw away when they had been received. The House of Lords agreed with the plaintiffs, seeing the subsequent disposal of the wrappers as irrelevant, since each wrapper in reality represented the profit on the sale of a bar of chocolate, and was therefore part of the consideration.

Adequacy is not determined solely by economic criteria. It is enough, for instance, that the promise is a promise to refrain from doing something which the promisor is legally entitled to do. It may be a promise not to take legal proceedings, or not to exercise a legal right such as a right of way. Even where the promise is related to a positive act the act may have little to do with anything capable of economic valuation, yet still be good consideration in the eyes of the law. A parent may undertake to pay a sum of money to a son or daughter in the event of them marrying, or graduating, and the marriage or graduation will be valid consideration in these circumstances.

Moreover it is not necessary that the promisor should obtain direct personal benefit from the consideration provided by the promisee. Thus a parent's promise to a son or daughter to pay them £10,000 to help them set up in business is enforceable if the business is established, whether or not the parent has a financial stake in it.

> The case of *Shadwell v. Shadwell (1860)* illustrates how the courts will accept as valuable consideration promises which cannot be valued purely economically. Here an uncle promised to pay his nephew a yearly sum in consideration of the nephew getting married. The nephew married, but the annuity fell into arrears. On his uncle's death the nephew brought action against the executors of the estate. They were held bound since, *inter alia,* the nephew's marriage was something of interest to the uncle.

The question of whether a forebearance will operate as adequate consideration may in particular cases be of some concern to those engaged in business and commercial activity. Suppose for example that the owner of the only retail travel agency in a small town is approached by a larger company, with a number of agencies in the area. The owner is told that in consideration of the payment of £30,000 by him to the company, it will not set up a competing business in the town. Would this be a valid agreement? In *Thorne v. Motor Trade Association (1937)* Lord Atkin, commented, "it appears to me that if a man may lawfully, in the furtherance of business interests, do acts which will seriously injure another in his business he may also lawfully, if he is still acting in the furtherance of his business interests, invite that other to pay him a sum of money as an alternative to doing the injurious acts".

3. CONSIDERATION MUST BE SUFFICIENT

Consideration is treated as insufficient, and therefore incapable of supporting a contract, when it involves the promisor undertaking to do something he is already obliged to do legally. The rationale here is that since the promisor is bound to carry out the promise anyway, there can be no true bargain in using performance of this promise to support another contract. Consideration is insufficient therefore in the following circumstances:

(a) Where the promisor has an existing contractual obligation to carry out the promise offered as consideration.

> In *Stilk v. Myrick (1809)* a promise by a ships captain to pay sailors an additional sum for working the ship on the return voyage was unenforceable, even though they had to work harder due to the desertion of two crew members. The court found that their existing contracts bound them to work the ship home in such circumstances, thus they had provided no new consideration to support the promise of extra wages.

In dramatically changed circumstances it may be possible to show that a fresh contract has been negotiated.

> In *Hartley v. Ponsonby (1857),* a ships crew was so depleted that the ship was dangerous to work. In these circumstances the promise of the captain to pay extra wages was held to be enforceable.

In addition there is an old common law principle that payment of a lesser amount to a creditor than the full debt due cannot discharge the debtor from liability for the full amount even though the creditor agrees it, and accepts the lesser amount. This is known as the rule in Pinnel's Case (1602). It is based upon the view that there can be no real bargain in a person agreeing to accept a lesser sum than they are legally entitled to. But if the varied agreement contains an additional element, such a promise to pay the reduced sum earlier than the date on which the full debt is due, then provided the creditor agrees it, this will be binding. It may be of considerable commercial advantage to receive a smaller amount immediately than have to wait for the full sum, where, for example, the creditor is experiencing cash flow problems.

In addition to early payment of a reduced amount if agreed by the creditor, there are certain other exceptions to the rule in Pinnel's case. They include:

(i) Substituted performance. This arises where the creditor accepts some other form of consideration instead of money, such as the delivery of goods. Alternatively payment of a lesser sum together with an additional element, such as a promise to repair the creditor's car, would suffice.

(ii) Payment of a lesser sum by a third party will discharge the full debt.

(iii) A creditor's composition. This occurs where two or more creditors whose full debts cannot be met by the debtor agree between themselves to accept a reduced payment, and the debtor pays this to each of them. Such an arrangement is an alternative to bankruptcy proceedings, or a winding up, and usually it will involve the debtor paying off the debts according to a fixed percentage, for instance, 50p in the £. Where a composition is made, creditors are precluded from subsequently pursuing the debtor for the outstanding amount.

(iv) Payment of a lesser sum where the debtor is disputing the value of the work that has been performed, and the creditor accepts the reduced amount. The reason why the creditor is bound by such an agreement is that if the dispute were to be resoved by court action, the court might determine the value of the work performed as worth even less than the debtor has offered to pay, hence accepting the reduced sum may be seen as a new bargain.

(v) When the equitable doctrine of promissory estoppel applies.

Points (iv) and (v) are examined in more detail in the discussion of discharge of contract in Chapter 4.

(b) Where the promisor has a public obligation to carry out the act.

Performance of a public duty as a means of furnishing consideration is insufficient to support the contract.

> This is demonstrated in the case of *Collins v. Godefroy (1831)*. The plaintiff had received a subpoena (a court order) to give evidence in court. He then agreed with the defendant to give the evidence in return for his expenses. The court held that there was no contract for the payment of expenses, as the promise of payment was not supported by sufficient consideration. The plaintiff was under an existing duty to give evidence.

However if the promisor performs some act beyond the public duty, this will operate as valid consideration.

> In *Harris v. Sheffield United F.C. (1987)* the football club challenged its contractual liability to pay for the policing of its football ground during home matches. It was held that the contract between itself and the police authority was valid. The number of officers provided was in excess of those who would have been provided had the police simply been fulfilling their public obligation to keep the peace and prevent disorder.

4. CONSIDERATION MUST BE LEGAL.

If it is illegal the whole contract will be invalidated.

5. CONSIDERATION MUST NOT BE PAST.

A party to a contract cannot use a past act as a basis for consideration. Therefore, if one party performs an act for another, and only receives a promise of reward after the act is complete, the past act would be past consideration. What is required is that the promise of one of the parties to the alleged contract is given in response to the promise of the other. If an act is carried out with no promise of reward having been made, it will be treated as purely gratuitous.

> In *Roscorla v. Thomas (1842)* the seller of a horse, after the buyer had purchased it, promised the buyer that it was sound and free from vice. It was not, and the buyer sued the seller on the promise. The action failed. The promise was supported by no new consideration. The principle established here may be of some concern in business life, for it is common to find statements that amount to promises, being given after the contract is concluded, for instance car salesmen giving undertakings after the customer has bought the vehicle and builders making claims about their properties to purchasers moving into the new house. In these circumstances the buyer may have protection under the Sale of Goods Act 1979 (see later).

There are three exceptions to the rule:

(a) where the work has been performed in circumstances which carry an implication of a promise to pay.

> In *Re Casey's Patents, Stewart v. Casey (1892)* the joint owners of a patent agreed with Casey that he should manage and publicise their invention. Two years later they promised him a third share in the patent, "in consideration of your services as manager". The court rejected the view that this promise was supported by past consideration from Casey. The request to him to render his services carried an implied promise to pay for them. The promise of a third share was simply the fixing of the price.

(b) where a debt, which has become unrecoverable by operation of the limitation period (i.e. statute barred) is revived by a subsequent acknowledgement of it by the debtor, which is made in writing. In such circumstances the Limitation Act 1980 states that no consideration of any kind need be sought to enforce the debt.

(c) under s.27 Bills of Exchange Act 1882, which provides that an antecedent debt or liability will support a bill of exchange.

6. CONSIDERATION MUST MOVE FROM THE PROMISEE

Only the parties to the agreement who have provided each other with consideration can sue on the contract. A person who has provided no consideration does not have the right to sue on the contract, for that person is not a party to it. This principle is known as privity of contract. It is examined in the next chapter.

INTENTION TO CREATE LEGAL RELATIONS

Having established the existence of a valid agreement supported by consideration, a contract may still fail unless it is able to satisfy a further legal test. The additional requirement is that the parties intended their agreement to have legal consequences. Many agreements are made in which it is abundantly obvious from the context of the event that it was never in the contemplation of the parties to bind themselves legally. How then can a court discriminate between those arrangements when the parties did intend their agreement to be legally enforceable, and those where this was not the intention? To answer this question the court will look at all the available evidence, and in particular whether the parties have expressly indicated their intention. For instance committing an agreement into written form may suggest a more formal type of relationship.

At common law there are certain presumptions to assist the court. If the subject matter of the agreement is of a social or domestic kind, where the context of the agreement or the relationship between the parties is such as to suggest an absence of full legal commitment, then the courts will presume there was no intention to create a contract. This does not mean, for example, that it is impossible for members of the same family to contract each with the other, and certainly many families are participants in joint business ventures such as partnerships which are founded on a contractual relationship. Rather it is simply a requirement of the common law that there is clear evidence of such an intention. This must be sufficient to rebut the presumption that the parties did not intend to contract.

> Thus in *Snelling v. John G. Snelling Ltd (1972)* the court had to identify the nature of an agreement between the plaintiff and his two brothers, who together were all directors of the defendant company. Each of them had provided loans to the company, and when they took a further loan from a finance company the brothers agreed not to reduce their own loan until the amount borrowed from the finance company had been repaid. By a separate agreement made between the three of them they undertook that if any of them resigned voluntarily as a director before repayment to the finance company had been made, repayment of the loan to the defendant company would be forfeited. The plaintiff voluntarily resigned and sued the company for the return of his money. The court held that the agreement between the brothers was intended to create legal rights, not least because it had emerged out of strong disagreements between the brothers. A further issue was whether the company itself was a party to the agreement, and could enforce the contract. It was held that the company had no enforceable rights under it, there being no privity of contract between it and the brothers on this issue.

In relation to commercial transactions the courts will presume an intention that they are intended to be legally binding. So whenever there is a business dimension to the agreement the only way in which it is possible to prevent the judicial presumption from operating is to indicate clearly that the agreement is not intended to be a contract. The inclusion of the phrase 'binding in honour' on a football coupon was held by the court in *Jones v. Vernons Pools Ltd. (1938)* to amount to clear evidence that there was no intention to create a contract.

> In *Rose and Frank Co. v. Crompton Bros. (1923)*, a written agreement entered into by two commercial organisations included the following clause "This arrangement is not entered into, nor is this memorandum written, as a formal or legal agreement . . . but . . . is only a definite expression and record of the purpose and intention of the . . . parties concerned, to which they each honourably pledge themselves". This clause, the court held, was sufficient evidence to overturn the presumption that the commercial agreement was intended to be legally binding.

Since "honour clauses" have the effect of making an otherwise legally enforceable agreement unenforceable by means of court action, they need to be treated with some care. There may appear to be sound reasons for their use in the right circumstances, but the inability to bring a claim for breach of the terms of the agreement before the courts does have the effect of leaving the parties commercially vulnerable. Suppose such a term is included in an agreement between the sole supplier of a particular type of goods and a customer who makes his profits from reselling these goods. The customer has no legal protection against the supplier unilaterally determining the agreement, leaving the customer with orders that cannot be met and the task of finding a new type of business. Of course the supplier may be just as vulnerable to unilateral action by the customer. If the customer ends the agreement, the supplier may be left with a large quantity of goods he will have to find new outlets for. This may be difficult or even impossible at short notice, however he will be unable to recover his losses by legal action.

It is important to bear in mind that a term which attempts entirely to exclude the court's jurisdiction will be void on the grounds that its effect would be to prevent a court from even determining the preliminary issue of the nature of the agreement itself. However it is quite legitimate to insert an arbitration clause into the contract. Arbitration clauses are a common feature of business agreements, for they provide a dispute solving mechanism which is generally cheaper, quicker and more private than court proceedings. (See Chapter 9)

Contractual intention is also of significance in relation to collective agreements. A 'collective agreement' is one between trade unions and employers or employers' organisations by which an agreement or arrangement is made about matters such as terms and conditions of employment. It is estimated that as many as 14 million employees within the United Kingdom are employed under contracts which are regulated in part by collective agreements. Section 18 of the Trade Union and Labour Relations Act 1974 provides that a collective agreement is presumed not to have been intended by the parties to be a legally enforceable contract unless the agreement is in writing and contains a statement that the parties intend it to be legally enforceable. Often the statutory statement of the particulars of the employment which the employee is legally obliged to give the employee will make express reference to a collective agreement in operation within the particular employment sector involved, and this will have the effect of incorporating it into the individual contract of employment. Once this has occured changes in the contract of employment created by re-negotiation of the collective agreement will automatically vary the individual employee's contractual relationship with the employer.

CAPACITY TO CONTRACT

Capacity is an expression that describes a person's ability to do something: in legal terms this covers the ability to make contracts, commit torts and commit crimes.

The general rule under English law is that anyone can bind himself by a contract, as long as it is not illegal, or void for public policy. There are however exceptions to the rule, of which the most significant are contracts made by corporations and contracts made by minors.

CORPORATIONS

The nature of corporate bodies is dealt with in Chapter 2, where it is noted that they are regarded as legal persons in their own right, thus enabling them to make contracts, commit torts (and some crimes), and hold land. Since they enjoy legal rights and are subject to legal obligations they can sue, and be sued, in respect of these rights and obligations.

Whilst corporations are created in different ways, for example by registration in the case of limited companies and by specific statute in the case of State corporations, they share common characteristics, and as far as their capacity is concerned they are all subject to the principle of ultra vires.

The doctrine of ultra vires

A corporation must be formed with stated objectives. These are located in the documents which create the organisation: its charter, the statute which establishes it; or its memorandum and articles of association. If the corporation acts outside these objectives it is said to be acting ultra vires — beyond its powers — and it cannot be bound. It lacks the capacity to do anything that its stated objectives do not authorise. Equally all activities falling within these objectives can be validly achieved, for they are intra vires — within the powers. No action can be brought to enforce a contract which is ultra vires a corporation: if there is any liability it will rest with those who have authorised or carried out the ultra vires activity. The issue of ultra vires will emerge either where a corporation is using it as a defence in circumstances where it is refusing to perform its contractual obligations, or where a challenge is being brought against the corporation by someone with a legal interest in doing so, in an attempt at preventing the corporation from carrying out an alleged ultra vires act. These two possibilities are illustrated in the following cases.

> In *Ashbury Railway Carriage and Iron Co. v. Riche (1875)* the company's objectives as expressed in the memorandum of association included the power to manufacture or sell railway rolling stock and to carry on business as mechanical engineers and general contractors. The company bought a concession to fully construct a railway line in Belgium from Antwerp to Tournai, and entered into an agreement with contractors, Messrs Riche, to carry out the work. The work was begun and money was paid to the contractors, but later as a result of shareholders action the directors of the company repudiated the contract, and the contractors sued for breach. The company claimed its contract with the contractors was ultra vires, and the House of Lords agreed. The action by the contractors failed.

> In *Attorney General v. Fulham Corporation (1921)* the corporation had power by statute to operate wash-houses where its inhabitants could wash their own clothes. The corporation established a municipal laundry, acting under these statutory powers, where the washing work could be carried out by employed staff. A ratepayer challenged the legality of this action, and through the Attorney-General proceedings were brought against the corporation. The Court held that the statutory powers did not extend to the running of a laundry, and therefore the activity was ultra vires. An injunction was granted restraining the corporation from running it.

A further possibility is the use of of ultra vires as a defence raised not by the corporation itself but by the other party.

> In *Bell Houses Ltd. v. City Wall Properties Ltd. (1966)* the objects clause in the memorandum of association of Bell Houses stated the principal object to be the developing of housing estates, but in addition it could "carry on any other business whatsoever which can, in the opinion of the board of directors, be advantageously carried out by the company in connection with or as ancilliary to the general business of the company". The company entered into a transaction with City Wall Properties to introduce it to a financier who would be able to provide financial help for property development. City Wall Properties refused to pay an agreed commission of £20,000 for the work done by the company on the grounds that the transaction was ultra vires the company. Bell Houses sued. The Court of Appeal held that the company was entitled to its fee, on the grounds that the agreement was within the company's powers provided the directors honestly believed it to be advantageous to the company, in relation to its principal business objects.

Limitations upon the ultra vires doctrine

Although the ultra vires doctrine is still of great importance in some spheres, notably the activities of central and local government, the impact on registered companies is no longer as significant as it used to be. This is because:

(i) the courts are prepared to recognise objects clauses which are broadly drafted. An example of such a clause is that used by Bell Houses (above).

(ii) the courts interpret objects clauses less strictly than they did in the past.

In *Re: New Finance and Mortgage Co. (1975)* the company's objects allowed it to carry on business as "Financiers, capitalists, concessionaires, bankers, commercial agents, mortgage brokers, financial agents and advisers, exporters and importers of goods and merchandise of all kinds and merchants generally". The company ran a filling station business, which owed Total £24,000 for petrol. The business went into liquidation. The liquidator claimed the business was an ultra vires activity, and refused to meet the payment. The court held the words "and merchants generally" to cover the running of a petrol filling station business, and thus that Total's claim was good.

(iii) s.35 Companies Act 1985 provides that "any transaction decided upon by the directors is deemed to be one within the capacity of the company in favour of a person dealing bona fide with the Company", even though the company's objects do not permit the activity. This provision grants a limited measure of protection to an outsider, who in the past was treated as having constructive (i.e. imputed) knowledge of the contents of the memorandum of association of the company (see Chapter 2).

(iv) the courts imply powers necessary for a company to achieve its stated objects.

In *Deuchar v. Gas Light and Coke Co. (1925)* the defendant company's main object was making and selling gas and the conversion of residual products into a marketable state. One residual product was napthalene which the company converted into beta-napthol which it sold commercially. The conversion required caustic soda, which the company originally bought from another company, however it realised that it would be more cost effective to manufacture the soda itself. This it started to do. Deuchar was the secretary of the company which had previously supplied the soda. It was aggrieved at the loss of its business with the defendant company, but had no means available to challenge the ending of the business relationship with the defendant company. Instead Deuchar bought shares in the company, and then sought an injunction, in his capacity as a member, to prevent the manufacture of the caustic soda which he claimed was ultra vires. The House of Lords held the activity to be intra vires on the grounds that the company had implied power to manufacture the products which were reasonably incidental to its express powers of converting residual products into a marketable state.

Ultra vires and local authorities

We have already seen that the same basic principles apply to local authorities as to registered companies. Local authorities are statutory bodies under the Local Government Act 1972 and the objects which such corporations may legitimately pursue must be ascertained from the Act itself. Over the years however, the ultra vires doctrine has not been applied rigidly to local authorities and the courts have consistently held that local authorities may not only do things for which there is express or implied authority, but also whatever is reasonably incidental to the doing of those things.

Thus in *Attorney General v. Smethwick Corporation (1932)* a resolution was passed by the corporation for the establishment of a printing and stationery work for the purpose of executing work required by them. An action was brought by the Attorney General on behalf of a ratepayer on the grounds that the proposal was ultra vires. The court held that the formation of this department was reasonably incidental or consequential upon the carrying out of the corporation's statutory duties and was not therefore ultra vires.

This common law rule was reflected in the general power to contract conferred on local authorities by virtue of s.111 Local Government Act 1972. This section provides that authorities are empowered to do anything (whether or not involving the expenditure, borrowing or lending of money or the acquisition or disposal of any property or rights) which is calculated to facilitate, or is conducive or incidental to, the discharge of any of their functions. Provided therefore that the activity carried on is related to the particular functions of the council in question it seems that it can be justified. This general power to contract conferred on local authorities is of course supplemented by a multiplicity of specific powers from various statutes. The Local Authority (Goods and Services) Act 1970 for instance, enables an authority to contract with other public bodies for the supply of goods and services.

MINORS

The law has always sought to protect minors from the consequences of entering into transactions which are detrimental to them. The aim has been to provide minors with some protection from their lack of commercial experience, whilst at the same time recognising circumstances in which it is entirely appropriate that they should be fully accountable for the agreements they make. The result is a mixture of common law and statutory rules which seek to achieve a balance between these conflicting objectives. The expression 'minor' refers to anyone under the age of eighteen, this being the age of majority under the Family Law Reform Act 1969. There are three categories of contracts which may be entered into by a minor. They are:

(i) valid contracts, which include beneficial contracts of employment, and contracts for necessaries. A beneficial contract of employment is one which is substantially for the minors benefit. This is invariably taken to mean that it must include some element of training or education, although this will probably be easily established. The court will set aside a contract of employment which viewed overall is not beneficial.

In *De Francesco v. Barnum (1890)* a minors contract of apprenticeship provided that she was to be totally at the disposal of her principal, who had no obligation to pay her. The court held the contract to be invalid, since its terms were harsh and onerous.

Necessaries are defined in s.3 Sale of Goods Act 1979 as "goods suitable to the condition in life of the minor . . . and to his actual requirements at the time of sale and delivery." This is a subjective test of the minors needs, found by reference to his economic and social status.

(ii) voidable contracts, which bind the minor until he repudiates them. This may be done before reaching majority or within a reasonable time thereafter. If repudiation has not taken place after this time the contract becomes valid. Contracts falling within this catagory are those of a long term nature, such as non beneficial contracts of employment, contracts for a lease, contracts to take shares in a company, and partnership agreements.

(iii) contracts of what have been described as a 'negatively voidable' kind, that is contracts which the minor can enforce to a certain extent, but which cannot be enforced against him. As a general principle contracts that do not come within the previous two categories fall within this one. In particular contracts for non-necessary goods, and contracts in which the minor has set up in business as a trader fall into this category. Originally the common law regulated the position regarding these contracts. Then the Infants Relief Act 1874 altered the common law in various ways. The present law is contained in the Minors Contracts Act 1987. This restores the original common law position by repealing the Infants Relief Act, and the law as it now stands regarding negatively voidable contracts is that:

(a) they are enforceable by the minor against the other party;

(b) they are not enforceable against him;

(c) property acquired by the minor under a contract in which he defaults can be reclaimed by the other party to the agreement if the court considers this to be "just and equitable". Alternatively a claim may be made for any property representing the property which is being sought, such as identifiable proceeds from the sale of goods. These provisions are not common law provisions, but are contained in s.3 of the 1987 Act. They apply whether or not the minor has acted fraudulently.

(d) a creditor can hold a minor bound, where the minor has either ratified the contract or has entered into a fresh agreement with the creditor after reaching the age of majority.

The lowering of the age of majority in 1969, together with the reluctance of many organisations such as mail order companies to deal with minors has meant that the law as it affects negatively voidable contracts is no longer of great commercial significance.

ASSIGNMENT — ARE WE AGREED?

You work as a legal assistant in the legal department of Anglo-Amalgamated Metal Industries plc. On returning from your summer holiday you find two files in your in-tray. They are accompanied by a memorandum from your superior, one of the company's lawyers, which states, "Please respond to the letters contained in the attached files. See me if you have any difficulties."

The first file contains the following letter from a solicitor:

> "I represent Miss Sally Goldwell. I understand from my client that she was recently interviewed for a clerical post with your company. Following the interview she was asked if she would be willing to accept the post, and she indicated that she would. Two days later, on 10th September 198x, she received a formal offer of the post from your company's Personnel Officer. She was asked to reply in writing within five days. She was ill at the time and arranged for a friend to notify you of her acceptance by phone. Her friend telephoned sometime after 7 pm on 13 September 198x. This was a Friday, and her friend had to leave a message on the Personnel Department's answerphone. I gather that the Personnel Department closes from 4.30 pm on Friday, until 8.30 the following Monday, and that the message only reached the Personnel Officer at midday on Monday 16th September. He had that morning telephoned another interviewee to offer her the job, which she accepted. My client subsequently heard from you that the post was no longer available for her.
>
> I am of the opinion that a contract exists between my client and yourselves, in respect of which you are in breach. I look forward to your prompt response.
>
> Yours faithfully,
> Roger Major."

The second file contained the following letter from one of the company's suppliers, Humberside Steels Ltd:

> "We refer to our offer to supply you with 40 tonnes reinforced steel bars, to which you responded with an order (68747/5/NX) for the goods to be delivered to you on 1st May. We replied immediately informing you that due to circumstances beyond our control delivery would be on the 24th May. We heard nothing from you, and delivered the goods on 24th May, only to find that you rejected them on the basis that they had not been ordered. We are at a loss to understand your action, particularly as we have often varied the delivery date with you in this way in the past, without complaint by you.
>
> We should be grateful therefore to receive your remittance in due course.
>
> Yours faithfully
> James Leach pp
> Humberside Steels Ltd."

TASKS

1. Draft replies to each of these letters, in which you state the legal basis upon which the company challenges the contractual claims they make.

2. In the form of a memorandum to your superior, Jane West, state the action you have taken, and indicate the weaknesses you believe exist in the company's legal position in respect of the two claims.

DEVELOPMENTAL TASK

The local citizens advice bureau has approached you to give a short talk to its voluntary workers concerning the way in which contractual agreements are made . Produce a short information sheet outlining the nature of a contract which you can give to the workers at the end of a meeting.

ASSIGNMENT — THE BROTHERS

Tim and Anthony O'Brien are brothers who set up together in business as builders a few years ago. The business was based in Dagenham where they both lived. In 1985 Tim married and moved some miles away to Colchester. As a result the business was dissolved, each brother re-establishing a business in his own right. Tim was more successful than Anthony, who was not such a good businessman. Anthony acquired a reputation as a bad credit risk, and found it increasingly difficult to find suppliers who were prepared to deliver building materials without payment in advance. He told Tim about the problem.

Tim's main supplier was a company called Anglian Associated Materials Ltd. Tim knew the managing director well, since they both belonged to the local golf club and were District Councillors together. Tim mentioned his brother's problem to Charlie, the managing director, and Charlie agreed to supply Anthony. "Obviously I'll see you alright Charlie, if anything goes wrong", responded Tim.

Earlier this year Anthony placed an order with Charlie's company for £2,000 worth of timber, and £4,000 of scaffolding. Due to acute cashflow problems he subsequently found himself unable to pay the full debt when it was demanded, and contacted Charlie direct to discuss the matter. Charlie reluctantly agreed to accept £1,000 for the timber, but insisted the scaffolding had to be paid for in full. Charlie then approached Tim, reminding him of his earlier promise, and requesting him to meet the outstanding £1,000 debt. Tim subsequently replied by letter as follows:

> "Dear Charlie,
> I have been advised that I have no legal liability towards payment of the outstanding amount of my brothers indebtedness to your company. However, in recognition of our friendship and all the help you have given me in the past I am prepared to make a payment of £250 towards the bill.
> Yours sincerely,
> Tim O'Brien.

later that week Tim wrote again:

> "Dear Charlie,
> I understand that my brother's business is in credit again. In the circumstances I feel I must withdraw my offer to you, and suggest that you pursue him for the outstanding amount.
> Yours sincerely,
> Tim O'Brien."

TASK

As an administrative assistant to the Company Secretary of Anglian Associated Materials Ltd you often deal with legal problems facing the company, and Charlie has asked you to consider whether the company has a legitimate claim for payment against either of the brothers.

Draft an informal report for the managing director in which you indicate the company's legal position in the matter.

Chapter 4

BUSINESS CONTRACTING II

In the last chapter the principal question being examined was establishing how and when a contract is made. It would be encouraging to say that no further contractual issues are ever likely to arise. The parties to the agreement having met the basic requirements and formed their contract then carry out their respective responsibilities to the satisfaction of each other, and performance is completed. This is what usually happens. The contract is made and performed. Each side is satisfied. The transaction is completed.

But this is not always so. Contracts can go wrong, sometimes for technical reasons and sometimes for practical reasons. Among the more common claims that arise are the following:

(a) that the contract is not binding because there was not true consent given to it. Such a possibility was mentioned in the discussion of freedom of contract. It may be alleged that the contract was induced by the making of false statements, that one or even both of the parties were mistaken in reaching their agreement. A further possibility is an allegation that one side exerted unfair influence over the other, or perhaps even made threats against the other.

(b) that the contract is invalid because its purpose is something contrary to the public interest, for instance because it imposes an unreasonable restraint upon trading freedom.

(c) that the obligations arising under the contract have not been performed either partially or in total, so that there has been a breach of contract.

(d) that some event has occured which has brought the contract to an end, without performance having been completed.

Of these various possibilities the most frequent are claims of breach of contract. Whatever the nature of the claim may be, however, it will always involve the innocent party seeking some remedy; perhaps financial compensation, a court order enforcing the performance of the contract, or a restoration of the parties to the position they were in before the contract was carried out.

In this chapter these further issues, concerning contractual rights and liabilities are examined under three sections. The first section considers the factors which can effect the validity of a contract. The second examines the contents of a contract, and the third looks at the way in which contractual liabilities are discharged, and the remedies available to an injured party if a contract is broken.

VALIDITY

Sometimes what appears superficially to be a properly constituted contract, proves on closer examination to contain some defect which was present when it was made. Certain defects of this kind the law recognises as sufficiently serious to either partially or wholly invalidate the contract. Such defects are referred to as vitiating (invalidating) factors. Those considered are misrepresentation, mistake, duress and undue influence.

MISREPRESENTATION

Before arriving at a contractual agreement the parties are invariably involved in a process of negotiation. Negotiations can range over any issues which the parties think are relevant to the protection of their interests, but they are certainly likely to cover questions of payment, when and how the contract is to be performed, and what terms will be attached to it. The aim of negotiating is both to obtain information and to drive a good bargain, and negotiating skill is a valuable quality in most areas of commercial and industrial life. Not all contracts are preceded by negotiations however, and as a general rule the more marked the imbalance in trading strength is between the parties the less likely serious negotiation of terms and conditions will be. Thus transactions between large organisations, and small organisations or private consumers tend to be characterised by the dominant party presenting the weaker party with a set of terms which are not open to discussion but have to be accepted in their entirety if a contract is to be made.

THE NATURE OF REPRESENTATIONS

Statements made during the bargaining process may become a part of the contract itself, that is, they may become terms of the contract and give rise to an action for breach of contract if they prove untrue. But in many cases there will be no intention by the maker of the statement that the statement should be absorbed into the contract at all. It will be made merely to induce the other party to make the contract. Statements of this sort are known as representations. If a representation is untrue for any reason it is referred to as a misrepresentation, and it will be actionable. The injured party (the misrepresentee) can base a claim not on breach of contract, but on the law applicable to misrepresentation. The reason is that the misrepresentation, whilst influential in the creation of the contract, has not been incorporated as a part of it. The contract itself has not been broken, but rather an assertion that was made in advance of it. It may however be possible to satisfy the court that in the particular circumstances a representation has become a contractual term, and in that event the action brought will be a contractual one. The important distinction between representations and terms is considered in more detail later in the chapter.

A representation is a statement or assertion of fact made by one party to the other before or at a time of the contract, which induces the other to enter into a contract. The statement can be in any form. Thus it can be in writing, such as a company prospectus containing details of the company's trading activities, or it can be spoken, or implied from conduct. The definition of a representation enables us to distinguish a number of statements whose form or content exclude them from being treated as representations.

(a) Statements of opinion

It frequently occurs that during the negotiating process statements are given which are based upon the opinion of the maker. Since the representation must be one of fact, a statement expressed as an opinion cannot become a representation. It can be a difficult task to clearly discriminate between what is, or can be fairly regarded as an issue of fact rather than opinion. The following cases illustrate the judicial approach to this question.

> In *Bisset v. Wilkinson (1927)* the vendor of some land in New Zealand told the purchaser that the land would carry his 1,000 sheep. The purchaser was aware that the vendor had no experience of sheep farming, and also that the

land had never carried sheep, but he went ahead and bought the land, only to find that it was too poor to support that number of sheep. He brought an action against the vendor for rescission, i.e. cancellation of the contract. His action failed. The court considered that the purchaser was not justified in treating the vendor's statement about the carrying capacity of the land as anything more than an expression of opinion. Of course, it would have been different if the vendor had been a sheep farmer himself, for then he would have been in a position to give accurate information.

In *Esso Petroleum Co. Ltd v. Mardon (1976)* Mardon took a tenancy of a filling station owned by Esso, having been given a forecast by an experienced Esso sales representative of the quantity of petrol the station could be expected to sell annually. This quantity was never reached during the four years Mardon remained as tenant, and the business ran at a loss. The Court of Appeal decided that the company had made a misrepresentation, since the sales representative's knowledge of such matters made the forecast a statement of fact rather than opinion, and the sales representative was acting in the capacity of an agent of the company. Mardon's claim for damages was successful. The misrepresentation was regarded as a negligent one, and the court also took the view that the representation amounted to a contractual warranty, that is a contractual promise. In his leading judgment Lord Denning MR commented: "it was a forecast made by a party, Esso, who had special knowledge and skill. It was the yardstick by which they measured the worth of a filling station. They knew the facts. They knew the traffic in the town. They knew the throughput of comparable stations. They had much experience and expertise at their disposal. They were in a much better position than Mr. Mardon to make a forecast. It seems to me that if such a person makes a forecast — intending that the other should act on it and he does act on it — it can well be interpreted as a warranty that the forecast is sound and reliable in this sense that they made it with reasonable care and skill. That warranty was broken. Most negligently Esso made a "fatal error" in the forecast they stated to Mr. Mardon, and on which he took the tenancy. For this they are made liable in damages".

Clearly it is not possible to avoid liability for a statement which is expressed as, or is subsequently claimed to be an opinion, when the knowledge and experience of the representor in the matter is far greater than that of the representee.

(b) Advertising and sales boasts

Although there is no rule of law which prevents such statements from amounting to representations they will be seen as no more than sales boasts, provided they are not capable of substantial verification. They do not attract any legal consequences. They are regarded simply as the over inflated belief the seller has in the product in his efforts at sales promotion. Examples include the estate agents, "most desirable residence", and the carpet company's "We cannot be equalled for price and quality." However to advertise that "interest free credit is available on all items bought this month", or that a motor vehicle has returned "31 mpg at a constant 75 mph" are clearly statements of fact. If untrue they give rise to an offence under the Trade Descriptions Act 1968 as well as amounting to misrepresentations.

(c) Statements of law

A false statement of law cannot constitute a misrepresentation. This is based upon the general legal proposition that ignorance of law does not excuse an otherwise unlawful act. The assumption is that the representee knows the law, and cannot therefore rely upon a plea that he relied upon inaccurate statements of law. Of course it would be quite different if these statements were being made by his legal adviser, upon whom he is placing reliance (see Chapter 6).

Distinguishing statements of law from statements of fact can in some cases be a difficult task. A single statement may be one of mixed law and fact. For example, to make a statement that a person is a tenant is both a statement of law, since the expression tenant carries a technical meaning which may or may not be accurate in this instance, and a statement of fact; either the individual is or is not a tenant. If a point of law is arrived at from a statement of the facts, then it seems the statement can be treated as one of law. An example would be a comment that, "since this contract was made by post it became binding when the acceptance was sent." Sometimes a statement may involve distinguishing between law, opinion and fact.

> In *Smith v. Land & House Property Corporation (1884)*, in a contract for the sale of a hotel the seller stated that it was leased to "a most desirable tenant." In fact the tenant was far from desirable and the purchaser attempted to terminate the contract on the grounds of misrepresentation. The court held that the statement was not of opinion but fact and constituted a misrepresentation. The statement was not one of law, for its principal observation was not the fact of the person being a tenant, but rather that the tenant was a person of value to the purchaser.

(d) Statements of future intention

A statement of future intention is not a statement of fact and is therefore not actionable. This is not the case however where the statement of future intention conceals the present state of mind of the misrepresentor which may constitute a fact.

> In *Edgington v. Fitzmaurice (1885)* the directors of a company invited a loan from the public to finance expansion. However their real intention was to use the money raised to pay off debts. This statement of intention was held to be a statement of fact which was false and actionable. Bowen LJ, in the course of his judgment, remarked "The state of a man's mind is as much as state of fact as the state of his digestion. It is true that it is difficult to prove what the state of man's mind at a particular time is, but if it can be ascertained it is as much a fact as anything else. A misrepresentation as to the state of a man's mind is, therefore, a misstatement of fact."

(e) Silence

It might be thought that a representation could not arise in a situation where no statements of fact are made. However, although generally a non-disclosure cannot amount to a representation, there are some important exceptions to this rule. In contracts uberimmae fidei (of the utmost good faith) duties of full disclosure are imposed.

The obligation of disclosure under such contracts is based on the nature of this particular class of agreement. They are in general contracts where one party only has full knowledge of all material facts. Insurance contracts and contracts for the sale of shares through the issue of a prospectus are examples of contracts uberrimae fidei. If full disclosure is not made in such cases the injured party can rescind the contract. Thus before entering into an insurance agreement the party seeking cover must disclose all facts which are material to the nature of the risk which is to be insured. In the case of a company issuing a prospectus the Financial Services Act 1986 s162 requires that the document must contain information prescribed under rules made by the Secretary for Trade and Industry (for instance the financial record of the company and details of contracts it has entered into.) A general duty of disclosure is laid down in s.163 which covers any information potential investors, or their professional advisers, would reasonably require in order to make an informed assessment of (a) the company's financial position and (b) the rights attaching to the shares to be issued. In determining what information comes within the general duty to disclose, the following matters are required by statute to be considered:

(i) the nature of the shares and who is issuing them,

(ii) the nature of those who are likely to acquire them,

(iii) the fact that certain matters (i.e. of an investment nature) may reasonably be expected to be known by the professional advisers likely to be consulted by the acquirers of shares, and

(iv) information available to investors or their professional advisers under statute.

In contracts for the sale of land the vendor is under an obligation to disclose any defects in his title, that is his ownership of the property, although this does not apply to defects in the property itself, for instance dry rot or damp.

If a statement is true when made but becomes untrue before the contract is concluded, the representor will be under a duty to disclose this alteration to the representor.

> In *With v. O'Flanagan (1936)* the purchaser of a doctor's practice was able to rescind the contract because, despite being told accurately during negotiations that the annual income of the practice was £2,000, he was not informed prior to the sale, which took place some months later, that the income of the practice had fallen sharply because of an illness which prevented the doctor from working.

The Financial Services Act 1986, also deals with this possibility in relation to the issue of a prospectus. It requires the issue of a supplementary prospectus if a "significant change" occurs or a "significant new matter" arises after the issue of the original prospectus, whilst the offer for shares is still open.

Inducement

The representation must induce the person to enter into the contract. There can be no inducement in cases where the other party is unaware of the representation or does not believe the statement, or has relied on his own skill and judgment. In such cases no action will lie in misrepresentation.

> In *Attwood v. Small (1838)*, during the course of negotiations for the sale of a mine, the vendor made exaggerated statements of its capacity. The buyers subsequently appointed their own experts to investigate the mine, and the agents reported back to the buyers that the vendors statements were true. As a result the buyers purchased the mine, only to discover that the statements were inaccurate. It was held that the buyers had no remedy in misrepresentation. They placed reliance upon their own independent investigation.

The representation need not be the sole or major inducement. It will be enough that it had a material affect upon the other persons mind, in their decision to reach an agreement.

TYPES OF MISREPRESENTATION

Actions for breach of contract and misrepresentation differ in an important respect. If a term of a contract is broken it is irrelevant to consider the state of mind of the contract breaker in establishing the existence and extent of liability. If however a mere representation has proved to be untrue i.e. it has become a misrepresentation, the effect this has on the liability of the misrepresentor depends on the state of mind accompanying it.

A misrepresentation may be made innocently, negligently or fraudulently.

A misrepresentation is innocent if the person making it had reasonable grounds for believing it to be true, and negligent where there was a lack of reasonable care taken to determine the accuracy of the statement. In contrast, a fraudulent misrepresentation is a representation which a person makes knowing it to be untrue, or believing it to be false, or which is made recklessly where the person making it does not care whether it is true or false. Thus it is a representation which is not honestly believed by the person making it, or where there has been complete disregard for the truth.

> Fraudulent misrepresentation was considered in the leading case of *Derry v. Peek (1889)*. Under a private Act of Parliament the company were granted power to operate horse-drawn trams, and could run steam powered trams with the Board of Trades' consent. This they applied for, and in the belief that the consent would be granted, they went ahead and offered shares to the public through a prospectus that stated the company had power to run trams by steam. Shares were taken up. The consent was not given, and in consequence the company was wound up, many investors losing their money. Action was brought against the directors in the tort of deceit. The House of Lords defined a fraudulent misrepresentation as stated above, and having found that the directors believed the consent was simply a formality, held that the tort had not been committed. The directors were inaccurate but not dishonest, and inaccuracy without more is not fraud. They were not liable to pay damages.

At common law it has been possible since 1964 to claim damages in the tort of negligence for a negligent misrepresentation under the principle laid down in *Hedley Byrne v. Heller (1964)*. This important case is considered extensively in Chapter 6, and it is appropriate here simply to note the main aspects of the decision. Hedley Byrne provides that where there is a "special relationship" between the persons making a statement and the recipient of it, a duty of reasonable care is owed in making it. If the duty is broken damages will be available, representing the loss suffered. The "special relationship" concept is central to the decision. The quality of this relationship was referred to by Lord Morris when he stated:

> "Where in a sphere in which a person is so placed that others could reasonably rely on his judgment or his skill or on his ability to make careful inquiry, a person takes it on himself to give information or advice to, or allows his information or advice to be passed on to another, who, as he knows or should know, will place reliance on it then a duty of care will arise".

The reliance placed on the statement by the recipient of it must be reasonable. In Hedley Byrne itself, the disclaimer of liability was enough to prevent reliance on the financial reference being reasonable. Following the decision in *Esso Petroleum v. Mardon (1976)* the Hedley Byrne principle has been extended to apply to a pre-contractual relationship, in addition to a non contractual relationship of the kind that appeared in Hedley Byrne.

REMEDIES AVAILABLE FOR MISREPRESENTATION

A variety of remedies are available to the misrepresentee. They include common law and equitable remedies, and the remedies available under the Misrepresentation Act 1967. At common law, as noted above, damages are available in the tort of deceit for fraudulent misrepresentation, and in the tort of negligence for negligent misrepresentation. In equity rescission is available in any case of misrepresentation. This is a remedy which seeks to put the parties back to their pre-contractual position. If this cannot be achieved, for instance where the subject matter of the contract has been altered, lost or sold to a third party, rescission is not available. Nor can it be claimed if it would be inequitable to grant it. Thus if a person in full knowledge of the misrepresentation affirms the contract, i.e. expressly or by implication indicates that he intends to continue, the right to rescind will be lost. Affirmation can occur through delay in bringing an action.

> In *Leaf v. International Galleries (1950)* the plaintiff bought from the defendants a picture described as a Constable, and was held unable to rescind the contract some five years later when he discovered on trying to re-sell it that it was not a Constable after all. The plaintiff also argued, unsuccessfully, that the contract was affected by mistake (see later). It can be of advantage to a plaintiff to plead alternative legal arguments in this way, for if one proposition fails the other might succeed, and clearly a plaintiff would not choose to bring two separate actions (or even more) if the matter can be dealt with in one trial.

Unlike the common law remedy of damages, which are available as of right once liability has been established, rescission, being an equitable remedy, is discretionary. The court exercises this discretion in accordance with certain principles, referred to as "equitable maxims." Essentially these principles are concerned with ensuring that in awarding equitable relief the court should be satisfied not only that the plaintiff has acted fairly, but also that the defendant will not be unfairly treated if the remedy sought by the plaintiff is granted. This is the justification for the restrictions on the granting of rescission, which are stated above.

Under statute damages are available under the Misrepresentation Act 1967 in respect of negligent and innocent misrepresentation. Under s.2(1) damages are available for negligent misrepresentation. It is a defence for the maker of the statement to show that up to the time of the contract he believed that the statement was true and that there was reasonable cause to believe this. Obviously such a belief will depend upon the steps taken by representor to verify the statement. There is an important difference between a claim brought for negligent misrepresentation under s.2(1), and a claim founded in the tort of negligence, which is that the burden of proof lies with the misrepresentor under s.2(1), but with the misrepresentee in negligence.

Under s.2(2), where a misrepresentation is a purely innocent one, damages may be awarded; however, the section requires that the party seeking relief must ask the court to rescind the contract. If the court is satisfied that grounds for rescission exist it may award damages instead, if it is of the opinion that it would be equitable to do so. The aim of this provision is apparently to cover cases where the misrepresentation is of a minor nature and give the court the discretion to award damages, whilst leaving the contract intact.

The diagram on the next page illustrates the remedies available for the different types of misrepresentation.

Under s.3 of the Act a person may not avoid liability in respect of claims brought under ss.2(1) and (2), unless the court, in its discretion, considers that reliance on a provision seeking to avoid such liability is fair and reasonable in the circumstances of the case. The case of *Howard Marine v. Ogden (1978)* provides an illustration of a claim brought under s.2(1), and the use of an exemption clause coming within s.3.

> The facts of *Howard Marine & Dredging Co Ltd v. A. Ogden & Sons*

Fig. 4.1 Remedies for misrepresentation

	Fraudulent misrepresentation	**Negligent misrepresentation**	**Innocent misrepresentation**
At Common Law	Damages in the tort of deceit	Damages in the tort of negligence under the rule in *Hedley Byrne v. Heller (1964)*, if a 'special relationship exists.	
In Equity	Rescission (and damages). If the contract is executory the fraud is a defence if the misrepresentator brings action for specific performance	Rescission	Rescission
Under Misrepresentation Act 1967		In addition to rescission, or, at the court's discretion instead of rescission, damages under s.2(1) if as a result of the misrepresentation of the innocent party has suffered loss. If the defendant can prove that up to the time of the contract he believed, with reasonable cause, that his statements were true, this will be a defence.	If the grounds for recission exist, the court, in its discretion, may award damages instead, under s.2(2).

(Excavations) Ltd (1978) were as follows. Ogdens agreed to hire two sea going barges from Howards, for the purpose of dumping earth at sea. Howards quoted a price in a letter to Ogdens, stating the cubic capacity of each vessel. At a later meeting Ogdens enquired of Howards representative what the carrying capacity of the vessels was in tonnes. The representative stated this to be about 1,600 tonnes. He made the statement honestly, based upon his recollection of the tonnage specified in Lloyds Register in London, which he had previously examined. He had also seen the shipping documents for the two vessels, which indicated the tonnage as 1,195 tonnes per vessel. This was in fact the correct figure, but all the representative remembered at the time of his statement was the Lloyds entry, which unusually was incorrect.

The lack of carrying capacity held up Ogden's work, and they refused to pay the hire charges. Howards withdrew the barges, and sued for damages. Ogdens counterclaimed, seeking damages under s.2(1) Misrepresentation Act 1967.

The agreement between the parties, referred to technically where a vessel is being hired as a charterparty, contained the following exemption clause: "Charterers acceptance of handing over the vessel shall be conclusive that (it is) in all respects fit for the intended and contemplated use by the Charterers and in every other way satisfactory to them ."

By a majority the Court of Appeal held that Howards were in breach of s.2(1), and that they could not rely on the exemption clause. Accordingly Ogdens could recover damages representing their losses. Bridge LJ stated: "In the course of negotiations leading to a contract the 1967 Act imposes an absolute obligation not to state facts which the representor cannot prove he had reasonable ground to believe." On the facts the representative was found by the court not to have established this "reasonable ground", for he had overlooked the disparity in tonnage between the shipping documents and the Register, recalling only the latter document with its inaccurate information.

On the issue of the exemption clause the court held that since its effect was to seek to exempt for negligent misrepresentation it was not a reasonable clause, and thus reliance on it was not fair and reasonable.

In cases of this kind, whilst the courts task is to apply the law to the facts, this will often involve issues of legal discretion. The courts are guided in their exercise of such discretion by recognising the commercial reality of the situation. In his dissenting judgment Lord Denning MR commented of the exemption, "The parties here were commercial concerns and were of equal bargaining power. The clause was not foisted by one on the other in a standard printed form. It was contained in all the drafts which passed between them, and it was no doubt given close consideration by both sides . . . It is a clause common in charterparty's of this kind . . . it is specially applicable in cases where the contractor has the opportunity of checking the position for himself. It tells him that he should do so; and that he should not rely on any information given beforehand, for it may be inaccurate. Thus it provides a valuable safeguard against the consequences of innocent misrepresentation."

MISTAKE

Traditionally the courts have shown reticence in treating mistake as a ground for the avoidance of contractual liabilities. We have already seen that a contract will remain valid despite its proving to be economically disadvantageous to one of the parties because of what is, in effect, a mistake as to the value or quality of the subject matter. *Haigh v. Brooks (1839)* provides a very useful illustration (see Chapter 3). It is not the responsibility of the courts to interfere with such agreements where the parties openly and voluntarily make their bargain. Where goods are the subject matter of the contract the common law rule was expressed as caveat emptor (let the buyer beware) and despite considerable erosion of this rule, principally through the passing of legislation such as the Sale of Goods Act 1979, aspects of it still remain. The purchaser of an item he believes is a valuable antique has no remedy when the mistake is discovered, finding he has paid far more than the item is worth. It may of course be different if the seller made false representations before the sale. The converse is also true where an item such as a painting, which is sold by its owner for next to nothing, subsequently realises many thousands of pounds at auction for its new owner. The original owner can only lament the error of judgment made in selling it in the first place. The caveat emptor rule is of considerable importance in private sales, but less so where the seller is a business.

The following types of mistake will not effect the validity of a contract:

(i) A mistake of law.

(ii) An error of judgment about the value of the subject matter of the contract, unless a misrepresentation was made.

(iii) A mistake about the meaning of a trade term. In *Harrison & Jones Ltd v. Bunten & Lancaster Ltd (1953)* a buyer purchased 100 bales of 'Sree brand' kapok from the seller. Both parties believed that this type of kapok was pure, but when the buyer discovered that Sree brand was a mixture of different types of kapok he claimed that the contract was void for mistake. The court, however, held that the contract was valid, being unaffected by the mistake.

(iv) A mistake about ability to perform the contract within a certain time. e.g. in a building contract.

Despite this wide range of mistake situations which are ignored in law, there are nevertheless circumstances where the mistake is regarded as of so funadmental a nature that the courts will treat it as affecting the contract. Such mistakes are known as operative mistakes, and they render the contract void. The following is an outline of the types of operative mistakes which are recognised.

MISTAKE ABOUT THE NATURE OF A SIGNED DOCUMENT

We are brought up on words of warning about care in signing documents, for good reason, since it will be no defence for the signatory to say he failed to read, or did not understand, the document. A defence known as non est factum (not my deed) is available, however, if the following conditions are satisfied:

(i) that the document signed is fundamentally or radically different from the one the signatory believed it to be; and

(ii) that the signatory exercised reasonable care in signing the document; and

(iii) that fraud was used to induce the signature.

In *Saunders v. Anglia Building Society (1974)* the House of Lords indicated the narrow limits of the defence of non est factum. The facts were that a 78 year old widow signed a document which a Mr. Lee had told her was a deed of gift of her house to her nephew. She did not read the document since, "at the time of signing her glasses were broken." The document in fact transferred her property to Lee, who subsequently mortgaged the property to a building society. The widow now sought to recover the deeds, pleading non est factum. The action failed. The document had been signed with carelessness, and furthermore it was not substantially different from the one she believed she was signing: they were both assignments of property.

There will sometimes be grounds other than mistake on which a person who has signed a contractual document can rely to avoid the contract. For example, in the case of consumer credit agreements such as hire-purchase agreements, the Consumer Credit Act 1974 grants a five-day period after the agreement is made within which the debtor can cancel the agreement, provided it was signed somewhere other than on the creditor's premises. Putting a signature to a contract which is void at law, such as an illegal contract, will incur no contractual liability.

MISTAKE AS TO THE IDENTITY OF THE OTHER PARTY

Mistake of this kind is usually unilateral, where only one of the parties is mistaken about the identity of the other party to the contract. When this occurs the contract will be void if the mistaken party can show that the question of identity was material to the making of the contract, and that the other part knew or ought to have known of the mistake. The majority of cases in which this type of mistake has occurred involve fraud, so the requirement of knowledge of the mistake will have been satisfied, and the mistaken party will be left with the difficult task of trying to show that he would not have made the contract if the true identity of the other party had been known.

> In *Cundy v. Lindsay & Co. (1878)* the respondents, a firm of linen manufacturers in Belfast, received an order for 250 dozen handkerchiefs from a rogue called Blenkarn whose address was 37 Wood Street, Cheapside. He signed the order to make it appear that it had come from a firm called Blenkiron and Company who traded at 123 Wood Street, Cheapside. The respondent knew Blenkiron and Company to be a reputable firm, and therefore sent the goods, together with an invoice headed Blenkiron and Company, to 37 Wood Street. Blenkarn then sold the goods to the appellant, who was unaware of the fraud. Lindsay and Company were held to be entitled to the goods since their contract with Blenkarn was void. His existence was entirely unknown to them; they intended to deal only with Blenkiron and Company
>
> If the parties deal face to face, mistake about identity will be far more difficult to establish. In a shop, for instance, the shopkeeper presumably intends a contract with the person on the other side of the counter, irrespective of what the person calls himself.
>
> In *Phillips v. Brooks (1919)* a rogue called North entered a jeweller's shop where he represented himself to be a gentleman called Sir George Bullough. He purchased a ring for £450, for which he gave the jeweller a worthless cheque. The following day North sold the ring to a firm of pawnbrokers. On discovering his loss later, the jeweller traced the ring to the pawnbrokers and sought to recover it from them, alleging that his original contract with North was void for mistake. The court disagreed, since the parties had dealt face to face. The contract was, however, voidable on the grounds of fraud. Unfortunately, this did not help the jeweller, as he had not taken steps to avoid the contract until after the ring had been purchased by the pawnbroker, who now had a good title (i.e. legal ownership) to it.

The expression "voidable" contract was considered in the last chapter. A voidable contract, such as one induced by fraud, gives the fraudulent party ownership of the goods until the innocent party takes action to avoid the contract, for example by informing the police of the loss. If before the contract has been avoided the rogue has sold the goods to a third party who buys in good faith and is unaware of the fraud, that third party becomes the owner of the goods, and the original owner cannot reclaim them. This was the position that Phillips the jeweller found himself in.

> An example of the limited extent to which a unilateral mistake may affect the validity of a contract is provided by *Centrovincial Estates PLC v. Merchant Investors Assurance Co. Ltd. (1983)* a case involving a business tenancy between the plaintiffs, the landlords and the defendants who were the tenants. The issue concerned the fixing of a new rent, under a rent review clause in the lease. The mistake in question was made by solicitors acting for the plaintiffs who wrote to the defendants on June 22 1982 asking them to agree to a new rent of £65,000 per annum to operate from the rent review date. The defendants were happy to agree to the new rent by letter the following day, for the figure suggested was a reduction of over £3,000 per annum on the current rent. The plaintiff's solicitors, when they discovered the error a few days later attempted to persuade the defendants to accept the true figure of £126,000 per annum. The plaintiffs claimed the mistake had prevented any consensus ad idem between the parties. The Court of Appeal, applying strict contract law, held that acceptance of an unambiguous offer resulted in a contrct. The mere assertion of a mistake, of which the offeree was unaware, did not affect the contract's validity.

BILATERAL MISTAKES

The instances of mistake considered so far concern mistakes made by just one of the parties. These are consequently known an unilateral mistakes. In cases of bilateral mistake both the parties are mistaken, either about the same thing (common mistake) or about something different (mutual mistake).

Mutual mistake

Where a mutual mistake occurs the parties are at cross purposes, and in cases of fundamental error arguably there can be no contract in existence anyway, on grounds of the uncertainty of their agreement. For example if one company agrees to sell a machine to another, and the description of it is so vague that the seller believes he is selling an entirely different machine to the one the buyer believes he is buying, there is no effective agreement within the process of offer and acceptance. The approach applied by the courts in these circumstances is an objective one.

> In *Raffles v. Wichelhaus (1864)* the buyer purchased a cargo of cotton from the seller, to arrive "ex Peerless from Bombay." Remarkably there were two ships named Peerless sailing from Bombay, one in October which the buyer had in mind and one in December which the seller had in mind. The court held that no contract had been entered into. Viewed objectively the facts denied the existence of an offer and an acceptance for there was no consensus ad idem.

Common mistake

> An example of a common mistake occurred in *Couturier v. Hastie (1856)*. A contract was made for the sale of some wheat which was to be shipped. Unknown to both parties, when they made the agreement the wheat had already been sold by the ship's captain because during the voyage it had started to overheat. The court held the contract to be void, since it was a contract of impossibility.

There are some significant exceptions to this type of claim. At common law relief from a contract affected by a common mistake will not be available where the mistake:

(i) occurs after the contract is made.

In *Amalgamated Investment & Property Co. Ltd v. John Walker & Sons Ltd (1976)* the defendants sold the plaintiffs a warehouse for £1.7m. The defendants knew the plaintiffs intended to redevelop the site, and both knew planning permission would be necessary. Contracts were exchanged on 25 September. On 26 September the defendants were informed by the Department of the Environment that the building had become "listed". This made development consent most unlikely, and without it the property was worth £200,000. The plaintiffs sought to rescind the contract. The Court of Appeal rejected the claim. There was no mistake in the minds of the parties when the contracts were exchanged sufficient to set the contracts aside.

(ii) is as to quality

An example of a mistake about quality is seen in *Leaf v. International Galleries (1950),* where the purchaser believed he was buying a Constable painting only to discover later that Constable was not the artist. The mistake was not operative, since the purchaser had received under the contract what he had bargained for, namely the painting.

A further illustration occurred in *Bell v. Lever Bros Ltd (1932)*. Bell, who was the managing director of a company controlled by Lever Bros Ltd, became redundant as a result of company amalgamations, and Lever Bros Ltd paid him £30,000 as compensation for his loss of office. It was subsequently discovered that as managing director he had committed serious breaches of duty by secret trading and could have been summarily dismissed without compensation. Although Bell had not revealed his misconduct to the company before he received the compensation, he was not acting fraudulently because he was unaware that what he had done rendered him liable to dismissal without compensation. The company sought to recover the compensation it had paid to Bell on the grounds of mistake. The House of Lords decided that it could not do so, since the company had paid the compensation in the belief that Bell was an employee who had carried out his duties in a proper way. They were therefore mistaken about the quality of their employee, which was insufficient to give rise to an operative mistake.

REMEDIES

At common law

The effect of an operative mistake at common law is to render the contract void 'ab initio' — from the outset. The true owner is thus entitled to the return of goods, or damages from whoever is in wrongful possession.

In equity

The position in equity is different however, for equity recognises certain types of operative mistake, which the common law does not grant relief for, in particular in cases involving mistake as to quality. The following cases illustrate the position.

In *Solle v. Butcher (1950)* the parties entered into a lease in the mistaken belief that, due to substantial improvements carried out to it, the flat concerned was not subject to rent control legislation. The tenant had been paying rent at the agreed rate of £250 p.a. when it was discovered that the flat was subject to rent control. The maximum rent recoverable was £140 p.a., although if the landlord had served a statutory notice on the tenant before the lease had been executed, he would have been entitled legitimately to charge £250 p.a., the extra amount representing the value to the tenant of the improvements. The tenant claimed the overpayment of rent. The landlord counterclaimed for possession. The Court of Appeal found itself unable to grant relief at common law for the mistake was one of quality. However exercising its equitable jurisdiction the court allowed the lease to be rescinded on condition that a new lease on the same terms at the higher rent be offered to the tenant, the new lease enabling the landlord to serve the relevant notice on the tenant.

In *Magee v. Pennine Insurance Co. Ltd (1969)* a proposal for insurance for a motor car had been incorrectly completed without the insured's knowledge. Following a crash, a claim was made and the insurance company agreed to pay £385 which the insured was willing to accept. On discovery of the material inccuracy in the policy however, the company withdrew their offer of payment for which they were then sued. The Court of Appeal held that under the common law the common mistaken belief that the policy was valid was inoperative and the contract of insurance was valid. In equity however the agreement to pay £385 would be set aside as there had been a fundamental misapprehension, and the party seeking to rescind was not at fault.

RECTIFICATION

In the context of considering equitable relief where parties to a contract have been in error, the equitable remedy of rectification is worth noting. Where it applies the court will rectify a written document so that it accords with the true agreement of the parties. For rectification to operate there must be:

(i) agreement on the particular aspect in question,

(ii) which is certain and unchanged at the time of writing, and

(iii) the writing must fail to express the agreement.

In *Craddock Bros. v. Hunt (1923)* an oral agreement for the sale of a house expressly excluded an adjoining yard and yet the later written agreement and conveyance included the yard. The court ordered a rectification of the documents in order to express the parties true original intention.

The equitable remedy of rectification will not be available however simply because one party has made a miscalculation and the agreement entered into does not express his intention.

In *Riverplate Properties v. Paul (1975)* the plaintiff granted a long lease of a maisonette to the defendant and had intended that the lessee should pay half the cost of exterior and structural repairs that were required. The lease however put the entire burden on the plaintiff. The defendant believed that she was not responsible for those repairs and the plaintiff claimed for rectification or rescission of the lease. The court held that a unilateral mistake of this kind could have no impact on the terms of the lease agreed by the parties. There was no justification for equity to disrupt the transaction actually entered into and the mistake was inoperative. The error in failing to include a suitable term in the lease was the plaintiffs.

DURESS AND UNDUE INFLUENCE

The term duress at common law involves coercion of a person into making a contract by means of actual or threatened violence to them. The threat must be illegal. The plea of duress is an extremely unusual one, although it was raised in a case that was heard by the Privy Council in 1976.

> *Barton v. Armstrong (1976)* involved death threats made by Armstrong against Barton, if Barton refused to purchase Armstrong's shares in a company of which they were both major shareholders. There was evidence that Barton regarded the acquisition as a satisfactory business arrangement in any event. He subsequently sought to have the deed by which he purchased Armstrong's share declared void. By a majority the court held the agreement to be void, although the minority view was that the claim should fail. This was because it seemed that although Barton took the threats seriously, the real reason for making the purchase was commercial.

A more subtle form of improper pressure is undue influence, which equity recognises gives the innocent party the right to rescind the contract. In some relationships a presumption of undue influence arises. This is the case where there is a fiduciary relationship, or where one person is in a position of dominance over the other e.g. parent and child, solicitor and client, doctor and patient, trustee and beneficiary. The dominant party who attempts to uphold a transaction entered into in such a relationship must rebut the presumption of undue influence by showing that he has not abused his position in any way. Evidence that the innocent party has taken independent advice will go a long way to rebutting the presumption and saving the contract.

> In *Lancashire Loans v. Black (1934)* the Court of Appeal recognised that the presumption of undue influence between a parent and a child can transcend the child marrying and leaving home. Here a married daughter, without independent advice, had contracted to pay off part of her mother's debts. The court held that the transaction could be set aside as the daughter had not exercised her free will but acted under the influence of her mother.

The courts are still prepared to recognise new relationships where the doctrine applies, for example an influential secretary companion and his elderly employee (Re Craig (1971)), and a banker who seeks to obtain a benefit from his customer (Lloyds Bank v. Bundy (1975).

> In *National Westminster Bank plc v. Morgan (1985)* a wife, as joint owner of the matrimonial home, had been advised to execute a second mortgage to refinance the old mortgage of the property. The advice had been given by the manager of the bank mortgagee who had assured the wife that the mortgage did not cover business debts. Although made in good faith this statement was untrue and the wife subsequently applied to have the mortgage set aside when the husband died, on the grounds of undue influence. The court held that the relationship had raised the presumption of undue influence as the manager's advice was relied on and the bank mortgagee had gained an advantage. Also the failure to suggest independent advice on these facts meant that the mortgage could be set aside on the ground of undue influence.

In modern times the courts have demonstrated an increased willingness to see the principles underlying duress and undue influence as elements in a broader principle of law which Lord Denning referred to in *Lloyds Bank v. Bundy (1975)* as "inequality of bargaining power." It may be useful to refer to his judgment, which is contained in Chapter 3. The idea of economic duress falls under this broad terminology. Two modern cases provide a clear illustration of situations in which the courts have recognised economic duress.

> In *Clifford Davies Management Ltd v. WEA Records Ltd (1975)*, two composer members of a pop group entered into an agreement with their manager to assign the copyright in all their work to him for a period of ten years, for a very small financial consideration and his promise to use his best endeavours to publish the work they composed. The Court of Appeal found that on the basis of bargaining inequality the contract could be set aside at the option of the composers. The factors cited by the court that pointed to the inequality were:
>
> (i) the overall unfairness of a ten year tie, supported by vague consideration offered in return by the manager;
>
> (ii) the conflict of interest arising from the manager acting as the business adviser to the composers, whilst at the same time representing his own company's interests in negotiating with them; and
>
> (iii) the absence of any independent advice available to the composers, and their reliance upon the manager who exerted undue influence over them.
>
> In *Universe Tankships Inc of Monrovia v. International Transport Workers' Federation (1982)* a ship the Universe Sentinal owned by Universe Tankships, was blacked by a union, the ITWF, which refused to make tugs available to assist in docking at Milford Haven. The blacking was based upon the ship sailing under a flag of convenience. Following negotiations between the parties, the ITWF agreed to lift the restriction in return for an undertaking from Universe Tankships to improve crew pay and conditions on the vessel and make a contribution to an ITFW fund — The Seafarers' International Welfare Protection and Assistance Fund. The company later sought to recover their $6480 contribution, and the House of Lords held they were entitled to its return, since it had been paid under economic duress. The agreement was voidable.

THE EFFECT OF PUBLIC POLICY ON CONTRACTS

It has previously been noted that whilst contracts are part of the private law, this does not mean contract making is the exclusive domain of the parties themselves, allowing them total freedom to make whatever type of contract they choose. At common law certain types of contract were regarded as illegal on the basis that they were contrary to public policy. The list of illegal contracts has been added to by statute.

Public policy is a vague term which has never been clearly defined. The legal writer Pollock saw it as "a principle of judicial legislation or interpretation founded on the current needs of the community." This appears to mean that it is concerned with the public good, rather than with what is politically appropriate; and in practice public policy involves the court in applying economic, moral and other criteria to the contract in question to decide whether it is desirable in the general public interest. By these means the courts have held many types of contract to be illegal including contracts to commit criminal and tortious acts, contracts for trading with the enemy in times of war, and contracts which oust the jurisdiction of the courts.

The effects of declaring a contract illegal will vary. Sometimes a party who is unaware of the illegality will be allowed to sue on the contract, but where the parties are fully aware of the illegal nature of the transaction the court will deny them any remedy.

> In *Foster v. Driscoll (1927)* a group of people entered into a partnership agreement in England, the object of which was to smuggle a ship-load of whisky into the USA. This was a violation of the prohibition laws then in force in the USA, so the partnership was illegal on the grounds of public policy, and it was held that no action could be brought in respect of any matter arising out of the agreement.

CONTRACTS IN RESTRAINT OF TRADE

One aspect of common law illegality which is of particular application within the sphere of business and commerce involves contracts that are regarded as being in restraint of trade, some of which are regulated by statute. The essence of such a contract is that it contains an agreement by one of the parties to it to restrict that party's freedom of trade with others outside the contract in the future. What constitutes such a contract can be discovered only by applying the principles set out by the courts, and in more recent times by Parliament. These are considered below. It should be borne in mind that because the doctrine of restraint of trade is guided by considerations of public policy, the categories of contract to which it applies alter as economic and social conditions change. Examination of the law regarding restraints tends to show that what the courts and Parliament are largely seeking to prevent are practices which restrict competition to the detriment of the public.

For convenience restraints are considered below under two headings:

(a) restraints controlled at common law; and

(b) restraints controlled by statute.

RESTRAINTS AT COMMON LAW

The leading authority here is the decision of the House of Lords in the Nordenfelt case.

> In *Nordenfelt v. Maxim Nordenfelt Guns & Ammunition Co. Ltd (1894)* the seller of a gun and ammunition manufacturing business agreed with the buyer not to manufacture guns or ammunition anywhere in the world, or compete in any way, for a period of 25 years. Although the undertaking not to compete in any way was considered unreasonable by the court as being too wide, it was severed from the rest of the restraint, which was considered to be a reasonable protection for the buyer. The seller, who was an inventor, had a worldwide reputation in the field of munitions, and this helped to explain the length and geographical location of the restraint clause. In the course of his judgment Lord Macnaghton laid down the following general principle:
>
> "The public have an interest in every person's carrying out his trade freely; so has the individual. All interference with individual liberty of action in trading, and all restraints of trade themselves, if there is nothing more, are contrary to public policy, and therefore void.'
>
> This is a prima facie presumption i.e. one made on first sight. It can be

rebutted where the restraint can be shown to be reasonable.

Restraints take many forms, but among the more important are the following:

(i) Restraints on employment. These are imposed by employers as a device to prevent employees from setting up in competition when they leave the employment.

(ii) Agreements between suppliers and retailers under which the retailer agrees to sell only the supplier's goods. Most cases have involved 'solus' agreements under which petrol stations have agreed to sell only the petrol and other products of a particular petrol company.

(iii) Price fixing agreements and agreements which seek to regulate or limit supplies of goods. Such agreements are governed by statute (see later).

As noted above, whilst there is an assumption that a contract in restraint of trade is void, if the restraint can be shown to be reasonable both in the interests of the parties to it and in the interests of the public generally, then it will be valid.

When an employer asks employees to covenant not to compete if they leave the employment, the restraint will usually specify the nature of the work that employees are prevented from carrying out, the geographical area over which the restraint is to operate, and the length of time that it is to run. Each of these elements must be reasonable. Generally if any part of the restraint is unreasonable this will render void the whole contract, but sometimes the court will be able to sever, i.e. cut out, the invalid part enabling the reasonable part to survive.

> In *Scorer v. Seymour-Jones (1966)* an employee of an estate agent who had offices in Kingsbridge and Dartmouth had entered into a contract not to carry on a business similar to that of his employer for a period of three years after leaving the employment, within a five-mile radius of the Kingsbridge and Dartmouth offices. He had been employed only at the Kingsbridge office. When he left his employer he set up in business as an estate agent within five miles of the Kingsbridge office, and his employer sought an injunction to restrain him from doing so. The injunction was granted by the court. The geographical area of the restraint was reasonable in the case of the Kingsbridge office, although there was no justification for the restraint regarding the Dartmouth office, since the employee had not worked there; however, it could be severed from the valid part of the contract.

The contemporary attitude of the courts in interpreting restraint clauses can be seen in the following decisions of the Court of Appeal.

> In the first case, *Littlewood's Organisation v. Harris (1977)* the defendant was employed as a Director by Littlewoods who compete with Great Universal Stores Ltd for the major share of the mail order business in the UK. The defendant agreed in his contract of employment that on its termination he would not for twelve months enter into a contract of employment with GUS Ltd or any subsidiary company. Littlewoods by such a restriction were seeking to protect confidential information of which the defendant was aware relating to the preparation of their catalogue, upon which the success of their business depended. As GUS Ltd operated all over the world it was argued that the restraint clause was wider than reasonably necessary to protect Littlewoods' interests in the UK. A majority of the court held however that the courts should interpret such clauses with regard to their object and intention and on a proper

interpretation the clause was intended to relate only to the UK mail order business and was therefore enforceable.

In the second case, *Greer v. Sketchley Ltd (1979)* the Court of Appeal was faced with a similar agreement. The plaintiff was a Director of the defendant's dry cleaning business with responsibility for the Midlands area. In his contract of employment he agreed that following its termination he would not for twelve months engage in employment anywhere in the UK in any business which could make use of secret processes carried on by his employer. In fact the defendants' business only operated in the Midlands and London area.

The court held that as the restraint clause purported to extend to areas where the defendants did not operate it was wider than reasonable necessary and therefore void. The court was not prepared to interpret the clause so that it applied only to the Midlands and London in a similar way that the clause in Littlewood's case was limited to the UK. In attempting to restrain the employee throughout the UK the employer was unfairly preventing competition and the free movement of labour.

As we have seen in the Nordenfelt case where a person sells a business the buyer will usually seek some form of protection to prevent the seller from setting up in competition. Restraints that are imposed in such cases are more likely to survive than whose imposed on employees, since the buyer and seller of a business will be negotiating on an equal footing nevertheless if the clause is too wide it will fail.

In *British Reinforced Concrete Engineering Co Ltd v. Schelff (1921)* the defendant who operated a business selling road reinforcements in the UK, sold his business to the plaintiff. In the contract of sale the seller agreed not to compete for a specified period in the 'sale or manufacture of road reinforcements' in the UK. The defendant took employment in the same type of business working for a competitor, and the plaintiff sued to enforce the restraint clause. The court held that had the clause been confined to 'sales' it would have been valid, but to include 'the manufacture of reinforcements' made the restraint wider than was reasonably necessary, and therefore void.

In the case of 'solus' and similar agreements there is no rule of law which prevents a supplier and a dealer from entering into an agreement under which the supplier is to be the retailer's sole supplier, but the duration of such an agreement must not be for an unreasonable length of time, or the restraint will be void as being against the public interest.

In *Esso Petroleum Co. Ltd v. Harpers Garage (Stourport) Ltd (1968)* Harpers Garage entered into a solus agreement with Esso for the supply of Esso petroleum to two garages owned by Harpers. They received a discount from Esso for agreeing to take only Esso petroleum and for undertaking to keep the two garages open at all reasonable hours. The House of Lords held that the restraint which tied one garage to the agreement for 4 years 5 months was valid, but the restraint which tied the other garage to take only Esso petroleum for 21 years, in return for a £7,000 loan to assist in the purchase and improvement of the garage, was too long and therefore invalid.

RESTRAINTS CONTROLLED BY STATUTE

Successive governments have used legislation to curb market practices which are considered to be anti-competitive and therefore contrary to the public interest. In a sense this gives rise to a curious situation in which the government attempts to limit trading freedom to make agreements which reduce competition, whilst at the same time encouraging a free market in which the stronger organisations inevitably seek to eliminate their competitors. Legislation in this field seeks to find a balance between these conflicting forces.

LEGAL CONTROL OF MONOPOLIES AND MERGERS

The first major piece of modern legislation was the Monopolies and Trade Practices Act 1948, which created the body now known as the Monopolies and Mergers Commission. Legislative powers were strengthened by the Monopolies and Mergers Act 1965. The Commission's main responsibility is to act as a watchdog enquiring into possible monopoly or oligopoly situations, reporting its findings to the government for possible further action. The Fair Trading Act 1973 repealed and re-enacted the 1948 and 1965 Acts and established the Office of the Director-General of Fair Trading. The Director-General was given authority to refer to the Commission possible areas where market concentration could be detrimental to the public interest, and was also given authority to assist the Commission in its investigation of such situations.

The 1973 Act:

(i) defines both a monopoly situation and a merger situation;

(ii) grants investigatory powers to the Monopolies and Mergers Commission;

(iii) grants powers to the Secretary of State for Trade and Industry to issue orders to deal with monopolies and mergers.

Under the 1973 Act a monopoly/merger situation exists if the following circumstances arise:-

either a single enterprise has (or through a merger, is likely to have) control of 25% of an individual market (a monopoly share);

or if the total assets of the merged organisation exceed £5m.

The Monopolies and Mergers Commission is technically independent of the government. It has the duty to "investigate and report on any question . . . with respect to the existence of a monopoly situation . . . or with respect to the creation of a merger situation." Both the Secretary of State and the Director General of Fair Trading can report matters to the Commission for investigation.

In its report the Commission will decide if either of the above circumstances exist and, if so, whether or not there are any factors which could justify the government in allowing them to continue. There are many instances of industries in which there is one company with more than 25% of the market, for instance in the biscuit market, United Biscuits have a 40% market share, and in baked beans, Heinz have a 64% market share. The fact that these have not been referred to the Commission reflects the belief of successive governments that competition was nonetheless adequate in these industries. If a referral is made, the Commission will consider whether or not the merger or the level of concentration operates in the public interest. To decide this, the Commission must bear in mind factors such as:

(i) the need to promote effective competition within the UK;

(ii) the need to protect consumers' interests regarding the price and variety of goods;

(iii) the need to minimise the costs of production;

(iv) the need to develop new techniques and products;

(v) the need to ensure unrestricted entry for new competitors into existing markets; and

(vi) the need to ensure a balanced distribution of industry and employment within the UK.

If the Commission's report indicates areas of concern, the Secretary of State for Trade and Industry on behalf of the government has the following options open to him. He may by order:

(i) require the transfer of property from one organisation to another;

(ii) require the adjustment of contracts;

(iii) require the reallocation of shares in an organisation;

(iv) prohibit a merger taking place.

The above orders are enforceable by court action through an injunction, that is a court order prohibiting or requiring specified action. Injunctions are examined later in the chapter.

The process described above is illustrated diagramatically in fig 4.2.

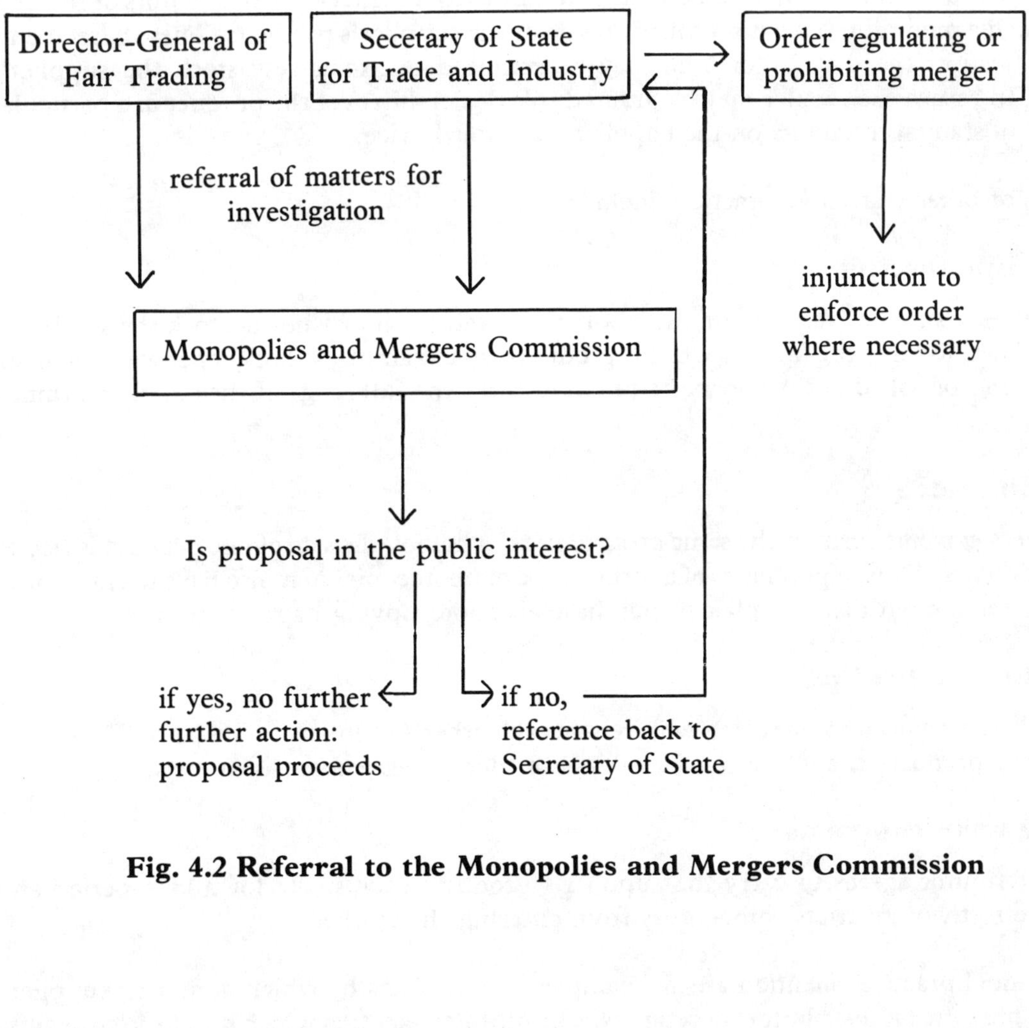

Fig. 4.2 Referral to the Monopolies and Mergers Commission

LEGAL CONTROL OF ANTI-COMPETITIVE PRACTICES

In order to make sense of the legislation designed to control trading practices regarded as anti-competitive, it is useful both to identify the parties involved in operating them, and the nature of the restraints imposed.

Restraints in the form of restrictive trade practices are commonly operated within agreements made between suppliers, and in agreements between suppliers and their distributors and retailers.

Agreements between suppliers

Suppliers often form agreements or associations with other suppliers in the same industry with the aim of either:-

(i) limiting the supply of goods or services;

(ii) fixing a standard price;

(iii) standardising contractual terms of sale;

(iv) purchasing raw materials through a "common pool" at an agreed price.

Agreements between suppliers and distributors or retailers

Suppliers who are dominant in a market may enter into agreements with distributors or retailers under which a minimum price is set for the resale of the supplier's products. These agreements may also restrict the distributor who may be required to exclusively stock the supplier's products. In return the retailer may be granted sole dealership over the product in a particular area and substantial discounts on the supplier's standard price.

Examples of other restrictive practices include:

(i) full line forcing

This involves a supplier requiring a distributor or retailer who wishes to stock the supplier's major product, to carry the full range of his products. For example, a shopkeeper wishing to sell a major brand of baked beans may be required to carry the full range of the supplier's tinned products.

(ii) tie-in sales

This is a less extreme form of the same arrangement, whereby the sale of one product is tied to the sale of others. Thus, a purchaser of a certain type of photocopier may also have to enter into a service agreement with the supplier to purchase all photocopying paper from him.

(iii) reciprocal trading

This involves organisations agreeing to purchase each other's products exclusively. Thus other competitor's products cannot be purchased where such an agreement is in force.

(iv) long term contracts

Here a distributor agrees to carry the supplier's products exclusively for a long period and therefore effectively restricts competitors from entering the market.

The individual practices mention are all examples of the means by which dominant suppliers may exert pressure on distributors or retailers. The ultimate sanction which may be used against distributors or retailers who fail to agree to such practices is a withdrawal of supplies.

The use of anti-competitive trading practices is not confined to the United Kingdom, such practices operate within the other member states of the European Community. In consequence legislative control of such practices is found both in domestic legislation and under Community law.

EEC Competition Law

The main provisions are found in Articles 85 and 86 of the Treaty of Rome, and they prohibit trade agreements that endanger freedom of trade between member states by preventing, restricting or distorting competition within the Common Market. Examples of such agreements are those which:

(i) fix prices or trading conditions;

(ii) limit production, markets, technical developments or investment;

(iii) share markets or sources of supply;

(iv) apply dissimilar conditions to equivalent transactions with other trading parties;

(v) make the conclusion of a contract subject to the acceptance of unconnected supplementary obligations.

Fines can be imposed by the EEC Commission on the parties to such an agreement. However, an agreement that otherwise infringes the Articles may be allowed to continue in certain circumstances, for example where the agreement exists in order to promote technical or economic progress which will also benefit consumers.

U.K. Competition Legislation

The Competition Act 1980 echoes the language of EEC competition legislation. Under the Act trade practices, other than those registerable under the Restrictive Trade Practices Act 1976, (see below) which "involve a course of conduct which has, and is intended to have the effects of restricting, distorting or preventing competition in connection with the production, supply and acquisition of goods and the securing of services in the UK" are treated as 'anti-competitive practices'. Whereas EEC legislation deals with competition within the broad geographical area of the Common Market, the 1980 Act is obviously restricted to UK markets.

A detailed investigation procedure is set out under the 1980 Act and is shown in the figure below (fig. 4.3). Essentially all the alleged anti-competitive practices are subject to preliminary investigation by the Director General of Fair Trading. If the practice is proven to be anti-competitive, action can be taken by the Secretary for Trade and Industry.

Particular practices by individual organisations may now be investigated and if necessary prevented without the need to investigate the industry as a whole. However, only large organisations are brought under scrutiny, that is companies with a turnover of more than £5m or more than a 25% share of their particular market.

Unlike the Restrictive Trade Practices Act 1976 (see below) there is no presumption under the 1980 Act that an agreement referred to the Commission operates against the public interest. In determining this question of public interest, the Commission simply takes into account all matters which appear to it to be relevant in the particular circumstances. For example, a manufacturer may offer his product to a supermarket at much bigger discounts than he offers to corner shops. The practice of offering such discounts could be referred to the Commission as being "anti-competitive" in that the number of corner shops is likely to be reduced because of this practice. The Commission in deciding the question of 'public interest', would have to balance the advantage to the consumer of obtaining lower-priced products against the convenience to the consumer of local shopping.

Having reached a conclusion on a reference, the Commission must then report to the Secretary

Fig. 4.3 Investigation procedure under the Competition Act 1980

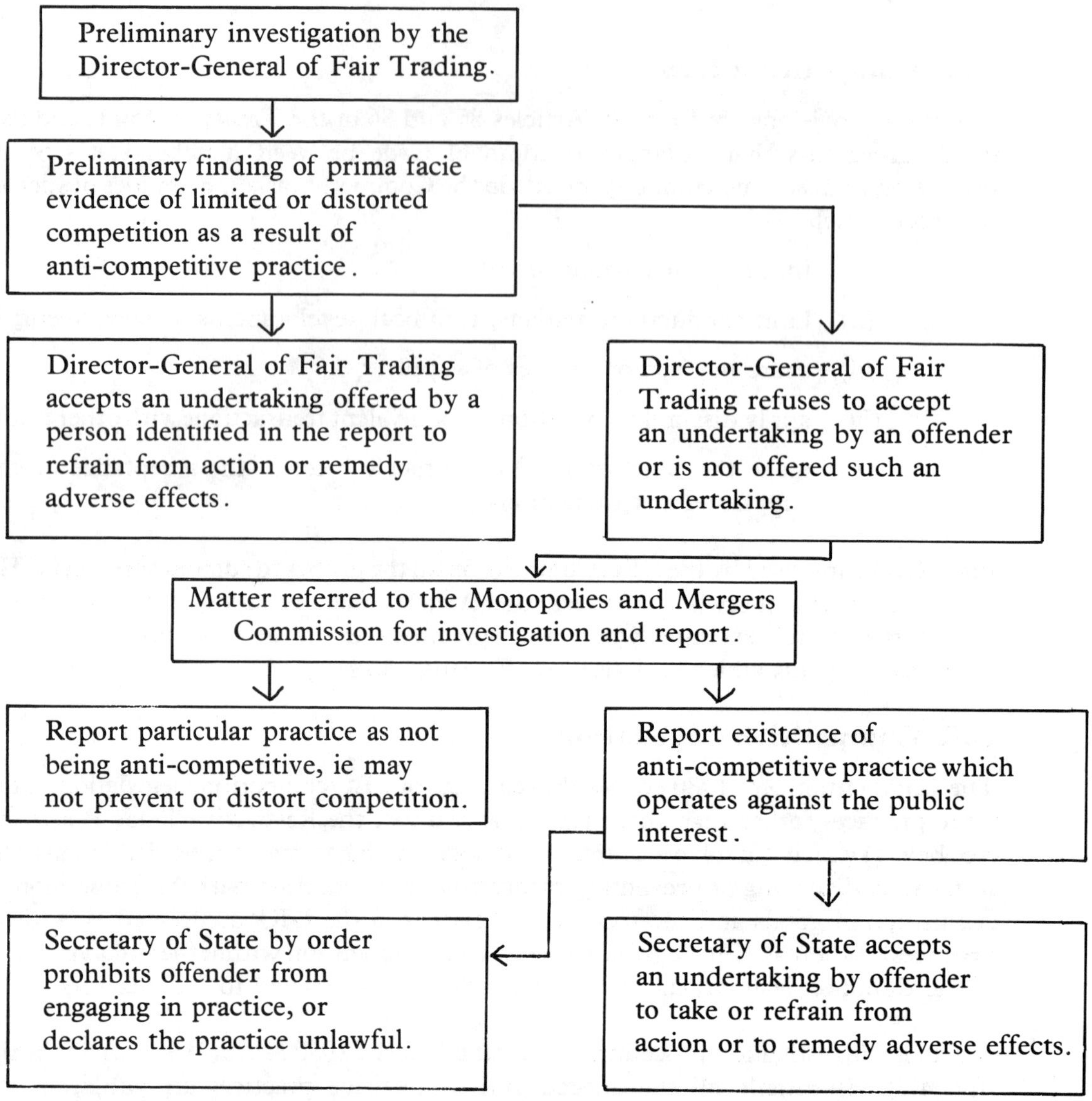

of State for Trade who has the power, by order, to declare an anti-competitive practice unlawful if the offender refuses to refrain from that type of conduct. The Act expressly excludes restrictive practices already registerable under the Restrictive Trade Practices Act 1976 to prevent an overlap of proceedings.

The types of practice which may be investigated by the Director-General of Fair Trading under the 1980 Act would include the giving of specific discounts, rebates and allowances, full-line forcing, tie-in sales, reciprocal trading and long-term contracts.

The Restrictive Trade Practices Act 1976

It was mentioned above that the Competition Act 1980 does not apply to agreements registered under the Restrictive Trade Practices Act 1976. Under this Act, duties are imposed on the Director-General of Fair Trading. He is required to compile and maintain a register of restrictive agreements, and also to bring such agreements before the Restrictive Practices Court, which has the function of deciding whether they are contrary to the public interest. The types of agreement registerable under the Act are those made by suppliers of goods which lead to a restriction relating to:

(i) the price charged for goods;

(ii) the terms and conditions of supply of goods;

(iii) the quantities or description of goods to be supplied;

(iv) the process of manufacture to be applied to any goods;

(v) those who may obtain the goods;

(vi) the area in which the goods may be obtained.

A registerable agreement is presumed to be contrary to public policy and it is for this reason the Director General of Fair Trading must bring such agreements before the Restrictive Practices Court. If the parties can satisfy the court that the agreement does not harm the public interest then it may be declared valid. To assist the parties there are eight grounds, called the "eight-gateways", set out in the Act. If they can establish any one of the gateways then the agreement will be treated as a valid one.

The gateways seeks to:

(i) protect the public against injury;

(ii) counteract restrictive measures taken by anyone not a party to the agreement;

(iii) enable the parties to negotiate fair terms with a monopolistic supplier or customer.

In fact, relatively few agreements have been approved by the court, and this indicates the tough line that it has taken with regard to restrictive practices.

> In *Re Net Book Agreement (1957)* the court considered an agreement by book publishers not to permit the retailing of books below published prices. The agreement was justified on the grounds that its removal could lead to unfair competition from large supermarkets and department stores only carrying a limited number of best-sellers, which could mean that the specialist book sellers were forced out of business.
>
> In *Chemist Federation Agreement (1958)* an agreement by the Federation to limit the sale of patent medicines to the public, only by qualified pharmacists, was declared void. The court was unimpressed by the argument that the restriction was necessary to protect the public against injury in view of the potentially dangerous nature of the goods being sold.
>
> The agreement itself does not need to be legally enforceable. In one case an arrangement between a group of contractors to delay submitting their individual tenders until they had met to discuss each others tenders was held to constitute a restrictive trading agreement (Re: *Installations at Exeter Hospital Agreement (1970)*.

The Resale Prices Act 1976

One of the most fundamental aspects of competition between retailers is that they should have the ability to charge whatever price they wish. Yet one of the most widely used restrictive agreements was the practice by dominant suppliers of imposing standard prices for their goods on all their retail outlets. These 'resale price maintenance' agreements were forced on distributors and retailers by suppliers, who could always threaten to withold supplies to ensure compliance. Such agreements were initially controlled by legislation in 1964, their regulation now being contained in the Resale Prices Act 1976. Under this Act it is unlawful for suppliers to make agreements to withhold supplies from, or supply on less favourable terms to, distributors who do not observe resale price conditions. As with other restrictive practices, the Restrictive

Practices Court has power to grant exemption on one or other of the grounds specified in the Act upon an application made by the Director-General of Fair Trading.

So far, only three exemptions have been made, relating to books, drugs and maps. Apart from these exemptions it is prima facie unlawful for a manufacturer to withhold supplies in an attempt to enforce a minimum resale price. Such a refusal to supply goods could, however, be justified if the producer shows that the dealer in question has, within the preceeding 12 months, been selling the same or similar goods as a 'loss leader', that is selling at a retail price below wholesale cost in order to attract custom for that and other products.

> In *Oxford Printing Ltd. v. Letraset Ltd. (1970)* the defendants withheld supplies from the plaintiffs, who had cut the price of the defendant's products and also used them to promote the sales of a competitor's product. Such withholding of supplies was held to be lawful in the circumstances.

At common law the difficulty of directly enforcing a resale price maintenance agreement can be seen in *Dunlop Pneumatic Tyre Co Ltd v. Selfridge and Co. Ltd (1915).*

> In *Dunlop v Selfridge (1915)*, Dunlop's sold tyres to a wholesaler on terms that he should resell them only at list price. He sold some of the tyres to Selfridges, who also agreed not to sell at below Dunlop's list price. However they subsequently did so and Dunlop sought an injunction against them and damages. The House of Lords held that their actions must fail, since there was no privity of contract between Selfridges and themselves. The terms of the sale read as follow:
>
> "Price Maintenance agreement is to be entered into by trade purchasers of Dunlop Motor Tyres
>
> (1) We will not alter or remove or in any way tamper with any of the manufacture marks or numbers on Dunlop covers or tubes.
>
> (2) We will not sell or offer any Dunlop motor tyres covers or tubes to any private customers or to any co-operative society at prices below those mentioned in the said price list current at the time of sale, nor give to any such customer or society any cash or other discounts, or advantages reducing the same. We will not sell or offer any Dunlop motor tyres, covers or tubes to any other person, firm or company at prices less than those mentioned in the said price list.
>
> (3) We will not supply any such goods to any person who supplies the Dunlop Company may decide to suspend nor to exhibit goods of Dunlop manufacture at any exhibition in the United Kingdom without the written consent of the Dunlop Company first had and obtained.
>
> (4) We will not export any tyres, covers or tubes supplied hereunder to any country outside the United Kingdom without the written consent of the Dunlop Company first had and obtained.
>
> (5) We agree to pay to the Dunlop Pneumatic Tyre Co., Ltd., the sum of £5 for each and every tyre, cover or tube sold or offered in breach of this agreement, as and by way of liquidated damages and not as a penalty, but without prejudice to any other rights or remedies you or the Dunlop Pneumatic Tyre Co., Ltd., may have hereunder."

PRIVITY OF CONTRACT

The doctrine of privity of contract has already been referred to, in the context of the principles applying to contractual consideration (see Chapter 3). The effect of the doctrine can be considerable as the Dunlop case demonstrates. The doctrine arises out of the contractual principle that consideration must move from the promisee, so that as a general rule the legal effects of a contract apply only to the contracting parties. The shareholder in a company is unable to take the benefit of a contract made by the company in the sense of obtaining personal rights under it, for the company and the shareholder are seperate persons. When a purchaser of a new vehicle discovered faults in it he has contractual rights against the garage which sold it, but not against the manufacturer. The manufacturer was not privy or party to the contract. The position would be different if the manufacturer issued a guarantee which the customer had completed and returned when the vehicle was purchased. If the faults were the cause of physical injury to the purchaser a remedy could be pursued in the tort of negligence.

There are a number of exceptions to the doctrine of privity of contract, where a person who has not provided consideration under a contract and is therefore a 'stranger' to it may nevertheless possess legal rights and obligations. They include the following:

(i) contracts made by an agent acting within his authority, but contracting on his principals behalf without indicating to the other party that he is an agent. In such circumstances the doctrine of undisclosed principal allows the principal to step in and sue, or be sued, on the contract.

(ii) where there has been an assignment of contractual rights, such as the right to a debt, the assignee can sue the original debtor under s.136 Law of Property Act 1925 if the creditor fails to notify the debtor that the assignment has been made, the debtor can validly discharge the debt by payment to the creditor rather than the assignee.

(iii) the holder for value of a bill of exchange can sue the acceptor and prior parties (see Chapter 8).

(iv) s.11 Married Womens Property Act 1882 enables the parties who benefit under a life policy if they are a surviving spouse and/or children of the insured to sue the insurance company on the policy.

(v) A further example of other parties than the insured being able to claim under an insurance policy that is not their own arises under the Road Traffic Act 1972, which enables a person driving a vehicle with the owners consent to cover under the owners insurance policy in certain circumstances. It also permits recovery of compensation to a third party injured by a driver in respect of his compulsory third party risks cover.

(vi) in respect of restrictive covenants imposed upon land subsequent purchasers will be bound to observe the covenant (see Chapter 8).

(vii) under the Resale Prices Act 1976 what the Restrictive Practices Court has exempted a resale price maintenance agreement, resale price maintenance conditions imposed by a seller will bind anyone obtaining the goods with a view to resale, if they have notice of the restriction.

Beyond these exceptions it seems that common law development to reduce the impact of the privity principle are unlikely. Lord Denning attempted to do so in *Jackson v. Horizon Holidays (1975)* . The plaintiff had booked a months holiday in Ceylon staying in an hotel. The defendant's brochure described the hotel facilities. These included a swimming pool, a mini-golf course and a hairdressing salon. The hotel in fact had none of these facilities and its food was poor. The Court of Appeal granted the plaintiff damages of £1,100. This represented not only his loss, but also that of his family who accompanied him, even though they were not parties to the contract. The court said that the plaintiff had made the contract partly for their benefit. The House of Lords in *Woodar v. Wimpey (1980)* criticised the Jackson decision. They rejected the view put forward in Jackson that there is any rule of English law enabling a contract made with A for the benefit of B, to entitle A to sue for damages suffered by B which B could have recovered if the contract had been made with him. Mr. Jackson's damages, said their Lordships, were increased because he not only suffered discomfort and disappointment personally, but witnessed his family similarly distressed.

CONTRACT TERMS

The terms of a contract are the obligations owed by the parties to each other under it. All contracts contain terms. In transactions involving large sums of money, or where the agreement is of a complex or technical nature, the terms are likely to be numerous and detailed. By inserting terms into the contract the parties will be trying to clarify their respective obligations towards each other, and to make provision for any possible contingencies that could arise after the contract has been concluded, such as shortages of labour or materials. Different types of contract obviously reflect different sets of terms appropriate to the nature and purpose of the agreement. For example if the contract involves the construction of a building or a ship its terms will seek to clearly identify the specifications involved. On the other hand the granting of a lease or tenancy will concentrate on matters such as who has responsibility for carrying out repairs, and how the property should be used. It is not only large organisations which are involved in detailed and technical contracts; even small organisations will encounter documents such as leases when they set up in business and seek accommodation. Clearly not all contracts contain detailed terms. In the simplest contracts terms will be single promises made by each party to the other. At the end of this chapter three sets of contractual terms are provided to help illustrate the way in which terms are applied in practice, and to give an opportunity for making comparisons between different types of contract and the terms they incorporate. The examples given are a contract of employment, a contract of sale, and a partnership agreement.

Standard form contracts

Clearly it makes commercial sense to set out precisely and exhaustively the terms which are to apply to the contract, and the means used by the majority of organisations to achieve this in the standard form contract. The standard form contract is a printed form consisting of a uniform set of terms for use by an organisation as the basis upon which it trades. A standard form agreement is of advantage in business in two ways:

(i) it helps to save time by removing the need for the regular negotiation of terms,

(ii) it will seek to provide the organisation with the maximum amount of commercial protection possible, by relying on terms which are entirely favourable to it, for instance, enabling it to cancel the agreement in specified circumstances, raise its price in line with increases in manufacturing costs, and so on.

We have already referred to the imbalance in trading strength that occurs in the majority of contracts which are made, with the dominant party dictating terms to the weaker party. Contracts, usually of a standard form kind, in which this dominance occurs are often referred to as contracts of adhesion, for the weaker party is unable to negotiate but must simply adhere to the stronger party's terms.

The use of standard form agreements does not always indicate a situation of dominance by one party over the other. In some areas of commercial and industrial activity standard terms are devised by organisations representing the interests of the sector generally. For example local authorities may together produce sets of terms which they can all use in their dealings with supplies of goods or services. In the building industry there are such arrangements. The present standard contract in use is the Joint Contracts Tribunal (JCT) form. Various versions of it are available to cover different types of building work. In transactions for the carrying out of construction work in the building trade the contract will usually commence with the Articles of Agreement in which the contractor expressly agrees to carry out the specified works as described and the employer agrees to furnish the 'contract sum' for the completion of the works. Here it is usual to identify the architect and surveyor and the procedure by which their replacements could be appointed. The Articles will also contain an arbitration clause for the settling of disputes and describing the circumstances and machinery for the appointment of an arbitrator. Usually a speciality contract is executed, for it gives the parties the added protection of a twelve year limitation period to take legal action following a breach. For a simple contract the limitation period is only six years, which in terms of building work is a relatively short period to discover defects.

A contract based upon the JCT form is likely to include the following terms, which are contained in it, and set out as contractual conditions:

a. the contractor's obligations to carry out the work and use the materials of the specified standard;

b. the payment of the contract sum and V.A.T.;

c. the duty of the contractor to comply with the architect's instructions and give him reasonable access to the site;

d. the specified materials and payment for them;

e. the statutory obligations in relation to such matters as the payment of fees and serving of notice that local authority inspection is required;

f. the payment of royalties for use of patented materials;

g. the power to vary the specified works and require defects to be remedied;

h. the power to appoint a clerk of the works;

i. the restriction on the parties right to assign;

j. the rights of the employer to take possession of completed parts;

k. the provision of insurance cover for injury to persons or property and the contractor's agreement to indemnify the employer;

l. the date of completion, possession, liquidated damages, time extensions, rights to determine on the happening of specified events;

m. the system of certificated payments by instalments as the work is completed in stages;

n. the definition of who is to be treated as nominated subcontractor or supplier.

THE CLASSIFICATION OF TERMS

The terms of a contract vary in importance. Sometimes the contract itself will say how much importance is attached to a certain term, while in other cases it may be left to the court to decide the question as the parties to the contract have not made it clear. The value that is attached to each term is of great significance because it determines what the consequences will be if the particular term is broken.

Major terms are called conditions. A condition is a term which is said to go to the root of the contract, and where performance is essential to the contract. If it is broken the innocent party has the right to treat the contract as repudiated and to refuse to perform his or her obligations under it. In addition he or she may sue for damages.

Minor terms are called warranties. They are terms which are said to be collateral to the main purpose of the contract. In consequence, if a warranty is broken the contract still stands, and the innocent party does not have the right to treat the contract as being at an end, merely the right to damages.

Where breach of a condition occurs the injured party is not bound to repudiate the contract. As an alternative the injured party can elect to treat the contract as subsisting, treating the breach of condition as if it were a warranty. The obligation that had been broken is then referred to as an ex post facto warranty, and only damages will be available to the injured party. There may be sound commercial reasons for treating a breach of condition as one of warranty, and letting the contract stand. The innocent party may realise that if the contract is repudiated it will be difficult to obtain an alternative supplier of the goods and services in question, or undue delay and inconvenience will be caused if the goods have to be disassembled, removed from the premises and returned to the supplier.

> Two similar cases illustrate the distinction between conditions and warranties. In *Bettini v. Gye (1876)* the plaintiff, an opera singer, agreed in writing to sing in various concerts and operas over a period of $3^1/_2$ months, and to be present at rehearsals for at least six days before the engagements were due to begin. Due to illness he arrived with only two days of rehearsals left, and as a result the defendant terminated the agreement. Looking at the contract as a whole, the court decided that the rehearsal clause was not a condition, but merely a warranty, for which damages alone was the remedy. The contract had been wrongfully terminated and the plaintiff could counter-claim for damages.
>
> In *Poussard v. Spiers and Pond (1876)* an opera singer was unable to take part in the first week of performances due to illness. In the mean time the management had engaged a substitute and refused the original singer the part when she arrived. They were held to be entitled to do so, for her non-attendance at the performances was a breach of a vital term of the contract.

Sometimes it is impossible to say whether a term is a condition or a warranty when it is first created because it will be so broadly framed that it could be broken in a major respect or a minor respect, and therefore it is only possible to say after the event what effect the particular breach should have on the contract. Such terms are referred to as 'innominate', meaning intermediate terms.

> The position is illustrated in *Hong Kong Fir Shipping Co. Ltd. v. Kawasaki Kaisen Kaisha Ltd (1962)*. Here a ship was chartered on terms that stated what it would be 'in every way fitted for ordinary cargo service'. Inefficient engine-room staff and old engines contributed to a number of breakdowns so that during the first seven months of the charter the ship was only able to be at sea for eight and a half weeks. The charterers repudiated the contract. The Court of Appeal decided that this particular breach did not entitle the charterers to repudiate. Diplock LJ stated that the terms in the contract were not really either a condition or a warranty but rather "an undertaking, one breach of which may give rise to an event which relieves the charterer of further performance . . . if he so elects and another breach of which may not give rise to such an event but entitle him only . . . to damages."

HOW TERMS ORIGINATE

So far the examples of terms that have been considered are those which have been expressly agreed between the parties. There are however two additional sources of contract terms, the courts and Parliament. Both these law making institutions are responsible for inserting terms into contracts, independent of the wishes of the parties involved, and the broad justification for doing so appears to be desire to enable the contract to 'work' and to achieve a level of protection for the consumer of goods and services. How contractual terms arise, is considered below.

Express terms

These are the terms which have been specifically detailed and agreed upon by the parties. The parties are free to classify them in advance as being conditions or warranties if they so wish. If they fail to do so it will be left to the court to decide how significant a particular breach is by looking at the term in relation to the contract as a whole.

We have already noted that some statements made prior to contract will constitute representations. Sometimes a representation will actually become a term of the contract. This being so, if the term is broken the innocent party will be able to bring an action for breach of contract, rather than for misrepresentation. It is often difficult to determine whether a representation has in fact become a term where there has been no express incorporation of it, and the courts will take into consideration a number of factors. For instance, a representation will be presumed not to have become a term if a formal written contract is executed after the representation and does not contain it. There is, however, one main test to be applied: whether the person making the statement was promising its accuracy. If so, the statement will become a contractual term.

> How difficult it can be to draw a distinction between representations and terms is illustrated by *Oscar Chess Ltd v. Williams (1957)*. The defendant wished to take a new car on hire-purchase terms from the plaintiffs, who were car dealers. In part exchange he offered them his own car, which was described in the log book as a 1948 Morris. He confirmed the vehicle to be a 1948 model, honestly believing this to be so, and received £290 part-exchange allowance. Eight months later the plaintiffs discovered that the car was a 1939 model, for which only £175 should have been allowed. They sued the defendant for the difference, i.e. £115. The Court of Appeal decided by a majority that the defendant's statement about the age of the car was not a term of the contract. Lord Denning made the point that, as motor dealers, the plaintiffs could without difficulty have checked the true age of the car with the manufacturers by giving them the engine and chassis numbers.

Terms implied by the courts

It is not the task of the courts to insert new terms into contracts, but rather to interpret those that already exist. But they will sometimes imply a term to give a contract 'business efficacy'. The rationale underlying such an approach is that since the parties clearly intended to create a binding agreement, they must have intended to include terms to make the contract 'work'.

> Thus in *Moorcock (1889)*, a term was implied by the court in a contract between a ship owner and a firm of wharfingers. The contract was to use their wharf on the Thames for the discharging and loading of his vessel, the Moorcock. He was going to pay a charge for the use of the cranes alongside the wharf. While the vessel was moored there she was damaged when the tide ebbed and she came to rest on a ridge of hard ground. The Court of Appeal held that the wharfingers were liable for breach of an implied term that the mooring was safe for the vessel. 'In business transactions such as this,' said Bowen LJ, 'what the law desires to effect by implication is to give such business efficacy to the transaction as must have been intended at all events by both parties who are businessmen.'

> In *Irwin v. Liverpool City Council (1977)*, the defendant council let a flat in an upper floor of a block of flats to the plaintiff tenant. A term was implied by the court into a tenancy agreement between the plaintiff and the defendant Council to the effect that the defendants had an obligation to keep in repair the stairs and the lift in the block of flats which they owned.

Two fields in which the courts have been active in implying terms are in the employment relationship, and in the landlord and tenant relationship. Thus at common law there are certain fundamental obligations owed by the employer to the employee and vice versa, which are implied by the courts. For instance the employee owes a duty of good faith to the employer at common law, whilst the employer has an obligation to provide for the employees safety. In the landlord and tenant relationship the common law imposes an obligation upon the tenant not to commit waste, ie physical harm, to the premises being occupied, and upon the landord to provide the tenant with quiet enjoyment, ie not to interfere with the tenants occupation of the premises. Significantly, in both these fields, Parliament has also legislated to insert terms, primarily with the view to protecting the weaker party from exploitation by the stronger.

Statutory implied terms

These are many and varied and, because they are statutory, the obligations they impose tend to be detailed. In many cases statutory terms are implied as a legislative attempt to counter-balance the inequalities that exist in particular bargaining situations, for example by restricting the ability of organisations which trade on the basis of their own standard form contracts to exclude liability for breaches of contract which they have caused. In other cases statutory terms can be seen as a vehicle for effecting profound social and economic change, such as the insertion of an equality clause in contracts of employment. Yet again, there are those statutory terms which simply represent a codification of judicially recognised mercantile custom, for example under the Sale of Goods Act 1979.

Statutory terms implied under the 1979 Act are considered in Chapter 5, in conjunction with an examination of other implied statutory terms which grant rights to consumers.

THE EXCLUSION AND RESTRICTION OF LIABILITY

We have seen how a contract creates obligations which the parties making it are obliged to meet, and that failure to do so constitutes a breach of contract which can possibly lead to a claim for damages. It follows that a prudent person, recognising the potential liabilities involved in entering into a contract, will try to reduce or entirely remove any such risk. How far this is possible depends upon whether the clause in the contract excluding or restricting liability is successfully incorporated into the contract, and if it has been whether it satisfied certain tests of validity laid down by both Parliament and the courts. The diagram below (fig. 4.4) indicates the questions which have to be answered in order to determine whether a clause excluding or restricting liability will work.

Incorporation and drafting of the terms

To become a part of a contract a term must be included in the contractual offer. We saw in Chapter 3 that a term is only valid if it is certain. In other words it must have a clear meaning which a court can, if needs be, specificially identify. So if a term does not form a part of the contractual offer, or is in some way unclear, it will be ineffective.

A good example of terms failing to become part of the contract occurs where the terms are introduced after the contract has been made.

> This happened in *Thornton v. Shoe Lane Parking (1971)*, where the terms of the contract were contained on the back of a parking ticket. They could only be read therefore after the customer had inserted the money into the

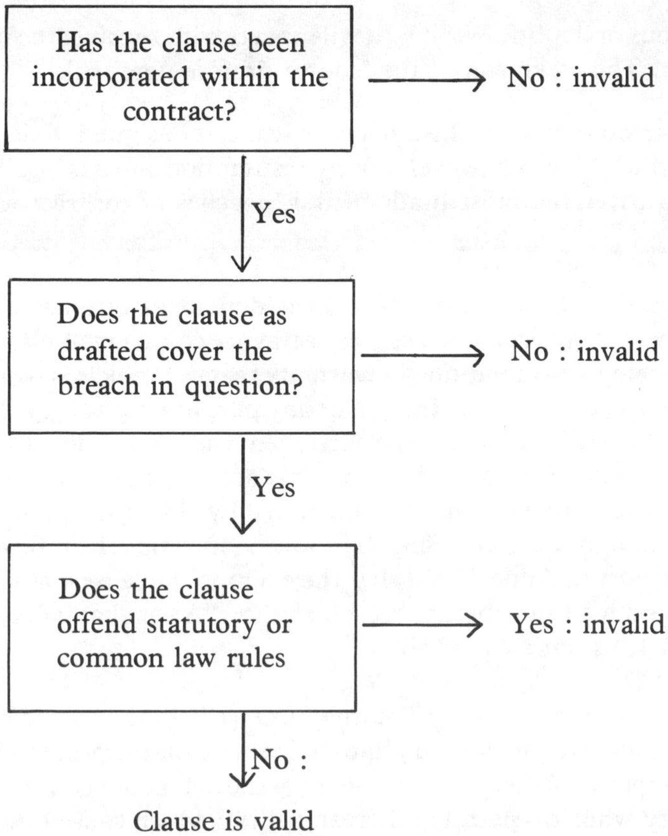

Fig. 4.4. The exclusion/restriction of contractual liabilities

machine, and thus subsequent to the making of the contract.

In *Olley v. Marlborough Court Hotel Ltd. (1949),* the plaintiff was staying in an hotel with her husband and her furs were stolen from their hotel bedroom. A notice on the back of the door stated that the hotel accepted no responsibility for lost or stolen items unless they were deposited with the manageress for safe keeping. The notice was held to be ineffective, since it was not brought to the plaintiff's attention until after she had booked the room at the reception desk.

Where the term is contained in an unsigned document, or on a notice, it will be effective only if the person relying on it took reasonable steps to bring it to the attention of the other party, and where the document or notice containing it might reasonably be regarded as contractual and likely to contain contractual terms. Of course if a document containing contractual terms has been signed then the signatory will be bound by its terms as was the case in *L'Estrange v. Graucob Ltd. (1934).*

The need to express contractual terms clearly is very important. This is especially so when the term is an attempt by one of the parties to exclude liability. As Scrutton LJ pointed out in *Alison (J. Gordon) Ltd. v. Wallsend Shipway and Engineering Co. Ltd. (1927),* "if a person is under a legal liability and wishes to get rid of it, he can only do so by using clear words."

The courts use the following tests for determining whether the exclusion clause is valid.:

(i) does it clearly and unequivocally cover the breach of contract is question. This is a rule of strict interpretation;

(ii) is it ambiguous or doubtful? If it is, it will be construed against the person who is relying on it. This is known as the 'contra proferentem' rule.

Furthermore it will be presumed that an exclusion clause was not designed to defeat the main purpose or object of the contract. This is however only a presumption and it is legally possible to draft an exclusion clause to cover the most fundamental breaches of contract. Compare the following cases.

> In *Karsales (Harrow) Ltd. v. Wallis (1956)*, the defendant purchased a second-hand car on hire-purchase terms from a finance company. A clause of the agreement stated "No condition or warranty that the vehicle is road-worthy or as to its age, condition or fitness for any purpose is given by the owner or implied therein". Following the agreement the car was delivered to the defendant at night. It was totally incapable of self-propulsion, and many parts were either missing or had been replaced by older parts. When the defendant found it in this condition the following morning, he refused to accept it. The Court of Appeal held that the exemption clause was not intended to cover such a fundamental breach as this. "A car that will not go" said Birkett LJ "is not a car at all".

> In *Photo Productions Ltd. v. Securicor Transport Ltd. (1980)*, the defendant company had contracted to provide a night patrol service for the protection of the plaintiff company's factory. An employer of the defendant company entered the factory while on patrol and created a fire which caused over £600,000 worth of damage. The defendant company sought to avoid liability by relying on a clause in the contract which excluded liability for "any injurious act or default by an employee of the company unless such an act or default could have been forseen and avoided by the exercise of due diligence on the part of the company" and "any loss suffered by the customer through . . . fire or any other cause, except in so far as such loss is solely attributable to the negligence of the company's employees acting within the course of their employment". The House of Lords held that the clause covered the breach of contract in question even though it was a fundamental one. The parties were in equal bargaining position and were therefore free to determine the extend of the obligations owed under the contract. The language of the exclusion was clear and it was not for the court to reject what the parties had agreed.

Statutory control of exclusion clauses

One of the most disturbing features of exclusion clauses is that they are a common feature of contracts of adhesion, the 'take it or leave it' contracts mentioned earlier in the chapter. A person who is in a weak bargaining position may have no effective control over the power of the stronger party to insert such exclusion clauses.

Under the Unfair Contract Terms Act 1977, Parliament has come to the aid of the weaker party. The Act applies not only to contractual exclusions but also tortious ones, for example a notice at the entrance of a public park that attempts to exonerate the council from liability for any harm suffered to the members of the public whilst in the park.

Under s.2 a person cannot, either by a contractual term or by notice, exclude or restrict his or her liability in contract or tort for death or personal injury arising from negligence. Liability for other loss or damage arising from negligence can still be excluded, provided the exclusion can be shown to be reasonable.

> An example of the second part of the section being constructed by the court is found in *Phillips Products v. Hamstead Plant Hire (1983)*. The hire company hired out a JCB to the plaintiffs under a standard term agreement. A driver was included, but the company excluded any liability in negligence for the driver's acts. In the event whilst he was working under the plaintiff's directions the driver damaged their factory through his own negligence. The court held the exclusion clause to be unreasonable and therefore invalid. It was unreasonable becaue the hire was for a short period giving the plaintiffs little opportunity to insure. They did not select, nor effectively control the driver, and moreover their experience of such hiring arrangements was very limited.

Under s.3, where a person inserts in their own written standard terms of business any term purporting to exclude or restrict liability for breach of contract, the term must satisfy the test of reasonableness. If the other contractual party is a consumer the rule applies, even if the contract is not based upon the other's written terms. An example of the application of this section would be where a time limit is placed upon the period for making claims.

Section 5 of the Act deals with guarantees. It provides that where goods are of a type ordinarily supplied for private use or consumption, a term contained in a guarantee of the goods cannot exclude or restrict liability for loss or damage caused by the negligent manufacture or distribution of the goods, where the defect occurs when the goods are in consumer use.

Finally section 6 deals with exclusions of the implied conditions of the Sale of Goods Act 1979. Originally it was quite permissible for a seller to exclude the statutory implied conditions from a contract of sale, but under the 1977 Act the position is very different. S.6 provides that if there is a sale to a consumer any clause excluding the terms implied by sections 12 to 15 of the Sale of Goods Act is ineffective. A person buys as a consumer if the goods are of a type ordinarily sold for private use or consumption by a seller in the course of business to a person who does not buy them in the course of business. In a non-consumer sale, for instance between two businesses, any attempt to exclude s.12 of the Sale of Goods Act is absolutely void, although sections 13, 14 and 15 can be excluded if the seller can show that this is reasonable. Whether it is reasonable to do so is determined by a number of guidelines laid down by the Act. These are:

a) The respective bargaining strengths of the parties relative to each other. This involves considering possible alternative sources of supply. For instance a monopolist seller may have difficulty in establishing the reasonableness of a widely drafted exclusion clause.

b) Whether the customer received an inducement to agree the term, or in accepting it had the opportunity of entering into a similar contract with other persons but without having to accept a similar term. The reference to other person involves account being taken of the suppliers within the market and their terms of trading. Sometimes suppliers combine to produce standardised terms of trading, giving buyers no opportunity of finding improved terms. An example of an inducement would be a reduction in price.

c) Whether the customer knew or ought reasonably to have known of the existence of the term. This involves the customer's knowledge of the trade in general, its terms and customs, and knowledge of the seller, with whom the customer may have previously traded on the same terms.

d) Where the term excludes or restricts any relevant liability if some condition is not complied with, whether it is reasonable at the time of the contract to expect that it would be practicable to comply with the condition. It might not be practicable, for example, to require the buyer to notify the seller of defects occurring in a large consignment of goods within a limited time period with a proviso that failure to notify in time will relieve the seller of any liability.

> In *George Mitchell Ltd v. Finney Lock Seeds Ltd (1983)*, a farmer purchased cabbage seed from a supplier. When the cabbages grew it became apparent

that they were of the wrong type and of inferior quality. The seed had cost Mitchells, the buyers, £192, but their loss was over £61,000, the profit they would have made on the years production. They were uninsured, and sued the sellers for the losses sustained. The defence put forward by the sellers was an exclusion clause limiting liability to either the cost of the seed, or its replacement value. The clause read:

". . . In the event of any seeds or plants sold or agreed to be sold by us not complying with the express terms of the contract of sale or with any representation made by us or by any duly authorised agent or representative on our behalf prior to, at the time of, or in any such contract, or any seeds or plants proving defective in varietal purity we will, at our option, replace the defective seeds or plants, free of charge to the buyer or will refund all payments made to us by the buyer in respect of the defective seeds or plants and this shall be the limit of our obligation. We hereby exclude all liability for any loss or damage arising from the use of any seeds or plants supplied by us and for any consequential loss or damage arising out of such use or any failure in the performance of or any defect in any seeds or plants supplied by us or for any other loss or damage whatsoever save for, at our option, liability for any such replacement or refund as aforesaid . . . "

The House of Lords affirmed the decision of the Court of Appeal that the clause did not enable the suppliers to avoid their full liability. In his judgment, the last he made before retiring, Lord Denning considered a number of questions relevant to the validity of the clause. The first was whether the clause was part of the agreement. It was found that it was, since such conditions were usual in the trade, and therefore well known, and in any event the clause was included on the back of the invoice. The second was the wording of the clause, and whether as drafted it covered and effectively limited the suppliers liability. It was found that the clause clearly did so. Finally the question arose as to whether the clause was a reasonable one. On this it was noted that such a term was effectively imposed by the supplier upon the buyer without negotiation, it was rarely applied by the suppliers, in practice, and the nature of the contract made the opportunity of discovering the defectiveness of the seed on the part of the buyer an impossibility at the time of purchase. In these circumstances the clause was found to be unreasonable applying the criteria which are now found in the Unfair Contract Terms Act 1977.

DISCHARGE OF CONTRACT

Since a contract gives rise to legally enforceable obligations, contracting parties need to know how and when these obligations have been discharged and cease to be binding on them. Only then have their duties been discharged. Discharge may occur in any of the following ways:

(a) DISCHARGE BY PERFORMANCE

The general rule is that complete performance, complying precisely to the contractual terms, is necessary to discharge the contract.

An illustration of this common law rule is the case of *Sumpter v. Hedges (1898)*. Here the plaintiff builder agreed to erect some houses for a lump sum of £565. Having carried out half the work to the value of £333 the builder was unable to complete the work because of financial difficulties. In an action by the builder to recover compensation for the value of the work done, the Court of Appeal confirmed that he was not entitled to

> payment. The legal position was expressed by Smith, LJ who stated "The law is that where there is a contract to do work for a lump sum, until the work is completed, the price of it cannot be recovered".

On the face of it this decision appears harsh in its effect upon the builder. In fact the difficulty for the court is that a single sum has been arranged in consideration for the completion of specified works. If these works are not completed in their entirety the court would be varying the clearly expressed intentions of the parties if it was to award the builder payment of a proportionate part of the lump sum. In other words, by agreeing a lump sum the parties have impliedly excluded that possibility of part payment for partially fulfilled building work.

The obligation on a contracting party to provide precise, complete performance of the contract before the contractual obligations can be treated or discharged can obviously produce injustice. There are however two exceptions that grant limited relief to the party obliged to perform.

(a) A Divisible Contract

In some circumstances the courts are prepared to accept that a contract is a divisible one where part of the performance of the contract can be set off against part of the consideration to be given in return. Had the parties in *Sumpter v. Hedges* agreed a specified sum to be paid on completion of certain stages of the house building, then the builder could have recovered compensation for part of the work done. In practice it is usual in a building contract to provide for payment of parts of the total cost at various stages of completion.

It is not necessary for the parties to formally specify that the contract is a divisible one, although in contracts involving substantial work, such as civil engineering operations, or shipbuilding, it would be most unusual not to find that the contract has not been split into stages, with payment due on completion of each stage. The courts seems willing to recognise a divisible contract wherever possible, and will, for example, regard a contract based upon an estimate or quotation given in advance, which itemises the work to be performed and with a breakdown of the costs as a divisible contract.

(ii) Substantial Performances

If a party to a contract has substantially performed his contractual obligations subject only to minor defects, the courts have recognised that it would be unjust to prevent him recovering any of the contractual price. Therefore under this exception the contractual price would be recoverable, less of course a sum representing the value of the defects. It must be stressed that the exception will only operate where the defects are of a trifling nature. This question is determined by considering not only the nature of the defects but also the cost of rectifying them in relation to the total contract price.

> A claim of substantial performance of the contract was made in *Bolton v. Mahadeva (1972)*. Here the plaintiff, a heating contractor, had agreed to install a central heating system in the defendant's house for £560. On completion of the work the system proved to be so defective that it would cost £174 to repair. The defendant refused to pay the plaintiff any of the cost of the work and the plaintiff sued. The County Court accepted the plaintiff's claim of substantial performance and awarded him the cost of the work less the cost of repair. On appeal however, the Court of Appeal held that in the circumstances the plaintiff had not substantially performed the contract and he was not therefore entitled to recover any of the cost of the work. The exception would not operate where there were numerous defects requiring a relatively high cost of repair.

From the consumer's point of view it can be difficult to ascertain whether incomplete performance of the contract is nevertheless sufficient on the facts to amount to substantial performance. A refusal of payment may well be met with a legal action by the contractor to recovee the debt owed, brought by the contractor. Further complications may be caused where the contractor has offered to remedy the customers complaint free of charge and the customer has refused to accept the offer. As we saw in the last chapter in the event of a dispute concerning the value of work performed, an offer of reduced payment by the debtor to the creditor will be binding on the creditor, an example of one of the exemptions to Pinnels case.

> In *Lawson v. Supasink Ltd (1982)* the plaintiff's employed the defendants to design, supply and install a fitted kitchen. The total cost was £1,200, and the plaintiffs had to pay a £200 deposit. After the kitchen untis had been fitted, but before work on the kitchen was completed, the plaintiffs informed the defendants of their dissatisfaction with the standard of workmanship. In response the defendants undertook to remedy the faults free of charge, but the plaintiffs later rejected this, asked for the units to be removed and for the return of their deposit. The defendants refused. The Court of Appeal, having accepted that the shoddy work did not amount to substantial performance, then considered the offer to remedy made by the defendants. The question was whether they had failed to mitigate their loss, that is minimise the damage they had suffered. In *Jayzu Ltd v. Saunders (1919)* Scrutton LJ commented, " . . in commercial contracts it is generally reasonable to accept an offer from the party in default," In Lawson the court held that the plaintiffs had not acted unreasonably for, in the words of Shaw LJ "I do not see how the plaintiffs could be required . . . to afford the defendants a second opportunity of doing properly what they singularly failed to do adequately in the first instance."

(iii) The Acceptance of Partial Performance

If a party to a contract partially performs his obligations and the other party accepts the benefit, then he is obliged to pay a reasonable price for it. Thus if a buyer in a sale of goods contract opts to accept rather than reject a delivery of less than the agreed quantity, then he is obliged to pay a reasonable price for it. In such circumstances the courts would allow an action on a quantum meruit basis (as much as he deserves). This exception however will only operate where the party receiving the benefit has the option of whether or not to accept or reject. In *Sumpter v. Hedges* the owner had no choice but to accept the work done on the half completed houses and was therefore not obliged to pay for it. In a situation like that in *Lawson v. Supasink* the units were capable of being removed and returned.

(iv) Where performance is prevented

Obviously if a party to a contract is prevented from fulfilling his contractual obligations by the other party then he will not be in default. If in a building contract the owner prevents the builder from completing, in these circumstances the builder can recover a reasonable price for the work done on a quantum meruit basis.

As well as the above exceptions to the general rule that the performance of contractual obligations must be precise, it is important to note that if a party to a contract makes a valid tender (offer) of performance this may be regarded as equivalent to performance. The refusal of the other party to allow performance to take place will discharge any further obligations on the part of the tenderers. Thus if a seller of goods attempts to deliver them at the agreed time and place and the goods meet contract description, the refusal of the buyer to accept them will

(i) amount to a valid tender of performance, and

(ii) entitle the seller to sue the buyer under s.50 Sale of Goods Act 1979 for damages for non-acceptance of the goods.

Despite the problems that can occur in performance, most contracts are satisfactorily discharged in this way.

(b) Discharge by Agreement

This method of discharge occurs where the parties to a contract agree to waive their rights and obligations under it. It is called bilateral discharge. To be an effective waiver the second agreement must be a contract, the consideration for which is the exchange of promises not to enforce the original contract. The situation however is more complex where one party to a contract has already executed or partly executed his consideration under it. Here for a waiver to be effective it must be embodied within a specialty contract or be supported by fresh consideration. This is called unilateral discharge and can only be achieved by accord and satisfaction. The accord is simply the agreement to discharge and the satisfaction is the consideration required to support it, e.g. X contracts to sell goods to Y for £50. X delivers the goods to Y and then hearing of Y's financial difficulties agrees to waive payment. Here the agreement of X to waive payment (the accord) is not enforceable unless supported by fresh consideration furnished by Y (the satisfaction). The fresh consideration of course must be of value but need not be adequate. As we saw in our examination of the principles of consideration, at common law the rule in Pinnels Case provides that there is no value in a creditor taking as satisfaction payment of a lesser sum than he was due under the original agreement.

> A creditors promise to accept a reduced amount may however be binding on him, through the operation of the equitable doctrine of promissory estoppel, established in *Hughes v. Metropolitan Railway Co (1877)* by the House of Lords, and by Denning J as he then was in *Central London Property Trust Ltd v. High Trees House Ltd (1947).* Here the defendant company took a 99-year lease on a block of flats from the plaintiff company at an annual rent of £2,500. The lease was granted in 1937. By 1940 the evacuation of large numbers of people out of London because of war meant that the defendant company was unable to let all the flats and could not meet the annual rent out of the profits it was making. As a result, the plaintiff company agreed to accept a reduced annual rent of £1,250. By the beginning of 1945 the flats were fully let again. An action was brought by the plaintiff company to recover the difference between the reduced rent and the full rent for the last two quarters of 1945. The action suceeded, for the court considered that the agreement of 1940 would continue only for as long as wartime conditions prevailed. The court also considered whether the plaintiffs could recover the remaining arrears from the defendants, relying on Pinnels Case. It took the view that such action would be inequitable, even though permissable at common law. In equity the creditor would be estopped, or denied the right of disowning his promise to accept the reduced amount, where the debtor had to the creditors knowledge relied on the promise, and acted on it to his detriment. This rule is consequently referred to as promissory estoppel. It was said in the later case of *Combe v. Combe (1951)* that the doctrine is a shield rather than a sword, meaning that the person receiving the promise cannot sue on it, the 'sword', but can raise it as a defence, 'the shield', if action is brought to recover the outstanding payment. The doctrine only arises within the context of a pre-existing contractual relationship, and does not remove consideration as a requirement of the simple contract.

It is worth pointing out that the High Trees decision is an authority which also supports the view that a deed can be varied by a simple contract. Prior to 1947 it had always been considered tht because a simple contract is inferior to the more formal deed, that only a deed could vary a deed.

Being a form of equitable relief, it is only possible for a person to raise promissory estoppel as a defence if he has acted in an equitable manner himself. In *D & C Buildiners v. Rees (1965)* Mr & Mrs Rees exorted a promise out of D & C Builders to accept a reduced amount than that originally agreed, for building work carried out to the Rees's home. They claimed the building work was substandard, but in fact they were simply attempting to escape the full payment due, using their knowledge that the builders were in financial difficulties and desperate for cash. The court refused to allow Mr & Mrs Rees the defence.

(c) Discharge by Breach

If a party to a contract fails to perform his obligations under it or performs his obligations in a defective manner then he may be regarded as being in breach of contract. Generally, the remedy of an innocent party to a contract who has suffered as a result of a breach is to sue for damages. For some breaches of contract however, the innocent party is given the additional remedy of treating the contract as repudiated, in other words terminated, and thus discharging himself from the obligations under it. As previously mentioned terms in a contract are classified into different categories and it is only when a condition has been broken that repudiatory breach has occurred. If a breach of contract occurs before the time set for performance of the contract it is called an anticipatory breach. This will occur where a party to a contract expressly declares that he will not perform his part of the bargain. Once an anticipatory breach has occurred the innocent party does not have to wait for the date set for performance but has the option of immediately suing for breach of contract.

> In *Hochester v. De La Tour (1853)* the defendant agreed in April to engage the plaintiff for work to commence in June. The defendant told the plaintiff in May that he would not require his services. The court held that a cause of action for breach of contract arose on the anticipatory breach in May. Thus in such circumstances the injured party can commence legal action at the time of the anticipatory breach. Alternatively he can wait until performance is due to see if it is infact carried out, and if it is not commence action thereafter.

(d) Discharge by Frustration or subsequent impossibility

A contract may be discharged by frustration where as a result of an event subsequent to making the contract, performance of the contract can no longer be carried out. The event must be subsequent to the contract for if the contract is impossible to perform at the time it is made there is no contract. Originally the common law did not take such a lenient view of changes in circumstances and required that the parties to a contract should provide for all eventualities. If because of a subsequent event performance of an obligation became impossible, the party required to perform the impossible obligation would be liable to pay damages for non performance.

> In *Paradine v. Jane (1647)* the King's Bench Court held a tenant liable to pay three years' arrears of rent to a landlord despite the fact that the tenant had been dispossessed of his house by soldiers during the Civil War.

Today however the courts recognise that certain supervening events may frustrate a contract and thus release the parties from their obligations under it. Were the facts of *Paradine v. Jane* to come before a modern court, the outcome would probably be quite different.

> In *National Carriers Ltd v. Panalpina (Northern) Ltd (1981)* the plaintiffs leased a warehouse in Hull to the defendants. The lease was for ten years, however for a period of 20 months the only access road to the premises was closed by the local authority due to the poor state of a listed building nearby. The defendants refused to pay any further rent to the plaintiffs. The House of Lords accepted the defendant's argument that a lease could,

in law, become frustrated, but felt that twenty months out of a ten year period, was not sufficiently substantial to frustrate the contract.

There are a number of grounds upon which a contract may become frustrated. They include:

(i) Changes in the Law

If because of new legislation performance of the contract would become illegal this would be a supervening event to frustrate the contract. In *Denny, Mott and Dickson Ltd. v. James B. Fraser Ltd (1944)* the House of Lords held that the contract for the sale of timber was frustrated because of the subsequent passage of various Control of Timber Orders rendering performance of the contract illegal.

(ii) Destruction of subject matter

If the subject matter or means of performance of the contract is destroyed this is an event which frustrates a contract. In *Taylor v. Caldwell (1863)* the plaintiff agreed to hire the defendant's music hall to give some concerts. Prior to performance the hall was destroyed by fire and this event, the court held, released the parties from their obligations under the contract.

(iii) Inability to achieve main object

If as a result of a change in circumstances performance of the contract would be radically different from the performance envisaged by the parties then the contract is frustrated. It must be shown that the parties are no longer able to achieve their main object under the contract. In *Krell v. Henry (1903)* the defendant hired a flat for two days to enable him to watch Edward VII's coronation procession. Due to the King's illness the Coronation was cancelled and the defendant naturally refused to pay. The Court of Appeal held that as the main object of the contract was to view the procession, and this could no longer be achieved, the foundation of the contract had collapsed. The contract was thus frustrated and the parties released from their obligations under it.

A further claim of frustration as a consequence of the cancellation of the Coronation was brought in *Herne Bay Steamboat Co. v. Hutton (1903).* here a steamboat had been chartered to watch the naval review as part of the Coronation celebrations and also for a day's cruise round the fleet. The Court of Appeal had to determine whether the cancellation of the naval review released the defendant from his obligation to pay the hire charge. The Court held that there had not been a sufficient change in circumstances to constitute a frustration of the contract. Here the defendant could have derived some benefit from the contract and was therefore liable to pay the hire charges. A further distinction between *Henry and Hutton* is that in Henry the claim was brought by a private individual whereas in Hutton the hirer was engaged in a commercial enterprise, using the hired boat to take trips of sightseers to Spithead. Frustration is not available in a commercial transaction where the contract turns out to be less profitable than one of the parties expected.

(iv) Death or illness

In a contract for personal services the death or illness of the person required to perform will frustrate the contract. Temporary illness or incapacity will generally not release a party from his obligations. The illness must be such that it goes to the root of the contract.

The common law doctrine of frustration will not apply in the following situations:-

(a) If performance of the contract has become more onerous on one party or financially less rewarding. In *Davis Contractors Ltd. v. Fareham U.D.C. (1956)* the plaintiff building company claimed that a building contract should be regarded as discharged by frustration due to the shortage of available labour and resultant increased costs. The House of Lords rejected the arguments that frustration had discharged the contract. Performance of the contract had simply been made more onerous than originally envisaged by the plaintiffs.

(b) If the parties to a contract have made express provision for the event which has occurred then the common law doctrine of frustration is inapplicable. The courts will simply give effect to the intention of the parties expressed in the contract.

(c) A distinction must be drawn between a frustrating event over which the parties have no control and a self-induced frustration. If it can be shown that a party to the contract caused the supposed frustrating event by his own conduct then there will be no frustration but there may be a contractual breach.

In *Maritime National Fish Ltd v. Ocean Trawlers Ltd. (1935)* the appellants had chartered a trawler from the respondents. The vessel was fitted with an otter trawl, which it was unlawful to use without a government licence from the Minister. The appellants used five vessels for fishing and applied for five licences, but were granted three and were allowed to nominate which vessels the licence would cover. They did not nominate the vessels chartered from the respondents, and refused to pay the charter fee. The Court held that they were liable to pay it. They could not claim frustration since it was a self-induced situation which prevented them from hiring the vessel.

Consequences of frustration of contract

To determine the rights and duties of the parties following frustration it is necessary to consider the position at common law and under statute. Frustration of course will terminate a contract. However under common law it does not discharge the contract ab initio (from the outset) but only from the time of the frustrating event. Therefore, if before that date work had been done or money transferred, the common law rule is simply that losses lie where they fall. It is thus not possible to recover money due or paid prior to frustrating events, except if there is a total failure or consideration, for example if there has been performance of consideration by one party and non performance of consideration by the other.

The common law position has been altered to some extent by the Law Reform (Frustrated Contracts) Act 1943. The Act however does not apply to certain contracts such as insurance, charter-parties (shipping contracts) and contracts for the sale of specific goods, so the common law position is still relevant. Under the Act the following conditions apply:-

(i) Money transferred prior to the frustrating event may be recovered.

(ii) Money due prior to the frustrating event is no longer due.

(iii) Expenses incurred prior to the frustrating event may be deducted from money to be returned.

(iv) Compensation may be recovered on a quantum meruit basis (as much as he deserves) where one of the parties has carried out an act of part performance prior to the frustrating event and thus conferred a benefit on the other party.

REMEDIES FOR BREACH OF CONTRACT

No account of the principles of the contract would be complete without some mention of the various remedies available to an innocent party in the event of a breach. The options available are to claim damages and/or treat the contract as discharged under the common law, or pursue an equitable discretionary remedy.

DAMAGES

The usual remedy is to sue for unliquidated damages under the common law. Unliquidated damages are damages whose level is determined by the court, exercising its own discretion. It is sometimes possible for a plaintiff to quantify the measure of damages being sought concisely, in which event the plaintiff will claim a liquidated amount e.g.: three weeks loss of salary where the salary is of a fixed amount.

Damages awarded under the unliquidated claim, should amount to a sum of money which will put the innocent party in the position he would have been had the contract been performed properly, that is the loss resulting from the breach directly and naturally. The courts have held however that it would be unfair to make a contract-breaker responsible for damage caused as a result of circumstances of which he was unaware.

> In *Hadley v. Baxendale (1854)* the plaintiff mill owner contracted with a defendant carrier who agreed to take a broken millshaft to a repairer and then return it. The carrier delayed in delivery of the shaft and as a result the plaintiff sought to recover the loss of profit he would have made during the period of delay. The court held that this loss was not recoverable as it was too remote. The possible loss of profit was a circumstance of which the carrier was unaware at the time of the contract. The result would have been different however had the plaintiff expressly made the defendant aware that this loss of profit was the probable result of a breach of contract.

The decision in *Hadley v. Baxendale* has been approved by the House of Lords on many occasions and knowledge of the circumstances which could produce the damage is still a crucial factor in determining the extent of the liability for breach.

> In *Czarnikow v. Koufos (The Heron II) (1969)*, a shipowner delayed in delivering a cargo of sugar to Basrah. The sugar was to be sold by the cargo owners at Basrah, where there was an established sugar market. During the nine days the ship was delayed the market price fell. The cargo owners successfully sued for their loss. The House of Lords considered that the loss ought to have been within the reasonable contemplation of the shipowners as a consequence of the delay. It was felt that the shipowners should have appreciated that a market for goods is something which by its nature fluctuates over time.

> In *Diamond v. Campbell-Jones (1961)* the defendant seller of premises wrongfully repudiated the contract of sale to a dealer and was held liable for the loss of profit that the dealer would have made on a resale. The fact that the seller was unaware that the purchaser intended to convert the premises before resale, in order to command a higher price, meant that the seller was not liable for the larger profit that the dealer would have made.

Quantification of damages in relation to goods or land is essentially a question of assessing the market price and then determining the actual loss. The Sale of Goods Act 1979 provides for a number of remedies, including damages, available to an injured party to a sale of goods transaction.

Remedies available to buyers and sellers

In the event of a breach of the obligations owed by one party to the other under a sale of goods contract the injured party may seek redress against the other. The principal obligations that arise may be summarised as follows:

(a) the seller must transfer ownership in the goods to the buyer; physically deliver them to the buyer unless the contract provides otherwise; fulfil the implied conditions and warranties contained in ss. 12-15 of the 1979 Act;

(b) the buyer must accept the goods and pay for them. Note that payment and delivery are concurrent obligations, unless the parties agree otherwise. This means they occur at the same time, for instance cash sales in shops.

The remedies of a seller

If the seller is owed money by the buyer the Act gives the seller the following rights, even if the buyer has become the owner of the goods:

(i) a lien over the goods, i.e. a right to retain possession until he is paid;

(ii) if the goods are in transit and in possession of a carrier, a right to regain possession of them during the transit if the buyer has become insolvent;

(iii) a right of resale in certain circumstances, for instance when the goods are of a perishable nature, or where the seller gives the buyer notice of the intention to resell and the buyer does not within a reasonable time pay for the goods. In the event of a resale the seller can claim damages representing any loss suffered. Such a loss could be the reduced profit on a resale because of a drop in the market price of the goods, including the cost of advertising them;

(iv) an action for the price of the goods;

(v) an action for damages where the goods are still owned by the seller and the buyer refuses or simply fails to accept them. Damages awarded will represent the loss directly and naturally resulting from the non acceptance. Prima facie, this will be the difference between the contract price, and the market or current price at the time when the goods should have been accepted, assuming of course there is an available market. So if supply exceeds demand and there is a fixed retail price for the goods damages will then represent the loss of profit that would have been made on the sale, but if demand exceeds supply then damages will only be nominal as the goods can be readily resold.

The remedies of a buyer

(i) an action to recover damages when the seller wrongfully fails or refuses to deliver the goods. Again damages are measured in the same way as outlined above in a seller's action for non-acceptance. It should be stressed that in the case of a non-delivery by the seller, or a non-acceptance by a buyer it is the market price when the breach occurs that is used to determine the measure for damages.

In *Pagnan v. Corbisa (1970)* Lord Justice Salmon made it quite clear that other market fluctuations are not relevant, ". . . the innocent party is not bound to go on the market and buy or sell at the date of the breach. Nor is he bound to gamble on the market changing in his favour. He may wait if he chooses; and if the market turns against him this cannot increase the liability of the party in default. Similarly, if the market turns in his favour, the liability of the party in default is not diminished".

(ii) recovery of the price paid if the goods are not delivered.

(iii) rejection of the goods where there has been a breach of condition, and damages for breach of warranty — the amount being the difference between the value of the goods as delivered, and their value if the warranty has been complied with. A buyer may elect to treat a breach of condition as a breach of warranty.

Other principles applicable to a claim for damages

Where a breach has occurred the innocent party, if he accepts that the breach discharges the contract, must take all reasonable steps to mitigate the loss resulting from the breach. There is no requirement for the injured party to act immediately or take on a risky venture but rather to act reasonably in order to minimise the loss rather than "sitting on the breach". For instance an hotel would be expected to try and relet a room that a customer, in breach of contract, had failed to use.

Damages are not limited to the pure economic cost of the loss of the bargain but may also be recovered for inconvenience, discomfort, distress or anxiety caused by the breach.

> In *Jarvis v. Swans Tours Ltd (1973)* the Court of Appeal held that the plaintiff was entitled to damages for mental distress and disappointment due to loss of enjoyment caused by breach of a holiday contract.
>
> Even the emotional distress caused to the employee in *Cox v. Philips Industries (1976)* when he was deemed in breach of a contract of employment was held to be quantifiable.

In substantial contracts involving large sums, e.g. building contracts, it is usual to attempt to liquidate damages payable in the event of a breach. This is achieved by the parties expressly inserting a clause into the contract providing for a sum of compensation to be payable on a breach. Generally, provided such clauses represent a genuine pre-estimate of the future possible loss rather than amounting to a penalty to ensure performance of contract, they are enforceable by the courts.

The right to treat a contract as discharged will depend upon the nature of the breach. For breaches of condition the innocent party may sue for damages and/or treat the contract as repudiated, whereas for less important terms the innocent party is limited to an action for damages.

Discretionary Remedies

These remedies are available because of the intervention of the Court of Chancery and include the injunction and specific performance. A prohibitory injunction is an order of the court commanding someone not to do something while specific performance is an order requiring an individual to do something. As equitable remedies, they are discretionary in nature, and are never granted where a common law remedy such as damages is sufficient to compensate the injured party. The injunction is sought as a remedy mainly in tort actions such as trespass or nuisance but could be used to prevent a threatened breach of contract. Specific performance has wider application in contract but is never granted to enforce contracts of personal service or contracts which require supervision to ensure that the work is properly carried out.

> In *Ryan v. Mutual Tontine Association (1893)*, the Court of Appeal held that despite the fact that a lessor of a service flat was in clear breach of his obligation to provide a porter who was "constantly in attendance", an application for specific performance of the lease was refused. This was on the ground that to ensure compliance constant supervision by the court would be required. Damages only were therefore awarded.

An example of the use of injuction can be seen in the *Harvela* case (see Chapter 3).

An injuction will not be granted if its effect would be to compel the party in breach to do something which he could not be ordered to do by a decree of specific performance.

> Thus in *Page One Records Ltd. v. Britton (1968)* an injunction was applied for to prevent the Troggs pop group from engaging anyone as their manager other than the plaintiff. An injunction on these terms was refused, for to grant it would indirectly compel the pop group to continue to employ the plaintiff.

ASSIGNMENT — THE PREMISES

Midlands & Northern Property Holdings plc is a company whose business involves the development of industrial and commercial sites for sale and for letting. R & C Enterprises Ltd, a small company based in Northampton, had been seeking commercial premises for some time when one of its directors became aware of an industrial unit that Midlands & Northern had available on a small development just outside town. Following a site visit and a meeting between the director and a representative of the property company, the director, Tom Armstrong raised with the rest of his board the possibility of taking a ten year lease of the premises, which Midlands & Northern were offering.

The company's main business is in coachworks, which involves it building and fitting different types of bodywork to lorry bases. Whilst the existing site was adequate for this work, the company had decided to diversify and use its skills and expertise in the construction of mobile buildings for schools and building sites. It was for this purpose that the new premises were required. Following a further meeting with the representative from Midlands & Northern, a number of questions were raised by Tom Armstrong. In particular he wanted to know if planning permission would be granted to use the premises in the way anticipated by the company; whether the large hardsurfaced area to the rear of the site was included in the lease; and whether the premises were suitable for the anticipated use. The representative wrote in reply; "I can assure you that planning content for the change of use of the premises will be forthcoming, following a conversation I have had with the Chief Planning Officer of the local authority. I can confirm that the premises include the hardsurfaced area referred to by you. I would add that the premises are entirely suited to the business operations planned by you, and that I see no reason why the business should not operate profitably."

R & C Enterprises Ltd leased the premises. A month after doing so planning consent for their proposed change was refused. The lease granted to them makes no reference to the hardsurfaced area to the rear of the premises, which is now being used by an adjoining owner, and the vehicular access to the premises is about to be cut off for a month for major works of repair and improvement to be carried out by sub-contractors acting for Midlands & Northern. You work for R & C Enterprises, and Tom Armstrong has asked you to produce a report for him, which indicates any possible legal action that may be taken against Midlands & Northern. In particular he is anxious to establish whether it is possible to terminate the lease. He has also given you a letter received from Midlands & Northern which states that due to an error by the company surveyor in correctly measuring the internal dimensions of the premises, the quarterly rental being charged is £1,000 less than it should be. The letter adds, "you were aware that the rental of the premises was based upon the number of square metres of floor space in the factory site, since this was discussed by us during negotiations". Tom is wondering how to respond to the letter.

TASK

Produce a report requested by Tom Armstrong, and draft a reply to the letter from Midlands & Northern, for Mr. Armstrong's approval, which rejects their claim, and contains a statement of the legal grounds for doing so.

ASSIGNMENT — A BAD WEEK AT BRITECH

The managing director of Britech Systems Ltd, an electronics company for which you work, has asked you to look into two problems facing the company which have blown up over the last week and are causing him considerable anxiety. The company is based to the west of London. One of these problems concerns a major contract negotiated between the company and an international telecommunications organisation ITTB. The contract involves the construction, installation and maintenance by the company of a highly sophisticated computer monitoring system to control signals beamed to and from the United Kingdom and North America using ITTB'S own satellite. The system was due to be installed and be fully operational by the beginning of December 198x., eight months away, but work has been halted due to the commercial collapse of Modem plc, which is the only UK supplier of certain vital microelectronic components used by Britech in the construction of the monitoring system. Modem went into liquidation two weeks ago, and it is unclear whether there is any chance of receiving the components ordered by Britech from Modem. ITTB, aware of the problem, is arguing that its contract with Britech has been frustrated, and has indicated that it is seeking another company to supply the system as a matter of urgency.

Additionally one of Britech's senior employees, who left the company six months ago, has just set up his own business as a Microelectronics Consultant, in Manchester. In common with other senior staff the employee, Gerry McBain, had agreed to a clause in his contract of employment which stipulated, "The employee agrees and undertakes that in the event of the termination of his/her employment with the company, he/she will not compete in any way with the business of the company or so act as to cause damage to the interests of the company, for a period of five years, to run from the date of termination such undertaking to extend to the whole of England and Wales."

The managing director of Britech has arranged to meet you tomorrow to discuss the legal position between the company, ITTB and Mr. McBain its former employee.

TASKS

Analyse the two situations described, and produce notes on them in which you seek to clarify the company's position, in order to advise the managing director (a) whether the company has a contractual claim against ITTB, and if it has what the measure of damages is likely to be, and (b) what the likelihood is of the company being able to successfully obtain an injunction to prevent the business operations of Mr. McBain.

Chapter 5

THE BUSINESS CUSTOMER'S RIGHTS AND ISSUES OF CONSUMER PROTECTION

This chapter aims to examine the contractual relationships arising between businesses and all those whom they supply. It is an area of critical importance in developing an understanding of business law, for it lies at the heart of commercial activity.

The primary objective of business activity is the provision of goods and services for consumers. Consumption of goods and services meets the private needs of individuals. All of us act as private consumers in this way. We make regular purchases of goods and services to satisfy our demand for a wide range of necessaries and luxuries, from food and clothing to motor cars, video recorders and holidays. Goods and services are also demanded by business organisations, who acquire them to meet their own internal requirements, as well as for the purpose of resale to other businesses in the chain of production or to consumers. The legal rules relating to interbusiness contracting are, in many cases, identical to those which apply where a business deals with a private consumer. However the law has increasingly sought to compensate for the relative economic weakness of individual consumers, by developing a framework of consumer protection.

The protection of the consumer has been sought by a combination of legal devices. These include:

(i) conferring remedies which are available by legal action in the civil courts, for example under the Sale of Goods Act 1979;

(ii) regulating certain types of trading activities, for instance through the licencing requirements under the Consumer Credit Act 1974; and,

(iii) imposing criminal liability in respect of certain types of unacceptable trading practices, for example under the Trade Descriptions Act 1968.

Fig 5.1 below is designed to provide an overview of the major features of consumer protection under the civil and criminal law.

Fig. 5.1 Consumer Protection under the Civil Law and the Criminal Law

	CIVIL LAW	CRIMINAL LAW
Enforcement	Rescission of contract. Sue for damages (or defence to an action for damages) in the County Court or High Court. Arbitration.	Local Authority: Trading Standards Department. Prosecution in the Magistrates and Crown Courts. Compensation orders under the Power of Criminal Courts Act 1973. Director General of Fair Trading
Defective Products	Sale of Goods Act 1979. Supply of Goods and Services Act 1982. Tort of negligence. Consumer Protection Act 1987. Codes of Practice.	Consumer Protection Act 1987. Food Act 1984. Road Traffic Act 1972 and other specific legislation. Health & Safety at Work Act 1974.
Defective Services	Supply of Goods and Services Act 1982. Professional Negligence. Regulation by trade or professional associations. Codes of practice.	Trade Descriptions Act 1968. Consumer Credit Act 1974. Health & Safety at Work Act 1974.
False Statements	Misrepresentation. Breach of contract. Negligent mis-statement. Tort of deceit.	Trade Descriptions Act 1968. Consumer Protection Act 1987. Weights & Measures Act 1985. Fair Trading Act 1973.
Exclusion of Liability	Common law rules of incorporation and interpretation. Unfair Contract Terms Act 1977.	Consumer Transactions (Restrictions on Statements) Order 1976 and (Amendment) Order 1978.

TYPES AND NATURE OF BUSINESS AGREEMENTS

In the previous two chapters we examined the legal rules relating to the formation of business contracts and the discharge of obligations arising under them. The remedies available in the event of one of the contracting parties non compliance with the contract were also considered. We shall now examine in more detail the various types of contract which are encountered in the business world and identify the features which distinguish them. Some types of contract involving the supply of goods, for example, which appear very similar, are nevertheless governed by different legal rules. The distinction between them may depend upon the provisions in the contract relating to the transfer of ownership or the time for payment and delivery. It is particularly important to be able to distinguish between the various types of contract otherwise there is a danger of applying the wrong legal rules.

1. CONTRACTS FOR THE SALE OF GOODS

Contracts for the sale of goods are perhaps the most significant category of business agreement because they are the type which are most commonly encountered in the commercial world. A sale of goods contract is basically one in which goods are exchanged for money. Examples of this type of contract range from the sale of a loaf of bread for fifty pence to the purchase of an aircraft for tens of millions of pounds.

The law relating to contracts for the sale of goods is contained principally in the Sale of Goods Act 1979. As a general rule the principle of freedom of contract applies to them. Essentially therefore the buyer and seller are free to negotiate the terms of the contract and make whatever bargain suits their own purposes. Many of the rules contained in the 1979 Act apply only where the parties have not expressly made their intentions clear on the matter in the contract. Some of the provisions in the Act, however, cannot be overidden by agreement between the parties.

A contract for the sale of goods is defined in s.2(1) which states that:

> "A contract for the sale of goods is a contract by which the seller transfers or agrees to transfer the property in goods to the buyer for a money consideration, called the price".

A closer consideration of the definition reveals the following:

(a) There must be "**a contract**". The formation of the contract is governed by the ordinary principles of the law of contract. No special formalities are required. The 1979 Act in s.4 states that:

> "a contract of sale may be made in writing (either with or without seal), or by word of mouth, or partly in writing and partly by word of mouth, or may be implied from the conduct of the parties".

(b) "**the seller transfers or agrees to transfer**". The Act distinguishes between "a sale" in which property is transferred to the buyer on the making of the contract and thus the seller's consideration is executed, and "an agreement to sell" in which property is transferred to the buyer at some future time and thus the seller's consideration is executory.

(c) "**property**". This means full legal ownership and is also sometimes referred to as "title". This must be distinguished from mere physical possession of goods which does not necessarily signify ownership.

(d) **"goods".** This includes any form of personal property which is tangible and moveable for example a motor vehicle, a computer or a ship. The definition does not extend to land or to intangible property rights such as intellectual property (see Chapter 8), shares or debts.

(e) "**money consideration**". In order for a contract to come within the definition in s.2(1) the price for the goods must include an element of money consideration. For this reason contracts of exchange or barter are not covered by the 1979

Act. However where goods are exchanged for a combination of money and other goods, a part exchange, the contract will come within the definition.

In *Aldridge v. Johnson (1857)* a contract for the exchange of 52 bullocks for a quantity of barley and a sum of money was held to be a contract for the sale of goods.

The importance of the definition in s.2(1) is that wherever there is a contract involving the exchange of ownership of goods for money the provisions of the Sale of Goods Act 1979 will apply to it.

2. AUCTION SALES

Where goods are sold at auction the contract of sale will be governed by the Sale of Goods Act 1979. In relation to the formation of the contract of sale the auctioneer makes an invitation to treat when asking for bids. Each bid is a separate offer and no contract is concluded until a bid is accepted by the auctioneer. The 1979 Act provides in s. 57 that:

> "a sale by auction is complete when the auctioneer announces its completion by the fall of the hammer, or in other customary manner; and until the announcement is made any bidder may retract his bid".

The section also allows the seller to place a reserve price on the goods and instruct the auctioneer not to sell below that price. The seller may bid himself up to the reserve price against any buyer. In each situation the seller must expressly reserve his right before the auction sale and bidders must be notified.

In an auction sale there are in fact three separate contracts: between the seller and the buyer; the seller and the auctioneer; and the buyer and the auctioneer.

(a) The contract between the seller and the buyer

This is a contract for the sale of goods and the provisions of the Sale of Goods Act 1979 apply to it except to the extent that they may have been varied by the express terms of the contract. When we examine the law relating to exclusion clauses in contracts below it will be seen that the buyer of goods at an auction sale can never "deal as a consumer" for the purposes of the Unfair Contract Terms Act 1977. This means that the stronger legal protection afforded to consumers will not be available to the buyer at an auction, even if he is in fact buying consumer type goods for his personal use.

Under the Auctions (Bidding Agreements) Acts 1927 and 1969 where the person to whom goods have been sold at an auction sale is a party to a bidding ring the contract is voidable at the option of the seller. A bidding ring is an arrangement between a person who attends auctions in the course of his business for the purpose of buying goods to resell (a dealer) and any other person, in which it is agreed that the parties within the bidding ring will not try to outbid each other. The objective of the agreement is that the price of particular items are not forced up by competitive bidding. Its effect is that the seller loses money. Usually those involved in the bidding ring will meet after the auction to divide their spoils. Under these Acts it is also a criminal offence for a dealer to offer or agree to give an inducement or reward to another person in return for their abstaining from bidding at an auction.

(b) The contract between the auctioneer and the buyer

This contract is governed by the common law rather than the Sale of Goods Act 1979. The rights and obligations of the parties are a matter for agreement between the auctioneer and the buyer. In practice this usually means that the terms of the contract are laid down in the auctioneer's printed auction conditions. The common law implies the following terms into this contract unless the parties have expressly agreed on contrary terms:

(i) the auctioneer has the seller's authority to sell the goods;

(ii) the auctioneer will give possession of the goods to the purchaser once the price is paid;

(iii) the auctioneer may retain possession of the goods until the full price is paid or tendered;

(iv) neither the auctioneer nor the seller will interrupt the buyer's quiet possession of the goods; and

(v) the auctioneer knows of no reason by which the seller is legally unable to sell the goods.

(c) The contract between the auctioneer and the seller

This contract is also governed by the common law and its terms will be those which have been agreed between the auctioneer and the seller. Again these will usually be laid down in the auctioneer's printed conditions of contract. In the absence of agreed terms to the contrary, the common law implies a promise on the part of the auctioneer that he will not give the buyer possession of the goods without receiving payment. He will be personally liable to the seller for the price if the buyer takes possession without making payment. The auctioneer has a common law lien on the proceeds of sale of the goods. This means that he is entitled to deduct his agreed fees from any sums which are due to the seller before making payment to him.

3. CONTRACTS OF BARTER

Barter is the method of trading used in the most primitive societies before the invention of money as a generally accepted medium of exchange. A contract of barter is one involving the exchange of goods for other goods or services in which no money actually changes hands. Such contracts are not governed by the Sale of Goods Act 1979 because of the absence of a money consideration.

A contract of barter or exchange is a "contract for the transfer of goods" as defined in Part 1 of the Supply of Goods and Services Act 1982.

4. CONTRACTS OF HIRE

The essence of a contract of hire is that the hirer, in return for some consideration, usually an agreed fee or the periodical payment of a sum of money, enjoys the possession and the use of goods belonging to someone else, the owner. It is never intended that the hirer shall become the owner of the goods himself under the terms of the contract. Contracts of hire are fairly common in the business world and the period of use by the hirer may range from hours to years. Examples of such contracts include the hire of a mobile crane for a specific task lasting two days; the rental of a household television set over a number of years; the hire of a car for a week whilst on holiday; and the hire of sports equipment at a sports centre. In recent times there has been a growth in the commercial leasing of plant and equipment, particularly motor vehicles, to businesses. Commercial leasing, which is a form of hiring, can be a tax efficient method of acquiring plant and equipment for use in a business.

Contracts of hire are governed partly by the Supply of Goods and Services Act 1982 and may also be regulated partly by the Consumer Credit Act 1974. In order to come within the 1974 Act the contract must be a "Consumer Hire Agreement". This is defined in s.15(1) of the 1974 Act as:

> "an agreement made by a person (the owner) with an individual (the hirer) for the bailment of goods, which:
>
> (a) is not a hire purchase agreement,
>
> (b) is capable of subsisting for more than three months, and
>
> (c) does not require the hirer to make payments exceeding £15,000".

Some of the language of Section 15(1) requires explanation:

(a) An agreement made "**by a person with an individual**". The Act distinguishes between a person and an individual. Whilst the owner may be a person, the hirer must be an individual before the agreement will be regulated by the Act. An individual is a flesh and blood person or an unincorporated association, such as a partnership. Persons, on the other hand, include, as well as individuals, legally created corporate entities such as limited companies or local authorities.

(b) "**for the bailment of goods**". The expression bailment describes a situation in which one person has possession of goods belonging to another. A contract of hire is one of several possible types of contract of bailment. Another example would be a contract under which goods are stored in a warehouse on behalf of a business.

(c) "**not a hire purchase agreement**". The nature of a hire purchase agreement is examined below. At this stage it is sufficient to note that an agreement will not be a consumer hire agreement if its real purpose is the eventual acquisition of ownership of the goods by the hirer. The basic idea of any contract of pure hire is that the hirer never becomes the owner of the goods. The goods revert to the possession of the true owner once the period of hire has expired.

Consumer hire agreements are regulated by the Consumer Credit Act 1974 which lays down strict rules as to their form and content. The agreement must be in writing and signed personally by the hirer. If either of these conditions is not fulfilled the owner has no right to sue the hirer under the agreement. The hirer must be given a copy of the agreement containing full information about his rights and duties and about the protection given to him by the 1974 Act. If any of these formalities are not complied with then no legal action can be taken against the hirer without the permission of the court.

5. CONTRACTS FOR THE SUPPLY OF SERVICES

A contract for the supply of services (or contract for services) usually involves the exchange of an individual's time skill or effort in return for money. A person providing a service could do so by engaging in such diverse activities as surveying a house, tuning a car engine, transporting commodities, or providing legal advice. The contract for services is distinct from the contract of employment (or contract of service) which we consider in Chapter 7. The basic obligations owed by those who provide services in the course of a business are outlined in Part II of the Supply of Goods and Services Act 1982.

6. CONTRACTS FOR WORK DONE AND MATERIALS SUPPLIED

Where services are provided and goods are supplied under the same contract, for example a contract to paint a portrait, to prepare and supply food or to service a motor vehicle, there may be some difficulty in classifying the contract. It could be a contract for the provision of services or a contract for the sale of goods. The court will decide into which category the contract falls by trying to identify the main purpose of the contract.

> In *Young and Marten v. McMannus Childs (1968)* the House of Lords held that a contract for the laying of tiles on the roof of a house was not a sale of goods contract even though the tiler supplied the tiles. The main purpose of the contract was the supply of services and so the contract was not within the Sale of Goods Act 1979.

> In *Robinson v. Graves (1935)* the Court of Appeal held that a contract under which an artist agreed to paint a client's portrait was not a contract for the sale of goods. The transfer of ownership of the canvas to the client was incidental to the main substance of the contract which was the provision by the artist of his skill, expertise and labour.

It may have been different if the client had selected a finished picture from the artist's studio and agreed to pay for it. Such an agreement is a contract for the sale of goods because the substance of the agreement is the transfer of ownership of a completed picture, not the provision of skill and labour by the artist. Parts I and II of the Supply of Goods and Services Act 1982 apply to contracts for work done and materials supplied.

7. CONTRACTS FOR THE SALE OR SUPPLY OF GOODS ON CREDIT TERMS

There are various forms of credit transaction which provide ways of getting goods on tick, ranging from contracts of hire purchase, credit sale and conditional sale agreements, to the use of "plastic money". Credit transactions were aptly characterised by one County Court Judge who complained that most of his time was taken up by:

> "people who are persuaded by persons whom they do not know to enter into contracts that they do not understand to purchase goods that they do not want with money that they have not got".

Although this statement is somewhat exaggerated, it helps to highlight some of the problems with which the law has had to deal arising from such agreements, and we shall examine the ways in which the courts and parliament have sought to provide solutions to those problems later in this chapter.

(a) Contracts of Hire Purchase

A contract of hire purchase, as its name suggests, combines elements of two types of contract. It is in effect a contract of hire which gives one party (the hirer or debtor) an option to purchase goods from the other (the owner or creditor) at the end of a period of hire. During the period of the agreement the debtor pays the creditor by instalments (usually monthly) and the ownership of the goods remains with the creditor. The agreement will contain a term giving the debtor an optional right to purchase the goods at a nominal price once all the instalments have been paid. Ownership of the goods will be transferred to the debtor if and when he exercises the option to purchase. He will invariably do this as soon as he has paid all of the instalments because the real point of the agreement, in practice, is to enable him to acquire ownership.

A hire purchase agreement is not a contract of sale falling within the Sale of Goods Act 1979. Many hire purchase agreements come within the definition of consumer credit agreements and these are regulated by the Consumer Credit Act 1974.

At first sight a hire purchase transaction appears to involve only two parties. In practice, however, the vast majority of hire purchase transactions involve a third party, a finance company. The person who supplies the goods may not be able to wait for his money and may require instant payment, while his customer wishes to have time for payment. The supplier will therefore sell the goods to a finance company, which will supply them to the customer on hire purchase terms under a separate contract.

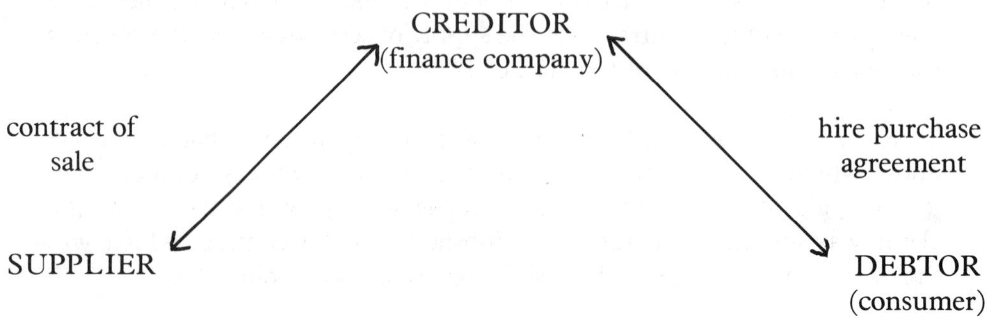

The supplier will have in his possession a stock of hire purchase forms belonging to the finance company with whom he usually deals. A customer wishing to take goods on credit will be asked to complete one of these forms and thus make a contractual offer to the finance company to take the goods on hire purchase. The supplier will complete a different form which will constitute a contractual offer to sell the goods to the finance company for cash. The supplier will forward both these offers to the finance company which will either accept or reject them both. If accepted, the supplier will be paid immediately by the finance company. The finance company becomes the owner of the goods and the customer will be bound by a contract of hire purchase with the finance company. Usually the customer will take possession of the goods from the supplier at this stage.

It would appear at first sight that there is no contract between the customer and the supplier where the finance company is involved in a credit transaction. If this were so, difficulties could arise for the customer, if, for example, he wished to sue the supplier for making false statements about the goods. The customer cannot at common law (though the position is different under the 1974 Act) rescind the contract with the finance company on the grounds that the supplier made a misrepresentation to him. However, the common law has recognised the existence of a contract between the customer and the supplier in these circumstances. The customer may sue the supplier for breach of this secondary or collateral contract.

> In *Andrews v. Hopkinson (1956)* the defendant car dealer showed a second hand car to the plaintiff and told him "it's a good little bus. I would stake my life on it". As a result the plaintiff entered into a hire purchase contract with a finance company. Soon afterwards he was injured in a collision caused by a failure of the car steering mechanism. It was held that the defendant was liable in damages to the plaintiff for breach of a collateral contract between them. The court was satisfied that each of the parties had given consideration to support the contract. On the part of the defendant, this was his statement, which amounted to a promise that the car was in good condition and reasonably fit for use. On the part of the plaintiff, his entry into the contract with the finance company was the consideration. It had been of direct benefit to the defendant as he was able to the sell the car to the finance company as a result.

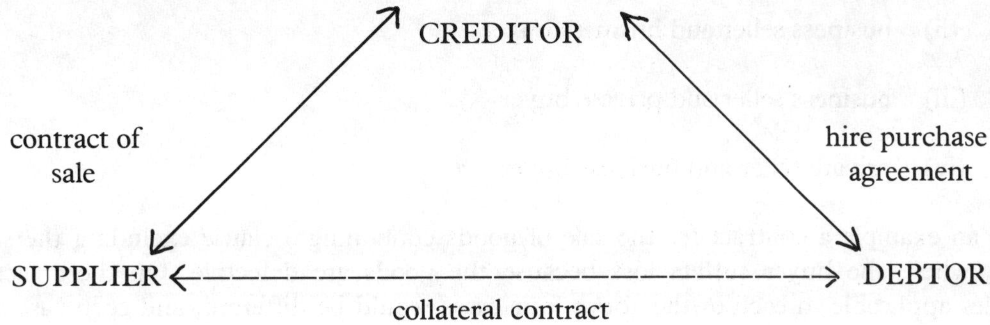

As we shall see later, where the supplier and creditor have a business connection, the debtor will be able to sue the creditor as well as the supplier in these circumstances.

(b) **Credit Sale and Conditional Sale Agreements**

Credit sale and conditional sale agreements are credit transactions under which the price of goods is payable by instalments. They will often be financed by a finance company in exactly the same way as hire purchase agreements.

At common law the credit sale agreement is broadly similar to the conditional sale agreement. Each is a contract for the sale of goods under which the buyer commits himself at the outset to the purchase. Theoretically, this is not the case with a hire purchase agreement. Here the customer has an option to buy but is not legally bound to exercise that option.

The main difference at common law between credit sale and conditional sale agreements is that:

(i) in a credit sale agreement ownership of the goods is transferred to the buyer as soon as the contract is made, whereas

(ii) in a conditional sale agreement ownership of the goods is not transferred to the buyer until some condition (usually the payment of the final instalment) is met.

While the instalments are being paid, the buyer is the owner of goods under a credit sale agreement; while the seller is the owner of goods under a conditional sale agreement. In this important respect a conditional sale agreement is similar to a hire purchase agreement. This is why many of the statutory rights of a consumer under a hire purchase agreement (such as the right of termination and the protected goods provisions, examined later), also apply to a conditional sale agreement. These rights do not arise in relation to credit sale agreement.

INTER-BUSINESS CONTRACTING AND CONSUMER CONTRACTING

The rights of the business customer and the degree of consumer protection available to him will vary considerably depending upon whether one or both of the parties are entering into the contract in the course of their business. Generally a greater degree of legal protection is available to a private individual than to a business. It is possible to envisage four different situations:

(i) private seller and private buyer

(ii) business seller and business buyer

(iii) business seller and private buyer

(iv) private seller and business buyer

Take as an example a contract for the sale of goods containing a clause excluding the seller's liability, where the buyer suffers loss because the goods are defective. On these facts the legal rules applicable in each of the above four cases would be different, and each case would not have the same outcome. It is important then to be able to distinguish between a situation where someone is acting in the course of a trade or business on one hand, or dealing as a consumer on the other.

DEALING AS A CONSUMER

In a broad sense anyone to whom goods or services are supplied can be regarded as a consumer and, as we shall see later, the law gives protection to all consumers. However, the protection available is greater in the case of the private consumer. The Fair Trading Act 1973 defines a private consumer in s.137 as:

> "the person to or for whom goods or services are, or are sought to be, supplied in the course of a business carried on by the supplier, and who does not receive or seek to receive the goods or services in the course of a business carried on by him".

The Unfair Contract Terms Act 1977 also provides a statutory definition of a private consumer. The Act states in s.12 that:

> "a party to a contract as a consumer in relation to another party if:
>
> (a) he neither makes the contract in the course of a business nor holds himself out as doing so; and
>
> (b) the other party does make the contract in the course of a business; and
>
> (c) where the contract involves the supply of goods, the goods are of a type ordinarily supplied for private use or consumption".

Three aspects of the transaction must be examined in order to see whether the buyer deals as a consumer: the buyer, the seller and the goods themselves. If the buyer buys for his business or from a private seller or if the goods are of a type which would not usually be purchased for private use then the buyer cannot deal as a consumer. The courts have been prepared to give a fairly wide interpretation of s.12:

> In *Peter Symmonds & Co. v. Cook (1981)* the plaintiffs were partners in a firm of surveyors and they bought a secondhand Rolls Royce in the partnership name with partnership money. The car was intended for use by one of the partners only. The High Court held that the plaintiffs were dealing as consumers in the purchase of the car even though it was to be used partly for business purposes.

The strained interpretation which the Judge placed upon the words of s.12 in this case demonstrates how far the courts are prepared to go in order to prevent unfairness where there is an inequality of bargaining strength and expertise between the parties to the contract.

Where the contract is made at auction or by competitive tender, the customer can never be regarded as dealing as a consumer for the purposes of the Unfair Contract Terms Act.

SUPPLYING IN THE COURSE OF A TRADE OR BUSINESS

Many of the legal rules which govern consumer protection apply only where goods or services are supplied in the course of a trade or business. There is no generally applicable precise definition of the expression "business", although there are a number of decided cases which give some guidance.

> In *Havering London Borough v. Stevenson (1970)* a car hire firm regularly sold its cars after a period of use in the business. A sale in these circumstances was held to be in the course of its trade or business as a car hire firm.
>
> On the other hand, in *Davies v. Sumner (1984)* the defendant was a self employed courier, who had a contract with a T.V. company to transport films and video tapes. He purchased a new car in June 1980, and travelled 118,000 miles in it before trading it in for another in July 1981. The mileometer had gone around the clock, and showed only 18,000 miles. The defendant did not disclose the true mileage, and was later charged with having applied a false trade description "in the course of a trade or business". The House of Lords held that he was not guilty, as this was a one-off sale which could not be regarded as an integral part of his business.
>
> In *Blakemore v. Bellamy (1983)* the defendant's spare time activity of buying, refurbishing and selling cars was held to be a hobby rather than a business. This was so even though he had sold eight different cars over a period of fifteen months and he had not driven them all himself or had them insured.

Business sellers may sometimes try to masquerade as private sellers for example by advertising in the small ad's in a newspaper. The purchaser may be misled by this and think that his legal remedies are limited because he has purchased from a private seller. In order to prevent such disguised business sales the Business Advertisements (Disclosure) Order 1977 was made under Section 22 of The Fair Trading Act 1973. Under this regulation it is a criminal offence for a trader or a businessman to advertise goods for sale without making it reasonably clear that the goods are being sold in the course of a business.

Where goods are sold by an agent in the course of his business for a private seller, the sale will be treated, for the purposes of the implied terms in s.14 of the Sale of Goods Act 1979, as a sale by a seller acting in the course of a business unless:

(a) the buyer knows that he is purchasing from a private seller, or

(b) reasonable steps are taken to bring it to his attention before the contract is made.

This could apply, for example, where goods are sold by a private seller at a public auction.

INTER-BUSINESS CONTRACTING

Where a contract is made between a business seller and a business buyer, the parties are allowed greater freedom of contract to agree their respective obligations by negotiation. The courts will be reluctant to interfere with the terms of a bargain made between contracting parties of equal bargaining power. Business consumers should be better placed in terms of their experience knowledge and bargaining power to look after their own interests than the private consumer would be. If there is unequal bargaining power, however, the courts may be prepared to step in and protect the weaker party to the transaction by invalidating part of the agreement under the Unfair Contract Terms Act 1977.

STANDARD FORM CONTRACTS

Standard form contracts covering many different types of transaction are in common use in the business world today. Standard form contracts are so called because the express terms of the contract are set out in a standard form or document which is used whenever an organisation enters into a contract with a customer. They are sometimes referred to as "contracts of adhesion" because in practice one of the parties is obliged to adhere to terms dictated by the other.

The advantages for a business organisation of using standard form contracts are that they are administratively convenient as each customer is contracting on the same terms, and more importantly that the terms are fixed in advance by the organisation. The terms will be drafted in such a way as to weight the commercial advantage in favour of the organisation and maximise any legal protection available to it.

The danger of this type of economic oppression was pointed out by Lord Diplock in *Schroeder Music Publishing Co. Ltd. v. Macauley (1974)* when he stated:

> "The terms of this kind of standard form of contract have not been the subject of negotiation between the parties to it, or approved by any organisation representing the interests of the weaker party. They have been dictated by that party whose bargaining power, either exercised alone, or in conjunction with others providing similar goods or services, enables him to say: "If you want these goods or services at all, these are the only terms on which they are available. Take it or leave it".

As we shall see, some of the more obvious abuses which were present at one time in this type of contract are now controlled by legislation; for example extortionate credit bargains by the Consumer Credit Act 1974, and exclusion or limitation of liability by the Unfair Contract Terms Act 1977.

Where parties of relatively equal bargaining strength deal with each other over a long period of time, standard form agreements may evolve by negotiation. Far from being oppressive, this type of standard form contract provides a framework of certainty for business transactions and an appropriate division of rights and responsibilities between the parties. It may take into account possible occurrences and contingencies. The apportionment of risks under it can be linked with the insurance arrangements of the parties. Such an agreement will be designed to avoid the risk of litigation between the parties, for example by use of arbitration and liquidated damages clauses.

A standard form contract for the sale of goods is set out in figure 5.2.

Fig. 5.2 Standard Form Contract for the Sale of Goods

1(a) THIS AGREEMENT is made the day of 19

BETWEEN of

(referred to in this agreement as "the seller") and

of

(referred to in this agreement as "the buyer")

WHEREBY IT IS AGREED that the seller shall sell and the buyer shall purchase the goods described in condition 2 in accordance with the terms of this contract.

(b) No amendments or modifications to these conditions and, in particular, no terms or conditions of purchase of the buyer shall form part of the contract or be binding upon the seller unless expressly agreed to in writing and signed by the seller.

2(a) Description of goods:

(b) The description of the goods in condition 2(a) above is believed to be correct as to weights, dimensions, capacity, composition, performance and otherwise. Any error, ommission or mis-statement therein (whether or not it materially affects the description of the goods) shall not annul the sale nor entitle the buyer to be discharged from the contract or to claim any compensation in consequence thereof. Provided that nothing in this condition shall oblige the buyer to accept any goods which differ substantially in any of the above-mentioned respects from the goods agreed to be sold if the buyer would be prejudiced by reason of such difference. In that event the buyer shall be entitled to rescind the contract and to claim repayment of the price, but the seller shall incur no further liability in respect thereof.

3(a) In addition to the price of the goods, the buyer shall pay

(i) VAT or other taxes payable in respect of the goods;

(ii) the cost of insurance under condition 8; and

(iii) the cost of delivery under condition 4.

(b) The price of the goods is :

add V.A.T. :

insurance :

delivery :

total amount due :

(c) Where the date of delivery specified in condition 4 is more than 6 months from the date of this agreement, the seller reserves the right to increase the price of the goods in proportion to any increase in costs to the seller of materials labour and other inputs between the date of this contract and the date of delivery.

(d) The buyer will pay the price of the goods and any other sums due to the seller under this contract within 30 days of the date of delivery. In the event of a failure to make payment by the due date interest at the rate of 10% per annum shall be payable on any sums outstanding.

4(a) The delivery date is   . This date is given by way of an estimate only and the seller shall not be liable for failure to deliver on time.

(b) Unless the seller is notified otherwise in writing at least 7 days before the delivery date, the seller shall deliver the goods to the buyer's place of business. The cost of transportation and insurance up to the time of actual delivery will be paid by the buyer in accordance with condition 3.

(c) The seller shall be entitled at its sole discretion to make partial deliveries or deliveries by instalments.

(d) Deviations in quantity of the goods delivered (representing no more than 10% by value) from that stated in condition 2 shall not give the buyer any right to reject the goods or to claim damages. The buyer shall be obliged to accept and pay at the contract rate for the quantity of goods delivered.

5(a) The seller reserves the right to modify the specification or design of the goods in whole or in part without prior notification to the buyer. The buyer shall accept such modified goods in performance of the contract.

(b) The buyer shall be deemed to have accepted the goods unless within 14 days of delivery written notice is received by the seller to the contrary.

6(a) The property in the goods shall remain with the seller until the seller has received payment in full for the goods and all other sums owing to the seller on whatever grounds.

(b) If the buyer sells the goods prior to making payment in full for them, the rights of the seller under this condition shall attach to the proceeds of sale or to the claim for such proceeds. The buyer shall, if required to do so by the seller, formally assign any such rights.

(c) For so long as the property in goods remains with the seller, the buyer shall store the goods separately so that they may readily be identified as the property of the seller. The seller shall during this time have the right to retake possession of the goods. For this purpose the buyer hereby irrevocably authorises the seller or his agents to enter upon any premises occupied by the buyer.

(d) The seller may maintain an action for the price notwithstanding that property in the goods may not have passed to the buyer.

7. The goods shall be at the risk of the buyer in all respects from the date of this contract or, if later, the date of manufacture by the seller.

8. Unless the buyer notifies the seller in writing to the contrary, the seller shall at the expense of the buyer insure the goods to the full replacement value thereof until the time of delivery.

9(a) In the event that the goods supplied to the buyer fail to comply with the terms of this contract, or prove to be defective, the liability of the seller is limited to the replacement of the goods or, at the seller's option, the refund of all payments made by the buyers in respect of those goods.

(b) Except as otherwise provided in condition 9(a), the seller shall be under no liability of whatsoever kind whether or not due to the negligence or wilful default of the seller or its servants or agents arising out of or in connection with any breach of the seller's obligations under this contract. All conditions, warranties or other terms, express or implied, statutory or otherwise, are hereby expressly excluded.

(c) Nothing in this condition shall exclude or restrict any liability of the seller for death or personal injury resulting from the negligence of the seller or its servants or agents.

(d) If it should be held in relation to any claim that the preceding provisions of this paragraph are ineffective, the buyer shall not be entitled to reject the goods and any damages recovered by the buyer shall be limited to the reasonable cost of remedying the breach of contract provided that the seller shall first be afforded the opportunity of itself carrying out such remedial work.

(e) Nothing in this condition shall exclude or restrict any liability of the seller for breach of its implied undertakings as to title; and, where the buyer deals as a consumer, any liability of the seller for breach of its implied undertakings as to description, quality, fitness for purpose, or correspondence with sample.

(f) In the case of transactions covered by paragraphs (4) and (5) of the Consumer Transactions (Restrictions on Statements) Order 1976 the provisions of this clause shall not affect the statutory rights of the consumer.

10. The seller shall not be liable for non-performance in whole or in part of its obligations under this contract due to causes beyond the control either of the seller or of the seller's suppliers including any Act of God, fire, flood, tempest, act of state, war, civil commotion, embargo, accident, plant breakdown, hinderence in or prevention from obtaining any raw materials or other supplies, interference by labour disputes, inability to obtain adequate labour, manufacturing facilities or energy, or any other like cause. If any such event continues for a period of more than 6 weeks, the seller may cancel this contract or vary condition 4(a) hereof by notice in writing to the buyer without liability on the part of the seller.

11(a) The seller shall have the right to terminate this contract by notice in writing in the event of the buyer's insolvency and the buyer shall indemnify the seller against all losses and damage suffered by reason of such termination.

(b) Termination of the contract under this condition shall not affect the accrued rights of the parties arising in any way out of the contract as at the date of termination.

(c) In the event of termination under this condition the seller shall have the right to enter any business premises occupied by the buyer and recover any goods which are the seller's property.

12. In the event of the cancellation of this contract by the buyer for whatever reason, the buyer agrees to pay 20% of the purchase price to the seller by way of liquidated damages.

13. The benefit of this contract shall not be assigned or transferred by the buyer without the prior written consent of the seller. The seller shall have the right to assign to any of its associated companies all of the rights, powers, duties and obligations under this contract without the consent of the buyer. In the event of any such assignment by the seller references in this contract to the seller shall be deemed to be references to any company taking under the assignment.

14. If any difference shall arise between the seller and the buyer upon the meaning of any part of this contract or the rights and liabilities of the parties hereto, the same shall be referred to the arbitration of two persons (one named by each party) or their umpire in accordance with the provisions of the Arbitration Act 1950 or any amending or substituted legislation for the time being in force.

SIGNED for and on behalf)
)
of the SELLER:)

SIGNED for and on behalf)
)
of the BUYER:)

The terms of the standard form contract in figure 5.2 were drawn up by the seller, and it is clear that most of its contents are weighted in his favour. We shall now examine selected clauses of the agreement in order to see what they are attempting to achieve, and comment on any legal rules which may affect their validity.

Clause 1(b) attempts to exclude any conflicting terms of business on which the buyer usually trades, or any other variation of the terms set out in the seller's standard form. As we noted in Chapter 3, where there is a battle of forms like the one which occurred in *Butler Machine Tool Co Ltd v. Ex-Cell-O Corporation Ltd (1979)*, the rules of offer and acceptance will determine whether clause 1(b) is actually effective.

Clause 2(b) is an attempt to deal with the problem posed by s.13 of the Sale of Goods Act 1979, which provides that compliance with description is a condition of the contract. Under s.13 anything less than strict compliance with the contract description gives the buyer the right to reject the goods and rescind the contract, even if he suffers no loss as a result. This happened for example, in *Re Moore & Landauer (1921)* and *Arcos v. Ronaasen (1933)*. Clause 2(b) is a limitation of liability and will be subject to the controls in s.6 of the Unfair Contract Terms Act 1977.

Clause 3(c) is a price variation clause. This type of clause is particularly significant when the rate of inflation is high. It allows the seller to pass on to the buyer any increase in costs between the date of the contract and the date of delivery. Increases cannot be passed on under clause 3(c) if delivery takes place within six months of the making of the contract. Obviously the longer the period of time between contract and delivery, the more the price will increase. A buyer faced with this type of term will usually try to negotiate an upper limit on any price increase if he cannot persuade the seller to withdraw it altogether.

Clause 3(d) provides for the payment of interest in the event of late payment of sums due to the seller from the buyer. This is an attempt by the seller to ensure a steady cash flow in his business. In the absence of a contractual right to interest:

(i) no interest will be payable by the buyer in respect of late payments, unless the seller actually issues legal proceedings against him to recover the debt; and

(ii) the buyer can avoid having to pay interest by paying the money at any time before legal proceedings are issued.

Clause 4(a) makes provision for the date of delivery. Under a commercial contract, the agreed delivery date is usually a condition rather than a warranty, unless the parties agree otherwise. This was established in the case *Hartley v. Hymans (1920)*. Under clause 4(a) the delivery date in any contract made by reference to these standard terms is a warranty only. The clause goes even further, however, and excludes the liability of the seller for failure to deliver on time. This exclusion of liability will be covered by s.3 of the Unfair Contract Terms Act 1977.

Clause 4(b) fixed the place of delivery. Where no provision is made for this in a contract, s.29 of the Sale of Goods Act 1979 provides that the place of delivery is the seller's place of business if he has one, and if not, his residence; except that, if the contract is for the sale of specific goods, which to the knowledge of the parties when the contract is made are in some other place, then that place is the place of delivery.

Clause 4(d) excludes the seller's laibility for delivery of the wrong quantity if the amount delivered is within 10% of the amount ordered, and obliges the buyer to take and pay for the quantity actually delivered. Without this clause, and clause 2(b) with which it overlaps, the buyer would be entitled, under s.30 of the Sale of Goods Act 1979, to choose, in the event of delivery of the wrong quantity, between:

(i) rejecting all of the goods delivered; or

(ii) rejecting any excess over the contractual quantity; or

(iii) accepting all of the goods delivered and paying for them at the contract rate.

Clause 5(b) limits the time during which the buyer can rescind the contract by rejecting the goods for breach of condition. Once a buyer has accepted goods, as we saw in the previous chapter, he is entitled to sue for damages only in the event of a breach of condition by the seller. Acceptance denies him the right of rescission.

Clause 6 is a retention of title clause. This type of clause is examined later in this chapter.

Clause 7 transfers risk to the buyer on the making of the contract. The transfer of risk is examined later in this chapter, and at this stage we need only comment that the buyer should insure the goods once risk is transferred to him: a matter which is provided for in clause 8.

Clause 9 is an elaborate limitation of liability clause designed to minimise the seller's liability for breach of contract. As such it is covered by s.3 and s.6 of the Unfair Contract Terms Act 1977. The purpose of each subclause should become clear when you have studied the text on exclusion clauses and the Unfair Contract Terms Act 1977 later in this chapter.

Clause 10 is a force majeure clause which aims to make provision for events which otherwise could frustrate the contract.

Clause 12 is a liquidated damages clause. This type of clause aims to quantify the amount recoverable by one of the contracting parties where the other is in breach of contract. At common law a liquidated damages clause is valid if it represents a genuine pre-estimate of the amount of money which would be lost in the event of a breach of contract. If, however, it provides for a payment which is out of proportion to the actual losses which are likely, the clause will be void as a penalty. In *Dunlop Pneumatic Tyre Co v. New Garage Motor Co (1915)*, Lord Dunedin stated that a liquidated damages clause:

> "will be held to be a penalty if the sum stipulated for is extravagant and unconscionable in amount in comparison with the greatest loss that could conceivably be proved to have followed from the breach."

Where the clause is held to be a penalty it is void and the innocent party can sue only for the loss actually sustained. On the other hand if the clause is valid and not a penalty, he can sue for the stipulated sum only, whether his actual loss is greater or smaller.

Clause 13 restricts the rights of the buyer to transfer the benefit of the contract. As we shall see in Chapter 8 the buyer's rights under the contract are a form of intangible business property (a chose in action) which can be sold or transferred to another person. Such a transfer would have to comply with the rules in s.136 of the Law of Property Act 1925, examined in Chapter 8.

Clause 14 is an arbitration clause. It enables either party to refer any dispute arising from the contract to arbitration. The process of arbitration is examined in Chapter 9, which also gives an assessment of the advantages and disadvantages of arbitration as compared to legal action in the courts.

TERMS IMPLIED BY STATUTE

In Chapter 4 we noted that obligations may arise under a contract in two different ways. First because the law imposes them, for example by Act of Parliament, and second because the parties expressly agree to them. In a contract for the sale or supply of goods the law imposes obligations on the supplier by the legal mechanism of implied terms in the contract of supply. These statutory implied terms operate as if the seller had said to the buyer "I promise you that . . .". Most of these terms are conditions, which, if broken, will give rise to the right to repudiate the contract and to damages (see Chapter 4). There are a small number of implied warranties also. The buyer's remedy in the event of a breach of warranty is damages.

The implied terms contained in Sections 12 to 15 of the Sale of Goods Act 1979 automatically become part of any contract for the sale of goods. These terms have been used as a model for incorporation by statute into all other contracts involving the supply of goods. Sections 8 to 11 of the Supply of Goods (Implied Terms) Act 1973 imply virtually identical terms in contracts of hire purchase. Sections 2 to 5 of the Supply of Goods and Services Act 1982 imply equivalent provisions into contracts for the transfer of goods, a term which includes contracts of barter and the supply of goods element of contracts for work done and materials supplied. Sections 7 to 10 of the 1982 Act also imply equivalent provisions into contracts for the hire of goods.

For convenience we shall refer to the 1979 Act for the purpose of examining the detailed content of the implied terms below.

IMPLIED TERMS RELATING TO TITLE (S12 OF THE 1979 ACT; S8, 1973 ACT; S2 and S7, 1982 ACT)

There is an implied condition that the seller has the right to sell the goods. If this is broken, for example because the goods belong to someone else, the buyer will be able to repudiate the contract and recover in full the price he paid.

> In *Rowland v. Divall (1923)* three months after buying a motor car the purchaser discovered that it had been stolen before it came into the seller's possession. The seller therefore had no right to sell it. The purchaser returned the car to its original owner and sued the seller under s.12. It was held that he was entitled to the return of the price because he had suffered a "total failure of consideration". The fact that the buyer had used the car for over three months did not affect his right to recover the full purchase price.

Where the seller is the true owner of the goods he may nevertheless have no right to sell them if for example they infringe intellectual property rights held by another person.

> In *Niblett v. Confectioners Materials Co. (1921)* the purchaser of a quantity of tins of preserved milk could not resell them without infringing the Nestle Company Trade Mark. This infringement arose because the labels placed on tins by the manufacturer bore the name "Nissly Brand". The seller was held to be in breach of s.12.

Under s.12 there is also an implied warranty that the goods are free from any potential claims by any third parties which had not been disclosed to the buyer. There is also an implied warranty that the buyer will enjoy quiet possession of the goods.

In *Microbeads v. Vinhurst Road Markings (1975)* the seller sold road marking machines to the buyer. After the sale a third party obtained a patent on the machine. The continued use of the machine by the buyer was then in breach of the third party's patent rights. The buyer sued the seller under s.12 claiming that he was in breach of the implied condition that he had the right to sell, and of the implied warranty that the buyer would enjoy quiet possession. The Court of Appeal held that there was no breach of condition. At the time of the sale there was no infringement of the patent and therefore the seller had the right to sell. However, the sellers were liable in damages for breach of the warranty that the buyer would enjoy quiet possession of the goods.

IMPLIED TERMS RELATING TO DESCRIPTION (S13 OF THE 1979 ACT; S9, 1973 ACT; S3 and S8, 1982 ACT)

Where there is a contract for the sale of goods by description there is an implied condition that the goods will correspond with the description. Whenever the buyer has not seen the goods before the contract is made the sale is obviously a sale by description. Also, if goods are packaged, for example food inside a tin or cardboard box, there is a sale by description. The buyer will only be able to see the goods after he has purchased them and opened the package. The vast majority of sales will be made by description. The 1979 Act provides in s.13(3) that a sale of goods is not prevented from being a sale by description by reason only that the goods are selected by the buyer after being exposed for sale, for example in a self-service store. The description can extend to such things as weight, size, quantity, composition and age.

In *Dick Bentley Productions Limited v. Harold Smith Motors Limited (1965)* a car dealer sold a secondhand car with a recorded mileage of 30,000. In fact the true mileage was nearer 100,000. The seller was held liable for a breach of s.13.

Similar conduct today could make the seller criminally liable under the Trade Descriptions Act 1968 (considered later in this chapter). One significant difference between the Sale of Goods Act and the Trade Descriptions Act is that the latter only applies where the sale is made in the course of a trade or business. Section 13 applies both to private and business sales.

In *Beale v. Taylor (1967)* the buyer purchased a car advertised as a 1961 Herald Convertible having had a trial run in it as a passenger. The buyer soon found the car to be unsatisfactory. On an examination by a garage it was discovered that the car had been made up of halves of two different cars. The rear portion was part of a 1961 Triumph Herald 1200 model while the front was part of an earlier 948 model. The two portions had been welded together unsatisfactorily into one structure, and the vehicle was unroadworthy and unsafe. The Court of Appeal held that the seller had broken the promise implied into the contract by s.13 and was liable in damages to the buyer.

A seller will be in breach of s.13 if he does not comply strictly with the contract description.

In *Arcos Ltd. v. E.A. Ronaasen & Son (1933)* the buyer agreed to purchase a quantity of wooden staves, half an inch thick, for making cement barrels. When they were delivered only 5% of them were exactly half an inch and the vast majority were nine sixteenths of an inch in thickness. An arbitrator found that the staves were still reasonably fit for making cement barrels. The House of Lords held that the buyers were entitled to reject the goods because the seller had not strictly complied with the contract description. Lord Atkin observed that:

> "a ton does not mean about a ton, or a yard about a yard. Still less when you descend to minute measurements does half an inch mean about half an inch. If the seller wants a margin he must and in my experience does stipulate for it".

Very small deviations from the contractual specification can however be disregarded for example where a delivery of 250 gallons of oil is 2 pints short.

Where the seller does not comply with the contract description the buyer is entitled to reject the goods even though he suffers no damage.

> In *Re: Moore & Co. Ltd. and Landauer & Co. (1921)* the buyer purchased a quantity of canned fruit. The contract stipulated that each case should contain thirty tins but on delivery about half the total quantity of tins were packed in cases of twenty four. The court held that the buyer was entitled to reject the goods, even though there was no evidence that the buyer would suffer any loss.

Buyers should beware when using specialised trade terms to purchase goods.

> The buyer in *Grenfell v. E.D. Meyrovitz (1931)* was held to have no remedy under s.13 when a quantity of glass he had purchased under the description "safety glass" proved unsuitable for use in goggles because it splintered under certain circumstances. The glass conformed with the technical meaning of safety glass.

> In *Peter Darlington Partners Limited v. Gosho Limited (1964)* the seller supplied canary seed to the buyer. The seed was sold on a "pure basis". In fact it was only 98% pure. This was the highest quality of purety possible, and the Court rejected the buyer's claim that the seller was in breach of s.13.

IMPLIED TERMS RELATING TO QUALITY AND FITNESS FOR PURPOSE (S14 OF THE 1979 ACT; S10, 1973 ACT; S4 AND S9, 1982 ACT)

S14(2) of the 1979 Act provides that:

> "Where the seller sells goods in the course of a business there is an implied condition that the goods supplied under the contract are of merchantable quality, except that there is no such condition:
>
> (a) as regards defects specifically drawn to the buyer's attention before the contract is made; or
>
> (b) if the buyer examines the goods before the contract is made, as regards defects which that examination ought to reveal".

The expression merchantable quality is defined in s.14(6) which provides that:

> "Goods of any kind are of merchantable quality if they are as fit for the purpose or purposes for which goods of that kind are commonly bought as it is reasonable to expect

having regard to any description applied to them, the price (if relevant) and all other relevant circumstances".

There are a number of important features of merchantable quality which should be noted:

(i) the seller must be a business seller. The implied condition does not apply to private sales;

(ii) the seller may be anyone in the chain of distribution, such as a manufacturer, wholesaler or retailer;

(iii) the condition does not apply where a defect has been drawn to the buyer's attention prior to the sale, or where the buyer has examined the goods before buying them and ought to have discovered the defect;

(iv) in order to comply with this section, some system of quality control will need to be introduced. This is particularly so where the seller is also the manufacturer;

(v) liability under the section is strict:

In *Frost v. Aylesbury Dairies Limited (1905)* the dairy supplied milk contaminated with typhoid germs. The dairy was held liable despite establishing that it had used all reasonable care to prevent such contamination.

Under the definition of merchantable quality, the standard expected of goods is a flexible one. They must be able to do the job they have been bought for, but only to the extent that this is consistent with:

(i) price

A person could not reasonably expect the same standard of quality and durability from a pair of shoes costing £5.00 as a pair costing £45.00, although if the shoes costing £5.00 had been reduced from £45.00 in a sale, the price would probably not be relevant in determining the standard of quality; and

(ii) description

Goods described as "shop soiled", "manufacturer's rejects", "seconds" or as "second hand" cannot be expected to demonstrate the quality of a new or perfect product.

In *Bartlett v. Sydney Marcus Limited (1965)* the seller, who was a car dealer, warned the buyer that a secondhand car had a defective clutch. The buyer was given the choice of purchasing it for £550 as it was, or £575 after the seller had repaired it. The buyer opted to take the car as it was. The repairs cost more than the buyer expected. He sued the seller alleging that, for this reason, the car was not of merchantable quality. The Court of Appeal held that the seller was not liable as there was no breach of the implied term.

In *Crowther v. Shannon Motor Company (1975)* it was held that a secondhand car which needed a replacement engine after three weeks was not of merchantable quality. The car had been described by the seller as being in excellent condition.

The requirement of merchantable quality extends not only to the goods themselves but also to their packaging and any instructions supplied with them.

> In *Wormell v. RHM Agriculture (East) Ltd. (1986)* the plaintiff was a farmer who purchased a chemical spray from the defendant in order to kill wild oats. The instructions provided with the spray indicated that its use outside a certain period carried the risk of injury to the crop. The plaintiff was aware of the warning and decided to take that risk. In fact, because of the late application, the spray was totally ineffective. The plaintiff claimed damages for the costs of the spray and the wasted labour in applying it. The seller was held liable because the Court found that the instructions were misleading and as a result the goods were not of merchantable quality or fit for the purpose for which they were supplied.

The wording of s.14(2) makes it clear that the obligation applies to all goods which are supplied under the contract.

> In *Geddling v. Marsh (1920)* mineral water was sold in bottles which were to remain the property of the manufacturer. The buyer was injured when a defective bottle burst. It was held that he was entitled to damages under s.14 even though the bottles were loaned rather than sold to him under the terms of the contract.

This rule applies even if the item which causes the harm was mistakenly supplied with the contract goods:

> In *Wilson v. Rickett, Cockerell and Co. Ltd. (1954)* a delivery of "Coalite" included a detonator from the mine, which exploded when it was put onto a household fire. The Court of Appeal held that the sellers were liable for a breach of s.14(2).

Goods may be unmerchantable even if they can easily be put right:

> In *Grant v. Australian Knitting Mills Ltd (1936)* the buyer purchased underpants which contained a chemical. This caused dermatitis, a skin disease, when the buyer wore them. The chemical would have been removed if the buyer had washed them before he wore them. It was held that the goods were not of merchantable quality, and the seller was liable.

The seller will not be liable, however, if the defect in the goods is caused by the way in which the buyer treats them.

> In *Heil v. Hedges (1951)* the buyer was infected with tapeworms after eating a pork chop which had been undercooked. It was held that the seller was not liable because the meat would have been quite safe if it had been properly cooked.

It appears that a seller will not be liable under this section solely because there are no spare parts available to service the goods which he has supplied.

> In *L. Gent v. Eastman Machine Co. Ltd. (1985)* the plaintiff purchased a knitting machine from the defendant. Not long afterwards spare parts were required and it took four months for the spares to be supplied. It was held that the knitting machine was not rendered unmerchantable by the seller's failure to be able to supply spare parts within a reasonable time.

In 1983 the Law Commission published a working paper, no. 85, on The Sale and Supply of Goods, followed by a Report (Cm 137) in 1987. This recommended a clarification of the seller's obligations in relation to the quality of goods supplied. The phrase 'merchantable quality' should be replaced with 'acceptable quality'. Goods would be of 'acceptable quality' if they were to be of a standard that a reasonable person would regard as acceptable, taking account of any description applied to them, the price, and all other relevant circumstances. Relevant circumstances would extend beyond the question of fitness of the goods for their common purposes, and include matters such as the appearance of the goods, their finish, suitability for immediate use, freedom from minor defects, safety, and durability. It is likely that legislation will incorporate the recommendations of the Law Commission eventually but, in the meantime, the Court of Appeal appears to have taken a lead in the same direction.

> In *Rogers v. Parish (Scarbrough) Limited (1987)* the plaintiff bought a new Range Rover from the defendant's garage. Although it was driveable and roadworthy the car had a number of defects in its engine, gearbox, oil seals and bodywork. The defendant argued that the car was of merchantable quality within the definition in s.14(6) as it could be driven in safety on a road and therefore was "fit for the purpose for which goods of that kind are commonly bought". The Court of Appeal rejected the defendant's argument on the grounds that it was based upon too narrow an interpretation of s.14(6). Mustill L.J., declared that:
>
> > "the purpose for which goods of that kind are commonly bought would include not merely the purpose of driving the vehicle from one place to another but of doing so with the appropriate degree of comfort, ease of handling, reliability and pride in the vehicle's outward and interior appearance".

Where the buyer requires the goods for a special or unusual purpose, the seller may be liable for a breach of s.14(3) if the goods are not fit for that purpose. Under s.14(3):

> "Where the seller sells goods in the course of a business and the buyer, expressly or by implication, makes known . . . to the seller . . . any particular purpose for which the goods are being bought, there is an implied condition that the goods supplied under the contract are reasonably fit for that purpose, whether or not that is a purpose for which such goods are commonly supplied, except where the circumstances show that the buyer does not rely, or that it is unreasonable for him to rely, on the skill or judgment of the seller".

Consumers sometimes place reliance on the expertise of the seller. For example when a customer goes into a shop and asks whether the shop has something that will perform a particular task, say fixing a broken ornament or removing stains from a carpet. A business may describe its accounting procedures to a supplier of office equipment, relying on the supplier to provide a suitable system to cope with these procedures. In these cases the seller will be liable under s.14(3) if the goods, even though of merchantable quality, do not fulfill the purpose for which the buyer requires them.

> In *Cammell Laird & Co. Ltd. v. Manganese Bronze & Brass Co. Ltd. (1934)* the buyers supplied the sellers with a specification for ships' propellers which they were to manufacture for the buyers. Reliance was placed upon the sellers regarding matters outside the specification, including the thickness of metal to be used. The propellers were found on delivery to be too thin. The buyer's action was successful on the ground that the unfitness concerned a matter on which the buyers had relied upon the seller's skill.

When the product only has one purpose the buyer will be held to have impliedly made known to the seller the purpose for which he wants the goods.

> In *Priest v. Last (1903)* the buyer was held to have made known impliedly to the seller the purpose for which he required a hot water bottle. The seller was liable under s.14(3) when the bottle burst after a few days injuring the plaintiff.

The seller will not be liable however, where the buyer does not tell him of any particular requirements.

> In *Griffiths v. Peter Conway Limited (1939)* the buyer, who had particularly sensitive skin, developed dermatitis as a result of wearing a coat which she bought from the defendant. The coat would not have had this effect on a normal person and the buyer had not told the seller about her sensitivity. It was held that the seller was not liable under s.14(3).

IMPLIED TERMS WHERE GOODS ARE SOLD BY SAMPLE (S15 OF THE 1979 ACT: S11, 1973 ACT; S5 AND S10, 1982 ACT)

Under s.15, where goods are sold according to a sample, there are implied conditions that:

(a) The bulk of the consignment will correspond with the sample in terms of quality;

(b) The buyer shall have a reasonable opportunity of comparing the bulk with the sample; and

(c) The goods shall be free from any defect rendering them unmerchantable which would not be apparent on a reasonable examination of the sample.

The function of a sample was described by Lord MacNaghten in *Drummond v. Van Ingen* (1887) when he stated:

> "The office of a sample is to present to the eye the real meaning and intention of the parties with regard to the subject matter of the contract which, owing to the imperfections of language, it may be difficult or impossible to express in words. The sample speaks for itself".

Many commercial and non-commercial transactions are made on the basis of samples, for example the purchase of a carpet or a made-to-measure suit by a consumer, or the purchase of raw materials by an industrial company.

CLAIMS BASED ON MORE THAN ONE GROUND

Where a person is injured by defective goods there may be a number of alternative grounds upon which he could sue. There is a considerable degree of overlap between s.14(2) and s.14(3), so that, for example the sellers in *Frost v. Aylesbury Dairies (1905)* and *Priest v. Last (1903)* were in breach of both implied conditions. The seller in *Beale v. Taylor (1967)* was found to be in breach of s.13, and would probably have been in breach of s.14 if he had sold the car in the course of a business. There is also a considerable overlap between the law of contract and the tort of negligence in this area. In *Grant v. Australian Knitting Mills (1935)* the retailer was liable because the goods were not of merchantable quality, and the manufacturer was liable in negligence.

In the next chapter a number of cases are examined in the field of product liability, for example *Lambert v. Lewis (1981)*, in which the injured party's claim is based both in negligence and in contract. Part 1 of the Consumer Protection Act 1987 gives additional remedies to persons who are injured by defective products. It is quite conceivable that an injured party would have a claim in contract, in negligence and under the 1987 Act. Figure 6.4 at the end of chapter 6 provides a comparison between these three alternatives. Of course the injured party can only recover damages once, but he may bring his claim under all of these headings by "pleading in the alternative". If he fails in one aspect of his claim, he can still recover damages if another succeeds.

The rule of privity of contract discussed in chapter 4 means that only the buyer can claim for breach of the implied terms. If this claim against the seller succeeds then liability can be passed down the line through the chain of distribution. The seller can sue his supplier for an indemnity based upon the supplier's breach of contract. He is in effect trying to drop out of the picture by saying "if I am liable then as my supplier you are liable on the same basis". This process, known as third party proceedings, continues until the manufacturer is sued. Only an effective exclusion of liability clause can break the chain of indemnity.

> In *Godley v. Perry (Burton & Sons Ltd., Third Party; Graham, Fourth Party) (1960)* a boy of six lost the sight of one eye when firing a catapult which he had bought for 6d from the defendant's shop. The catapult fractured below the point where the handle joined the fork. The evidence showed that it was made of cheap brittle polystyrene, indifferently moulded and containing internal voids. The retailer had purchased the catapult from a wholesaler who had purchased it from an importer. The importer had bought the goods from a manufacturer in Hong Kong. The plaintiff sued the defendant shopkeeper who issued third party proceedings against the wholesaler. The wholesaler in turn claimed against the importer. The court decided that the catapult was not of merchantable quality, and that the retailer was liable to the purchaser. Liability passed up the line so at the end of the day the importer (or his insurers) were left either to bear the loss or pursue the manufacturer in the Hong Kong courts.

IMPLIED TERMS IN CONTRACTS FOR THE SUPPLY OF SERVICES

The Supply of Goods and Services Act 1982 sets out terms which will be implied both into contracts for the supply of services and into contracts for work done and materials supplied. These terms will apply, for example, to contracts for dry cleaning, entertainment and professional services, home improvements and motor vehicle maintenance. The major areas of concern in relation to this type of contract were identified in a report of the National Consumer Council in 1981 entitled "Services Please". These concerns were quality of service, delay in performance and cost. They are all dealt with by the 1982 Act. The aim of this part of the 1982 Act is simply to codify the common law without changing it. The NCC believed that this was necessary for three reasons: certainty and clarity; ease of reference, and in order to focus attention on the existence of the obligations owed by those who supply services.

Implied duty to use reasonable care and skill

The 1982 Act in s.13 provides that:

> "In a contract for the supply of a service where the supplier is acting in the course of a business, there is an implied term that the supplier will carry out the service with reasonable care and skill".

Exemptions from the operation of this section have been made for company directors, who, as we have seen, have a duty to use such care as they would use in relation to their own personal affairs in performance of their duties as directors. A solicitor acting as an advocate before a court is also exempted from the section because of the rule that advocates cannot be made liable for professional negligence (see *Rondel v. Worsley* (1969) discussed in chapter 6). The section has no application where services are provided for a client by a barrister, because the barrister does not have a contract with his client. A number of the cases discussed in relation to professional negligence in the next chapter provide good illustrations of the application of s.13.

The section extends beyond professional services:

> In *Curtis v. Chemical Cleaning and Dyeing Company (1951)* the plaintiff took a wedding dress to the defendant dry cleaners for cleaning. When she came to collect the dress she found that it had been stained. It was held that the company were liable for the damage to the dress which had been caused by their failure to take care of it.
>
> In *Lawson and Lawson v. Supasink Limited (1984)* the plaintiffs employed the defendant company to design, supply and install a fitted kitchen at a price of £1,200. Plans were drawn up and agreed but the company did not follow them when installing the units. The plaintiffs complained about the standard of work before the installation was complete. After taking independent expert advice the plaintiffs demanded the return of their deposit and asked the defendants to remove the kitchen units. The defendants refused and the plaintiffs sued. The Judge found that the kitchen was installed in "a shocking and shoddy manner" and that the work was "beyond redemption". He awarded damages of £500 for inconvenience and loss of the use of the kitchen; damages of the difference between the cost of equivalent units and the contract price; and the return of the deposit. On appeal the defendants argued that they had substantially performed the contract and were therefore entitled to the contract price less the cost of remedying any defects. This was rejected by the Court of Appeal on the grounds that the standard of workmanship and design was so poor that the doctrine of substantial performance could not be applied, having regard to the large sums which would have to be spent to remedy the defects.

The contract in the Supasink case was a contract for work and materials. Section 13 of the 1982 Act applies to the work element in such a contract. In some cases it may be important to know whether the defect complained of is due to fault in the materials themselves or the supplier's failure to take care in doing the work. This is because the nature of the liability for each of the two elements of the contract is different. In relation to the supply of materials, the supplier will be strictly liable, even if he is not at fault (like the defendant in *Frost v. Aylesbury Dairies (1905)* above). If the work is defective the supplier will only be liable if he has failed to take reasonable care. Another reason why the distinction may be important is that different controls on the use of exclusion clauses are applied by the Unfair Contract Terms Act 1977 to each element of contracts of this type (see below).

Where services, or goods and services, are supplied by any person taking on work in connection with the provision of a dwellinghouse, s.1(1) of the Defective Premises Act 1972 imposes a duty of care on that person. He has a duty to see that the work is done in a workmanlike or professional manner with proper materials so that, in relation to the work he has taken on, the dwelling will be fit for habitation when it is completed.

Implied terms relating to time for performance

Section 14 of the 1982 Act provides that:

> "Where, under a contract for the supply of a service by a supplier acting in the course of a business, the time for the service to be carried out is not fixed by the contract, . . . there is an implied term that the supplier will carry out the service within a reasonable time. What is a reasonable time is a question of fact".
>
> In *Charnock v. Liverpool Corporation (1968)* the plaintiff recovered damages for the defendant's unreasonable delay in performing a contract. The defendant took eight weeks to repair the plaintiff's car when a reasonably competent repairer would have completed the repairs within five weeks.

If a reasonable time has elapsed within which the contract should have been performed, the customer is entitled unilaterally to serve a notice fixing a time for the performance of the contract. The new time limit must be reasonable. If the supplier fails to meet it, the Court of Appeal held in *Charles Rickards Limited v. Oppenheim (1950)* that the customer is entitled to withdraw from the contract without penalty.

If the time for performance of the contract has been agreed then s.14 does not add an additional requirement that the services should be provided within a reasonable time.

Implied terms relating to the cost of the service

Section 15 of the 1982 Act deals with the cost of services supplied. It provides that:

> "Where under a contract for the supply of a service, the consideration for the service is not determined by the contract, . . . there is an implied term that the party contracting with the supplier will pay a reasonable charge. What is a reasonable charge is a question of fact".

Section 15 does not enable a customer to reopen an agreement on the grounds that the charge for the service is unreasonably high, if the customer originally agreed to pay that charge. Only where there is no mechanism in the contract for determining the price the section applies and limits the amount recoverable to a reasonable sum.

EXCLUSION CLAUSES

Legal liability can arise in a variety of different ways, for example through misrepresentation, breach of contract or negligence. One way of trying to reduce or extinguish this liability is by the use of exclusion or limitation clauses. An exclusion clause in a contract is an express term which attempts to exempt one party from all liability for failure to perform some part of the contract. An example of an exclusion clause in a contract for the supply of goods is: "the seller hereby excludes all liability for breach of any express or implied condition, term or warranty". A limitation clause on the other hand is slightly different for it aims to reduce rather than extinguish the liability. It could be drafted so as to place an overall financial limit on the liability of one party for breach of contract, to limit liability to the replacement of goods supplied; or to deprive the other of a particular remedy for the breach. In this text we will be dealing with the legal principles which apply both to the exclusion and limitation of liability, but, for convenience, we will refer to exclusion only and this can be taken to mean total or partial exclusion of liability.

The principle of freedom of contract permits the use of exclusion clauses, although the courts developed a number of common law principles which were designed to rob them of effect in certain circumstances. These principles were developed because the courts recognised that the use of exclusion clauses could result in unfairness to one of the contracting parties. Judicial controls were developed largely by the application of pre-existing principles of contract law and are therefore limited in scope. It was not until the 1970's that legislation was introduced. The Unfair Contract Terms Act 1977 now provides a comprehensive set of rules which regulate the use of exclusion clauses in contracts and the use of non-contractual notices.

In determining the validity of an exclusion clause, several legal principles have to be applied. The first step is to make sure that legal liability of one type or another would arise if the exclusion were not present. Next the common law rules of incorporation and interpretation (discussed below) must be applied. If the exclusion survives the application of the common law rules, we must then apply the provisions of the Unfair Contract Terms Act 1977. Figure 5.3 summarises these steps in diagrammatic form.

Fig. 5.3

COMMON LAW CONTROL OVER EXCLUSION AND RESTRICTION OF CONTRACTUAL LIABILITY

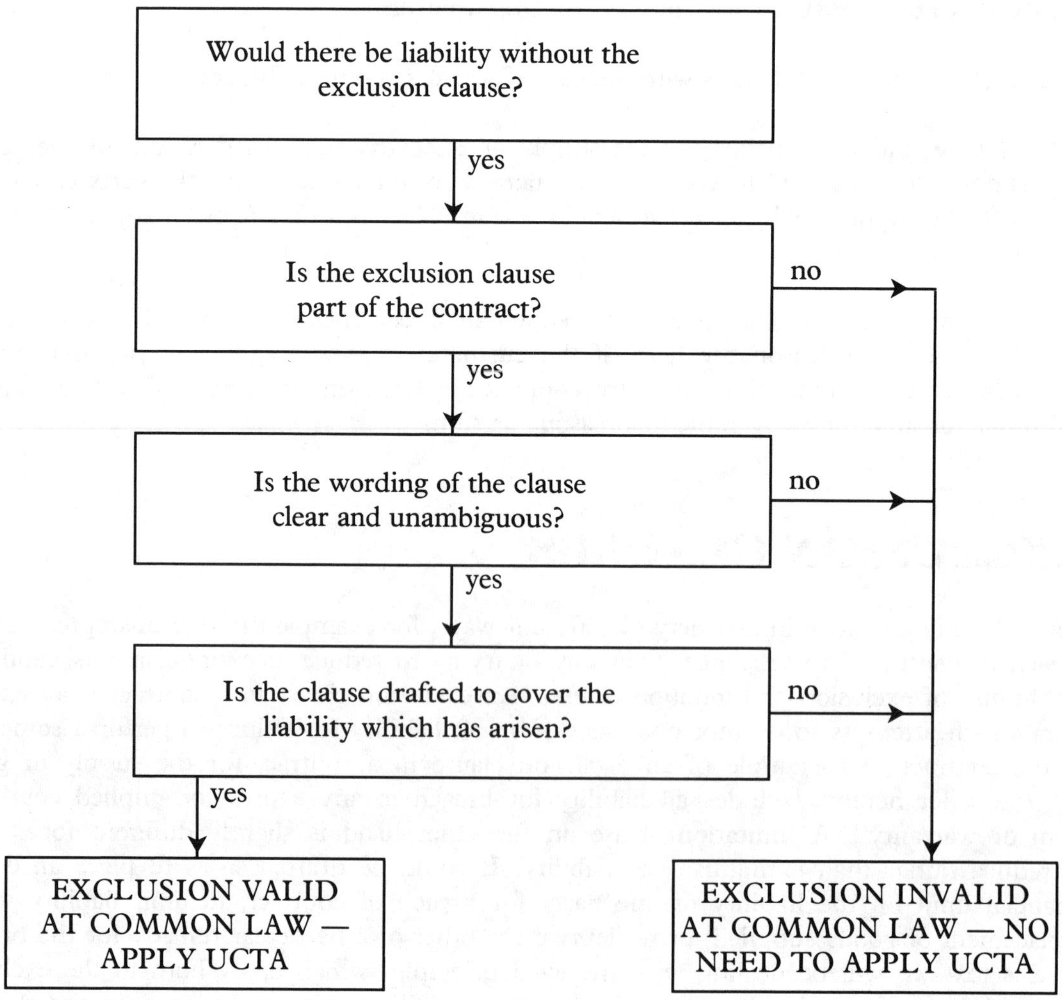

INCORPORATION — IS THE TERM PART OF THE CONTRACT?

(a) Signed Documents

Where a person has signed a document containing an exclusion clause he will be bound by the terms contained in the document whether or not he has read or understood them. The only exceptions to this rule are where the signature is induced by fraud or misrepresentation. Otherwise the exclusion clause will automatically be part of the contract.

> In *L'Estrange v. Graucob (1934)* the plaintiff, who was the proprietress of a cafe, bought a vending machine under the terms of a sales agreement which she signed without reading. The contract contained a clause excluding the seller's liability, among other things, for breach of the implied terms under the Sale of Goods Act. The vending machine was defective. The Court of Appeal held that the plaintiff had no remedy against the seller because she was bound by the terms of the exclusion clause in the document which she had signed.

> In *Spriggs v. Sotheby Parke Bernet and Co. Ltd. (1984)* the plaintiff deposited a diamond with Sotheby's to be auctioned. He signed a document, without reading it, and put it straight into his wallet. The document contained details of the agreement and a declaration in bold type immediately above the space for the plaintiff's signature. The declaration stated "I have read and agree to the instructions for sale as detailed on the reverse of this form". On the reverse of the form there was an exclusion clause. It was held that the clause had been validly incorporated into the contract.

Where the contents of the document have been misrepresented before it is signed, an exclusion clause in the document will not be effective to the extent that the effect of the clause was misrepresented.

> In *Curtis v. Chemical Cleaning and Dyeing Co. (1951)* the plaintiff took a wedding dress to the defendant company for cleaning. An assistant asked her to sign a receipt, and before she signed she was told that the effect of her signature was to exclude the cleaner's liability for damage to any beads or sequins on the dress. In the process of cleaning the dress was stained, although no damage was done to the beads and sequins. In fact the signed receipt had excluded the defendants' liability for any damage to the dress "howsoever caused". The Court of Appeal held that the defendants were liable for the damage to the dress and could not rely on the full exclusion clause because they had misrepresented its effect to the plaintiff.

(b) Unsigned Documents

Where the term is contained in an unsigned document, or displayed on a notice, it will be effective only if the person relying on it took reasonable steps to bring it to the attention of the other party, and where the document or notice might reasonably be regarded as likely to contain contractual terms.

> In *Chapelton v. Barry U.D.C. (1940)* the plaintiff hired a deck chair from the defendant for use on a beach. He paid an attendant and was given a ticket in return. He was injured when the chair collapsed as he sat down on it. There was an exclusion clause printed on the back of the ticket which the plaintiff had not read. The Court of Appeal held that

the ticket was merely a receipt and not the sort of contractual document which a reasonable person might have expected to contain contractual terms. The exclusion clause was therefore ineffective and the defendants were liable.

(c) Terms introduced after the Contract is made

An exclusion clause will not be effective unless it is adequately brought to the attention of the other party before the contract is made. It must be part of the contractual offer, and the rules of offer and acceptance can be used to determine whether the clause is actually part of the contract.

> In *Olley v. Marlborough Court Hotel Limited (1949)* the plaintiff booked into an hotel and paid for the room in advance. She went up to her hotel room where there was a notice which stated "The proprietors will not hold themselves responsible for articles lost or stolen unless handed to the Manageress for safe custody". The plaintiff left her fur coat in the room and it was stolen. The Court of Appeal held that the defendant was not entitled to rely on the exclusion clause as it was not a term of the contract. The contract was concluded at the reception desk and the plaintiff had no notice of the clause at that stage.
>
> In *Thornton v. Shoe Lane Parking (1971)* the plaintiff drove into a car park which he had not used before. At the entrance there was a machine which issued a ticket to him before raising a barrier to allow entry. On the back of the ticket there was a statement that it was issued subject to terms and conditions displayed within the car park. One of these conditions purported to exclude the defendant's liability for injury to customers howsoever caused. The plaintiff was injured by the defendant's negligence when he came to collect his car. The Court of Appeal held that the exclusion clause was ineffective because it had been introduced after the contract was concluded. Lord Denning analysed the process of contract formation in the following way:
>
>> "The customer pays his money and gets a ticket. He cannot refuse it. He cannot get his money back. He may protest to the machine, even swear at it; but it will remain unmoved. He is committed beyond recall. He was committed at the very moment when he put his money into the machine: the contract was concluded at that time. It can be translated into offer and acceptance in this way. The offer is made when the proprietor of the machine holds it out as being ready to receive the money. The acceptance takes place when the customer puts his money into the slot. The terms of the offer are contained in the notice placed on or near the machine stating what is offered for the money. The customer is bound by these terms as long as they are sufficiently brought to his notice beforehand, but not otherwise. He is not bound by the terms printed on the ticket, if they differ from the notice, because the ticket comes too late. The contract has already been made".

Where there is a previous course of dealing between the parties the court may be prepared to recognise the incorporation of an exclusion clause into a contract even though it was not specifically referred to at the time the contract was made. This will occur where the past dealings between the parties have consistently been made on the same terms and with the exclusion clause.

In *Spurling v. Bradshaw (1956)* the plaintiffs were warehousemen who had dealt with the defendant for many years and always on the plaintiff's standard contractual terms. These terms excluded the plaintiff's liability for "negligence, wrongful act or default". The defendant delivered eight barrels of orange juice to the plaintiff for storage and a few days later received an acknowledgement which referred to the standard terms of contract. When the defendant came to collect the barrels they were found to be empty. He refused to pay the storage charges and the plaintiff sued. It was held that the exclusion clause, although on this occasion introduced after the contract was made, was part of the contract. This was because the parties had regularly dealt with each other in the past and had done so consistently on the same contractual terms. The defendant was therefore well aware of these terms when he deposited the goods. The exclusion of liability was valid and the plaintiff's claim for storage charges succeeded.

(d) **Overriding Oral Promise**

An exclusion clause may be overridden by a later statement made by the seller to the buyer.

In *Harling v. Eddy (1951)* the plaintiff bought a heifer at a cattle auction. One of the auctioneer's printed conditions of sale stated that no warranty was given in respect of any animal sold. When the heifer was put up for sale little interest was shown and no bids were made until the auctioneer said "there is nothing wrong with her. I will guarantee her in every respect and I will take her back if she is not what I say she is". The plaintiff bought the animal which died of tuberculosis four months later. It was held by the Court of Appeal that the verbal statement overrode the exclusion clause in the printed conditions, and the plaintiff's claim succeeded.

INTERPRETATION AND DRAFTING OF EXCLUSION CLAUSES

An exclusion clause must be drafted carefully. It must be clear and unambiguous, and it must cover the liability which has arisen. The clause will be interpreted narrowly against the party seeking to rely on it. This is known as the "contra proferentem" rule.

In *Andrews Ltd v. Singer and Co. Ltd. (1934)* the plaintiffs agreed in writing to buy a "new Singer car". The contract contained a clause which excluded the defendant's liability for breach of "all conditions, warranties and liabilities implied by statute, common law or otherwise". The car delivered to the plaintiff had in fact done a considerable number of miles. It was held that the seller was in breach of an express condition that the car would be new. He could not therefore rely on an exclusion of implied terms, and was liable to the plaintiff.

In *Baldry v. Marshall (1925)* the plaintiff told the defendant that he required a car suitable for touring. The defendant was a car dealer and, on his recommendation, the plaintiff bought a Bugatti from him. The written contract of sale excluded the seller's liability for breach of any "guarantee or warranty, statutory or otherwise". The car proved unsuitable for touring. It was held that the seller was in breach of the implied condition under s.14 of the Sale of Goods Act that the car would be suitable for a purpose made known to the seller. The exclusion clause was ineffective because it excluded only guarantees or warranties and did not exclude liability for breach of a condition of the contract.

Exclusion clauses are sometimes introduced by words which indicate that the party imposing them will take all reasonable care or will make every effort to perform his obligations. This type of wording may be interpreted by the courts as imposing a pre-condition for the operation of the exclusion clause. If the party relying on the clause does not fulfil the pre-condition he cannot take the benefit of the exclusion.

> In *B & S Contracts Limited v. Victor Green Publications Limited (1984)* the plaintiffs were contractors who traded on standard terms which excluded their liability for non-performance which resulted from industrial action by their workforce. The exclusion clause began with the words "Every effort will be made to carry out the contract, but . . ." The Court of Appeal held that the contractors were obliged to take reasonable steps to perform the contract before they could rely on the exclusion clause. They failed to prove that they had done this and were therefore unable to rely on the exclusion clause.

The approach of the courts to the interpretation of exclusion clauses has changed with the introduction of the statutory controls contained in the Unfair Contract Terms Act 1977. Before the 1977 Act the courts had few means of invalidating exclusion clauses in contracts and, because of the potential injustice which they caused, were prepared to interpret such clauses in a hostile manner. Judges would sometimes place a strained meaning on the words of the clause in order to deprive it of effect. However since the introduction of the 1977 Act, the potential unfairness of such clauses has been reduced greatly and the courts are now able to adopt a less hostile approach in interpreting their wording.

> In *Photo Productions Limited v. Securicor Transport Limited* (1980) the defendant contracted to provide security services, including night patrols, at the plaintiff's factory. While on patrol one of the defendant's employees deliberately lit a small fire which got out of control and destroyed the factory and its contents. The contract, which was on Securicor's standard terms, contained the following condition:
>
> > "Under no circumstances shall the company (Securicor) be responsible for any injurious act or default by any employee of the company unless such act or default could have been foreseen and avoided by the exercise of due diligence on the part of the company as his employer; nor, in any event, shall the company be held responsible for; (a) any loss suffered by the customer through burglary, theft, fire or any other cause, except insofar as such loss is solely attributable to the negligence of the company's employees acting within the course of their employment . . ."
>
> The House of Lords held that the exclusion clause was effective. It was clear and unambiguous and it covered the breach of contract complained of. Lord Diplock stated that
>
> > "in commercial contracts negotiated between businessmen capable of looking after their own interests and of deciding how risks inherent in the performance of various kinds of contract can be most economically borne (generally by insurance) it is, in my view, wrong to place a strained interpretation on words in an exclusion clause . . ."

CONTROL OF EXCLUSION CLAUSES BY LEGISLATION

The **Unfair Contract Terms Act 1977**, which is examined in detail below, is the major legislation which controls the use of exclusion clauses across a wide spectrum of business liability. There are, however, a number of specific provisions in other Acts which apply in particular situations to restrict or prevent the use of such clauses.

The **Defective Premises Act 1972**, in s.6(3) renders invalid any term of an agreement which (i) tries to exclude or restrict the duty arising under the Act or (ii) attempts to limit any liability for breach of the duty. The duty is owed by anyone taking on work in connection with the provision of a dwelling house, including the builder, architect, surveyor and any subcontractors, and the duty is to build dwelling houses properly.

The **Consumer Protection Act 1987**, in s.7, invalidates any attempt to exclude liability arising under Part I of the Act for injuries caused by defective products. Additionally, under s.41 of the 1987 Act there can be no exclusion of liability for breach of statutory duties in relation to consumer safety.

The **Consumer Credit Act 1974**, in s.173, forbids the inclusion in any agreement regulated by the Act of any term which attempts to diminish the protection which the Act affords to the consumer.

Under the **Misrepresentation Act 1967**, s.3, any contract term excluding or restricting liability for misrepresentation will be invalid unless it is shown to be reasonable, applying the reasonableness test in s.11 of the Unfair Contract Terms Act 1977.

THE UNFAIR CONTRACT TERMS ACT 1977

The Unfair Contract Terms Act 1977 is the first attempt by Parliament to deal with exclusion and limitation of liability in a comprehensive way. There are provisions in the Act which control attempts to exclude or limit liability in relation to negligence, contractual obligations, indemnities, guarantees, implied terms in contracts to supply goods and misrepresentation. For the purposes of the 1977 Act, exclusion or restriction of liability is widely defined so as to include:

(a) making enforcement of a remedy subject to restrictive conditions, for example a requirement that notice of loss or damage must be given within a specified time or in a specified manner,

(b) excluding or restricting any right or remedy, for example taking away the right to reject goods for breach of condition and confining the buyer's remedy to damages only,

(c) restricting the liability, for example to a maximum amount recoverable,

(d) restricting the time within which the remedy may be claimed, for example by specifying that no claim may be made more than 28 days after the date of the contract,

(e) preventing liability arising in the first place, for example by including a term which provides that the seller does not give any warranty or undertaking that the goods are fit for any purpose.

The Act only applies to "business liability". This is defined as liability for breach of obligations arising from things done in the course of a business or from the occupation of premises used for business purposes. The meaning of the term business was discussed earlier, and for the purposes of this Act it includes a profession, and the activities of any government department or local or public authority. The Act provides varying degrees of protection against exclusion clauses and notices. Some are totally invalidated, others are subjected to a test of reasonableness, and there are others to which the Act does not apply at all.

Exclusion clauses to which the Act does not apply

The Act does not apply in the following situations. In these cases the exclusion will be subject only to the common law rules discussed above:

(a) where the liability in question is not a "business liability", for example liability arising from the defective state of a private house;

(b) where the situation falls outside the wording of a particular section of the Act. A verbal contract in which neither party deals as a consumer is, for example, outside the scope of s.3;

(c) where the Act specifically states that it does not apply. Schedule 1 tells us that the Act, in whole or in part, does not extend to the following types of contract:

(i) insurance contracts

(ii) contracts involving land

(iii) contracts dealing with intellectual property

(iv) contracts relating to the formation or dissolution of business organisations

(v) contracts involving the creation or transfer of securities

(vi) in relation to contracts of employment, s.2 does not apply except in favour of the employee.

The Reasonableness Test

Where the Act subjects an exclusion clause to the reasonableness test, the burden of proving that the contract term or notice is reasonable lies with the party seeking to rely on the exclusion. The test in relation to a contract term is that the term shall have been a fair and reasonable one to be included in the contract, having regard to the circumstances which were or should have been known to the parties at the time when the contract was made. In relation to a non-contractual notice the test is whether it would be fair and reasonable to allow reliance on it, having regard to all the circumstances at the time when the liability arose. An example of a non-contractual notice would be a notice displayed at the entrance to a public park.

Schedule 2 of the Act lays down guidelines which the court can take into account in determining whether a contract term satisfies the requirement of reasonableness. The guidelines are discussed below in connection with s.6 and s.7.

EXCLUSION OF LIABILITY FOR NEGLIGENCE

In dealing with exclusion of liability for negligence, the Act defines the term 'negligence' to cover the following:

(a) contractual negligence, or the breach of any duty to use reasonable skill and care in the performance of a contract,

(b) common law negligence, for example under the rule in *Donoghue v. Stevenson* (1932) discussed in the next chapter, and

(c) liability for breach of the common duty of care, owed to visitors by an occupier of premises, under the Occupier's Liability Act 1957.

Section 2 of the Act provides that:

> "(1) A person cannot by reference to any contract term or to a notice given to persons generally or to particular persons exclude or restrict his liability for death or personal injury resulting from negligence.
>
> (2) In the case of other loss or damage, a person cannot so exclude or restrict his liability for negligence except insofar as the term or notice satisfies the requirement of reasonableness".

This gives us two important basic rules. First that it is not possible to exclude liability for death or personal injury resulting from negligence. The case of *White v. Blackmore* (1972), considered in the next chapter, gives an example of a notice which, before the Act, effectively excluded negligence liability for death or personal injury. Such a notice is now invalid. The plaintiff in that case would have succeeded had the Act been in force at the time of the negligent act. Furthermore in *Thornton v. Shoe Lane Parking* (1971) discussed above, the exclusion of liability for personal injury would have been wholly ineffective under the 1977 Act, if it had actually been part of the contract.

The second rule is that liability for loss or damage other than death or personal injury cannot be excluded unless the exclusion is reasonable. This would apply, for example, to clauses which excluded liability for damage to property or financial loss caused by negligence. Under this provision the exclusion clauses in cases like *Spurling v. Bradshaw (1956)* and *Olley v. Marlborough Court Hotel (1949)* would be subject to the reasonableness test. In the next chapter there are a number of examples of cases in which the reasonableness test has been applied, for example *Smith v. Eric S. Bush (1987)*, *Stevenson v. Nationwide Building Society (1984)* and *Yianni v. Edwin Evans (1981)*.

> In *Spriggs v. Sotheby Parke Bernet and Co. Limited (1984)*, considered earlier in the chapter, the plaintiff, who was a businessman, deposited a diamond with Sotheby's to be auctioned. He signed a document which, among other things, excluded Sotheby's liability for negligence. He was given the opportunity to insure the diamond but did not do so. Whilst the diamond was on view prior to the auction, it was stolen despite the defendant's fairly comprehensive security system. The plaintiff sued for negligence and the defendants relied on the exclusion clause. Under s.2(2) the clause is only valid if the defendant can show that it is reasonable. The court held that the clause in this case was reasonable and valid. The plaintiff was a successful and experienced businessman and no doubt was used to contracts containing exclusion clauses. He could not be regarded as having unequal bargaining power. The risk was one which could have been covered by insurance but the plaintiff turned down the opportunity to take this precaution.
>
> In *Phillips Products v. Hampstead Plant Hire (1983)* the defendant hired out a JCB to the plaintiffs under a standard term agreement. They supplied

the driver but excluded any liability in negligence for his acts. Whilst he was working under the plaintiff's direction, the driver damaged their factory through his own negligence. It was held that the exclusion clause was unreasonable and invalid. This was because the hire was for a short period and the plaintiffs had little opportunity to insure. They did not select, nor effectively control the driver. Their experience of such hiring arrangements was very limited.

An exclusion of liability for negligence is sometimes contained in a guarantee given by a manufacturer or distributor of goods. Such a guarantee will usually offer to repair or replace faulty goods such as televisions, washing machines and other electrical goods, free of charge within a specified time period commencing with the date of purchase; and will often be subject to stated exceptions, for example that the defect is not due to misuse, accidental damage or attempted repair by an unqualified person. In some cases, however, a guarantee may attempt to do more than qualify the benefit which it gives. It may purport to take away other rights of the consumer which are independent of the guarantee, such as the right to sue the manufacturer in the tort of negligence. This could be done by supplying a postcard with the goods which the consumer is asked to fill in and send to the manufacturer within a specified time in order to "preserve his rights under the guarantee". The postcard would then refer to the rights under the guarantee and contain an exclusion clause limiting the consumer's other rights.

In relation to exclusion clauses in guarantees, s.5(1) provides that:

"In the case of goods of a type ordinarily supplied for private use or consumption, where loss or damage:

(a) arises from the goods proving defective while in consumer use; and

(b) results from the negligence of a person concerned in the manufacture or distribution of the goods, liability for the loss or damage cannot be excluded or restricted by reference to any contract term or notice contained in or operating by reference to a guarantee of the goods".

For these purposes the goods are "in consumer use" when a person is using them or has them in his possession for use, otherwise than exclusively for the purposes of a business; and a "guarantee" includes anything in writing which contains some promise or assurance (however worded or presented) that defects will be made good by repair, replacement, financial compensation or otherwise. This Section does not apply where the guarantee is given by the seller as part of the contract of sale with the buyer. In such a case other provisions of the Act would apply. Figure 5.4 below illustrates the combined effect of S2 and S5 of the Act.

EXCLUSION OF LIABILITY FOR BREACH OF CONTRACT

Section 3 of the Act applies where one of the parties to a contract deals a consumer (see above), or where the contract is made on written standard terms of business. In either of these situations, the section subjects to the test of reasonableness any term in which the other party:
in which the other party:

"(a) when himself in breach of contract, excludes or restricts any liability of his in respect of the breach; or

(b) claims to be entitled —

(i) to render a contractual performance substantially different from that which was reasonably expected from him, or

EXCLUSION OF LIABILITY FOR NEGLIGENCE

Section 2 and Section 5 Unfair Contract Terms Act 1977

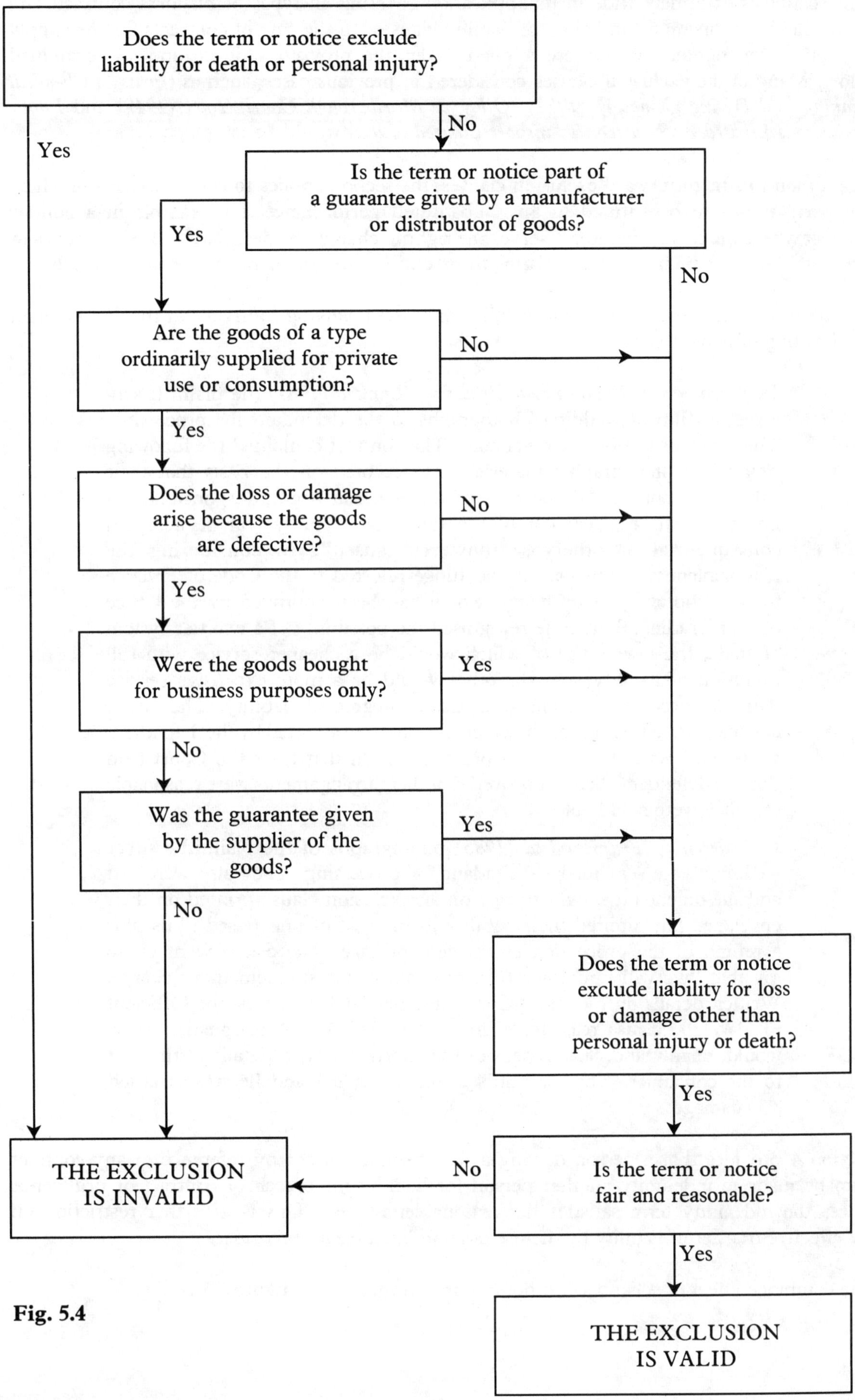

Fig. 5.4

> (ii) in respect of the whole or any part of his contractual obligation, to render no performance at all".

This section is extremely wide in its application covering all types of business contract, and all manner of exclusion or limitation of liability clauses. In the case of contracts for the supply of goods, even tighter controls are applied under the provisions of s.6 and s.7, examined below. Many of the exclusion clauses considered in previous cases, such as *Curtis v. Chemical Cleaning and Dyeing Company (1951), Olley v. Marlborough Court Hotel (1949)* and *Photo Productions Limited v. Securicor Transport Limited (1980)* would be caught by s.3.

In addition to straightforward exclusion clauses, the section applies to contract terms in which one party claims to be entitled to give substituted performance, for example in a holiday contract where the travel operator reserves the right to change the destination. It also applies to contract terms in which one party claims to be entitled to render no performance at all.

The application of s.3 can be seen in the following cases involving contracts for the development and printing of photographs.

> In *Woodman v. Photo Trade Processing Limited (1981)* the plaintiff sent a reel of film of wedding photographs to the defendant for processing. The film was lost by the defendant. The contract contained the following clause "all photographic materials are accepted on the basis that their value does not exceed the cost of the material itself. Responsibility is limited to the replacement of the films. No liability will be accepted consequential or otherwise, however caused". In considering the reasonableness of this clause, the Judge referred to the Code of Practice for the Photographic Industry, which had been approved by the Office of Fair Trading. This code recognised the possibility of a two tier system of trade, the lowest tier of which would be a cheaper service with full exclusion of liability; and the other would be a more expensive service with the processors accepting a greater degree of liability. The Judge concluded that this approach, which had not been adopted by the defendant, would be both reasonable and practicable. On that basis the Court held that the defendants had not proved that their arrangements were reasonable and they were held liable.
>
> In *Warren v. Truprint Ltd (1986)* photographs of the plaintiff's silver wedding were sent to the defendant for processing. They also were lost and the defendant sought to rely on an exclusion clause printed on their envelope. This limited their liability to the cost of unexposed films plus a refund of the processing charge and postage. The clause went on to say that "we will undertake further liability at a supplementary charge. Written details on request". The Court held that this was not sufficient to make the clause reasonable under the 1977 Act. A reasonable clause would, plainly and clearly, set out the alternative with details of the cost to the consumer. The plaintiff's claim succeeded and he was awarded £50 damages.

Section 4 provides that a person dealing as a consumer cannot by reference to any contract term be made to indemnify another person for liability for breach of contract or negligence unless the indemnity term satisfies the reasonableness test. This is a further restriction on the effective transfer of liability by the use of an indirect exclusion clause.

The combined effect of s.3 and s.4 of the Act are summarised in figure 5.5 below.

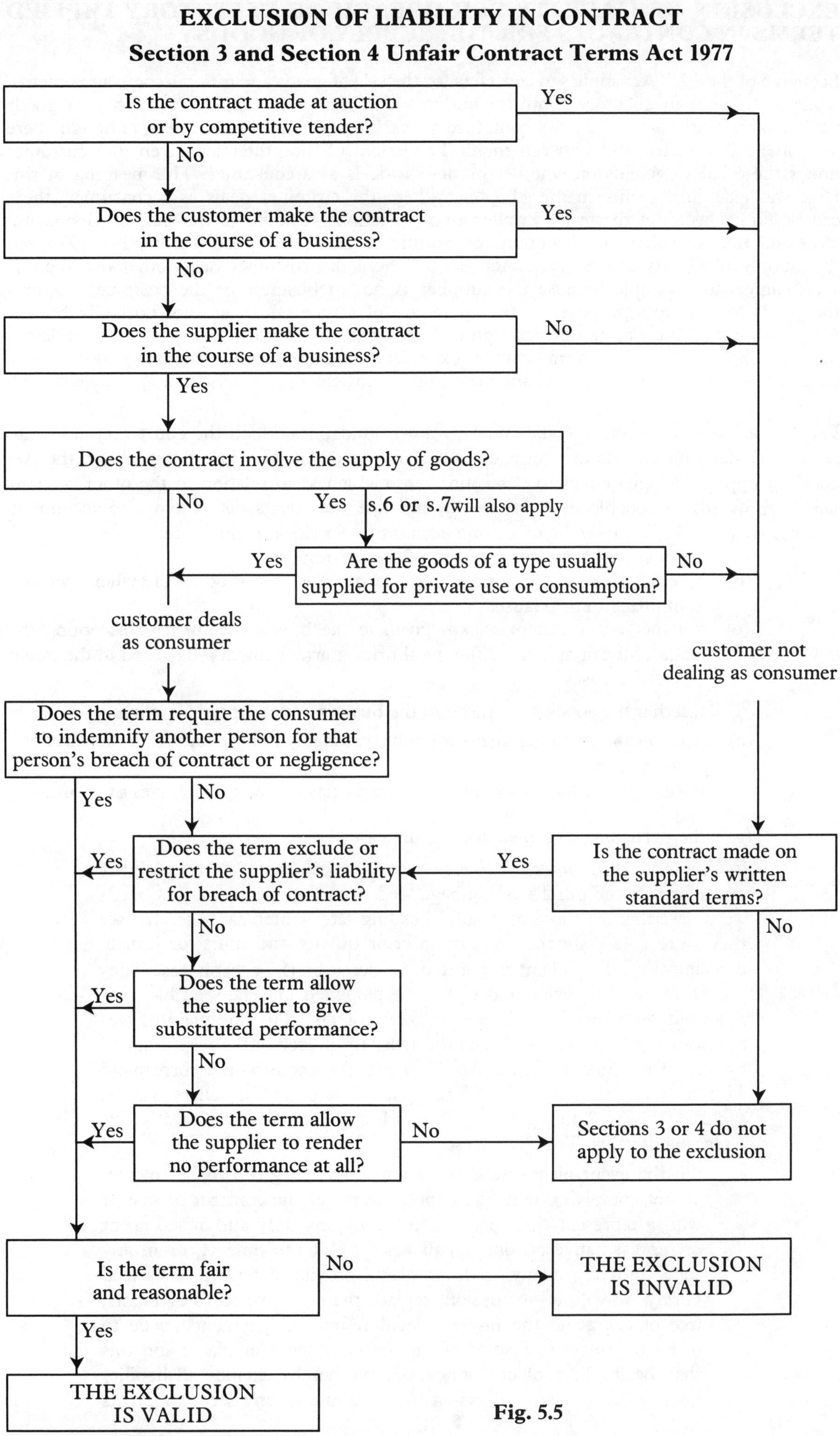
EXCLUSION OF LIABILITY IN CONTRACT
Section 3 and Section 4 Unfair Contract Terms Act 1977
Is the contract made at auction or by competitive tender?
Yes
No
Does the customer make the contract in the course of a business?
Yes
No
Does the supplier make the contract in the course of a business?
No
Yes
Does the contract involve the supply of goods?
No
Yes
s.6 or s.7 will also apply
Are the goods of a type usually supplied for private use or consumption?
Yes
No
customer deals as consumer
customer not dealing as consumer
Does the term require the consumer to indemnify another person for that person's breach of contract or negligence?
Yes
No
Does the term exclude or restrict the supplier's liability for breach of contract?
Yes
No
Is the contract made on the supplier's written standard terms?
Yes
No
Does the term allow the supplier to give substituted performance?
Yes
No
Does the term allow the supplier to render no performance at all?
Yes
No
Sections 3 or 4 do not apply to the exclusion
Is the term fair and reasonable?
No
Yes
THE EXCLUSION IS INVALID
THE EXCLUSION IS VALID

Fig. 5.5

EXCLUSION OF LIABILITY FOR BREACH OF STATUTORY IMPLIED TERMS IN CONTRACTS FOR THE SUPPLY OF GOODS

Section 6 of the 1977 Act applies to contracts for the sale of goods and hire purchase agreements, while s.7 applies to all other contracts under which the possession or ownership of goods passes to the customer. The rules contained in each section are very similar, although there are some minor differences between them. The extent of the protection given to a customer under these rules depends on whether or not he deals as a consumer. The meaning of this term was examined earlier in this chapter. Where the customer deals as a consumer, there can be no exclusion of the terms implied under Sections 12 to 15 of the Sale of Goods Act 1979 and the equivalent provisions in the Supply of Goods (Implied Terms) Act 1973 and the Supply of Goods and Services Act 1982. Where the customer deals otherwise than as a consumer, for example because the supplier is not in business or the customer requires the goods for business purposes or the goods are of a type which are not normally bought for private use, there can be no exclusion of liability for breach of the implied terms relating to title. The other implied terms can be excluded as against such a customer, but only if the clause satisfies the test of reasonableness. Figure 5.6 below summarises the application of s.6 and s.7.

For the purpose of s.6 and s.7, the Act lays down guidelines which the court may take into account in determining whether an exclusion clause is reasonable. Strictly speaking, the Act does not apply these guidelines to determine reasonableness in relation to the other sections which apply the reasonableness test, but in practice the courts take them into account in those cases also. The factors to be taken into account under the guidelines are:

(a) the relative bargaining strength of the parties;
(b) whether there was an opportunity to purchase the product elsewhere without submitting to the clause;
(c) whether any inducement was given to the buyer in return for accepting the clause, for example the differential pricing arrangements suggested in the photo processing cases;
(d) whether the goods were made to the buyer's design or specification;
(e) whether the customer knew or ought reasonably to have known of the existence of the clause;
(f) the extent to which it was open for the parties to cover themselves by insurance; and
(g) the particular circumstances of the case.

In *George Mitchell Limited v. Finney Lock Seeds Limited (1983)* the plaintiff was a farmer who purchased cabbage seed from the defendant. The seeds were described as those of a solid heading late winter cabbage. In fact they were of a different type, of inferior quality and unfit for human consumption. The plaintiff planted 63 acres of these cabbages. They proved to be of no value and had to be ploughed in. The seed had cost £192 but the plaintiff's loss was in excess of £61,000. The plaintiff was not insured for this loss and sued the seller for breach of the term implied by s.13 of the Sale of Goods Act 1979 that the goods would correspond with their description. The defence put forward by the sellers was an exclusion clause limiting liability to either the cost of the seed or its replacement value. The clause read:

> "in the event of any seeds or plants sold or agreed to be sold by us not complying with the express terms of the contract of sale or with a representation made by us or by any duly authorised agent or representative on our behalf prior to, at the time of, or in any such contract, or any seeds or plants proving defective in varietal purety we will, at our option, replace the defective seeds or plants, free of charge to the buyer or will refund all payments made to us by the buyer in respect of the defective seeds or plants and this shall be the limit of our obligation. We hereby exclude all liability for any loss or damage arising from the use of any seeds or plants

EXCLUSION OF LIABILITY FOR BREACH OF STATUTORY IMPLIED TERMS IN CONTRACT FOR THE SALE AND SUPPLY OF GOODS
Section 6 and Section 7 Unfair Contract Terms Act 1977

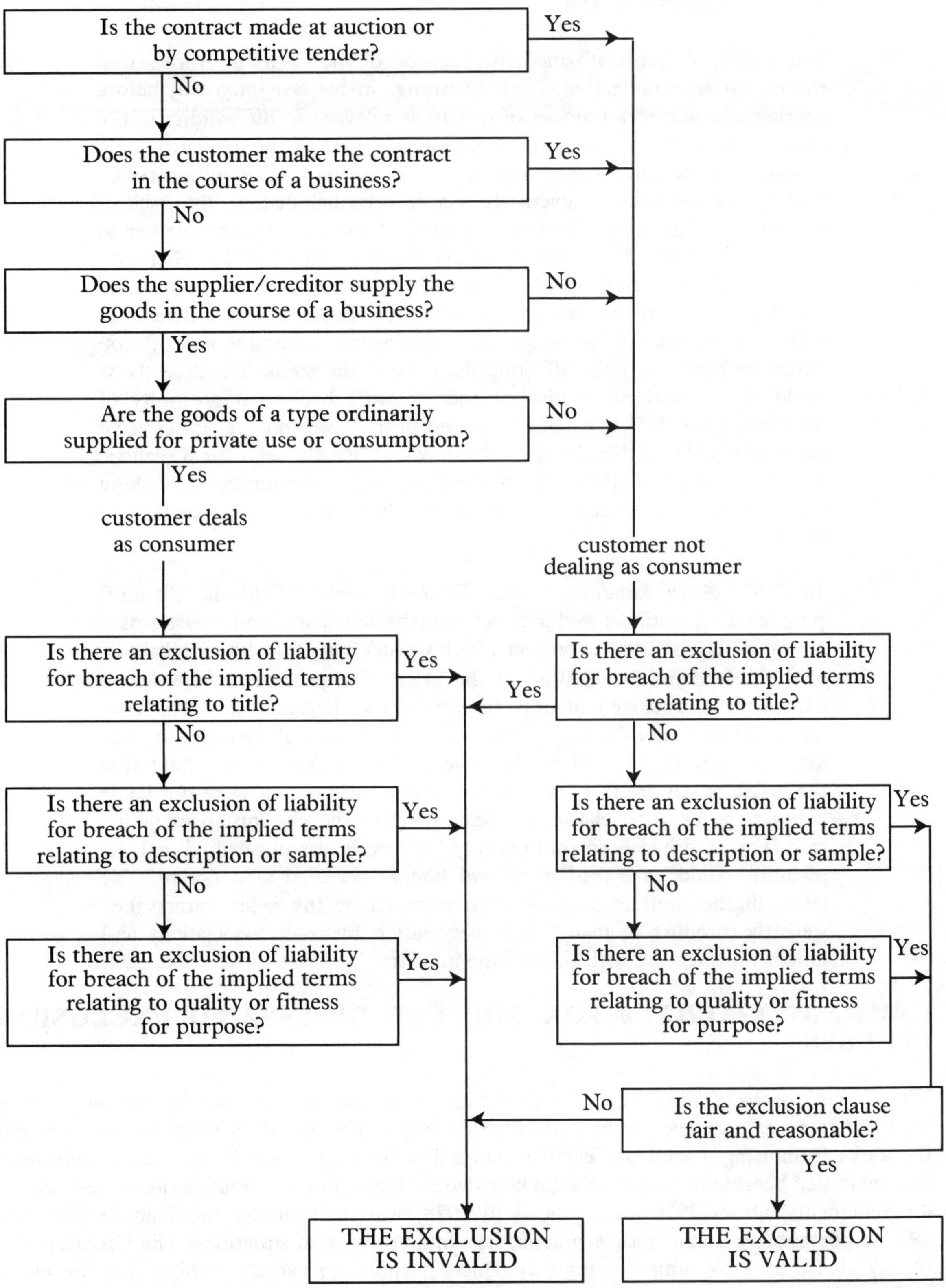

Fig. 5.6

> supplied by us and for any consequential loss or damage arising out of such use or any failure in the performance of or any defect in any seeds or plants supplied by us or for any other loss or damage whatsoever save for, at our option, liability for any such replacement or refund as aforesaid".

The House of Lords affirmed the decision of the Court of Appeal that the clause was ineffective. Lord Denning, in his last judgment before retiring, considered a number of questions relevant to the validity of the clause. The first was whether the clause was part of the agreement. He found that it was since such conditions were usual in the trade, and therefore well known, and in any event the clause was included on the back of the invoice. The second was the wording of the clause, and whether as drafted it covered and effectively limited the supplier's liability. He found that the clause clearly did so. Finally the question arose as to whether the clause was a reasonable one. It had been imposed by the defendant without negotiation. The seedsmen could insure against the risk of crop failure without materially affecting the price of the seeds. The defendants could have tested the seeds but the plaintiffs had no opportunity of discovering the defectiveness of the seed until it was too late. In addition there was evidence that the defendants would usually negotiate a realistic settlement where a claim was justified in similar circumstances. Taking these factors into account the clause was held to be unreasonable and invalid.

In *R.W. Green Limited v. Cade Brothers Farms (1978)* the plaintiffs purchased a quantity of seed potatoes from the defendants under the terms of a written standard form contract which included a clause limiting liability of the defendants to a refund of the price. The potatoes were infected with a virus which could only be detected at harvest time. The crop failed and the plaintiffs sued the defendants for breach of the terms implied into the contract by s.14 of the Sale of Goods Act. It was held that the defendants were in breach of the implied terms, but were not liable because the exlusion clause was reasonable in the circumstances of the case. The seed had been sold cheaply because it was uncertified and the plaintiffs could have paid more and bought certified seed potato. The terms of the contract had not been imposed by the seller, rather they were the product of many years negotiation by trade associations and unions representing both sides of the industry.

CRIMINAL LIABILITY FOR THE USE OF INVALID EXCLUSION CLAUSES

The Unfair Contract Terms Act 1977 invalidates many exclusion clauses so that they cannot be relied upon as a defence to an action for damages. The Act does not, however, prevent the trader from using invalid clauses. The clause may have no legal validity, but the consumer may be misled because of his lack of legal knowledge. The Consumer Transactions (Restrictions on Statements) Order 1976 (as amended in 1978) was made under the Fair Trading Act 1973 to prevent this unfair trading practice in a limited range of situations. The Order applies to any clause in a consumer transaction which purports to exclude liability for breach of Sections 13, 14 or 15 of the Sale of Goods Act 1979. Under the Order it is a criminal offence for a person, in the course of a business, to do any of the following:

(a) display a notice of such a clause at a place where consumer deals are likely to be made,

(b) publish any advertisement to supply goods which includes such a clause,

(c) provide the consumer with a written contract or other document containing such a clause, or

(d) supply goods bearing any statement about the seller's liability in relation to description quality or fitness for purpose, unless the statement makes it clear that it does not affect the statutory rights of the consumer.

TRANSFER OF OWNERSHIP AND RISK IN CONTRACTS FOR THE SALE OF GOODS

TRANSFER OF OWNERSHIP

The transfer of ownership, or passing of property, or title, must be distinguished from the transfer of physical possession of goods. As a general rule, s.28 of the Sale of Goods Act 1979 provides that, unless otherwise agreed, the buyer is entitled to delivery only upon payment for the goods. Ownership, on the other hand, can be transferred at any time depending upon the terms of the contract. It may be at the time of making the contract, or after the buyer has paid the price, or at some other time.

It is important to know exactly when ownership of goods is transferred under a contract of sale for a number of reasons:

(a) under s.20, the risk of accidental loss or damage is transferred to the buyer when property passes to him, unless otherwise agreed. The party which bears the risk of accidental loss or damage will probably wish to insure the goods;

(b) under s.49 the seller can normally only sue for the price after property has passed to the buyer;

(c) in considering whether the contract has been frustrated due to perishing of the goods. The contract cannot be frustrated if property has passed to the buyer before the goods perish;

(d) in the event of the insolvency of the buyer, the seller may be able to retake possession of the goods if property has not passed to the buyer; and

(e) if the buyer resells the goods immediately, as a general rule, the sub-buyer will get a good title only if property had previously passed to the buyer.

In order to determine when property passes in a contract for the sale of goods, it is of crucial importance to decide whether the goods are specific, unascertained, or ascertained.

Specific goods are defined in s.61 of the Act as:

"goods which are identified and agreed upon at the time the contract for sale is made".

Goods which are not singled out in this way at the time of contracting are unascertained goods. Ascertained goods are those which were unascertained and are subsequently set aside for the performance of the contract. Goods which were not identified and agreed upon at the time of the contract can never become specific goods.

> In *Kursell v. Timber Operators Limited (1927)* under a contract for the sale of uncut timber standing in a forest, the buyers were entitled to cut and remove, within 15 years, all timber above a certain minimum size. The forest was subsequently nationalised and the Court had to determine whether the ownership of trees fitting the contract specification had passed to the buyer. It was held that property had not passed because the trees were unascertained goods. They could not be specific goods because trees fitting the contract description were merely identifiable. They had not actually been identified.

At the time the contract is made, the goods can only be one of two types, specific or unascertained. If the particular goods to be used in performance of the contract are identified and agreed upon at that time, the goods are specific. If not the goods are unascertained. Unascertained goods cannot subsequently become specific goods. They will become ascertained goods after they have been identified.

PASSING OF PROPERTY IN SPECIFIC GOODS

The general rule is contained in s.17 of the Act which provides:

> (1) Where there is a contract for the sale of specific or ascertained goods the property in them is transferred to the buyer at such time as the parties to the contract intend it to be transferred.
>
> (2) For the purpose of ascertaining the intention of the parties regard shall be had to the terms of the contract, the conduct of the parties and the circumstances of the case.

This allows the parties to make whatever agreement they think fit in relation to the passing of property in the goods. Many standard form contracts include a retention of title clause under which property does not pass to the buyer until the purchase price has been paid. Such clauses, examined later, are permitted by s.17.

Where no provision is made in the contract and it is not clear from the circumstances what the parties' intentions are, s.18 provides a number of rules which can be applied in order to determine when property passes.

> **Rule 1:**
> "Where there is an uncondition contract for the sale of specific goods in a deliverable state, the property in the goods passes to the buyer when the contract is made and it is immaterial whether the time of payment or the time of delivery, or both, be postponed".

Under this rule the ownership of goods may be transferred to the buyer even though they are still in the seller's possession.

> In *Tarling v. Baxter (1927)* the seller sold a quantity of hay to the buyer, but the hay remained on the seller's land pending collection. Before it was collected it was destroyed by fire. It was held that property passed to the buyer when the contract was made. The loss was therefore his as he carried the risk of accidental destruction.
>
> In *Dennant v. Skinner & Collom Limited (1948)* a rogue successfuly bid for a car at auction and was allowed to take it away after paying by cheque. After the sale was complete, he signed a form agreeing that ownership of the vehicle would not pass to him until the cheque was

> cleared. He quickly resold the car to the defendant. When the cheque was dishonoured the original seller sued the defendant for the return of the car. It was held that the terms in the document signed by the rogue were introduced after the contract had been made at the auction. That contract was complete on the fall of the hammer. As no reference had been made to the retention of title clause prior to that moment, the clause was not part of the contract. Property therefore passed to the rogue on the making of the contract under s.18 r.1. He passed a good title to the defendant when he resold the vehicle. The plaintiff's claim therefore failed.

The goods must be in a "deliverable state" before r.1 will apply. Under s.61(5):

> "goods are in a deliverable state . . . when they are in such a state that the buyer would under the contract be bound to take delivery of them".

> In *Underwood v. Burgh Castle Brick and Cement Syndicate (1922)* the plaintiff sold a condensing engine to the defendants. The engine weighed over 30 tons and was cemented to the floor of the plaintiff's premises. It had to be dismantled and detached from the floor and the seller agreed to do this. The engine was damaged in the process. It was held that property had not passed to the buyer at the time it was damaged as the goods were not then in a deliverable state. The risk was therefore with the seller who had to bear the loss.

Goods are not in a deliverable state merely because they are transportable. Whether goods are in a deliverable state will depend in each case on the terms of the contract. Where specific goods are not in a deliverable state at the time the contract is made, r.2 may apply.

> **Rule 2:**
> "Where there is a contract for the sale of specific goods and the seller is bound to do something to the goods for the purpose of putting them into a deliverable state, the property does not pass until the thing is done and the buyer has notice that it has been done".

This rule will apply if, for example, a contract for the sale of a motor vehicle contained a term that the seller would replace the exhaust system before delivery to the buyer. The ownership of the car would not be transferred until the work had been done and the buyer had been notified.

> **Rule 3:**
> "Where there is a contract for the sale of specific goods in a deliverable state but the seller is bound to weigh, measure, test or do some other act or thing with reference to the goods for the purpose of ascertaining the price, the property does not pass until the act or thing is done and the buyer has notice that it has been done".

This rule, like r.2, only applies where it is the seller who must do something to the goods. If something must be done by the buyer rather than the seller, property will pass under s.18 r.1 on the making of the contract.

> In *Turley v. Bates (1863)* a contract for the sale of clay provided that the buyer had to weigh it in order to determine the price. It was held that property passed to the buyer when the contract was made.

Figure 5.7 summaries the rules relating to the passing of property in specific goods.

PASSING OF PROPERTY IN SPECIFIC GOODS

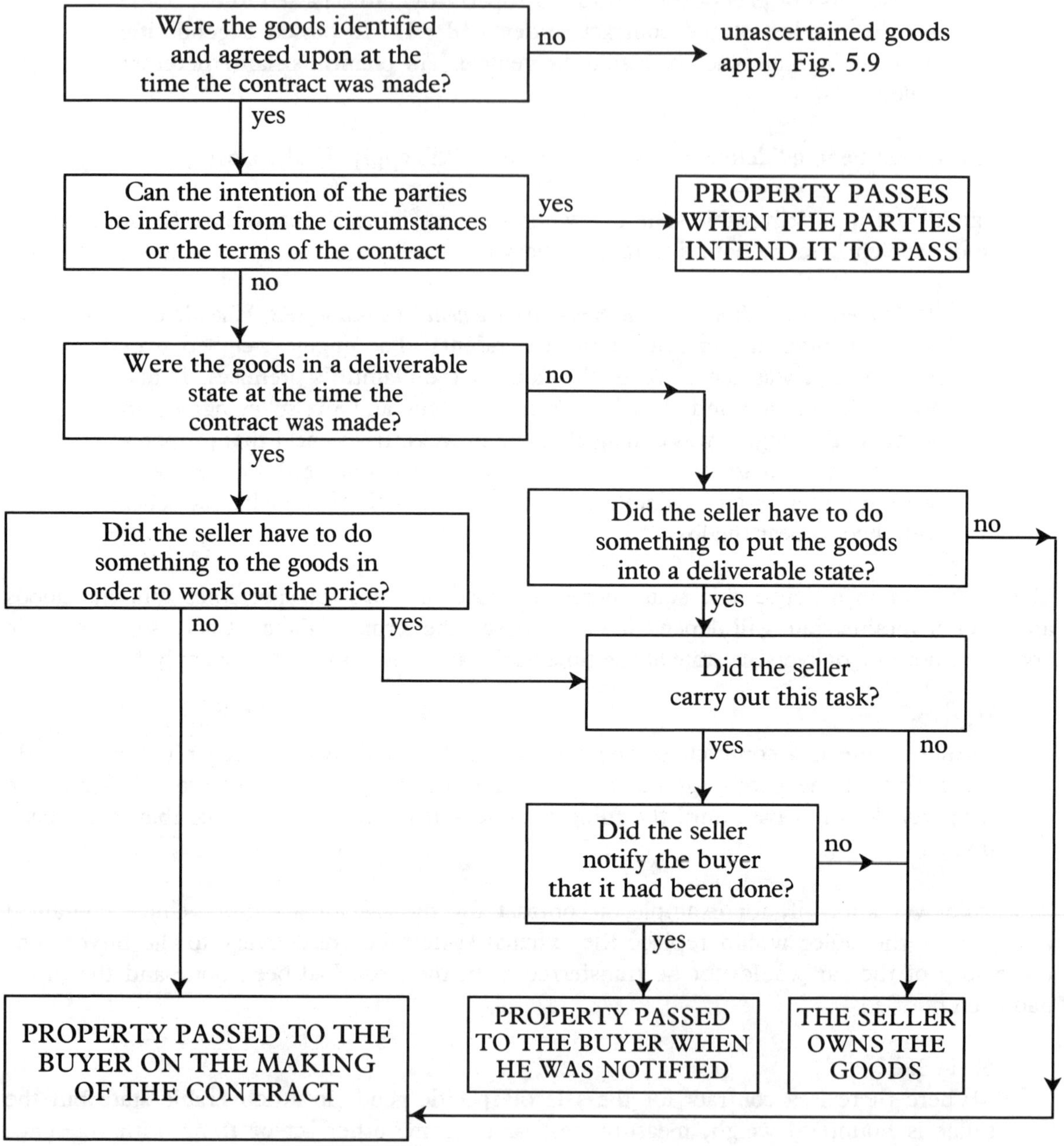

Fig. 5.7

PASSING OF PROPERTY WHERE GOODS ARE DELIVERED ON SALE OR RETURN

Section 18 rule 4 applies where goods are delivered to the buyer on approval or on sale or return terms. It is unnecessary for the purposes of r.4 to decide whether the goods are specific or unascertained.

> **Rule 4:**
> "When goods are delivered to the buyer on approval or on sale or return or other similar terms, the property in the goods passes to the buyer:
>
> (a) when he signifies his approval or acceptance to the seller or does any other act adopting the transaction;
>
> (b) if he does not signify his approval or acceptance to the seller but retains the goods without giving notice of rejection, then, if a time has been fixed for the return of the goods, on the expiration of that time, and, if no time has been fixed, on the expiration of a reasonable time".

Any act of the buyer, such as using or selling the goods, which is inconsistent with the ownership of the original seller, will be "an act adopting the transaction" for the purposes of r.4(a).

> In *Kirkham v. Attenborough (1897)* the plaintiff gave goods to a customer on sale or return terms. He pawned the goods. The plaintiff was never paid and claimed the goods from the pawnbroker. It was held that he could not recover them because the pawning of the goods was "an act adopting the transaction". Ownership passed to the customer as a result and he transferred it on to the pawnbroker.
>
> In *Weiner v. Gill (1906)* the plaintiff delivered goods to his customer on sale or return under a standing contract which provided that "goods had on approbation or on sale or return remain the property of Samuel Weiner until such goods are settled for or charged". The goods were pawned with the defendant, from whom the plaintiff sought to recover them. It was held that s.18 r.4 did not apply. It was overridden by the express term in the contract, which, under s.17, governed the transfer of ownership. The rules in s.18 apply only where no intention has been made clear by the parties. Under the express terms of the contract the goods remained the property of the plaintiff. (Despite this, however, the defendant actually did get a good title under s.2 of the Factors Act 1889, discussed later in this chapter).

If the customer is unable to return goods within the approval period for a reason outside his control, for example because they have been stolen or accidentally destroyed without any fault on his part, he will not be deemed to have adopted the transaction and property will not pass to him.

If goods have been sent to the customer without his asking for them, the Unsolicited Goods and Services Act 1971 may apply (see later in this chapter). Under this Act the goods will become the property of the customer as an unconditional gift after the expiration of the time limit specified in the Act.

Figure 5.8 summarises the rules relating to the passing of property where goods are delivered on approval or on sale or return.

PASSING OF PROPERTY WHERE GOODS ARE DELIVERED ON APPROVAL OR ON SALE OR RETURN

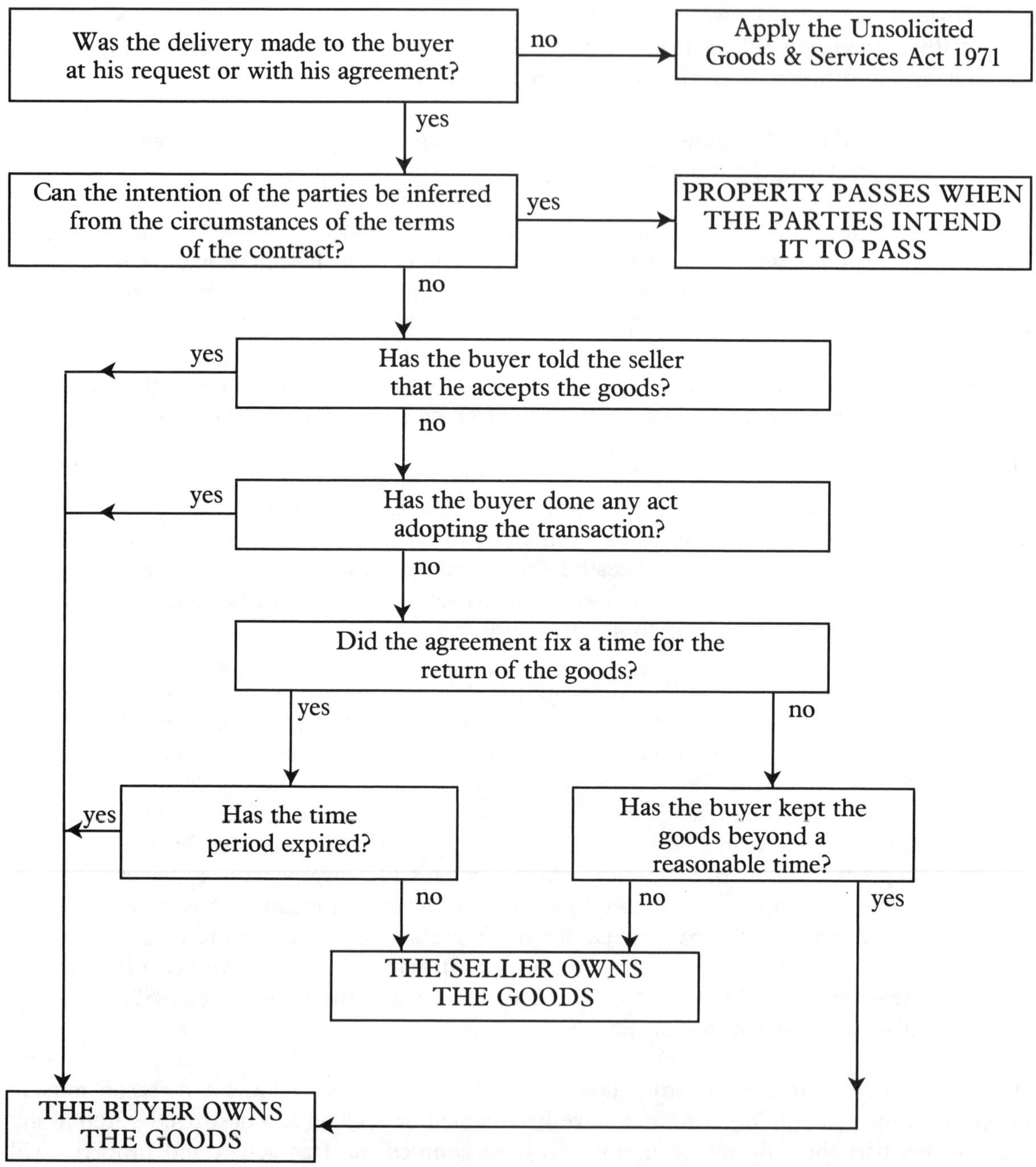

Fig. 5.8

PASSING OF PROPERTY IN UNASCERTAINED GOODS

Until the parties have identified which goods are the subject of the contract, property cannot pass from the seller to the buyer.

Section 16 provides that:

> "Where there is a contract for the sale of unascertained goods no property in the goods is transferred to the buyer unless and until the goods are ascertained".

This section cannot be used to determine when property passes to the buyer, it only tells us that property cannot pass until the goods have been ascertained. Once this has occurred s.17 will apply if there is evidence of the parties' contractual intention, otherwise rule 5 of s.18 must be applied. The following case provides an example of the application of s.16:

> In *Healey v. Howlett & Sons (1917)* the defendant ordered twenty boxes of mackerel from the plaintiff, who was a fish merchant. One hundred and ninety boxes were dispatched by rail, and railway officials were instructed to set aside twenty boxes for the defendant. The train was delayed and, before twenty boxes were set aside, the fish deteriorated. It was held that property in the goods remained with the plaintiff at least until they were set apart. They were therefore at the seller's risk when they deteriorated.

Once goods are ascertained, it is a question of contractual intention under s.17 as to when ownership is transferred. If, for example, the contract contains a retention of title clause, this will govern the passing of property. Where no contractual intention appears, however, s.18 r.5 provides that:

> "Where there is a contract for the sale of unascertained or future goods by description, and goods of that description and in a deliverable state are unconditionally appropriated to the contract, either by the seller with the assent of the buyer or by the buyer with the assent of the seller, the property in the goods then passes to the buyer; and the assent may be exprssed or implied, and may be given either before or after the appropriation is made".

Figure 5.9 summarises the requirements for the passing of property in unascertained goods.

Property cannot pass under s.18 r.5 unless the goods are in a deliverable state. It was noted earlier that goods are in a deliverable state when they are in such condition that the buyer would be bound to accept them under the terms of the contract.

> In *Philip Head and Sons Ltd. v. Showfronts Ltd. (1970)* the plaintiff sold carpeting under a contract which required them to lay it in the defendants' premises. Carpeting which was delivered for this purpose was stolen before it could be laid. The plaintiff sued for the price. It was held that the carpet was not in a deliverable state, as the seller was bound to lay it under the terms of the contract. The seller owned the carpet at the time it was stolen and had to bear the loss.

The expression "unconditional appropriation" is not defined in the Act. For an appropriation to be unconditional, the seller or the buyer must set goods aside irrevocably for the performance of the contract.

> In *Carlos Federspiel & Co. v. Charles Twigg and Co. Ltd. (1957)* the sellers

PASSING OF PROPERTY IN UNASCERTAINED GOODS

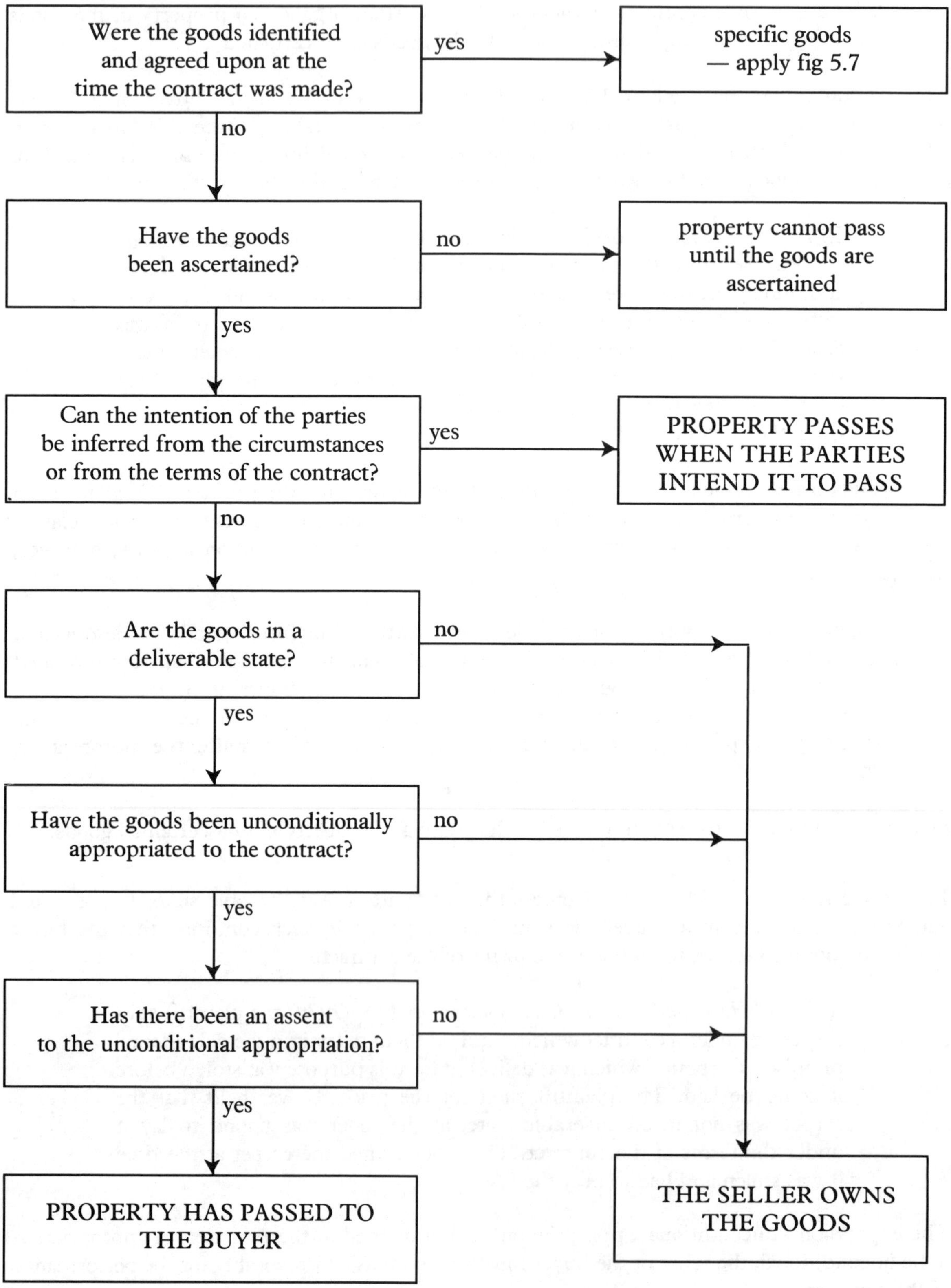

Fig. 5.9

manufactured goods for the buyers. The goods were packed in containers with the buyer's name and address on them. The sellers became insolvent. The buyers claimed that the ownership of a number of containers, still in the seller's possession, had passed to them under rule 5. It was held that there had not been an unconditional appropriation of the goods and therefore they were still in the seller's ownership. Pearson, J., stated that:

> "a mere setting apart or selection by the seller of the goods which he expects to use in performance of the contract is not enough. If that is all, he can change his mind and use those goods in performance of some other contract and use some other goods in performance of this contract. To constitute an appropriation of the goods to the contract the parties must have had, or be reasonably supposed to have had, an intention to attach the contract irrevocably to those goods, so that those goods and no others are the subject of the sale and become the property of the buyer".

Rule 5(2) provides that:

> "where in pursuance of the contract, the seller delivers the goods to the buyer or to a carrier for the purpose of transmission to the buyer, he is deemed to have unconditionally appropriated the goods to the contract".

There must be an assent to the appropriation before property will pass to the buyer. Rule 5 provides that an assent may be express or implied and may be given either before or after the appropriation is made.

In *Pignatoro v. Gilroy and Son (1919)* there was a contract for the sale of rice, which the buyer had agreed to collect. The seller packaged the rice and informed the buyer that it was ready for collection. The buyer delayed for over three weeks before coming to collect. By this time the rice had been stolen. It was held that property had passed to the buyer under r.5 and he must bear the loss. His delay and the failure to object to the appropriation within a reasonable time was evidence of an implied assent.

RETENTION OF TITLE

The 1979 Act in s.17 envisages that the parties may make express provision in the contract for the transfer of ownership. A retention (or reservation) of title clause is an express term which provides that ownership of goods will not be transferred to the buyer until payment has been made. The major advantage of retention of title, from the seller's point of view, is that the goods belong to him until he receives payment for them.

If the buyer becomes insolvent after delivery but before payment, the seller will be able to reclaim the goods because they belong to him. Without a retention of title clause the goods belong to the buyer. They will be available for distribution to the buyer's creditors on insolvency. The seller will be in the position of an unsecured trade creditor and therefore low down in the order of priority for repayment of debts. A retention of title clause effectively places the seller first in the order of priority in relation to goods which are still in the buyer's possession.

In *Aluminium Industrie Vaassen BV v. Romalpa Aluminium Limited (1976)* the seller sold aluminium foil to Romalpa, an English company for use in its manufacturing processes. At the time of manufacture the foil became mixed with other materials. The written contract contained a retention of title clause, under which ownership of the aluminium foil would be transferred to Romalpa when it had paid all sums owing to the seller. The clause went on to reserve ownership over any goods which were mixed with the aluminium foil. Romalpa became insolvent and a receiver was appointed. The seller claimed the ownership of aluminium foil still held by the company; and the proceeds of resale of unmixed foil sold by the receiver to third parties. No claim was made in respect of mixed goods or the proceeds of sale of mixed goods. The Court of Appeal held that the retention of title was valid and the seller's claim succeeded in full.

TRANSFER OF RISK

The party who carries risk must bear the loss where goods deteriorate or are stolen, damaged or destroyed in circumstances where no-one else can be made liable for the loss. The party who carries risk will usually protect himself by insurance.

Under a contract for the sale of goods risk can be transferred from the seller to the buyer at any time. If the parties make no express provision for the transfer of risk, it will take place at the same time as the transfer of ownership. The 1979 Act in s.20(1) provides:

> "Unless otherwise agreed, the goods remain at the seller's risk until the property in them is transferred to the buyer but when the property in them is transferred to the buyer the goods are at the buyer's risk whether delivery has been made or not".

Many standard form contracts transfer risk to the buyer on the making of the contract, or relate it to the transfer of possession.

It is possible that goods may be exposed to additional risks if one of the contracting parties does not comply with his obligations. To cover this possibility, the 1979 Act in s.20(2) provides that:

> "where delivery has been delayed through the fault of either the buyer or seller the goods are at the risk of the party at fault as regards any loss which might not have occurred but for such fault".

In *Demby Hamilton v. Barden (1949)* there was a contract for the sale of thirty tons of apple juice by sample. The buyer agreed to take delivery in weekly loads. The seller crushed all thirty tons of juice at once in order to ensure correspondence with the sample. The buyer took delivery of the first few instalments and then took no further deliveries for a period of time, during which the juice went off. It was held that the buyer must bear the loss. Risk transferred to him under s.20(2) even though property remained with the seller.

TRANSFER OF TITLE BY A NON-OWNER

Under a contract of sale, the principal obligation of the seller is to transfer the ownership of goods to the buyer. Clearly this presents no difficulty where the seller actually owns the goods or has the authority of the owner to sell them. However where the goods are stolen or where the seller holds them under the terms of a hire purchase agreement, in an attempted sale the seller does not have the legal right to transfer ownership. A person who buys such goods will not acquire a good title to them because the seller cannot pass on to the buyer that which he does not have. This rule is expressed in the latin maxim "nemo dat quod non habet". This means no-one can give what he has not got.

The rule is embodied in s.21 of the Sale of Goods Act 1979, which provides that:

> "Where goods are sold by a person who is not their owner, the buyer acquires no better title to the goods than the seller had".

A thief has no legal title to goods and a purchaser from a thief acquires no better title. The thief could be prosecuted under s.1 of the Theft Act 1968 for the offence of theft. He could also be sued by the owner for damages, under the Torts (Interference with Goods) Act 1977.

If the purchaser knew that the goods were stolen at the time he bought them, he could be prosecuted under the Theft Act 1968 for the offence of handling stolen goods. He could also be sued by the owner for damages, or for an order of specific delivery, under the Torts (Interference with Goods) Act 1977. In turn, he could sue the thief for breach of the implied terms relating to title, under s.12 of the Sale of Goods Act 1979 provided he purchased the goods innocently.

Where the purchaser acts in complete innocence and the thief disappears with the purchase money, the owner and the purchaser are left in dispute about the ownership of the goods. Each has some justification for his claim. In these circumstances the law has recognised that some balance must be struck between the protection of the property rights of the original owner, and the protection of the legitimate claim of a purchaser acting in good faith.

In *Pearson v. Rose and Young Limited (1951)* Lord Denning summed up the difficulty of striking a fair balance between two innocent victims:

> "In the early days of the common law the governing principle of our law of property was that no person could give a better title than he himself had got, but the needs of commerce have led to a progressive modification of this principle so as to protect innocent purchasers . . . the cases show how difficult it is to strike the right balance between the claims of true owners and the claims of innocent purchasers".

In an attempt to strike this balance, a number of exceptions to the general rule have been evolved. The principal exceptions are:

(a) estoppel;

(b) sale under common law or statutory powers, or by court order;

(c) sale in market overt;

(d) sale under a voidable title;

(e) sale by a seller in possession;

(f) sale by a mercantile agent;

(g) sale by a buyer in possession; and

(h) sale of a motor vehicle subject to a hire purchase agreement.

ESTOPPEL

This exception is contained in s.21 of the 1979 Act which, after stating the general rule that a buyer can acquire no better title to goods than the seller had, continues with the words:

> ". . . unless the owner of the goods is by his conduct precluded from denying the seller's authority to sell".

An estoppel arises where the owner of goods, by his conduct, has allowed the purchaser to believe that the seller has a right to sell them. The true owner is prevented (or "estopped") from denying to the purchaser that the seller had authority to sell.

> An example of conduct amounting to an estoppel can be seen in *Eastern Distributors Limited v. Goldring (1967)* where the owner of a van wished to raise a loan. He got together with a car dealer in order to deceive a finance company by making it appear that the dealer owned the van and the original owner wished to acquire it from him on hire purchase. The standard forms were forwarded to the plaintiff finance company who received them in good faith believing that the van belonged to the trader. The plaintiff bought the van and let it to the original owner on hire purchase. The original owner did not pay his instalments and subsequently sold the van to the defendant, an innocent purchaser. The finance company sued the ultimate purchaser of the van claiming ownership. It was held that the conduct of the original owner in making it appear that the car dealer owned the vehicle, acted as an estoppel. Thus he was prevented from denying that the finance company had the ownership of the van. This meant that the original owner could not transfer a good title to the ultimate purchaser. The van therefore belonged to the plaintiff finance company.

SALE UNDER COMMON LAW OR STATUTORY POWERS, OR UNDER THE ORDER OF A COURT

Such a sale will vest a good title in the purchaser, regardless of whether or not the original owner authorised or approved of it, so long as the power of sale exists and is properly exercised.

SALE IN MARKET OVERT

Market overt is the term used to describe any open, public and legally constituted market in England. There are no markets overt in Wales or Scotland. In the City of London all shops are market overt.

The 1979 Act, in s.22 provides that:

> "Where goods are sold in market overt, according to the usage of the market, the buyer acquires a good title to the goods, provided he buys them in good faith and without notice of any defect or want of title on the part of the seller".

Goods must be sold according to the usage or usual customs of the market, otherwise the buyer will not get a good title. Generally goods must be on display and sold in a public part of the market or shop, and the sale must take place during normal business hours between sunrise and sunset.

> In *Bishopsgate Motor Finance Co. v. Transport Brakes Ltd. (1949)* a customer acquired a motor car on hire purchase from the plaintiffs. Before completing

the repayments under the agreement, the customer took it to Maidstone Market where he instructed an auctioneer to sell it. The car did not reach its reserve price and he sold it privately to the defendant who bought it in good faith and had no knowledge of the hire purchase agreement. The Court held that a private sale was within the usage of the market and therefore the defendant obtained a good title to the car. In the course of his judgment, Lord Denning summed up the problem of conflicting legal principle which a court has to deal with where there is a sale by a non-owner :

> "In the development of our law, two principles have striven for mastery. The first is for the protection of property: no-one can give a better title than he himself possesses. The second is for the protection of commercial transactions: the person who takes in good faith and for value without notice should get a good title. The first principle has held sway for a long time, but it has been modified by the common law itself and by statute".

SALE UNDER A VOIDABLE TITLE

A contract may be voidable at the option of one of the contracting parties, for example where the buyer is induced by misrepresentation to make the agreement. The contract is binding until the buyer chooses to avoid it or set it aside. Similarly, where the buyer fraudulently persuades the seller to accept a cheque which is subsequently dishonoured, the contract is valid until the seller does some overt act evidencing an intention to avoid it.

Property may pass to a buyer under a voidable contract. His title to the goods is also voidable and will be lost if the seller avoids the contract. If the buyer resells the goods before the seller avoids the contract, the new buyer will obtain title. If the resale takes place after the seller avoids the first contract, the new buyer does not have title and the original seller can recover the goods from him.

This is provided for in s.23 of the 1979 Act, which states:

> "When the seller of goods has a voidable title to them, but his title has not been avoided at the time of the sale, the buyer acquires a good title to the goods, provided he buys them in good faith and without notice of the seller's defect of title."

In *Phillips v. Brooks (1919)* a rogue obtained a ring worth £450 from a jeweller. The rogue had a voidable title to the ring and subsequently pawned it with the defendant pawnbroker. In an action by the jeweller to recover the ring from the pawnbroker, it was held that the pawnbroker had a good title to it. The jeweller had not avoided his contract with the rogue at the time the ring was pawned.

A contract can be avoided by informing the other party that the contract is at an end. This may not be possible however where the other party has made off with the goods dishonestly. In such a case the seller must do some other act evidencing his intention to avoid the contract, for example informing the police of the fraud.

In *Car and Universal Finance Co. v. Caldwell (1963)* the plaintiff sold a car to a buyer, who fraudulently induced him to accept a cheque in payment. The cheque was dishonoured. The plaintiff contacted the police and the A.A. and asked them to recover the car for him. Subsequently

> the buyer resold the car to the defendant, from whom the plaintiff reclaimed it. It was held that the contract between the plaintiff and the buyer was voidable. The plaintiff's act of informing the police and the A.A. was sufficient to evidence an intention to avoid it. This had occurred before the buyer's resale to the defendant and therefore the car belonged to the plaintiff.

SALE BY A SELLER IN POSSESSION

This exception, contained in s.24 of the 1979 Act, applies where a seller has sold goods to a buyer (B1) to whom property has passed. The seller, still in possession of the goods, resells them to a second buyer (B2). Applying the general principle, B2 would not obtain ownership because the seller has already transferred it to B1. However, if the conditions laid down in s.24 are satisfied, B2 will obtain a good title.

The 1979 Act, in s.24 provides:

> "Where a person having sold goods continues or is in possession of the goods, or of the documents of title to the goods, the delivery or transfer by that person, or by a mercantile agent acting for him, of the goods or documents of title under any sale, pledge, or other disposition thereof, to any person receiving the same in good faith and without notice of the previous sale, has the same effect as if the person making the delivery or transfer were expressly authorised by the owner of the goods to make the same".

B2 will get a good title if he is acting honestly and does not know of the previous sale to B1. There must be an actual delivery of the goods or documents of title to him. B1 will be left with the right to sue the seller for damages for breach of contract. He will have no rights against B2 or against the goods.

> In *Pacific Motor Auctions Ltd. v. Motor Credits (Hire Finance) Limited (1965)* the seller, a car dealer, sold a number of cars to the plaintiffs (B1) under a "display agreement" whereby the seller remained in possession of the cars for display in his showroom. He was paid 90% of the purchase price and was authorised to sell the cars as the plaintiff's agent. The seller got into financial difficulties and the plaintiffs cancelled his authority to sell the cars. Disregarding their instructions, he sold a car to the defendant (B2) who took it in good faith and without notice of the previous sale. The Court held that the defendant, who had taken delivery of the car, obtained a good title to it by virtue of s.24.

Figure 5.10 summarises the requirements of s.24 in a diagrammatic form.

SALE BY A MERCANTILE AGENT

A mercantile agent, or factor, is a person who, in the ordinary course of his business, buys, sells or otherwise deals with goods on behalf of others. A sale of goods by a mercantile agent will usually pass a good title to the purchaser under s.2 of the Factors Act 1889 even if the agent has no express authority to sell the goods.

The 1889 Act in s.2(1) provides that:

> "Where a mercantile agent is, with the consent of the owner, in possession of goods or of the documents of title to goods, any sale, pledge, or other disposition of the goods, made by him when acting in the ordinary course of business of a mercantile agent,

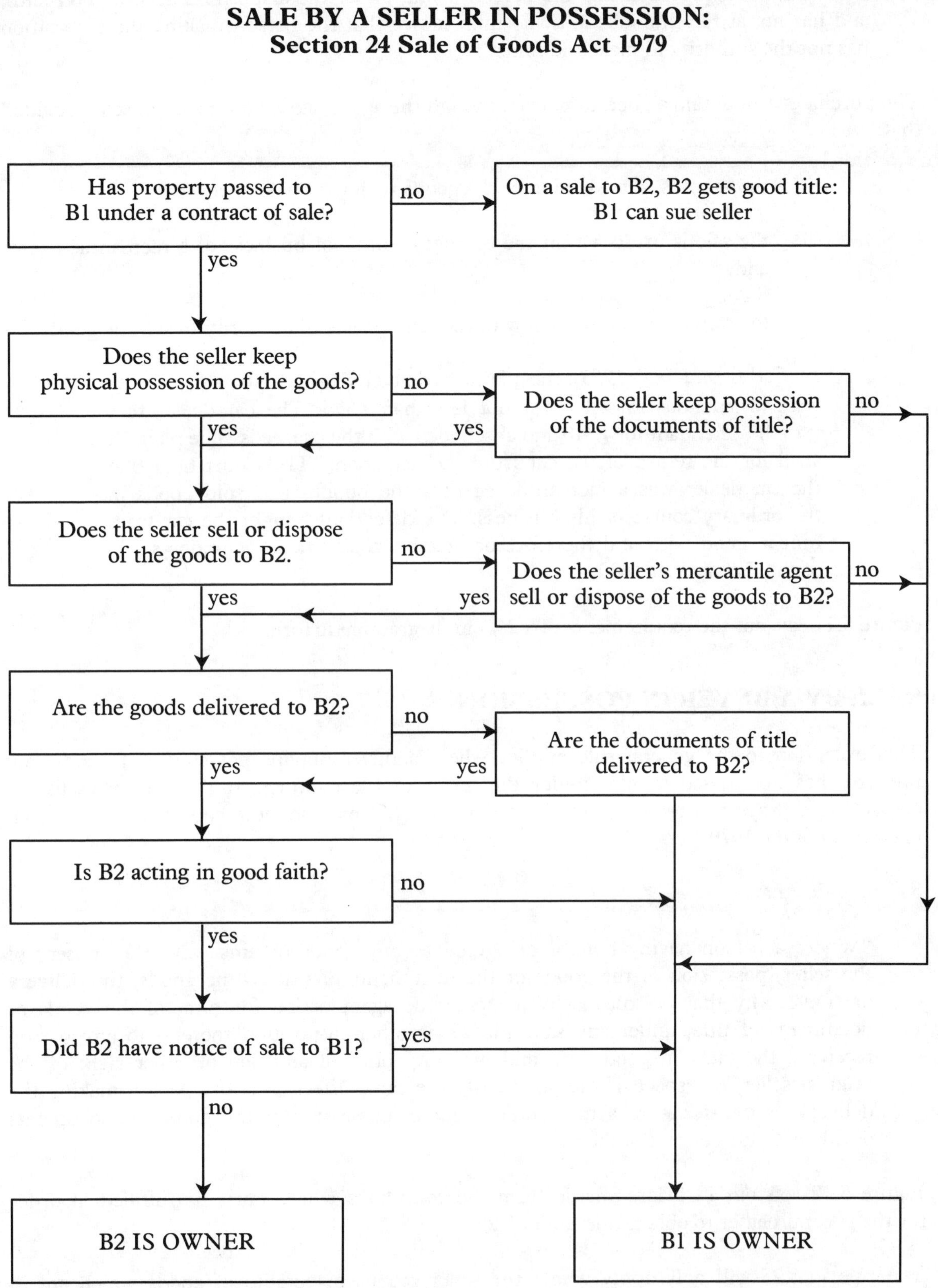
SALE BY A SELLER IN POSSESSION:
Section 24 Sale of Goods Act 1979
Has property passed to B1 under a contract of sale?
no
On a sale to B2, B2 gets good title: B1 can sue seller
yes
Does the seller keep physical possession of the goods?
no
Does the seller keep possession of the documents of title?
no
yes
yes
Does the seller sell or dispose of the goods to B2.
no
Does the seller's mercantile agent sell or dispose of the goods to B2?
no
yes
yes
Are the goods delivered to B2?
no
Are the documents of title delivered to B2?
yes
yes
Is B2 acting in good faith?
no
yes
Did B2 have notice of sale to B1?
yes
no
B2 IS OWNER
B1 IS OWNER

Fig. 5.10

shall . . . be valid as if he were expressly authorised by the owner of the goods to make the same; provided that the person taking under the disposition acts in good faith, and has not at the time of the disposition notice that the person making the disposition has not the authority to make the same".

The purchaser will obtain a good title, even though the agent had no authority to sell, provided that:

(i) the agent is in possession of the goods with the owner's consent;

(ii) the sale is made within the ordinary course of business of a mercantile agent; and

(iii) the purchaser did not know of the agent's lack of authority to sell the goods.

In *Folkes v. King (1923)* the plaintiff delivered his car to a car dealer with instructions to sell it for not less than £575. The car dealer sold it to the defendant for £340 and absconded with the proceeds. The plaintiff sued for the return of the car from the defendant. The Court held that the car dealer was a mercantile agent as he bought and sold goods in the ordinary course of his business. The defendant bought the car from him in good faith and therefore obtained a good title to it under s.2(1) of the Factors Act 1889.

Figure 5.11 sets out the requirements of s.2(1) in diagrammatic form.

SALE BY A BUYER IN POSSESSION

This exception to the general rule applies where a buyer obtains possession of goods, but property has not passed to him under the terms of the contract. If the buyer resells the goods before property passes to him, the sub-buyer (B2) may obtain a good title to the goods under s.25 of the 1979 Act.

S25 provides that:

"Where a person having bought or agreed to buy goods obtains, with the consent of the seller, possession of the goods or the documents of title to the goods, the delivery or transfer by that person, or by a mercantile agent acting for him, of the goods or documents of title, under any sale, pledge or other disposition thereof, to any person receiving the same in good faith and without notice of any lien or other right of the original seller in respect of the goods, has the same effect as if the person making the delivery or transfer were a mercantile agent in possession of the goods or documents of title with the consent of the owner".

Figure 5.12 sets out in diagrammatic form the conditions which must be fulfilled in order for the sub-purchaser to obtain title under s.25:

The rule in s.25 will only apply where the seller retains ownership of goods which are in the buyer's possession after a contract of sale. This situation could occur under s.18 r.2 or r.3, although more usually it would be one in which there is a retention of title clause in the contract.

In *Newtons of Wembley Ltd. v. Williams (1964)* the plaintiff sold a car to a rogue and was paid by cheque. The parties expressly agreed that

SALE BY A MERCANTILE AGENT IN POSSESSION: S2(I) Factors Act 1889

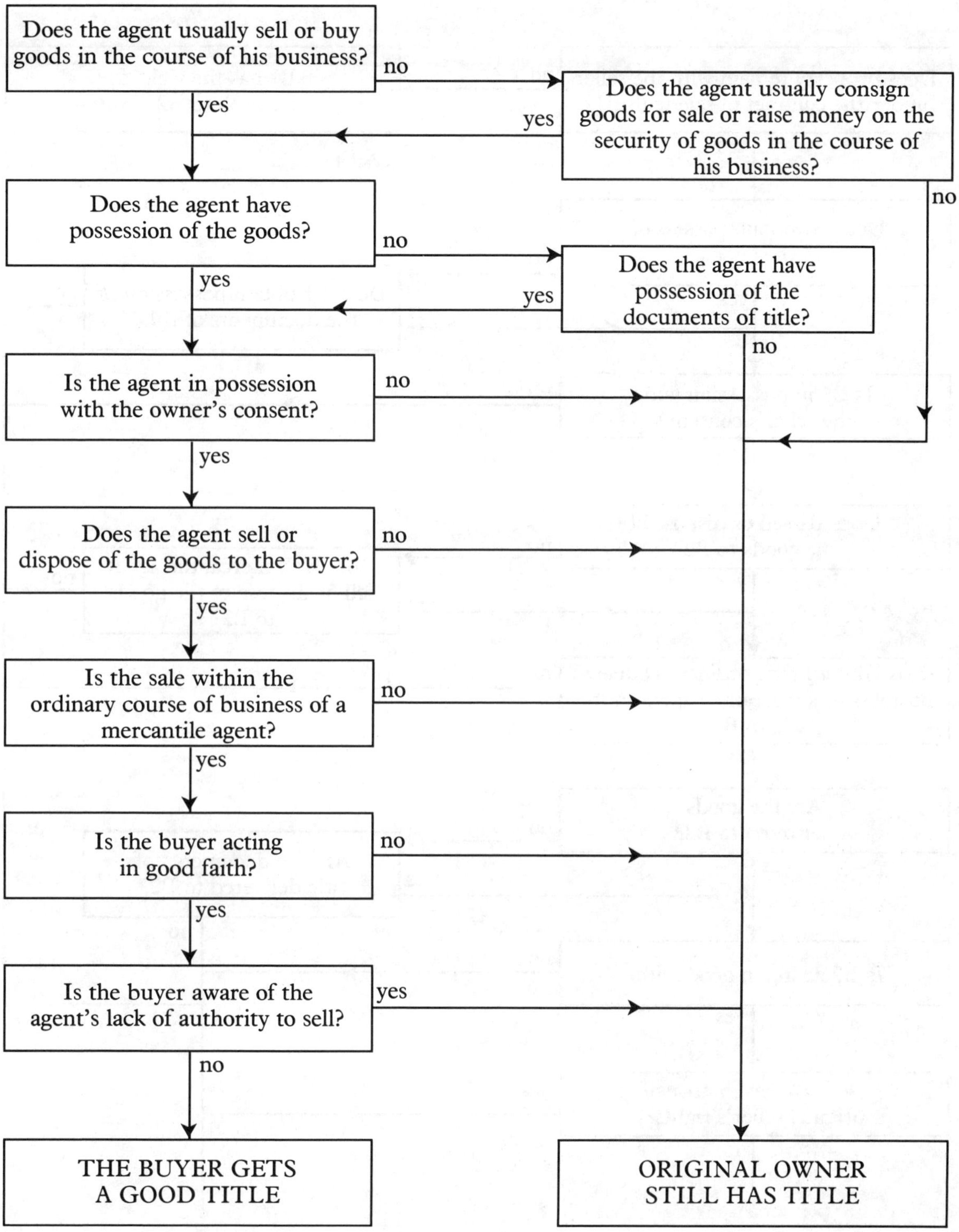

Fig. 5.11

SALE BY A BUYER IN POSSESSION
S25 SALE OF GOODS ACT 1979

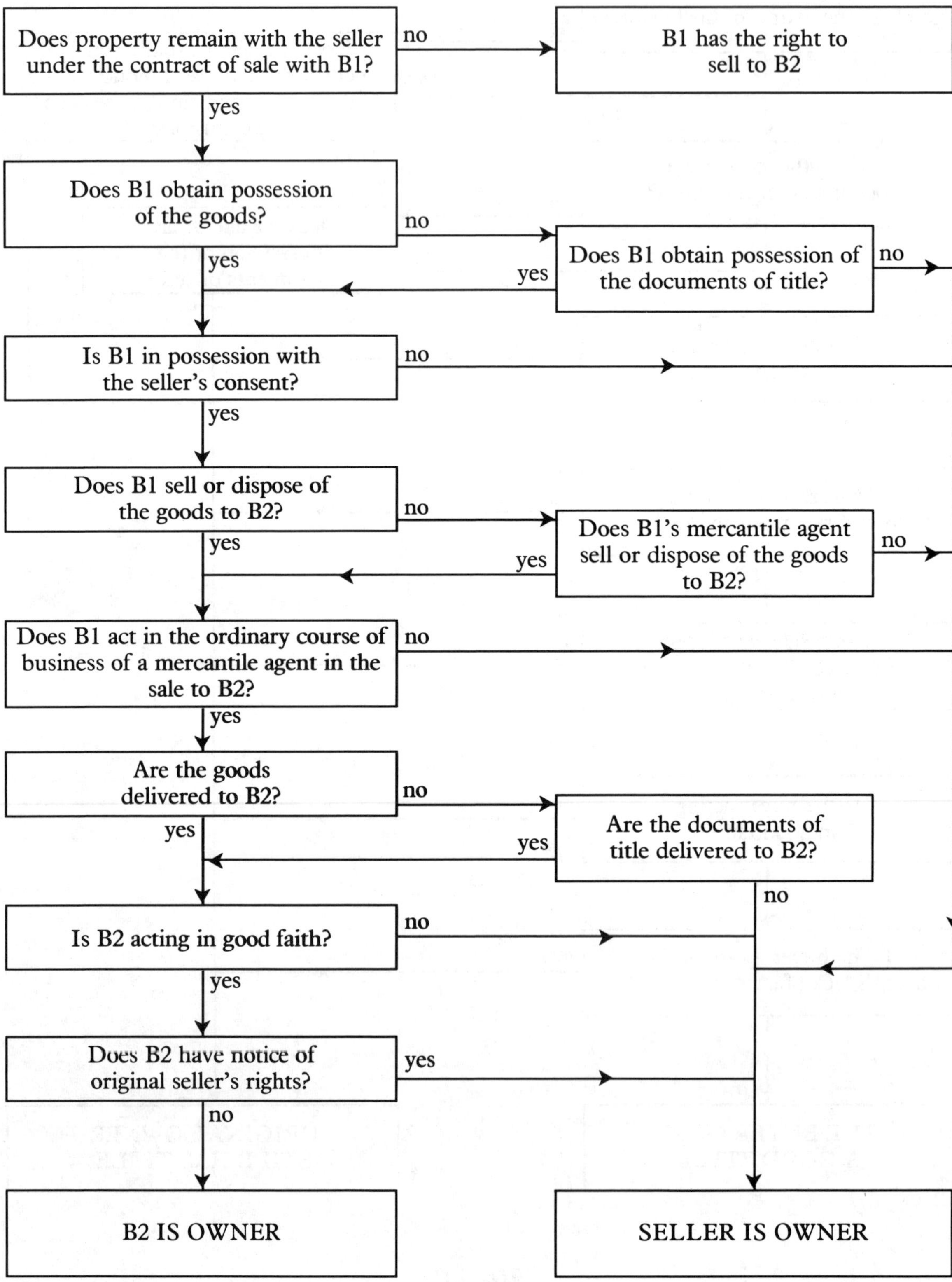

Fig. 5.12

> ownership of the car would remain with the plaintiff until the cheque was cleared. The rogue took the car, with its registration book, and resold it to the defendant in Warren Street, London, a recognised second hand car market where dealers regularly operated. The defendant purchased the car in good faith and without notice. The rogue's cheque was dishonoured and the plaintiff claimed the car from the defendant. The Court of Appeal held that the rogue was a buyer in possession under s.25. The requirements of the section were satisifed and the defendant obtained a good title to the car.

> In *Four Point Garage Ltd. v. Carter (1985)* the seller sold a car to B1, who resold it to B2, the defendant. Each contract contained a retention of title clause. The defendant paid B1 for the car. B1, who became insolvent, had not paid the plaintiff. It was held that, although property had not passed to B1, he was a buyer in possession and the defendant obtained good title to the car under s.25.

Where the original seller has a defective title to goods, it appears that B2, the sub-buyer from the buyer in possession, will not obtain title under s.25. The Court of Appeal has recently held that the section does not have the effect of perfecting the defective title.

> In *National Employers Mutual General Insurance Association Limited v. Jones (1987)* the defendant, B2, bought a car in good faith from an intermediate buyer, B1, who had purchased it, also in good faith, from a thief. The original owner sued for the return of the car, but the defendant claimed to have acquired a good title to it under s.25. The Court of Appeal, by a majority, held that no purported sale by a thief, or by a person who acquired goods from him, could transfer a good title to a sub-purchaser under s.25. The plaintiff was therefore entitled to the return of his car.

SALE OF A MOTOR VEHICLE SUBJECT TO A HIRE PURCHASE AGREEMENT

This exception is contained in Part III of the Hire Purchase Act 1964. It applies where the debtor under a hire purchase or conditional sale agreement disposes of a motor vehicle before property passes to him under the terms of the credit agreement. The exception applies to motor vehicles only and not to goods of any other type.

The Hire Purchase Act 1964, in s.27 provides that:

> "Where a motor vehicle has been let under a hire purchase agreement, or has been agreed to be sold under a conditional sale agreement, and, at a time before the property in the vehicle has become vested in the hirer or buyer, he disposes of the vehicle . . . to a private purchaser . . . in good faith and without notice of the hire purchase agreement or conditional sale agreement, that disposition shall have effect as if the title of the owner or seller to the vehicle had been vested in the hirer or buyer immediately before that disposition.

Only a private purchaser of a motor vehicle is protected by s.27. A "trade or finance purchaser", for example a garage or finance company, is not protected by the section because there are facilities, within these trades, to check up on the existence of an outstanding credit agreement relating to any motor vehicle. However, where a trade or finance purchaser buys a motor vehicle and then resells it, the first private purchaser to buy it will obtain the original creditor's title under s.27.

A private purchaser will be protected by s.27 so long as he acts in good faith and has no notice of the rights of the original creditor.

> In *Barker v. Bell (1971)* the debtor had a car on hire purchase from a finance company. Before he paid off the sums due under the hire purchase agreement, he sold the car to an innocent private purchaser. He told the purchaser that the car had been subject to a hire purchase agreement which was paid off, and showed him a receipt marked with the words "final payment". The Court of Appeal held that property passed to the purchaser by virtue of s.27 of the 1964 Act. The finance company's argument that the purchaser had notice of the hire purchase agreement was rejected. In his judgment, Lord Denning stated that:
>
> > "A purchaser is only affected by notice if he has actual notice that the car is on hire purchase. He is not affected merely by being told that it was previously on hire purchase which has now been paid off".

Figure 5.13 sets out in diagrammatic form the requirements of s.27 of the 1964 Act.

CONSUMER CREDIT

The Consumer Credit Act 1974 was introduced with the aim of ensuring "truth in lending". The Act applies to a wide range of types of credit agreement and places strict controls upon persons who provide credit facilities in the course of their business. Overall responsibility for administering the Act lies with the Director General of Fair Trading. The Act creates many criminal offences and enforcement in relation to these is by local authority Trading Standards Officers.

Agreements regulated by the Act fall within two broad categories, consumer hire agreements (defined above), and consumer credit agreements. Under s.8:

> "A consumer credit agreement is an agreement between an individual (the debtor) and any other person (the creditor) by which the creditor provides the debtor with credit not exceeding £15,000".

The agreement must be for the provision of "credit". This is defined in wide terms by s.9(1) to include "cash loans and any other form of financial accommodation". Hire purchase, conditional sale and credit sale agreements will all be consumer credit agreements if they satisfy the other elements of the definition. Certain types of credit agreement, particularly those concerned with the purchase and development of land and buildings, are excluded from the operation of the Act and are not consumer credit agreements.

An agreement will not be a consumer credit agreement where:

(a) the debtor is a limited company, and therefore not "an individual" (a flesh and blood person), or

(b) the amount of credit provided is in excess of £15,000.

In these cases most of the provisions of the Act will not apply and the agreement will be governed by common law principles.

**SALE OF MOTOR VEHICLE WHILE ON HP:
PART III Hire Purchase Act 1964**

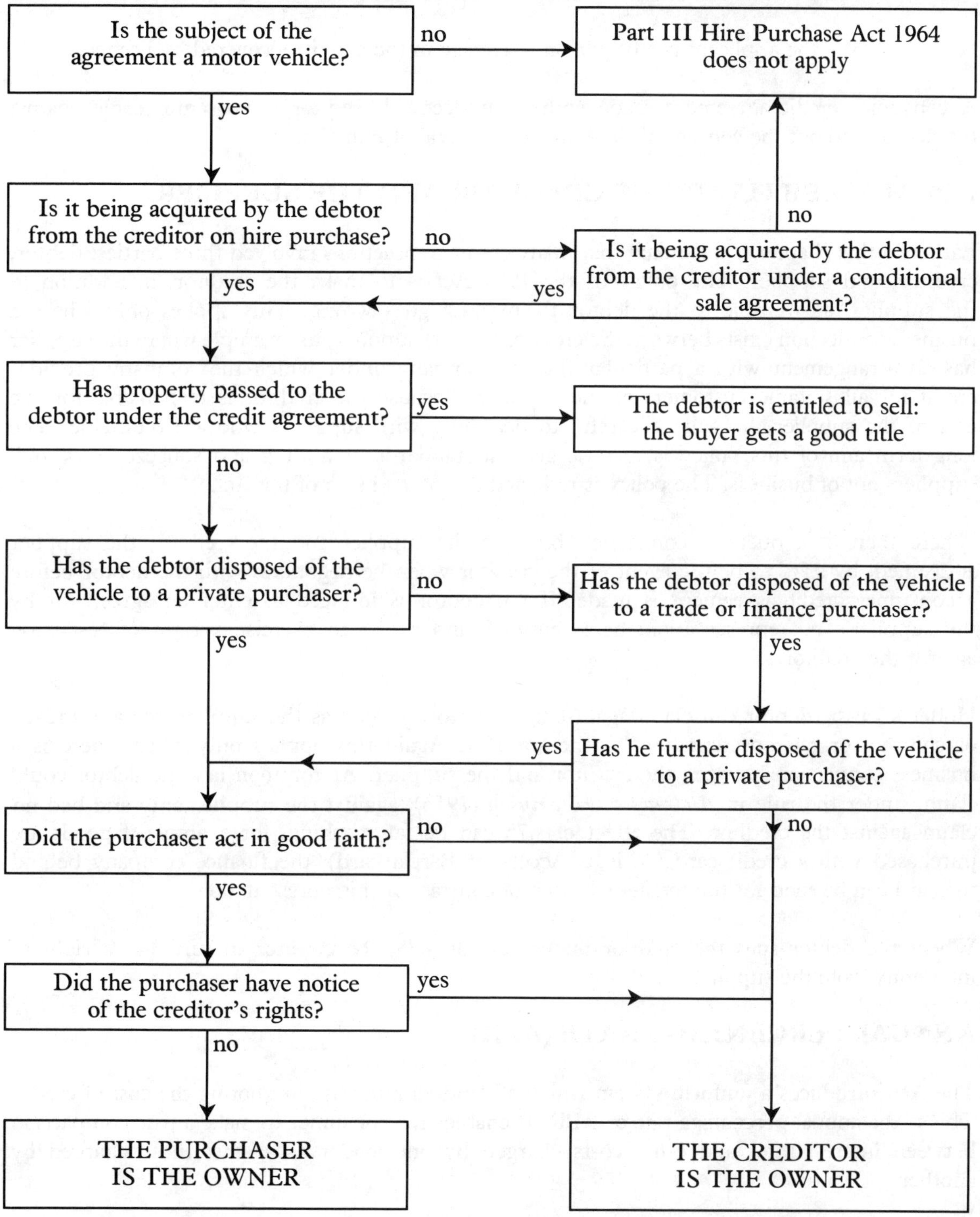

Fig. 5.13

LICENSING OF CREDITORS

Any person who intends to carry on the business of providing credit cannot do so unless he first obtains a licence from the Director General of Fair Trading. The Director General must grant a licence to any person who makes an application, provided he is satisfied that:

(a) the name under which the business is operating is neither misleading nor undesirable, and

(b) the applicant is a fit person to engage in the activities covered by licence.

A consumer credit agreement made with an unlicenced creditor is not enforceable against the debtor without the consent of the Director General of Fair Trading.

EQUAL LIABILITY OF THE CREDITOR AND THE SUPPLIER

Earlier in this chapter it was noted that many credit transactions involved three parties: debtor, creditor, and supplier. The policy of the 1974 Act is to make the creditor, in addition to the supplier, answerable to the debtor if anything goes wrong. This applies only where a business connection exists between the creditor and the supplier, for example where the supplier has an arrangement with a particular finance company under which the company provides credit for all suitable customers of the supplier. Because the creditor is responsible for the acts of the supplier, he will be careful to deal only with suppliers who are reputable. The long term aim of this policy is to raise general standards of trading and squeeze "cowboy" suppliers out of business. The policy is reflected in s.56 and s.75 of the Act.

Where there is a business connection between the supplier and the creditor, the supplier is deemed, by s.56, to be the agent of the creditor when he negotiates with the debtor before a consumer credit agreement is made. If the debtor is induced to enter an agreement by the supplier's misrepresentation, he is entitled under s.56 to exercise a right of rescission against the creditor.

Under s.75 the debtor can claim against the creditor, as well as the supplier, for any breach of contract or misrepresentation by the supplier. Again this applies only where there is a business connection between the creditor and the supplier. At common law the debtor could claim, under the rule in *Andrews v. Hopkinson (1956)*, against the supplier only and had no claim against the creditor. The effect of s.75 can be far reaching, for example if goods are purchased with a credit card (such as Access or Barclaycard), the finance company behind the card can be sued for the retailer's breach of contract or misrepresentation.

Where the debtor sues the creditor under s.56 or s.75, the creditor in turn has a right of indemnity from the supplier.

ANNUAL PERCENTAGE RATE (APR)

The Act introduces a uniform system which all lenders must use in quoting the cost of credit. This is the annual percentage rate or APR. It enables the consumer to make a true comparison between interest rates and other costs charged by one lender as against those charged by another.

Prior to the introduction of APR there was no standard method of calculating the percentage rate. At that time loans on identical terms in relation to interest and other costs could be advertised at widely varying rates, depending upon the statistical method used to calculate the rate. Consumers therefore had no reliable yardstick against which the different deals on offer could be measured.

All traders must now calculate the cost of credit using the statistical method laid down by the Act. The APR, arrived at in this way, must be shown on certain types of credit advertisement, for example in newspapers, catalogues or shop windows. In addition, the consumer has the right to ask for a written quotation of credit terms, which must specify the APR, where a trader advertises that credit is available.

FORM AND CONTENT OF CONSUMER CREDIT AGREEMENTS

The Consumer Credit Act lays down strict rules governing the form and content of agreements. The object of the rules is to protect the debtor by giving him the fullest possible information about his rights and obligations.

The agreement must be in a form which complies with regulations made under the Act. It must contain details of such things as:

(a) the names and addresses of the parties

(b) the APR

(c) the cash price

(d) any deposit

(e) the amount of credit

(f) the total amount payable

(g) the amount of each payment

(h) repayment dates

(i) sums payable on default

(j) certain rights and protections under the Act.

The agreement must be in writing and signed personally by the debtor. If either of these requirements is not met, the creditor will be unable to sue the debtor if he defaults, for example by stopping his payments.

The debtor must receive a copy of the agreement when he signs it, and a further copy as soon as it has been signed by the creditor. If this requirement is not complied with, the creditor cannot sue the debtor, or enforce the agreement in any other way, for example by repossession, unless he previously obtains the permission of the court.

CREDIT REFERENCE AGENCIES

A credit reference agency is an organisation which collects financial information about individuals. This includes a person's record in paying off debts and previous credit agreements, and outstanding judgments recorded against them in the county court. Creditors will usually consult credit reference agencies before entering into agreements with new customers. There are two national credit reference agencies.

These are: CCM Systems limited,
Talbot House,
Talbot Street,
Nottingham NG1 5HF.

and Credit Data Limited,
Regency House,
38 Whitworth Street,
Manchester M60 1QH.

In addition there are a number of local agencies. Where an individual applies for credit he may require the trader to provide him with the name and address of any credit reference agency which has been consulted about him.

An individual has the right, under s.158 of the 1974 Act, to know what information is being held about him by a credit reference agency. He also has the right to correct any false information in the file kept by the agency. To exercise this right he must make a written request, containing sufficient particulars to enable the agency to identify the file, and accompanied by a fee of £1.

The agency must supply the individual with a copy of any file which it keeps relating to him. The copy must be in plain English and accompanied by a notice of the individual's right to correct false information. If the agency does not keep a file relating to the individual, it must write informing him of that fact.

If any of the information in the file is incorrect, the individual can ask the agency to correct it. If the agency refuses to alter the file to the satisfaction of the individual, or if it does not reply within 28 days of a request, the individual can write a note of correction of up to 200 words. The agency must add the note of correction to the file. It also has a duty to send details of the correction to anyone who obtained information from the file within the previous 6 months.

An agency will be guilty of a criminal offence if it fails to comply with a duty imposed on it by the 1974 Act.

COOLING OFF AND CANCELLATION

It is a well established principle of the law of contract that once an agreement has been entered into, cancellation by one of the parties is a breach of contract which entitles the other to sue for damages. The Consumer Credit Act 1974 provides an important exception to this principle.

An agreement will be cancellable under the Act where:

(a) statements are made by the trader in the presence of the debtor prior to making the agreement, and

(b) the debtor signs the agreement at a place other than the trader's place of business, for example at home.

The right of cancellation typically applies to credit transactions entered into with doorstep salesmen, although the right exists whenever the above conditions are fulfilled. Where an agreement is cancellable, it must contain a notice informing the debtor of his right to cancel. The agreement can be cancelled at any time up to the end of the fifth full day after it has been signed by both parties.

Notice of cancellation must be given in writing. It can be expressed in any manner, so long as it indicates an intention to withdraw from the agreement. Where a debtor exercises the right to cancel, he ceases to be liable under the agreement and is entitled to the return of all sums paid by him.

DEFAULT BY THE DEBTOR

(a) default notice

Where a debtor is in breach of a consumer credit agreement, the creditor cannot terminate the agreement or demand early payment or recover possession of goods until a "default notice" has been served on the debtor. The notice must in the form prescribed by the Act. It must specify the nature of the breach, the action required to remedy it, and the date (giving at least 7 days) by which remedial action must be taken.

The creditor cannot take any steps to enforce an agreement until the date specified in the notice has passed. If the debtor complies with a default notice within the required period, the breach of agreement by him is treated as not having occurred.

(b) protected goods

Where the debtor under a hire purchase or conditional sale agreement has paid at least one third of the total price, the goods are "protected goods". If the debtor is in default of the agreement, the creditor at common law has an unrestricted right to repossess the goods because at this stage he still owns them. However, under s.90 of the 1974 Act, the creditor cannot retake possession of protected goods without either a court order or the debtor's permission. If he does so the agreement terminates. The debtor is released from all liability under it. In addition he is entitled to recover from the creditor all sums previously paid by him under the agreement.

> In *Capital Finance v. Bray (1964)* a finance company repossessed a car without a court order. As the debtor had repaid more than one third of the total price, the car was covered by the protected goods rules. The company, realising its mistake, returned the car to the debtor by leaving it outside his house. The debtor used the car for several months but refused to make any further payments. The finance company sued for payment. The debtor counterclaimed for the return of all money paid by him under the agreement. It was held that the finance company had wrongfully repossessed the car and could not correct the mistake by returning it to the debtor. The debtor was entitled to repayment of all sums which he had paid under the agreement.

EXTORTIONATE CREDIT BARGAINS

Under s.137 of the 1974 Act, the courts have power to re-open any credit agreement, whether or not it is a consumer credit agreement, which is part of an extortionate credit bargain, and relieve a debtor from payment of any sum in excess of that which is fair and reasonable. The courts have wide powers under this section and can order a creditor to repay all or part of any sum already paid; or set aside any obligation imposed on the debtor, or alter the agreement in any other way in order to do justice between the parties.

A credit bargain is extortionate under the Act if it requires the debtor to make payments which are "grossly exorbitant" or which otherwise "grossly contravene the ordinary principles of fair dealing". In order to determine whether a credit bargain is extortionate a number of factors will be taken into account, including:

(a) interest rates prevailing at the time it was made;

(b) the age, experience, business capacity and state of health of the debtor;

(c) the degree and nature of any financial pressure on the debtor when the bargain was made;

(d) the degree of risk accepted by the creditor and his relationship to the debtor;

(e) whether or not a cash price was quoted;

(f) how far any linked transaction was reasonably required for the protection of the creditor, or was in the interest of the debtor.

In *A. Ketley v. Scott (1981)* the defendant borrowed £20,500 in order to enable him to complete the purchase of a house. The money was released by the plaintiff on the same day that he was approached for the loan. The defendant did not tell him that his bank account was £2,000 overdrawn, the bank had a first mortgage on the house, and he was also liable under a £5,000 guarantee. Nor did he disclose that the house had been valued at £24,000. The loan was for three months at an annual rate of interest of 48%. At the expiry of its term the plaintiff sued for repayment of capital and interest. The defendant counterclaimed for the re-opening of the agreement as an extortionate credit bargain. It was held that the plaintiff was entitled to enforce the agreement. This was not an extortionate credit bargain because the lender had taken a considerable risk; obtained little security; had been deceived by the defendant; had no time to check the defendant's financial position, and advanced the money with extraordinary speed.

TERMINATION BY THE DEBTOR

A debtor under a hire purchase or conditional sale agreement may terminate the agreement under s.99 at any time before the final payment falls due. He must give notice in writing to the creditor, or to any person authorised to receive payment on the creditor's behalf. The debtor must return the goods to the creditor.

Under s.100 the debtor's liability on termination is limited to:

(a) any sums already due for payment before the date on which he exercises the right of termination; and

(b) a further sum to bring his total payments up to one half of the total price (or less if the agreement so provides) or any lesser sum which in the opinion of the court represents the creditor's loss on termination; and

(c) if he has broken an obligation to take reasonable care of the goods, compensation for this.

CONTRACTING OUT

Under s.173 of the 1974 Act it is not possible to insert a term into a consumer credit agreement which takes away any of the protection given to the debtor by the Act. Contracting out is absolutely prohibited.

ADMINISTRATIVE MACHINERY OF CONSUMER PROTECTION

Both central and local government have important roles to play in the field of consumer protection. The major role of central government is the promotion and implementation of legislation, whilst the enforcement of this legislation is mainly the responsibility of local government.

The role of central government in consumer protection

The consumer protection responsibilities of central government are spread across a number of departments, many of which have a junior minister with responsibility for consumer affairs.

The Home Office has responsibility for liquor licensing, dangerous drugs and poisons; as well as explosives and firearms.

The Department of Trade's responsibilities in the field of consumer protection include weights and measures, consumer credit, fair trading, consumer safety, trading standards, and monopolies, mergers and restrictive practices. The Department is also responsible for a number of national consumer protection bodies, including:

(a) the Office of Fair Trading

(b) the Monopolies and Mergers Commission

(c) the British Hallmarking Council

(d) the National Consumer Council

(e) the Consumer Protection Advisory Committee

(f) the Nationalised Industry Consumer Councils

and

(g) the British Standards Institution.

The Ministry of Agriculture Fisheries and Food looks after food and drugs, food additives, pesticides, and public health standards in slaughterhouses.

THE OFFICE OF FAIR TRADING

The Office of Fair Trading, created by the Fair Trading Act 1973, has a significant national role in relation to the broad task of protecting the interests of the consumer. The 1973 Act created the post of Director General of Fair Trading. The Director has wide powers under the 1973 Act and other legislation, notably the Consumer Credit Act 1974 and the Estate Agents Act 1979.

The duties of the Director are:

(a) to review commercial activities and report to the Secretary of State;

(b) to refer adverse trade practices to the Consumer Protection Advisory Committee;

(c) to take action against traders who are persistently unfair to consumers;

(d) to supervise the enforcement of the Consumer Credit Act 1974 and the administration of the licensing system under that Act;

(e) to arrange for information and advice to be published for the benefit of consumers in relation to the supply of goods and services and consumer credit;

(f) to encourage trade associations to produce voluntary Codes of Practice; and

(g) to superintend the working and enforcement of the Estate Agents Act 1979.

Review of commercial practices

Under this general heading the Director has three functions:

(i) to keep under review commercial activities in the U.K. relating to the supply of goods and services to consumers; and to collect information about these activities in order to become aware of practices which may adversely affect the **economic interests** of consumers;

(ii) to receive and collect evidence of commercial activities which he thinks are adversely affecting the **general interests** of consumers, for example on economic, health or safety grounds;

(iii) to supply information relating to adverse trade practices to the Secretary of State and make recommendations as to any action which the Director considers necessary to combat them.

Referral of adverse trade practices to the Consumer Protection Advisory Committee

The Director has power to refer to the Consumer Protection Advisory Committee any consumer trade practice which in his opinion adversely affects the economic interests of consumers. The type of activity which can give rise to such a reference include trade practices relating to:

(i) the terms or conditions on which the goods or services are supplied,

(ii) the manner in which those terms or conditions are communicated to the consumer,

(iii) promotion of the goods or services by advertising, labelling or marking of goods or canvassing,

(iv) methods of the salesmanship employed in dealing with consumers,

(v) the way in which goods are packed, or

(vi) methods of demanding or securing payment for goods or services supplied.

A reference by the Director may include proposals for the creation of delegated legislation by the Secretary of State. The Director has power to make such proposals where he considers that a consumer trade practice is likely to have any one of the following effects:

(i) misleading consumers as to their rights and obligations under the transaction; or

(ii) withholding adequate information on the rights and obligations of consumers; or

(iii) subjecting consumers to undue pressure to enter into transactions; or

(iv) causing the terms of the consumer transactions in question to be so adverse as to be oppressive.

The Consumer Protection Advisory Committee must report to the Secretary of State, usually within three months, indicating whether it agrees with the Director's proposals as they stand, or in a modified form. If so the Secretary of State may make regulations giving effect to the proposals. Under s.22 of the 1973 Act it is a criminal offence to contravene any such regulations.

Examples of regulations made under this procedure include the Consumer Transactions (Restrictions on Statements) Order 1976 and (Amendment) Order 1978, and the Business Advertisements (Disclosure) Order 1977, which were examined earlier in this chapter. Another example is the Mail Order Transactions (Information) Order 1976, which applies to goods sold by mail order which have to be paid for in advance. Under the regulations, any advertisement for such goods must state the true name or company name of the person carrying on the mail order business, as well as the true address of the business. Thus, for example, an advertiser giving only a P.O. Box number would be committing an offence.

Taking action against persistently unfair traders

The Director has power to bring proceedings in the Restrictive Practices Court against any person who persistently maintains a course of conduct which is unfair to consumers. Before making a reference to the Court, the Director must first attempt to obtain a written assurance from the trader that he will refrain from the unfair trade practice. If the trader refuses to give an assurance, or breaks an assurance once it has been given, the Director must apply for an order restraining the continuance of the unfair conduct. If the trader does not comply with the order, he will be in contempt of court and liable to imprisonment.

A course of conduct will be regarded as being unfair to consumers if it involves a breach of any legal obligations, either criminal or civil, by the trader. Examples of unfair conduct include persistently giving short measure or applying false trade descriptions, or repeatedly delivering unmerchantable goods.

Encouraging voluntary Codes of Practice

The Director has a duty to encourage trade associations and other organisations to prepare Codes of Practice and circulate them to their members. The codes should be designed to give guidance to traders relating to the safeguarding and protection of the interests of consumers.

A code of practice is a statement by a trade association which aims to establish and define the standards of trading which it expects from its members. Voluntary codes of this type have been introduced, following consultation with the Office of Fair Trading, to cover many areas of business. Such codes often provide a mechanism for the arbitration (see chapter 9) of consumer complaints as an alternative to legal proceedings in the courts.

Figure 5.14 is an extract from the Office of Fair Trading leaflet "Cars" which gives details of the Codes of Practice agreed with four trade associations in the motor industry.

Codes of practice provide a means whereby, in effect, a sector of industry or commerce can regulate itself. There are a number of costs and benefits to this. The main advantages are:

(a) a code can encourage a positive approach to trading standards and set high standards in excess of the legal minimum;

(b) a code can be changed fairly quickly in order to meet changing circumstances;

(c) a code can be expressed in non-technical language and interpreted positively according to its spirit;

Cars, like any other complex piece of machinery, can go wrong. They're costly to buy and have repaired or serviced. You want to be sure of getting a fair deal.

Apart from the protection of the law there are Codes of Practice promoted by the motor trade associations and supported by the Office of Fair Trading.

Codes lay down standards of service which members of the trade associations ***must*** follow. They give you benefits over and above your legal rights. You will know you are covered by a Code when you see one of the trade association's symbols (see back panel). All car manufacturers and importers follow a Code and expect their franchised dealers to do the same.

It makes sense to use a reputable garage or dealer, particularly one who follows a Code of Practice (in this leaflet they're called 'Code traders').

Buying a new car

- Check all the documents before you buy.
- Find out the total cost of putting the car on the road. Code traders must tell you this on the order form.
- When you take delivery of your car make sure you are given any **Pre-Delivery Inspection Checklist.** Code traders must see that this inspection is carried out properly and that you get a copy of the standard checklist. This may form part of the handbook or service booklet.
- Read the terms of the **Manufacturer's Warranty** (or guarantee) carefully. Make sure you know how to make best use of its benefits; it is a bonus and does not take away your legal rights.
- Get the **Car Handbook** from your code trader at the time of sale.
- Follow the manufacturer's running-in and other instructions.
- Have your car serviced as recommended by the manufacturer – if you don't, the terms of the warranty may not apply.
- If the manufacturer advises you of a safety recall, it is in your own interest to react quickly and to have your vehicle checked and rectified, if appropriate, by your dealer.

Buying a used car from a dealer

- Check that the dealer is a Code trader.
- Any approved checklist must be prominently displayed. Any defects must be clearly shown on the checklist, and a copy given to you when you buy.
- Check that all the important facts about the car (price, condition, mileage) are in writing.
- Carry out an independent inspection of the car prior to the sale. Seek help from an AA or RAC expert or from a competent friend or mechanic.
- Code traders should wherever possible obtain a signed statement from the previous owner about the car's mileage. If they cannot verify it, they must say so, or put a disclaimer notice over the mileometer.

Buying a used car privately

- **Be Careful** – you have fewer rights buying from a private individual than you would from a trader. The law says only that the car must be 'as described'. Your rights depend a lot on what the seller tells you about the condition and value of the car.
- Take along someone as a witness to what is said in case problems arise with the car. These statements along with any written description must be true.
- If the car turns out faulty you might be able to sue the seller for misrepresentation for what he said about the quality. Ask a consumer adviser first.
- Have the car inspected by the AA, RAC or other expert.

The **Vehicle Registration Document** is not proof of ownership. If you doubt that the seller either owns the car or has the legal right to sell it, ***don't*** buy it. An MOT certificate is not a guarantee that the car is roadworthy.

Beware of motor traders pretending to be private sellers!

They operate from home and use small ads in newspapers because they want you to think that you have fewer rights than when buying from traders.

If you buy a faulty car through a small ad and you suspect the seller is a trader in disguise, tell a local authority trading standards officer, who may prosecute him. Once you can show he isn't selling privately, you can make a claim just as if he had been operating openly.

Watch out at auctions!

You do not always have the same legal rights when buying at motor auctions as when you buy directly from a garage or dealer, so follow three golden rules:

1 Before you make a bid, visit some auctions to see how they work.

2 Read any notices and the auctioneer's terms and conditions carefully.

3 You have to decide on the condition of the car, and whether you are getting value for money. Good looks aren't necessarily a guide to a car's condition.

An auctioneer may legally 'contract out' of his responsibilities under the Sale of Goods Act. But you could challenge him in court if it seems unreasonable of him to rely on any statement denying responsibility.

How the law protects car buyers

Under the **Sale of Goods Act 1979,** if you buy a new or used car (even an 'old banger') from a trader, it must be of 'merchantable quality'. This means that it must be reasonably fit for its normal purpose when account is taken of such things as the price paid and how it was described to you. The car must also be 'as described' and 'fit for any particular purpose' you told the seller about.

The seller cannot use small print in his contact with you to avoid these obligations and, if a car does not satisfy any one of these conditions, you might be entitled to a refund, or the cost of the repairs. A lot will depend on the kind of fault and how long you used the car. But you will not be entitled to a refund for any specific fault you were told about, or if you examined the car when you bought it and the faults were so obvious you should have noticed them.

Under the **Trade Descriptions Act 1968** new and used cars must be described accurately, whether in writing, speech or by illustration. For example, if a car is said to have done 20,000 miles, this must be true unless the dealer makes it absolutely clear to you that he has not been able to verify the reading on the clock.

The act is enforced by Trading Standards (or Consumer protection) Officers. Tell them if you suspect the law is being broken. They may prosecute. If convicted, the trader can be fined or imprisoned. In England, Wales and Scotland the courts can award you compensation if you have suffered as a result of the offence.

Please note
The Act does not apply to private sales.

Under the **Road Traffic Act 1972,** it is an offence for anyone (trader or private individual) to sell an unroadworthy car – unless he makes it clear that it is suitable only for breaking up. Tell the police if you have be sold an unroadworthy car – the seller could be fined or you could sue him.

The **Unfair Contract Terms Act 1977** protects you from many 'exclusion clauses', which traders sometimes use in their notices, forms or invoices. Any clause about not accepting responsibility for loss or damage to your property through their negligence will be effective only if the trader can prove in court that the clause is reasonable. If, for example, a garage damages your car while it is in for a service, don't accept what any small print or notice says – get advice from your consumer adviser. Notices cannot limit the trader's responsibility if personal injury or death is caused through his negligence.

The trade associations

These are the trade associations which have agreed the Codes of Practice described in this leaflet. The first three have a common Code – the Code of Practice for the Motor Industry. The fourth has a code which deals only with the vehicle body repairs for cars and caravans. Contact the relevant trade association if you have a problem which you have been unable to resolve with a Code trader, or if you would like a copy of their Code. Remember, they will only be able to help you with a complaint about a Code trader.

The Conciliation Service
Motor Agents Association Ltd
73 Park Street
Bristol
BS1 5PS
For all complaints in England, Wales and Northern Ireland, except those about new cars

Customer Complaints Service
Scottish Motor Trade Association Ltd
3 Palmerston Place
Edinburgh
EH12 5AQ
For all complaints in Scotland, except those about new cars

The Customer Relations Adviser
Society of Motor Manufacturers and Traders Ltd
Forbes House
Halkin Street
London
SW1X 7DS
For all new-car complaints

SMMT

The Conciliation Service
The Vehicle Builders & Repairers Association
Belmont House
Gildersome
Leeds
LS27 7TW
For all complaints about their members' work

For further information contact:

Prepared by the Office of Fair Trading and the Central Office of Information, July 1986.
Printed in the UK for HMSO. Dd 8934507 FAIR JO148AR

Fig. 5.14

(d) a code normally deals only with one type of business or product. It can be drawn up to meet particular problems which are likely to arise in the limited area which it covers. Legislation, on the other hand, usually applies to all sectors of business;

(e) a code can clarify the rights and obligations of the trader and the customer in simple language;

(f) a code can provide procedures and remedies which are appropriate to its subject matter in a more flexible way than legislation.

There are, however, a number of drawbacks associated with self regulation by Codes of Practice. These include:

(a) Limited sanctions are available in the event that a trader does not comply with the provisions of a code. The ultimate penalty is usually expulsion from the trade association. In some sectors at least, this is not a very real punishment.

(b) The trade association may be in a position of conflict of interests when drawing up a code. Its principal function is the protection of the interests of its members.

(c) The consumer may not be aware of the existence of a code or the remedies which it offers.

(d) A code will not apply to a trader who is not a member of the trade association. In some sectors, particularly where the trade association has a high profile, for example A.B.T.A. in the travel trade, most traders are members. In other sectors, however, only a minority of traders belong to a trade association.

This final point is perhaps the most significant disadvantage of the system of self regulation by codes of practice. In a discussion paper issued by the Office of Fair Trading in 1986, entitled "A general duty to trade fairly", this problem was recognised. It was proposed that new legislation should be introduced to impose a duty on all traders, regardless of their membership of trade associations, to trade fairly. Compliance with a relevant code of practice would be enforced by the criminal law. As we shall see later, this model has been adopted by the Consumer Protection Act 1987 in relation to misleading price indications.

THE ROLE OF LOCAL AUTHORITIES IN CONSUMER PROTECTION

Responsibility for the enforcement of most consumer protection legislation, other than that which gives the consumer a right to sue for damages, rests with Local Authorities. It is carried out by trading standards or consumer protection departments. In practice, these departments see their major role as one of giving guidance to traders. This is done by a combination of education and persuasion. Prosecution for criminal offences is seen as a last resort when other measures fail.

Another important aspect of the work of these departments is the verification of weights and measuring apparatus, and the analysis of samples. They also act as a channel of information from members of the public to the Office of Fair Trading about unfair trade practices.

Trading standards officers have wide investigatory powers to enable them to carry out their enforcement functions effectively. They can make sample purchases of goods or services; enter premises; require suppliers to produce documents; carry out tests on equipment; and seize and detain property. A person who obstructs a trading standards officer, or makes a false statement to him commits a criminal offence.

Many Acts of Parliament and regulations made under them are enforced by trading standards officers. A number of these are examined below, including the Consumer Credit Act 1974, the Food Act 1984, parts of the Road Traffic Act 1972, the Trade Descriptions Act 1968, the Weights and Measures Act 1985, the Unsolicited Goods and Services Act 1971, and the Consumer Protection Act 1987. Before we consider this legislation in detail we shall examine the power of the criminal courts to award compensation to the consumer following the conviction of a trader for a criminal offence.

CONSUMER PROTECTION BY MEANS OF THE CRIMINAL LAW

Most, but not all, of the criminal offences designed to protect the consumer apply only to persons supplying goods or services in the course of a trade or business. Enforcement of the criminal law in this area is, as we have seen, primarily the function of trading standards departments. Traders who are charged with criminal offences will be prosecuted in the Magistrates or the Crown Court. If convicted, they will be liable to a fine or, in some cases, imprisonment. Following a conviction the criminal courts also have power to make a "compensation order" to the victim of the crime. In this context the victim will be the consumer who has suffered loss as a result of the offence.

The power to make a compensation order is contained in s.35 of the Powers of Criminal Courts Act 1973. This provides that any court convicting a person of an offence may, in addition to its sentencing power, make an order requiring the offender to pay compensation for any personal injury, loss or damage resulting from the offence or any other offence taken into consideration.

In deciding whether to make an order the court must take account of the ability of the defendant to pay. There is a limit of £1,000 compensation for each offence of which the accused is convicted. Under s.67 of the Criminal Justice Act 1982 the power to make compensation orders was extended. They may now be made "instead of or in addition to" a fine.

The power to make compensation orders is particularly useful from the point of view of the consumer. It saves him the trouble and expense of bringing proccedings in the civil courts. It will be used only in relatively straightforward cases, however. It is not designed to deal for example with complicated claims involving issues of causation or remoteness of damage.

The Director General of Fair Trading, Sir Gordon Borrie, in the Hamlyn Lecture in 1984, gave the following figures relating to the number of compensation orders made under the Trade Descriptions Act and the average amount of compensation awarded:

Year	No. of Compensation Orders Made	Average Amount of Compensation
1978/79	194	£147
1979/80	138	£173
1980/81	107	£183
1981/82	94	£308

SPECIFIC CONSUMER PROTECTION LEGISLATION

Some of the more significant Acts of Parliament creating criminal offences in the field of consumer protection are examined below.

THE FOOD ACT 1984

The principal objectives of the Food Act 1984 (previously the Food and Drugs Act 1955) are to prohibit the sale of food which is adulterated or which contains harmful additives, foreign bodies or mould. The Act also prohibits misleading advertising or labelling of food, and lays down standards of quality for certain foods.

The Food Act, in s.2 makes it an offence for a person to sell to the prejudice of the purchaser:

> "any food which is not of the nature, or of the substance, or of the quality, of the food demanded by the purchaser".

> In *Meah v. Roberts* (1978) an employee of a brewery cleaned the beer pumps and taps in a restaurant with caustic soda. He placed the remaining fluid in an empty lemonade bottle labelled "cleaner" which he left for use by the restaurant. The caustic soda was mistakenly served to a customer who ordered lemonade. The customer became seriously ill as a result. It was held that the restaurant proprietor was guilty of an offence under s.2 because the food was not of the nature demanded.

Liability under s.2 is strict and the trader may be guilty even though he has taken reasonable care.

> In *Smedleys Limited v. Breed (1974)* a customer was supplied with a tin of peas which contained a small green caterpillar. The caterpillar had been sterilised in the defendants' processes and did not constitute a danger to health. The defendants had an extremely efficient system for eliminating foreign bodies from their products. They were found to have taken all reasonable care to avoid the presence of the caterpillar in the tin. Nevertheless, their conviction for an offence under s.2 was upheld by the House of Lords.

The sale of food which is unfit for human consumption is an offence under s.8 of the 1984 Act, which provides that:

> "A person who . . . sells, or offers or exposes for sale, or has in his possession for the purposes of sale . . . any food intended for, but unfit for, human consumption is guilty of an offence . . ."

> In *David Greig Ltd. v. Goldfinch (1961)* a trader was convicted of an offence under s.8 when he sold a pork pie which had small patches of mould under the crust, even though the mould was not particularly harmful to human beings.

THE WEIGHTS AND MEASURES ACT 1985

The 1985 Act provides for the inspection and testing of weighing and measuring equipment in use for trade. Under s.17 of the Act it is an offence to use for trade, or to have in one's possession for use in trade, any weighing or measuring equipment which is false or unjust. It is also an offence under s.28 to give short weight or short measure.

The Act restricts the units of measurement which can lawfully be used by a trader. It lays down detailed requirements as to the packing, marking and making up of certain types of goods; and provides that, in relation to pre-packed or containerised goods, a written statement must be marked on the container giving information about the net quantity of its contents.

CONSUMER CREDIT ACT 1974

Schedule 1 of the Consumer Credit Act 1974 contains a list of over 35 criminal offences associated with contraventions of the Act. These include, for example, trading without a licence; failure to supply copies of consumer credit agreements; refusal of a trader to give the name of a credit reference agency which he has consulted; failure by a credit reference agency to correct information on its files; and obstruction of enforcement authority officers.

ROAD TRAFFIC ACT 1972

The Road Traffic Acts, and regulations made under them, contain a large number of criminal offences designed to ensure consumer safety. Examples include offences relating to the construction and use of motor vehicles and the safe loading of vehicles. Under s.60 of the 1972 Act it is an offence for any person, whether or not he is a trader, to sell or supply a motor vehicle which is unroadworthy. This offence will be committed where, for example, a vehicle is sold with defects in its braking or steering system or in its tyres. It is also an offence under s.60 to fit defective or unsuitable parts to a motor vehicle; and under s.33 to sell a motor cycle crash helmet which does not comply with safety regulations.

THE UNSOLICITED GOODS AND SERVICES ACT 1971

This Act was passed to impose criminal and civil liability on traders carrying on the practice of "inertia" selling. This involves sending goods or providing services which have not been ordered and demanding payment or threatening legal action if payment is not made. The Act provides that unsolicited goods or services need not be paid for, and unordered goods may be retained by the recipient if they are not collected by the sender within six months of delivery. It is an offence for the sender to demand payment for unsolicited goods or services.

THE TRADE DESCRIPTIONS ACT 1968

In an earlier part of this chapter we examined the circumstances in which a person would be regarded as transacting in the course of a trade or business. An important application of this question arises in relation to criminal liability under the Trade Descriptions Act 1968. With one exception, discussed below, there can be no liability under the 1968 Act unless the person applying the false description does so within the course of a trade or business. This is one reason why the Business Advertisements (Disclosure) Order 1977 requires a trader to identify himself as such when he advertises in the classified advertisements in newspapers.

Where there is a genuine private sale and, for example, the seller falsely describes the goods, the buyer's remedy will be rescission. He may also claim damages in a civil law action for misrepresentation or breach of the term implied into the contract by s.13 of the Sale of Goods Act 1979. A buyer from a business seller can also exercise these remedies, but in addition may report the trader to the trading standards department with a view to a prosecution under the 1968 Act.

Two principal offences under the Trade Descriptions Act 1968 relate to false description of goods, and making misleading statements about services. A number of defences are also provided for. Further offences of giving misleading price indications were originally contained in s.11 of the Act, and the Price Marking (Bargain Offers) Order 1979 made under the Prices Act 1974. These offences have been replaced by others under Part III of the Consumer Protection Act 1987, and are considered separately below.

False Description of Goods

The 1968 Act provides, in s.1(1) that:

> "Any person who, in the course of a trade or business:
>
> (a) applies a false trade description to any goods; or
>
> (b) supplies or offers to supply any goods to which a false trade description is applied;
>
> shall, subject to the provisions of this Act, be guilty of an offence".

Two different types of conduct will amount to offences under this section. The first is where the trader himself applies the false trade description contrary to s.1(1)(a). This offence could be committed, for example, by a trader who turns back the mileometer of a car to make it appear that the car has not travelled as many miles as it actually has. The second, under s.1(1)(b), involves supplying or offering to supply goods to which a false trade description has been applied by another person, for example where a retailer sells a garment to which the label "pure new wool" has been attached by the manufacturer, where the garment is partly composed of manmade fibres.

In relation to the s.1(1)(b) offence, the trader will not be able to rely on a *Fisher v. Bell* type defence where he displays goods for sale.

> In *Fisher v. Bell (1961)*, a shopkeeper who displayed flick knives for sale was acquitted of an offence of "offering to supply" them on the grounds that the display was an invitation to treat rather than a contractual offer.

The 1968 Act, in s.6, closes this loophole by providing that

> "a person exposing goods for supply or having goods in his possession for supply shall be deemed to offer to supply them".

A false trade description may be applied verbally or in writing, for example in a label on goods or in an advertisement. The statement must be false to a material degree in order to contravene the Act.

The meaning of the term "trade description" extends, by s.2, to statements relating to quantity, size, composition, method of manufacture, fitness for purpose, place or date of manufacture, approval by any person or other history including previous ownership of goods.

> In *Sherratt v. Geralds The American Jewellers Ltd. (1970)* the defendant sold a watch described by the maker as a diver's watch and inscribed with the word "waterproof". The watch filled with water and stopped after it had been immersed in water. It was held that the defendant was guilty of an offence under s.1(1)(b).

> In *Robertson v. Dicicco (1972)* a secondhand motor vehicle was advertised for sale by a dealer and described as "a beautiful car". The car, although having a visually pleasing exterior was unroadworthy and not fit for use. The defendant was charged with an offence under s.1(1)(a). He argued that his statement was true as he had intended it to refer only to the visual appearance of the vehicle. It was held that he was guilty because the description was false to a material degree. A reasonable person would

have taken it to refer to the mechanics of the car as well as its external appearance.

A similar approach was taken in *Kensington and Chelsea Borough Council v. Riley (1973)* where the trader was convicted of an offence under s.1(1)(a). It was held that the description "in immaculate condition" was false when applied to a car which required repairs costing £250 to make it roadworthy.

In *Routledge v. Ansa Motors (Chester-le-Street) Limited (1980)* a Ford Escort motor car which was manufactured in 1972 was first registered in 1975. Subsequently it was advertised by the defendant as "a used 1975 Ford Escort". It was held that the defendant had applied a false trade description to the car, contrary to s.1(1)(a).

In *Cadbury Ltd. v. Halliday (1975)* the word "extra value" had been printed on the wrappers of chocolate bars. It was held that these words did not constitute a trade description under the Act because the definition of that expression in s.2 covered only matters of verifiable fact. The expression extra value involved a matter of opinion rather than fact, and therefore no offence had been committed.

In order to be guilty of an offence under s.1, the trader must make the statement in connection with a sale or supply of goods.

In *Wickens Motors (Gloucester) Ltd. v. Hall (1972)* the purchaser of a car from the defendant complained about its performance. The complaint was made 40 days after the car had been supplied to him. The defendant told him that there was nothing wrong with the car, although this was untrue. It was held that the defendant was not guilty of an offence under s.1(1)(a) because there was insufficient connection between the false description and the sale.

An offence under s.1 may be committed by "any person". This is not limited to the seller, but may include the buyer, particularly where he is an expert in relation to the subject matter of the contract.

In *Fletcher v. Budgen (1974)* a car dealer bought an old car from a customer for £2, saying that it was only fit to be scrapped. In fact the dealer repaired the car and advertised it for a resale for £135. It was held that he was guilty of an offence under s.1(1)(a) because he applied a false trade description to the car when he bought it in the course of his business.

Where defects in goods are disguised and the trader has no reason to realise or suspect that they are present, he will not be guilty of an offence under s.1(1)(b).

In *Cottee v. Douglas Seaton Ltd. (1972)* the bodywork of a car which had been in very poor condition was repaired using plastic body filler. This was smoothed down and the car repainted before it was sold to the defendant. The defendant was unaware of the fact that the bodywork was defective. He resold the car to a purchaser who subsequently discovered the defect. It was held that the disguised defects amounted to a false trade description as the goods, in effect, told a lie about themselves. The defendant was not guilty of an offence, however, because he was unaware that the description had been applied to the goods.

A person may be guilty of an offence under s.1(1)(b), even though he does not know the description is false, provided he knows that the description has been applied to the goods by another person. This situation may arise for example where a car dealer sells a car which records an incorrectly low mileage on its mileometer. If a dealer is uncertain as to the accuracy of the recorded mileage, he may try to ensure that a false trade description is not applied by displaying a notice disclaiming the accuracy of the mileage reading.

> In *Norman v. Bennett (1974)* a customer bought a secondhand car with a recorded mileage of 23,000 miles. In fact the true mileage was about 68,000 miles. He signed an agreement containing a clause which said that the reading was not guaranteed. It was held that this was not an effective disclaimer. Lord Widgery, the Lord Chief Justice, stated that, in order to be effective, a disclaimer:
>
> > "must be as bold, precise and compelling as the trade description itself and must be as effectively brought to the notice of any person to whom the goods may be supplied. In other words, the disclaimer must equal the trade description in the extent to which it is likely to get home to anyone interested in receiving the goods".

The use of a disclaimer will be an effective defence provided it complies with the test laid down in *Norman v. Bennett.* The Motor Trade Code of Practice, approved by Director General of Fair Trading in 1976, recommends the use of the following form of wording in these circumstances:

> "We do not guarantee the accuracy of the recorded mileage. To the best of our knowledge and belief, however the recording is correct/incorrect".

Clearly a disclaimer will only be an effective defence to a charge under s.1(1)(b). If the trader himself has turned back the mileage he will be unable to rely on this defence. It should also be appreciated that a disclaimer of this type is an exclusion clause and, in any civil claim by the customer, would be subject to controls, discussed earlier, under the common law and the Unfair Contract Terms Act 1977.

False statements relating to the provision of services, accommodation or facilities

Suppliers of services, such as holiday tour operators, hairdressers, estate agents, and drycleaners will be liable to prosecution under s.14 of the Trade Descriptions Act 1968 if they make false statements knowingly or recklessly in the course of their business. Under s.14(1):

> "It shall be an offence for any person in the course of any trade or business:
>
> (a) to make a statement which he knows to be false; or
>
> (b) recklessly to make a statement which is false;
>
> as to any of the following matters:
>
> (i) the provision . . . of any services, accommodation or facilities;
>
> (ii) the nature of any services, accommodation or facilities . . .
>
> (iii) the time at which, manner in which or persons by whom any services, accommodation or facilities are provided;

(iv) the examination, approval or evaluation by any person of any services, accommodation or facilities;

or (v) the location or amenities of any accommodation . . ."

In order to obtain a conviction under s.14, the prosecution must show either that the trader knew that the statement was false, or that he was reckless as to its truth or falsity. A statement is made recklessly if it is made regardless of whether it is true or false. It need not necessarily be dishonest. The knowledge or recklessness must be present at the time the statement is made.

> In *Sûnair Holidays Ltd. v. Dodd (1970)* the defendant's travel brochure described a package holiday in a hotel with "all twin bedded rooms with bath, shower and terrace". The defendant had a contract with the hotel owners under which they were obliged to provide accommodation of that description. A customer who booked the package was given a room without a terrace. The defendant had not checked with the hotel to make sure that its customers were given the correct accommodation. It was held that the statement was not false when it was made, and therefore the defendant was not guilty of an offence under s.14.

It must be shown that the trader, at the time the statement is made, either knows that it is false or is reckless as to its truth or falsity; and that the statement actually is false. Subsequent developments are irrelevant if these elements are present at the time the statement is made.

> In *Cowburn v. Focus Television Rentals Ltd. (1983)* the defendant's advertisement stated: "Hire 20 feature films absolutely free when you rent a video recorder". In response to the advertisement a customer rented a video recorder. The documentation supplied with it indicated that he was entitled only to 6 films, and that they were not absolutely free because he had to pay postage and packing. When he complained, the defendant refunded his postage and packing and supplied 20 free films to him. It was held that the defendant was guilty of an offence under s.14 because the statement in his advertisement was false and recklessly made. The fact that he subsequently honoured the advertisement provided no defence, as this was done after the offence had been committed.

> In *Wings Ltd. v. Ellis (1984)* the false nature of a statement in their travel brochure was not known by a tour operator when its brochure was published. When the mistake was discovered, reasonable steps were taken to remedy it. Despite this, a holiday was booked by a customer on the basis of the false information. It was held by the House of Lords that the tour operator was guilty of an offence under s.14 because the statement was made when the brochure was read by the customer, and at that time the defendant knew that it was false.

Defences under the Trade Descriptions Act 1968

It is a defence to any charge under the 1968 Act that the defendant innocently published a misleading advertisement received by him for publication in the ordinary course of his business. This defence, available for example to newspapers, is provided by s.25.

A number of separate defences are contained in s.24. These are available to a defendant who can prove.

"(a) that the commission of the offence was due to a mistake or to reliance on information supplied to him or to the act or default of another person, an accident, or some other cause beyond his control; and

(b) that he took all reasonable precautions and exercised all due diligence to avoid the commission of such an offence by himself or any person under his control".

In order to have an effective defence under s.24, the onus is on the defendant to prove any one of the reasons listed in paragraph (a) and all of the elements in (b). He must also supply to the prosecution, at least 7 days before the hearing, a written notice giving such information as he has to enable the other person to be identified.

> In *Baxters (Butchers) v. Manley (1985)* the defendant was accused of offences under the 1968 Act in relation to the pricing and weight of meat exposed for sale in his butcher's shop. He claimed that the offences were due to the act or default of the shop manager. This claim was accepted by the court, but the defence under s.24 failed because he was unable to prove that he had taken reasonable precautions to avoid the commission of the offence by his manager. In particular he had failed to give the manager any detailed instructions or guidelines on the requirements of the Act; there was no staff training; and the standard of supervision by a district manager was inadequate.

> In *Lewin v. Rothersthorpe Road Garage (1984)* the s.24 defence was raised in response to a prosecution for selling a motor car to which a false trade description had been applied. The defendant was a member of the Motor Agents Association, and had adopted the code of practice drawn up by the Association in consultation with the Office of Fair Trading. Staff had been instructed in the contents of the code of practice. The court held that he had taken reasonable precautions to avoid the commission of an offence by his employee.

Where an offence has been committed under the 1968 Act due to the act or default of another person, the other person may be prosecuted under s.23. This is the only situation under the Act where a person can be guilty of an offence even though he is not acting in the course of a trade or business.

> In *Olgeirsson v. Kitching (1986)* the defendant was a private individual who had owned a Ford Granada car. It had previously belonged to Humberside police and whilst in their ownership required a new mileometer. At that stage the car had travelled 64,000 miles. When the police sold it to the defendant the recorded mileage was 10,500 miles, although the true mileage was disclosed. The defendant later sold the car to a garage, telling them that it had only travelled 38,000 miles. The car was resold on that basis. Later the truth was discovered and the defendant was charged under s.23. It was held that he was guilty. The fact that he was not a trader did not bring him outside the scope of the offence.

In relation to enforcement of the 1968 Act, as we have seen, wide investigatory powers are conferred on local authority trading standards officers. Before a prosecution is brought, however, the local authority is required to inform the Department of Trade. This is to prevent numerous unnecessary prosecutions for the same false trade description.

> The legality of bringing a second prosecution where there are a number of complaints in relation to the same false statement was at issue in *R.*

> *v. Thomson Holidays Limited (1973).* In this case a misleading statement in a travel brochure constituted an offence under s.14. The Court of Appeal held that a separate offence was committed every time someone read the brochure, and that it was not necessarily improper to bring more than one prosecution in these circumstances.

MISLEADING PRICE INDICATIONS:

PART III OF THE CONSUMER PROTECTION ACT 1987

New provisions in the Consumer Protection Act 1987, s.20 to s.26, replace both s.11 of the Trade Descriptions Act 1968 and the Price Marking (Bargain Offers) Order 1979. The previous provisions had proved to be badly drafted and difficult to enforce.

A new offence of giving a misleading price indication is contained in s.20 of the 1987 Act, which provides that:

> "A person shall be guilty of an offence if, in the course of any business of his, he gives (by any means whatever) to any consumers an indication which is misleading as to the price at which any goods, services, accommodation or facilities are available".

The types of statements which would be caught by s.20 include:

(a) false comparisons with recommended prices, for example a false claim that goods are £20 less than the recommended price; or

(b) indications that the price is less than the real price, for example where hidden extras are added to an advertised price; or

(c) false comparisons with a previous price, for example a false statement that goods were £50 and are now £30; or

(d) where the stated method of determining the price is different to the method actually used.

Failure to correct a price indication which initially was true, but has become untrue, is also an offence under s.20.

The Secretary of State has power, after consulting the Director General of Fair Trading, to issue a code of practice designed to give practical guidance on the requirements of s.20. Its aim will be to promote good practice in relation to giving price indications. Breach of the code will not, of itself, give rise to criminal or civil liability, but may be used as evidence to establish either that an offence had been committed under s.20, or that a trader had a defence to such a charge.

The following cases, decided under previous legislation, illustrate the type of behaviour which will be contrary to s.20.

> In *Richards v. Westminster Motors Ltd. (1975)* the defendant advertised a commercial vehicle for sale at a price of £1,350. When the buyer purchased the vehicle he was required to pay the asking price plus VAT, which made a total price of £1,534. It was held that the defendant was guilty of giving a misleading indication as to the price at which he was prepared to sell goods.

In *Read Bros. Cycles (Leyton) v. Waltham Forest London Borough (1978)* the defendant advertised a motor cycle for sale at a reduced price of £540, £40 below the list price. A customer agreed to purchase the motor cycle and negotiated a £90 part exchange allowance on his old vehicle. The defendant charged him the full list price for the new cycle, and stated that the reduced price did not apply where goods were given in part exchange. It was held that the defendant was guilty of giving a misleading price indication.

In one signifcant respect the offence under s.20 is narrower than the offences which it replaced. This is that s.20 only applies to consumer transactions. For the purpose of s.20, the expression "consumer" means:

(a) in relation to any goods, any person who might wish to be supplied with the goods for his own private use or consumption;

(b) in relation to any services or facilities, any person who might wish to be provided with the services or facilities otherwise than for the purposes of any business of his; and

(c) in relation to any accommodation, means any person who might wish to occupy the accommodation otherwise than for the purposes of any business of his.

A consequence of the narrowing down of the offence is that misleading price indications to business customers will not be caught by it. On the facts of *Richards v. Westminster Motors*, for example, the defendant would not now be guilty of an offence under s.20 because the customer was not a consumer.

CONSUMER SAFETY : PART II CONSUMER PROTECTION ACT 1987

Part II of the Consumer Protection Act 1987 implements proposals contained in a White Paper on the safety of goods published in July 1984 (cmnd 9302). This part of the 1987 Act consolidates, with amendments, previous legislation on consumer safety including the Consumer Safety Act 1978 and the Consumer Safety (Amendment) Act 1986.

The 1987 Act creates a new offence, in s.10, of supplying consumer goods which are not reasonably safe. An offence is also committed by offering or agreeing to supply unsafe goods or exposing or possessing them for supply.

In deciding whether goods are reasonably safe, the court must examine all the circumstances, including:

(a) the way in which the goods are marketed;

(b) the use of any mark, for example indicating compliance with safety standards;

(c) instructions or warnings as to the use of the goods;

(d) whether the goods comply with relevant published safety standards;

(e) whether there is a way in which the goods could reasonably have been made safer.

The offence in s.10 can be committed only in relation to consumer goods. Consumer goods are goods which are ordinarily intended for private use or consumption, with the exception of food, water, gas, motor vehicles, medical products and tobacco.

The Secretary of State has power, under s.11, to make regulations for the purpose of ensuring that goods of any particular type are safe. Safety regulations can cover the design, composition or finish of goods; and ensure that appropriate information is given in relation to them. They may also restrict the distribution of particular types of goods or prohibit their supply or exposure for supply.

A considerable number of regulations, made under previous legislation, are still in force. These relate for example to aerosols, babies' dummies, balloons, cosmetics, electrical goods, nightdresses, toys and many other types of product. Breach of safety regulations is an offence under s.12 of the 1987 Act.

Under s.41 of the 1987 Act any person who suffers injury or loss as a result of a breach of the safety regulations has the right to sue the trader for damages for breach of statutory duty. This right cannot be restricted or excluded by any term or notice in any contract.

The Secretary of State also has a number of other powers under the 1987 Act. He may, for example, serve a "prohibition notice" on a trader requiring him to stop trading in unsafe goods of a particular description. Alternatively, where a trader has distributed goods which are unsafe, the Secretary of State may serve on him a "notice to warn". This requires the trader, at his own expense, to publish warnings about the unsafe goods to persons to whom they have been supplied.

Power is also given to local authorities under the Act, to serve a "suspension notice" on any trader. This in effect freezes the goods in the hands of the trader for up to six months. The power to serve a suspension notice arises if the authority has reasonable grounds for suspecting that the goods are not reasonably safe under s.10, or are in breach of safety regulations. A trader who fails to comply with a suspension notice is guilty of a criminal offence.

A magistrate's court has power to order the forfeiture of goods where there has been a contravention of the safety provisions of the 1987 Act. Where goods are forfeit they must, under s.16, either be destroyed, or released for the purposes of being repaired, reconditioned or scrapped.

ASSIGNMENT — A GOOD LITTLE RUNNER

You are a voluntary worker at your local citizens advice bureau. You work at the bureau on a part-time basis. Each month the organiser of the bureau arranges a case study meeting for all workers, in which one of them is asked to present a case study based upon an actual problem he or she has actually encountered in the bureau, and this month your turn has arrived to give the presentation. You have decided to tell the story of the sale of a motor vehicle, which you had to deal with earlier in the year. The case centred upon a Mr. Tony Livingstone. The facts were as follows:

Tony Livingstone is in full time employment as a clerk in a firm of turf accountants. His spare time activity is the acquisition of motor cars which he fixes up, runs around in for a while, and resells at a profit. He usually has two or three cars at any given time, and at the time in question had sold twelve vehicles through the classified columns of his local newspaper during the past eighteen months, in each case giving the impression that he was selling the family car.

Livingstone bought a 1978 Ford Escort for £800 in February. The bodywork of the car was thin and rusty in places, and he repaired it using plaster filler and fibreglass patches. He repainted the car completely after smoothing down the repairs. He advertised the car for sale at £1,600, describing it as "a good little runner, in excellent condition for its age."

The advertisement was replied to by Mary Walsh. After a test drive and some negotiation she agreed to buy the Escort for £1,450.

Mary became extremely dissatisfied with the car. Within a month of purchase the plaster filler and fibre glass patches started showing through the paintwork. More seriously, she discovered that the car was in fact two halves of different cars welded together, the front being part of a 1978 Escort and the rear part of a slightly older model. The mechanic in her local garage, whose examination of the car revealed this, told her that the car was unroadworthy because of it.

Mary responded by writing the following letter:

> *Dear Mr. Livingstone,*
>
> *About the car you sold me five weeks ago. You said it was a good little runner. Well I took it to the garage the other day and the mechanic told me its total rubbish – made up from bits of other cars! I paid you £1,450 for that car and I can tell you I expect a lot more for my money! The rust is coming through and its quite obvious you just bodged it up. You said it was your family car for years. You must have known it had been in an accident or something. Anyway, I've been round to the trading standards people at the council. They say you'll have to give me my money back. And they're looking into it further. They've heard of you before and you could get prosecuted. I'll be coming round to your house on Saturday morning to bring the car back so you better have my money ready.*
>
> *Mary Walsh.*

Mary had not in fact been to the council. A friend had suggested that she should mention the trading standards department in her letter. When she arrived at Tony Livingstone's house on the Saturday she was met with abuse and threats. In a distressed state she was interviewed by you later that day, when you advised her of the legal position.

TASKS

Prepare a handout for your fellow workers in which you clearly analyse for them the extent of Tony Livingstone's civil and criminal liability in respect of the sale of the Ford Escort. The handout will be given to them after you have given your presentation.

ASSIGNMENT — DAVID AND CHRISTINE GEARY

Ian Trodd who runs a smallholding, placed the following advertisement in the local newspaper:

> "FOR SALE': six Aberdeen Angus bull calves, four Hereford calves, up to five weeks old; quantity of hay and straw."

David Geary, a local farmer, responded to the advertisement and agreed to buy the six Aberdeen Angus bull calves and two of the Hereford heifers at an inclusive price of £850. David noticed that none of the calves had ear tags and Ian susbequently agreed to tag them ready for collection by David the following morning.

David also agreed to buy 500 of the 2,000 bales of hay in Ian's barn for £750 and all of the straw bales in the same barn at a price of £40 per ton. The straw was to be loaded onto David's wagon the next day and weighed by him at a nearby public weighbridge. When David arrived the following morning he found that Ian's barn and all of its contents had been destroyed by a fire in which all of the Aberdeen Angus and Hereford calves have perished.

TASKS

1. David Geary is a member of the National Farmers Union (the NFU), and has sought the Union's advice concerning his agreement with Mr. Trodd. You are an officer employed by the NFU, and have been asked to telephone Mr. Geary to explain to him his position in this matter. Prepare notes prior to making the telephone call, which identify clearly and precisely the legal issues raised by it. Bear in mind that Mr. Geary will wish to know exactly how he should be proceeding.

2. Following your telephone conversation with David Geary he raises a further issue with you, on which he seeks your help. His wife Christine runs a pottery business, supplying her products to sales outlets, usually craft shops, on a sale or return basis. Last month she supplied pottery to The Craft Corner, a shop in Bury St. Edmunds, and to Flair, a specialist china and pottery shop in Exeter. She has learnt that The Craft Corner has now closed down and sold all its stock to Suffolk Art Supplies, and that her pottery has been stolen from the shop in Exeter. David asks if you will write informing Christine of any rights she has to payment from Suffolk Arts Supplies, and from Flair, since she believes she will have to personally bear the loss. Write a suitable letter to Christine.

DEVELOPMENTAL TASK

Draw up a set of standard trading terms for use by anyone operating a business which involves the supply of goods on sale or return. The terms should reflect the commercial protection necessary in such a trading activity, taking into account in particular (i) transfer of ownership, (ii) risk, (iii) insurance, and (iv) time limits for the return of goods.

ASSIGNMENT — AN INCIDENT AT ASHBURNE POOL

Ashburne District Council owns and operates a sports complex in Ashburne town centre. A notice at the main entrance to the centre states:

> *"The Council can accept no responsibility for loss or damage to visitors personal possessions within this complex, howsoever arising."*

A notice at the bottom of the steps in the main pool leading to the high diving board states:

> *"Divers: you use the diving board at your own risk."*

Peter and his sister Mary visited the leisure complex in order to swim. They paid ten pence each for keys to the cubicles in the changing rooms and locked the doors when they left. Whilst Mary swam in the pool Peter climbed the ladder to the diving board. The non-slip coating on the board had worn. Peter lost his footing and plunged into the pool injuring himself. He was rushed to hospital.

When Mary subsequently returned to collect their clothes from the cubicles she found the doors open and the clothes gone. She angrily complained to the changing room attendant who explained that he had left his desk to see what was happening when Peter had his accident, and could only assume that during this time someone had used the master keys from behind the desk to gain access to the cubicles. Changing room attendants are under strict instructions from the council never to leave the desk unattended.

The theft was reported to the police who a week later during a routine inspection of market stalls in Ashburne market, identified Mary's jewellery being worn by Phyllis, one of the stall-holders. During an interview with the police Phyllis revealed that she had purchased the items earlier in the day from Joe, another stall-holder. Peter's watch had not yet turned up.

TASKS

1. You work as a clerical assistant in Ashburne Leisure Services Department. The Director of Leisure Services is seeking your advice concerning the potential legal liability faced by his department for the injury suffered by Peter and the losses sustained by Peter and his sister. He has asked you to prepare him a report which analyses the situation. Produce the report requested by the Director, and in it identify (a) the validity of the notices; and (b) the legal effectiveness of the council's instructions to the changing room attendant.

2. Phyllis, who belongs to the same squash club as you, has mentioned the problem concerning the jewellery. Provide her with advice on the matter, indicating whether she has a good title to the jewellery.

Chapter 6

THE BUSINESS CUSTOMER'S RIGHTS: ISSUES OF NEGLIGENCE

THE NATURE OF LIABILITY IN NEGLIGENCE

Liability in the tort of negligence arises where foreseeable damage to the plaintiff is caused by the defendant's breach of a legal duty to take care. The tort has wide application and includes liability for losses or injuries suffered at work, on the roads, in dangerous premises, or as a result of medical accidents, professional malpractice or defective products.

A central feature of liability in negligence is that liability is fault-based. A defendant will be liable only if the court is satisfied that he failed to take reasonable care. Negligence provides a mechanism for loss distribution and the apportionment of the risks inherent in activities likely to result in loss or injury. It can be argued that a fault-based system is far from ideal as a means of ensuring fair treatment and proper financial assistance to those who are injured or disabled through no fault of their own. Indeed it has often been said that the law of negligence is like a lottery in which a few successful litigants are handsomely rewarded. Many other claimants are unable to obtain compensation due to a lack of evidence of fault, a lack of a substantial defendant to pursue or a refusal of the court to impose liability in the circumstances of the case.

One alternative to a system of fault-based liability is the introduction of strict liability for injuries sustained either generally or in particular categories of situation. Under a system of strict liability the injured party should find it much easier to obtain compensation because he will not need to prove a failure to take care on the part of the defendant. Such a system could be financed centrally through taxation, for example an additional tax on petrol to finance a scheme for road accidents. Alternatively it could be funded by compulsory insurance for those who would be exposed to liability, for example medical practitioners in respect of medical accidents. A further alternative is to have a combination of both methods of funding. However the likelihood of the widespread introduction of strict liability for these and other categories of personal injuries in the foreseeable future is remote.

A notable exception is the introduction of strict liability for injuries caused by defective products to the consumer in the Consumer Protection Act 1987. This is examined in a later part of this chapter. The effect of the 1987 Act will be to increase substantially the number of successful claims against manufacturers of defective products. The Act, however, does not impose an obligation on those affected to insure against the liability it creates, nor does it provide an independent source of funds to compensate claimants. It falls upon the individual businessman to make sure that his own insurance arrangements are adequate to cover the additional liability which he is likely to face.

THE SIGNIFICANCE OF NEGLIGENCE LIABILITY FOR THE BUSINESSMAN

The businessman is exposed to potential claims in negligence from a number of diverse sources. He is especially vulnerable because, under the rules of vicarious liability examined in Chapter 7 he is liable as an employer for wrongful acts committed by his employees in the course of their work. The prudent businessman will wish to take steps to minimise the liabilities to which he would otherwise be exposed. There are two things which he can do. First he can try to ensure that his business practices and the systems under which his employees operate are tightly structured and controlled so as to reduce the risk of injury and thereby prevent claims arising. Second he would be well advised to maintain an appropriate range of insurance policies to cover those risks which are most likely to affect his particular type of business.

TYPES OF INSURANCE COVER AVAILABLE

Insurance companies usually offer a wide range of policies and will arrange the cover available to meet the requirements of the individual business. Some types of cover are compulsory and therefore all businesses affected must have them; whilst others, although not compulsory, are such that no prudent businessman would consider it worthwhile to operate without them. Most businesses would be covered by all or most of the following types of policy:

(a) employers liability — in Chapter 7 we consider the duty of care owed by the employer at common law to provide a safe system of work, safe equipment and premises and safe fellow employees; and examine the employer's liability in negligence for injury to an employee caused by a breach of any of these duties. Under the Employers Liability (Compulsory Insurance) Act 1969 all employers other than Local Authorities and nationalised industries are required to insure against the risk of personal injury to their employees. The insurance must be contained in an approved policy which has prescribed contents. The policy must be issued by an authorised insurer.

(b) motor vehicles — under the Road Traffic Act 1972 the driver of a motor vehicle is required to be insured against third party personal injury risks. Most businesses running motor vehicles, and indeed most other motorists, obtain insurance cover well beyond the minimum laid down by the Act. Additional cover beyond the statutory minimum could include third party property risks; the risks of fire, or theft of the vehicle itself, or full comprehensive cover which would include losses of the insured persons vehicle or property caused by his own fault.

(c) product liability — a policy of this type is designed to cover liability for injury or losses caused by defective products manufactured or supplied by the insured in the course of his business. It should cover liabilities arising in contract, negligence or under the Consumer Protection Act 1987.

(d) public liability — product liability cover is often included in this type of policy. The policy generally includes loss or injury sustained by a member of the public as a result of the activities of the business, for example liability under the Occupiers Liability Act 1957 for injury to a customer caused by the unsafe state of the business premises, or the organisation's liability in negligence resulting from an accident caused by an employee in failing safely to carry out his duties.

(e) premises and stock — this provides insurance against loss of or damage to business property caused by fire, theft or negligence.

(f) professional indemnity — a policy of this type covers the insured for claims made against him in respect of professional negligence for example a claim against an architect for miscalculating the depth of the foundations of a multistorey building or specifying inadequate reinforcements for the structure. In some professions, for example, solicitors, professional indemnity insurance is in effect compulsory because the professional body will refuse to issue a Practising Certificate without evidence of premium payment on an appropriate policy.

(g) legal expenses insurance — this is a relative newcomer to the UK insurance market and provides the insured with a full indemnity for legal costs incurred in engaging in legal action in the civil or criminal courts.

Having identified some of the major types of insurance cover available to protect the businessman from losses which could otherwise be incurred by the business, it is worth pointing out that the levels of cover, in terms of the financial limits on the claims that the insurer would satisfy, are a matter of commercial judgement which will depend on the nature of the business concerned.

Additionally, the businessman entering into a contract of insurance must disclose all material facts which could affect the insurer's assessment of the risk. He would also be well advised to examine carefully the detailed wording of the policy in order to be certain that he is actually getting the cover which he wants.

It is interesting to notice that, because of the universal use of insurance by businesses, many of the commercial cases litigated before the courts are in reality disputes between insurance companies standing in the shoes of the named plaintiffs and defendants who have often already been paid out by the insurance companies.

ESSENTIAL ELEMENTS OF LIABILITY IN NEGLIGENCE

In order to succeed in a claim in negligence the plaintiff will have to prove three things:

(a) that the defendant owed him a legal duty of care,

(b) that the duty was broken, and

(c) that the defendant's breach of duty resulted in foreseeable loss or damage to the plaintiff.

Once the plaintiff has established these elements there are a number of defences available to the defendant. He may try to establish:

(a) that the plaintiff contributed to his injury by his own negligence — the defence of Contributory Negligence.

(b) that the plaintiff had voluntarily assumed the risk of injury — a defence based on consent known technically as of volenti non fit injuria, or

(c) that the plaintiff's claim is out of time and therefore statute-barred under the Limitation Act 1980 (as amended).

We shall now examine in more detail the elements of liability and the defences available in a negligence claim.

LEGAL CHANGE AND THE DEVELOPMENT OF THE DUTY OF CARE IN NEGLIGENCE

The tort of negligence is an area of legal liability which has been developed by the common law through the decisions of judges in individual cases over the centuries. The process is a continuing one and significant developments have taken place in recent years particularly in relation to the question of when a duty of care is owed by a defendant to the plaintiff.

Recent important decisions of the House of Lords and Court of Appeal, in cases which have raised issues relevant to the area of professional negligence, have been marked by some judicial disagreement as to the pace and shape of legal change. The role of the judges as lawmakers in bringing about such change and the extent to which the judiciary should confine their role to the application of legal principles to factual situations rather than concern themselves with the shaping of policy when deciding cases has, as we shall see, also been the subject of some debate.

THE APPROACH OF THE COURTS BEFORE 1932

The major milestone in the evolution of the law of negligence is the decision of the House of Lords in *Donoghue v. Stevenson (1932)* in which Lord Atkin laid down general principles which could be applied to any situation in order to determine whether a duty of care is owed. Before 1932 there were no legal principles of general application which defined the circumstances in which a person could be liable for loss or injury caused by his carelessness to another. Indeed the courts were reluctant to recognise or develop such principles.

> In *Winterbottom v. Wright (1842)*, for example, the defendant was a coachbuilder who contracted to supply a coach on hire to the Postmaster General for the delivery of mail. The contract of hire required the defendant to maintain the coach "in fit, proper, safe and secure state and condition". The plaintiff, who was the driver of the coach, was permanently disabled when the coach broke down throwing him from his seat. The plaintiff's claim alleged that the defendant had "improperly and negligently conducted himself . . . utterly disregarded . . . wholly neglected and failed to perform his contractual duties". The plaintiff's claim failed on the grounds that he was not a party to the contract between the defendant and the Postmaster General, and whilst the defendant had broken his duty to maintain the coach in a safe condition, that duty was owed to the Postmaster General and not to the plaintiff.
> In the course of his judgment Lord Abinger stated that:
>
> "There is no privity of contract between these parties; and if the plaintiff can sue, every passenger, or even any person passing along the road, who was injured by the upsetting of the coach, might bring a similar action. Unless we confine the operation of such contracts as this to the parties who entered into them, the most absurd and outrageous consequences, to which I can see no limit, would ensue."
>
> Alderson, B. expressed a similar opinion:
>
> "If we are to hold that the plaintiff could sue in such a case, there is no point at which such actions would stop. The only safe rule is to confine the right to recover to those who enter into the contract: if we go one step beyond that, there is no reason why we should not go fifty."

The decision of the court in this case was clearly influenced by the fear of "opening the floodgates of litigation" by creating a legal principle which could impose open-ended liability on one defendant to numerous potential plaintiffs for a single negligent act. Throughout the development of the concept of duty in negligence we shall see that this reluctance to create open ended liability, particularly in respect of losses other than personal injuries, is a recurrent theme in judicial decision making and a factor which strongly influences the scope of the legal principles which emerge from the cases.

Whilst liability for negligent acts existed prior to 1932 outside the framework of contract, there was no unified structure of legal principles which could be applied in any given case. Instead there were a number of categories of situation in which a duty of care was recognised, for example as between doctors and patients; road users and other road users; occupiers and persons invited into premises. In order to succeed in an action the plaintiff had to bring his case within one of the recognised categories, otherwise the courts would hold, as in the case of *Winterbottom v. Wright,* that no duty of care was owed.

An early attempt to lay down a general principle governing all negligence cases was made by Lord Esher (who was then known as Lord Justice Brett, the Master of the Rolls) in *Heaven v. Pender (1883).*

> The facts of *Heaven v. Pender* are that the defendant was the owner of a dry dock used for the painting and repair of ships. The plaintiff was employed by a master painter to paint a ship and was injured when a defective rope, supporting the cradle from which he was working, broke, throwing him to the ground. The cradle had been erected by the defendant as part of the staging surrounding the ship. The Court of Appeal held that the defendant was liable. The judgment of Cotton, L.J. with which Bowen L.J. agreed, was based on the grounds that the defendant as occupier of the premises owed a duty of care to the plaintiff because the source of danger was within the defendant's control. This was an existing recognised category of negligence. Lord Esher, however, based his decision in favour of the plaintiff on much broader grounds. He examined the existing categories of cases in which negligence liability was recognised, and from these he formulated in general principle:
>
> "The proposition which these recognised cases suggest, and which is, therefore, to be deduced from them, is that whenever one person is by circumstances placed in such a position with regard to another, that every one of ordinary sense would at once recognise that if he did not use ordinary skill and care in his own conduct with regard to those circumstances he would cause danger or injury to the person or property of the other, a duty of care arises to use ordinary care and skill to avoid the danger".
>
> This approach was roundly rejected by Cotton and Bowen L.L.J. on the grounds that it created an "unnecessarily large" principle which was inconsistent with a number of existing precedents, and was not followed in subsequent cases.

DONOGHUE V. STEVENSON AND THE NEIGHBOUR PRINCIPLE

> The facts of *Donoghue v. Stevenson (1932)* are that the plaintiff's friend bought her a bottle of ginger beer in a cafe. The ginger beer was in an opaque bottle and, after pouring some of it and drinking from her glass, the remainder was poured from the bottle into the glass. This was found to contain the remains of a decomposed snail, the sight of which caused the plaintiff to suffer shock and become ill. As the drink was a gift from her friend, the plaintiff had no contract with the seller. She therefore sued the manufacturer claiming that he owed a duty of care to her to ensure that his

> product was not contaminated during the process of manufacture. The defendant argued that he owed no legal duty to the plaintiff because there was no contract between them and the case fell outside the existing recognised categories of duty. The House of Lords rejected the defendant's arguments and, by a slim majority of three judges to two, found for the plaintiff.

This case is important for two reasons. First in the field of product liability, examined later in this chapter, the decision is important because Lord Atkin's judgment defines the duty of a manufacturer of a product towards a person injured by a defect in the product. In this respect the decision represents an effective reversal of the rule in *Winterbottom v. Wright*. In the context of legal change it can be noted that economic conditions had changed considerably in the 90 years between the two decisions. With the increase in size of manufacturing companies there was a consequent improvement in the ability of the manufacturer to meet the cost of such claims and ultimately to pass those costs on to the consumer. By 1932 it was no longer usual for the producer to sell his goods direct to the consumer as the patterns of trading activity had moved towards the increasing use of middlemen. One effect of this movement was to decrease the likelihood that the injured consumer would have a contractual remedy against the producer. The creation of the manufacturer's duty in negligence therefore filled a gap which had been opening up in the range of remedies available to a person injured by a defective product.

The second reason why the decision in *Donoghue v. Stevenson* is important is a reason of far greater significance in the context of the development of the law of negligence as a whole. It is because Lord Atkin, in formulating the neighbour principle, laid down a unifying principle of liability for harm caused unintentionally by the defendant. For this reason the decision in Donoghue is often regarded as marking the birth of negligence as a tort. In the celebrated passage from his judgment Lord Atkin said:

> "The rule that you are to love your neighbour becomes in law, you must not injure your neighbour; and the lawyers question, Who is my neighbour? receives a restricted reply. You must take reasonable care to avoid acts or omissions which you can reasonably foresee would be likely to injure your neighbour. Who, then, in law is my neighbour? The answer seems to be — persons who are so closely and directly affected by my act that that I ought reasonably to have them in contemplation as being so affected when I am directing my mind to the acts or omissions which are called in question."

The defendant's duty is a duty to take reasonable care to avoid causing foreseeable harm and it is owed to anyone closely and directly affected by the defendant's conduct. The close relationship necessary between the defendant and plaintiff in order for a duty to exist is often referred to as a relationship of proximity between the parties.

> The status of the neighbour principle as a rule of general applicability was underlined by the House of Lords in *Home Office v. Dorset Yacht Co (1970)*. Here the plaintiff's yacht was damaged by borstal trainees who had escaped while on a training exercise on an island. They had been carelessly left unsupervised by their guards. Applying the neighbour principle, it was held that the defendant owed a duty of care to the plaintiff whose yacht had been moored between the island and the mainland, as it was reasonably foreseeable that the trainees might use the yacht as a means of escape. The defendant was vicariously liable for the failure of its employees to supervise the trainees. This breach of duty caused the plaintiff's loss for which the Home Office was liable.

In a leading judgment, Lord Reid stated:

> "*Donoghue v. Stevenson* may be regarded as a milestone, and the well known passage in Lord Atkin's speech should I think be regarded as a statement of principle. It is not to be treated as if it were a statutory definition. It will require qualification in new circumstances. But I think that the time has come when we can and should say that it ought to apply unless there is some justification or valid explanation for its exclusion."

RESTRICTIONS ON THE APPLICATION OF THE NEIGHBOUR PRINCIPLE

Lord Reid's statement implies that there may be cases in which a straight application of the neighbour principle will suggest the existence of a duty of care, but nevertheless the court would refuse to recognise a duty because there are valid justifications for failing to impose liability. The justifications which are used in these circumstances are often referred to as considerations of public policy. We can interpret this expression as meaning reasons based on judicial perceptions of what may or may not be in the best interests of the community at large. It is inevitable that policy issues arise in the course of deciding cases in negligence. This is because Parliament has rarely intervened to influence the direction of legal developments in this field by passing legislation. The judges have, therefore, found it necessary to make decisions on policy issues as part of the process of deciding cases and developing an acceptable coherent and workable body of legal rules.

Evaluating the processes of legal change under the common law reveals the constitutional dilemma in which the judiciary finds itself. In former times judges refused to admit that they were making new law when deciding novel cases. It was claimed that they were merely declaring rules of the common law which had already existed but had never previously been stated. This 'declaratory theory' was based in part on a desire not to be seen to be challenging the functions of the legislature by openly creating new laws. In reality of course it is inescapable that the process of deciding a case on a novel point involves the creation of a new precedent which, as we saw in Chapter 1, becomes a new and binding rule of law. One concern in the conclusion that judges do create law is the absence of direct effective accountability to the community for the decisions which they make. In a civilised democratic society one would expect such accountability to go hand in hand with the considerable power of the law maker. This helps to explain the unease expressed by some judges in cases where the application of the neighbour principle has been restricted or denied on grounds of public policy.

In *McLoughlin v. O'Brien (1982)*, for example, Lord Scarman expressed the view that the judges should not concern themselves with issues of public policy. He argued that their function and expertise concerned the logical development of legal principles and the application of these principles to factual situations. The question of whether the application of the neighbour principle should be restricted or denied on grounds of policy is one which, in Lord Scarman's view, should be answered by Parliament. The reason for this is that the judicial process is not well equipped to make decisions involving political, social or economic issues:

> "I am persuaded that in this branch of the law it is not for the court but for the legislature to set limits, if any be needed, to the law's development. This case raises directly a question as to the balance in our law between the functions of judge and legislature. The common law covers everything which is not covered by statute. It knows no gaps. The function of the court is to decide the case before it, even though the decision may require the extension or adaptation of a principle or in some cases the creation of new law to meet the justice of the case. But, whatever the court decides to do, it starts from a baseline of existing principle and seeks a solution consistent with or analogous to a principle or principles already recognised.

> By concentrating on principle the judges can keep the common law alive, flexible and consistent, and can keep the legal system clear of policy problems which neither they, nor the process which it is their duty to operate, are equipped to resolve. If principle leads to results which are thought to be socially unacceptable, Parliament can legislate to draw a line or map out a new path.
>
> The problem in this case is one of social, economic, and financial policy. The considerations relevant to a decision are not such as to be capable of being handled within the limits of the judicial process."

Lord Scarman's view, however, has not found favour with the majority of senior judges. They are prepared to accept that policy issues are constantly being resolved by the courts and that this is inevitable, given that Parliament is not likely to produce legislation on a subject in which there is little immediate political impact. In any event Parliament would be able to step in and legislate if there was major dissatisfaction with the decisions which the courts were making.

The views expressed by Lord Reid in *Home Office v. Dorset Yacht Co. (1970)* about the significance of the neighbour principle were supported by the House of Lords in *Anns v. London Borough of Merton (1977)*. Lord Wilberforce, in a statement which can be regarded as a further milestone in development of the law of negligence, explained the approach which a court should take in determining whether a duty of care exists in any given case:

> ". . . the position has now been reached that in order to establish that a duty of care arises in a particular situation, it is not necessary to bring the facts of that situation within those of previous situations in which a duty of care has been held to exist. Rather the question has to be approached in two stages.
>
> First, one has to ask whether, as between the alleged wrongdoer and the person who has suffered damage there is a sufficient relationship of proximity or neighbourhood such that, in the reasonable contemplation of the former carelessness on his part may be likely to cause damage to the latter, in which case a prima facie duty of care arises. Secondly, if the first question is answered affirmatively, it is necessary to consider whether there are any considerations which ought to negative, or to reduce or limit the scope of the duty or the class of person to whom it is owed or the damages to which a breach of it may give rise".

It should be appreciated that in the majority of claims for personal injuries or damage to property, for example in the field of product liability, there will not be any special considerations restricting the application of the neighbour principle in order to establish that a duty of care exists. It is in relation to claims for financial loss, for example in the area of professional negligence, that policy considerations — such as the fear of creating open-ended liability — will be relevant in applying the second stage of Lord Wilberforce's test.

The introduction of Lord Wilberforce's two stage test led to a reassessment of the existence and scope of the duty of care in some situations. Some judges believed that it relieved them of the obligation to follow restrictive pre-1977 precedents and allowed them re-assess those situations having regard only to the two-stage test. An example of this approach is provided by the decision of the High Court in the case of *Ross v. Caunters (1980)* which is examined in more detail in the context of professional negligence later in this chapter. In this case the High Court felt able to disregard a decision of the House of Lords in 1861 and decide that a solicitor was liable in negligence to a beneficiary under a will who lost a legacy because of a mistake by the solicitor.

The House of Lords has recently sought to curtail the tide of judicial creativity which followed the judgment of Lord Wilberforce in *Anns v. Merton*. In *Leigh & Sillavan Ltd. v. Aliakmon*

Shipping Co. Ltd, The Aliakmon (1986), Lord Brandon, delivering a judgment with which the other presiding Law Lords were in complete agreement, took the view that the test applied only to novel types of factual situation and that the test was not to be applied where the situation was already covered by pre-1977 precedents. Referring to the two stage test, Lord Brandon stated that it:

> ". . . does not provide, and cannot in my view have been intended by Lord Wilberforce to provide, a universally applicable test of the existence and scope of a duty of care in the law of negligence. In this connection I would draw attention to a passage in the speech of Lord Keith in *Governors of the Peabody Donation Fund v. Sir Lindsay Parkinson & Co Ltd (1984)* . After citing a passage from Lord Wilberforce's speech in the *Anns* case now under discussion, he said:
>
> 'There has been a tendency in some recent cases to treat these passages as being of themselves of a definitive character. This is a temptation which should be resisted.'
>
> Lord Wilberforce was dealing, as is clear from what he said, with the approach to the question of the existence and scope of a duty of care in a novel type of factual situation which was not analogous to any factual situation in which the existence of such a duty had already been held to exist. He was not, as I understand the passage, suggesting that the same approach should be adopted to the existence of a duty of care in a factual situation in which the existence of such a duty had repeatedly been held not to exist."

It will be interesting to see what weight is given, in future cases, to Lord Brandon's view; and in particular to see what impact this passage will have on the rate of legal change in the development of the duty of care in negligence.

BREACH OF DUTY

Once it has been established that the defendant in a given situation owes a duty of care to avoid injury to the plaintiff, the next question which falls to be decided is whether the defendant was in breach of that duty. It should be stressed that these are two separate issues and only after the court is satisfied that a duty exists will it go on to consider the question of breach. A breach of duty is a failure to take reasonable care. This involves a finding of fault on the part of the defendant.

In the words of Alderson B. in *Blyth v. Birmingham Waterworks Co. (1856)*:

> "Negligence (in the sense of a breach of duty) is the omission to do something which a reasonable man, guided upon those considerations which ordinarily regulate the conduct of human affairs, would do, or something which a reasonable and prudent man would not do."

The duty of care is broken when a person fails to do what a reasonable man would do in the same circumstances. The standard of care required of the defendant in a particular case will vary according to the circumstances of the case and the skills which the defendant holds himself out as possessing. Thus a surgeon carrying out an operation is required to demonstrate the skills and knowledge of a reasonably competent surgeon. On the other hand the degree of care expected of a hospital porter is not so exacting. Whilst the standard of care required of a skilled defendant such as a professional person will be high, the reverse cannot be said to be true. An inexperienced or unskilled defendant will not be able to argue that the standard of care which he is required to demonstrate is correspondingly low.

> Thus in *Nettleship v. Weston (1971)* the Court of Appeal held that a learner driver was in breach of her duty of care to the plaintiff, a passenger, for failing to demonstrate the driving skills of a reasonably competent qualified driver and was liable for the injuries sustained by the plaintiff as a result.
>
> More recently in *Wilsher v. Essex Area Health Authority (1986)* the Court of Appeal held that the inexperience of a junior doctor was no defence to an action in medical negligence. A premature baby suffered near blindness as a result of receiving excess oxygen. This was given because a junior doctor failed correctly to carry out a test to determine the level of oxygen in the baby's blood. The court held that the defendant was vicariously liable for the junior doctor's negligence in failing to display the skill of a fully qualified and reasonably competent doctor.

In determining whether a duty of care has been broken the court must assess the conduct of the defendant and decide whether he acted reasonably or unreasonably. This assessment allows the judge a large measure of discretion in an individual case, although it could be argued that it also produces some uncertainty in the law. The main factors which the court will take into account in deciding whether there has been a breach of the duty of care are:

(a) the extent of the risk created by the defendant's conduct — whether the risk was serious or obvious;

(b) the nature of the harm which is likely to be caused to the plaintiff;

(c) the practicability and expense of taking steps to minimise the risk; and

(d) the particular circumstances of the case.

A good example of the way in which the courts attempt to balance these factors is provided by the case of *Bolton v. Stone (1951)*.

> In *Bolton v. Stone* the plaintiff was standing on the highway outside her home and was struck by a cricket ball hit by a visiting batsman off the pitch of the local cricket club. She sued the members and committee of the cricket club. The ground had been used for cricket since 1864, well before the surrounding houses were built. Balls were rarely hit out of the ground and onto the highway, perhaps only six times in the previous thirty years, and there was no record of any previous accident. The ball in question had travelled seventy eight yards before passing over the fence and about twenty-five yards further before hitting the plaintiff. The top of the fence was seven feet above the highway and seventeen feet above the pitch. The House of Lords held that the defendants were not liable because they had taken reasonable care. The chances of such an accident were so slim that the reasonable man would have done no more than the defendants had done to prevent it from happening. In the course of his judgement, Lord Ratcliffe stated:
>
> "A breach of duty has taken place if the defendants are guilty of a failure to take reasonable care to prevent the accident. One may phrase it as 'reasonable care' or 'ordinary care' or 'proper care' — all these phrases are to be found in decisions of authority — but the fact remains that, unless there has been something which a reasonable man would blame as falling

> beneath the standard of conduct that he would set for himself and require of his neighbour, there has been no breach of legal duty. It seems to me in this case that a reasonable man, taking account of the chances against an accident happening, would not have felt himself called upon either to abandon the use of the ground for cricket or to increase the height of his surrounding fences."

In Chapter 7 we examine a number of cases involving a breach of the employer's duty of care for the safety of his employees — see for instance *Latimer v. AEC (1953)* and *Paris v. Stepney Borough Council (1951)*. Consideration of those cases will further demonstrate the approach of the courts in balancing the factors which are relevant to the question of breach of duty.

PROOF OF THE DEFENDANT'S BREACH OF DUTY

The normal rule in a civil case is that the plaintiff must adduce evidence to prove his case on balance of probabilities. It will therefore be the plaintiff's job, in a negligence case, to show that the defendant did not act in a reasonable way. If he is unable to do this his claim will fail.

> In *Wakelin v. London and South Western Railway Co. (1886)* the body of the plaintiff's husband was found near a level crossing on a railway. He had been hit by a train but there was no evidence to suggest what had happened. The accident could have been his own fault or it could have been attributable to the fault of the defendant. As the plaintiff was unable to prove that the defendant acted in an unreasonable manner, her claim failed.

The difficulty involved in proving that a defendant is in breach of the duty of care is illustrated by the legal claims arising from the injuries caused to unborn children by the drug Thalidomide. Although legal proceedings were issued in the UK, none of the claims were ever brought before the courts. There were two main legal reasons for this. Firstly because it was not certain that a duty of care could be owed to an unborn child (this has since been established by legislation under the Congenital Disabilities (Civil Liability) Act 1976). Secondly because the plaintiffs would probably have been unable to prove that the defendants had failed to take reasonable care. The drug had undergone extensive testing before it was released onto the market. Although it had not been tested on pregnant women, it is not clear that a reasonable drug manufacturer would have tested a drug of that type — a tranquilliser — for its effect upon the developing child within the womb of the pregnant woman, given the state of scientific knowledge within the pharmaceutical industry at the time. After protracted negotiations an out of court settlement was reached between the parties on terms dictated by the defendants. The levels of agreed compensation were widely regarded as being well below those which might have been awarded at the conclusion of a successful trial. Some observers believe that the defendants would not even have agreed to settle the claims on those terms had it not been for the considerable pressure of public opinion and the efforts of a well organised group of the defendant company's own shareholders on the plaintiff's behalf.

RES IPSA LOQUITUR

In some cases the plaintiff may be relieved of the burden of proving negligence if the court accepts a plea of res ipsa loquitur (the thing speaks for itself). This is a rule of evidence which applies where the plaintiff's injury is one that would not in the ordinary course of events have happened without negligence and there is no satisfactory alternative explanation for the injury other than negligence by the defendant.

The effect of the rule is that the court will infer negligence on the part of the defendant without the need for the plaintiff to pinpoint the cause of the injury or explain how the defendant failed to take reasonable care. The defendant will be liable unless he furnishes evidence to show that his negligence did not cause the plaintiff's loss.

The rule will be of great assistance to the plaintiff where it seems to be obvious that the defendant was negligent but the plaintiff is unable to pinpoint the exact nature of the defendant's breach of duty.

> In *Scott v. London and St. Catherine Docks Co. (1865)* a customs officer was injured when six sacks of sugar fell on him as he was passing the defendant's warehouse. The court held that the res ipsa loquitur rule applied and inferred negligence on the part of the defendant which it was unable to disprove. During the course of his judgement, Erle, C.J. stated:
>
> "Where the thing is shown to be under the management of the defendant, or his servants, and the accident is such as, in the ordinary course of things, does not happen if those who have the management use proper care, it affords reasonable evidence, in the absence of explanation by the defendant, that the accident arose from want of care."
>
> In *Cassidy v. Ministry of Health (1951)*, the plaintiff was injured in a surgical operation on his hand. Denning, L.J. asserted that the res ipsa loquitur rule enabled the plaintiff to say, in effect:
>
> ". . . I went into hospital to be cured of two stiff fingers. I have come out with four stiff fingers, and my hand is useless. That should not have happened if due care had been used. Explain it, if you can."
>
> The defendant was held liable as he was unable to explain how such a result was consistent with the use of reasonable care.
>
> In *Ward v. Tesco Stores (1976)* the plaintiff was injured when she slipped on a pool of yoghurt which had previously been spilled onto the floor of the defendant's supermarket and had not been cleaned up. The Court of Appeal supplied for the res ipsa loquitur rule and the defendant was held liable as it was unable to show that it had taken reasonable care.

FATAL ACCIDENTS

Where the defendant's breach of duty has resulted in death, legal action may be brought on behalf of the estate of the deceased person under the Law Reform (Miscellaneous Provisions) Acts 1934 and 1970. The dependants of the deceased will have a separate claim under the Fatal Accidents Act 1976 as amended by the Administration of Justice Act 1982.

We shall consider each type of claim in turn:

(a) The personal representatives may pursue any claim which the deceased person would have had if he had survived. Here damages are restricted to items of loss which arose between the injury and the death. The claim could include pain and suffering, loss of earnings and medical expenses, in each case up to the time of death. Funeral expenses are also recoverable but losses or notional losses in respect of the years after the death cannot be claimed in an action by the deceased's personal representatives.

(b) Certain relatives who were financially dependent on the deceased person are entitled to claim against the defendant. These are his spouse, parents, grandparents, children, grandchildren, sisters, brothers, aunts and uncles, and their issue. In addition, any co-habitee who lived with him as husband or wife for at least two years immediately before the death may claim. The aim of the court will be to provide maintenance for those relatives who have lost the financial support which he provided before his death. In order to succeed, the plaintiff must show:

(i) that he is a relative,

(ii) that there is actionable negligence, and

(iii) that he was a dependant and has suffered financially as a result of the death.

In addition, a claim for a bereavement award for suffering and grief, which is for a fixed sum of £3,500, may be made by the spouse of the deceased or the parents of a child under 18 who is killed.

RESULTING DAMAGE

The third essential element of liability in negligence is that the defendant's breach of duty resulted in foreseeable loss or damage to the plaintiff. In reality this involves two separate issues — the issues of causation and remoteness of damage:

1. CAUSATION OF DAMAGE

The causation issue is concerned with the question of cause and effect: was the defendant's breach of duty the operative cause of the plaintiff's loss. The plaintiff's claim will fail if he is unable to prove this link. He must show that but for the defendant's negligence his loss would not have occurred.

> In *Barnett v. Chelsea and Kensington Hospital Management Committee (1969)* the plaintiff's husband was a night watchman, who called at the defendant's hospital in the early hours of the morning complaining of vomiting. He was sent home without being examined and was told to contact his own doctor later that day. He was suffering from arsenic poisoning and died a few hours later. The court held that the defendants were in breach of their duty of care, but the claim failed because the negligence of the hospital had not caused the death. It would not have been possible to save the life of the plaintiff's husband even if he had been examined and treated at the hospital because there is no cure for arsenic poisoning.

Two further cases — *JEB Fasteners Ltd v. Marks Bloom & Co. (1983)* and *Shankie Williams v. Heavey (1986)* — which were decided on the issue of causation are examined later in this chapter.

2. REMOTENESS OF DAMAGE

Where the plaintiff proves that his injuries were caused by the defendant's breach of duty, he can recover damages provided that his injuries were not too remote a consequence of the breach. The law does not necessarily impose liability for all of the consequences of a negligent act. Some damage may be too remote. Only damage which was reasonably foreseeable at the time of the negligent act can be recovered by the plaintiff.

> In *The Wagon Mound (1961)* a large quantity of fuel oil was carelessly spilled by the defendant's employees while a ship was taking on fuel in Sydney Harbour. Some of the oil spread to the plaintiff's wharf where welding operations were taking place. The plaintiff stopped welding

temporarily, but recommenced after receiving expert opinion that fuel oil would not ignite when spread on water. Two days later the oil ignited when a drop of molten metal fell onto a piece of waste floating in the oil, causing extensive damage to the plaintiff's wharf. The court found as a fact that it was not reasonably foreseeable that the oil would ignite in these circumstances. It was held that the damage to the wharf was too remote, and the plaintiff's claim failed.

The plaintiff's damage may be held to be too remote where an unforseen new independent act, outside the defendant's control, intervenes to break the chain of causation. If the plaintiff's damage is caused by such a 'novus actus interveniens' the defendant will not be liable for it. For example an employer's liability for injury suffered by an employee at work will not extend to further injuries received in the course of negligent medical treatment in hospital.

In *Cobb v. Great Western Railway (1894)* the defendant allowed a railway carriage to become overcrowded. As a result the plaintiff's pocket was picked and he lost nearly £100. It was held that the act of the thief was a novus actus interveniens and therefore that the plaintiff's loss was too remote.

DEFENCES TO A NEGLIGENCE ACTION

CONTRIBUTORY NEGLIGENCE

Where the plaintiff has successfully established all of the elements of a negligence action, but has in some way contributed to his injuries by his own negligence, the defendant may raise the defence of contributory negligence.

Section 1(1) of the Law Reform (Contributory Negligence) Act 1945 provides:

"Where any person suffers damage as the result partly of his own fault and partly of the fault of any other person or persons, a claim in respect of that damage shall not be defeated by reason of the fault of the person suffering the damage, but the damages recoverable in respect thereof shall be reduced to such extent as the court thinks just and equitable having regard to the claimant's share in the responsibility for the damage."

The effect of this provision is simply that the plaintiff's damages will be reduced in direct proportion to the extent to which he is to blame for his injuries.

In *Davies v. Swan Motor Co (Swansea) Ltd (third party James) (1949)* the plaintiff's damages were reduced by 20% when he was held to be contributorily negligent. He was riding on the back of a dust lorry contrary to his employer's instructions and was injured when the dust lorry was in collision with a bus.

In *Stapley v. Gypsum Mines (1953)* the plaintiffs were miners who, contrary to specific instructions by their employer, worked under a dangerous roof. They were injured when the roof collapsed and fell in on them. Their damages were reduced by 80% for contributory negligence.

In *Froom v. Butcher (1976)* it was held that the failure to wear a seat belt was contributory negligence and that the appropriate reduction in damages was 25% if the seat belt would have prevented the injury altogether, or 15% if it would merely have reduced the extent of the injury.

In *Sayers v. Harlow UDC (1958)* the plaintiff became locked inside a public lavatory because of the defendant's negligence in failing to maintain the door lock. After failing to attract attention or assistance, she attempted to climb out over the top of the door. In doing so she fell and was injured. It was held that the defendant was liable in negligence, but the plaintiff's damages were reduced by 25% for contributory negligence.

VOLUNTARY ASSUMPTION OF RISK (VOLENTI NON FIT INJURIA)

This defence, which is universally referred to by its latin name volenti non fit injuria, is available to the defendant where the plaintiff freely and voluntarily accepts a risk of which he has full knowledge. In modern times the courts have been reluctant to apply the defence, which has the effect of completely defeating the plaintiff's claim, other than in exceptional circumstances. The reason for this is that the type of behaviour which would come within the defence would also usually amount to contributory negligence. The courts probably take the view that a more just outcome can be achieved by applying the rules of contributory negligence.

In *Smith v. Charles Baker & Sons (1891)* the plaintiff was employed in the excavation of a railway cutting. He was injured by a stone which fell from an overhead crane. He had known that there was an element of risk in working beneath the crane but had not objected to his employer. As a defence to his action for compensation, the employer argued that the plaintiff had voluntarily undertaken the risk of injury. The House of Lords held that the employer was liable. The defence failed because mere knowledge of the risk was not the same as consent to the danger. Lord Herschell stated the volenti rule in the following terms:

"One who has invited or assented to an act being done towards him cannot, when he suffers from it, complain of it as a wrong" and he continued "if then, the employer thus fails in his duty towards the employed, I do not think that because (the employee) does not straightaway refuse to continue his service, it is true to say that he is willing that his employer should act thus towards him. I believe it would be contrary to the facts to assert that the plaintiff in this case either invited or assented to the employers negligence."

In *Bowater v. Rowley Regis Corporation (1944)* the plaintiff was employed as a carter, and was ordered to take out a particular horse to pull his cart. He protested because the horse was known to be vicious but his protests were in vain. He was injured by the horse and in an action for damages the defendant raised the defence of volenti non fit injuria. It was held that the defence was inapplicable because the plaintiff had not genuinely consented to run the risk — in reality he had little choice but to take out the horse.

The defence of volenti non fit injuria will not usually be available where the plaintiff has been injured while attempting to rescue someone from a peril created by the defendant's negligence. In these circumstances the rescuer cannot normally be regarded as having freely consented to the risk of injury.

In *Haynes v. Harwood (1935)* for example, a policeman was injured while stopping a runaway horse and cart which endangered the safety of the members of the public, including children, in a busy street. It was held that, in the circumstances, he had at least a moral duty to intervene, and his claim for damages succeeded.

> By way of contrast in *Cutler v. United Dairies Ltd (1933)* the plaintiff intervened to stop a runaway horse within a field. It posed no risk of injury to anyone. The plaintiff was unable to recover damages for the injuries which he sustained as the court held that he had voluntarily assumed the risk of injury.

EXCLUSION OF LIABILITY FOR NEGLIGENCE

Under the rules of common law it used to be possible for a defendant to exclude his liability for negligence, either by including an appropriately worded term in a contract, or by displaying a notice to that effect.

> In *White v. Blakemore (1972)*, for example, the plaintiff's husband, a member of a racing club, stood next to the ropes near a stake watching a race. The wheel of a racing car caught on the rope pulling the stake out of the ground. The stake killed the plaintiff's husband. Notices had been displayed by the defendant in prominent positions excluding all liability for accidents howsoever caused. It was held that the notices were effective to protect the defendant from liability.

Since the introduction of the Unfair Contract Terms Act 1977 (examined in Chapter 5), however, the scope of the common rules have been considerably cut down. You will recall that under Section 2 of the 1977 Act liability for death or personal injury caused by negligence cannot be excluded, but that it may be possible to exclude liability for other types of damage or loss. Such an exclusion will only be effective however if the defendant can prove that it is fair and reasonable to allow reliance on it in the circumstances of the case.

TIME LIMITS FOR CLAIMS IN NEGLIGENCE

The Limitation Act 1980, as amended by the Latent Damage Act 1986, provides that no legal action may be taken in respect of certain types of claim unless proceedings are issued within the limitation period. After this time the claim is said to be statute barred and the court will refuse to entertain it. The limitation period varies according to the legal basis of the claim and the type of injury or damage suffered by the plaintiff.

(a) Personal injuries or death

Personal injury claims in negligence (and in contract) are subject to a limitation period of three years. Time starts to run either on the date on which the right to sue first arises, or, if later, on the date on which the plaintiff is aware:

(i) that he has suffered significant injury,

(ii) that this is attributable to the defendant's negligence or breach of contract, and

(iii) of the identity of the defendant.

Where this formula applies there is no final long term cut off date after which the plaintiff's claim cannot be brought. The plaintiff will usually use this formula when he is suing for injuries which did not manifest themselves at the time of the negligent act. This could apply if, for example, the plaintiff contracted a lung disease through exposure to industrial dust from asbestos or coal, and the disease did not become apparent for a number of years.

(b) Claims other than personal injury

In the case of a claim which does not involve personal injury, for example for property damage or financial loss, the limitation period both in negligence and in contract is six years from the date on which the right to sue first arises. In the case of a negligence claim for this type of loss the Latent Damage Act 1986 enables the plaintiff to commence legal proceedings outside the six year period (nb the 1986 Act does not apply to a contract claim). Under the Act the claim must be made within three years of the date on which the plaintiff became aware:

(i) that the damage was significant,

(ii) that it was attributable to the negligence of the defendant, and

(iii) of the identity of the defendant.

Under the 1986 Act, however, the limitation period cannot be extended beyond 15 years of the date of the event which constituted the defendant's breach of duty. As we noted above there is no such 'long stop' date beyond which the period for bringing a personal injuries claim cannot be extended.

One of the principal reasons for the introduction of the Latent Damage Act 1986 was to provide an effective remedy for a person in the situation of the plaintiff in the case of *Pirelli v. Oscar Faber*.

> In *Pirelli General Cable Works Ltd v. Oscar Faber & Partners (1983)* the defendants were consulting engineers who advised the plaintiffs on the design and erection of a large chimney for the boiler at their factory. The design was defective and expert evidence showed that internal cracks had occurred within the chimney before April 1970. The damage was not discovered, however, until 1977 and the plaintiff did not commence legal proceedings until 1978. The House of Lords held that the six year limitation period began to run as soon as the damage occurred and therefore the claim was statute barred. The limitation period had expired even before the plaintiffs knew that they had suffered any damage.

Under the provisions of the 1986 Act the issue of limitation would have been decided in the plaintiff's favour on the facts of the Pirelli case. The Act is designed to eliminate this type of injustice.

PROFESSIONAL NEGLIGENCE

The field of professional negligence is a growth area within the law of negligence. It operates in a situation where a client or a third party suffers loss or damage as a result of the failure by a person to exercise care in carrying out his profession. Where this occurs, the injured party may have a number of avenues of redress open to him, in addition to legal action in the courts.

ALTERNATIVES TO COURT ACTION

Most professionals, for example, lawyers, doctors, architects, surveyors and accountants, are regulated by professional associations. These bodies are almost invariably authorised, through contractual conditions of membership or by Act of Parliament, to exercise disciplinary powers over members of the profession. These disciplinary powers are usually exercised, in the more serious cases, by a domestic tribunal. The tribunal will act rather like a court and will hear formal complaints against members of the profession. If a complaint is proven, the tribunal will have power to impose punishments ranging from a simple reprimand to the imposition of a fine or the suspension or withdrawal of the right to practice as a member of the profession.

In addition to disciplinary tribunals, many professional bodies sponsor arbitration schemes which provide a means by which compensation claims can be adjudicated without reference to the courts. One example is the Solicitors Arbitration Scheme set up by the Law Society in 1986. The scheme is run by the Chartered Institute of Arbitrators. In order to use the scheme both the solicitor and the claimant must agree. They will be bound by the decision of the arbitrator and neither party can subsequently take the matter to court. The arbitrator will look at written submissions by the parties and other supporting documents. He will decide whether the claim is valid and fix the amount of compensation to be awarded. In exceptional cases, where it appears that a decision cannot be made on the examination of documents alone, there is provision for a verbal hearing with the agreement of both parties. Each party must pay a registration fee of £46 but this fee will be refunded to the successful party. The remaining costs of the scheme are paid by the Law Society itself. The process of arbitration is examined further in Chapter 9.

THE LEGAL BASIS OF A PROFESSIONAL NEGLIGENCE CLAIM

The vast majority of professional negligence claims are made by clients of the professional, rather than by third parties who have no contractual relationship with him. Most claims will therefore be based upon an allegation of a breach of contract. The professional has a contractual duty to his client to take reasonable care in providing professional services. This is recognised in Section 13 of the Supply of Goods and Services Act 1982 which provides that:

> "In a contract for the supply of a service where the supplier is acting in the course of a business, there is an implied term that the supplier will carry out the service using reasonable skill and care."

We have already examined a number of cases coming within the scope of this contractual duty in the context of consumer protection in the previous chapter. The duty is also significant in relation to professional negligence. We may use the term contractual negligence to refer to liability for breach of this duty. A small number of exceptions to the duty are provided for by section 12(4) of the 1982 Act. These include the duties owed by company directors and barristers and are examined more closely elsewhere in this text.

Where the plaintiff has no contractual relationship with the professional, he will have to establish that a duty of care is owed to him under general principles of the tort of negligence. Without a contract he will obviously be unable to rely on Section 13 of the 1982 Act. The term 'third party negligence' may be used for the sake of convenience to distinguish this situation from one of contractual negligence. It used to be the case that where the plaintiff had a claim in contract the courts would not recognise the existence of a right to sue the defendant in tort. In *Esso Petroleum Ltd v. Mardon (1976)*, however, the Court of Appeal held that where there is a contract between two parties, an action in tort may be brought in addition to a claim in contract. This view now appears to be well established so that for example in *Midland Bank Trust Co Ltd v. Hett, Stubbs and Kemp (1979)* (discussed more fully below) the High Court refused to follow its own previous decision in *Clark v. Kirby Smith (1964)* and allowed a claim in tort against a solicitor who had negligently performed a contract with his client.

There are a number of important differences between contractual negligence and third party negligence. Where the plaintiff has a contract with the professional he may sue alternatively in contract and in tort. He may therefore take advantage of whichever set of rules are most favourable to his claim. Where there is no contract however only the rules of the tort of negligence will apply to the claim. Figure 6.1 below summarises the major differences between the two alternative bases of claim.

Professional negligence : main differences between claims in contract and tort.

	contract	tort
who can sue	client only	client or third party
type of loss recoverable if not too remote	all types of loss	see Figure 6.2
test for remoteness of damage	Hadley v. Baxendale (i) damage arising in the ordinary course of events (ii) unusual losses if known to be likely at time of contract	The Wagon Mound damage of a type which was reasonably foreseeable at the time of the breach of duty
time limits for claims	(i) time runs from breach (ii) Latent Damage Act 1986 does not apply (iii) see Figure 6.4 for time limits	(i) time runs from damage (ii) Latent Damage Act 1986 applies (iii) see Figure 6.4 for time limits
exclusion of liability	s.2 and s.3 Unfair Contract Terms Act 1977	s.2 Unfair Contract Terms Act 1977

Fig. 6.1

FINANCIAL LOSS CAUSED BY PROFESSIONAL NEGLIGENCE

Where the plaintiff is suing for contractual negligence there will be little difficulty in establishing liability for financial loss caused by the defendant's breach of contract, provided that the loss is not too remote. The rules of remoteness of damage in contract were laid down in *Hadley v. Baxendale (1854)* and were examined in Chapter 4.

Where the claim is based upon tortious or third party negligence, the plaintiff may have more difficulty in establishing that the defendant owed a duty of care to avoid causing his financial loss. A claim for financial loss (sometimes referred to as economic loss) usually takes the form of a claim for the loss of profits which the plaintiff would have made but for the defendant's negligence or the loss of money invested as a result of advice or information given by the defendant. As we previously noted when examining the development of the duty of care, the duty can readily be established by applying the neighbour principle where the claim relates to personal injury or property damage. Where the plaintiff's loss is financial, however, considerations of public policy may come into play in determining the existence and scope of the duty of care, and Lord Wilberforce's two stage test will have to be borne in mind.

Across the spectrum of professional activities it is possible to distinguish two broad categories of claim for financial loss:

(1) financial loss caused by negligent statements

(2) financial loss caused by negligent acts.

The basis and scope of the duty of care will vary according to which of these categories the plaintiff's claim comes within. We shall examine the basic ground rules for each category, returning to them later when we consider the liability of members of some particular professions for negligence.

1. FINANCIAL LOSS CAUSED BY NEGLIGENT STATEMENTS

Prior to the decision of the House of Lords in *Hedley Byrne v. Heller (1964)* it was well settled law that there could be no liability in tort for financial loss caused by negligently made statements. In *Candler v. Crane, Christmas & Co (1951)* for example the Court of Appeal by a majority held that a false statement, carelessly made, was not actionable in the tort of negligence. Lord Denning dissented and was prepared to recognise the existence of a duty of care where the defendant had some special knowledge or skill upon which the plaintiff relied. He stated that:

> "From early times it has been held that persons who engage in a calling which requires special knowledge and skill owe a duty of care to those who are closely and directly affected by their work, apart altogether from any contract or undertaking in that behalf."

The judgment of Lord Denning was approved by the House of Lords in *Hedley Byrne v. Heller,* and the decision of the majority in the Candler case was overruled.

> In *Hedley Byrne & Co v. Heller and Partners Ltd (1964)* the plaintiffs were advertising agents whose clients, Easipower Ltd, were customers of the defendant merchant bank. The plaintiffs had been instructed to buy advertising space for Easipower's products on television and in the newspapers. This involved them in the expenditure of large sums of money. Never having dealt with Easipower before, the plaintiff's sought a reference as to their creditworthiness to the extent of £100,000 from the defendant. The reference was given 'without responsibility on the part of the bank' and stated with reference to Easipower: "Respectably constituted company, considered good for its ordinary business

> engagements. Your figures are larger than we are accustomed to see". In fact Easipower had an overdraft with the bank, which ought to have known that the company would have difficulty meeting payments to the plaintiff. Within one week of giving the reference the bank was pressing Easipower to reduce its overdraft. Relying on the reference the plaintiffs incurred personal liability by placing advertising contracts. Easipower then went into liquidation due to insolvency and as a result the plantiffs lost over £17,500. The actual decision in the case was that the defendant was not liable as the disclaimer of responsibility was effective to prevent the bank from assuming a duty of care.

The principal importance of the decision, however, is that the House of Lords recognised the existence, in certain circumstances, of a duty of care in relation to financial loss caused by negligently made statements. Lord Morris stated that:

> "if someone possessed of a special skill undertakes, quite irrespective of contract, to apply that skill for the assistance of another person who relies upon such skill, a duty of care will arise."

Lord Pearce expressed the view that the duty would only arise in relation to a statement about "a business or professional transaction whose nature makes clear the gravity of the inquiry and the importance and influence attached to the answer".

For reasons of public policy, the scope of the duty and the class of persons to whom it is owed was restricted by the House of Lords. The main policy reason for this was a reluctance to create open ended liability by exposing a defendant to claims by numerous plaintiffs for a single instance of negligence. In Lord Reid's view the danger of 'opening the floodgates' in this way was particularly acute for a number of reasons:

> "I would think that the law must treat negligent words differently from negligent acts . . . Quite careful people often express definite opinions on social or informal occasions even when they see that others are likely to be influenced by them; and they often do so without taking that care which they would take if asked for their opinion professionally or in a business connection. . . . But it is at least unusual casually to put into circulation negligently made articles which are dangerous. . . . Another obvious difference is that a negligently made article will only cause one accident and so it is not very difficult to find the necessary degree of proximity or neighbourhood between the negligent manufacturer and the person injured. But words can be broadcast with or without the consent or the foresight of the speaker or writer. It would be one thing to say that the speaker owes a duty to a limited class, but it would be going very far to say that he owes a duty to every ultimate 'consumer' who acts on those words to his detriment."

For these reasons the House of Lords held that in order for a duty to arise there must be a 'special relationship of reliance' between the parties. It was characterised by Lord Devlin as "a relationship equivalent to a contract" (albeit lacking the essential ingredient of consideration discussed in Chapter 3). The most authoritative definition of the special relationship of reliance was given by Lord Reid who said that it included:

> ". . . all those relationships where it is plain that the party seeking information or advice was trusting the other to exercise such a degree of care as the circumstances required, where it is reasonable for him to do that, and where the other gave the information or advice when he knew or ought to have known that the inquirer was relying on him."

Clearly there would be no special relationship of reliance in respect of casual remarks in the course of conversation on a social or informal occasion. In any event the person who is asked for information or an opinion could refuse to give it; make clear that it was given without careful consideration, or, as happened in the Hedley Byrne case, disclaim responsibility for it. In Lord Reid's opinion:

> "A reasonable man, knowing that he was being trusted or that his skill and judgment were being relied on, would, I think, have three courses open to him. He could keep silent or decline to give the information or advice sought: or he could give an answer with a clear qualification that he accepted no responsibility for it or that it was given without that reflection or inquiry which a careful answer would require: or he could simply answer without any such qualification. If he chooses to adopt the last course he must, I think, be held to have accepted some responsibility for his answer being given carefuly, or to have accepted a relationship with the inquirer which requires him to exercise such care as the circumstances require."

Where the person making the statement excludes liability for it or states that it is given without responsibility, the Unfair Contract Terms Act 1977 applies with the result that the disclaimer will be invalid unless the person who made the statement proves that it is fair and reasonable in the circumstances to allow reliance on the disclaimer. It may be then that a case with similar facts to those of *Hedley Byrne v. Heller* would be decided differently if it came before the courts today.

The test for determining whether a duty of care exists outside a contract in relation to careless statements causing financial loss is whether a special relationship of reliance exists between the parties. This is narrower in its scope than the neighbour principle and under it the duty will be established if the plaintiff can prove:

(i) that the defendant possessed special skill or knowledge,

(ii) that the plaintiff relied on the defendant to exercise care,

(iii) that the defendant knew or ought to have known that the plaintiff was relying on him, and

(iv) that reliance by the plaintiff was reasonable in the circumstances.

We have already seen in Chapter 4 that damages for loss caused by a careless statement may be recovered under the Misrepresentation Act 1967 where the statement is a negligent misrepresentation which induces a person to enter a contract. When we considered liability for negligent misrepresentation many of the cases which we examined were argued on the basis both of the Misrepresentation Act and of the Hedley Byrne principle. It may be useful to refer in particular to *Esso Petroleum Co Ltd v. Mardon (1976)* and *Howard Marine and Dredging Co v. Ogden (A.) & Sons (Excavations) (1978)*.

2. FINANCIAL LOSS CAUSED BY NEGLIGENT ACTS

It has been a longstanding principle of the law of negligence that pure financial (or economic) loss caused by a negligent act rather than a statement is not recoverable.

> Thus for example in *Weller Co v. Foot & Mouth Disease Research Institute (1965)* the defendants carried out research into foot and mouth disease, a highly infectious disease affecting cattle. The virus escaped from their premises and affected cattle in the surrounding area. As a result restrictions on the movement of cattle were introduced and two cattle markets belonging to the plaintiff auctioneers had to be closed. The plaintiffs sued for loss caused to their business. It was held that, because

the loss was purely financial and not connected with any physical harm caused to the plaintiffs or their property, no duty of care was owed by the defendants to the plaintiffs, and the claim failed.

The major policy reason for refusing to recognise a duty of care for pure financial loss is that it could lead to open ended liability. In the Weller case, for example, the closure of the markets would have affected the businesses of all those who transported cattle to and from the markets; of the shops, cafes and public houses in the vicinity of the markets; of the banks which would have handled the money in the sale and purchase of cattle; and the destruction of cattle caused by the escape of the virus could have adversely affected the economic interests of cattle feed suppliers, agricultural workers and milkmen, with substantial knock-on effects throughout the local economy. If the defendants were not to be liable for all of these consequences, the line of legal liability has to be drawn restrictively. Thus claims can be brought for injury to the person and damage to property, and for financial losses which are closely associated with such injury or damage. However, with one exception discussed below, claims for pure financial loss caused by the defendant's negligent act are not allowed. The extent of a plaintiff's financial loss may not readily be foreseen by the defendant before the negligent act occurs and the plaintiff will be in the best position to assess the extent and insure against the risk of financial loss.

Financial loss directly associated with physical injury may be referred to as 'consequential' rather than 'pure' financial loss. Here the defendant may owe a duty to the plaintiff under the neighbour principle. An example of the distinction between these types of financial loss can be seen in *Spartan Steel v. Martin.*

In *Spartan Steel & Alloys Ltd v. Martin & Co (Contractors) Ltd (1972)* the defendant's employee, while digging up a road with a mechanical excavator, carelessly damaged an electricity supply cable and cut off the power to the plaintiff's factory. In order to prevent damage to a furnace, the molten metal in it had to be poured off before it solidified. The melt was damaged to the value of £368, and the plaintiffs lost the profit of £400 which they would have made had the process been completed. The electricity supply was cut off for 14 hours during which four additional melts could have been processed. The profit on the additional melts would have been £1,767. The Court of Appeal held that the first two items claimed were recoverable — these were damage to property and consequential financial loss. The loss of profits on additional melts, however, was a pure financial loss not sufficiently connected with the physical damage and therefore not recoverable.

A 1982 decision of the House of Lords has created an exception to the rule that no duty can be owed in respect of pure financial loss unassociated with physical damage.

In *Junior Books Ltd v. Veitchi Co Ltd (1982)* the plaintiff engaged a main contractor to build a new factory. The main contractor, at the request of the plaintiff, engaged the defendant to lay the floor of the building. The defendant was therefore a nominated subcontractor and had no contractual relationship with the plaintiff. Due to the defendant's failure to mix and lay the floor with reasonable care, the floor began to crack up leaving the plaintiff with an unserviceable building bearing high maintenance costs. The plaintiff ceased production, had the floor relaid and sued the defendant for all the costs and losses incurred by him.

The claim was made up as follows:

		£
(i)	replacement of floor	50,000
(ii)	storeage of stock	1,000
(iii)	removal of machinery	2,000
(iv)	loss of profits	45,000
(v)	employee wages thrown away	90,000
(vi)	overheads thrown away	16,000
(vii)	investigation of defects in floor	3,000
	Total claim	207,000

The defendant denied that he owed a duty to the plaintiff in respect of that part of the claim which represented pure financial loss. The House of Lords, by a majority, held the defendant liable for the full claim, including the element of pure financial loss. The duty of care in this case was thus extended beyond one of preventing physical harm being done by faulty work to a duty to avoid the presence of defects in the work itself and to avoid the resultant financial losses. Lord Fraser, in his judgment, stressed that he was deciding the case "strictly on its own facts. I rely particularly on the very close proximity between the parties." After discussing the floodgates argument Lord Fraser continued: "The proximity between the parties is extremely close, falling only just short of a direct contractual relationship. The injury to the plaintiff was a direct and foreseeable result of negligence by the defendants. The plaintiffs nominated the defendants as specialist subcontractors and they must therefore have relied on their skill and knowledge."

The Junior Books case has been treated in subsequent cases as laying down a narrow exception to a general principle, rather than as a springboard for the extension of liability. Thus in *Muirhead v. Industrial Tank Specialties (1985)*, discussed below in the context of product liability, the Court of Appeal refused to extend the duty to a manufacturer of defective electric motors which caused financial loss to the ultimate consumer. The decision was made on the grounds that there was not a sufficient degree of close proximity between the plaintiff and the defendant to give rise to a duty of care to avoid causing financial loss.

More recently in *Leigh & Sillavan Ltd. v. Aliakmon Shipping Co Ltd, The Aliakmon (1986)* the House of Lords held that the buyer under an export contract to whom the ownership of the goods had not passed, but to whom the risk of accidental destruction had been transferred by the terms of the contract, could not sue the shipowner in negligence for pure financial loss caused to him by the fact that the goods were damaged whilst in transit on board ship.

Figure 6.2 provides a summary of the types of loss which can be sued for in a claim involving professional negligence and the test which the court will apply in deciding whether a duty of care exists.

Establishing a duty of care to avoid causing various types of loss by professional negligence

Type of loss	Duty in contractual negligence	Test to be applied for duty in tort
death or personal injury	duty implied if no express term	neighbour principle — proximity of plaintiff and foreseeability of harm
loss of or damage to property	duty implied if no express term	neighbour principle
financial loss caused by negligent statement	duty implied if no express term	special relationship of reliance — Hedley Bryne v. Heller
negligent act causing financial loss consequential upon physical damage	duty implied if no express term	neighbour principle — Spartan Steels v. Martin
negligent act causing pure financial loss	duty implied if no express term	no duty — Weller v Foot & & Mouth Research Institute unless very close proximity Junior Books v Veitchi

Figure 6.2

PROFESSIONAL NEGLIGENCE LIABILITY AND SPECIFIC PROFESSIONS

We shall now consider the way in which the courts have applied the principles outlined above in a variety of circumstances involving allegations of negligence against members of a number of specific professions. In doing so we should bear in mind that the rules laid down in relation to one profession can often be applied to other professions. You may find it useful, in relation to each case, to attempt to identify the essential elements of each negligence action as they arise, and to analyse each decision so as to pinpoint the element which is at the centre of the dispute.

1. MEDICAL PRACTITIONERS

Most claims against members of the medical profession arise as a result of personal injuries suffered by patients in their care. Establishing the existence of a duty of care will usually present few difficulties for the plaintiff. However his task of proving a breach of duty may be more problematic.

> In *Bolam v. Friern Hospital Management Committee (1957)* the plaintiff broke his pelvis during electro-convulsive therapy treatment at the

> defendant's hospital. He claimed that the doctor was negligent principally because he failed to exercise any manual control over the plaintiff during treatment beyond merely arranging for his shoulders to be held, the chin supported, a gag used, and a pillow put under his back. Informed medical opinion consisted of two schools of thought regarding the use of restraint in these circumstances, one view favouring restraint, the other against it. It was held that there had been no breach of duty by the defendants.

McNair J., discussing the standard of care required of a professional man, stated:

> ". . . where you get a situation which involves the use of some special skill or competence, then the test as to whether there has been negligence or not . . . is the standard of the ordinary skilled man exercising and professing to have that special skill. A man need not possess the highest expert skill; it is well established law that it is sufficient if he exercises the ordinary skill of an ordinary competent man exercising that particular art . . .
>
> . . . A doctor is not guilty of negligence if he has acted in accordance with a practice accepted as proper by a responsible body of medical men skilled in that particular art. Putting it the other way round, a man is not negligent, if he is acting in accordance with such a practice, merely because there is a body of opinion who take a contrary view."

The statements of McNair J., were approved by the House of Lords in *Whitehouse v. Jordan.*

> In *Whitehouse v. Jordan (1981)* a senior hospital registrar in charge of a difficult birth used forceps to assist in the birth. The use of forceps was unsuccessful and the baby was eventually delivered by Caesarian section. The baby was born with brain damage. It was alleged that this resulted from the defendant's negligence in pulling too hard and too long with the forceps. The Court of Appeal held that the defendant was not liable in negligence even though he had made an error of judgment. Lord Denning, M.R., in a statement which was not accepted as valid by the House of Lords, asserted that:
>
> "we must say, and say firmly, that, in a professional man an error of judgment is not negligent".
>
> The House of Lords, whilst confirming the decision of the Court of Appeal, disagreed with the statement by Lord Denning. Lord Fraser stated that:
>
> ". . . I think that Lord Denning M.R. must have meant to say that an error of judgment 'is not necessarily negligent". . . . Merely to describe something as an error of judgment tells us nothing about whether it is negligent or not. The true position is that an error of judgment may, or may not, be negligent; it depends on the nature of the error. If it is one that would not have been made by a reasonably competent professional man professing to have the standard and type of skill that the defendant held himself out as having, and acting with ordinary care, then it is negligent. If, on the other hand, it is an error that a man, acting with ordinary care, might have made, then it is not negligence."

In relation to the liability of medical practitioners for professional negligence reference can be made to the cases of *Cassidy v. Ministry of Health (1951)* and *Wilsher v. Essex Area Health Authority (1986)* examined earlier in this chapter. It is also significant that on the 10th July 1987 the High Court awarded a record sum in damages of £1,032,000 to a patient, Mr Samir Hosn following incorrect medical treatment which left him with a mental age of two and the ability to walk only with the greatest difficulty.

2. ACCOUNTANTS

It was estimated by one writer in the New Law Journal (August 2 1985) that the total outstanding claims against accountants in the UK for professional negligence was in excess of £500 million. Such claims are invariably for financial loss and are governed by the rules of contractual negligence or by the principles laid down by the House of Lords in *Hedley Byrne v. Heller (1964)* or both. In the discussion of the Hedley Byrne case earlier in this chapter, reference was made to the dissenting judgment of Lord Denning in *Candler v. Crane Christmas (1951).*

> In *Candler v. Crane Christmas & Co (1951)* the plaintiff proposed to invest £2,000 in a company, but before making the investment he wished to examine the company's accounts. The defendant accountants were in the course of preparing the accounts. They were instructed by the managing director of the company to complete their work quickly and to show the accounts to the plaintiff. On the strength of the accounts the plaintiff invested his money in the company. The accounts were carelessly prepared and gave a wholly misleading picture of the state of the company, which was wound up within a year. The plaintiff lost his investment and sued the accountants for professional negligence. In a majority decision which has since been overruled by the House of Lords, the Court of Appeal held that the defendant owed no duty of care to the plaintiff. The dissenting judgment of Lord Denning is very significant in the current debate as to the extent of the accountant's liability to third parties for professional negligence. It is worth quoting at some length from the judgment of Lord Denning. He stated that a duty to use care in making statements was owed by:
>
> "those persons such as accountants, surveyors, valuers and analysts, whose profession and occupation is to examine books, accounts, and other things, and to make reports on which other people — other than their clients — rely in the ordinary course of business. Their duty is not merely a duty to use care in their reports. They also have a duty to use care in their work which results in their reports." and he continued "to whom do these professional people owe this duty? I will take accountants, but the same reasoning applies to the others. They owe the duty, of course to their employer or client; and also I think to any third person to whom they themselves show the accounts, or to whom they know their employer is going to show the accounts, so as to induce him to invest money or take some other action on them. But I do not think the duty can be extended still further so as to include strangers of whom they have heard nothing and to whom their employer without their knowledge may choose to show their accounts. Once the accountants have handed their accounts to their employer they are not, as a rule, responsible for what he does with them without their knowledge or consent."
>
> . . . It will be noticed that I have confined the duty to cases where the accountant prepares his accounts and makes his report for the guidance of the very person in the transaction in question. That is sufficient for the decision in this case. I can well understand that it would be going too far to make an accountant liable to any person in the land who chooses to rely on the accounts in matters of business, for that would expose him to "liability "in an indeterminate amount for an indeterminate time to an inde- "terminate class"."

> . . . My conclusion is that a duty to use care in statement is recognized by English law, and that its recognition does not create any dangerous precedent when it is remembered that it is limited in respect of the persons by whom and to whom it is owed and the transactions to which it applies.
>
> One final word: I think that the law would fail to serve the best interests of the community if it should hold that accountants and auditors owe a duty to no one but their client. Its influence would be most marked in cases where their client is a company or firm controlled by one man. It would encourage accountants to accept the information which the one man gives them, without verifying it; and to prepare and present the accounts rather as a lawyer prepares and presents a case, putting the best appearance on the accounts they can, without expressing their personal opinion of them. This is, to my way of thinking, an entirely wrong approach. There is a great difference between the lawyer and the accountant. The lawyer is never called upon to express his personal belief in the truth of his client's case; whereas the accountant, who certifies the accounts of his client, is always called on to express his personal opinion as to whether the accounts exhibit a true and correct view of his client's affairs; and he is required to do this, not so much for the satisfaction of his own client, but more for the guidance of shareholders, investors, revenue authorities, and others who may have to rely on the accounts in serious matters of business. If we should decide this case in favour of the accountants there will be no reason why accountants should ever verify the word of the one man in a one-man company, because there will be no one to complain about it. The one man who gives them wrong information will not complain if they do not verify it. He wants their backing for the misleading information he gives them, and he can only get it if they accept his word without verification. It is just what he wants so as to gain his own ends. And the persons who are misled cannot complain because the accountants owe no duty to them. If such be the law, I think it is to be regretted for it means that the accountants' certificate, which should be a safeguard, becomes a snare for those who rely on it."

Following the decision in *Hedley Byrne v. Heller (1964)* these passages from Lord Denning's judgment have the approval of the House of Lords. The Hedley Byrne case itself established the 'special relationship of reliance' as the test to be applied in determining whether a duty of care is owed by a person making a careless statement, for example an accountant carelessly preparing misleading accounts, and causing financial loss.

More recently, however, the Court of Appeal appear to have disregarded this test for determining whether an accountant owes a duty of care in such circumstances.

> In *JEB Fasteners Ltd v. Marks Bloom & Co (1983)* the plaintiff proposed to take over another company called B.G. Fasteners Ltd. The principal reason for the takeover was that the plaintiff wished to acquire the services of the two directors of the target company. A copy of the audited accounts of the target company had been certified by the defendant accountants, without qualification, as giving a true and fair view of the state of the company. The accounts were relied upon by the plaintiff, which acquired the entire share capital of B.G. Fasteners. The accounts had been carelessly prepared and gave a misleading picture as to the value of the company. At the time the accounts were audited the defendants had no knowledge of the plaintiff or its intentions, and were not aware that a takeover from any source was contemplated.

The Court of Appeal held:

(a) that the defendants owed a duty of care to the plaintiff even though it was a complete stranger to them at the time of the audit. The defendants ought to have foreseen that B.G. Fasteners would require funds from money lenders or investors in the short term and that such persons were likely to rely on the audited accounts;

(b) that the defendants were in breach of the duty of care as the accounts did not provide a true and fair view of the company. In particular there was a gross overvaluation of stock which caused the profit and loss account to show a profit when in reality the company had made a loss in excess of £13,000; and

(c) that the plaintiff's claim failed on the issue of causation of loss. The evidence clearly indicated that, even if the plaintiff had known the true financial position of the target company, it would nontheless have gone ahead with the takeover. This was because the plaintiff's overriding object was to acquire the services of the two directors of B.G. Fasteners. Therefore the defendant's negligence was not the operative cause of the plaintiff's loss.

The importance of the decision in the JEB Fasteners case is that the Court of Appeal approached the question of duty by applying the broad test of reasonable foresight of harm — the neighbour principle — rather than the more restrictive test of whether there was a special relationship of reliance between the parties. The Court of Appeal felt able to do this, despite the considerable authority of the Hedley Byrne decision, by applying the two stage test laid down by Lord Wilberforce in *Anns v. Merton (1977)* discussed in detail earlier in this chapter. The point is still very much an open one, however, particularly in the light of the observations by Lord Brandon in *Leigh and Sillavan Ltd v. Aliakmon Shipping Co Ltd, The Aliakmon (1986)* on the status and use of Lord Wilberforce's two stage test.

Until there is a new decision by the House of Lords on this issue, it is unclear which is the proper test to apply in determining whether a duty of care is owed by an accountant in these circumstances. In view of the extent of outstanding claims against accountants for professional negligence, it would not be surprising if the question does come up for consideration by the House of Lords in the near future.

3. SURVEYORS

In Chapter 8, we examine the process of conveyancing in relation to the acquisition of land and premises by a business, and look at the role of the surveyor within that process. A surveyor, in carrying out a survey of a dwellinghouse which is being purchased with the aid of a Building Society mortgage, owes a duty of care to the purchaser of the property to carry out a reasonably careful visual inspection. This was established by the decision of the High Court in *Yianni v. Edwin Evans (1981)*.

The Yianni case was recently confirmed by the Court of Appeal in *Smith v. Bush.*

In *Smith v Eric S. Bush (a firm) (1987)* the defendants were engaged by the Abbey National Building Society to carry out a survey and valuation of a house as required by s.13 Building Societies Act 1986. The plaintiff, who intended to purchase the house, paid for the inspection. She later purchased without the benefit of any structural survey. Eighteen months after the purchase part of the house fell in because the flues in the attic were left unsupported when the chimney breast in the room below had been taken out: a defect which the defendants had overlooked when surveying

> the house. The Court of Appeal held that the defendants were in breach of the duty which they owed to the plaintiff to carry out a reasonably careful visual inspection of the premises. Lord Justice Dillon described the duty of the surveyor in the following terms:
>
> "it was no part of the defendants duty to carry out a full structural survey of the house, and this was understood by the plaintiff. She knew that she was taking a chance on their being no hidden defects in the house which would not have been apparent on a reasonably careful visual inspection of the house. . . . The surveyor's obligation is merely to carry out a reasonably careful visual inspection."
>
> The court also had to deal with another major legal issue in this case. The copy of the surveyor's report, which had been given to the plaintiff, contained a disclaimer of liability: "The surveyors have made this report without any acceptance of responsibility on their part to you". The Court of Appeal took the view that the disclaimer would have been effective but for the operation of s2(2) of the Unfair Contract Terms Act 1977 (see Chapter 5). Under s2(2) a disclaimer is valid only if the defendant can prove that it is fair and reasonable to allow reliance on it. On the issue of reasonableness, Lord Justice Dillon expressed the opinion that:
>
> "where the surveyor is dealing with a property at the lower end of the market and he knows that the purchaser is likely to rely on his report, and not instruct his or her own surveyor, I find it very difficult to see why it should be fair and reasonable to allow him to rely on an automatic blanket exclusion of all liability for negligence if his visual inspection of a property turns out to not to have been reasonably careful."
>
> The plaintiff's claim was therefore successful as the disclaimer of liability was held to be unreasonable and ineffective.

The reasonableness of a disclaimer of liability in similar circumstances to Smith v. Bush was considered in *Stevenson v. Nationwide Building Society (1984)*. In Stevenson's case, however, the purchaser was an estate agent who was well familiar with the difference between a valuation and a structural survey. It was held that the disclaimer was reasonable and effective to protect the defendant, when its staff surveyor failed to notice a substantial structural defect during the course of a visual inspection.

The extent of the surveyor's liability to third parties for reports to their clients was recently tested in the case of *Shankie-Williams and others v. Heavey (1986)*.

> In this case the defendant was employed by Mr. & Mrs. Shankie-Williams (the first and second plaintiffs) to carry out a survey for dry rot on a flat that they intended to buy. The surveyor wrongly reported that there was no dry rot and the purchase went ahead. The third plaintiff saw the report and, believing that it referred to the whole building, bought the flat immediately above. In fact both flats were badly affected by dry rot. The Court of Appeal held that the defendant owed no duty of care to the third plaintiff. The claim of the first and second plaintiffs also failed on the issue of causation. A duty of care was owed to them but the court was satisfied that, on the evidence, they would have purchased the flat without a reduction of the purchase price had they known of the dry rot. The surveyor's negligence therefore was not the operative cause of their loss.

4. THE LEGAL PROFESSION

In Chapter 1 we noted the fact that the legal profession in the UK is divided into two distinct branches and commented upon the roles of solicitors and barristers in the legal process. In relation to that part of their work which involves the presentation of cases before a court, members of both branches of the legal profession enjoy an immunity from liability for professional negligence, for reasons which we will consider below. This immunity is of particular significance for the barrister, as most of his work will involve advocacy in the courts.

(a) BARRISTERS

> In *Rondel v. Worsley (1967)* the plaintiff, who had been convicted of causing grievous bodily harm, sued his barrister for professional negligence. He claimed that the defendant barrister had failed to take reasonable care in the conduct of his criminal defence and that he would have been acquitted if the case had been properly handled. The House of Lords held that the plaintiff's claim failed. A barrister's conduct of a case in court could never give rise to a claim in negligence.

The decision was made on the grounds of public policy. It would be contrary to the public interest to allow such a claim for the following reasons:

(i) A barrister owes a duty not only to his client but also to the court, for example he has a duty not to mislead the court. These twin duties could, on occasion, conflict with each other. He should not be placed, under the pressure of a potential negligence claim, in a position in which he might be tempted to disregard his duty to the court.

(ii) A finding of negligence would necessarily involve a finding that the case in question had been wrongly decided. Thus the negligence proceedings would amount to a retrial of the original case and cast uncertainty on the finality of the previous decision.

(iii) The judge in the original case has a duty to ensure a fair trial and will intervene if necessary to ensure that all of the relevant issues are properly considered.

(iv) Barristers have no choice but to accept a client provided the proper fee is paid.

The immunity of the barrister in these circumstances was said by the majority of the Law Lords in Rondel's case to extend to solicitors engaged in litigation before the courts.

> The scope of the barrister's immunity was further considered by the House of Lords in *Saif Ali v. Sydney Mitchell & Co (1978)*. A barrister failed to advise the plaintiff to bring proceedings against the correct defendant in a personal injuries claim within the three year limitation period. The House of Lords held that the barrister was not immune from proceedings in negligence in these circumstances because the immunity only extends to matters of pre-trial work which are intimately connected with the conduct of the case in court.

In relation to work carried out by a barrister which is not connected with litigation, for example giving opinions and drawing up wills, he may be liable for professional negligence under the principles laid down by the House of Lords in *Hedley Byrne v. Heller (1964)*.

(b) SOLICITORS

A solicitor can be liable to his client for contractual negligence and may also be liable to third parties in negligence.

In *Ross v. Caunters, (1979)*, for example, a solicitor drew up a will and sent it out for his client to sign. The solicitor gave instructions for the signing and witnessing of the will but forgot to warn his client that if the will was witnessed by a beneficiary or the spouse of a beneficiary then the gift would be invalidated. The will was witnessed by the husband of the plaintiff and the mistake was not discovered until after the client's death. The plaintiff, who was a beneficiary under the will, lost her gift and sued the solicitor for the financial loss caused by his negligence. It was held that the solicitor owed a duty of care to the plaintiff and was liable as his failure to take care had caused her loss.

In *Midland Bank Trust Co Ltd v. Hett, Stubbs and Kemp (1979)* the defendant solicitors carelessly failed to register as a land charge an option to purchase a farm granted to their client. The client's right to exercise the option to purchase was defeated, because of the failure to register, on the sale of the farm to a third party. The client sued in negligence and the court held that the solicitors were in breach of their duty of care to the client both in contract and in tort under the Hedley Byrne principle. It was essential to the success of the claim that the court recognised the existence of a duty in the tort of negligence in addition to the contractual duty. This is because the plaintiff's claim in contract was statute-barred under the Limitation Act as more than six years had elapsed since the breach of contract by the solicitors. The limitation period in the tort of negligence, however, does not begin to run until the damage has occurred, in this case the date on which the farm was sold to the third party. As this was within six years of the commencement of proceedings in this case, the claim in the tort of negligence was not time-barred.

PRODUCT LIABILITY IN NEGLIGENCE

It was seen in Chapter 5 that the right to make a product liability claim in contract is confined to an injured person who actually buys the goods himself. The contract claim can be brought against the supplier of the goods only. The supplier is strictly liable, even if he is not at fault. In negligence anyone injured by the product can sue anyone who has failed to take reasonable care in relation to it thereby causing the injury.

We shall now examine those elements of negligence liability which are particularly significant in defective product claims:

1. THE DUTY OF CARE

In relation to liability for manufactured products we have seen that it was not until as late as 1932 that it was recognised that a general duty of care was owed by manufacturers to consumers. This was established by the decision of the House of Lords in the case of *Donoghue v. Stevenson (1932)* the facts of which were described earlier. The importance of the decision in the field of product liability lies in the fact that, in his leading judgment, Lord Atkin described the duty of a manufacturer in the following terms:

> ". . . a manufacturer of products, which he sells in such a form as to show that he intends them to reach the ultimate consumer in the form in which they left him with no reasonable possibility of intermediate examination, and with the knowledge that the absence of reasonable care in the preparation or putting up of the products will result in an injury to the consumer's life or property, owes a duty to the consumer to take that reasonable care."

Although this statement has been developed by subsequent interpretation it can still be regarded as the framework within which a court will decide whether a duty of care exists. Four elements within the framework require closer examination:

(a) Who can be sued

Lord Atkin's reference to 'a manufacturer of products' embraces everyone involved in the manufacturing enterprise from design to distribution. It also extends to others who have worked on the goods at any time.

> In *Stennet v. Hancock (1939)*, for example, the plaintiff was a pedestrian who was injured when part of the wheel of a lorry broke away whilst the lorry was being driven. The defect in the wheel was the result of a repair which had not been carried out properly. The court held that the repairers were liable under Lord Atkin's manufacturing principle.

(b) What type of defects will give rise to liability

Lord Atkin referred to products which the manufacturer sells "in such a form as to show that he intends them to reach the ultimate consumer in the form in which they left him with no reasonable possibility of intermediate examination." This has been interpreted as limiting the application of the duty to products with latent defects. Latent defects are faults which are not apparent on an examination of the goods. Lord Wright in *Grant v. Australian Knitting Mills Ltd (1936)* stated that:

> "The principle of Donoghue's case can only be applied where the defect is hidden and unknown to the consumer . . . the man who consumes or uses a thing which he knows to be noxious cannot complain in respect of whatever mischief follows, because it follows from his own conscious volition in choosing to incur the risk or certainty of mischance."
>
> This interpretation of Lord Atkin's principle was followed in the case of *Crow v. Barford (Agricultural) Ltd. and H.B. Holttum & Co. Ltd. (1963)*. The plaintiff bought a rotary lawn mower known as a Barford Rotomo from Holttum after it was demonstrated to him at home. The machine was designed in such a way that the guard for the blades had an opening to allow the grass to be expelled as it was being cut. To start the lawn mower the user's foot had to be placed on the casing containing the blade. While starting the Rotomo the plaintiff's foot slipped into the opening and two of his toes were cut off.
>
> The claim against the manufacturer was made on the basis of the principle in *Donoghue v. Stevenson* but the Court of Appeal decided that this did not apply because the danger was "perfectly obvious" and not hidden or unknown to the plaintiff. The claim in contract against the retailer was also unsuccessful because the plaintiff had inspected the lawn mower during the demonstration before he purchased it. This brought the case within the exception contained in s14(2) of the Sale of Goods Act that the seller does not promise that the goods are of merchantable quality in relation to defects which ought to have been revealed by the buyer's prior examination of the goods.

(c) To whom is the duty owed

Lord Atkin tells us that the duty of care is owed to the "ultimate consumer" of the product. This expression has been interpreted widely so as to include the purchaser, any person injured while using or consuming the product and any other person, such as the plaintiff in *Stennett v. Hancock*, who is injured by the product in circumstances where injury to him ought reasonably to have been foreseen.

> For example, in *Lambert v. Lewis (Lexmead Ltd, third party; Dixon Bate Ltd, fourth party) (1982)* the driver of a car and his son were killed and the plaintiffs, his wife and daughter, were injured when their car was hit by a trailer which had become detached from a farmer's Land Rover and careered across the road into the path of their car. The accident was caused by a design defect in the towing hitch, which was unable to cope with the stresses to which it was subjected in normal use. The evidence showed that part of the towing hitch had been missing for a number of months before the accident and that the farmer should have realised this.
>
> The trial judge decided that the manufacturer was 75% to blame for the accident and that the farmer was 25% to blame and apportioned liability accordingly. The farmer issued third party proceedings against the retailer from whom he had purchased the towing hitch. He was seeking indemnity for the damages for which he was liable and basing his claim in contract on the retailer's breach of the implied terms in Section 14 Sale of Goods Act. The retailer in turn issued fourth party proceedings against the manufacturer in contract and in negligence. On appeal the House of Lords decided that the retailer was not liable to the farmer because the farmer's own negligence, rather than the retailer's breach of contract, was the operative cause of his loss. The fourth party proceedings were consequently dismissed because the retailer had no liability to pass on to the manufacturer.

(d) What type of damage is recoverable

In his statement of the duty of care owed by a manufacturer, Lord Atkin confines the scope of the duty to "injury to the consumer's life or property". Within this damages are recoverable for death, personal injury or damage to property, including damage to the product itself.

One category of loss which cannot always be sued for in negligence, as we have seen, is purc financial loss. A 1985 case provides a good illustration of this rule in the context of product liability.

> In *Muirhead v. Industrial Tank Specialists (ITT Marlow, third party; Leroy Somer Electric Motors Ltd, fourth party) (1985)*, the plaintiff was a wholesale fish merchant who installed in his premises a large seawater tank in which to store lobsters. The seawater had to be filtered, oxygenated and recirculated. This was done by a series of pumps working 24 hours per day. The tank and pumps were installed by I.T.S. Ltd. The pumps were manufactured by Leroy Somer Electric Motors Ltd and supplied to the plaintiff by ITS Ltd through other suppliers in the chain of distribution. The pumps constantly broke down and on one occasion the recirculation of water was affected so that the plaintiff lost his entire stock of lobsters. The plaintiff successfully sued I.T.S. Ltd in contract but the company went into liquidation unable to satisfy the judgment against it. The plaintiff then proceeded with action against the manufacturers claiming damages for:
>
> (a) cost of pumps: £4,284.46
>
> (b) additional labour in boiling and refrigerating salvaged dead lobsters, estimated: £500.00

(c) additional costs of electrical engineers to attend to pumps, estimated £500.00

(d) additional working time and labour for attendance upon pumps to check, correct tripping out, etc., estimated: £1,500.00

(e) loss of interest on capital deployed and/or loss of availability of working capital: to be quantified

(f) loss of profit on intended sales, estimated: £127,375.00

(g) loss of lobsters at cost, estimated: £11,000.00

The vast bulk of the claim was for the loss of profits on intended sales but the Court of Appeal decided that this was pure financial loss and therefore not recoverable in a negligence action. The rest of the plaintiff's claim succeeded.

2. BREACH OF DUTY

Once it has been established that the manufacturer in a given case owes a duty of care to avoid injury to the plaintiff, the second major element of negligence liability which the plaintiff must prove is that the manufacturer was in breach of that duty. A breach of duty is a failure to take reasonable care and involves a finding of fault on the part of the manufacturer. In many cases the task of proving this may be a difficult one for the plaintiff, involving a detailed investigation of the defendant's processes of manufacture design and testing and a comparison with procedures adopted by other producers in the same field. The plaintiff will need to employ expert witnesses who can analyse these processes and procedures and pinpoint any lack of care which may have caused the defect in the product and therefore caused the injury. If the plaintiff is unable to prove a breach of duty he may have to bear the loss himself without compensation, unless there is another available legal basis for his claim.
A breach of the duty of care may occur outside the process of development design and manufacture.

In the case of *Vacwell Engineering v. BDH Chemicals Ltd (1971)* for example, the manufacturer of a chemical produced for industrial use was held liable in negligence for a failure to give proper and adequate warnings that the chemical would explode when mixed with water. This should have been achieved by clear labelling of the product.

In *Walton v. British Leyland (UK) Ltd (1978)* the failure of British Leyland to recall the Austin Allegro car after a large number of 'wheel drift' faults had been reported to the company was held to be a breach of the duty of care. Leyland were held liable to the plaintiffs who were severely injured when the wheel of their Allegro came off as the vehicle was travelling at 60 mph on a motorway. The Judge, Willis J., in the High Court stated:

"The duty of care owed by Leyland to the public was to make a clean breast of the problem and recall all cars which they could in order that safety washers could be fitted . . . The company seriously considered recall and made an estimate of the cost at a figure (£300,000 in 1974) which seems to me to be in no way out of proportion to the risks involved. It was decided not to follow this course for commercial reasons. I think this involved a failure to observe their duty of care for the safety of the many who were bound to remain at risk . . . "

Res ipsa loquitur

In the context of product liability the principle of res ipsa loquitur is of considerable signficance. The tendency in recent times has been for the courts to allow the plaintiff to rely on the rule in many cases involving defective products. Res ipsa loquitur is considered in detail earlier in this chapter. Here we may note its application in product liability cases.

> In *Chaproniere v. Mason (1905)* the plaintiff broke a tooth when eating a bread bun which was found to contain a pebble. He pleaded res ipsa loquitur and the defendant baker was held to be liable because he was unable to prove that he had not been negligent.

Where the plaintiff pleads res ipsa loquitur, the manufacturer will need to produce strong evidence if he is to satisfy the court that the injuries were not caused by his negligence. It will not be sufficient for him to show that he has a good system of work and provides adequate supervision during the process of manufacture.

> In *Grant v. Australian Knitting Mills (1936)* the plaintiff contracted dermatitis because of the presence in his underwear of excess sulphite after the process of manufacture by the defendant. The defendant's evidence was that he had manufactured over four and a half million pairs of underpants and had received no other complaints. Nevertheless he was held liable because the probability was that someone in his employment for whose acts he was legally responsible had failed to take care.

> In *Hill v. James Crowe (Cases) Ltd (1978)* the plaintiff, a lorry driver, was injured when he fell off a badly nailed wooden packing case on which he was standing in order to load his lorry. The manufacturer of the packing case gave evidence that the standards of workmanship and supervision in his factory were high and argued that he had not failed to fulfil his duty to the plaintiff to take reasonable care in producing the case. The Court held that the defendant was liable for the bad workmanship of one of his employees even though, in general terms, he had a good production system. He had not proved that the plaintiff's injuries were not due to the negligence of one of his employees.

This above case provides us with an example of the manufacturer's liability for a foreseeable misuse of his product.

The extremely high standard of care which the courts are prepared to impose on a manufacturer can be seen in *Winward v. TVR*.

> In *Winward v. TVR Engineering (1986)* the defendants were in the business of producing specialist sports cars. They were responsible for the design and assembly of the vehicles using components bought in from other sources. The car in question incorporated a Ford engine which was supplied to the defendants fitted with a Weber carburettor. The carburettor had a basic design fault which ultimately caused petrol to leak from it. The plaintiff's wife was injured when leaking petrol came into contact with the hot engine. The defendants argued that it was reasonable for them to rely on the expertise of their supplier, particularly as the design fault had never previously manifested itself. The Court of Appeal held that the defendants were in breach of their duty through their failure to test the component and modify its design.

STRICT LIABILITY UNDER PART I OF THE CONSUMER PROTECTION ACT 1987

The Consumer Protection Act 1987 was part of a large crop of legislation which was rushed through at the end of Mrs. Thatcher's second term of office. Part I of the Act, which introduces a framework of strict liability for defective products, was passed in order to fulfill U.K. obligations under the EEC Directive on Product Liability (85/374/EEC).

Legal Change and the EEC Directive

We saw in Chapter 1 that a consequence of our membership of the EEC is that we are obliged to implement legal changes agreed in principle within the Community. One method of achieving legal change is through the use of the directive. A directive is binding as to the result to be achieved but allows the member state to choose the precise content of the rules. The directive on product liability is set out below in figure 6.3.

The preamble to this Directive tells us that it has a two-fold purpose:

(i) to establish a uniform system of product liability within the EEC in order to remove distortions of trade and competition which arise because of the differences between the laws of member states in this field; and

(ii) to solve the problem of a fair apportionment of the risks inherent in modern technological production.

There were lengthy negotiations between the EEC member states on the terms of the Directive. Final adoption in July 1985 was only possible because of an agreement to differ on some of the sticking points in the negotiations.

This gave rise to a number of optional provisions in final text of the Directive and means that full harmonisation of some aspects of product liability law throughout the EEC will not have been achieved. A practical consequence of this may be 'forum shopping' by the injured party. Where there are two possible defendants, each in a different EEC country, the forum shopper will bring his claim in the country in which he stands the best chance of success, having regard to the options adopted there.

The Directive provides for a review of the working of the optional provisions in 1995 in order to reconsider the question of full harmonisation after that review.

The UK response to the three options which were available under the Directive has been:

(i) to incorporate the development risks defence;

(ii) to exclude unprocessed agricultural produce and game, and

(iii) to reject an overall financial limit (£41m) for damage caused by identical products with the same defect.

THE CONSUMER PROTECTION ACT 1987

The Consumer Protection Act comes into effect on a day to be appointed. In order to comply with the terms of the Directive the Act will have to be brought into effect on or before 30th July 1988.

The Act does not apply to any product which is put into circulation before it comes into force.

THE EUROPEAN PRODUCT LIABILITY DIRECTIVE

The official complete text

COUNCIL DIRECTIVE of 25 July 1985

on the approximation of the laws, regulations and administrative provisions of the Member States concerning liability for defective products

(85/374/EEC)

THE COUNCIL OF THE EUROPEAN COMMUNITIES,

Having regard to the Treaty establishing the European Economic Community, and in particular Article 100 thereof,

Having regard to the proposal from the Commission[1],

Having regard to the opinion of the European Parliament[2],

Having regard to the opinion of the Economic and Social Committee[3],

Whereas approximation of the laws of the Member States concerning the liability of the producer for damage caused by the defectiveness of his products is necessary because the existing divergencies may distort competition and affect the movement of goods within the common market and entail a differing degree of protection of the consumer against damage caused by a defective product to his health or property;

Whereas liability without fault on the part of the producer is the sole means of adequately solving the problem, peculiar to our age of increasing technicality, of a fair apportionment of the risks inherent in modern technological production;

Whereas liability without fault should apply only to movables which have been industrially produced; whereas, as a result, it is appropriate to exclude liability for agricultural products and game, except where they have undergone a processing of an industrial nature which could cause a defect in these products; whereas the liability provided for in this Directive should also apply to movables which are used in the construction of immovables or are installed in immovables;

Whereas protection of the consumer requires that all producers involved in the production process should be made liable, in so far as their finished product, component part or any raw material supplied by them was defective; whereas, for the same reason, liability should extend to importers of products into the Community and to persons who present themselves as producers by affixing their name, trade mark or other distinguishing feature or who supply a product the producer of which cannot be identified;

Whereas, in situations where several persons are liable for the same damage, the protection of the consumer requires that the injured person should be able to claim full compensation for the damage from any one of them;

Whereas, to protect the physical well-being and property of the consumer, the defectiveness of the product should be determined by reference not to its fitness for use but to the lack of the safety which the public at large is entitled to expect; whereas the safety is assessed by excluding any misuse of the product not reasonable under the circumstances;

Whereas a fair apportionment of risk between the injured person and the producer implies that the producer should be able to free himself from liability if he furnishes proof as to the existence of certain exonerating circumstances;

Whereas the protection of the consumer requires that the liability of the producer remains unaffected by acts or omissions of other persons having contributed to cause the damage; whereas, however, the contributory negligence of the injured person may be taken into account to reduce or disallow such liability;

Whereas the protection of the consumer requires compensation for death and personal injury as well as compensation for damage to property; whereas the latter should nevertheless be limited to goods for private use or consumption and be subject to a deduction of a lower threshold of a fixed amount in order to avoid litigation in an excessive number of cases; whereas this Directive should not prejudice compensation for pain and suffering and other non-material damages payable, where appropriate, under the law applicable to the case;

Whereas a uniform period of limitation for the bringing of action for compensation is in the interests both of the injured person and of the producer;

Whereas products age in the course of time, higher safety standards are developed and the state of science and technology progresses; whereas, therefore, it would not be reasonable to make the producer liable for an unlimited period for the defectiveness of his product; whereas, therefore, liability should expire after a reasonable length of time, without prejudice to claims pending at law;

Whereas to achieve effective protection of consumers, no contractual derogation should be permitted as regards the liability of the producer in relation to the injured person;

Whereas under the legal systems of the Member States an injured party may have a claim for damages based on grounds of contractual liability or on grounds of non-contractual liability other than that provided for in this Directive; in so far as these provisions also serve to attain the objective of effective protection of consumers, they should remain unaffected by this Directive; whereas, in so far as effective protection of consumers in the sector of pharmaceutical products is already also attained in a Member State under a special liability system, claims based on this system should similarly remain possible;

Whereas, to the extent that liability for nuclear injury or damage is already covered in all Member States by adequate special rules, it has been possible to exclude damage of this type from the scope of this Directive;

Whereas, since the exclusion of primary agricultural products and game from the scope of this Directive may be felt, in certain Member States, in view of what is expected for the protection of consumers, to restrict unduly such protection, it should be possible for a Member State to extend liability to such products;

Whereas, for similar reasons, the possibility offered to a producer to free himself from liability if he proves that the state of scientific and technical knowledge at the time when he put the product into circulation was not such as to enable the existence of a defect to be discovered may be felt in certain Member States to restrict unduly the protection of the consumer; whereas it should therefore be possible for a Member State to maintain in its legislation or to provide by new legislation that this exonerating circumstance is not admitted; whereas, in the case of new legislation, making use of this derogation should, however, be subject to a Community stand-still procedure, in order to raise, if possible, the level of protection in a uniform manner throughout the Community;

Whereas, taking into account the legal traditions in most of the Member States, it is inappropriate to set any financial ceiling on the producer's liability without fault; whereas, in so far as there are, however, differing traditions, it seems possible to admit that a Member State may derogate from the principle of unlimited liability by providing a limit for the total liability of the producer for damage resulting from a death or personal injury and caused by identical items with the same defect, provided that this limit is established at a level sufficiently high to guarantee adequate protection of the consumer and the correct functioning of the common market;

Whereas the harmonization resulting from this cannot be total at the present stage, but opens the way towards greater harmonization; whereas it is therefore necessary that the Council receive at regular intervals, reports from the Commission on the application of this Directive, accompanied, as the case may be, by appropriate proposals;

Whereas it is particularly important in this respect that a re-examination be carried out of those parts of the Directive relating to the derogations open to the Member States, at the expiry of a period of sufficient length to gather practical experience on the effects of these derogations on the protection of consumers and on the functioning of the common market.

HAS ADOPTED THIS DIRECTIVE:

Article 1

The producer shall be liable for damage caused by a defect in his product.

Article 2

For the purpose of this Directive 'product' means all movables, with the exception of primary agricultural products and game, even though incorporated into another movable or into an immovable. 'Primary agricultural products' means the products of the soil, of stock-farming and of fisheries, excluding products which have undergone initial processing. 'Product' includes electricity.

Article 3

1. 'Producer' means the manufacturer of a finished product, the producer of any raw material or the manufacturer of a component part and any person who, by putting his name, trade mark or other distinguishing feature on the product presents himself as its producer.

2. Without prejudice to the liability of the producer, any person who imports into the Community a product for sale, hire, leasing or any form of distribution in the course of his business shall be deemed to be a producer within the meaning of this Directive and shall be responsible as a producer.

3. Where the producer of the product cannot be identified, each supplier of the product shall be treated as its producer unless he informs the injured person, within a reasonable time, of the identity of the producer or of the person who supplied him with the product. The same shall apply, in the case of an imported product, if this product does not indicate the identity of the importer referred to in paragraph 2, even if the name of the producer is indicated.

Article 4

The injured person shall be required to prove the damage, the defect and the causal relationship between defect and damage.

Article 5

Where, as a result of the provisions of this Directive, two or more persons are liable for the same damage, they shall be liable jointly and severally, without prejudice to the provisions of national law concerning the rights of contribution or recourse.

Article 6

1. A product is defective when it does not provide the safety which a person is entitled to expect, taking all circumstances into account, including:
(a) the presentation of the product;
(b) the use to which it could reasonably be expected that the product would be put;

Fig. 6.3

(c) the time when the product was put into circulation.

2. A product shall not be considered defective for the sole reason that a better product is subsequently put into circulation.

Article 7

The producer shall not be liable as a result of this Directive if he proves:
(a) that he did not put the product into circulation; or
(b) that, having regard to the circumstances, it is probable that the defect which caused the damage did not exist at the time when the product was put into circulation by him or that this defect came into being afterwards; or
(c) that the product was neither manufactured by him for sale or any form of distribution for economic purpose nor manufactured or distributed by him in the course of his business; or
(d) that the defect is due to compliance of the product with mandatory regulations issued by the public authorities; or
(e) that the state of scientific and technical knowledge at the time when he put the product into circulation was not such as to enable the existence of the defect to be discovered; or
(f) in the case of a manufacturer of a component, that the defect is attributable to the design of the product in which the component has been fitted or to the instructions given by the manufacturer of the product.

Article 8

1. Without prejudice to the provisions of national law concerning the right of contribution or recourse, the liability of the producer shall not be reduced when the damage is caused both by a defect in the product and by the act or omission of a third party.

2. The liability of the producer may be reduced or disallowed when, having regard to all the circumstances, the damage is caused both by a defect in the product and by the fault of the injured person or any person for whom the injured person is responsible.

Article 9

For the purpose of Article 1, 'damage' means:
(a) damage caused by death or by personal injuries;
(b) damage to, or destruction of, any item of property other than the defective product itself, with a lower threshold of 500 ECU, provided that the item of property:
 (i) is of a type ordinarily intended for private use or consumption, and
 (ii) was used by the injured person mainly for his own private use or consumption.

This Article shall be without prejudice to national provisions relating to non-material damage.

Article 10

1. Member States shall provide in their legislation that a limitation period of three years shall apply to proceedings for the recovery of damages as provided for in this Directive. The limitation period shall begin to run from the day on which the plaintiff became aware, or should reasonably have become aware, of the damage, the defect and the identity of the producer.

2. The laws of Member States regulating suspension or interruption of the limitation period shall not be affected by this Directive.

Article 11

Member States shall provide in their legislation that the rights conferred upon the injured person pursuant to this Directive shall be extinguished upon the expiry of a period of 10 years from the date on which the producer put into circulation the actual product which caused the damage, unless the injured person has in the meantime instituted proceedings against the producer.

Article 12

The liability of the producer arising from this Directive may not, in relation to the injured person, be limited or excluded by a provision limiting his liability or exempting him from liability.

Article 13

This Directive shall not affect any rights which an injured person may have according to the rules of the law of contractual or non-contractual liability or a special liability system existing at the moment when this Directive is notified.

Article 14

This Directive shall not apply to injury or damage arising from nuclear accidents and covered by international conventions ratified by the Member States.

Article 15

1. Each Member State may:
(a) by way of derogation from Article 2, provide in its legislation that within the meaning of Article 1 of this Directive 'product' also means primary agricultural products and game;
(b) by way of derogation from Article 7 (e), maintain or, subject to the procedure set out in paragraph 2 of this Article, provide in this legislation that the producer shall be liable even if he proves that the state of scientific and technical knowledge at the time when he put the product into circulation was not such as to enable the existence of a defect to be discovered.

2. A Member State wishing to introduce the measure specified in paragraph 1 (b) shall communicate the text of the proposed measure to the Commission. The Commission shall inform the other Member States thereof.

The Member State concerned shall hold the proposed measure in abeyance for nine months after the Commission is informed and provided that in the meantime the Commission has not submitted to the Council a proposal amending this Directive on the relevant matter. However, if within three months of receiving the said information, the Commission does not advise the Member State concerned that it intends submitting such a proposal to the Council, the Member State may take the proposed measure immediately.

If the Commission does submit to the Council such a proposal amending this Directive within the aforementioned nine months, the Member State concerned shall hold the proposed measure in abeyance for a further period of 18 months from the date on which the proposal is submitted.

3. Ten years after the date of notification of this Directive, the Commission shall submit to the Council a report on the effect that rulings by the courts as to the application of Article 7 (e) and of paragraph 1 (b) of this Article have on consumer protection and the functioning of the common market. In the light of this report the Council, acting on a proposal from the Commission and pursuant to the terms of Article 100 of the Treaty, shall decide whether to repeal Article 7 (e).

Article 16

1. Any Member State may provide that a producer's total liability for damage resulting from a death or personal injury and caused by identical items with the same defect shall be limited to an amount which may not be less than 70 million ECU.

2. Ten years after the date of notification of this Directive, the Commission shall submit to the Council a report on the effect on consumer protection and the functioning of the common market of the implementation of the financial limit on liability by those Member States which have used the option provided for in paragraph 1. In the light of this report the Council, acting on a proposal from the Commission and pursuant to the terms of Article 100 of the Treaty, shall decide whether to repeal paragraph 1.

Article 17

This Directive shall not apply to products put into circulation before the date on which the provisions referred to in Article 19 enter into force.

Article 18

1. For the purposes of this Directive, the ECU shall be that defined by Regulation (EEC) No 3180/78[4], as amended by Regulation (EEC) No 2626/84[5]. The equivalent in national currency shall initially be calculated at the rate obtaining on the date of adoption of this Directive.

2. Every five years the Council, acting on a proposal from the Commission, shall examine and, if need be, revise the amounts in this Directive, in the light of economic and monetary trends in the Community.

Article 19

1. Member States shall bring into force, not later than three years from the date of notification of this Directive, the laws, regulations and administrative provisions necessary to comply with this Directive. They shall forthwith inform the Commission thereof[6].

2. The procedure set out in Article 15 (2) shall apply from the date of notification of this Directive.

Article 20

Member States shall communicate to the Commission the texts of the main provisions of national law which they subsequently adopt in the field governed by this Directive.

Article 21

Every five years the Commission shall present a report to the Council on the application of this Directive and, if necessary, shall submit appropriate proposals to it.

Article 22

This Directive is addressed to the Member States.

Done at Brussels, 25 July 1985.

For the Council
The President
J POOS

References
[1] OJ No C 241, 14.10.1976, p.9 and OJ No C 271, 26.10.1979, p.3
[2] OJ No C 127, 21.5.1979, p.61
[3] OJ No C 114, 7.5.1979, p.15
[4] OJ No L 379, 30.12.1978, p.1
[5] OJ No L 247, 16.9.1984, p.1
[6] This Directive was notified to the Member States on 30 July 1985.

Fig. 6.3

This means that businesses which are affected by the Act will have some time in which to make any adjustments which they consider necessary in order to protect their position before the Act is operational.

Liability under s2(1) of the Act arises "where any damage is caused wholly or partly by a defect in a product". In order to succeed in a claim, the plaintiff must prove two things:

(a) that the product was defective, and

(b) that the defect caused the injury or damage.

If the plaintiff can prove these things, the defendant will be liable even though he took all possible care in relation to the product. This is the crucial difference between strict liability under the Act and liability based upon negligence which, as we have seen, depends upon proof of fault by the defendant.

WHO IS LIABLE?

Liability falls upon all or any of the following persons:-

(a) the **producer** — this term is defined in s1(2) and includes the manufacturer of the product, the producer of any raw materials or the manufacturer of a component part.

(b) the **'own brander'** — any person who, by putting his name on the product or using a trade mark or other distinguishing marks in relation to it, has held himself out to be the producer of the product.

(c) the **importer into the EEC** — a person importing the product into the Community from a non Community state for the purpose of supplying it in the course of his business.

(d) any **supplier** who cannot identify the person who produced the product, or supplied it to him. In such circumstances that person will be liable, regardless of whether he was a business supplier provided he supplied the product to someone else, and the following conditions are met:

    (i) he is requested by a person suffering any damage to identify any producer, own brander or importer into the EEC;

    (ii) the request is made within a reasonable time after the damage occurs;

    (iii) at the time of the request it is not reasonably practicable for the injured party to identify all of the potential defendants; and

    (iv) he fails, within a reasonable time, to comply with the request or to identify the person who supplied the product to him.

Thus it will be imperative, where litigation is threatened, for businesses to be able to identify the supplier of the products or component parts used in any goods sold by the business. It will be particularly important to differentiate, by product coding for example, between the products of two or more suppliers who are supplying identical components for incorporation into the same type of finished product. This will apply to all component parts ranging from electric motors to nuts and bolts.

Where two or more persons are liable for the injury each can be sued for the full amount of the damage. The party who is sued may be entitled to a contribution or indemnity from anyone else who is liable, under the Civil Liability (Contribution) Act 1978. Of course the injured person can only recover compensation once, regardless of the number of possible defendants or the legal basis of his claim. The injured person will usually choose to sue the defendant against whom liability can most easily be established and who is most likely to be able to afford to pay the damages or to have insurance cover.

WHEN IS A PRODUCT DEFECTIVE?

In order to succeed in a claim the plaintiff will have to prove that his injury was caused by a defect in the product. S3 tells us that a product will be regarded as defective when "the safety of the product is not such as persons generally are entitled to expect". It is clear that the lawnmower in *Crow v. Barford and Holttum* above would be defective under this definition. The question of when a product is defective is likely to be central to much of the litigation under the Act. Section 3(2) gives us some guidance as to the factors which will be relevant in deciding whether a product is defective. It provides that:

> "In determining what persons generally are entitled to expect in relation to a product all the circumstances shall be taken into account, including —
>
> (a) the manner in which, and purposes for which, the product has been marketed, its get-up, the use of any mark in relation to the product and any instructions for, or warnings with respect to, doing or refraining from doing anything with or in relation to the product;
>
> (b) what might reasonably be expected to be done with or in relation to the product; and
>
> (c) the time when the product was supplied by its producer to another person;
>
> and nothing in this section shall require a defect to be inferred from the fact alone that the safety of a product which is supplied after that time is greater than the safety of the product in question."

Clearly it is very important for any business to ensure that the packaging of their products is such that it does not suggest or imply that the product can be used in a manner or for a purpose which is unsafe. Appropriate warnings of the dangers associated with the use or foreseeable misuse of the product must be amply displayed on the packaging and, where necessary, on the goods themselves. A further precaution which may be taken by the producer of goods is the date coding of products in order to take advantage of the defence suggested by the final part of s3(2). Thus if a safer product is subsequently developed and put onto the market, the level of safety provided by the original product cannot be judged solely by reference to improved safety features in the new product.

DEFENCES

A number of specific defences are provided for in Section 4 of the Consumer Protection Act. These are in addition to the obvious defences that the product was not defective or that it was not the cause of the plaintiff's loss. Thus it is a defence to show:

(a) that the defect was attributable to the defendant's compliance with a legal requirement, or

(b) that the defendant did not supply the goods to anyone.

In this connection it is interesting to notice s1(3) which says that where a finished product incorporates component products or raw materials, the supplier of the finished product will not be treated as a supplier of the component products or raw materials by reason only of his supply of the finished product. Thus, for example, a builder using high alumina cement could argue that he was not a supplier of that cement for the purposes of the Act. He could invoke this defence if the building subsequently deteriorated due to defects in the cement.

(c) Section 4 also enables the defendant to escape liability if he can show that he had not supplied the goods in the course of his business and that he had not own branded, imported into the EEC, or produced the goods with a view to profit.

This defence could be invoked, for example, in relation to the sale of home made jam at a coffee morning in aid of charity.

(d) The nature of the fourth defence under Section 4 depends upon whether the defendant is a producer, own brander or importer into the EEC. If he is, he can escape liability by proving that the defect was not present in the product at the time he supplied it. If he is not, he must show that the defect was not present in the product at the time it was last supplied by any person of that description.

(e) Section 4 provides the 'development risks defence' that, given the state of scientific and technical knowledge at the time the product was put into circulation, no producer of a product of that kind could have been expected to have discovered the defect if it had existed in his products while they were under his control.

The development risks defence has provoked much discussion. Its adoption was optional under the terms of the directive. It is argued that the defence reduces the strictness of liability by introducing considerations which are more relevant to negligence. Its main impact will be seen in those areas which are at the forefront of scientific and technical development. The pharmaceutical industry, for example, could benefit from it in relation to the development of new drugs. It may seem ironic that if an event like the Thalidomide tragedy were to re-occur the victims could be prevented from recovering compensation because of the operation of this defence. The tragedy was in fact a major cause of pressure for the introduction of strict product liability laws throughout Europe.

(f) Where the defendant is a producer of a component product, he will have a defence under Section 4 if he can show that the defect in the finished product is wholly attributable to its design or to compliance with instructions given by the producer of the finished product.

DAMAGE

Assuming the plaintiff succeeds in his claim, the question arises as to the types of loss he will be compensated for. Under Section 5 damages are recoverable for death or for personal injury. This includes any disease or other impairment of a person's physical or mental condition. The plaintiff will also be able to claim compensation for damage to his property. However, exceptions to this provide significant limitations on liability under the Act. There is no liability for loss of or damage to:

(a) the product itself,

(b) any property in respect of which the amount of the claim would be below £275,

(c) any commercial property — property of a type which is not ordinarily intended for private use, occupation or consumption and which is not actually intended by the plaintiff for his own private use, occupation or consumption.

Any of these excluded losses could of course be the subject of a claim in contract or negligence. Figure 6.4 below provides a comparison of the alternative forms of legal liability for damage caused by defective products.

Section 7 of the Consumer Protection Act provides for an absolute prohibition on the limitation or exclusion of liability arising under the Act.

COMPARISON OF ALTERNATIVE FORMS OF LEGAL LIABILITY INJURIES CAUSED BY DEFECTIVE PRODUCTS			
	Contract	**Negligence**	**Consumer Protection Act**
who is liable	seller; he may claim an indemnity from the previous seller in the chain of distribution	manufacturer; includes designer, repairer, processor and other persons working on goods	producer, own brander, importer into EEC, supplier who refuses to identify previous supplier or producer
who can claim	buyer only	ultimate consumer provided injury to him is foreseeable	any person injured by a defect in the product
basis of liability	strict; if goods not reasonably fit for usual or notified special purposes	fault; failure to take reasonable care in relation to the product	strict; where the product does not provide the safety which persons are entitled to expect
types of loss	personal injury death damage to property financial loss	personal injury death damage to property financial loss in exceptional cases	personal injury death damage £275 + to consumer property other than product
ex-clusion of liability	prohibited if buyer dealing as consumer otherwise possible if exclusion is reasonable	prohibited if death or personal injury otherwise possible if exclusion is reasonable	prohibited in all cases
time limit for claims	personal injury; 3 years from the date on which the plaintiff had knowledge of the material facts giving rise to the claim other claims; 6 years from the date on which cause of action arose; or, in negligence cases only, (if later) 3 years from the date of plaintiff's knowledge of the material facts if within 15 years of the negligent act		3 years from the date on which the plaintiff was aware of the damage the defect and the identity of the defendant if no more than 10 years since the product was put into circulation

Fig. 6.4

TIME LIMITS FOR CLAIMS

The limitation period provided for in the Act, regardless of the type of damage, is three years from the later of:

1. the date on which the right to take action arises, or
2. the date on which the plaintiff is aware:
   (a) that he has suffered significant damage,
   (b) that the damage is attributable to a defect in the product, and
   (c) of the identify of the defendant.

There is an overall cut off point 10 years after the product is put into circulation. After the 10 year period has elapsed no new claims can be made although any proceedings which have already been started may continue.

ASSIGNMENT — THE NEW COMPLAINTS DEPARTMENT

Spicer and Sharp PLC is an expanding company based in the West Midlands. The company is engaged in the production of power tools, D.I.Y. equipment and accessories. Most of its products, or their components, are actually manufactured by subcontractors and supplied to Spicer and Sharp's main works in Kings Norton, where they are assembled and packaged in the distinctive style of the company under the Spicer and Sharp brand name. The company's expansion is based on an aggressive marketing strategy which aims to establish strong product identity and brand loyalty in order to capture a major share of the UK market.

With the introduction of the Consumer Protection Act 1987, the company is facing an increase in the number of customer complaints and product liability claims against it. This is imposing a considerable strain on the resources of the company's small legal department. The directors have decided to establish a new consumer complaints department to act as a filtering mechanism, dealing with less serious complaints and referring on to the legal department those which are likely to result in substantial claims against the company. In relation to the more serious complaints, the task of the consumer complaints department will be to obtain as much relevant information as possible from the complainant and from internal sources within the company; to make a preliminary assessment of the legal basis of the claim and any defences which may be available to the company; and to make broad recommendations as to any action which should be taken by the company, for example in relation to its quality control procedures, in order to prevent further similar claims. A report dealing with all of these matters must be prepared by the department, and copies given to the legal department and to Mr. Philip Sharp, the director to whom the department will be responsible.

Having been in post as a legal assistant in Spicer and Sharp's legal department for three years, you have been appointed to set up and run the new consumer complaints department. Your first task is to deal with a complaint which has recently been received relating to injuries sustained by Andrew Tucker while using a circular saw fitted with a Spicer and Sharp circular saw blade and belonging to his brother Alan. Alan purchased the new blade for his Spicer and Sharp circular saw from Sedgewick's Home Handyman Stores and loaned it to Andrew who was constructing built-in wardrobes in his daughter's bedroom.

While Andrew was using the saw, the blade shattered when it was applied to a piece of second hand timber which contained a number of old nails. Part of the blade flew up hitting Andrew who suffered facial injuries and may be disfigured permanently as a result. It appears likely that the steel used in the blade had been subjected to excessive hardening in the process of production with the result that it was unusually brittle and more likely to shatter in these circumstances.

Sedgewick's Home Handyman Stores purchased the saw blade from Spicer and Sharp as part of a larger consignment of the company's products. Unfortunately there is no certain means of establishing the identity of the supplier of the defective saw blade to Spicer and Sharp because three separate suppliers are under contract to supply identical blades to the company. However, detailed records of the initial testing and subsequent random testing of each of the three supplier's products are on file in the quality control department at Kings Norton. Examination of the records gives no indication that this type of defect had ever come to light in respect of any of the blades which had previously been tested.

TASK

Prepare a report for circulation to the legal department and to Philip Sharp, in which you indicate:

1. whether Andrew would have a viable claim against the company in the tort of negligence or under Part 1 of the Consumer Protection Act 1987;

2. the nature of any defences which may be available to the company in the event of any claim;

3. whether any steps should be taken in relation to circular saw blades still in the possession of the company or its retails customers, given that three further complaints hae been received involving circular saw blades within a month of the complaint by Andrew Tucker.

DEVELOPMENTAL TASK

As part of the process of setting up the consumer complaints department, you are required to design an incident report form to send out as part of the company's initial response to a complaint. The form should be designed to enable you to obtain the material facts about the case from the complainant.

ASSIGNMENT — AN ARABIAN TALE

Thompsons Importers was a business owned and managed by Michael Thompson. Michael had decided to sell the business, having reached an age at which he felt he ought to be taking life more easily. The major activity carried on by Thompsons was the import into the United Kingdom of luxury goods from the Middle East and India.

The business was put on the market, and one of Michael's trading competitors, Arabia Exportex Ltd expressed an interest in acquiring it. The managing director of the company, Alan Naseem, indicated to Michael that the company would require a report on the condition and future prospects of the business and Michael agreed to this.

The report was prepared by Rupert Gray, an accountant with Frayne and Company a reputable firm of accountants in Birmingham. Alan Naseem happened to know Rupert Gray, and encouraged him to make the report, "as pessimisstic in assessing the future prospects of Thompsons as you feel truth will permit."

Rupert Gray's report contained a number of reasons for doubting the future viability of Thompsons. In particular it contained statements that: "the business in unlikely to withstand competition from foreign competitors whose profit margins and overheads are lower, and who are attracting an increasing share of the market"; and "import duties on luxury goods from outside the EEC are to be increased from next year."

Rupert Gray actually had no knowledge or information about foreign competition either for the present or the future, but had relied on observations made by Alan Naseem during a conversation with him. He had however read an article in Accountancy World in which it was stated that "import duties on some luxury items brought into the United Kingdom from outside the EEC are to be revised." Arabia Exportex Ltd sent a copy of the report to Michael Thompson, who in consequence dropped his price by £100,000. Arabia Exportex Ltd purchased at the lower price.

Two years after selling out to Arabia Exportex Ltd, Michael happened to meet a former business colleague who knows the import business well. Michael discovered that no changes had been made to import duties since he sold the business, and the foreign competition referred to in the report had not materialised. Following an angry phone call to Alan Naseem, Mr. Naseem has revealed the instruction he gave to Rupert Gray regarding the report, and says his company cannot be held responsible for a report produced by an independent professional.

TASK

You are employed by a large firm of accountants who for many years have handled Michael Thompson's affairs. You are called upon to provide legal advice from time to time, and the senior partner has passed on to you the situations described above, as told to him by Michael Thompson. The senior partner suggests that probably a solicitor needs to be involved, but has asked you to arrange to meet Mr. Thompson to discuss the matter when he calls in to the office next week, or alternatively to write advising him.

Prepare notes on the issues involved as a preliminary to meeting and discussing the matter with Mr. Thompson.

Chapter 7

EMPLOYING THE WORKFORCE

All business organisations engaged in the production of goods or the provision of services will have a workforce to enable them to fulfil their objectives. For the vast majority of organisations the makeup of its workforce, ranging from managerial staff to blue collar workers, is the single most important feature of the business. To enable the business to flourish there must be a willing workforce able to contribute skill, expertise and work in return for a wage or salary. At first sight the wage/work bargain negotiated between an employer and employee seems to give rise to a relatively straightforward relationship, however the reality is quite different. Over the last twenty-five years there has been substantial development in the legal regulation of the employment relationship.

It is not the province of a business law text of this nature to carry out a detailed examination of employment law generally, but rather to deal with those areas of greatest significance for the businessman. It is proposed therefore to examine the nature of employment relationships, distinguishing between the employee and the self employed contractor; to consider health and safety obligations and the extent to which an employer may be made liable for the actions of his workforce; and finally to deal with the right of employees when the demands for their services have ceased or diminished. It has already been noted that employment law is a broad and detailed field of legal study. Readers who wish to examine other aspects of the employment relationship may find it useful to refer to 'Core Studies for BTEC National' which considers in particular the formation and content of the contract of employment, sex and race discrimination and unfair dismissal.

EMPLOYMENT RELATIONSHIPS

There are an infinite variety of terms and conditions under which one person will do work for another. The requirements of employers will range from the need to engage full-time employees where a long standing relationship with their employees is envisaged, characterised by mutual trust and confidence between the parties, to the use of temporary workers engaged to complete a particular task. It may be that the temporary worker, such as the accountant or draftsman, provides a specialist skill which is required by the employer only on an intermittant basis. Alternatively temporary and casual employment may only be offered because of economic necessity or the expansion or contraction of the size of the workforce in line with demand. Independent contractors (or self employed workers) are now well established as a substantial proportion of the workforce of some industries, for instance, the media, catering and construction. Of the million or so construction workers, well over half a million are self employed. This form of employment has many advantages for both sides. The employer 'gets the job done' and the contractor is normally well paid in return. A criticism of the system is that it provides no support for the older or infirm worker, no security of employment and may lead to a general reduction in health and safety standards.

There are a large number of legal and economic consequences stemming from the distinction between employed and self employed status. For this reason it is necessary to be able to identify the status of the employment relationship that has been entered into. Employment legislation and the common law both recognise the distinction between employment under a contract of service and self employment under a contract for services. The distinction is a relatively straightforward one to make in the majority of cases. It is only in a small proportion of cases that difficulties arise, often where employers or those they employ are seeking contractor status for economic advantage or in order to evade legal responsibilities. In the following tables there is a summary of the major legal and economic consequences of the employment classification.

LEGAL AND ECONOMIC CONSEQUENCES OF EMPLOYMENT CLASSIFICATION

CONTRACT OF SERVICE (EMPLOYED PERSONS)	CONTRACT FOR SERVICES (SELF EMPLOYED PERSONS)
LIABILITY	
An employee may be made liable for the wrongful acts of employees committed during the course of their employment.	As a general principle an employer may not be made liable for the wrongful acts of contractors he employs other than in exceptional cases.
HEALTH AND SAFETY	
A high standard of care is owed by an employer both under statute and the common law with regard to the health and safety of his employees.	While both the common law and statute recognise the existence of a duty of care by an employer in relation to the contractors he employs at common law it is of a lesser standard than the duty owed to employees.
STATUTORY EMPLOYMENT RIGHTS	
A large number of individual employment rights are conferred on employees by statute which generally arise after a period of service eg the right to unfair dismissal protection, redundancy payments, to belong to a trade union and take part in trade union activities, to protection in the event of the employers insolvency, to guarantee payments, to security of employment after maternity leave, to statutory maternity pay, to a written statement of the main terms and conditions of employment and the right not to be discriminated against on the grounds of sex, race or marital status.	Contractors are effectively excluded from the mass of individual employment rights conferred by statute. One notable exception however is the legislation in relation to sex and race discrimination which protects the self employed when they are providing personal services.
INCOME TAX	
The income tax payable by an employee is deducted at source by the employer under the pay as your earn scheme ie P.A.Y.E. (Schedule E).	The income tax of a self employed person is payable by the taxpayer and not his employer on a lump sum preceding year basis (Schedule D). Apart from the obvious advantage of retaining the tax until it falls due at the end of the year it is also felt that such a taxpayer has more favourable treatment of reasonable expenses when assessed for tax.
WELFARE BENEFITS	
Under the Social Security Act 1975 both employer and employee must contribute to the payment of Class I National Insurance contributions assessed on an earnings related basis which entitles the employee to claim all the available welfare benefits eg unemployment benefit, statutory sick pay, industrial disablement benefit, state retirement pension.	Under the Social Security Act 1975 a self employed person is individually responsible for the payment of lower Class 2 National Insurance contributions and has only limited rights to claim welfare benefits eg statutory sick pay.

DISTINGUISHING BETWEEN THE EMPLOYED AND SELF EMPLOYED

Over the years a number of tests have been formulated by the courts to attempt to determine any given worker's status. Originally the courts would only consider the level of control over a worker by an employer. In *Performing Rights Society Ltd. v. Mitchell and Booker (1924)*, McCardie J. said that "the final test, if there is to be a final test, and certainly the test to be generally applied, lies in the nature and degree of detailed control over the person alleged to be a servant" If an employer could tell his workers not only what to do, but also how and when to do it, then the worker was regarded as an employee, employed under a contract of service. Today the courts adopt a much wider approach and applying the mixed or multiple test take account of all the circumstances to determine a worker's status. This is not to say that control is no longer a significant factor for it would be difficult to imagine a contract of service where the employer did not have the authority to control the work performed by the employee. Control is of course a less obvious feature the more specialised, skilled or trusted the workers becomes, for example a surgeon.

> In *Ready Mixed Concrete Ltd. v. Ministry of Pensions (1968)* under a peculiar procedure laid down in National Insurance legislation Mackenna J, a single judge of the Queens Bench Division of the High Court, sat as the final appellate court to decide the employment status of a driver for the plaintiff company. This was in order to determine the employer's responsibility in relation to the National Insurance contributions of his drivers. The Ministry of Pensions had rejected the employers contention that its drivers were self employed, despite the existence of written contracts of employment (30 pages long) which had attempted to create a contract for services rather than contracts of service. The declaration that the driver was self employed was not decisive and all aspects of his job were considered, for instance the fact that the driver purchased the lorry from the company; had to maintain it; pay was calculated on the basis of the concrete carried; and the driver could in some circumstances delegate the driving. These factors pointed to the driver being a contractor, whilst others pointed to his status as an employee. He had to paint the lorry in the company colours, he had to use it exclusively for company business and he was required to obey reasonable orders. MacKenna J. stated that there is a contract of service if an individual agrees to provide his own work, submits to his employers control and in addition the majority of the contractual provisions are consistant with a contract of service. This approach has since been referred to as the mixed and mutliple test. On the facts the power to delegate work was regarded as a decisive indication that the drivers were self employed under a contract for services.

The status of self employment cannot be achieved simply by including an express provision in a contract. The courts will look to the substance of an employment relationship rather than the label applied by the parties in order to decide a worker's status.

> In *Ferguson v. John Dawson Ltd., (1976)* the plaintiff, a builder's labourer, agreed to work as a 'self employed labour only sub contractor', an arrangement commonly known as 'the lump'. When working on a flat roof he fell and suffered injuries. No guard rail had been provided, in breach of the duty to employees owed under the "Construction (Working Places) Regulations 1966. The High Court decided that the employer was in breach of this statutory duty towards the plaintiff and damages of over £30,000 were awarded. On appeal the employer argued that as the plaintiff

> was self employed the statutory duty was not owed to him. It was the plaintiff's responsibility to ensure that the guard rail was in place. The Court of Appeal held, by a majority, that the plaintiff was in reality an employee and so entitled to the compensation awarded. The 'lump' was no more than a device to attempt to gain tax advantages and whilst a declaration as to employment status may be relevant it is not the conclusive factor to determine the true nature of the relationship.

> A difficult case to reconcile with the decision in *Ferguson (1976)* is *Massey v. Crown Life Insurance Co., (1978)*. Here a branch manager of an insurance company, who also acted as a general agent, decided to become 'self employed' on his accountant's advice, despite the fact that his duties remained unchanged. The Court of Appeal concluded that a change of employment status had in fact taken place so that he was unable to bring a claim for unfair dismissal. Ld. Denning M.R. stated that if there is ambiguity in the relationship then this can be resolved with a declaration one way or the other.

Whilst there was a degree of ambiguity in the above case in the branch manager's original position as manager/agent it was significant that here there was a professional man, having considered independent advice, making a declaration which he believed would be to his benefit. This is in contrast to the labourer in Ferguson 1976 who was unadvised and could not be said to have consciously chosen to be a contractor with all the legal consequences that this involves.

> Consider also the decision of the Employment Appeals Tribunal in *Thames Television v. Wallis (1979)*. Here a researcher, and later a reporter for a T.V. company was taxed under Schedule D and treated as self employed. This was despite the fact that there was detailed control over her work over which her employer had exclusive access. On her dismissal she claimed compensation for unfair dismissal alleging that in reality she had been employed under a contract of service. The EAT agreed stating that the original declaration as to status was "only one consideration that had to be taken into consideration in determining her status". It was found possible to distinguish the decision in Massey 1978 on the grounds that in Massey (1978) there had been a deliberate change in status whereas in Wallis (1978) the researcher's status was ambiguous from the outset.

Despite the existence of a clear agreement between the employer and the worker that he should be treated as self employed this may nevertheless be regarded by the courts as a false designation and overturned.

> In *Young v. Wood Ltd., v. West (1980)* West, a sheet metal worker, asked his employer if he could be treated as self employed. This was accepted and despite the fact that there was no difference between his working conditions and those of P.A.Y.E. workers West was paid without deduction of tax and was not given holiday entitlement or sick pay. Furthermore the Inland Revenue had accepted the change resulting in an estimated tax advantage of about £500 over five years because of assessment under schedule D rather than schedule E. Stephenson L.J. seemed to cast doubt on Lord Denning M.R.'s approach in Massey 1978 by stating that "It must be the court's duty to see whether the label correctly represents the true legal relationship between the parties". The Court of Appeal found that as it was impossible to regard West as in 'business on his own account' he was not self employed but remained an employee. Consequently the tribunal had jurisdiction to hear his complaint of unfair dismissal.

By asking the question whether the worker is "in business on his account" or under the control of an employer under a continuing business relationship, the Courts have found it possible to conclude that a relationship that was traditionally regarded as self employment was in reality a contract of service.

> So in *Airfix Footwear Ltd. v. Cope (1978)* the court held that homeworkers, employed to assemble shoe parts for a company using equipment supplied by them, were not contractors but employees. While the work was provided on a regular basis the employer argued that there was no obligation to provide work and the worker could also refuse it. In the present case the employment relationship had continued over the seven year period. In reality the employer decided on the things to be done, the manner, means, and the time and place of performance. The homeworker should therefore be regarded as an employee.
>
> In *Nethermere (St. Neots) Ltd. v. Taverna and Another (1984)* the position of homeworkers was once again considered. Here a trouser manufacturer had paid a piece rate to homeworkers over a number of years. Machines for home use had been installed by the employer and work delivered daily. Following a dispute about holiday pay, the arrangement was terminated, and a claim for unfair dismissal brought by the workers. While the Court of Appeal confirmed that the law required mutual obligations for a contract of service in this situation, such mutuality was present in the continuing obligation of the employer to provide and pay for work and the employees obligation to accept and perform it. Despite the absence of strict legal obligations to offer and carry out the work, by evaluating the practices which reflected the economic realities of the situation (economic and psychological pressures) the majority of the Court of Appeal concluded that the applicant homeworkers were employees.
>
> Reliance on a pool of casual workers has long been a tradition in some sectors of business including the catering industry and the legal status of so called 'regular casuals' was put to the test in *O'Kelly and Others v. Trusthouse Forte plc (1983)*. A banqueting department run by the employer was staffed in part by full time employees but mainly by so called 'casuals'. Among the casuals were 'regulars' who were given preference when work was available, often expected to work very long hours and consequently had no other employment. The applicants in this case were 'regulars' but when they became Trade Union shop stewards they were told by the employer that their services would no longer be required. In a claim for unfair dismissal brought by the applicants the first issue the Industrial Tribunal had to deal with was whether they were employed under a contract of service and so protected by the unfair dismissal legislation. In determining their employment status the tribunal acknowledged that its role was to "consider all aspects of the relationship, no feature being itself decisive, each of which may vary in weight and direction and, having given such balance to the factors as seem appropriate determine whether the person was carrying on business on his own account". Applying this mixed or multiple test the tribunal isolated factors consistent with a contract of service such as substantial control, the lack of capital equipment and the lack of power to delegate. Factors inconsistent with a contract of service included the lack of mutual obligations on the part of the employer to provide work and on the part of the worker to offer services (referred to as mutuality of obligation). In addition there was the custom and practice of the catering industry to employ large numbers on a casual basis. By placing most emphasis on the inconsistent factors the tribunal found that the applicants were not employees and therefore not entitled to statutory protection. The Court of Appeal later confirmed the tribunal's decision.

While there is no doubt that the decision in O'Kelly supports the custom and practice of the hotel and catering industry and confirms the fact that a fundamental feature of the contract of employment is the requirement to provide work and offer services it is nevertheless difficult to reconcile with previous decisions in particular Ferguson 1976. The reality of O'Kelly is that the regular casuals were subject to the same control as full time employees. They often worked longer hours than full time staff and a failure to work when required had the dramatic consequences of removal from the regular casuals lists. Having no alternative employment, capital equipment or profit sharing it would be difficult to describe them as business people working on their 'own account'.

> The lack of a binding obligation to accept work highlighted in O'Kelly was also apparent in *Wickens v. Champion Employment (1984)*. Here the EAT examined the employment status of 'agency temporaries'. These are individuals who are employed to provide secretarial services to clients of their agent. On a claim for unfair dismissal the question arose as to the status of the relationship between the agency and the client and the EAT found it to be one of self-employment. This was despite the large degree of control over the 'temps', the fact that the documentation referred to them as employees and the growing practice of agencies of giving employment status to temporaries.
>
> The significance of 'mutality of obligations' for the purpose of identifying a contract of service re-emerged in *Hellyer Brothers Ltd. v. McLeod (1987)*. The question faced by the Court of Appeal was whether trawlermen who had sailed exclusively for the same employer for a number of years were entitled to redundancy payments now that their services were no longer required. The difficulty for the crewmen was that according to the custom and practice of the industry each voyage was covered by a separate crew agreement which was terminated by mutual consent on completion of each voyage. The crewmen invariably returned to the same employer for the next voyage despite being under no legal obligation to do so. To qualify for redundancy payments however they had to show that they were continuously employed under one overall contract of employment. Due to the lack of mutuality of obligation over the period of employment both the EAT and the Court of Appeal held that there was no overall contract of service and so no entitlement to redundancy payments.

The fact that there has been so much litigation on the employed/self employed distinction suggests that in the borderline cases in particular, decisions are by no means clear.cut. The courts are faced with the difficult task of maintaining a balance between the freedom of employers to offer employment on the terms that best suit their interest and the rights of workers, for the most part in an unequal bargaining position, to obtain the benefits of employed status.

HEALTH AND SAFETY AT WORK

The law relating to health and safety at work can be said to have two major objectives:

a) To minimise the risk of injury to and enhance the welfare of those at the work place by imposing legal duties on employers, employees, contractors, manufacturers and other which are enforced by means of criminal sanctions, and

b) To provide the means by which those who suffer injury at work may be able to recover compensation.

THE CRIMINAL CODE

The criminal code in relation to health and safety has its origins in early nineteenth century legislation and until 1974 progress had been made by means of piecemeal legislation applying to particular industries and different workplaces, e.g. mines, factories, offices, shops,, railways and agriculture. The report of the Roberts Committee on Safety and Health at work in 1972 criticised the then fragmented state of the legislation and subsequently the Health and Safety at Work Act 1974 was passed. The aims of the Act were to

a) lay down general duties applicable across the industrial spectrum;

b) provide a unified system of enforcement under the control of the health and Safety Executive and local authorities.

The Act was designed to promote a constructive attitude to health and safety in the working environment and created the Health and Safety Commission to assist in this process. The Commission was given the task of producing detailed regulations, applicable to each industrial sector backed up by codes of practice designed to give guidance as to how general duties and specific regulations could be satisfied. At the heart of the 1974 Act are the detailed regulations laying down specific health and safety requirments. For instance, welders in the shipbuilding industry must by regulations be provided with certain safety equipment by their employers. Furthermore a code of practice, although not law, gives guidance to an employer as to how this regulation may be fulfilled. In the above example the code will prescribe safety equipment to be worn such as goggles, boots, spats etc. It should be stressed that failure to comply strictly with a code of practice does not necessarily constitute a failure to comply with a statutory regulation and consequently may not constitute breach of the law. Such a failure could however be used as evidence in a criminal prosecution to support an allegation that a regulation has been broken.

ENFORCEMENT

Enforcement of the safety legislation is in the hands of the Health and Safety Executive and local authorities which have a number of powers at their disposal. The breach of a general duty or a specific regulation under the 1974 Act is a criminal offence. This can lead to a prosecution in the criminal courts. Less serious offences are dealt with summarily in the Magistrates Court and those of a more serious nature are tried on indictment in the Crown Court. Conviction carries a fine or a term of imprisonment which for an indictable offence can be up to two years imprisonment. The fundamental aim of those enforcing the 1974 Act is to encourage a positive attitude to health and safety at the workplace rather than to take numerous employers through the criminal courts. There is no doubt however that some employers resent the economic cost of health and safety and it may only be the threat of criminal prosecution that will cause the more recalcitrant employers to respond.

One of the major innovations of the Act was the introduction of constructive sanctions. A Health and Safety Inspector who believes that an employer is contravening one of the statutory provisions may serve on that person an improvement notice requiring that the contravention be remedied within a specified period. In cases where the contravention involves an immediate risk of serious injury the inspector may serve a prohibition notice which will direct that the particular activity is terminated until the contravention is rectified. Failure to comply with a prohibition notice, for example by using a machine which as been identified as a serious source of danger, is an offence triable on indictment in the Crown Court.

An example of a specimen improvement notice which may be served by the Health and Safety Executive on an individual or organisation is shown below.

HEALTH AND SAFETY EXECUTIVE
Health and Safety at Work etc. Act 1974, Sections 21, 23, and 24

IMPROVEMENT NOTICE

SPECIMEN

Name and address (See Section 46) — To Abbotsfield Furniture Ltd
Sandyford Way, Abbotsfield, West Midlands

(a) Delete as necessary — (a) Trading as ....

I (b) Howard Gemmell

(b) Inspector's full name — one of (c) H.M.Factory Inspectorate

(c) Inspector's official designation — of (d) Grosvenor House, Union Street,
Abbotsfield Tel no. 021 482 7319

(d) Official address — hereby give you notice that I am of the opinion that at

(e) Location of premises or place and activity — (e) Abbotsfield Furniture Ltd(above address)

you, as (a) an employer, ~~self-employed person/a person wholly or partly in control of the premises~~

(f) Other specified capacity — (f) ....

(a) are contravening/~~have contravened in circumstances that make it likely that the contravention will continue or be repeated~~

regulations relating to the storage of dangerous gases (namely oxygen andacetylene)

(g) Provisions contravened — (g) see attached sheet

The reasons for my said opinion are – dangerous gases stored in compound in proximity to highly flammable materials

and I hereby require you to remedy the said contraventions or, as the case may be, the matters occasioning them by

(h) Date — (h) 24th March 1983

(a) in the manner stated in the attached schedule which forms part of the notice.

Signature Howard Gemmell Date 24th Feb 1983

Being an inspector appointed by an instrument in writing made pursuant to Section 19 of the said Act and entitled to issue this notice.

(a) An improvement notice is also being served on ....

of ....

related to the matters contained in this notice.

Serial No. I

NOTES

1 Failure to comply with an Improvement Notice is an offence as provided by Section 33 of this Act and renders the offender liable to a fine not exceeding £400 on summary conviction or to an unlimited fine on conviction on indictment and a further fine of not exceeding £50 per day if the offence is continued.

2 An Inspector has power to withdraw a notice or to extend the period specified in the notice, before the end of the period specified in it. You should apply to the Inspector who has issued the notice if you wish him to consider this, but you must do so before the end of the period given in it. *(Such an application is not an appeal against this notice.)*

3 The issue of this notice does not relieve you of any legal liability resting upon you for failure to comply with any provision of this or any other enactment, before or after the issue of this notice.

4 **Your attention is drawn to the provision for appeal against this notice to an Industrial Tribunal.** Details of the method of making an appeal are given below *(see also Section 24 of the Health and Safety at Work etc. Act 1974)*.

(a) Appeal can be entered against this notice to an Industrial Tribunal. The appeal should be sent to: –

(for England and Wales) The Secretary of the Tribunals
Central Office of the Industrial Tribunals
93 Ebury Bridge Road LONDON SW1W 8RE

(for Scotland) The Secretary of the Tribunals
Central Office of the Industrial Tribunals
Saint Andrew House
141 West Nile Street GLASGOW G1 2RU

(b) The appeal must be commenced by sending in writing to the Secretary of the Tribunals a notice containing the following particulars: –

(1) The name of the appellant and his address for the service of documents.

(2) The date of the notice or notices appealed against and the address of the premises or place concerned.

(3) The name and address *(as shown on the notice)* of the respondent.

(4) Particulars of the requirements or directions appealed against.

and (5) The grounds of the appeal.

A form which may be used for appeal is attached.

(c) **Time limit for appeal**
A notice of appeal must be sent to the Secretary of the Tribunals within 21 days from the date of service on the appellant of the notice or notices appealed against, or within such further period as the tribunal considers reasonable in a case where it is satisfied that it was not reasonably practicable for the notice of appeal to be presented within the period of 21 days. If posted, the appeal should be sent by recorded delivery.

(d) The entering of an appeal suspends the Improvement Notice until the appeal has been determined, but does not automatically alter the date given in this notice by which the matters contained in it must be remedied.

(e) The rules for the hearing of an appeal are given in

The Industrial Tribunals (Improvement and Prohibition Notices Appeals) (S1 1974 No. 1925) for England and Wales.

and The Industrial Tribunals (Improvement and Prohibition Notices Appeals) (S1 1974 No. 1926) for Scotland.

An example of a specimen prohibition notice which may be served by the Health and Safety Executive on an individual or organisation is shown below.

HEALTH AND SAFETY EXECUTIVE
Health and Safety at Work etc. Act 1974, Sections 22—24

PROHIBITION NOTICE

Serial No. **P**

Name and address (See Section 46) To Abbotsfield Furniture Ltd, Sandyford Way
Abbotsfield Industrial Estate. AF2 3Pc

(a) Delete as necessary *(a)* Trading as ....

I *(b)* Howard Gemmell

(b) Inspector's full name one of *(c)* H.M. Factory Inspectorate

(c) Inspector's official designation of *(d)* Grosvenor House, Union St
Abbotsfield tel no. 021 482 7319

(d) Official address

hereby give you notice that I am of the opinion that the following activities,
namely – manufacturing process involving
welding and the storage of dangerous gases
in proximity to the company paint store.

which are *(a)* being carried on by you/~~about to be carried on by you/under your control~~

(e) Location of activity at *(e)* Abbotsfield Furniture (above address)

involve, ~~or will involve~~ *(a)* ~~a risk~~/an imminent risk, of serious personal injury.
I am further of the opinion that the said matters involve contraventions of the following statutory provisions: –
see attached sheet

because ....

and I hereby direct that the said activities shall not be carried on by you or under your control *(a)* immediately/~~after~~

(f) Date *(f)* 24th March 1983

unless the said contraventions and matters included in the schedule, which forms part of this notice, have been remedied.

Signature Howard Gemmell Date 24th March 1983

being an inspector appointed by an instrument in writing made pursuant to Section 19 of the said Act and entitled to issue this notice.

NOTES

1 Failure to comply with a Prohibition Notice is an offence as provided by Section 33 of this Act and renders the offender liable to a fine not exceeding £400 on summary conviction or to an unlimited fine or to imprisonment for a term not exceeding two years or both on conviction on indictment and a further fine of not exceeding £50 per day if the offence is continued.

2 An Inspector has power to withdraw a notice or to extend the period specified in the notice, before the end of the period specified in it. You should apply to the Inspector who has issued the notice if you wish him to consider this, but you must do so before the end of the period given in it. *(Such an application is not an appeal against this notice.)*

3 The issue of this Notice does not relieve you of any legal liability resting upon you for failure to comply with any provision of this or any other enactment, before or after the issue of this notice.

4 **Your attention is drawn to the provision for appeal against the notice to an Industrial Tribunal.** Details of the method of making an appeal are given below *(see also Section 24 of the Health and Safety at Work etc. Act 1974)*.

(a) Appeal can be entered against this notice to an Industrial Tribunal. The appeal should be sent to: –

(for England and Wales) The Secretary of the Tribunals
Central Office of the Industrial Tribunals
93 Ebury Bridge Road LONDON SW1W 8RE

(for Scotland) The Secretary of the Tribunals
Central Office of the Industrial Tribunals
Saint Andrew House,
141 West Nile Street GLASGOW G1 2RU

(b) The appeal must be commenced by sending in writing to the Secretary of the Tribunals a notice containing the following particulars: –
(1) The name of the appellant and his address for the service of documents.
(2) The date of the notice or notices appealed against and the address of the premises or place concerned.
(3) The name and address *(as shown on the notice)* of the respondent
(4) Particulars of the requirements or directions appealed against.
and (5) The grounds of the appeal.
A form which may be used for appeal is attached.

(c) Time limit for appeal

A notice of appeal must be sent to the Secretary of the Tribunals within 21 days from the date of service on the appellant of the notice or notices appealed against, or within such further period as the tribunal considers reasonable in a case where it is satisfied that it was not reasonably practicable for the notice of appeal to be presented within the period of 21 days. If posted the appeal should be sent by recorded delivery.

(d) The entering of an appeal does not have the effect of suspending this notice. Application can be made for the suspension of the notice to the Secretary of the Tribunals, but the notice continues in force until a Tribunal otherwise directs. An application for suspension of the notice must be in writing and must set out –

(a) The case number of the appeal, if known, or particulars sufficient to identify it and

(b) The grounds on which the application is made. It may accompany the appeal.

(e) The rules for the hearing of an appeal are given in: –

The Industrial Tribunals (Improvement and Prohibition Notices Appeals) Regulations 1974 (S1 1974 No. 1925) for England and Wales.

and

The Industrial Tribunals (Improvement and Prohibition Notices Appeals) (Scotland) Regulations 1974 (S1 1974 No. 1926) for Scotland.

GENERAL DUTIES

Most of the general duties contained in the 1974 Act impose a standard of care based on the idea of reasonable practicability. The most important general duty is that contained in s.2(1) and imposes on employers a duty to ensure, so far as is reasonably practicable, the health safety and welfare of their workers. More specifically this duty involves under s.2(2) in so far as is reasonably practicable:

a. providing and maintaining safe plant and save work systems;

b. making arrangements for the use, handling, storage and transport of articles and substances;

c. providing any necessary information, instruction, training and supervision;

d. maintaining a safe place of work and a safe access to and exit from it;

e. maintaining a safe working environment.

The scope of the general duty contained in s.2, qualified by the words "reasonably practicable" is difficult to determine and little guidance has been provided by the courts. However the meaning of this phrase is obviously crucial in determining the scope of an employer's duty. It would be wrong to assume that it imposes a standard of care comparable with the duty to take reasonable care at common law. The statutory duty requires the employer to take action to ensure health and safety unless on the facts it is impracticable in the circumstances.

In *Associated Dairies v. Hartley (1979)* the employer supplied his workers with safety shoes which they could pay for at £1 per week. An employee who had not purchased the shoes suffered a fractured toe when the wheel of a roller truck ran over it. There was an obvious risk to workers from roller trucks in the employer's warehouse. Accordingly an improvement notice was served on the employer requiring him to provide his employers with safety shoes free of charge (estimated cost £20,000 in the first year and £10,000 per annum thereafter). The Court of Appeal held that while such a requirement was practicable in all the circumstances of the case it was not reasonably so bearing in mind the cost in relation to the risk of injury. The improvement notice was therefore cancelled, the court confirming that in relation to the general duty practicability alone is not the test for it is qualified by the term 'reasonable'.

The issue of 'practicability' under s.2 and its scope in relation to an employer with a large workforce working with contractors was raised in *R v. Swan Hunter Shipbuilders Ltd., and Telemeter Installation Ltd., (1981).* Here eight men had been tragically killed by a fire which broke out on a ship under construction on the River Tyne. The fire had been fueled by an oxygen enriched atmosphere caused by the failure of an employee of a sub-contractor (Telemeter) to turn off the oxygen supply over night. Both the employer and the sub-contractor were convicted of offences under the Act in the Crown Court and subsequently appealed to the Court of Appeal. The employer argued that the duty to provide a safe system of work to persons other than their own employees imposed an intolerable burden where there was a large workforce with many different direct employers. The court however having examined the wording of s.2(1) and 2(2) decided that providing employees with a safe system of work may involve a duty to an employer to provide instruction and information to persons other than their own employees about potential dangers. Such instructions need not be given if the employer can show on the balance of probabilities that it was not reasonably practicable in the circumstances. Here the employer was

> aware of the dangers and by sub-contracting the work they were under a duty to 'inform and instruct'. In the words of Dunn L.J. "If the provision of a safe system of work for the benefit of his own employees involves information and instruction as to potential dangers being given to persons other than the employer's own employees, then the employer is under a duty to provide such information and instruction. His protection is contained in the words 'so far as is reasonably practicable' which appear in all the relevant provisions. The onus is on the defendants to prove on the balance of probabilities that it was not reasonably practicable in the particular circumstances of the case".

The fact that a working practice adopted by employers is universal within the industry is not conclusive evidence that the general duty under s.2(1) has been discharged. The High Court in *Martin v. Boulton and Paul (Steel Construction) Ltd (1982)* held that a universal practice whilst of great weight is not conclusive evidence that it was not reasonably practicable to use some other and safer method.

A further requirement of s.2 for employers is the obligation to prepare and revise a written statement of their general policy on health and safety and bring this statement to the notice of their employees. The statement should be more than a bland statement of responsibilities but rather a genuine attempt to identify specific health and safety problems of the employer in question and the arrangements that have been made to deal with them. Matters to be included would include, inspection procedures, emergency arrangements, safety precautions, consultative arrangements and training. Safety representatives may be appointed by recognised trade unions in which case s.2. further provides that it is the duty of an employer to consult with such representatives in order to promote health and safety at the workplace. In many cases this will involve consultations with safety committees which have the function of reviewing measures taken to ensure health and safety at work. It is worth noting that the general duties owed under s.2 apply to employees only and this would not include those training under a Youth Training Scheme as they are not treated as person's working under a contract of service. Following the Health and Safety (Youth Training Scheme) Regulations 1983 however, trainees on Y.T.S. are brought under the umbrella of the Act.

Both employers and those who are self employed are required, in the words of s.3, to "conduct their undertakings in such a way, in so far as is reasonably practicable", to protect persons other than their own employees from risks to their health and safety". This would require an employer to give anyone who may be affected, information relating to health and safety risks arising from the way in which the business is run.

> Guidance as to the interpretation of s.3 was provided by the Court of Appeal in *R. v. Mara (1987)*. Here the defendant Mr. Mara, a director of a cleaning company called CMS Ltd., was convicted of an offence in that he had permitted a breach of his company's duty under s.3. The company had failed to conduct its undertaking in such a way as to ensure that persons not in its employment were exposed to health and safety risks. The facts were that the cleaning company had contracted to clean premises owned by International Stores plc on weekdays. This involved using electrical cleaning machines. As the loading bay could not be cleaned because it was in constant use it was agreed that employees of International Stores should do the work using CMS Ltd., equipment. One Saturday morning whilst using a CMS cleaning machine a Store's employee was electrocuted due to the defective condition of the machine's cable. Mr. Mara was convicted and fined for an offence under s.3. On appeal however it was submitted that as the incident occurred on a Saturday morning, when the cleaning company did not work, it was not 'conducting its undertaking" at all, and so could not be in breach of its duty. The Court of Appeal rejected the

> submission however, holding that s.3 could not be limited to situations where a company's undertaking is in the process of actively being carried on. The way in which CMS Ltd. conducted its undertaking was to clean during weekdays and leave their equipment for use by their client's employees, at weekends. By failing to ensure that its equipment was safely wired the company was in breach of its s.3 duty to its client's employees. Consequently the director had rightly been convicted of an offence.

By virtue of s.4 a general duty is imposed on those who control work premises to ensure so far as is reasonably practicable the safety of the premises, any means of access and exit from the place of work, and of any plant or substance provided for use on the premises. This general duty is similar to the common duty of care owed by the person in control of premises to any visitor under the Occupiers Liability Act 1957. The duty is to take such care as is reasonable in the circumstances to ensure that the visitor is reasonably safe in using the premises for the purpose for which he is entitled to enter.

A further general duty imposed under s.5 on those who control work premises is to use the best practicable means to prevent the emission of offensive substances and to render harmless and inoffensive those substances emitted. Again there is an overlap between this duty and obligations owed under the Control of Pollution Act 1974 and the Public Health Act 1936.

Those who design, manufacture, import or supply any article for use at work are required under s.6 in so far as in reasonably practicable to ensure the articles safety, to carry out necessary testing and examining and provide sufficient information about the use of the article at work to render it safe and without risks to health. Finally there is a general duty imposed by s.7 on every employee while at work to take reasonable care for the health and safety of himself and of other persons who may be affected by his acts or omissions at work and to cooperate with employers in the discharge of their health and safety duties.

COMPENSATION

A further major objective of the law relating to health and safety at the workplace is to provide a means by which those who have suffered injury may recover compensation. Since the mid nineteen sixties state benefit has been available for employees who suffer injury from accidents arising out of and in the course of employment or contract prescribed industrial diseases. If injury is caused through fault however, whether of the employer or a fellow worker, an injured person can bring a claim for damages through the courts. If it can be shown that injury has occurred as a result of a failure to comply with a regulation under the Health and Safety at Work Act 1974 or some other statutory obligation, for instance under the Factories Act 1961, then a claim could be brought for damages under a civil action for breach of statutory duty. This action has status as a separate tort and can provide a means of redress for persons who suffer harm as a result of the breach of a duty imposed by statute. An analogous position applies to consumer safety so that if an individual suffers harm as a result of failure to comply with safety regulations made under the Consumer Protection Act 1987, they may bring an action for breach of statutory duty under s.41. (see Chapter 5).

A further alternative for an employee who has suffered harm due to the fault of his employer or a fellow employee is to base a claim on common law negligence. Under the common law an employer owes a legal duty of care to ensure the health and safety of his employees and this duty takes effect on an implied term of the contract of employment. An employer is required to take reasonable care with regard to the safety of his employees by providing a safe system of work. The provision of a safe system of work involves an obligation to provide safe fellow employees, safe plant and equipment, safe working premises and safe working methods. It should be stressed however that the common law duty is not one of strict liability but rather a duty to take reasonable care in the circumstances.

> In *Latimer v. AEC (1953)* after a factory was flooded the employer asked his workforce to return, warning them of the dangerous state of the factory floor. Sawdust had been used to cover most of the damp areas but not enough was available and the plaintiff slipped and was injured. To determine whether the employer had broken the common law duty of care he owed to his employees the court weighed the cost of avoiding the injury against the extra risk of injury and held that the employer had acted reasonably in the circumstances.

The common law duty encompasses an obligation to provide safe plant and appliances. If an employer was aware that machinery or tools are not reasonably safe, and an employee is injured as a result, the employer will be in breach of his duty.

> In *Bradford v. Robinson Rentals (1967)* the employer provided an unheated van for the employee to make a 400 mile journey during the winter. The court held that the employer was liable for the employee's frost bite which was reasonably forseeable.

In the past an employer could satisfy his duty by showing that he purchased equipment from a reputable supplier and had no knowledge of any defect. Now, however, following the Employer's Liability (Defective Equipment) Act 1969 injury occuring to an employee under those circumstances may be attributed to the deemed negligence of the employer. If damages are awarded against the employer, then it is up to him to seek a remedy from the supplier of the defectve equipment. Since the Employer's Liability (Compulsory Insurance) Act 1969 requires all employers to insure against the risk of causing personal injury through fault of their employees an injured employee can be generally confident that damages awarded to him will be met.

The employers duty also imposes an obligation to provide safe working methods and safe working premises. To determine whether an employer is providing safe working methods, it is necessary to consider a number of factors including the layout of the work place, training and supervision, warnings and whether protective equipment is provided. It should be stressed that the common law duty on an employer is to take reasonable care, and if he gives proper instructions which the employee fails to observe then the employer will not be liable if the employee is then injured.

> In *Charlton v. Forrest Printing Ink Co. Ltd. (1978)* the employer gave proper instructions to an employee who was given the job of collecting the firm's wages. The instructions required the employee to vary his collecting arrangements to prevent robbery. The employee failed to do this and suffered severe injury when he was robbed. The Court of Appeal held that the employer was not liable as he had taken reasonable steps to cut down the risk. The normal industrial practice of firms of that size in that area was to make their own payroll collection rather than employ a security firm.

In addition, the standard of care owed by an employer will vary with regard to each individual employee. A young apprentice should be provided with effective supervision while this may not be required for an experienced employee.

> In *Paris v. Stepney BC (1951)* the plaintiff, a one-eyed motor mechanic, lost the sight of his good eye while working at chipping rust from under a bus. Despite their being no usual practice to provide mechanics with safety goggles, the court decided that they should have been provided to the plaintiff. The defendants were liable as they could foresee serious consequences for the plaintiff if he suffered eye injury.

An employer must take reasonable care to ensure that he provides his workers with safe fellow workers. To engage an employee who has a past record of dangerous behaviour could put the employees at risk and constitute a negligent act on the part of the employer for which he could be made directly liable. Certainly if an employer is aware of an employee who by incompetence or practical jokes is creating a dangerous situation at work he should take steps to discipline him and if necessary dismiss him. Moreover the legal responsibility of an employer covers the situation when an employee under his control causes harm to a fellow employee or a third party by some wrongful act. This is by virtue of the doctrine of vicarious (substituted) liability.

VICARIOUS LIABILITY

There are some situations where the law is prepared to impose vicarious (substituted) liability on an individual who is not at fault for the commission of the wrongful (tortious) act of another. The best known example of this situation is the common law rule which imposes vicarious liability on employers in respect of torts committed by their employees during the course of their employment. Accordingly, if one employee (Jones) by his negligent act causes harm to a fellow employee (Smith) then in addition to the possibility of (Smith) pursuing a legal action against (Jones) he may have the further option of suing his employer who will have become vicariously liable if the negligent act occurred during the course of Jone's employment. The same principle applies equally where the injuries are caused by an employee to some third party. However, while employers have a choice as to whether they insure against the risk of injury to third parties, under the Employer's Liability (Compulsory Insurance) Act 1969, an employer is required to insure himself in respect of injuries caused by his employees to their colleagues. The imposition of vicarious liability does not require proof of any fault on the employer's part, or any express or implied authorisation to commit the wrongful act. All that must be proved for the purpose of vicarious liablility is:

(1) an actionable wrong committed by the worker;

(2) that the worker is an employee;

(3) that the wrongful act occurred during the course of his employment.

What then is the theoretical basis for imposing liability in these circumstances? A number of reasons have been suggested, ranging from the view that he who creates and benefits from a situation should assume the risk of liability arising from it, to the idea that if an organisation embarks on an enterprise and as a result harm is caused by one member it should be the responsibility of the organisation to compensate for the harm. It is after all the employer who selects and controls the employees who work for him. The employer has the responsibility of training staff and can of course dismiss those whose work is performed incompetently. The practical reason for vicarious liability is of course that if the employee were solely liable he would have to insure himself, and the cost of this would be indirectly borne by the employer in the form of higher wages. Under the present system insurance costs are borne directly by the employer who, as a principle of sound business practice, will normally carry adequate insurance. (see Chapter 6).

To determine an employers liability it is first necessary to establish the employment status of the worker who is alleged to have committed the wrongful act. This is because the legal position differs dramatically depending on whether the worker is employed as an employee under a contract of service rather than as a contractor under a contract for services. Usually this issue may be settled without argument but in the small proportion of cases where there is doubt the courts are left with the task of identifying the true contractual status of the worker by applying the tests discussed earlier in the chapter. It is convenient to deal with the legal position of employees and independent contractors separately.

EMPLOYEES

As a general principle an employer is vicariously liable for the tortious act of his employees committed during the course of their employment. The phrase 'course of employment' has produced numerous interpretations in the courts, but essentially it concerns the question of whether the employee was doing his job at the time of the tortious act. It should be emphasised that an employee will have both express and implied authority to perform work for his employer and while he will have no authority to commit torts he may nevertheless be guilty of a tortious act in the performance of his authorised duties.

> In *Century Insurance Ltd. v. Northern Ireland Road Transport Board (1942)* a tanker driver while delivering petrol at a garage, lit a cigarette and carelessly threw away the lighted match which caused an explosion and considerable damage. His employer was held to be vicariously liable for his negligence as the employee had acted within the course of his employment. By supervising the unloading, the employee was doing his job, but by smoking, he was doing it in a grossly negligent manner.

If an employee is doing something of purely personal benefit at the time of the negligent act then he may be regarded, to quote from the colourful language of the Victorian era as "off on a frolic of his own", and his employer will not be responsible.

> In *Hilton v. Thomas Burton (Rhodes) Ltd. (1961)* the plaintiff's husband was a demolition worker who was killed through the negligent driving of one of his colleagues. The defendent employer denied vicarious liability as at the time of the accident the van was being driven from a cafe on an unauthorised break. The court held that although the van had been driven with the permission of the employer, at the time of the incident the driver was not doing that which he was employed to do. Accordingly the employer was not liable for the negligent driving.

The extent to which an express prohibition by the employer will prevent vicarious liability will depend upon the nature of the prohibition. If it merely attempts to instruct the employee how he is to do his job the employee may still be within the course of his employment for the purposes of vicarious liability.

> In *Rose v. Plenty (1976)* a milkman, contrary to an express prohibition, engaged a thirteen year old boy to help him deliver the milk. The boy was subsequently injured by the milkman's negligent driving and sued both the milkman and his employer. The Court of Appeal held that despite the prohibition of the employer, he remained vicariously liable as the milkman had acted within the course of his employment. Scarman L.J. having considered the prohibition stated that "There was nothing in the prohibition which defined or limited the sphere of his employment, the sphere of his employment remained precisely the same after as before the prohibition was brought to his notice. The sphere was as a roundsman to go the rounds delivering milk, collecting empties and obtaining payment. Contrary to instructions the roundsman chose to do what he was employed to do in an improper way. But the sphere of his employment was in no way affected by his express instructions".

It seems therefore that only an express prohibition which effectively cuts down the 'sphere of employment' will prevent the establishment of vicarious liability. The fact that contemporary courts seem to favour the idea of a very wide sphere of employment in individual cases severely limits the opportunity of employers to restrict liability by express instruction. It is only by deciding the authorised perameters of an individual's job, and deciding that the act complained of fell outside these perameters that vicarious liability can be successfully denied.

In *Joseph Rand v. Craig (1919)* Carters employed to take rubbish to a tip were subject to an express prohibition against tipping other than on the authorised dump. On the question of liabiility for unauthorised tipping the court held that as the carters were employed to transport the rubbish to and from defined places, by unauthorised tipping they had stepped outside the course of their employment and so their employer could not be held liable for their conduct. If the act is done on the employers premises with the employers interest in mind the employer may be made liable provided the act has a close connection with the employee's job.

In *Kay v. ITW Ltd. (1968)* the employer was vicariously liable for the negligent driving of a forklift truck driver who, without authority, attempted to drive a five-ton diesel lorry which was blocking his way.

Similarly in *Compton v. McClure (1975)* the employer was held to be vicariously liable for the negligence of an employee who when late for work caused an accident when driving negligently on the factory road.

Even the manager in a public house in *Stone v. Taffe (1974)* was held to be within the course of his employment when he negligently failed to ensure that a stairway was properly lighted for a customer, despite the fact that the injury occurred two and a half hours after licensed closing time.

While it may be reasonable for an employee to use a degree of force in protection of his employer's property, or to keep order, an employee who commits an assault which has no connection with his work will be solely liable for his conduct.

So in *Warren v. Henleys Ltd. (1948)* the employer was held not to be vicariously liable for a physical attack by a petrol pump attendant on one of his customers. The claim that the attendant was acting within the scope of his employment was rejected, for while the attack developed out of an argument over payment for petrol it was in reality motivated by an act of private vengeance.

PRIMARY NEGLIGENCE

It is important to draw the distinction between vicarious liability and the direct or primary liability of an employer.

In *Carmarthenshire County Council v. Lewis (1955)* a child at a local authority nursery school wandered from the school yard onto the highway and caused the death of a lorry driver who swerved to avoid the child. An action was brought against the council in negligence on the grounds that the child's teacher had left her unattended for a short time. In fact at the relevant time the teacher was attending to the needs of another child. The court held that the teacher had in fact fulfilled the common law duty of care required of her by acting as a prudent parent would in the circumstances. Consequently there could be no vicarious liability imposed on her employer. However the fact that the child could reach the street so easily indicated that the council were failing in their legal duty to operate a safe system at the school and so were held to be directly liable for their primary negligence.

> A more recent example of the distinction between the direct and vicarious liability of an employer is provided by the decision in *Nahhas v. Pier House (Cheyne Walk) Management (1984).* Here the tenant of a luxury flat deposited the key with a porter during a stay in hospital. This was the normal system operated by the owners, but unfortunately a porter, one of their employees, used the key to steal jewellery from the plaintiff's flat. In fact the porter had a long criminal record involving eleven prison terms of which his employer, the owners, were unaware. The court held that while the system of depositing keys was not negligent, the failure by the employer to thoroughly check the porter's background constituted a breach of the legal duty of care owed to the tenants which resulted in damage. Consequently the employers were liable for their primary negligence and also responsible vicariously for the criminal act of the porter carried out during the course of his employment.

Certainly to impose liability on an employer for the tortious or criminal acts of an employee under his control there must be a connection between the act complained of and the circumstances of employment. The fact that employment gives the employee an opportunity to commit the wrongful act is insufficient to impose vicarious liability on the employer.

> Recently in *Heasman v. Clarity Cleaning Co. (1987)* the Court of Appeal found it possible to absolve the defendant cleaning company from liability for the acts of one of their cleaners who while employed on the plaintiffs premises used the plaintiff's telephone to make international telephone calls amounting to £1411. The mere fact that the cleaners employment provided the opportunity to fraudulently use the plaintiff's telephone was of itself insufficient to impose liability on the defendant.

LOANED EMPLOYEES

Occassionally the courts have been faced with the issue of vicarious liability for the tortious acts of an employee committed when he has been hired out by his primary employer to another employer.

> In *Mersey Docks and Harbour Board v. Coggins & Griffith Ltd. (1947)* a crane and its driver had been hired out by one employer to another. The question before the House of Lords was which employer should be made liable for its negligent operation by the cranedriver. Their Lordships held that while the cranedriver remained an employee of his primary employer, for the purpose of vicarious liability responsibility depended upon whether a sufficent degree of control over his acts had passed to the primary employer. "The workman may remain the employee of his general employer, but at the same time, the result of the arrangements may be that there is vested in the hirer a power of control over the workman's activities sufficient to attach to the hirer responsibility for the workman's acts and defaults and to exempt the general employer from that responsibility". In this case control had passed over and consequently it was the hirer of the crane who was made liable.

A further difficulty in relation to the loaned employee is the question as to which employer is responsible if he suffers injuries due to the negligence of a fellow employee. In such cases the employee is usually advised to sue both his general employer and the employer to whom he was loaned.

This was the situation in *Thompson v. T. Lohan (Plant Hire) Ltd. and J. W. Hurdiss Ltd. (1987)* where an action was brought by Mr. Thompson's widow alleging that her husband's death was due to the negligence of a fellow worker. Mr. Thompson, who was employed by the first defendants (the plant owners) as a JCB driver, was killed as a result of an incident which occurred whilst he and his machine were on hire to the second defendants (the hirers). The High Court held that the claim in negligence had been proved and Mr. Thompson's employer, (the plant owners), were liable for damages. A major point of issue however was whether the plant owners were entitled to be indemnified against liability by the hirers because of certain clauses in the hire contract to that effect. All hirings by the plant owners were made subject to the terms of the Contractors Plant Association conditions of hire, two of which were relevant in this case. Condition 8 provided that: "When a driver or operator is supplied by the owner of the plant . . . such person shall be under the direction and control of the hirer . . . Such drivers or operators shall for all purposes in connection with their employment in the working of the plant be regarded as the servant or agents of the hirer . . . who alone shall be responsible for all claims arising in connection with the operation of the plant by the said drivers or operators". Condition 13 went on to provide that: "During the continuance of the hire period, the hirer shall . . . fully and completely indemnify the owner in respect of all claims by any such person whatsoever, for injury to persons or property caused by or in connection with or arising out of the use of the plant and in respect of all costs and charges herewith whether arising under statute or common law". In the light of the above clauses the High Court held that the hirers should indemnify the plant owners against the damages and costs recovered by Mrs. Thompson. On further appeal to the Court of Appeal however it was argued that the indemnity clause was in fact inoperative as it conflicted with s.2(1) of the Unfair Contract Terms Act 1977 which states that "A person cannot by reference to any contract term or to a notice given to persons generally or to particular persons exclude or restrict his liability for death or personal injury resulting from his negligence (see Chapters 4 & 5). The Court of Appeal held that as the intention of this clause was to protect the victims of negligence, there was nothing in s.2(1) to prevent a person at fault making arrangements with others to share or bear the burden of compensating those victims of negligence. The plaintiff was in no way prejudiced by the operation of the contract clauses which operated to require the hirer to indemnify the plant owner against the damages and costs recovered by the plaintiff.

INDEPENDENT CONTRACTORS

Generally vicarious liability has been confined to the employer/employee relationship and where contractors are employed responsibility for their wrongful acts is solely their own. The justification for not extending vicarious liability to employers of contractors other than in exceptional cases stems from the fact that the contractor is not subjected to his employer's control in the same way as an employee. One important exception which in recent times has assumed significance is the situation where the contractor has been employed to carry out a statutory duty imposed on the employer. This is because of the recent move towards requiring public bodies to put out many of their statutory functions for competitive tender among contractors and so the possibility of imposing liability on employers for the tortious acts of a contractor have increased significantly. The law in this area is not new.

> The case of *Hardaker v. Idle District Council (1896)* remains the leading authority in relation to the delgation of statutory duties. The council acting under a statutory power to construct a sewer employed a contractor to carry out the work. The contractor negligently pierced a gas main and the plaintiff's property was damaged by the resultant explosion. In an action by the plaintiffs against the contractor and the council employer the court held that in exercising their statutory power the council owed an overriding duty to the public. This duty was to construct a sewer so as not to damange the gas main and put the public at risk. The council could not discharge this duty by simply employing a contractor to carry out the work, and accordingly they remained responsible to the plaintiff for its breach.

There are then certain legal duties that cannot be delegated, and if the wrongful act of a contractor constitutes a breach of such a duty, owed by an employer to a third party, then the contractor's employer may be made vicariously liable for the default.

> In *Rogers v. Nightriders (a firm (1983)* a mini cab firm undertook to provide a hire car to the plaintiff for a journey and did so by engaging a contractor driver. The plaintiff was injured in an accident caused by the negligent maintenance of the mini cab by the contractor. In an action against the mini cab firm the court held that they were not liable as an employer could not be made vicariously liable for their contractor's default. On appeal however it was held that as the employer had undertaken to provide a vehicle to carry the plaintiff, and since they ought to have forseen harm to the plaintiff if the vehicle was defective, they owed a duty of care to the plaintiff to ensure that the vehicle was reasonably fit. Such a duty could not be delegated to a contractor and accordingly the employers were liable for breach of the primary duty that they owed to her.

This case is a further example of the distinction that must be drawn between vicarious and direct or primary liability previously considered. By providing a negligent contractor the employer in Roger v. Nightriders had failed to fulfil a direct duty of care he owed to those he could reasonably foresee being affected.

EMPLOYEES' RIGHTS ON THE TERMINATION OF A BUSINESS ENTERPRISE

There may be many reasons why an employer decides to terminate all or part of a business enterprise. The decision to close down may be one imposed upon the employer, for instance because of insolvency leading to bankruptcy or a winding up. Alternatively the decision could be a voluntary one, made in the interests of good business practice, possibly to shut down a less lucrative part of the business enterprise. Whatever the reason for the termination it will most certainly have impact on the employees, some of whom may be offered alternative employment, a different place of work, or be told that they are now surplus to requirements and that their employment is terminated. In this part of the chapter it is proposed to examine the employer's situation in these circumstances particularly in relation to redundancy payments.

When the employers cessation of business is due to insolvency the law attempts to assist employees in relation to sums owing from the employer. Arrears of wages have been regarded as a priority debt for many years and the Employment Protection (Consolidation) Act 1978 ss.121, 122 give further sums owed priority status. These include payment for time off to look for work, payment for time off during authorised trade union activities and payments in respect of suspension on medical grounds. A further right is to apply to the Secretary of State alleging an employers insolvency, and claiming arrears of wages, notice payment, holiday pay, unfair dismissal compensation etc. The Secretary of State has a discretion to make these and other payments out of the Redundancy Fund. Complaints that the Secretary of State has not made a payment can be made to an Industrial Tribunal which has power to make a declaration.

'Redundancy' is simply the term used to describe the reason for dismissing a worker whose job has now ceased or the employer's requirements for it to be performed have now diminished. In relation to unfair dismissal rights (considered in Core Studies for BTEC National), redundancy is one of the statutory reasons for dismissal contained in the Employment Protection (Consolidation) Act 1978 (EPCA 1978) upon which an employer can rely. If redundancy is the true reason for dismissal, and the selection process is a fair one and reasonable in the circumstances, then the dismissal may be held to be justifiable and fair. The issue that we are concerned with here however is whether an employee dismissed by reason of redundancy is entitled to a statutory redundancy payment.

REDUNDANCY PAYMENTS

The right to a redundancy payment for qualified workers dismissed because there is no longer a demand for their services was first introduced in 1965 under the Redundancy Payments Act. The 1965 Act was the first major statutory intervention in the individual employment relationship since the nineteenth century. Its provisions are now consolidated in the EPCA 1978. The original idea was that the provision of lump sum severance payment to redundant employees would encourage a shake out of underemployed labour in industry generally with less risk of industrial action and encourage mobility of labour. Under the original scheme every employer makes contributions to the Redundancy Fund and received a rebate of 35% from the fund for any payment made so long as notice was given to the Department of the Environment. The rebate was abolished from October 31 1986 except for those who employ a staff of less than ten. To fall within the present scheme it is necessary to have worked as an employee for the same employer for at least sixteen hours a week for an unbroken period of two years after the age of eighteen. Excluded categories include: workers at retirement age, workers covered by a more suitable scheme contained in a collective agreement which had been approved by the Secretary of State, registered dock workers; civil servants and national health workers; independent contractors.

DISMISSAL FOR REDUNDANCY

To qualify for a payment the employee must have been dismissed for reason of redundancy. Redundancy occurs when a employee is dismissed because his employer has discontinued or intends to discontinue the business for which he was employed or because the needs for his particular services have diminished. Alternatively the employee may qualify for a payment if he is laid off or kept on short term working for four consecutive weeks or six or more weeks in a thirteen week period and also complies with the requirements of the Act.

A fundamental requirement for a successful claim is that there has been a dismissal. This can occur expressly by the employer terminating the contract of employment; impliedly where a fixed term contract expires; constructively where there has been such a dismissal or by operation of the law when the employer had died or been dissolved. If an employee leaves employment prematurely in a redundancy situation without waiting to be dismissed then he may prejudice the success of his claim.

> *In Morton Sundour Fabrics v. Shaw (1966)* the employee in question, having been warned of the possibility of redundancy left to take other employment. The court held that as he had not been dismissed, he was therefore not entitled to a redundancy payment.

In *Marriott v. Oxford District Co-op Soc. Ltd. (1979)* a foreman supervisor was told by his employer that the position of foreman was no longer required and that his wage would be reduced by £1 per week to reflect his loss of status. The employee continued to work under protest for three weeks before terminating his employment by notice, claiming redundancy. The Court of Appeal held that there had been not true consent to the contractual variation and the contract of employment had been terminated by reason of redundancy so that the employee was entitled to a redundancy payment.

More recently in *Caledonian Mining Co. Ltd. v. Bassett and Steel (1987)* a sympathetic approach was taken by the Employment Appeal Tribunal to employees who in a redundancy situation had written to their employer terminating their employment. The men had originally been told that manpower on their site would be reduced, and asked whether they would be interested in alternative employment. Despite an expression of interest by the men the employer did not respond and failed to offer alternative work. The men did receive an offer from the National Coal Board which they accepted. This led to the letter of termination which the employer argued constituted a resignation, and as there had been no dismissal in law there was no right to a redundancy payment. The EAT agreed with the IT however and held that the men had been encouraged to resign and take another job with the intention of avoiding redundancy payments. The true position here was that the employer had caused the men to resign and in reality the employer was terminating the contract. Accordingly the employees were dismissed in law and entitled to a redundancy payment.

A further contentious issue is whether an employee who offer to take what is described as 'voluntary redundancy' has been dismissed for the purposes of the EPCA 1978.

In *University of Liverpool v. Humber and Birch (1984)* the EAT held that the employees in question could not be regarded as dismissed, rather their contract had been terminated by mutual agreement when they applied for and received early retirement. Here the employees had made an express offer to retire which had been accepted by the employer and this was not regarded as a redundancy dismissal. It is still possible however for an employee to volunteer to place himself amongst those who may be dismissed for redundancy.

In *Morley v. C.T. Morley Ltd. (1985)* it was held that three company directors could be dismissed by the company of which they were joint owners and the fact that they had volunteered for redundancy did not prevent there being a redundancy dismissal.

It is significant that the EPCA 1978 expressly provides in s.91(2) that unless the contrary is proved there is a presumption that a dismissal is by reason of redundancy. It would be for the employer to show therefore that the dismissal was due to incompetence or misconduct to escape the obligation of a redundancy request. Furthermore in s.81(2) the Act states that dismissal wholly or mainly attributable to a cessation of business, a transfer of the place of work, a cessation or discontinuation of requirements for that type of employee, will constitute redundancy under the Act. To require employees to change their place of employment therefore without authorisation in their contracts of employment could amount to redundancy.

> In *O'Brien v. Associated Fire Alarms Ltd. (1968)* the Court of Appeal held that men who had homes in Liverpool, and were employed there, could be impliedly required to work anywhere in the Liverpool area. An attempt to require them to work outside the area, in particular in Barrow in Furness, was not authorised by their contract. Redundancy had thus occurred therefore when the men were dismissed for there was a reduction in the work requirements at their place of employment in the case of the Liverpool area. The men were entitled therefore to redundancy payments.

Whether a reduction in the requirements of the employer for a type of employee constitutes redundancy is a complex issue. The approach to be adopted is to analyse the requirements of the existing contract of employment. It is by assessing the contractual position of the employee in question, rather than the job he actually does, that it is possible to determine whether the employer's requirements for the employee have ceased or diminished. Consequently there is less likely to be a redundancy situation under a contract which provides that the employee can be required to perform many duties.

> In *Haden Carrier Ltd. v. Cowen (1982)* the Court of Appeal considered the position of Mr. Cowen who had been employed as a Divisional Contracts Surveyor to assist the Divisional Manager. When work fell off he was declared redundant on the grounds that the requirements of the business for work of the kind carried on by Mr. Cowan had ceased or diminished. In a claim for unfair dismissal the applicant contended that he was not redundant, for an express term in his contract provided that he could be "required to undertake, at the direction of the Company, any and all duties which reasonably fall within the scope of his responsibilities". As there was not a reduction in the requirements of the Company for employees to carry out any and all the duties which fell within the scope of Mr. Cowans former responsibilities, the Court of Appeal agreed with the EAT and held him not to be redundant.

The case therefore confirms the view that it is not sufficient to ask whether the same number of employees are needed to carry out the work that they were actually doing. What must be decided is whether there has been a diminution in demand for employees to carry out the work they could be obliged to carry out under the terms of their employment. This strict contractual approach can lead to somewhat surprising results.

> In *Pink v. White and White and Co. (Earls Barton) Ltd. (1985)* the employee in question was engaged in a shoe factory as a machining and finishing room operative although the task he actually performed was that of a sole layer/pre sole fitter. Despite their being no reduction in requirements for the job he actually did the fact that there was a diminution of the work of the closing and finishing room meant that the applicant could be regarded as redundant.

In situations where an employee's skills have become outdated because of new working methods and he is dismissed there may be conflicting views as to whether the dismissal is for redundancy or incapability.

A controversial decision on the point in that of *Hindle v. Percival Boats (1969)*. Here the applicant was skilled and built and repaired wooden boats. His employer began to specialise in the production of fibreglass boats and the demands fo the applicants work were greatly reduced. Eventually he was dismissed as unsatisfactory when he refused to take on less skilled work. The majority of the Court of Appeal held that the man was not entitled to a redundancy payment as the type of work in which he was engaged was still in existance. Had there been a genuine rundown with the applicant's job swallowed up then the court might have been convinced of a redundancy situation. Ld. Denning M.R. however delivered a strong dissenting judgement. He firmly believed that the employer had failed to rebut the presumption of redundancy by showing that the dismissal was due to some other cause.

SUITABLE ALTERNATIVE EMPLOYMENT

A final point to stress is that under s.82(5) there can be no redundancy if the employer makes an offer of suitable alternative employment which the employee unreasonably rejects. The offer will be suitable if:

a. the provisions of the new contract are similar to the previous contract; or

b. the provisions of the new contract do differ but the offer constitutes an offer of suitable alternative employment.

Whether the offer is suitable or not will depend on examining the circumstances of the particular case, e.g. work, pay, hours, conditions, travelling, fringe benefits, accommodation, social and family links, children's education.

In *Devonald v. J.D. Insulating Co. Ltd. (1972)* the applicant was required to move from a factory in Bootle to another in Blackburn. He refused, and on his claim for redundancy the tribunal held that suitable alternative employment had been offered as he was already required under his present employment to do outside contract work.

Also in *Fuller v. Stephanie Bowman Ltd. (1977)* the applicant typist refused to move from Mayfair to a new office in Soho. She found the move distasteful particularly as the new office was above a sex shop. The tribunal found that the refusal to move was unreasonable in the circumstances, as it was based on undue sensitivity and consequently the claim for redundancy must fail.

The decision of the EAT in *Gloucestershire County Council v. Spencer (1985)* supports the view that it is for management to set the appropriate standard of work to be achieved. Here the number of cleaners at a school had been reduced from five to four and the hours of work of the remaining employees cut by 45 minutes. The employer recognised that standards would drop but maintained nevertheless that the new terms constituted an offer of suitable alternative employment. This offer was rejected by the remaining cleaners on the grounds that they felt they could not continue to do a satisfactory job. The Industrial Tribunal agreed and found that while the alternative jobs were "suitable" within the meaning of the section, the employees refusal to accept the new terms was not unreasonable as they could not do the new jobs adequately. The EAT on the other hand held that the Tribunal was in error, for the standard of work set by the managemet cannot be reasonably objected to by employees as a ground for refusing to work. Accordingly the offer of suitable alternative employment had been unreasonably rejected and the applicants were not entitled to redundancy payments.

REDUNDANCY PROCEDURE

The 1978 Act lays down the procedure to be followed in a redundancy situation particularly where an independent trade union is involved. It involves consultation, advance warnings, written notice to the Secretary of State, the trade union being given certain details surrounding the redundancy and individual employees being given time off to seek new employment. Certain details must be disclosed by the employer to trade union representatives and these include the reasons for redundancies, numbers involved and how they are selected. The duty to consult the authorised bargaining representatives of a recognised Trade Union is contained in s.98 of the Employment Protection Act 1975. Such consultation should begin at the earliest opportunity. This must be at least 90 days before the first dismissal if 100 or more are to be dismissed at one establishment and 30 days before the first dismissal if the redundancy involves between 10 and 100 dismissals. Certain information must be given to the representatives including the reasons for the proposals, numbers and descriptions of employees who are to be dismissed, the method of selection and the method of dismissal. If the employer fails to comply with the consultation process than a complaint may be made to an industrial tribunal which has power to make an award of up to 90 days wages depending on the circumstances.

The law relating to the process by which a redundancy situation is dealt with is supplemented by codes of practice. The A.C.A.S. code on discipline and dismissal includes a section on redundancy. The matters dealt with by the code include consultation, selection procedures, alternative employment, appeal procedure and redundancy counselling. Codes of Practice as we have seen don't constitute rules of law but their importance was re-emphasised by the House of Lords in West Midlands Cooperative Society v. Tipton 1986.

The A.C.A.S. Code stresses the need for the fullest consultation between employers and employees or trade unions in advance of a redundancy situation. They should produce agreed selection and appeal procedures. Failure to warn and consult may of course render a redundancy dismissal unfair. To make a selection based on 'attitude to work' without any warning or consultation was held to be unfair in Graham v. ABF Ltd. 1986. This was despite the fact that a full consultation may well have produced the same result. For the purpose of selection the Code advocates objective criteria including skill, age, length of service, standard of performance and future requirements for employees.

REDUNDANCY CALCULATION

To calculate the amount of a redundancy payment it is necessary to establish the following:-

i. 'the relevant date', i.e. the date that the contract of employment terminated;

ii. 'week's pay', i.e. the minimum remuneration to which the employee is entitled in the week preceeding the relevant date (maximum of £158);

iii) 'years of continuous employment', i.e. the number of years of employment calculated in weeks in which the employee works 16 hours minimum. Certain matters will break the continuity such as long absence through illness and certain periods, although not breaking continuity, will not count, e.g. periods of absence due to strikes or lock outs after July 1964.

Having established the above matters, the calculations of redundancy payment is as follows:-

For each year employed between the age of:	Amount of Redundancy Payment:
18-21	Half Week's Pay x No. of Years Worked
22-40	One Week's Pay x No. of Years Worked
Men 41-65 Women 41-65	One and a Half Week's Pay x No. of Years Worked.

The maximum length of reckonable service is 20 years and the maximum week's pay is £158, e.g. maximum payment under the scheme is for a man over 60, with 20 years continuous service, on a wage of £158 per week:-

$$20 \times 1.5 \times 158 = £4740$$

When making the payment the employer should give the employee a written statement of how it has been calculated and details of any lump sum given to a redundant employee. Failure to provide such a statement could lead to the payment being regarded as voluntary rather than a redundancy payment. It should be noted however that much larger sums are payable under private schemes for redundancy payments entered into by employers and Trade Unions.

ASSIGNMENT — THE FAULTY TRIMMER

Market Product Testing Ltd. is a marketing company specialising in assessing the market potential of products of various manufacturers. For this purpose the company employs 43 full-time interviewers who work a minimum of 35 hours per week interviewing members of the public in their homes, usually after an appointment has been made by telephone. The company has a further 67 part-time workers who telephone members of the public and occasionally act as interviewers should demand require it. Caroline is classified as a part-time employee but for the last eighteen months she has been engaged exclusively as an interviewer, invariably working for between 40 and 50 hours per week. All interviewers are under the same degree of control by the company. They are given a list of clients. Time is allocated to the interviewer for presenting the product for use by the client, followed by an interview some weeks later on its performance. While the company employs the full-time staff under contracts of service, the part-time staff are classified as casual workers and are self-employed.

Last summer the company contracted with a manufacturer to test the market for electic hedge trimmers. Caroline was involved in the marketing campaign. Interviewers are under strict instructions from the company never to interfere with manufacturers products. When asked to do so by a client Caroline fitted an electric plug to a trimmer. The plug was wired wrongly by Caroline and consequently the client received an electric shock when he used the trimmer. Furthermore the client suffered injuries to his hip when he dropped the appliance on suffering the shock. The injured client has subsequently sought legal advice from his solicitor who now intends to take the matter up with the company.

TASKS

You are an administrative officer in Market Product Testing Ltd, and act as an assistant to the Managing Director. He has received a letter from the solicitor whose client was injured by the hedge trimmer. The Managing Director has sent you the following memorandum.

From: Managing Director	Ref: BR/JC/2405
To: Admin. Officer	Date: 24 May 19xx

There is a board meeting in two weeks time, in which there is an agenda item concerned with the employment status of interviewers. Prepare an infomal report for me in which you identify the advantages and disadvantages to the company of employing all these staff as self-employed workers. Since there appears to be a strong view already within the company in favour of self-employed status for interviewers, outline in the report how this can be lawfully achieved.

Coincidentally I received yesterday a letter from a firm of solicitors who allege that we are responsible for injuries caused to one of their clients. Indicate to me in your report whether you feel that a legal claim against the company would have any merit. Could the company be made liable for any negligence it has shown, or any negligence by the interviewer in question?

1. Produce the report required by the managing director.

2. Draft a simple contract that could be used by the company for the purpose of employing interviewers on a self-employed basis.

DEVELOPMENTAL TASK

Prepare a short address to be delivered by the managing director to a meeting of the interviewers, in which he will seek to persuade them of the advantage of self-employed status.

ASSIGNMENT — LEN THE PRINTER

Len is 47 and for the last 23 years has been employed as a printer by Fulton Printers Ltd., a small printing and typesetting business located in Bradford. For the last fourteen years Len has been foreman printer and his present gross wage is £187 per week. Since 1984 the management of the business has been effectively in the hands of Tim Fulton, the eldest son of the company's founder. Tim is concerned that the business has become less profitable as a whole and for some time has maintained only a steady turnover with a general increase in wage levels. On the printing side, old fashioned machinery and outdated methods contribute to a nett loss making exercise. Tim has convinced his fellow directors, his father included, that the printing side of the business should be terminated. Typesetting on the other hand, which is much more lucrative, is to be substantially developed with investment in new technology. The business will then become a specialist typesetter, servicing printing firms throughout the Bradford area. Len is told the news on his 48th birthday in a personal letter from Tim. As a loyal servant of the business, Len is offered, in Tim's words "the opportunity to meet the challenge of retraining as a typesetter on his present wage and so secure his future with the business". The letter goes on to point out that "the only alternative is to leave and take your chances in the job market". Len is aware that his employment prospects as a printer are not good but is uncertain whether he can cope with what is effectively a different job requiring different skills. He is also concerned that his employer does not operate a redundancy scheme with its employees.

TASKS

You are employed by the Union of British Printworkers, at their headquarters in Birmingham, where you deal with employment problems being experienced by union members.

Len is a member of the union, and he has written to it seeking help in relation to his situation at Fultons. The letter has been passed to you from your senior, for immediate attention. In it Len writes:

"I really don't know whether I have actually been made redundant at my place of work, and whether I am entitled to a redundancy payment. I have wondered about taking up the company's offer and retraining, but my worry is that I might find myself unable to cope with new demands, and have to leave anyway. I suppose if this happened I would lose any rights to a redundancy payment."

1. Produce notes on Len's redundancy dilemma's, to be attached to the file that has been opened for Len, in which you

    (a) identify whether if he leaves Fultons it will be by reason of redundancy;

    (b) state whether he is entitled to a redundancy payment if he does leave through redundancy;

    (c) explain whether Len is correct in his view that by leaving after retraining he will lose his rights to redundancy pay, and

    (d) calculate the redundancy payment Len would receive if he were regarded as a redundant worker.

2. Write a reply to Len in which you clearly but briefly explain to him, in simple terms, his legal position. The letter will incorporate your findings which have been recorded on the entry you have made to the file. Len's address is 18 Ulverston Terrace, Bradford, West Yorkshire.

DEVELOPMENTAL TASK

Undertake a role play exercise in which you simulate an interview between Tim and Len, with yourself as Len's representative. The aim of the interview is to allow a full and frank exchange of views regarding Len's position.

Chapter 8

ACQUISITION AND USE OF PROPERTY

THE NATURE OF PROPERTY

THE RIGHTS OF AN OWNER

A business may own a wide range of property, taking many different forms and performing many different functions. A glance at the balance sheet of any business will reveal the major types of property — or assets — commonly used by the trading organisation.

Under the heading *'fixed assets'* are found those items of property of a relatively permanent character which are acquired for use in the business. These may be tangible assets such as plant and machinery, vehicles and premises, or intangible assets such as patents, trademarks and goodwill. The balance sheet will also show the *'current assets'* of the business which will include raw materials, work in progress, stock, debtors and cash.

The legal rules which regulate ownership, use and disposal of these different forms of business property vary according to the nature of the property itself and the legal category into which it falls.

The ownership of property brings with it certain legal rights and duties. The rights include the right to use and enjoy physical possession of the property, to consume it, alter it, destroy it or dispose of it by transferring ownership of it to another person by way of gift or sale. Ownership also brings with it the risk of loss or damage by accidental destruction. The business will usually safeguard itself against this risk by insurance. To enforce these rights the law provides a range of remedies to the property owner. These are considered later in this chapter.

CLASSIFICATION OF PROPERTY

Real Property and Personal Property

Most legal systems distinguish between two main types of property, *movable* and *immovable*. This distinction is based upon the nature and characteristics of the property itself. Movable property includes goods and chattels, shares, debts and cheques; while immovable property is land and the things which go with land such as buildings and rights of way.

The English legal system, however, does not adopt this approach and, for historical reasons, makes a primary distinction between *real* and *personal* property. Real property is simply freehold land. All forms of property other than freehold land are categorised as personal property.

Fig 8.1 below sets out a classification of business property in diagrammatic form.

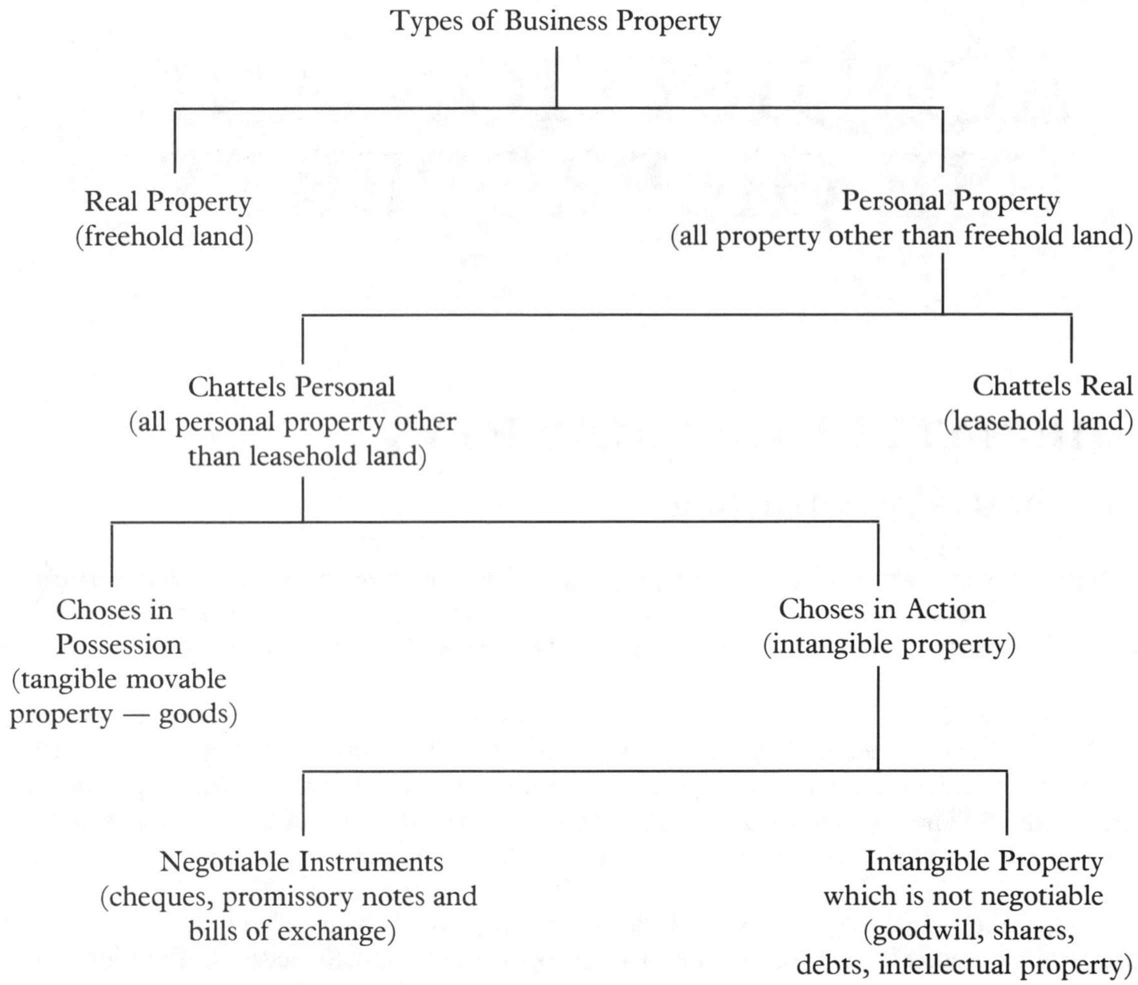

The historical reason for this distinction is that, in the early days of the common law, a form of legal action known as a *'real'* action could be used by a dispossessed owner of freehold land in order to repossess his land in the common law courts. This remedy was not available to an owner of any other type of property, not even to a holder of leasehold land, and such owners could only take an action in court to recover damages or financial compensation from the person who had taken their property because the court had no power to order the restoration of their property to them. Thus real property was that property which could be recovered by taking a 'real' action in the courts and all other property was classified as personal property. The classification survives today even though the powers of the courts have changed over the centuries and it is now perfectly possible for a court to make an order restoring personal property to its true owner.

Chattels Real and Chattels Personal

All types of personal property are known as *chattels. Chattels* is an old English word, meaning goods, derived from the word for cattle, which were in those days the most valuable form of personal property. Land and buildings held under the terms of a lease are chattels real. They are the form of personal property (chattels) most closely resembling freehold land (real property) and derive their name accordingly. All other forms of personal property are known as chattels personal.

Chattels personal are those forms of property, tangible and intangible, which other systems would classify as movable property, such as plant and equipment, vehicles, patents and debts.

A further division or classification of chattels personal is made between *'choses in possession'* and *'choses in action'* depending on whether they are tangible or intangible.

Choses in Possession and Choses in Action

Choses is a French word meaning things. *Choses in possession* or things in possession are literally those things or objects which we can physically possess. Choses in possession therefore are items of physical movable property for instance 'goods' within the meaning of the Sale of Goods Act 1979 such as books, machinery, cars or desks.

Choses in action or things in action differ from choses in possession in that they have no physical existence. Choses in action are intangible forms of personal property such as goodwill, patents and debts, the rights in which can only be asserted by taking legal action.

There may be some physical or tangible evidence of the existence of the property rights in question but the rights themselves are intangible. For example, a share certificate is a tangible piece of paper, but its value lies in the legal rights which it represents, rights to vote at meetings of the company, rights to receive dividends and rights to share in the ultimate division of the property of the company on winding up once prior claims have been met.

Negotiable Instruments

Negotiable instruments such as cheques, bills of exchange and promissory notes are choses in action which represent the right to receive the payment of sums of money. They are considered later in this chapter.

LAND

Land is the most permanent and often the most valuable asset which a business can own. For legal purposes, the buildings and other fixtures such as fences and trees on the land are treated as being part of it, and thus the ownership of business premises is regarded by the law as the same thing as the ownership of the land on which those premises stand. The airspace above and the soil below the land are also treated as being part of the land.

The premises from which businesses operate may be owned by the business outright. This is referred to as freehold ownership. On the other hand the premises may be rented from some other person or organisation. This is referred to as leasehold ownership. Technically all land in England and Wales is owned by the Crown and individuals or business organisations may only hold an *'estate'* in land. The expression "estate in land" refers to the measure of a person's interest in land from the point of view of time.

> Under s.1 of the Law of Property Act 1925, only two legal estates can exist in land:
>
> (a) the fee simple absolute in possession (the freehold estate); and
>
> (b) the term of years absolute (the leasehold estate).

FREEHOLD LAND

The *fee simple absolute in possession* is the freehold estate in land which effectively represents absolute ownership. The expression 'fee' refers to the fact that the estate is inheritable; 'simple' means that there are no restrictions on who may inherit; 'absolute' refers to the fact that the grant in unconditional and 'in possession' means that the grant is to take effect immediately.

The freehold owner is entitled to immediate possession of his land and this entitlement cannot be brought to an end except by the owner himself. He is entitled to pass on his ownership by sale to another or by inheritance to any of his heirs.

The only practical effect of the Crown's technical ownership of land is that the land will pass to the Crown as *'bona vacantia'* in the unlikely event that the freehold owner dies without any next of kin whatsoever and without a will giving the property to a named beneficiary.

For all practical purposes the freehold owner is an absolute owner of his land. Having said this there are many legal restrictions on his right to do as he pleases with his land, imposed both by Acts of Parliament and by the common law. These restrictions, examined later in the chapter, also apply to the rights of an owner of leasehold land.

LEASEHOLD LAND

Where a business operates from premises which are rented, the business will be a tenant and own a leasehold estate in the land. The landlord will be the owner of the freehold estate. A leasehold estate (or 'term of years absolute') is created when the freeholder grants a lease to a tenant for certain term. This will include a lease for a time period which is fixed for example a seven year lease. Alternatively the term of the lease could be made certain by the service of a notice to quit for instance a monthly tenancy. The lease gives the business tenant the right to occupy the land and premises to the exclusion of all others (including the landlord) in return for the payment of rent. When the period of the lease comes to an end the landlord is entitled, at common law, to regain possession of his property. By Act of Parliament, however, the tenant will usually have the right of security of tenure. This right to stay in possession will override the landlord's common law right to regain possession, and will enable the tenant to extend his period of occupation by virtue of a new lease on terms which are reasonably equivalent to the terms contained in the original lease.

THE TERMS OF A BUSINESS LEASE

A business lease will normally be granted by deed and will outline the rights and obligations of the landlord and the tenant in the form of *covenants*. A covenant is simply a contractual promise made by deed.

Leases of business premises will usually contain the following covenants:

(a) **By the tenant**

- (i) to pay rent and rates (there may also be a rent review clause under which the amount of the rent may be increased from time to time);
- (ii) to keep the premises in a good state of decorative repair;
- (iii) to permit the landlord to enter the premises from time to time in order to view the state of repair;
- (iv) not to carry out alterations to the premises without the landlord's consent;
- (v) not to assign, sublet or otherwise part with possession of the premises;
- (vi) not to use the premises for any purpose other than that stated in the lease.

(b) **By the landlord**

(i) not to interfere with the tenant's quiet enjoyment of the property;

(ii) to insure the premises;

(iii) to keep the main structure and exterior of the premises in good repair.

STATUTORY RIGHTS OF THE TENANT

In addition to his rights under the express terms of the lease, a tenant of business premises has certain statutory rights under the Landlord and Tenant Acts 1927 and 1954. Three of the major statutory rights of the business tenant under the Landlord and Tenant Acts are:

(a) security of tenure,

(b) compensation for improvements, and,

(c) in certain circumstances, compensation for disturbance.

(a) **Security of tenure**

By virtue of Part II of the Landlord and Tenant Act 1954 a business tenancy does not automatically come to an end when the contractual period of the tenancy expires. The tenancy continues automatically even though its term has expired, unless and until it is brought to an end by one of the methods stipulated by the Act. The tenant has the right to remain in possession of the premises on new terms which, if they cannot be settled by agreement between the parties, will be fixed by the court. If the landlord requires possession of the premises he cannot evict the tenant against his will except by an order of the court. Such an order will only be granted if the landlord establishes one of the limited grounds laid down in the Act. Broadly the landlord will be granted possession if he can show either that the tenant has failed during his tenancy to comply with the covenants under the lease for example, if he has persistently delayed in the payment of rent; or where the landlord himself requires possession of the premises in order to redevelop or reconstruct them, or for his own business or residential use.

(b) **Compensation for disturbance**

If the landlord is granted possession on the grounds that he requires them for redevelopment or reconstruction, or for his own business or residential use, the tenant will be entitled to financial compensation in order to assist with removal expenses. The compensation is not related to the actual expenses incurred by the tenant, however, it is fixed by reference to the rateable value of the property and the length of the tenancy.

(c) **Compensation for improvements**

Where the tenant increases the value of the premises during the tenancy by making improvements, for example, by erecting a new building, or extending the existing premises or putting in a new drainage system, he will be entitled to compensation on leaving the premises, provided that he obtained either the consent of the landlord or the approval of the court before he actually carried out the improvements. The amount of the compensation will relate to the increase in letting value of the premises.

ACQUISITION OF LAND

The acquisition of land involves the transfer of property rights in land which is usually achieved by the formal process of conveyancing. In Chapter 3 it was noted that contracts involving the sale of land are only enforceable if the requirements of s.40 Law of Property Act 1925 are complied with. There does not have to be a formal written contract in order to comply with s.40, but rather written evidence which supports the existence of the contract. This must be signed by the party against whom it is to be used as evidence (or his agent) and contain details of the essential terms of the contract. The essential terms which the document must contain are:

(a) the names of the vendor and purchaser;

(b) the identity of the land;

(c) the price to be paid by the purchaser.

THE PROCESS OF CONVEYANCING

The process of conveyancing is concerned with the legal mechanics of the sale or purchase of land or of an interest in land. The process is basically the same for all land regardless of the purpose for which it is used, be it a private house, an office, a factory or farmland. There may be some variation in the detail of the process, however, depending upon (a) whether the freehold or the leasehold estate is being transferred and (b) whether the title to the land is registered at the Land Registry, or is unregistered. We need not examine the detail of these variations and shall simply consider the basic process in outline.

The process is divided into two stages — the periods *before* and *after* an exchange of contracts.

Prior to an Exchange of Contracts

A person who wishes to sell land may either advertise the property himself or employ an estate agent to act on his behalf in negotiating the sale. When a purchaser is found, an agreement will be made in principle for the sale of the property at an agreed price, and it is then that the vendor and the purchaser will instruct their respective solicitors. At this stage the transaction is 'subject to contract'.

'Subject to Contract'

A contract for the sale of land is unenforceable unless it is evidenced in writing under s.40 Law of Property Act 1925. A purchaser and vendor will not usually wish to be legally bound until a formal exchange of contracts has been made. This is because the purchaser will have to conclude his financial arrangements and fully investigate the property before he commits himself, and the vendor may wish to arrange the purchase of a new property to take effect at the same time as his sale is completed. The parties or their representatives will, however, need to communicate with each other in writing but will not wish, at this stage, to provide each other with a signed letter which could be used as evidence for the purposes of s.40. For this reason all correspondence passing between the parties or their representatives should be marked with the words 'subject to contract'. It is well established by usage and case law that any documents so marked will not be accepted by the courts as sufficient evidence for the purposes of s.40.

The following matters will need to be dealt with before an exchange of contracts can take place.

(a) Draft contracts

The vendor's solicitor will obtain the title deeds relating to the property and, using information gathered from the deeds and from the vendor himself, will draw up a draft contract with an identical counterpart which will be submitted to the purchaser's solicitor for approval.

(b) Enquiries and searches

The purchaser's solicitor will make investigations about the property by:

(i) visiting the property and inspecting it;

(ii) sending a standard form of preliminary enquiries containing questions about physical and legal aspects of the property to the vendor's solicitor;

(iii) making enquiries to the Local Authority to discover what information it has relating to it or to proposals which may affect it, for example demolition orders or road improvement schemes;

(iv) making a search in the Register of Local Land Charges to determine whether any matter registered there affects the property.

(c) Finance

Prior to an exchange of contracts the purchaser will wish to conclude his financial arrangements so that he can satisfy himself that once he is legally bound he is able to raise the full amount of the purchase price. The majority of domestic purchases are made with the aid of a building society mortgage, and it is at this stage in the process that confirmation is required from the mortgagee that the necessary funding will be available to finance the purchase. The purchase of business premises are often funded, at least partly, by a mortgage also, but from a commercial bank rather than a building society. The nature of a mortgage, and the rights and obligations of the mortgagor and the mortgagee are considered later. Before lending money on the security of a mortgage, the mortgagee will wish to be satisfied firstly that the borrower has the ability to repay. He will do this enquiring of the employer of a private individual borrower, or assessing the accounts of a business borrower covering the last three financial years. Secondly he will wish to be sure that the property itself is sufficiently valuable to provide full security in the event of default by the borrower. This will usually be done by instructing an independent surveyor to give a valuation of the property.

(d) Survey

A contract for the sale of land is governed by the common law principle *'caveat emptor'* or 'let the buyer beware'! There are no statutory implied terms of quality or fitness for purpose. The purchaser takes the property as he finds it and must therefore satisfy himself about its physical condition and the state of any buildings before an exchange of contracts with the vendor.

A purchaser will usually employ a surveyor to act on his behalf in inspecting the property in order to find out whether there are any structural defects or other problems such as dry or wet rot, rising damp or woodworm. If any problems of this nature are detected while the purchase is *'subject to contract'*, the purchaser is free to look for another property, or to re-negotiate the price. If the defects become manifest after he has purchased, he will not usually be able to sue the vendor because of the *'caveat emptor'* rule.

Where the purchaser is financing the purchase with a loan raised on the security of a mortgage of the property, the mortgagee will usually arrange a survey himself, at the purchaser's expense, before agreeing to advance the money. If the mortgagee is a building society, then under Building Societies Act 1986, it *must* arrange a survey for the purposes of valuation. As we have seen, a surveyor, acting for a building society in these circumstances owes a duty to the borrower to take reasonable care in carrying out a visual inspection of the property.

In *Yianni v. Edwin Evans & Sons (1981)* the plaintiffs were buying a house for £15,000 with the aid of a £12,000 building society mortgage. The building society instructed the defendant surveyors to carry out a valuation of the property. After an inspection of the house the defendants reported to the building society that in their opinion the house was adequate security for a loan of £12,000. The plaintiffs completed the purchase of the property and soon afterwards discovered serious cracks in the foundations. They sued the defendants for £18,000 which was the estimated cost of repairing the foundations. The court held that the defendants owed a duty of care to the plaintiffs and that they were liable to pay the £18,000 damages in the tort of negligence for a breach of that duty of care.

Exchange of contracts to completion

Once the parties are satisfied that all the preliminary matters outlined above have been satisfactorily sorted out, they will be clear to enter into a legally binding contract. They will sign identical counterparts of the formal contract and the purchaser's solicitor will deliver his client's signed part along with a deposit representing 10% of the purchase price to the vendor's solicitor. In exchange he will receive the vendor's signed part of the contract. At this point the parties are legally bound by the contract. It will usually be a matter of three or four weeks before the sale is finally completed. The 10% deposit paid by the purchaser on exchange is a sign of his good faith and will be forfeit if he subsequently withdraws from the contract without justification.

Once contracts have been exchanged, the purchaser has an insurable interest in the property and should take out a policy of insurance immediately. He will not, however, be in full possession of the property until completion takes place.

In the time before completion, the purchaser's solicitor will examine the title deeds to the property and investigate the vendor's title in order to be absolutely certain that the vendor is able to give full ownership to the purchaser without any possibility of a claim by any other person. For this purpose the purchaser's solicitor also makes further searches in central registers. It is possible for a person with legal rights over the property, such as a second mortgage, to protect his rights by registering them in a central register. The effect of such a registration is that the person to whom the property is conveyed will take subject to those rights unless they are discharged before completion by the vendor, for example by redeeming the second mortgage out of the proceeds of sale.

The purchaser's solicitor prepares the formal deed of conveyance in readiness for completion. Where the vendor conveys the land to the purchaser as a 'beneficial owner' the following covenants are implied by s.76 of the Law of Property Act 1925:

(i) that the vendor has a good right to convey the property;

(ii) that the purchaser will enjoy quiet possession of the property;

(iii) that the property will be free from claims or demands by any other person;

(iv) that the vendor will, if necessary, at a future date, remedy any defect in the present conveyance.

Completion of the transaction

On the day of completion the purchaser will pay the balance of the purchase price (90%) to the vendor in return for the title deeds to the land, including the conveyance to himself, and the keys to the property. The property now fully belongs to the purchaser and he may take up possession.

RESTRICTIONS ON THE USE OF LAND

As previously mentioned a freehold owner is for all practical purposes regarded as the absolute owner of the property. Such ownership carries with it a number of rights, although these rights are in some circumstances qualified by statutory and common law restrictions. A leaseholder is in a similar position, although such a person has of course to observe the covenants contained in the lease. The main rights and restrictions of landowners are as follows:

(a) the right to develop the land

A landowner is subject to the control of the local planning authority under the Town and Country Planning Act 1971 in relation to any proposed development of the land. Planning permission is required for any material alterations of buildings on land or the use to which they are put. If an individual is considering acquiring a piece of land, there is a means by which he can obtain outline planning permission for any proposed development to ascertain whether full planning permission is likely to be granted.

If an owner carries out development without permission, the local planning authority may serve an *enforcement notice* on him requiring the works to be removed or the new use to be discontinued. If the enforcement notice is not complied with the authority may enter the land and restore it, charging the cost to the owner and alternatively, or in addition, may take proceedings in the magistrates' court against the owner. The magistrates may impose a fine of £1,000 and a further penalty of £50 per day thereafter while the contravention continues.

Under the Building Act 1984, formerly the Building Regulations 1965 and 1976, plans for the construction of new buildings or for the structural alteration of existing buildings must be approved by the local authority. The purpose of the Building Regulations is to ensure that building construction is carried out in accordance with good building and design principles. Building inspectors may inspect the building works as they continue in order to see that the approved plans are adhered to.

(b) the right to retain ownership

Wide powers are conferred on local authorities and other bodies with regard to the compulsory purchase of land. A freeholder can be required to sell his interests in the land to a body exercising compulsory purchase powers, usually in order to facilitate some development scheme. An owner can, of course, object to a compulsory purchase order and then a Public Local Inquiry will have to be held to consider the views of those affected. Such inquiries are conducted by an inspector who will recommend a course of action to the appropriate Minister (the Secretary of State for the Environment) and his decision is final.

(c) the right to natural resources

An owner has full mineral rights, however by statute certain natural mineral resources such as gas, oil and coal belong to the government or one of its agencies. Thus coal is in the ownership of British Coal, a state corporation.

(d) the right to water

The owner of land adjoining a river enjoys certain common law rights. These riparian rights as they are known, allow him to take water for ordinary purposes connected with the land. This right however is substantially modified by the Water Resources Act 1963, which operates a licencing system for the extraction of water.

(e) rights in relation to the use of land

As a general proposition a landowner, subject to planning control, can use the land as he likes. However the ability of the businessman to operate any business he chooses is subject to a number of restrictions. These restrictions can arise by an agreement, or be imposed by law.

(i) restrictions arising by agreement

Whether an individual occupies premises as a business tenant or a freeholder there could be some restriction on his rights to use the property for business purposes.

In a business lease the deed creating it will contain a number of covenants. As we have seen there is normally a covenant restricting business use, and this could come in a positive or negative form. It could restrict the tenant to carrying on a particular business or using the property for a particular purpose, for instance carrying on the business of a retail travel agent. Alternatively the covenant could prevent the tenant from carrying on a particular form of trade or any activity causing a nuisance or annoyance, such as a public house. Both the landlord and tenant have bound themselves personally by the covenants in the lease and will retain this contractual liability throughout its term. Covenants which restrict use may also apply to a freeholder. Such restrictive covenants could originate from a transaction under which one landowner, Smith sold part of his land to a purchaser, Jones. In the deed conveying the land to Jones, Smith may for the benefit of land retained by him, have extracted a promise from Jones not to use the land for anything except residential purposes. Thus if Jones now attempts to break the covenant by setting up a business, Smith can seek an injunction to prevent him. Of course it is not always the seller who abstracts the promise, it could be the purchaser who imposes a restriction on the seller.

A major feature of such covenants is that they will become attached to the land that they are to benefit and also the land which carries the burden. This mens that successive purchasers may enjoy the benefit or bear the burden of the covenant and so enforce it. Where the character of a neighbourhood changes or it becomes obvious that the covenant impedes some reasonable use of the land it is possible to apply to the Lands Tribunal which has power to modify or discharge it.

(ii) restrictions imposed by law

At common law an owner may be restrained by injunction from using his land in such a way as to cause a nuisance to his neighbour. He may also be liable in damages in the torts of nuisance or negligence, under the rule in *Rylands v. Fletcher*, or under the Occupiers Liability Acts 1957 and 1984 for injury or loss caused to others by unreasonable or unlawful use of his own land.

For a detailed examination of these torts students should refer to 'Core Studies for BTEC National'.

Other restrictions arise under statute. For instance, under the Public Health Act 1936, a local authority has an obligation to inspect its area to ascertain whether there are any *'statutory nuisances'* and to take action to see that they are abated. Section 92 of the Act defines the following as statutory nuisances:

"(i) premises which are in such a state as to be prejudicial to health or a nuisance;

(ii) an animal kept in such a place or in such a manner as to be prejudicial to health or a nuisance;

(iii) an accumulation or deposit which is prejudicial to health or a nuisance;

(iv) dust or effluvia caused by any trade, business, manufacture or process and being prejudicial to the health of, or a nuisance to, the inhabitants of the neighbourhood;

(v) a workplace which is not provided with sufficient means of ventilation, or in which sufficient ventilation is not maintained, or which is not kept clean or which is so overcrowded while work is carried on as to be prejudicial to the health of those employed therein".

Where it is satisifed that a statutory nuisance exists, the local authority may serve an *abatement notice* on the person or organisation responsible for the nuisance, requiring that person to take specified action in order to bring the nuisance to an end. If an abatement notice is not complied with, the local authority may, in certain circumstances, carry out the specified action itself and recover the cost from the person responsible. The authority may also apply to the Magistrates' Court for a *'nuisance order'* requiring compliance with the terms of the abatement notice, and the Court has power additionally to impose a fine.

Under the Health and Safety at Work Act 1974, previously examined in Chapter 7, an employer has a duty to ensure, so far as is reasonably practicable, the health and safety of his employees by maintaining a safe place of work and a safe working environment. Use of land by a business in circumstances contravening the Health and Safety at Work Act 1974 could render the business liable to face a criminal prosecution.

(f) the right to freedom from unlawful interference

Interference with the right of an owner of land to enjoy quiet possession of his land may be actionable under the civil law as the tort of trespass. Any person who, without lawful authority, enters or remains upon the land of another, or places or throws any physical object on to such land, is a trespasser.

An occupier of land may use reasonable force, if necessary, to eject a trespasser, but only after asking him to leave and allowing him a reasonable opportunity to do so.

An occupier of land may also sue a trespasser for damages and does not have to prove that he suffered any loss as a result of the trespass. He may apply for an injunction in order to prevent the continuation or repetition of the trespass.

An owner or occupier of land may also be able to sue in the torts of nuisance or *Rylands v. Fletcher* either for an injunction or for damages in circumstances where his enjoyment of his own land is interfered with as a result of activities carried on by his neighbours which amount to an unreasonable or unlawful use by his neighbours of their land.

LAND AS SECURITY

The value to a business of its freehold or leasehold land extends beyond the intrinsic value of such property as a place from which the business is conducted, or a resource in the production process. The business may also use the land as a means of raising finance by obtaining a loan secured by a mortgage of the land.

A mortgage is simply a transaction under which a borrower, the mortgagor in return for a loan from the lender, the mortgagee gives security in the form of property which is usually land. Domestic mortgages are most commonly created when a building society, bank, insurance company or local authority lends money towards the purchase of a home. For business premises a commercial mortgage will usually be arranged through a mortgage broker with a bank or finance company. In the business context the mortgage transaction can provide the means by which either:

(a) commercial premises are acquired from which the business activity is carried on, or

(b) additional funds are raised to finance business activity.

To create a formal or "legal" mortgage of a freehold or leasehold two methods are available under the Law of Property Act 1925. The first method involves the transfer of a lease (usually for 300 years) from the mortgagor to the mortgagee subject to a clause that the lease is to terminate when the loan is repaid. This is called a provision for cesser on redemption. If the property to be mortgaged is leasehold then a sub lease is granted for a shorter period than the original lease. While the lease is merely notional and no rent is payable under it, it does provide a means by which the mortgagee can if necessary enforce his security. The second method available is simpler, more popular with institutional lenders and is known as the "charge" method. Here the mortgagor charges his land with the repayment of the debt by the means of a short deed expressed to be a charge by way of legal mortgage. The main difference between a charge and a mortgage is that under the charge the borrower retains ownership in the property and the lender is given certain rights over it. Under the mortgage however some ownership of the property is transferred to the lender for the purposes of providing security for the loan.

An alternative to the legal mortgage is the less formal "equitable" mortage. An equitable mortgage arises where no mortgage deed is executed and the borrower merely deposits the title deeds of the property with the lender. While there is no transfer of ownership to the lender under such an arrangement the borrower is effectively prevented from selling or re-mortgaging the land. A weakness of the equitable mortgage is that if a subsequent legal mortgage were to be created over the land, that mortgage would take preference if the mortgagee had no knowledge of the equitable mortgage.

Where a legal mortgage is created, this must be done by deed. The deed must comply with the Law of Property Act 1925. The mortgage deed will set out the rights and obligations of the mortgagor and mortgagee, which will usually include the following:

The rights of the mortgagor

(a) **The right to redeem the mortgage** — the mortgage deed will provide for the repayment of the amount borrowed (the capital sum) with interest by instalments over a definite period of time which is usually a number of years. The mortgagor has the right to be discharged from his obligations under the mortgage deed once the capital sum has been repaid with interest; and he has the right to make a full repayment at any time, even before the date specified in the mortgage, and thereby redeem his property. Generally the courts have sought to protect the right of the mortgagor and have not allowed mortgage terms which unreasonably prevent or postpone the mortgagor's right to redeem the mortgage.

In *Fairclough v. Swan Brewery Co. Ltd. (1912)* a twenty year mortgage term postponed the right to redeem for nineteen years and forty six weeks. This postponement was held to make the mortgage virtually unredeemable and so declared void.

(b) **The right to enjoy the use of his land** during the repayment period, without any interference by the mortgagee, so long as he (the mortgagor) is fulfilling his obligations under the mortgage and repaying the instalments as they fall due. In these circumstances the mortgagor has full use of his property though there may be some restrictions, for example on structural alterations without the consent of the mortgagee since these could affect the value of the security.

The rights of the mortgagee

The principal right of the mortgagee is to the repayment of the capital sum with interest in accordance with the terms of the mortgage. If the mortgagor defaults in his obligation to repay, the mortgagee can rely on one or more of the following rights.

(a) **The right to sue the mortgagor** The mortgagor is under a contractual obligaton to repay the full amount of the loan with interest. If he is in arrears he may be sued personally by the mortgagee for the full amount and not merely for the outstanding instalments. Usually, however, the mortgagee will prefer to enforce his rights against the property because the mortgagor is not likely to be able to satisfy a judgement debt if he is in such financial difficulty as to be unable to repay the mortgage instalments.

(b) **The right to take possession of the property** if the mortgagor defaults in the repayment of the loan. This right will be contained in the mortgage deed and will usually be exercised by the mortgagee as a preliminary step, prior to exercising a power of sale, in order to obtain vacant possession of the property.

(c) **The power of sale** This power may be exercised by the mortgagee where at least two months' interest is overdue and where he has served notice on the mortgagor requiring him to repay the mortgage debt in full and the mortgagor has failed to do so within three months. The mortgagee may then sell the property over the head of the mortgagor, take out all sums due to him from the proceeds of sale and pay any remaining monies back to the mortgagor.

(d) **Foreclosure.** This amounts to the transfer of the mortgaged property to the mortgagee absolutely and may only be done by an order of the court, which is obtained in two stages.

The first stage involves an application to the court, where the mortgagor is substantially in arrears, for an order requiring him, within a specified time, to repay the loan and redeem the mortgage.

If the mortgagor fails to redeem the mortgage, the second stage involves a further application to the court for a final order of foreclosure terminating the mortgagor's right of redemption and transferring the ownership of the land absolutely to the mortgagee.

PROPERTY OTHER THAN LAND

CHOSES IN POSSESSION

Earlier in this chapter it was noted that choses in possession are items of personal property which have a physical existence and can be touched or moved. In other words they are goods. Chapter 5 deals with the legal rules relating to contracts for the sale of goods and other contracts involving the transfer of ownership of goods from one party to another. The detailed regulation of such transactions simply reflects the fact that the production and distribution of goods is the lifeblood of the majority of business organisations in the commercial world.

We shall now consider the legal consequences, both under the criminal law and under the civil law, of the unlawful interference by one person with the goods of another.

CRIMINAL LIABILITY FOR INTERFERENCE WITH GOODS

A person who interferes with the property of another may be liable, under the criminal law, to punishment in the form of a fine, or imprisonment, or both. The main offences relating to such interference are contained in the Theft Act 1968 and the Criminal Damage Act 1971.

Theft

By section 1 of the Theft Act 1968 a person is guilty of theft if he dishonestly appropriates property belonging to another with the intention of permanently depriving the other of it.

'Property', for the purposes of this offence, is defined in s.4 of the Act to include "money and all other property, real and personal, including things in action and other intangible property", although the section goes on to exclude land from the definition except in one or two specified instances. Theft, like most other criminal offences, contains two main elements:

(a) the mental element or guilty mind, called 'mens rea'

(b) the physical element or guilty act, called 'actus reus'.

The guilty act is the 'appropriation'. This involves taking or otherwise assuming the rights of an owner of property belonging to another. The mental element of the offence is the dishonesty of the accused, and his intention to permanently deprive the owner of his property. Without an intention to permanently deprive the owner of his property the offence is not committed. The dishonest borrowing of property belonging to another is not theft, but a separate offence is created by the Theft Act 1968, s.12, of taking a conveyance such as a motor car without lawful authority and this offence may be committed without an intention to permanently deprive the owner of his conveyance.

Criminal Damage to Property

By section 1 of the Criminal Damage Act 1971 a person who without lawful excuse destroys or damages any property belonging to another, intending to destroy or damage such property or being reckless as to whether any such property would be destroyed or damaged is guilty of an offence.

Property, for the purposes of this offence, is defined by the Act as 'property of a tangible nature, whether real or personal, including money'. Because of the nature of the offence, choses in action are not included in the definition, although clearly land and buildings are included as well as goods and money. The guilty act which constitutes the offence is the damage or destruction caused to another's property. If this is done by fire then the offence is known as arson. The mental element is the intention of the accused or his recklessness as to whether the property is damaged or destroyed.

CIVIL LIABILITY FOR INTERFERENCE WITH GOODS

The civil law remedies available to a person whose goods have been wrongfully interfered with are contained in the Torts (Interference with Goods) Act 1977. The Act applies to goods, which are defined by s.14 to include "all chattels personal other than things in action and money". The Act therefore applies to choses in possession but not to choses in action.

Section 1 of the Act defines 'wrongful interference with goods' to mean:

(a) conversion of goods,

(b) trespass to goods,

(c) negligence so far as it results in damage to goods,

(d) any other tort so far as it results in damage to goods.

Conversion of Goods

Conversion of goods is the denial of an owner's title to goods. Such a denial may take the form of wrongfully taking them away from the owner, keeping them, destroying them or disposing of them to a third party.

Trespass to Goods

Trespass to goods is denying the owner of goods the right to possession of them by wrongfully removing them or damaging them without depriving the owner of them completely.

Negligence

Negligence involves a failure to take reasonable care which results in foreseeable damage to the goods.

The remedies available under the Act are contained in s.3 which provides for:

(a) damages alone; or

(b) damages in addition to an order for specific delivery of the goods. An order for specific delivery is discretionary and may be refused, or, if granted, may be subject to conditions imposed by the court; or

(c) an order that the defendant pay the value of the goods to the plaintiff instead of specific delivery.

INTANGIBLE PROPERTY (CHOSES IN ACTION)

Earlier in this chapter it was seen that choses in action are forms of personal property which have no physical existence, although they may be evidenced by some physical thing such as a share certificate or a mortgage deed. The essential characteristic of a chose in action is that it is a property right which can, if necessary, be asserted by taking legal action in the courts.

Choses of action are an important form of business property. They include the following:

(a) debts owed to the business;

(b) shares held in a business;

(c) business goodwill;

(d) intellectual property, including patents, copyright and trademarks; and

(e) negotiable instruments, such as cheques and bills of exchange.

THE NATURE OF CHOSES IN ACTION

Because of the intangible nature of this form of property the law has recognised that in some cases special protection is needed to prevent infringement of the owner's rights in relation to it. This can be seen particularly in respect of intellectual property.

The legal nature of the various forms of intangible property are considered below:

(a) debts. A debt is a legal right to receive payment. In a business context this will usually involve the right to payment for goods and services provided to a customer. The business owns the right to payment. This creates an asset, which appears in the balance sheet. As an item of business property a debt can be sold. Some organisations actually specialise in purchasing debts, at a discount. Unless they are in need of immediate funds businesses will not usually sell their debts. However where a debtor is in financial difficulties, and the chances of enforcing the debt through court action are small the business may be glad to cut its losses and sell the debt at a heavy discount. Debt recovery presents a major problem for all businesses, especially small businesses which have limited funds available to them, and can easily experience cash flow difficulties. It is not unusual for small organisations with a full order book but with many outstanding debts to 'go under'.

(b) shares. This form of property is dealt with in Chapter 2.

(c) business goodwill

Business goodwill is the term used to describe the most fundamental asset of any business organisation, its reputation. The reputation of any business operating in a market is measured by the extent to which its goods and service have achieved public respect. This respect is normally built up over a number of years so that a regular custom develops to ensure a steady level of business. To obtain a good reputation it is necessary for a business to recruit a skilled and loyal workforce and in many cases maintain a high level of research and development into its products. A number of factors contribute therefore to establishing and maintaining the goodwill of a business includes its custom, workforce and future plans for the goods and services it provides. There is normally no need to place a monetary value on business goodwill and therefore it will not usually appear in the assets column of the Balance Sheet when yearly accounts of a business are drawn up. Unlike tangible assets however, if it is lost it cannot be easily replaced so that many businessment would regard it as the most priceless asset of the business. The necessity to value business goodwill arises when there is a change in the ownership of a business. On the introduction of a new partner into a partnership it may be necessary to value the goodwill to determine his or her capital contribution. If a business is sold as a going concern then the business goodwill is valued as the sum of money that the purchase price exceeds the value of the tangible assets of the business;

(d) intellectual property;

(e) negotiable instruments.
These two aspects of intangible property are dealt with in detail below.

INTELLECTUAL PROPERTY

The expression 'intellectual property' is used to describe a group of tangible rights in personal property e.g. patents, copyright, registered designs and trade marks.

PATENTS

A patent may be described as the exclusive right to make use of, develop or sell an invention. It is conferred on a person who produces an original process or machine and is obtained by registration at the Patent Office. The objective is to encourage full disclosure of a new invention and protect the inventor's interest by conferring on him a legal monopoly of exploitation, usually for twenty years.

The grant of a patent arises under s.1 of the Patent Act 1977, if the invention is new, involves an inventive step and is capable of industrial application. The patent will be taken to be capable of industrial application if it can be made or used in any branch of industry including agriculture. The Patent Act 1977 also provides that a patent must not encourage offensive, immoral or anti-social behaviour, it must not consist of a scientific theory, mathematical method or computer programme or be of a literary dramatic musical or artistic work most of which are protected by copyright. If an invention is made at the workplace by an employee then patent rights and other benefits belong to him or her. However if the invention arises from the employee's normal duties the invention may belong to the employer under the Act.

> In *Reiss Engineering Co. v. Harris (1985)* an employee had invented a new valve, after receiving notice of redundancy, but before his employment had terminated. His employers' claim that they owned the invention was

rejected, for the employee was not employed to design or invent and nor could an invention reasonably be expected to result from his normal duties.

In cases where an invention is lawfully patented by the employer an employee can still apply to the High Court for a fair share of the money derived from a patent which proves to be of 'outstanding benefit' to the employer. The aim of this provision is to ensure that employees are given a fair reward for inventions.

Infringement of a patent is actionable in the High Court where the patent holder could obtain the remedy of damages and/or an injunction. Goods which infringe the patent may be ordered to be delivered up or destroyed.

COPYRIGHTS

A copyright is under s.2 Copyright Act 1956 the ownership of an original work that is of a literary dramatic, musical or artistic nature. 'Artistic work' includes under s.3 painting, sculptures, drawings, engravings, photographs and works of architecture. Copyright exists therefore in books, magazines, sound recordings, films, television and radio broadcasts and following the Cable and Broadcasting Act 1984, cable programmes.

In *Express Newspapers v. Liverpool Daily Post and Echo (1985)* the expression 'literary work' for the purpose of copyright was considered. Here there was a claim that the game 'Millionaire of the Month' published in a daily newspaper involved skill and labour in its production and so constituted a literary work for the purposes of copyright proceedings. Cards carrying a five letter code had been distributed to the public at random and to participate in the game these cards had to be checked against a grid of letters published daily in the plaintiff's national newspaper. These letter grids were then published in the defendant's local newspaper and the plaintiffs sought an injunction claiming infringement of copyright. The court held that copyright existed in each of the grids as 'literary works' and the injunction was granted.

A copyright holder has the exclusive right to authorise another person to reproduce or publish the work and can profit through the printing sales and copying of that work. This right arises at the time the work is created and lasts until the end of fifty years from the date of publication or fifty years from the death of the originator whichever is later. It is possible to publish a book of course after the author's death! As with patents the copyright of written work produced in the course of employment belongs to the employer.

The rights of a copyright holder would be infringed by any unauthorised act in relation to the material, such as reproducing or publishing the work or performing or broadcasting the work in public. The Copyright Act 1956 provides civil remedies in the form of damages and a court injunction where copyright has been infringed and in serious cases criminal proceedings may also be brought.

It should be noted that there can be circumstances where the courts recognise that a technical breach of copyright has occurred but decide that in the public interest the injured party should not be provided with a remedy.

In *British Leyland Motor Corp.Ltd. v. Amstrong Patents Co. Ltd. (1986)* a majority of the House of Lords held that by copying the plaintiff's exhaust system the defendants had infringed the plaintiff's copyright in the design drawings which constituted an "artistic work". To provide the plaintiffs with an injunction however would effectively prevent competing manufacturers from providing spare parts for the plaintiff's vehicles and so deprive car owners from access to a free market for these spare parts. The copyright breach was regarded as subordinate to the rights of vehicle owners and so the plaintiffs were not entitled to enforce their copyright in a manner so as to maintain a monopoly in the supply of spare parts for their vehicles.

REGISTERED DESIGNS

A design is the artistic shape or pattern which has been applied to an article and appeals visually, for instance, curtain material or wallpaper. An original design can also become protected property under the Registered Design Act 1949 by registration with the Registry of Designs. This gives protection for a five year period and again infringements are actionable in the High Court by a claim for damages and/or an injunction.

The owner of a patent copyright or registered design can of course grant permission for the work to be used on payment of royalties. This can be a particularly lucrative source of income and a large number of organisations produce goods on licence paying royalities on each item made.

TRADE MARKS

Under the Trade Marks Act 1938 a trade mark is simply a mark on goods to show to the world at large that there is a connection between the goods and the producer or supplier. They are a means by which organisations establish product identity. The identity may be assisted by the manufacturer's name such as Hoover, Polaroid, Coca-Cola or Levi Strauss or more usually it could appear under a brand label such as Persil or Weetabix. Identity could also be associated with a symbol or logo used by the organisation, for instance, VW for Volkswagen.

In *Re Coca-Cola Co's Application (1986)* the House of Lords held that the Coca-Cola company were not entitled to register their distinctively shaped coke bottle as a trade mark. A mark has to be something distinct from the thing being marked and a bottle is simply a container rather than a mark.

A register of trade marks is maintained at the Patent Office, registration entitling the owner to exclusive use of the mark in relation to certain goods. Following the Patents, Design and Marks Act 1986, the register of marks, designs and patents may now be kept on computer so making the process of searches and obtaining copies of entries quicker and less costly.

The owner of a trade mark can bring an action for damages and/or an injunction against another individual or organisation who without authority uses the name or a similar trade mark in relation to goods of the same description.

In *Mitsubishi v. Fiat (1987)* the plaintiffs manufactured cars and used the word "Lancia" as a trade mark. They sought to prevent the defendants from using the word "Lancer" as a name for one of their cars. While the words sounded similar the two trademarks looked completely different. The Court of Appeal held that in all the circumstances there was no risk of confusion between the two trademarks and the defendants could go ahead and register "Lancer" as a trademark.

Furthermore an organisation which represents its goods, either innocently or intentionally, to be those of another organisation may be made liable for the tort of passing off. The injured party would be entitled to damages and/or an injunction.

> In *McDonald's Hamburgers v. Burgerking (U.K.) (1986)* the defendants advertised their "whopper" hamburger stating "It's Not Just Big, Mac" and "Unlike some Burgers, it's 100 per cent, pure beef, flame grilled, never fried, with a unique choice of toppings". The plaintiffs claimed amongst other things, that reading the advertisement the public would think that the burger was an improvement of their "Big Mac" burger, and available at the defendant's premises. The court agreed and an injunction was granted restraining the tort of passing off.

NEGOTIABLE INSTRUMENTS

The most important types of negotiable instruments are *bills of exchange* and *cheques,* although many others may be encountered in the commercial world, such as *promissory notes, bank notes, bankers' drafts, treasury bills and dividend warrants.* For the business community the cheque is the most commonly used method of payment, and an appreciation of the rules concerning the use of cheques is of prime importance. All negotiable instruments have the following special characteristics, which are not shared by other choses in action, and are referred to collectively as *negotiability*.

These are that:

(a) ownership is transferred by delivery alone if the instrument is payable to bearer, or by endorsement and delivery if payable to order;

(b) a transferee taking in good faith and for value who is a 'holder in due course' acquires a good title despite any defects in the title of the transferor;

(c) the holder of a negotiable instrument can sue on it in his own name whether or not he is a party to it;

(d) on assignment of the instrument there is no need to notify the person who will eventually have to pay out on it.

BILLS OF EXCHANGE AND CHEQUES

A bill of exchange is "an unconditional order in writing, addressed by one person to another, signed by the person giving it, requiring the person to whom it is addressed to pay on demand, or at a fixed determinable future time, a sum certain in money to, or to the order of, a specified person, or to bearer". The person who gives the order, or draws up the bill, is known as the *'drawer'*. The person who is ordered to pay is known as the *'drawee'*, and the person to whom payment is to be made is known as the *'payee'*.

A cheque is a bill of exchange drawn on a banker payable on demand.

A cheque is therefore an unconditional order in writing, signed by the person giving it (the drawer or customer), requiring the banker to whom it is addressed (the drawee) to pay on demand a sum certain in money to, or to the order of, a specified person (the payee), or to bearer.

Cheques are widely used in the commercial world because, as an alternative to cash, they are much more convenient both in terms of the security risks involved in carrying around large sums of cash and because they provide a record of payment for accounting purposes and evidence of payment for legal purposes.

Cheques are not, however, legal tender and there is no obligation to accept a cheque in payment of a debt. A person or organisation who is owed money can refuse to accept a cheque and insist on payment in cash.

In order to encourage the use of cheques and to make them more acceptable in the ordinary course of business, banks issue bankers cards to their customers which effectively guarantee that a person accepting a cheque up to the value of £50 will be paid by the bank.

Bills of exchange are used mainly in the field of foreign trade and they can be used as a means of allowing a buyer time to pay for the goods. A bill of exchange may look like this:

> Durham. October 10th, 198X
>
> £5,000
>
> Six months after date pay C Ltd. (payee) the sum of five thousand pounds.
>
> (signed) A Ltd. (drawer)
>
> To B Ltd. (drawee)
Sydney Australia

Where A Ltd. sells goods to the value of £5,000 to B Ltd. in Australia, and A Ltd. owes £5,000 to C Ltd. who is also in Australia, A Ltd., by drawing a bill of exchange on B Ltd. is effectively instructing B Ltd. to pay C Ltd. the money A Ltd. owes C Ltd., and is avoiding the necessity of physically transporting those sums of money back and forwards to Australia.

NEGOTIATION — THE TRANSFER OF OWNERSHIP

The method of transferring ownership of negotiable instruments is known as *negotiation* and its form depends upon whether the instrument is made payable to bearer, or to order. For the purposes of simplicity we shall refer here only to cheques, although what is said will also apply to bills of exchange generally.

A cheque payable to bearer is negotiated by simple delivery. Thus if a cheque is drawn in favour of "*John Smith or bearer*" and John Smith hands over the cheque to Tom Brown in settlement of a debt, ownership of the cheque is transferred to Tom Brown by the act of handing it over without any other action being taken.

A cheque payable to order is negotiated by indorsement and delivery.

An indorsement is simply the signature of the payee on the back of the cheque. If a cheque is drawn in favour of "*John Smith or order*", to negotiate the cheque to Tom Brown, John Smith must sign the back of the cheque and then hand it over to Tom Brown. Whether the cheque will be a bearer cheque or an order cheque in the hands of Tom Brown will depend upon the form of the indorsement.

If John Smith signed his name on the back of the cheque without naming a new payee this is known as an *indorsement in blank* and has the effect of converting the cheque into a bearer cheque.

If, on the other hand, John Smith has named a new payee by writing *'Pay Tom Brown or order'* or simply *'Pay Tom Brown'* on the back of the cheque and then signed it, this is known as a *special indorsement* and the cheque remains an order cheque.

EFFECT OF FORGED OR UNAUTHORISED SIGNATURE

The general rule is that a forged signature is wholly inoperative. Where a signature is forged or unauthorised, it is as though that signature was not there at all on the cheque. As there can be more than one signature on a cheque, it is necessary to distinguish the consequences of forgery of particular signatures.

Forgery of the drawer's signature

Since a cheque is an unconditional order in writing *'signed by the person giving it'*, where the signature of the drawer is forged, and therefore *wholly inoperative,* the document is not a cheque or a bill of exchange. It is therefore entirely worthless, and no-one can acquire any rights under it.

Forgery of an indorsement

(a) **Order Cheques**

Where a cheque is drawn payable to order, the payee must indorse it before he can negotiate it to someone else. Similarly, where a cheque has been negotiated and, by special indorsement, is made payable to another person, known as the indorsee, that other person must himself indorse the cheque before he can negotiate it further. In each case, because the cheque is an order cheque, the indorsement is *essential* if the negotiation is to transfer ownership validly.

Where an essential indorsement on an order cheque is forged, no subsequent party can acquire ownership of the cheque.

For example, A draws a cheque on B bank in favour of C or order. C indorses it and negotiates it to D. A thief steals the cheque, forges D's indorsement and negotiates it to E. E indorses the cheque and negotiates it to F.

A ⟶ C ⟶ D // E ⟶ F

There is a break in the chain and D is the true owner. D can recover the cheque from F, suing in tort if necessary.

Whilst title does not pass under a forged indorsement, persons subsequent to the forgery may have certain rights as between themselves so that in the example above F could sue E.

(b) **Bearer Cheques**

In the case of bearer cheques an indorsement is not essential to valid negotiation because ownership of a bearer cheque passes by delivery alone. Therefore, if an indorsement on a bearer cheque is forged, the forgery does not affect the subsequent negotiation of the cheque.

Rights of the Holder

We noted earlier that one of the characteristics of a negotiable instrument was that in certain circumstances the person receiving the instrument can acquire a better title to it than the person who transferred it to him. This rule applies to a person who receives a cheque or bill of exchange as a *holder in due course.*

A holder in due course is one who has taken a cheque:

(a) complete and regular on the face of it;

(b) before it was overdue (i.e. in circulation for 10 days or more);

(c) without notice that it had been previously dishonoured, if that is the case;

(d) in good faith and for value;

(e) without notice of any defect in the title of the person who negotiated it to him.

A holder in due course can sue, in his own name, any or all of the parties to a cheque.

This does not apply, however, in relation to an order cheque which bears a forged essential indorsement because no party subsequent to the forgery can acquire title to the cheque, and therefore no such party can be a holder in relation to the cheque.

A holder who is not a holder in due course will still be able to sue on the cheque.

CROSSED CHEQUES

The object of crossing a cheque is to convey instructions to the banker as to the manner of payment. Cheques can be crossed simply by drawing two parallel lines across the face of the cheque.

The effect of crossing a cheque is that it must be paid through a bank account. The payee or bearer will not be able to obtain cash for it across the counter in a bank.

This provides some safeguard in the case of stolen cheques because a thief will not wish to be traced by putting a cheque through his account and because the processing of the cheque will allow a time delay during which the cheque could be stopped.

General crossing

Two parallel lines are drawn across the face of the cheque. The words *'and company'* in full or abbreviated may be written between the lines but this is not essential. The effect of a general crossing is that the cheque is payable only through a bank account. The cheque cannot be paid over the counter.

Special crossing

The name of a particular bank or branch is written between the parallel lines. The effect of a special crossing is that that cheque must be paid into the named bank or branch.

Not negotiable

The words *'not negotiable'* may be written between the parallel lines. The effect of these words is to remove the characteristics of negotiability from the cheque. Although it is still transferable, the holder of such a cheque can obtain no better title to it than the person from whom he took it. There can be no *'holder in due course'* in relation to a cheque with a not negotiable crossing.

Account Payee

This crossing does not prevent the cheque from being transferred or from being negotiable. It is an instruction to the banker who may be liable in negligence if he collects the money for some account other than that of the person named as payee.

In the interests of business security the most effective combination of crossings is a general crossing to which the words 'not negotiable' are added.

TRANSFER OF INTANGIBLE PROPERTY

Unlike negotiable instruments, ownership of most types of choses in action cannot be transferred by delivery alone. A formal assignment of the benefit of most intangible property rights is required in order for the transfer of ownership to be fully effective.

If, for example, A owes B £500 and B wishes to transfer the rights to receive that money to C, B will have to make a formal assignment of the debt to C.

This must comply with s.136 of the Law of Property Act 1925, which provides that an assignment of a debt or chose in action will transfer to the assignee all the rights of the assignor if:

(a) the assignment is absolute and not merely partial;

(b) it is in writing and signed by the assignor;

(c) written notice is given to the debtor or other person liable on the chose in action.

If the assignment from B to C was of a debt, and was made in a document signed by B, it will effectively transfer B's debts to C provided that A was given written notice of the assignment.

ASSIGNMENT — WHAT'S IN A NAME?

In the last fifteen years Ricca has become a household name in fabrics and furniture design. To have Ricca furnishings in your home is for many people the mark of success.

When the young designers Richard and Catherine Bratton formed their Ricca company in 1969 they had no idea that their upmarket products would become the basis of a £50 million business by the mid nineteen eighties, or that their distinctive style and Ricca logo would become internationally known.

In 1984 when the company went public, it was already an organisation employing four hundred staff at its main premises in Derby. You work in its small legal department at Derby, as an assistant to one of the two company lawyers, Michael Richardson. Your department deals with a wide range of legal matters, and at the moment you are working on three separate issues which Michael has asked you to look over, prior to discussing them with him. These issues are briefly described below.

The Ricca name and logo. A newly formed company that is competing in the same market as Ricca, is regarded by the Ricca board of directors as having unreasonably infringed Ricca's business interests, by incorporating in the name of Reeca Ltd, and selling a range of furniture described as the 'Celeste range'. Ricca produced a range called 'Celestial', a term which the company has registered as a trade mark. The two furniture ranges are of a different style however, and whilst the logo of each company is a design based upon the letter 'R', which incorporates a similar typeface, the Ricca logo is circular, whereas the Reeca logo is triangular.

The design director. Following an internal disagreement with other members of the board, the design director, Milos Kasna left the company earlier this year and set up his own business designing and printing fabrics. His company is already selling fabrics which are based upon a design started by Mr. Kasna after he resigned from the company,but was still working out his notice. Additionally he is selling a fabric which he designed for Ricca four years ago, but which the company stopped producing after one year because of poor sales.

The lease. Part of the Derby premises, housing the furniture division of the company, is held on a ten year lease which is due to expire in eight months time. There is evidence that the landlord, wishes to expand his business, which adjoins the furniture division and may oppose the renewal of the lease.

TASKS

1. Examine the situations involving the competition from Reeca Ltd and Milos Kasna's new company, and produce a written document for Michael Richardson which advises him of Ricca's legal rights, and how the company should proceed.

2. Produce a report for the board of directors which outlines the rights of the company in relation to the renewal of its business lease.

Chapter 9

THE RESOLUTION OF BUSINESS DISPUTES

In this chapter it is proposed to examine the machinery which exists for resolving legal conflict in the business world. While the High Court has an important role to play in hearing civil disputes concerning large sums of money the vast majority of civil legal actions are dealt with at County Court level. The use of arbitration and tribunals, in particular the industrial tribunal for employment disputes, is also widespread in the business world. This chapter will consider therefore the various sources of legal advice and information, the process of suing in the County Court and making an application before an Industrial Tribunal, and the use of arbitration as a means of resolving business disputes without recourse to the courts.

SOURCES OF LEGAL ADVICE AND INFORMATION

Many sources of legal advice and information are available to a trader who has a legal problem. He may be able to research it himself by looking at law books in a library, but more usually he will seek outside help. If he is a member of a trade or professional association or trade union it is probable that he will be able to obtain legal guidance from such a body, particularly if the question is one which is closely associated with the operation or regulation of his business.

In relation to legal enquiries of a general nature, the Citizen's Advice Bureau may be able to point the trader in the right direction, or provide the information which he requires. In addition, there are a number of law centres which provide a similar, though more specialist, role in giving legal advice and acting on behalf of clients. Law centres, however, tend to deal with legal problems arising in relation to social issues such as housing, immigration, consumer and employee rights. They do not usually take on the role of advising businessmen in relation to commercial matters.

The most obvious source of advice and legal information is the solicitor. Larger business organisations may have their own legal department or in-house solicitor to provide a comprehensive legal service for the business, by dealing with such matters as conveyancing, drawing up contracts, registering intellectual property rights, advising management on day to day legal matters, designing procedures to ensure compliance by the business with its legal requirements and conducting litigation on its behalf.

Smaller business organisations cannot usually justify the expense of a legal department and will use solicitors in private practice to deal with their legal affairs. Solicitors are the general practitioners of the law, although within any particular firm individual solicitors will usually specialise in one or two areas of law. If a businessman refers a legal problem to a solicitor and the solicitor requires further specialist help or advice in order to deal with it, the solicitor can obtain the opinion of a barrister. The barrister, or counsel, usually specialises in a much narrower field of law than the solicitor. A businessman cannot approach a barrister directly for legal help but must first use a solicitor. The solicitor can refer the matter to a barrister if he feels that it is necessary. The main functions of the barrister are to provide legal opinions, to draw pleadings in preparation for litigation, and to act as an advocate in court. A solicitor cannot always act as an advocate without a barrister because the solicitor has only limited rights of audience before the courts. He is allowed to appear before a Magistrates Court, a County Court and, in certain circumstances, a Crown Court without a barrister. He is unable to appear in the High Court or any of the appeal courts and must use a barrister if he intends to conduct a case in one of these courts.

Communications between a client and a solicitor or barrister are subject to legal professional privilege. This means that the lawyer is duty bound not to disclose the communication to any other party without the authority of the client. In practice the effect of legal professional privilege is that the client can disclose all of the information which is relevant to his legal problem without fear that the information may be used against him at some later stage. The purpose of the rule is to ensure that the client does not hold back information which might be relevant to the legal problems which has arisen. This allows the lawyer to have all of the facts and to make a proper decision as to the course of action which is in the client's best interests.

Under the Legal Aid Scheme an individual may be entitled to receive help with his legal problem. Depending upon his financial circumstances, all or part of the cost of legal help will be paid by the state. This can extend to representation before a court. In order to qualify for free legal aid the individual's resources must be very low, both in terms of capital and income. If he is not entitled to free legal aid because he has more than the minimum resources he may still get some help from the legal aid scheme but he will have to make a contribution towards his own costs. If the individual has capital assets or average income, however, he may be caught in the "middle income trap". This is described as a trap because he will be too well off to obtain legal aid but will not be sufficiently well off to be able to afford the costs of litigation himself. He may therefore have to decide not to take legal action in the courts.

SUING IN THE COUNTY COURT

Before the businessman takes a decision to sue in the County Court, for example for an outstanding debt, there are a number of matters which he must consider carefully. Probably the most important factor will be that of cost, both in terms of money and in terms of the time and resources which must be invested in legal proceedings. Most of the plaintiff's costs will eventually be payable by the defendant if the plaintiff wins his case. However the plaintiff has a contract with his solicitor and is bound under that contract to pay the solicitors fees, and disbursements such as court fees, regardless of the outcome of the case. The plaintiff must therefore spend all of this money himself in the hope of later recovering it from the defendant. Even if the plaintiff is successful, he may not be able to obtain an order that the defendant pays all of his legal costs because a defendant can challenge the amount of a successful plaintiff's legal bill. This is done in a "taxation of costs" in which the court will require the defendant to pay only those costs which were reasonably and necesssarily incurred by the plaintiff in the action. After a taxation, the plaintiff will usually have to pay some part of his own legal costs. These in effect are deducted from whatever damages he has recovered from the defendant.

Another important consideration, closely associated with the question of costs, is whether the defendant will actually be able to satisfy any judgment which is eventually made against him. If the defendant is a "man of straw", and has no resources, the plaintiff will be wasting his money by pursuing him in the courts. He may end up by having to pay all of his own legal costs and by getting them back from the defendant by instalments of £1 a month, or by not getting them back at all. For this reason it is essential that the financial circumstances of the potential defendant are investigated before proceedings are issued against him. There is no formal procedure for this type of investigation, so the plaintiff will simply have to conduct it in the best way that he can.

In making the decision to sue someone, the businessman must also be aware that the legal process is slow. It may take 1 to 4 years to obtain judgment against a defendant, depending on the complexity of the case and its particular circumstances. In extreme cases, litigants have suffered mental illness or depression as a result of involvement with litigation. There is recognised mental condition called litigation nuerosis. Involvement in litigation over a long period of time is certainly a drain on the resources of the parties in terms of time, money and mental energy.

Publicity is another important factor. Proceedings before the courts are held in public and can be attended by anyone, including the press. Depending on the circumstances, the businessman may be inviting adverse publicity and a loss of goodwill by taking legal proceedings. If the legal action is being taken against an important customer, the damage to ongoing business relationships can be considerable.

In addition to these factors, it almost goes without saying that the plaintiff must have a sound legal basis for his claim and sufficient evidence to support it. This evidence may be documentary or may be provided by witnesses. In the case of the verbal evidence by witnesses, the credibility of the witnesses will be an important consideration. It may also be necessary to employ expert witnesses if the subject matter of the dispute is technical in nature, for example if it centres around a mechanical or electrical problem.

NEGOTIATION, COMPROMISE AND SETTLEMENT

For one or more of the reasons given above, the parties to a dispute will usually try to reach a settlement without the necessity of taking legal proceedings. Negotiations will take place before legal proceedings are issued and will usually continue as an ongoing process right up to the date of the trial. If both parties are prepared to litigate, this is probably an indication that there is some merit in the case that each of them is arguing. If a compromise can be agreed this will probably result in the saving of costs, time and adverse publicity.

COUNTY COURT PROCEDURE

Once the decision to sue has been taken, the plaintiff must decide in which court to issue proceedings. Where the action is based on contract or tort, and the amount claimed is £5,000 or less, the County Court has jurisdiction to hear the claim. If the claim is above £5,000, the case must be heard in the High Court, although that court may also hear smaller claims. The procedures in both courts are broadly similar, although in the High Court the procedure tends to be more complicated. In this chapter we shall examine County Court procedures only.

Assuming that the case is to be brought in the County Court, the plaintiff must decide which County Court to use. The claim must usually be brought in the district in which the defendant lives or carries on business or in the district in which the cause of action arose (for example where the contract was made).

The procedure for the conduct of the action is laid down in the County Court Rules. These are designed to ensure fairness between the parties. This is achieved by ensuring that the matter in dispute is understood by the parties and by the court, and that neither party is taken by surprise at the trial by the introduction of any new matter which ought to have been disclosed to him before the trial. The Rules also give time limits within which procedural steps must be taken by each party. These are designed to ensure that there is no unnecessary delay in the conduct of the case.

Letter before action

The first step which must be taken by the plaintiff is to send a "letter before action" to the defendant. In it the plaintiff will state his claim, invite the defendant to comply with his demands within 7 days, and inform him that court proceedings will be taken if he fails to do so. A letter before action gives the defendant the opportunity to meet the plaintiff's claim without incurring legal costs, or to state any legitimate grounds of defence which are available to him, and which may give rise to negotiations for settlement of the claim. If the plaintiff does not send a letter before action, and the defendant meets his demands as soon as proceedings are issued, the plaintiff will be unable to recover costs from him.

Issuing a summons

Within a fortnight of sending a letter before action, if there is no positive response to it, the plaintiff may request the court to issue a summons against the defendant. There are two types of summons, the default summons and the fixed date summons. A default summons is used whenever the plaintiff is claiming money, either a fixed sum or one which includes an element of damages which must be assessed by the court. A fixed date summons will only be used when the plaintiff claims a non-money remedy, such as an injunction, the possession of land or the recovery of goods. In this text we shall be examining the procedure which applies to a default summons, because this type of summons is most often used by the businessman. The procedure for a fixed date summons is broadly similar.

The plaintiff must file a request for the issue of a default summons, together with the summons itself at the County Court office. In addition he must provide two copies of the particulars of claim, one for the court and one for the defendant. In the particulars of claim the plaintiff must specify the legal basis of his claim and remedy which he seeks. He will also include a brief description of the material facts surrounding his claim. The particulars of the claim and summons will be served on the defendant by the court together with forms on which the defendant can either make an admission and a proposal for payment or put forward a defence and/or a counterclaim.

Judgment in default

If the defendant fails to respond within 14 days of receiving the summons the plaintiff may request the court to enter judgment against him. The plaintiff has in effect won his case by default, and can enforce the judgment against the defendant if he fails to pay.

Admission and offer of payment

On receiving the summons however the defendant may have decided to admit the claim in part or in full, and make an offer to pay the amount due either immediately or by instalments. If the defendant requests time to pay, he must provide the court with details of his financial circumstances and the exact terms of his proposals for payment. These will be forwarded by the court to the plaintiff, who will decide whether or not to accept the offer of payment. If he accepts, judgment will be entered in the terms of the agreement. If the plaintiff does not accept the defendant's proposals, the court will fix a date for a hearing before the Registrar for a decision on the terms of payment. The decision of the Registrar will be binding on both parties and judgment will be entered.

If the defendant fails to keep up payment, enforcement action may be taken against him by the plaintiff.

Defence

If the defendant believes he has a valid defence to the plaintiff's claim, he must file particulars of the defence in the County Court Office within 14 days of receiving the summons, in order to prevent judgment being entered against him in default.

MAIN STEPS IN A DEFAULT ACTION IN THE COUNTY COURT

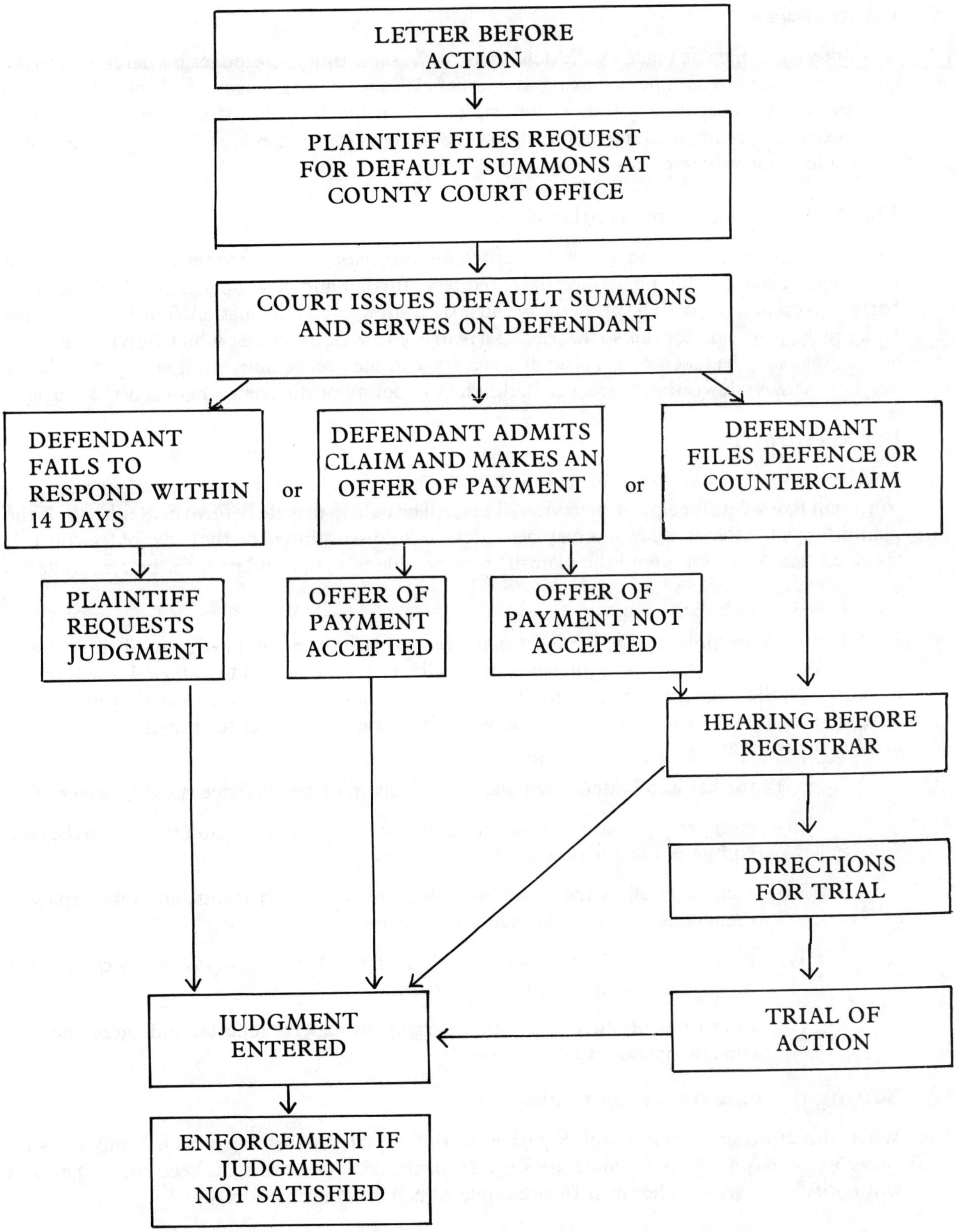

If he feels that he has insufficient information about the plaintiff's claim to set out his defence in full or if he does not have time to prepare a full defence, but still wishes to defend the action, he may lodge a "holding defence" with the court within the time period and give "further and better particulars" of his defence at a later date when he is requested to do so by the plaintiff. A holding defence is simply a statement denying any indebtedness to the plaintiff.

Counterclaim

A counterclaim may be made by the defendant at the same time as he lodges his defence with the court. In a counterclaim he is making a separate claim for damages against the plaintiff, which will survive as a separate action if the original claim by the plaintiff is withdrawn. Where circumstances permit, a counterclaim should be made as it provides a useful bargaining tool in negotiations for settlement.

Further and better particulars

If either of the parties feels that he has insufficient information relating to the claim or defence of the other, he may, within prescribed time, request "further and better particulars" of the other party's claim or defence. The other party must then supply the information. The County Court Rules make provision for this so that each party may know the exact case which he has to answer, and neither may be taken by surprise at a late stage in the proceedings. In this way the process helps to narrow down the issues and highlight the points of difference between the parties.

Pre-trial review

Once the initial exchange of information about each party's side of the case has taken place, the court will fixe a date for a pre-trial review. This will be held in private before the Registrar. If the plaintiff fails to attend, the action may be struck out or discontinued on the order of the court. If the defendant does not attend the plaintiff may be able to obtain judgment if he can prove his case.

If both parties are present, the Registrar will seek to clarify the points at issue, if there is any doubt about them. He may also explore the possibility of a settlement at this stage. If the action is to go to trial, the Registrar will give directions to the parties as to the things that they must do in order to prepare the case for trial. Directions given by the Registrar at the pre-trial review may include orders that:

(i) further and better particulars of the claim or the defence must be given;

(ii) each party prepare a list of the documents in their possession relating to the case and give it to the other;

(iii) each party allow the other to inspect the listed documents, and take copies of them (this is called 'discovery of documents');

(iv) the parties try to agree matters which are not disputed, to save the necessity and expense of proving them in court; and

(v) the parties produce plans, photographs or experts reports, and agree on their contents if possible.

Setting the case down for trial

When the directions given by the Registrar at the pre trial review have been complied with, either party may apply to the court to fix a date for the trial. Once this has been fixed, the court will notify the parties, who must then complete their final preparations.

The trial

Many cases are settled on the doorstep of the courtroom before a trial takes place. This is because the pressure for settlement builds up to a peak when the parties are faced with the reality of a trial. They may be aware of some weakness in their case, or may doubt the ability of a key witness to appear credible and resolute in the face of cross examination. Even at this late stage considerable savings of costs can be made by settling the case.

The proceedings in a County Court trial are conducted in a formal manner. The plaintiff will have to present his evidence first, and any witnesses may be cross examined by the defence, or questioned by the judge. The plaintiff's lawyers can re-examine any of his witnesses, but must confine their questioning to matters already raised by them. Thus they could, for example, clarify any points which may have become confused in cross examination, or emphasise any important points which may have been obscured. Next it is the turn of the defence to present its evidence, and again there may be cross examination and re-examination.

Legal argument may then take place, followed by a summing up of each party's case. The judge will usually deliver judgment at the end of the trial, but may reserve judgment, particularly if there are difficult points of law to consider. If judgment is reserved the parties will have to attend court at a later date when judgment will be given.

Costs

As we noted above, the party who loses the case will have to pay the winner's costs, in addition to his own. He can however, challenge the amount of the other party's bill by applying to the court for a taxation of costs.

Appeal

An appeal can be made from a decision of the County Court to the Court of Appeal. The appeal may be on a question of law or a question of fact, and must be lodged within specified time limits. The costs involved in making an appeal will be very high and careful thought should be given before this step is taken.

ENFORCEMENT OF A JUDGMENT

If judgment is given against a defendant, payment is due immediately unless the court has made an order for payment by instalments or has otherwise postponed payment. If the judgment debtor does not make payment when it is due, steps can be taken to enforce the judgment. There are a number of alternative methods of enforcement, and it will be important to choose a method which will bear fruit having regard to the particular circumstances of the judgment debtor.

Oral examination

To assist in making an informed choice as to the method of enforcement, the party entitled to payment may make an application to the court for an order that the judgment debtor be orally examined before the court as to his means. The order may include provision for the production of books, accounts or other documents. The judgment debtor will be liable to imprisonment if he fails to attend. At the oral examination he will be cross examined on oath, as to his means and resources, by the registrar and the applicant. It can be established, for example, whether he has any investments, bank accounts, savings or other assets such as a house or a car; or if he is working, the name and address of his employer and details of his salary and any other source of income. Armed with this information, a decision can be taken as to the most effective method of enforcement. The following are the principal methods.

Warrant of execution

A warrant of execution directs the County Court bailiff to seize any goods belonging to the judgment debtor, and to sell them to raise money to pay the creditor. It will be useful, at the oral examination, to establish what goods belong to the debtor and where they are located, in preparation for the issue of a warrant of execution.

Attachment of earnings

If it has been established that the judgment debtor has regular employment, the plaintiff can apply for an order under the Attachment of Earnings Act 1971. This is in effect a direction to the employer to deduct a specified sum from the debtor's wages each week, and pay it direct to the court, which will forward the money to the plaintiff.

Garnishee orders

If the plaintiff discovers, at the end of the oral examination, that the debtor is owed money by a third party, he may apply for a garnishee order. The effect of the order is to require the third party to pay the money direct to the plaintiff, or at least so much of it as will satisfy the judgment debt and costs. This type of order is particularly useful where, for example, the judgment debtor has money in a bank account or some other similar form of savings.

Charging order

The plaintiff can apply for a charging order on land held by the debtor or on any shares owned by him in a company. This gives him security for the judgment debt which can ultimately be enforced by the sale of the property in question.

Bankruptcy proceedings

As we saw in Chapter 2, the creditor will have grounds to petition for the bankruptcy of the debtor if a judgment debt of £750 or more remains outstanding after a warrant of execution has been issued but returned unsatisfied. In practice the threat of bankruptcy proceedings is a powerful stimulus to make a defaulting debtor find the money to pay the debt.

BRINGING A CLAIM BEFORE AN INDUSTRIAL TRIBUNAL

Any claim to enforce a statutory employment right, such as the right not to be unfairly dismissed, must be presented before an industrial tribunal within the appropriate time limit. In a case involving unfair dismissal the claim must be presented within three months of the effective date of the termination of employment. The Tribunal does have a discretion to allow an application out of time where it was not reasonably practicable to present it before the end of the three months period. In practice Tribunals rarely hear applications presented out of time however and in *Swainston v. Hetton Victory Club Ltd (1983)* the fact that the application was only one day late was sufficient for the Tribunal to refuse to hear the claim.

PRESENTING A CLAIM

To present a claim it is usual to complete and submit an IT1 form to the Regional Office of Industrial Tribunals (ROIT). Use of the IT1 form is not a statutory requirement and it would be sufficient to make a claim in writing containing a statement of the grounds upon which unfair dismissal is claimed.

The ROIT acknowledges receipt of the IT1 by sending an IT5 form to the employee. This form confirms that the application has been made, states that copies of the IT1 have been passed on to the employer and the Advisory, Conciliation and Arbitration Service (ACAS) and informs the employee that notice of the hearing will be sent at a future date. The employer (respondent) is sent a copy of the IT1 by the ROIT as well as formal notice that the application has been made, known as an IT2, and a blank form IT3 which is technically known as a 'notice of appearance'. Having examined the details contained in the IT1 and the IT2 and checked their accuracy, in particular whether the applicant has the required period of continuous service to bring a claim, the employer has then 14 days to 'enter an appearance'. It is at this stage that the respondent should attempt to clarify the legal position, consider the evidence and if necessary apply to the ROIT for an extension of time before entering an appearance by returning the IT3. If the respondent requires further clarification of the applicants' ground for the claim he can make a request for further particulars. Whether or not the respondent wishes to resist the claim he must complete the notice of appearance IT3 form and return it to the ROIT. If the respondent has failed to provide sufficient particulars of his ground for resisting the claim he can be required to do so by the tribunal. A copy of the IT3 is then sent to both the applicant and ACAS.

Soon after the IT3 has been returned to the ROIT a notice of hearing IT4 is sent to both parties. This sets a date for the hearing but in practice a postponement can be applied for in writing and is normally granted when requested. It may be that the respondent disputes that the applicant is qualified to bring the claim, perhaps in relation to the employee's period of continuous employment for the purpose of unfair dismissal. In these circumstances it is usual to request a preliminary hearing to determine the issue.

CONCILIATION

The role of a conciliation officer in an unfair dismissal claim is to endeavour to promote a settlement of the complaint without the dispute having to go to an Industrial Tribunal. The officer is required to promote a settlement if requested to by either party or if he feels he could act with a reasonable prospect of success. For this purpose the officer should seek to promote the reinstatement or re-engagement of a dismissed employee on equitable terms or if this is not practicable, attempt to persuade the employer to agree to make the employee a compensation payment. His function is not to negotiate with the parties but rather to act as a channel of communication through which the parties do their bargaining.

The conciliation officer has vast experience of course and if asked to do so he can draw on this experience to give an impartial opinion as to the position. If a settlement is reached, and this happens in over 50% of cases, it is usual for it to be arranged through the conciliation officer. This would be enforceable in the same way as an award by the Tribunal, whereas a private settlement would not prevent an employee from still presenting a claim before the Tribunal.

PRE-HEARING ASSESSMENT

Either party may apply for a pre-hearing assessment to take place, or the tribunal may arrange an assessment in the absence of an application. The pre-hearing assessment is carried out by a full tribunal examining the papers, assessing the strength of the applicant's claim and whether the respondent's defence has any merit. No evidence from witnesses is heard but the tribunal may take account of any written applications and the argument of the parties or their representatives. If an opinion is reached that either party's case is particularly weak then the tribunal will issue a warning that if the party concerned proceeds to a full trial an order for costs may be made against him. While the tribunal rarely awards costs they do have a discretion to do so where a party, in bringing the proceedings has acted frivolously, vexatiously or otherwise unreasonably. By proceeding with a claim after a pre-trial assessment has decided that it is particularly weak, a party would be regarded as acting unreasonably. In addition an employee who brings a claim without any substance, with the aim of harassing his employer, acts frivolously or vexatiously and could have costs awarded against him. If the case proceeds to a full hearing then it is heard by a differently constituted tribunal who are not made aware of the opinion reached at the pre-hearing assesssment.

THE HEARING

Each Industrial Tribunal is made up of three equal members one of whom is a legal chairman and must be a barrister or solicitor of at least seven years standing. The chairman sits with two lay members, from both sides of industry, and each member is given an opportunity to express opinions as to the decision and their reasons for it.

A tribunal hearing is not conducted with the same degree of formality as a trial in a court of law. The Rules of Procedure regulations make it clear that a tribunal may conduct a hearing in a manner most suitable to clarify the issues without the need to comply strictly to the normal rules relating to the admissibility of evidence. This makes it more possible for lay representation, often by a trade union official. Legal aid is not available for legal representation before most tribunals, including the industrial tribunal. The degree of formality will depend very much on the legal chairman whose main responsibility is to ensure that the proceedings are conducted fairly. Tribunal members must be impartial and have no interest in the matter before them. Both parties must be heard and made fully aware of all the allegations made against them so that evidence may be brought to refute them if necessary.

REMEDIES

There are a number of remedies available to a successful applicant to a tribunal depending upon the nature of the claim.

(a) Declarations — as to the legal right of the parties

(b) Monetary awards — to compensate the complainant

(c) Orders — to require a course of action, such as reinstatement

(d) Recommendations — that a party should take a course of action.

A declaration as to legal rights will rarely be of relevance in a claim of unfair dismissal and is more likely where there has been a finding of persistant racial or sexual discrimination or non compliance with an improvement or prohibition notice under the Health and Safety at Work Act 1974 (see Chapter 7). A monetary award is made in the vast majority of cases. Compensation for a successful applicant in an unfair dismissal claim may be comprised of several separate elements, for example the basic award, compensatory award, additional award and special award. The most important orders a tribunal can make in an unfair dismissal claim are re-engagemet and reinstatement.

Re-engagement requires an employer to re-employ the dismissed applicant, though not necessarily on the same terms as before. Reinstatement orders the employer to restore the ex-employee to his former position and treat him as if he had never been dismissed. A recommendation is a remedy applicable mainly to cases of discrimination where the employers are advised of a course of conduct which would negative the impact of a discrimating practice.

ENFORCEMENT

Surprisingly an Industrial Tribunal has no jurisdiction to enforce its own remedies so that if a non-money order is not complied with, for instance for reinstatement or re-engagement it is then reduced to a monetary award. Although it is rarely necessary to do so a monetary award can be enforced in the County Court. If an IT financial award is not complied with within a reasonable time, for instance two weeks, the employee should contact the employer and attempt to discover his intentions. The employer has 42 days from the date of the decision to lodge an appeal. The effect of an appeal will be to hold in abeyance any award until the appeal has been heard. If there are no proposals from the employer and no appeal is made within 42 days, then the employee should normally write a letter threatening legal proceedings without further notice if the sum is not paid within seven days. Then finally if the letter does not meet with a response the employee should issue proceedings in the County Court. The action is for the sum claimed plus court fees and is made by way of an originating application supported by a sworn statement (known as an affidavit). County Court proceedings for debt and enforcement are considered earlier in the chapter.

There is no point suing however if the employer becomes bankrupt or goes into liquidation. In such a case an application for payment should be made to the administrative receiver, the receiver, liquidator or trustee. If there is no payment, or only partial payment is made, the applicant can made a claim for payment from the Secretary of State for Employment. The Secretary of State has power to pay certain tribunal awards in full out of the redundancy fund.

Main Steps in an Application Brought before an Industrial Tribunal

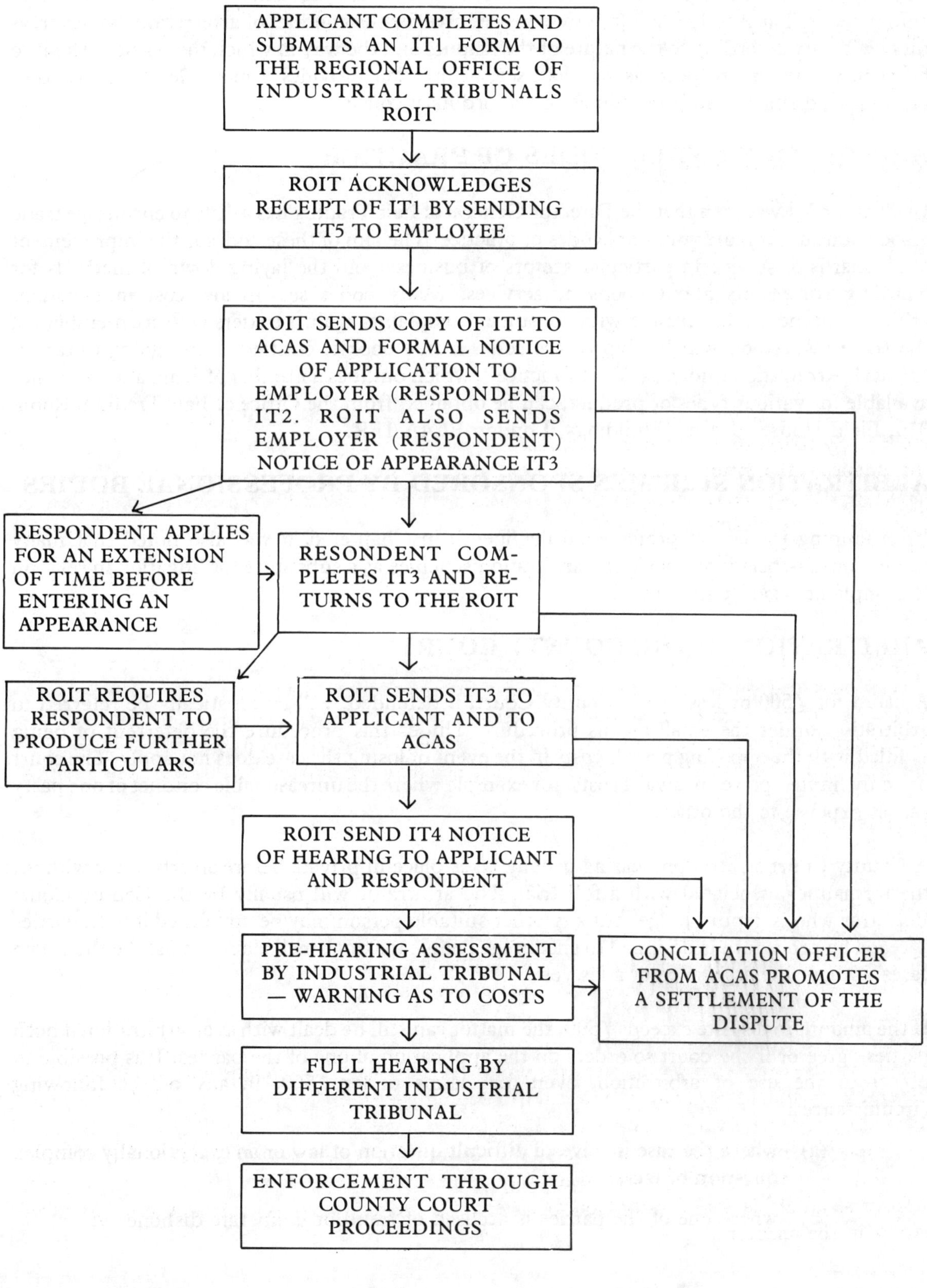

ARBITRATION

Arbitration is a means of resolving a dispute without recourse to the courts. An arbitrator is a person to whom both sides of the dispute put their case. He will consider the evidence and make a decision by applying ordinary rules of law to the facts before him. The decision of an arbitrator can be enforced in the courts, if necessary.

The legal framework within which arbitration operates is contained in the Arbitration Act 1950. This deals with matters such as the effect of arbitration agreements, awards, costs and enforcement. The Act does not lay down procedures for the conduct of arbitration, however, as these will vary according to the nature of the dispute and the way in which the parties wish it to be handled. In this respect, as we shall see, arbitration provides a more flexible method of resolving a dispute than proceedings in the ordinary courts.

ARBITRATION UNDER CODES OF PRACTICE

In Chapter 5 it was seen that the Director General of Fair Trading has a duty to encourage trade associations to promote voluntary codes of practice. The aim of these codes is the improvement of standards of service in particular sectors of business; and the laying down of methods for handling complaints about goods or services. Many codes set up low cost independent arbitration schemes for dealing with consumer complaints against traders who are members of the trade association which adopted the code. A free booklet entitled "I am going to take it further!: Arbitration under Codes of Practice", which outlines a number of arbitration schemes available for various types of product, can be obtained from the Office of Fair Trading, Room 310, Field House, Bream's Buildings, London EC4A 1PR.

ARBITRATION SCHEMES SPONSORED BY PROFESSIONAL BODIES

In examining the law of professional negligence in Chapter 6, it was also noted that many professional associations sponsored arbitration schemes as a substitute for litigation in relation to complaints against their members.

ARBITRATION IN THE COUNTY COURT

A claim for £500 or less in the County Court, if defended, will automatically be referred to arbitration under the small claims procedure. Under this procedure the deterrent of being saddled with the opposing party's costs in the event of losing the case does not apply. The court has only limited power to award costs, for example where the unreasonable conduct of one party causes expense to the other.

A County Court arbitration hearing usually takes place in private before an arbitrator without the formalities associated with a full trial. The arbitrator will usually be the County Court Registrar who is deputy judge, but any other suitable person may be appointed if both parties agree. The procedure is designed to encourage people making small claims to handle their own cases without the assistance of a lawyer.

If the amount in dispute exceeds £500, the matter can still be dealt with as an arbitration if both parties agree or if the court so orders on the application of one of the parties. It is possible to object to the use of arbitration, even for claims under £500, in any of the following circumstances:

(a) where the case involves a difficult question of law or an exceptionally complex question of fact;

(b) where one of the parties is accused of fraud or deliberate dishonesty;

(c) where the parties both agree that normal court proceedings shall apply;

(d) where it would be unreasonable for the claim to be heard as an arbitration having regard to its subject matter or the interests of any other person likely to be affected, for example where the decision will, in practice, create a precedent which will be followed in a number of similar cases.

Where a dispute is dealt with by way of arbitration in the County Court, the hearing will usually be informal and strict rules of evidence will not apply. The arbitrator may adopt any method of proceeding which he considers to be convenient, so long as it affords a fair and equal opportunity to each party to present his case. The case could be dealt with by an exchange of documents for example rather than a hearing with the parties present in person.

ARBITRATION CLAUSES IN CONTRACTS

Many standard form contracts contain an arbitration clause. This is an agreement to submit any differences or disputes which may arise in relation to the contract to arbitration. An example of such a clause can be found in the standard form contract contained in figure 5.2 in Chapter 5. Condition 14 of the agreement gives the parties the power to choose arbitration as a means of resolving any dispute. Some standard form contracts contain conditions under which any dispute must be submitted to arbitration. This can be done by adopting the wording of an arbitration clause which was held to be valid in the case of *Scott v. Avery (1856)*. Under such a clause the right of action in court only arises after an award has been made by an arbitrator.

SUBSEQUENT AGREEMENT TO ARBITRATION

Even where there is no arbitration clause in the contract, parties to a dispute can agree at any time to submit the dispute to arbitration. The agreement may be made after the dispute has arisen and any agreement to submit to arbitration operates as a binding contract.

An arbitration agreement comes into being where two or more persons agree that an existing or potential dispute between them shall be resolved in a legally binding way by one or more persons in a judicial manner. Under s.32 of the Arbitration Act 1950 an arbitration agreement must be in writing. If an arbitrator is appointed under a verbal agreement he will usually invite the parties to enter into a written agreement, in order to bring the arbitration within the 1950 Act. The arbitration agreement may incorporate such matters as the method of appointment of the arbitrator and the procedural rules governing he conduct of the arbitration.

THE UNIQUE FEATURES OF ARBITRATION

Where the parties have not laid out in advance any particular procedure, there is a large degree of flexibility in the way in which the arbitration can be concluded. With the agreement of the parties the arbitrator can adopt whatever procedure appears most appropriate. The case may be decided upon documentary evidence alone; or documents and written representations; or a site visit; or the examination of any goods which are at the centre of a dispute. Alternatively there could be a formal hearing of the case with expert witnesses and lawyers in attendance.

In addition to the flexibility of choosing an appropriate procedure, there is flexibility in relation to the location and time of any hearing. The arbitration can be heard at any place which the parties choose. The could, for example, be in a location near the site of the dispute. The hearing could take place at a weekend, for example, and thereby avoid the loss of time during working hours.

In a dispute involving matters of a technical nature, an appropriately qualified independent expert could be appointed as arbitrator. This may enable a swifter conclusion to be reached in the case.

Probably the single most important factor in the mind of a businessman who chooses to refer a dispute to arbitration is that the proceedings are totally private. Adverse publicity can therefore be avoided, and so can the public disclosure of confidential information or trade secrets. The advantage of privacy may be lost, however, if there is an appeal against the decision of the arbitrator.

Appeal against the decision of an arbitrator can be made on the grounds either that the proceedings were not conducted fairly, or that the decision contains an error of law. An arbitration award will only be set aside on grounds of unfairness if the arbitrator has failed to comply with the rules of natural justice. These are that he must be, and be seen to be, impartial and unbiased; and that each party to the dispute must be given a fair opportunity to present his own case and to answer the case put forward by his opponent.

One of the parties may suspect that the arbitrator has made an error of law in reaching his decision, but be unable to confirm that suspicion because the arbitrator has not given full reasons for his decision. In such a case that party can apply, under s.1 of the Arbitration Act 1979, to the High Court for an order requiring the arbitrator to give full reasons.

Arbitration is often a less expensive method of resolving business disputes than litigation in the ordinary courts. In some cases, however, where formal procedures are adopted, arbitration may actually be more expensive than litigation. One reason for this is that the cost of the actual hearing must be borne by the parties. This will include, for example, the arbitrator's fee, the cost of accommodation for the hearing, and of recording evidence. In most cases these costs are more than compensated for by the speed with which a case can be dealt with, the informality of procedures and the fact that the arbitrators award is final and cannot, except in the limited circumstances discussed above, be the subject of an appeal.

One of the disadvantages of arbitration is that an arbitrator, having reached a decision and made an award, is unable to enforce that award. In the event that the award is not complied with, it can only be enforced by taking action in the courts. The agreement to submit a claim to arbitration is a binding contract and failure to comply with an arbitrator's award is a breach of contract which can be the subject of proceedings in the County Court or the High Court. A simple procedure for enforcement is provided for in s.26 of the 1950 Act. Under this the award may be enforced in the same way as a court order with the permission of the High Court. This involves an application to the High Court for the enforcement of the arbitration award. If the court is satisfied that the award is valid it will enter judgment in favour of the successful party. The award can then be enforced in the same way as any other judgment of the court.

ASSIGNMENT — TO SUE OR NOT TO SUE

David Adams and Frank Bartlett are partners in a firm of accountants which carries on business in Dartley, a small market town in the North West. Their work is almost exclusively confined to preparing accounts and advising on tax matters for clients who operate small businesses in the local area. The business has a clientele of between seventy and eighty, providing a turnover of around £95,000. When you bear in mind that the firm has a staff of three employees, an accounting assistant and two secretaries, it is not difficult to appreciate that bad debts are to be avoided at all costs. Unfortunately the firm has had an unpaid bill of £2,340 on its books for the past eighteen months. The bill relates to work done in 1986 for a new client, Andrew Davies, a building merchant in Dartley. Despite three reminders from the firm and a solicitor's letter threatening legal action no payment has yet been received. This is despite the fact that Davies' 1986 accounts showed a healthy profit and it is common knowledge in Dartley that Davies is expanding into bigger premises. Frank Bartlett has also heard on the grapevine that Davies is now using a rival firm of accountants.

Six months ago the accountancy firm purchased an electronic typewriter with a memory and visual display facility from Bolton Office Supplies Ltd for £454. The typewriter developed an electronic fault which has rendered the display facility unreliable. The firm sought to reject the machine when the fault was discovered, however the supplier refused to take it back, and offered instead to deliver the typewriter to the manufacturer for repair under the terms of the manufacturer's guarantee. David Adams wrote to the supplier and rejected this suggestion pointing out that Bolton Office Supplies Ltd were legally responsible for the defects in the typewriter. He again demanded a full refund of the purchase price and requested the supplier to take the machine back. The letter was posted three weeks ago and no response has been made by the supplier.

Yesterday Frank Bartlett, the senior partner, received a letter from a firm of solicitors requesting a statutory statement of the reason or reasons for dismissing Sarah Tindley an ex-employee. Sarah had worked as a secretary for the firm for the past eleven years but three weeks ago was summarily dismissed with wages paid in lieu of the three months notice that she was entitled to. The decision to dismiss Sarah instantly was taken by Frank after Sarah had admitted that she had used the fourteen pounds in the firm's petty cash to purchase a pair of shoes which were on 'sale' at a local store.

You are James Morris a trainee accountant who has just completed a stage of your accountancy examinations in which you studied business law. Frank Bartlett has discussed with you the various matters above and asked for your opinion on how the firm should proceed. You decided to impress your employer with an informal report in which you deal with each matter in turn.

TASK

Indicate in the report:

1. Whether legal proceedings to recover the debt are worthwhile and the legal process involved in taking county court action for debt recovery.

2. Whether the firm is within its contractual rights to repudiate the contract for the typewriter (See Chapter 5) and if legal proceedings are taken how they differ from the debt action.

3. If Sarah decides to pursue a claim for unfair dismissal indicate the steps which the firm would need to take should they decide to defend the claim.

INDEX